STUDIES IN HISPANIC AMERICAN AFFAIRS

Edited by
A. CURTIS WILGUS

Volume IV
COLONIAL HISPANIC AMERICA

Colonial Hispanic America

EDITED BY

A. CURTIS WILGUS

NEW YORK

RUSSELL & RUSSELL · INC

1963

PREFACE

THE Fourth Annual Seminar Conference on Hispanic American Affairs at The George Washington University was held from July 1 to August 9, 1935. The lectures here published were presented during this period. As in previous Seminar Conferences, the lectures were so arranged as to give continuity to the treatment of the general subject under discussion. At various times during the course guest speakers read papers dealing with special subjects within the field of colonial Hispanic American affairs. But in order not to break the thread of unity of the scheduled speakers, these lectures have been printed as appendices. Unlike previous volumes, this one contains maps and extensive bibliographies, which are added in order to give the work greater value as a reference, and perhaps as a textbook.

The editor has been assisted in reading proof by Professor George Howland Cox, Dr. Raul d'Eça, Dr. Philip Ainsworth Means, and Miss Catherine Phelps. As in the past, the book has been guided through the various stages of printing by Mr. Henry W. Herzog. The index has been prepared by Dr. d'Eça. Editorial work has been confined chiefly to securing uniformity of presentation.

A. CURTIS WILGUS,
Director of the Center of Inter-American Studies.

TABLE OF CONTENTS

[vii]

CHAPTER ONE

THE SIGNIFICANCE OF HISPANIC AMERICAN COLONIZATION

By James Alexander Robertson

THIS discussion is concerned not so much with the facts of the colonization of Hispanic America as with certain deductions that may be made from such facts. The facts themselves can be obtained from general reading and from the chapters which follow. But it is hoped that what is here said will suggest something of the milieu and inheritance that made the colonization possible, and some of the processes of that colonization.

I

The Europe of 1450 was painfully struggling toward a larger and more complex life. The horizon of its knowledge was, and had been for some time, changing in force and direction. The Crusades, Venetian trade, the rise of the Turk with his threat to Europe, the tales of such travelers as John of Carpini and Marco Polo, and, too, the brighter dawn of study and learning, were all parts of a larger whole. Moreover, the use of gunpowder in battle had added a destructive power that was revolutionizing warfare.

By 1450 much of Europe had become conscious of India and the Far East. The nearer East was better, but unfavorably, known, for the Turk and Arab had closed the overland way in part of that region to India and its fabulous riches and the spices that took the place in those days of ice for the preservation of food. To Spain, and indeed, to Portugal, regions of the nearer East were unfavorably known, for out of it had come the Arab and his allies of north Africa into the Iberian Peninsula, and for seven centuries the Spaniards especially had fought intermittently against the invading Moor.

By about 1450 Gutenberg had perfected the first printing press and had printed the first book with movable types. The day of the laboriously wrought manuscript, although it lingered on, was definitely over. This was an impetus to progress than which few have been greater.

By 1450 Prince Henry the Navigator, who had begun his despatch of expeditions down along the African coast at least as early as 1421, had still ten years left of his active life.[1] The Europe of his time and later owed him much for his forward vision, his energy, his unconquerable spirit, and his intelligence. Because of the impetus he gave to geographical discovery, he rightfully has a place in the history of America. Before 1450, the Portuguese had rediscovered and planted colonies in the Madeira, Azores, and Cape Verde islands. Almost simultaneously with the Portuguese discoveries began the slave trade from Africa.[2]

The second recorded European discovery of western lands beyond the islands off the European and African coasts—forty-two years after 1450 —was no slight achievement. It had been prepared directly by the exploring activities of Prince Henry the Navigator; and the discovery was inevitable in this period. It was the merest chance, however, that the discovery was made by a Spanish, and not a Portuguese, expedition. As it is, historians must eternally wonder whether some Portuguese had not already glimpsed the possibility of a western land mass from evidence furnished by the sea itself. Be that as it may, the Portuguese, following the impetus given by Prince Henry, held themselves after his death to the African and Oriental discoveries, pushing ahead from promontory to promontory, from river to river, until in 1488 Bartolomé Diaz rounded the Cope of Good Hope, and ten years later, Vasco da Gama reached India—the consummation of a quest that had lasted wellnigh a century. Portuguese colonization and exploitation of mainlands and islands followed and endured until they were challenged in certain regions by the Spaniards, the Dutch, and the English, and to some little extent, by the French. This was mainly a colonization among peoples of advanced civilization and culture. It was, moreover, a colonization in regions whence had formerly come, via Arabian traders, the coveted wealth of spices, silks, and other merchandise. It meant the passing of a trade monopoly that had formerly belonged to Venetian traders, although the rise of the Turks had already spelt its ruin to the Portuguese who sought the goods either at their source or in the large Oriental emporiums just as the Arab had done.

In 1450 the Turk's throttlehold on Europe was but three years away, when the capture of Constantinople made an European power out of a race nomadic and Asiatic in its origin. For some time these virile people had been thundering at the gates of Europe.

It was a changing world. Spain's seven-century contest with the

---

[1] See Edgar Prestage, *The Portuguese pioneers* (London, 1933).

[2] González de Repáraz, *Historia de la colonización* (Barcelona, 1933), 270-272.

Moor—though intermittent—with final victory in 1492, released the energies of a people, not yet a solidified nation, for other tasks. By finally taking up the proposals of Columbus, which Portugal had rejected, the Catholic Kings, Ferdinand and Isabella, made it possible for Spain to acquire an empire such as the world has rarely seen.[3] Thus Portugal lost a great opportunity. And yet, it is proper to ask just what the Portuguese could and would have done with the western lands had they acceded to the importunities of Columbus. They were already engrossed in the African and Oriental project, and could have ill-spared any men to colonize in another direction. If one may reason from their tardiness in coming to an appreciation of possible opportunities in Brazil, one may easily come to the conclusion that the western lands would have continued to lie fallow for many years, so far as Europe was concerned, unless another nation had wrested control from the Portuguese; and the western Indies might have been held merely as an outpost of empire had they learned the secret of the Pacific. The matter is open for speculation, but it would seem that it would have been physically impossible for the small country of Portugal, already so involved in the Orient in point of men and expense, to have done more than it was doing. Indeed, it was only when its Oriental colonies began to suffer from other nations and when other nations began to cast envious eyes upon Portuguese America, that Brazil was given any great amount of consideration. At the same time, the honor of recorded discovery was denied the people who seemed, from the standpoint of experience, to be most fitted to make it, and came to a people who had had little experience in large maritime ventures.

With the discovery, Spain was faced with new responsibilities and new opportunities. Whatever the lands in the west might prove to be —whether a part of Asia or unrecorded regions—the responsibilities were the same if Spain decided to hold them, while the opportunities depended on the attitude toward utilization. If the lands were a part of Asia, then it might be expected that people of a certain culture, refinement, and civilization might be encountered. If the lands were those hitherto completely unknown, what might they have from which Spain might benefit?

---

[3] Roger B. Merriman, *The rise of the Spanish empire in the old world and the new*, IV, 400, says: "Measured by the extent of the territory over which he theoretically held sway, Philip was the most powerful monarch that the world has ever known." This statement might, of course, be considered in connection with the power and empire of Ghengis Khan.

Undoubtedly, the discovery was one of the great moments of the world. Just how important it was, the discoverer never knew—and he was not alone in his ignorance. It took long years to lay bare the geographical secrets of the western land mass and even of the islands near its coasts. Geographical fantasies were to be conceived and to persist for many years before the truth was established. The search for mythical straits and islands and locations was long continued, and map makers laid down with great regularity various geographical errors long after actual exploration had separated fancy from reality. It must ever be a question whether Columbus had any doubts that the continental land mass he saw and reached on his third and fourth voyages, and whose immensity he guessed dimly from the pathway in the sea made by the Orinoco, was Asia or some entirely new region, although he did call it "another world." Yet not until 1513 did Balboa, "silent upon a peak in Darien," behold, first of recorded Europeans, the Pacific, and not until 1520, did Magellan, a Portuguese sailing in Spanish service, pass through the strait that bears his name; although some years before either event, the name "America" had been given to a region in the southern continent and had been slowly extended to the whole Western Hemisphere.

II

Historians are accustomed frequently to speak of the three periods of discovery, conquest, and colonization in Spanish and Portuguese America as if they were three separate and distinct entities. The fact is, however, that the three processes were almost simultaneous and proceeded side by side to what has been called the end of the period of the conquest. When Columbus returned from his first voyage, he left a small nucleus for a colony in Isla Española (modern Hispaniola), and on his second voyage he took seventeen vessels and 1,500 people with the intention of forming a permanent colony; while on his third voyage he took 200 colonists. When Nicolás de Ovando went out to take possession of his government, he was accompanied by 2,500 persons, including 73 families. Diego Velázquez, who went to Cuba in 1511, explored, conquered, and colonized that island, and later, although he was deprived of the reward of his foresight, visualized the conquest of Mexico. Cortés, the greatest of all the *Conquistadores,* founded the city of Vera Cruz almost as soon as he reached the shores of the promised land. Francisco Pizarro, Pedro de Alvarado, the cruel Pedrarias, Benalcázar, Pedro de Valdivia, and others of the exploring *Conquistadores* established settlements. Asunción in Paraguay was founded before the surrounding territory had been conquered. In territory now a part of the United States, the lack of readily found treasure and other factors prevented the forming of settlements for many years. Narváez, Soto, and Coronado were conquerors only, although, had they found treasure and an easy conquest, they would perhaps have founded colonies. Luna y Arellano actually founded a settlement in what is now Alabama, but it failed. But there was a different tale in Florida where the great Asturian navigator, Pedro Menéndez de Avilés founded St. Augustine—the first permanent settlement in the lands north of the Rio Grande—almost as soon as he reached the northern mainland.

Of course, the early settlements were primarily military in character and were formed to act as bases for further conquest, or, as in the case of Florida, to forestall other nations and prevent them from reaching the rich colonies. But it is true that from the very first, Spain showed a desire to colonize. Its very title to the new lands, obtained from the pope in 1493, obliged it to colonize and evangelize as the price of conquest. Conquest and colonization were living forces existing side by side, and almost each new conquest was preceded and followed by exploration. It is true, however, as Roscher so sapiently remarks, that while the conquest was progressing, the government could do little more than to gradually develop its system of colonization and administration.[4]

Portugal, fully occupied with its Oriental colonies, did not evince the same eagerness in early years to colonize Brazil, their first recorded American discovery made in 1500. Its urge for colonization came only about 1525, when the Portuguese had to choose between taking real possession of Brazil or of abandoning it. Three facts, indeed, decided Portugal to take possession of this vast colony: the Spanish conquests and the riches of Spain's new colonies; various Spanish expeditions, including those of Solís and Magellan, the search for spices, and the discovery of the Pacific; and the presence of French vessels and pirates in American waters.[5] Before 1530 Portuguese attempts were but slight, being, indeed, little more than the occasional cutting of dyewood. By 1535, moreover, only twelve *capitaneas* had been created, each having a frontage of fifty or sixty leagues and an indeterminate depth, and each of which became a focus of settlement.[6] The mineral wealth of Brazil

---

[4] *The Spanish colonial system* (New York, 1904), 2. This is Bourne's translation.

[5] González de Repáraz, *Historia de la colonización*, 285-286.

[6] *Ibid.*, 287-288; and Chapman, *Colonial Hispanic America* (New York, 1933), 72 ff.

2

was slow in developing, so that the colonists did not have the same urge as the Spaniards to desert their settlements. They began, therefore, to cultivate the soil, and the early introduction of sugar cane into the colony determined in large measure that the form of the colony should be agricultural and commercial. The result was that although many of the same factors were found in Brazil as in the Spanish colonies, there were also great differences. The successful cultivation of sugar made necessary considerable slave labor. The same inroads were made on the Indians as in the Spanish colonies, but very early Portugal turned to the negro, with whom so much contact had already been had in Africa, and the negro slave trade became a powerful factor in Brazil.

Among early settlers in Brazil were many Jews who sought relief from religious persecution in Portugal; and in common with many of the early colonization practices, there were contingents of convicts. There was considerable absentee landlordism, and notwithstanding frequent friendly relations with the Indians each settler had to be ready to bear arms in case of hostilities. Nevertheless, as in the Orient, the Portuguese were chiefly interested in the trade aspects of their colony in America, while the Spaniards, on the other hand, were conquerors.

Turning now to early Spanish efforts, it will be seen that it was no fault of Columbus or Ovando that the colonists they brought, fired by an ancient lore, abandoned the colony and rushed off in quest for gold and other treasure. Rather was it the fault of human nature—a phenomenon that has been seen times innumerable. The quiet development of a stable colony and agricultural pursuits had little appeal to men who had either fought against and looted the Moor, or who had been reared in such an atmosphere. The gambler's chance of finding treasure ready at hand was more powerful than the forcing of the mind to the quiet tasks of development and the establishing of homes for the growth of a stable society. At a later period, the French *coureurs des bois* wandered off into the trackless forests of Canada and what is now northern United States, filled with the same restlessness of spirit that could not brook the idea of quiet development. It was the same desire for sudden wealth, the same dislike of hard work, that drove La Salle's men to mutiny in the Texas wilderness near the end of the seventeenth century. The same phenomena have appeared in the gold rushes of California, Australia, South Africa, the Klondike, and Alaska. The Spaniard was, moreover, by training and disposition, a gentleman adventurer.

Certainly, in their colonization, Spain and Portugal had little or no model to follow, nor overmuch experience to point the way. Colonies had been established, it is true, in the Canaries, the Madeiras, the Azores, and the Cape Verde Islands, but these islands were relatively near home and only moderately extensive. Each country had certain institutions and methods of administration that were naturally transplanted into the new lands, and from them, as was most natural, evolved new applications. This was the case also in the English colonies.

It was, after all, the accident of circumstances that determined at least one direction of the activities attending the conquest and colonization both of Spanish and Portuguese regions in America. The Spaniards found gold, silver, and other treasure; the Portuguese in the early days found little or none. Lured on by their early successes in Isla Española, relatively modest though they were, the Spaniards were eager in their search for easy wealth. Each new region seemed to their excited fancy a land of riches beyond compare. Mexico and Peru whetted their appetites. So the acquisition of treasure—at first wrested from the Indians who had won it from the soil, rivers, and mines, and later directly won from the mines, not through Spanish labor, but through that of the Indians—became the *sine qua non* of the conquest. It is proper to ask how long the English would have maintained stable settlements had they found gold and silver at their doorsteps or how scrupulous they would have been had they had Indians to impress. English corsairs and pirates were not averse to filching Spanish gold and other treasure when opportunity offered, nor was this looked at askance in England. Hope of riches led Narváez, Soto, and Coronado on their wonderful explorations, and it certainly was one of the considerations that moved the brilliant Valdivia.

Thus, the Spaniards sought wealth in many regions. The result was the penetration, exploration, and conquest of vast tracts of land. On the other hand, the Portuguese, confronted by what they thought to be a dearth of treasure, perforce settled down on the lands to a tamer sort of existence—that of tilling the soil. Rather stable settlements or settled regions were the result in various part of Brazil.

While the Spaniards made entrances or raids for gold and silver, the Portuguese made raids for slaves to work their plantations—a practice of which the Spaniards were also guilty on more than one occasion. The Spaniards were called *Conquistadores,* the Portuguese *Bandeirantes*—from their custom of carrying a banner *(bandeira)* in front of them when they went on their raids. The English colonists, who were not averse to working on the lands themselves and who, moreover, had indentured servants to mistreat and no great body of docile Indians, had a much more efficient and less troublesome method—they simply killed off the Indians when they got in the way; and Anglo-Americans followed in their footsteps. The story of the Spanish *Conquistador* has been told in English many times, but the latest and one of the best books is that of F. A. Kirkpatrick, *The Spanish Conquistadores* (London, 1934). The adequate history of the *Bandeirantes* in English is still to be written.

It was the accident of circumstances also that determined the treatment of the Indian both in the Spanish and in the Portuguese colonies. Columbus had not counted on the deeply moral nature of Isabella when he caught a number of Indians and took them as slaves to Spain, and he was doubtless extremely surprised when the queen ordered them released forthwith. Ferdinand was not so squeamish, and when he came into more exclusive control of affairs of state after Isabella's death, his policy was largely based on whether any certain action would affect his revenues adversely. The moral right of the Spaniards to enslave the Indians, first introduced by Isabella's condemnation of it, was discussed earnestly for many years. The problem of the Indian vexed Spain sorely. It led to much speculation—and the Spaniard has always been given to philosophical speculation—on the nature of the Indian, and the question of whether he possessed a soul was gravely discussed. If he had no soul, but was akin to the beasts and so possessed of no moral nature, why bother about him? If, on the other hand, he possessed a soul, then he had a moral nature and should be answerable for his conduct and should not be enslaved, although laws governing his conduct should be made. The Laws of Burgos of 1512 and their clarification of 1513 failed to define adequate stable and workable conditions governing the treatment of the Indian. Finally, that great defender of the Indian, Bartolomé de las Casas, won a signal victory in the enactment of the New Laws of 1542. His many years of earnest work, his thundering against the cruelties practiced on the Indians by the *Conquistadores*, his charges carried to the court of Spain itself, where he was pitted in his arguments against the great jurist, Ginés de Sepúlveda, his tracts written with all the precision of a lawyer's brief, especially the one entitled *Brief relation of the destruction of the indies* (published later in 1552), the earnestness of his single-track mind—all gained him his reward. But it was, after all, an empty reward, for the New Laws could not be put into practice against the clamor of public opinion, and in some regions no attempt was even made to carry them out lest the Spaniards mutiny. So they remained a dead letter.

Strangely enough, Casas, with his exaggeration and over-emphasis became in later days the chief argument and incentive for the Dutch, French, and English attacks on the Spaniards and their colonies. Perhaps he did, after all, as much harm as good.

The Indian problem continued. Before the law, the Indian was proclaimed to be the equal of the Spaniard, and many humane laws were framed. In reality, being the weaker part of society, he was treated as a minor to the last days of Spanish possession in America. He has had his revenge. His blood flows through perhaps a majority of the people of Hispanic America. There are many books that deal with this matter, both in Spanish and in English. The latest volume in English is that by Lewis Hanke, *The first social experiments in America,* which was published by the Harvard University Press in 1935.

Spain's promise (really an obligation) to furnish religious instruction to the heathen inhabitants of the New World was probably better kept than could or would have been the case with any other nation. This arose from the religious background of the Spanish people from the sovereign down, from the seven-century conflict with the Moor, from the hatred of heresy, and from a desire for solidarity of religious belief. It was all this that finally determined, in spite of all the cruelty of the conquest, in spite of the tribute and the *mita,* and in spite of all the other hardships visited on the Indian, the humane laws that were made, the restrictions laid on the *Conquistadores* and *encomenderos,* and the spread of Christianity over all the colonies. The mission annals are filled with the heroic and self-sacrificing deeds of the missionaries. These men, with unswerving loyalty, stood between the Indian and rapacious Spaniards. To them much was due. Although the evangelization was often only a veneer and is still so to this very day among the Indian populations—so strong is the persistence of religious belief—yet it did something to the native Indian. What matter though the ideal was that of parents toward minor children? Perhaps no other method would have worked. At any rate, the work of the missionaries, in spite of all its faults, stands out in bold relief. It is an honorable chapter in the colonial life of three centuries.

In Brazil there was no such urge as was manifested in the Spanish colonies. The Indian was exploited even more than by the Spaniards. He represented just so much good human material from which a labor supply could be drafted for work on the plantations; and it was only when the Indians became scarce and it was cheaper to import the more satisfactory negro slaves from Africa that raiding expeditions against the Indians tended to lessen. Jesuit missionaries strove to diminish the hard lot of the Indians and to teach them something of Christianity, and the Jesuits stood firmly against the exploitation of the Indian. Yet the mission movement in Brazil never attained a tenth of the importance it reached in the Spanish colonies.

A pleasing result of the mission movement, both in the Spanish and the Portuguese colonies, was, however, the compilation of grammars and vocabularies of the native languages and the translation into various Indian languages of the Christian doctrine, catechisms, prayers, and other things so that today these represent all we know of some of the languages. Various chronicles by missionaries in various regions are in some cases almost the only record known of certain Indians. On the historical and linguistic sides, as well as on the religious side, much is owed to the missionaries.

III

It is proper at this point to inquire about the methods of administration practiced in the New World. The possession of new lands overseas necessitated some method of administration if the new dominions were to be held. As knowledge of the real extent of the western Indies broadened by virtue of discovery, exploration, and conquest, and as new settlements were made, some evolution in the methods employed naturally occurred. In the case of Spain, that country was called on almost overnight to devise some sort of plan for the administration of new lands, the extent of which could not be estimated. Spain approached its task with a splendid daring and even enthusiasm that have few, if any, equals, and without shrinking; and in its deliberations there was at least a quasi maturity that one would not ordinarily have expected. It was an unusual situation. Spain itself was in the very process of formation politically. The country was by no means a well-correlated unit. A successful war had just been fought, and many home questions were awaiting solution. Yet here was this new country with a distant colony on its hands which might prove an asset or a liability. Spain took a chance.

The capitulations made with Columbus before his initial voyage were in the main what that astute person demanded. But his second voyage proved him to be a poor administrator, and the year following his ignominious return to Spain in 1499—an indignity placed on him by his successor, Bobadilla—he was deprived of all administrative powers, and these were never regained. It was probably Portuguese influence that induced him to produce a colony based on the African slave trade—a proposal which Isabella indignantly rejected, and which was not seriously broached again until Las Casas proposed negro slavery as a substitute for Indian slavery. However poor an administrator Columbus was, the New World is indebted to him for the first transference of seeds and animals to America—one of Spain's greatest gifts to the New World.[7]

Spain was not organized for expansion overseas. It had, perforce, to operate with what it had, or to adapt Spanish organisms to the new conditions. Ferdinand had visualized a trading colony, perhaps after the manner of the Portuguese colonies in the Orient, but this was when little was known of the New World and it was believed that it might be a part of Asia. Columbus reasoned correctly that there should be at least a certain amount of agriculture. The trouble was with the Spaniards themselves. The soldier disdained to work with his hands if he could get some one else to work for his support while he gave his attention to conquering the country, and the Spanish farmer only too often ran off to the mines, or became a soldier. The Spaniards were too independent to be controlled, and this trait has remained a chief characteristic of their descendants in Hispanic America to this day.

It was soon realized in Spain that there must be some sort of permanent home organization to despatch expeditions, receive incoming vessels, and attend to all the other business connected with the new venture. Juan de Fonseca, the Archdeacon of Seville, was able, with what help could be furnished him, to look after these matters in the time of Columbus. His office expanded into the House of Trade of the Indies *(Casa de Contratación de Indias)*, with headquarters in Seville, whence all expeditions were despatched until the silting of the Guadalquivir River and the increased size of ships forced vessels to clear from and enter into Cádiz. This organization, modeled more or less on the Portuguese House of Trade, became very important and had considerable influence, both political and economic. Not only did it have charge of shipping, but as well of charts and maps, of *derreteros* or logs, of ship's instruments, and many other activities. The chief pilot was stationed here, and one branch was really a school for pilots. The *casa* was ordered, among its various other duties, to lay down a model chart for navigators, which was never to leave the offices, but of which copies were to be made

[7] See Robertson, "Some notes on the transfer by Spain of plants and animals to its colonies overseas" in *The James Sprunt Historical Studies*, XIX, No. 2 (Chapel Hill, 1927), 7-21.

for Spanish navigators. Extra care was taken that such charts should not fall into the hands of foreigners, so fearful were the Spanish monarchs lest the secrets of the Indies be known. It was this that led the Catholic Kings to throw all sorts of restrictions about their American colonies in order that they might be kept one hundred per cent Spanish. The liberal laws or inclinations of Charles V were forgotten by succeeding monarchs. Among other duties, the *Casa de Contratación* had to administer the trading laws, it had to see that no persons considered dangerous or subversive entered the colonies, and it had to see that the king duly received his fifth on gold and other treasure. It was in reality a colonial office.

The House of Trade and the other home organization, the Council of the Indies *(Consejo de Indias)*—the nucleus of which first appeared in 1511, and which was primarily organized to consult over and advise the sovereign with respect to proposed legislation, and so forth, for the Americas—were the principal entities in Spain concerned with the colonies. For the colonies themselves, administrational forms already familiar in Spain were simply transferred to the new lands. Thus, the *cabildo* became the organ for municipal government, and as new settlements were founded, boards of aldermen and their presidents were appointed. The *cabildo* in Spain, at the time of the colonization in America, had already lost much of its traditional power and importance because of the aggressive policy of the crown. Notwithstanding this, its transfer to the Indies provided a governing element that retained certain of the principles of democracy which were not without effect when the time came for independence. Columbus appointed such a body at the founding of Santo Domingo; the first action Cortés took when he founded Vera Cruz was the appointment of a *cabildo;* and the same procedure was followed in all newly created settlements, even in the Philippines.

Leaders of expeditions of discovery, exploration, and conquest, to whom royal patents were granted, were usually given the title of governor and captain-general of the territory discovered and conquered, and often the title of *adelantado*. Their patents carefully set forth the conditions of the conquests and the rewards. Frequently, the royal fifth was reduced or excused entirely for a certain definite period. In case of success, the reward and profit might be of moment. Failure meant loss, for leaders generally conducted expeditions at their own expense. From the successful ventures colonies usually arose.

By the transfer of the *audiencia,* or high court, to its colonies, the

Spanish monarch, always fearful lest his officials, especially those at such a distance as the Indies, acquire too great power, provided a check, often salutary, on his governors and viceroys. Possessing administrative and legislative, as well as judicial, power, this tribunal often served its purpose admirably, but as the records abundantly show it was not always an unmixed blessing. The same was true of the *residencia,* or official inquisition, which each governor and viceroy had to undergo at the end of his term.

By the inauguration in 1529 of viceregal government in Spanish America (although Mendoza, the first appointee, did not actually assume office until 1535), Spain attempted to institute in the colonies the same absolutism as in Spain itself. Notwithstanding, however, that the viceroy was the direct representative of the monarch, the same degree of absolutism that existed in Spain could not be reached in America. Distance from the court, the immense size of the New World, and various developing factors which gave a new outlook on life, prevented the complete realization of the king's intentions. As an administrational policy, the appointment of viceroys in the American colonies was a move of great significance. It meant, with its almost immediate extension from New Spain to Peru, the gradual cessation of the civil wars of various *Conquistadores.* It meant the orderly development of Spanish authority. By bringing to the colonies the formalism and ostentation of the Spanish court, it provided, among other things, that psychological factor for which most governments strive—a factor which had thitherto been lacking. It meant ultimate authority, and the viceroy occupied the pinnacle of colonial government.

Official life in the colonies was vitiated by the purchase and sale of public posts, both municipal and provincial, at public auction to the highest bidder. This led not only to inefficiency but also to petty and major peculation and graft. The effect on municipal and provincial administration can well be imagined.

The possession by the Spanish monarch of the right of the royal patronage *(patronato real)* gave him considerable power in ecclesiastical affairs in the colonies. The concordat between himself and the pope transferred to him certain attributes normally residing in the vicar of Christ. The king was thus authorized to appoint to all ecclesiastical positions in the colonies up to archbishops. The tithes collected from the faithful were paid, not directly to the church but to the king, who could dispose of them as he pleased, although they were supposed to be used for ecclesiastical purposes. He also received the proceeds from the sale of the bulls of the crusade, which amounted annually to a large sum. So complete was the control of the king in the ecclesiastical realm that no religious could go to America without his permission or order, and, conversely, no one could return except by his authority. In reality, the Spanish church was in some ways little short of a national church. It might easily be argued that the general result was to make more *pro forma* an ecclesiastical system already in many ways formal. Yet the connection between church and state was so close that one could scarcely tell where one ended and the other began. After the acquisition of independence by the Spanish colonies, the *patronato real* became a matter for serious discussion between the papacy and several of the new states.

From the very beginning of its colonization, Spain, induced thereto by its conflict with the Moor, its fear of the Jews within its borders, and its hatred of heresy—mixed political and religious factors—insisted on purity of blood *(limpieza de sangre)* in all emigrants to the New World. New Christians *(nuevos cristianos)*, that is, newly baptized Moors or Jews, were debarred and the taint of blood was extended to two generations. It is vastly to the credit of Spain that when the Inquisition was introduced into the colonies, the Indians were especially exempted from its jurisdiction. Perhaps because of the insistence on *limpieza de sangre* in emigrants, the rôle of that tribunal in the New World was comparatively small.

How colonists were to live was early considered. In 1497 appeared the germ of the later homestead of the United States, and under Columbus, Bobadilla, and Ovando came the beginning and early development of the *repartimiento* system and its successor, the *encomienda* system.[8] The *encomienda* was a peculiar reward granted to a *Conquistador,* and certain injunctions, including the providing of religious instruction to the Indians, were prescribed by special laws. Human nature being what it is, one need not wonder that the laws governing the system were more often than not evaded or simply ignored. In the United States we are too close to the eighteenth amendment to our own Constitution to be surprised at the evasion of basic laws which may be unpopular. Later chapters in this volume will explain the *repartimiento* and *encomienda* in sufficient fullness and nothing more need be said of them here. Suffice it to say that the *encomendero,* as a constituent part of the population, occupied an important position in the country.

---

[8] See Lesley B. Simpson, *The encomienda in New Spain* (Berkeley, 1929), and José María Ots, *Instituciones sociales de la América española en el período colonial* (La Plata, 1934), chapter I.

As the Spaniards succeeded in their conquests and in the founding of colonies, a *mestizo* population came into existence. Comparatively few Spanish women came to the colonies in the early days, and the union of Spanish soldiers and colonists with Indian women was encouraged. From all-white families, the Creole population of the Indies began to develop, and both the *mestizo* and Creole elements in the population were to became important factors as the independence struggle neared, both because, and in spite, of Spain's characteristic policy of "divide and rule." With the introduction of negro slavery into the colonies, many other degrees of mixture began to appear in the population, the results of which can be easily detected in the modern inhabitants of some of the states developed from the former colonies. Populations, their growth or increase, the diseases affecting them, the economic, cultural, and other factors involved, are matters to which special attention should be devoted. Emeterio S. Santovenia, writing of the colonization of Cuba, but whose observation can be extended to all of Spanish America, remarks that "the human material constituted by the colonizers was heterogeneous." [9]

Trade between Spain and its colonies, the restrictions with which it was hedged about, the trading and treasure fleets, the fairs, the monopolies, the trading companies, and other trade factors can be no more than mentioned. These will all be discussed in later chapters. The same is true of education and general culture, and the formation of society. But as an introduction to the economic aspects of Spanish colonization, one should read carefully Haring's *Trade and navigation between Spain and the indies in the time of the Hapsburgs* (Cambridge, 1918), and Hamilton's *American treasure and the price revolution in Spain, 1501-1560* (Cambridge, 1934).

IV

Turning now to colonization in Brazil, it will be evident that that colony exhibited in its development many factors similar to those found in the neighboring Spanish colonies; but in certain aspects, on the contrary, it showed wide divergence. There existed, in general, the same trade restriction, economic short-sightedness, and monopolistic tendencies. But Brazil was not free from foreign attempts to colonize until after the middle of the seventeenth century, although the first governor-general, Thomé de Sousa, had been appointed in 1549. Colonization

---

[9] "La colonización de Cuba—organización institucional" in *Revista Cubana,* Havana, I, no. 1 (January, 1935), 14.

passed through the three phases of agriculture, stockraising, and mining, but the comparatively late discovery of precious metals and diamonds, and the profitable cultivation of the sugar cane, gave a certain trend to the colony that made for stable growth. There was no proscription of Jews and no test for purity of blood. Heresy seems not to have been feared.

When the exploitation of native peoples failed to furnish sufficient labor, Portugal turned to negro labor, and until almost the eve of emancipation the importation of negro slaves was of the highest importance. Indeed, as has been often remarked, without the importation of slaves, Brazil could not have existed. Miscegenation of the Portuguese with the Indians formed a new element in society called Mamelukes, who in their turn were active in making raids. After the arrival of negroes, miscegenation between them and the Portuguese, the Indians, and the Mamelukes was common.

The country was colonized in various regions in quite separate fashions, which is still visible today. Any cruelty toward the Indians as exhibited in the Spanish colonies can be matched with equal cruelties in Brazil. But because there were no discoveries of gold and other treasure in the early days, the colonization proceeded along solid lines in which success was the result of hard and continuous work.

The conquest and colonization of Brazil cannot compare in brilliancy with those of Spanish America. The results in Brazil, owing to the steady, quiet persistence of the colonizers, have been solid and even stupendous, and bear comparison with the results attained in the Spanish colonies. Only of late years have students in the United States begun to study the conquest and colonization of Brazil with anything like the care they have given to the Spanish colonies, owing among other things to the language barrier. This is now changing, and the next decade bids fair to extend our knowledge materially. Many monographs and careful studies are necessary before it can be said that we have anything like an adequate knowledge of Brazil's past as a colony. There is need of another Bourne who can write for us an acceptable volume on "Portugal in America." The significance of Hispanic American colonial history is to be found in the present countries that have been formed out of the old colonies. But that significance will be further unrolled in the following chapters which discuss backgrounds, conquest and settlement, government, the church and other institutions, society, intellectual life, international relations, and the revolutionary era, out of which developed the present Hispanic American states.

CHAPTER TWO

GEOGRAPHICAL BACKGROUND OF THE COLONIAL PERIOD IN CARIBBEAN AMERICA

By CLARENCE F. JONES

CARIBBEAN America embraces Mexico, the Central American states, the Greater Antilles, the Lesser Antilles, and Colombia and Venezuela. In this discussion, however, Colombia and Venezuela will be omitted. Caribbean America thus delineated includes an area of approximately 1,055,500 square miles. This is only one-seventh of the area of the vast continent of South America. But the much smaller area in the tapering southern portion of North America and the island-dotted fringe of the northern and eastern margins of the Caribbean Sea present just as striking geographical contrasts as the continental expanse of South America. Furthermore, the significance of the area cannot be measured fully in terms of land area, for the placid blue waters of the Caribbean Sea and the Gulf of Mexico constituted theatres of far greater activity than some sections of the mainland. From the reef fringed shores of Barbados to the rugged coast of Lower California the region covers nearly sixty degrees of longitude. It extends from temperate northern Mexico in thirty-two degrees north latitude to the tropical shores of southern Panama in seven degrees north latitude.

I. LOCATION AND COMMERCIAL ROUTES

The location of Caribbean America gave it a combination of conditions that set the stage for significant precolonial developments and made it an important theatre throughout the colonial period. In colonial times the control of the Caribbean gave access to the gold, silver, and glory of not only the Caribbean Sea area but also southern North America and western South America.

The location of the region in the path of the north equatorial current and the northeast trades was a big factor in bringing Columbus and his followers to its shores. Though he did not realize it, Columbus on his first voyage really made three great discoveries. They were (1) the New World, (2) the best route for sailing vessels from Europe to the West Indies, North America, and nothern South America, and (3) the best route for sailing vessels from the West Indies and North America

[17]

to Europe.[1] Thus he blocked out in the North Atlantic the routes that were to become the chief paths of commerce for centuries. Within the Caribbean and the Gulf of Mexico, the currents and the winds favored early exploration of all the shores. Within thirty years of Columbus' first voyage most of the islands and shores of the Caribbean and Gulf were fairly well charted. Only short voyages led the Spaniards from the Greater Antilles to the mainland. The southern portion of North America being narrow soon led to the discovery of the Pacific and to the development of important transcontinental or isthmian routes.

The establishment of commercial routes in Caribbean America shows striking relationships to the location and shape of lands and seas of the area. Nearly all of the colonial traffic of Spain was focussed on, or went through, the Caribbean. Even after the discovery and settlement of Peru, Chile, Paraguay, and Argentina, the motherland compelled all shipments to and from these lands to go via Panama and the Caribbean. Although eastern Argentina faced the Atlantic, Spain compelled her subjects to make the long haul over the plains, mountains, and deserts of the Andes, thence north along the west coast of the continent[2] to two great isthmian routes: the San Juan-Atrato River route across northern Colombia and the Old Gold Road across Panama from Old Panama to Puerto Bello. The trade moved in this direction because of several conditions. The cold stormy waters of the South Atlantic and South Pacific restricted the use of the Cape Horn route, and the South Atlantic for a long time was really a Portuguese sea because of their control of Brazil and the Cape of Good Hope route to the Indies. During the rainy season the San Juan-Atrato route was practically an all-water route, only a short portage being necessary. The route across Panama was short, and the Old Gold Road was paved with stones and logs. Thus, in spite of the heat, humidity, insects, and diseases, these routes across the isthmus were preferred in getting precious cargo from the Pacific to the Atlantic.

Another great line of trade, the trans-Pacific trade with the East Indies, was developed over the trade wind route across the Pacific and

---

[1] E. C. Semple and C. F. Jones, *American history and its geographic conditions*, 10.

[2] In the first settlements in eastern Argentina established without direct order from the crown, trade directly to Spain was prohibited by the ban of 1599 under penalty of death and forfeiture of property. Only through Lima and Panama could settlers lawfully communicate with Spain. See *Documentos para la historia argentina*, Buenos Aires, 1915, *Tomo* V, "Comercio de Indias" (1713-78), 41-48; Clarence F. Jones, *South America*, 305-307.

by the use of the westerlies on the return voyage to the shores of southern California and Mexico. This trade, which flourished for more than a century, moved across the continent on three routes: from Acapulco on the west coast of Mexico to Mexico City and Vera Cruz, across Nicaragua by way of the lakes and the San Juan River, and from Old Panama to Puerto Bello on the Old Gold Road.

On the Atlantic side several strategic points and significant routes developed. Vera Cruz, the Bay of Honduras, Puerto Bello, Cartagena, Santa Marta, and La Guaria all became important outlets for trade from the Pacific or the mainland. Ships leaving these points moved to strategic points in the Greater Antilles, like Havana, Port-au-Prince, San Juan, or St. Thomas. After being placed under the protection of convoys, the cargo ships, laden to their water line with silver, spices, dyewoods and hides, moved to Europe by way of the route of the westerlies. Thus most of Spain's trade with her colonies entered and left the Americas through the Caribbean area. Consequently, it actually became the key to the colonial empire of Spain.

The physical conditions of this region played a vital part in directing the course of events during precolonial and colonial times. The relief, rainfall, temperature, winds, plant life, animal life, and the mineral resources affected in many ways the advance of the Indians, the Europeans, and the negroes. In the islands and the hot humid plains of Central America the seminomadic Indians had not advanced beyond the archaic stage of culture. In the subtropical to temperate highlands of Mexico and Central America the Indians had become sedentary, had developed agriculture, irrigation, metal working, and manufacturing, and had attained a high degree of culture. During colonial times these contrasted areas played very different rôles. Though the human element in those areas certainly may have been an important factor, the material and cultural advance of the regions depended to a large extent upon the combination of physical conditions.

II. Physical Conditions and Responses in the Islands and Humid Lowlands

For convenience in analyzing the environmental conditions and responses in these two contrasted types of areas, one may discuss the latter type in three divisions: the Lesser Antilles, the Greater Antilles, and the Caribbean lowlands of Central America.

The Lesser Antilles. The Lesser Antilles stretch in a broad arc from the Dutch West Indies off the north coast of Venezuela to the Virgin

Islands east of Puerto Rico. In this arc of more than twelve hundred miles lie more than a dozen significant islands and numerous islets that are simply dots in a vast sea of turquoise blue. Excepting Trinidad, only Guadeloupe embraces more than five hundred square miles. All the major islands, with the exception of Trinidad, Barbados, Curaçao, and the eastern half of Guadeloupe, are the tops of old volcanoes. Some are surrounded by coral reefs, while most of the smaller islands and the exceptions noted above are coral limestone. The rugged relief of most of the volcanic islands rises abruptly from the sea to elevations of 3,000 to 5,000 feet.[3] Most of these lands are in steep mountain slopes; only in a few places have even small plains areas been built up by streams washing down the steep mountain valleys. All these islands are tropical. Even the higher elevations only slightly alleviate the enervating effects of constantly high temperatures.[4] On the other hand, the refreshing trade winds, coming over the near-by waters, make them infinitely more comfortable places in which to live than are the vast interior lowlands of South America. These same winds and convection bring to the high and larger islands a heavy precipitation, but the low and smaller islands are dry.[5] In the rugged islands the windward sides or the higher parts receive much more rain than the leeward side or lower portions. In general, the windward sides lack a dry season, whereas the leeward sides

---

[3] Soufrière in Guadeloupe rises to 4,869 feet above sea level; Mt. Diablotin in Dominica 4,740 feet; Mt. Pelé in Martinique 4,430 feet; Soufrière in St. Lucia about 4,000 feet; and Mt. St. Catherine in Grenada 2,749 feet.

[4] The following table shows especially well the temperatures characteristic of those islands; figures are mean monthly temperatures:

Station	Jan.	Feb.	Mar.	Apr.	May	June	July	Aug.	Sept.	Oct.	Nov.	Dec.	Annual
Kingstown, St. Vincent	77.0	77.3	77.0	78.5	79.2	79.7	80.1	80.8	81.0	80.1	79.2	77.8	79.0
Bridgetown, Barbados	76.3	76.5	77.0	78.4	80.0	80.3	80.0	80.0	79.8	79.3	78.6	77.2	78.6
Castries, St. Lucia	75.6	75.8	77.0	78.1	79.8	80.4	80.4	80.6	80.6	79.6	78.6	77.0	78.6
Camp Jacob, Guadeloupe	69.4	68.8	69.4	71.6	73.3	73.8	74.0	74.8	74.6	73.8	72.2	70.4	72.2

The highest temperature recorded at Kingstown was 91° F. and the lowest 64° F.

[5] Mean monthly rainfall:

Station	Jan.	Feb.	Mar.	Apr.	May	June	July	Aug.	Sept.	Oct.	Nov.	Dec.	Annual
Kingstown, St. Vincent	5.42	4.00	3.59	4.08	4.52	8.68	9.42	10.68	10.06	11.97	12.60	5.78	90.80
Bridgetown, Barbados	2.06	1.70	1.64	1.67	1.82	4.36	4.84	6.81	6.60	6.03	4.58	3.47	45.58
Castries, St. Lucia	5.68	3.89	4.12	4.01	6.88	8.98	9.73	10.45	9.73	10.28	9.29	7.96	91.00
Camp Jacob, Guadeloupe	9.49	6.73	7.48	7.99	15.39	14.17	20.20	16.73	17.09	14.61	16.50	9.84	156.22
Celcour, Guadeloupe	4.07	2.56	2.96	3.03	4.22	4.62	5.43	6.37	6.27	6.42	6.20	4.57	56.72

may have a distinct dry season,[6] which favors the ripening and harvesting of several tropical crops. Most of these islands lie in the zone of West Indian hurricanes which do a tremendous amount of damage to crops, roads, homes, and shipping whenever they strike. All the people live in fear of them. In response to the relief, temperatures, and heavy precipitation evenly distributed throughout the year, the high parts of all the islands and the rainy lower slopes support a dense tropical rain forest. The small and low dry islands are almost treeless and support only a thorn forest or savanna type of vegetation. Also the dry islands, in contrast to most of the arid parts of the mainland, lack even meager supplies of water for irrigation.

These physical conditions set the stage for a rather backward existence of the native population. At the time of their discovery most of the large islands and many of the smaller ones were inhabited by small groups of Arawak and Carib Indians, chiefly Caribs, who had not advanced beyond the hunter-and-fisher stage of culture. Although the islands offered havens for small groups, a single semi-sedentary group could easily be dispersed and driven onto the sea or back into the deep forested valleys.

These people practiced little or no agriculture. On the rainy islands the preparation of the soil is difficult. The heavy red clays are hard to work. Giant trees have to be felled, and fast growing bushes kept down by organized effort. The hillsides cleared of the forests erode rapidly. Furthermore, the early people lived on what they could gather. These areas had a variety of products that could be utilized. Among them are the tubers, the manioc, *malanga,* and sweet potatoes. Among the food products from trees are the alligator pear, the soursap, the sweetsap, the *chirimoya,* the star apple, the *níspero,* the mammey apple, Barbados cherry or nance, the *guava,* the *jocote,* and others.[7] The islands lacked

---

[6] Woodford Hill and Batalie illustrate the rainfall of a windward station and a leeward station (both at low altitudes) in the island of Dominica. Figures are for mean monthly rainfall:

Station	Jan.	Feb.	Mar.	Apr.	May	June	July	Aug.	Sept.	Oct.	Nov.	Dec.	Annual
Woodford Hill	7.58	4.40	3.08	6.19	9.40	10.14	9.63	9.86	9.80	11.53	10.98	9.36	103.44
Batalie	2.08	1.75	2.40	1.09	7.80	8.20	9.43	7.38	8.35	7.21	8.31	5.92	69.92

The rainfall at the following two stations on the southwestern side of Basse Terre, Guadeloupe illustrates the effect of altitude. Bologne is on the coast and Camp Jacob is at 1,750 feet elevation. Figures are for mean monthly rainfall:

Station	Jan.	Feb.	Mar.	Apr.	May	June	July	Aug.	Sept.	Oct.	Nov.	Dec.	Annual
Bologne	2.24	2.17	2.63	1.67	2.72	6.09	5.39	6.86	6.83	4.88	5.03	2.55	49.06
Camp Jacob	9.49	6.73	7.48	7.99	15.39	14.17	20.20	16.73	17.09	14.61	16.50	9.84	156.22

[7] H. J. Spinden, "The origin and distribution of agriculture in America," *Proceedings of the International Congress of Americanists,* (1917), 275.

large animals that could be used for food,[8] but fowl and fish, both of which are abundant, were fairly easily taken with bow and arrow and other means. The forests also supplied logs for dugout canoes that afforded the only means of moving from island to island, bark woven shirts and trousers, brush shelters, and blowpipes and clubs used in waging tribal warfare. Though stones were abundant and were used for simple artifacts, the Indians did not build any bridges, buildings, or temples. Also, in all the volcanic and coral islands no gold, silver, or other minerals, useful to early peoples, are present. The debilitating and enervating climate, and diseases and pests added to the difficulties of maintaining life even at a low stage of culture. Food could not be kept long so that the people had to be almost constantly employed in obtaining food. Also the outbreak of plagues and the scarcity of food at certain periods in the year caused frequent migrations of family groups and tribes.

With the advent of the Spaniards, the human element in the Lesser Antilles changed rapidly. After establishing themselves in the Greater Antilles, the Spaniards made frequent raids on the smaller islands for Indians to work in the fields and in the mines. Not being accustomed to the hard labor imposed upon them, and subject to the many diseases of the region, the Indians died by the thousands. The small area of the islands made the capture of the coastal-dwelling Caribs relatively easy. Fifty years from the time of Columbus' first landfall the Indian populations of most of the Lesser Antilles had almost entirely disappeared. None of the Lesser Antilles was settled permanently in the sixteenth century. These small detached areas without gold, silver, and sedentary populations held little of value for the Spaniards during the first century of Spanish activity in America. But it was during the latter part of the sixteenth century that stories reached England of the valuable treasures moving out of the Greater Antilles and the mainland to Spain. Then pirates and buccaneers of England, France, and Holland began to prey upon the treasure laden ships. For the work of these daring sea robbers the protected harbors of some of the Lesser Antilles made ideal havens of safety, whence they could pounce upon cargo ships and into which they could scurry when chased by Spanish vessels.

In the colonizing period of the seventeenth and eighteenth centuries the Lesser Antilles held a great attraction for the Europeans in search

---

[8] A species of *Agouti*, found in St. Vincent, St. Lucia, and other islands of the Lesser Antilles, is the largest native mammal of the group.

of sugar colonies. The drier islands and the less rainy portions of the others were in many respects almost ideal for sugar culture. Also the wind-swept drier islands were less ridden with mosquitoes and other insects and diseases that played havoc with many early attempts at colonization. The English[9] established a colony in St. Christopher in 1623 and one in Barbados in 1624-1625; the French established a colony in St. Christopher in 1625. The Dutch established colonies in St. Eustatius and Curaçao between 1632 and 1634. The Lesser Antilles received settlements from every colonizing power of that period. At the conclusion of each war, the powers usually exchanged a few islands. The great esteem in which these islands were held is shown by the difficulty that Benjamin Franklin had in persuading the British to take Canada instead of Guadeloupe[10] in 1763 at the end of the Seven Years War and by the fact that New York was traded for Dutch Guiana. In this period the wealth of these islands was their trade in sugar, rum, and slaves. Also, they served as bases for operations farther afield. But the small size, scattered nature, and lack of a variety of resources of the Lesser Antilles restricted the rôle they could play during the colonial period.

The Greater Antilles. The different rôle played by the Greater Antilles grew out of their location, larger area, contrasted physical conditions, and greater resources.

The Greater Antilles, embracing Cuba, Jamaica, Hispaniola, and Puerto Rico, have an area of 81,500 square miles,[11] an area more than ten times that of all the Lesser Antilles combined, and an area only slightly larger than that of Great Britain. These islands have rugged mountain interiors of crystalline and plutonic rocks of granite, porphyry, and basalt, all much older than the eruptive rocks of the Lesser Antilles and nowhere showing traces of craters or recent volcanic activity. The older rocks, richer in minerals than the volcanic rocks and coral formations of the Lesser Antilles, stand at heights of 7,870 and 7,380 feet in Cuba and Jamaica, 10,300 feet in Hispaniola, and nearly 4,000 feet in Puerto Rico. They are flanked by rolling hills and level plains of white limestone which is so widely distributed in all the islands.

---

[9] All the British Leeward Islands, except Dominica (1761), were settled between 1623 and 1650; the Windward Islands were conquered between 1762 and 1803 by the British. See F. W. Pitman, *The development of the British West Indies,* opposite page 1.

[10] Pitman, 345-356.

[11] Cuba has an area of 44,160 square miles, Jamaica 4,450, Hispaniola 29,530, and Puerto Rico 3,435.

Though always warm, the islands are refreshed by the strong trade winds, and the temperatures of the winter months are distinctly lower than those of August and September. The large area, the high mountains, and the strong trade winds give distinct windward and leeward sides to the islands. This gives great contrasts in rainfall in short distances. In general, the windward sides, cloud-bathed and frequently showered upon, are damp and dripping. The leeward sides are bright with sunshine and very dry. While these islands have dry and wet seasons, on the windward sides the dry season is really not dry but only less wet, but the leeward sides have a pronounced dry season.[12] This is especially true in Puerto Rico and Jamaica, but less well marked in central Cuba where the mountain backbone is not so high. These climatic changes from season to season and the contrasts tend to alleviate the enervating effects of high temperatures and high humidity of a tropical location.

The rainy and dry seasons, differences in altitude that affect the temperatures and the amount of rainfall, and the differences in rocks and soils, combine to make contrasts in plant life. On the windward slopes with continuous rains are tropical rain forests. In areas with a short rainy season and a long dry season there are scattered trees and thickets of thorn forest almost impossible to penetrate. Over the broad limestone plains with a long rainy season and a marked dry season are broad savannas interspersed here and there with scattered solitary palms and clumps of other trees. All the Greater Antilles have considerable expanses of these three major types of vegetation.

While the indigenous fauna of the Greater Antilles is poor compared to the neighboring mainland, it is somewhat richer than that of the Lesser Antilles. There were no monkeys, jaguars, pumas, tigers, wild dogs, sloths, ant-eaters, or armadillos. The *iguana,* native to the Greater Antilles, has been used for food from early times. Nearly one hundred and eighty distinct kinds of birds are peculiar to the Greater Antilles. Fish and turtles abound in the coastal waters.

With this physical setting as a background, the native Indians had not advanced to a high stage of material and intellectual culture, but they were in many respects superior to the Indian groups of the Lesser Antilles. The Arawaks, known by different tribal names in different

---

[12] Mean monthly precipitation:

Station	Jan.	Feb.	Mar.	Apr.	May	June	July	Aug.	Sept.	Oct.	Nov.	Dec.	Annual
San Juan	4.15	2.71	2.98	4.10	5.28	5.31	5.68	5.99	6.20	5.58	6.86	5.80	60.64
Ponce	1.03	0.97	1.42	2.14	2.91	3.85	2.89	4.19	4.92	6.72	3.47	1.36	35.83

islands, constituted the dominant Indian tribe, but the Caribs, rather late invaders from South America, settled in coastal locations and by their frequent raids made life miserable for the other Indians. The Arawaks practiced agriculture in a crude fashion, making use of manioc, *malanga,* corn, beans, squashes, tobacco, cotton in some places, and many fruits from the forest trees. They developed weaving, made pottery, hewed dugouts, and fashioned bows and arrows. They made simple artifacts from stones and wood, but they did not erect huge stone structures and they made little use of the minerals, found especially in Hispaniola and to a smaller extent in Puerto Rico and Cuba.

The first permanent settlement by the Spaniards at Isabella in northern Española (Hispaniola) in December 1493 marked the beginning of the important part the Greater Antilles were to play during colonial times. On his first voyage, Columbus learned the difficulty of obtaining provisions from the Indians because of their hostile nature and because the regions were notably poor in food plants and domesticable animals. Consequently, in planning his second voyage and the establishment of a colony, he brought horses, cattle, sheep, goats, pigs, chickens, seeds of vegetables, oranges, lemons, melons, rice, and even sugar cane.[13] Thus he introduced two important aids to advancing culture—domestic animals and a greater variety of food plants. These laid the foundation for the utilization of the broad savannas and fertile soil areas of the Greater Antilles since all the early settlements in the Greater Antilles had stockraising and agriculture as basic activities. From the islands these animals and food plants were soon taken to the mainland.

At this first settlement the Spaniards learned something of the debiliating effects of the hot, humid climate and of insect pests and diseases that were to take a tremendous toll of nearly every early expedition to Caribbean America. Within a month from the founding of the settlement there was hardly a well man among the hundreds of colonists of the expedition; not even Columbus escaped.[14] Also, within a month after settlement placer gold was discovered in the gold-bearing streams of the interior. The spread of the news of the discovery of gold stimulated interest in the New World as nothing else could have done. The Europeans were not fitted for the hard labor in the gold washings. The Indians were as little adapted to continuous strenuous effort in the hot humid tropics as the Spaniards, but the Indians were enslaved and put

---

[13] E. G. Bourne, *Spain in America,* 35-37.

[14] Las Casas, *Historia de las indias,* II, 21-22.

to hard work.[15]   The gold washings were in the rugged interior and away from the sweep of the refreshing trade winds, a characteristic feature of the native coastal habitat of the Arawaks and Caribs. The mining districts had enervating heat, high humidity, heavy precipitation, insect pests, and tropical diseases. Unaccustomed to strenuous work, subjected to long hours of toil and cruel treatment, and poorly fed, the Indians perished very rapidly or fled to the innermost recesses of the highland forests. The Spaniards raided all the Caribbean islands and even the mainland to replenish the fast disappearing native population of the Greater Antilles. It is estimated that the Indian population of Hispaniola, in spite of repeated importations, declined from sixty thousands in 1507 to five thousand in 1548.[16] To replace the declining native population, negroes were imported. The first slaves arrived from the Gold Coast of Africa as early as 1501.[17] In 1510, two hundred and fifty were brought in. Importation of slaves increased rapidly. Later the cultivation of sugar and other crops became the basis for the greatest traffic in human souls the world has ever known.[18]

Once established in the Greater Antilles, it was inevitable that the Spaniards would soon attempt the conquest of the mainland. Long narrow Cuba points like a finger across the narrow passage to the shores of Yucatan and Central America. Lured by the desire to discover the spice islands and by the fantastic tales of gold and great empires that reached the Spaniards in the Greater Antilles, they were willingly wafted by the currents and winds toward the west. The Greater Antilles be-

---

[15] John Fiske, *The discovery of America*, II, 440-450.

[16] Sir Spencer St. John, *Haiti or the black republic* (1889), 30; Otto Schoenrich, *Santo Domingo* (1918), 20.

[17] Fiske, II, 457.

[18] The Spaniards got their first negro slaves from the Portuguese; the slave trade was formally legalized by 1518. Later they brought many themselves and obtained more from the Portuguese, pirate traders of all nations, and the organized slave trading companies of Portugal, Holland, and England. Sir John Hawkins' celebrated voyage took place in 1562, but probably not until 1631 did a regular chartered English company undertake to carry on the trade. "In the twenty years from 1713 to 1733 fifteen thousand slaves were annually imported into America by the English, of whom from one-third to one-half went to the Spanish Colonies." See W. E. B. Du Bois, *The suppression of the African slave-trade to the United States of America* (1904), 2. Between 1680 and 1786 the total importation of slaves into all the British American colonies has been estimated at 2,130,000, or an annual average of 20,095. See Bryan Edwards, *History of the British colonies in the West Indies*, Book II, page 65. Between 1702 and 1775 inclusive, Jamaica imported annually 6,725 slaves and exported 1,853. See Pitman, 79, 391-392. Between 1708-1767 Barbados received 3,000 annually, and between 1720 and 1755 the Leeward Islands received 2,680 annually.

came the center of colonial activity. From Cuba, Hispaniola, and Puerto
Rico expeditions were sent out in all directions to explore new territories and conquer empires. Because of early settlement,[19] large areas
of savannas and forests, and early developed agriculture, the Greater
Antilles had the resources, provisions, and man power for outfitting
these expeditions.[20] For the first half of the sixteenth century they
were the focal points through which passed the flower of Spain, bearing
the Old World culture to the utmost corners of the colonial empire. For
a much longer period they served as the gathering points for the Spanish
galleons from northern South America, Central America, and Mexico;
they served as the points for the organization of the convoys of the
treasure laden ships en route to Spain via the route of the westerlies;
they became rendezvous and especially fertile fields for the activities of
the gold-and-blood-thirsty buccaneers and pirates; they became important focii (especially Jamaica) for the African slave trade; and
later they became the most important Spanish, English, and French
sugar colonies. Thus, the Greater Antilles played a much greater rôle
in early colonial times than the Lesser Antilles and even the eastern
lowlands of Central America and Mexico.

The Eastern Lowlands of Central America and Mexico. In many
respects the eastern lowlands of Central America and Mexico are less
favorable for human settlement and advance than even the Lesser
Antilles. Like the vast Amazonian lowland, these plains do not have a
single one of the factors that have favored the advance of primitive
peoples and of settlement in colonial and modern times.[21]

The lowlands stretch for fifteen hundred miles from southern Mexico
to southern Panama. Though very narrow in places, they broaden out to
a width of eighty miles in Nicaragua and Honduras and to more than
one hundred and fifty miles in southern Mexico. Along much of the
coast is a fringe of coral islands or low sandy beaches backed by lagoons.
Nearly everywhere the coastal stretches are low and swampy. On the

---

[19] In 1509 Ponce de León began the conquest of Puerto Rico and in 1511 San
Juan was founded. Under orders from Diego Columbus, Juan de Esquivel began
the conquest of Jamaica in 1509. Diego de Velásquez de León began the occupation of Cuba in 1511; within three years Santiago was founded, and in 1515 a
settlement was made at Havana.

[20] Hundreds of fortunate adventurers had accumulated fortunes in the placers of
Hispaniola, and with a view of repeating their success on the mainland, solicited
and obtained from the Spanish Crown a grant to explore a portion of the mainland. T. C. Dawson, *The South American republics,* II, 404.

[21] Griffith Taylor, *Environment and race* (London, 1927), part IV, pages 301-
341.

western side, the lowlands are bordered by the high and rugged Cordilleras, which increase the difficulty of crossing the lowland. In only a few places do river valleys make easy the access to the highlands; such places are the Motagua, the San Juan (Nicaragua), Reventazón, and Chagres valleys.

Everywhere the plains are hot and rainy all of the time. At Belize, British Honduras, the mean temperature of the warmest month, August, is eighty-two and six-tenths degrees and for the coldest month, January, seventy-four and eight-tenths degrees.[22] In the summer months many portions in the central part of the United States have higher temperatures, but in these lowlands the heat and humidity are continuous day in and day out, month in and month out. Based on the mean, the difference between the hottest and coldest months is only seven and eight-tenths degrees at Belize, and only three degrees at Colon. The difference between day and night is greater than that between winter and summer. These lowlands are very rainy and have no dry season; the season locally called the dry season is merely less wet than the remainder of the year.[23] Thus, no dry season favors the ripening and harvesting of crops. The plant cover is always wet, and clothes and shoes mold unless put in the sun each day or put into a "dry closet" where an electric light keeps them from molding.

The vegetative response to this continuous heat and moisture is the tropical rain forest. This is a dense growth of tall trees, underbrush, and vines, crowding for space on the ground and for light through the canopy of leaves. To traverse these forests, man has to go by the rivers or cut his way with a *machete*. Although rich in tropical timbers, the forests provide only a meagre food supply even for primitive people. Yet these forests harbor many animals not found on the Greater or Lesser Antilles—monkeys, jaguars, wild pigs, tapir, deer, and ant-eaters. The *iguana*, native to the region, was valued as an article of food by some of the aborigines. Many species of birds inhabit the forests, and the coastal waters and streams are rich in fish, shell-fish, alligators, and

---

[22] Mean monthly temperatures:

Station	Jan.	Feb.	Mar.	Apr.	May	June	July	Aug.	Sept.	Oct.	Nov.	Dec.	Annual
Belize	74.8	76.6	79.2	79.9	81.9	82.4	82.6	82.6	82.0	79.3	76.1	73.6	79.3
Colon	79.3	79.2	79.8	80.5	79.8	79.4	79.4	79.3	79.5	79.0	78.1	79.0	79.3

[23] Mean monthly precipitation:

Station	Jan.	Feb.	Mar.	Apr.	May	June	July	Aug.	Sept.	Oct.	Nov.	Dec.	Annual
Belize	7.44	3.22	2.47	2.23	4.91	7.86	8.23	8.27	9.38	10.58	13.29	6.65	84.53
Bluefields	9.86	6.93	3.61	3.12	8.08	17.00	28.58	16.07	8.74	11.22	11.40	14.28	138.89
Limón	14.57	6.45	7.06	10.62	8.50	6.22	16.87	12.23	5.69	5.01	11.86	16.64	121.72
Colon	3.69	1.62	1.57	4.35	12.48	13.39	15.89	15.07	12.51	14.94	21.02	11.32	127.85

turtles. But of more concern to man in many ways is the insect life, so abundant and so pestiferous.

Considering this combination of environmental conditions there is little wonder that the Indians of these lowlands made little progress. With the exception of the Old and New Mayan Empires in the coastal plain of the peninsula of Yucatan,[24] the Indians were less advanced than those of the Greater Antilles. The forests were very sparsely inhabited by small groups of Indians in the lowest of the archaic stage of culture. They gathered a meagre subsistence from forest and stream, practiced almost no agriculture, dwelt in crude brush shelters, slept in the ashes *may*. of their fires, practiced promiscuous intermarriage and cannibalism, and waged frequent tribal warfare. Though these lowland Indians had a number of food plants, they made little use of them. The high humidity, very heavy precipitation, and the lack of a dry season made agriculture almost impossible. Because of the rapid growth of vegetation the only means of clearing was by burning off the trees and brush, and in the continuous dampness this was difficult. The burning consumed the humus of the soil[25] and thus added to the rapid leaching of the heavy rain in lowering the fertility of the sandy and heavy clay soils of the lowland. Added to these difficulties were the many insect pests and diseases that were always sapping the strength and even taking the lives of the people dwelling there. Whenever a plague broke out, the Indians had only one means of escape and that was for the well ones to pick up and migrate to a new area. While the backward lowland Indians left no records of any pestilences, the Mayas left abundant evidence of the visitation of plagues and their effects.[26]

---

[24] The high development of the Maya in the tropical rain forest area of Mexico and Guatemala has not been completely explained. Attempts have been made to explain the Old Empire decline on the bases of a change of climate and the rise of the New Empire farther north in a region with a rhythm in rainfall. See E. Huntington, "Maya civilization and climatic changes," in *International Congress of Americanists*, XIX (1917), 150-164, and S. G. Morley, "The inscriptions at Copan" (Washington, 1920), 447-452.

[25] O. F. Cook, "Vegetation affected by agriculture in Central America," in United States Bureau of Plant Industry, *Bulletin 145*, (1909), 11-13.

[26] A few years before the Spaniards arrived, the Mayas in Yucatan were visited by a plague that killed hundreds of thousands, caused many migrations, and instigated intertribal wars. "A great pestilence came on the peninsula. Those who touched the dead were also in a few hours dead. The pestilence spread far and wide, afflicting not only the Maya but their very crops according to the tradition that the Spaniards found. The very fruit mottled with a strange fungoid mildew, poisonous and burning to the taste. Amidst streets and fields dead and unburied bodies, hideously swollen, burst open, displaying the intestines filled with maggots.

With this physical and human background the hot, humid lowlands held little attraction for the Spaniards. As a matter of fact, they were avoided as much as possible after the Spaniards learned of the terrible toll of life they took from each expedition sent into their fastnesses.[27] In the entire stretch of one thousand five hundred miles of coast line only a few settlements were made. These served especially as trans-shipment points and points providing contact with the highlands of Mexico and Central America. Even after four hundred years and with improved commercial contacts and political conditions, these lowlands remain very sparsely inhabited. Except in the ports and in a few areas of plantation agriculture, the lowlands are still inhabited by backward Indians and negroes who eke out a subsistence living in the face of adverse environmental conditions and who gather a few forest products for export.

III. Physical Conditions and Responses in the Highland Basins of Mexico and Central America

Standing out in striking contrast to the hot, humid lowlands in physical makeup and in human responses, are the highland basins and plateaus of Central America and Mexico. What conditions in the physical makeup of these selected spots, in relation to human advance, set them off so strikingly from the Lesser Antilles and the eastern lowlands of Central America? These embrace the largest area of Caribbean America and historically by far the most significant. The highland zone extends almost uninterrupted from the southern border of the United States to the rain forests of lowland Panama, a distance of more than two thousand miles. In places the highland zone is five hundred miles wide. But not all of this area has favored man. From northern Mexico to Costa Rica, many small sheltered basins and plateaus afforded almost ideal spots for germinating civilizations.

Much of the highland area is young geologically. In many places, dormant and active volcanic peaks rise into the zone of eternal snows.[28]

No doubt, wherever the plague touched on temple altar or temple cess-pool, in that land without sanitation and with hideous blood-rites, the plague was kindled afresh. The peace of thirty years vanished with the coming of the plague. . . . Banked-up hatreds were released and old wrongs remembered. . . . With the plague there came on the Cocomes either a fresh upstirring of hate—or else an overmastering desire for fresh fish. War began." J. Leslie Mitchell, *The conquest of the Maya,* 228-229.

[27] T. C. Dawson, *The South American republics,* II, 404-406; J. L. Mitchell, *The conquest of the Maya,* 231-267; E. G. Bourne, *Spain in America,* 104-114.

[28] The volcanic peak of Orizaba rises to 18,700 feet above sea level, Popocatepetl to 17,880 feet, and Tacana and others in Guatemala to more than 13,000 feet.

Out over the valleys and basins these volcanoes have repeatedly poured sheets of lava and spread thin mantles of volcanic ash which have broken down into very fertile soils. Fertile mountain-rimmed basins were easily defended from outside warlike tribes. The fertile waste-filled and gently rolling surfaces of the basins were easily tilled.

Lying between 3,800 and 9,000 feet above the sea, the basins are free from the enervating heat of the lowlands and they have a more distinct rhythm in temperatures[29] which stimulates activity on the part of both man and beast. The basins are semiarid to arid; although there are great differences in short distances, in general they receive annually from twenty to sixty inches.[30] The long rainy season, from May to October, gets from two-thirds to four-fifths of the total annual rainfall. Thus, the rains come in the warmer months when plants can make most use of them. The dry season favors the ripening and harvesting of crops and makes necessary the storing up of provisions to last over the very dry season, which in places is almost rainless. In the sections of lower rainfall, irrigation is necessary.

In response to temperatures and rainfall, the vegetation consists of either grasses, open woodlands, or thorn forests. Because of less rain and a marked dry season, the plants store up more concentrated food than plants in the hot humid areas. A thin grass-covered or open woodland area is much more easily brought under cultivation than a portion of a tropical rain forest or savanna, and the fertility is more easily retained.

Though these basins had no domesticable animals except the dog, there was a great variety of animals that could be killed for food—pumas, tigers, foxes, deer, rabbits, and rodents. These animals were hunted by individuals and large organized parties with bows, darts, nets, traps, and blowguns. Many birds,[31] fish, reptiles, and clams added to

---

[29] Mean monthly temperatures of San José (3,760 feet), Quezaltenango (7,710 feet), and Mexico City (7,434 feet):

Station	Jan.	Feb.	Mar.	Apr.	May	June	July	Aug.	Sept.	Oct.	Nov.	Dec.	Annual
San José	67.3	68.7	70.2	70.5	70.7	69.2	69.1	68.8	68.6	68.4	68.3	66.9	68.9
Quezaltenango	51.8	53.4	57.8	60.1	62.3	61.9	60.4	60.0	60.2	59.4	56.9	52.7	58.1
Mexico City	54.1	57.0	60.6	63.9	64.9	63.9	62.1	62.1	61.0	59.0	56.5	54.0	59.9

[30] Mean monthly precipitation of San José, Quezaltenango, and Mexico City:

Station	Jan.	Feb.	Mar.	Apr.	May	June	July	Aug.	Sept.	Oct.	Nov.	Dec.	Annual
San José	.60	.18	.77	1.76	9.04	9.53	8.27	9.53	12.04	11.78	5.75	1.59	70.84
Quezaltenango	.04	.14	.02	.59	5.13	6.18	3.26	3.86	4.75	3.54	.47	.21	28.19
Mexico City	.20	.20	.50	.80	1.90	3.90	4.50	4.60	3.90	1.60	.50	.20	22.80

[31] The Aztecs reached great heights in many arts and attainments. Their feather-work was magnificent, and to supply the feathers necessary for ornaments and

the food supply and materials. Many ingenious methods were used to capture fowl, snakes, and alligators. The highland areas lack many of the insect pests and diseases that so handicap life in the hot, humid lowlands. It is difficult for those who have not experienced some of the debilitating effects of malaria, tropical diseases, and insect pests to appreciate the full advantages of an area that is largely free from them.

In addition to these favorable factors, the mineral resources of the highland areas add materially to the raiment, abode, and general well-being of the inhabitants. Few regions possess a greater variety of stones and clay[32] that could be utilized by early peoples for artifacts, implements, and buildings and temples. Gold, silver, copper, and zinc are found in many areas throughout the highland area. In the more arid sections salt, a commodity in great demand by primitive peoples, is easily produced around the margins of lakes and along the coast.

This combination of physical conditions in the highland basins of Central America and Mexico set a stage, in many respects similar to that of the valleys and high plains of the Central Andes, for the rise of several very advanced cultures. It is not pertinent to this discussion to analyze the different degrees of material and intellectual advance attained by many of the early tribes or even those of the later Mayas, Toltecs, and Aztecs. But some of the activities of these later people in relation to the environmental complex of the highland basins and plateaus should be pointed out. In the evolution of culture, it was the sedentary peoples who developed the highest cultures and attained to civilization. It is fairly well established that the Mayas, Toltecs, and Aztecs were semisedentary before they entered the regions which saw the blossoming and flowering of their cultures.[33] For obtaining food, clothing, shelter, artifacts, implements, and other necessities by a seden-

---

garments they maintained immense aviaries of bright plumaged birds whose feathers were plucked at regular intervals. The rulers, priests, and officials wore clothing and mantles of featherwork which aroused the wonder and admiration of the Spaniards. See A. H. Verrill, *Old civilizations of the new world* (1929), 160-161, and Lucien Biart, *The Aztecs* (1900), 93-94.

[32] Agate, topaz, sapphire, quartz, amethyst, and practically every precious and semi-precious stone known to Mexico were carved, cut, polished, and perforated by the Aztecs. The Aztec art in obsidian or volcanic glass, one of the hardest and most refractory of minerals, is remarkable. They used it for knives, arrow-heads and spearheads, mirrors, and for many ornamental purposes. A. H. Verrill, *Old civilizations of the new world,* 161-162.

[33] "It is known that, during the long journey which brought the Aztecs from their primitive country to the shores of the lake where they founded their capital, they tilled the soil wherever they sojourned and lived upon the crops."—Biart, 254.

tary population, the highland basins fostered agriculture, irrigation, transportation, mining, the construction of temples and buildings, the development of the arts, and a strong family, tribal, and empire organization.

Agriculture has been named the antecedent condition for all the high cultures of the New World.[34] It is believed for many reasons that agriculture in the New World originated in the high basins of Mexico. How did this region favor the origin of agriculture? Agriculture would be more likely to originate under rather hard conditions of life than under those that were easy. A semiarid environment fostering a healthy and hungry population would offer special inducements to people to take up agriculture to appease the pangs of hunger. The loose, fertile, alluvial, and volcanic soils would be easy to prepare, and irrigation would make such people complete masters of the all-important question of securing enough to eat. Screening and washing seeds at springs, along the shores of lakes, and on the banks of streams, would almost inevitably result in volunteer crops and lead to artificial watering of plants. The pressure of population on food supply is greater in a semiarid environment than in hot, humid regions where foodstuffs may be gathered, but where at the same time diseases, pests, and a debilitating climate operate to decrease the numbers and the efficiency of groups of people. In the semiarid region, the clearing of the land for crops is much less laborious than in the rain forests, and the control of the water supply makes man the master of the entire life of the community. However, the highland basins are not without their handicaps, for droughts, locusts, and, in the higher ones, frosts may destroy the crops and cause great suffering for want of food.[35] This region has a variety of plants easily adapted to cultivation and production of rather abundant food. Maize, one of our most widespread and useful plants, seems to have been developed from a wild grass in the Mexican highland. Early cultivated also were beans, squashes, pumpkins, melons, sage, *Capsicum Annum,* tomatoes, peanuts, *huauhtli,* now a forgotten cereal, other dry seeds of a similar type,[36]

---

[34] H. J. Spinden, "The origin and distribution of agriculture in America," in *Proceedings of the Nineteenth International Congress of Americanists* (1917), 269.

[35] Records give evidence of disastrous droughts in the Valley of Mexico which caused famines, migrations, and wars. During the reign of the eighth Toltec king, several years of drought and an invasion of locusts destroyed all their crops. From 1450 to 1454 severe frosts followed by drought destroyed nearly all the crops of the Aztecs and caused them to emigrate in numbers.—Biart, 40, 77.

[36] W. E. Safford, "A forgotten cereal of ancient America," in *Proceedings of the Nineteenth International Congress of Americanists* (1917), 286-297.

and *agave*. *Agave* in early times supplied all the needs of the poor; it supplied food, drink, clothing, shelter, artifacts, and medicine.

The Aztecs had a well-developed agriculture. Having no plow and possessing no domestic animals strong enough to help, they tilled the fields with incessant labor. For digging the soil they used a copper mattock with a handle. An efficient network of canals carried the water from the mountain streams out over the fields. Lands were allowed to lie fallow; the weeds were burned to keep up the soil fertility. They built watchtowers where a man drove the flocks of birds away with a sling. They built huge granaries for storing the harvests.

Time and space will not allow a discussion in detail of other different lines of development of the Mayas, Toltecs, or Aztecs. All wove textiles of hair, or fibers; all skillfully wove feathers into clothing, mantles, and hats; all used gold, silver, copper, and many kinds of stones and performed wonders in working them; and all were immensely rich in gold, silver, and precious stones, although these were valued for their beauty and for ornamental purposes. They had developed excellent systems of irrigation and constructed remarkable forts and defenses placed in strategic positions and designed with bastions, salients, moats, and even loopholes. They carried out feats of bridge and aqueduct building, roadmaking, and transportation. They built up an extensive system of commerce. They conquered and confederated many diversified tribes and maintained their rulers, priests, temples, armies, and religion chiefly through an intricate system of taxation over a large area. Truly, these are great achievements for ancient peoples to have attained. But these achievements were realized under environmental conditions more or less propitious to groups of Indians with the ability and the desire to make use of the resources of the highland basins and plateaus.

The same environmental conditions that fostered the rise of native cultures in these areas held an attraction for the Spaniards. The Spaniards were accustomed to semiarid and arid areas. The civilized groups of wealthy sedentary Indians whetted the avarice of the Spanish adventurers and soldiers as nothing else could have done. The accumulated wealth of the Indians, their buildings, lands, mines, and even the Indians themselves became the property of the Spaniards. In the highlands of Mexico and Central America were established nearly all the chief centers of Spanish colonial activity of the mainland of Caribbean America.

CHAPTER THREE

GEOGRAPHICAL BACKGROUND OF THE COLONIAL PERIOD IN SOUTH AMERICA

By CLARENCE F. JONES

ALTHOUGH the Indians of South America and the introduced peoples were dominant factors in shaping the course of events during the colonial period, the physical conditions of the continent acted as the stage on which the drama of events unfolded through the centuries. The relief, rainfall, temperature, plant life, animal life, diseases and pests, and the mineral resources either favored or hindered the advance of the Indians, the Europeans, and the negroes. In precolonial days the degree to which the natives obtained material and intellectual attainments depended, in no small measure, on the environmental conditions of the areas in which they lived. In broad areas the nomadic people had not advanced beyond the hunter-and-fisher and the archaic stage of culture. In others, they had become sedentary, had made much use of the resources, and had attained a high degree of culture. The areas that harbored the more advanced peoples not only provided a greater variety of resources, but in addition they had conditions that even ancient people regarded as affording tolerable comfort. These areas, throughout colonial times and even down to the present time, have held the greatest attraction for the Europeans.

In a discussion of the geographic background of the colonial period in South America it seems advisable to point out some of the chief characteristics of the environmental factors of the continent as a whole, and then discuss the influence of these factors as a group in retarding advance in certain regions and in furthering advance in others.

I. CONDITIONS FOR APPROACHING AND ENTERING THE CONTINENT

The persistence, strength, and annual north-south shift of the northeasterly trade winds and the westward flowing currents favored the early discovery and exploration of the northern and northeastern coasts of South America by Columbus,[1] Cabral, and others. These winds and

---

[1] Columbus, in setting out on his third voyage, naturally followed the custom, then so common, of running to the parallel on which he intended to sail, and he proceeded to the Cape Verde Islands. Sailing to the southwest from there he en-

the location of the Caribbean coast of the continent in the direct line of
Spanish activity westward caused early and frequent activity on the
northern coast. The far eastward extension of the Brazilian coast and
its resources of Brazilwood, a valuable dyewood, caused the early Portuguese settlement of this coast and its establishment as an important
way station on the Cape of Good Hope route to the spice islands of the
East.[2] But the approach to other portions of the continent involved grave
difficulties, weighty considerations, and the failure of many early expeditions. Though Magellan in October and November 1520, favored by
wind and weather, threaded his way in five weeks through the strait that
bears his name, the strait never became a practical route until after the
introduction of steam. In the one hundred years following the discovery, owing to the stormy waters of this region and those along the western coast of southern South America, not half a dozen ships reached
the Pacific around South America.[3]   Practically, the Pacific was accessible only by the long journey around the Cape of Good Hope or over
the Isthmus of Panama. Panama thus became the focus of the trade
of western South America and even of Argentina.

Once having attained the margins of the continent, the first voyagers
encountered additional problems, many of which have in no wise diminished in their retarding effects. This is so, particularly in the tropical lands, where swamp, pestilence, and impenetrable forest curb human
activities. In addition, few valuable indentations break the coast line,
the regular outline giving way to numerous island and promontory protected harbors only in the largely unexploitable Chilean archipelago.
Few large, deep estuaries lead far into the continent, as is the case in
more fortunate Europe and North America. Here no drowned river

---

tered the belt of calms for nine days and drifted to the northwest. He then *"caught
the trade-wind on the starboard quarter"* and *"after a brisk run of ten days"*
reached Trinidad and later the Venezuelan coast. John Fiske, *The discovery of
America,* I, 488-496.

[2] In March 1500, Pedro Alvarez Cabral, sailing for the East Indies, was instructed, "after passing the Cape Verde Islands in 14° N., to sail directly south,
as long as the wind was favorable. If forced to change his course, he was ordered
to keep on the starboard tack, even though it led him southwest." He was to
continue on this course until he reached the latitude of 34° S.; this would place
him in the zone of the westerlies and aid him in rounding the Cape of Good Hope
and would cause him to miss the doldrums and the southeast trades along the
west coast of Africa. In forty-two days after leaving Lisbon, Cabral, by following these instructions, accidentally discovered Brazil. T. C. Dawson, *The
South American republics,* I, 295-297.

[3] Dawson, I, 20-22.

mouths afford such facilities as are enjoyed by London or New York. On the east coast, Rio de Janeiro's splendid harbor is the result of a purely local development of the Serra do Mar. Elsewhere, shallow waters are the rule. Buenos Aires maintains a narrow channel by unceasing and costly dredging. At the one great indentation on the north coast, Lake Maracaibo, large ocean vessels are kept out by the bar; consequently, freight and passengers for the lowland are transferred at Curaçao to vessels drawing not more than eleven feet of water. Vessels calling at Georgetown time their arrival so as to cross the bar at the mouth of the Demerara at high tide. In northern Colombia, vessels cannot enter the Magdalena because of the shallow water in the mouths of the river. All freight must be moved by rail a short distance from the Caribbean to the lower Magdalena ports. On the important stretches of the west coast, no indentations compare with those on the east. Only Valparaiso offers docking facilities to large vessels; but even here the open harbor—a characteristic of the west coast—permits strong winds periodically to wreak havoc among craft at anchor or at dock.

Compared to Europe and North America, with respect to rivers permitting access to the interior, South America shows striking shortcomings. The north and east coasts have only four rivers serving as important water highways to the interior. The west coast has none; the giant cordillera system limits navigable stretches of Pacific streams to only a few miles.

The greatest of these natural channels, the Amazon, is without parallel in the world as regards river navigability. But it has widely fluctuating waters; the difference between high and low water at Pará amounting to thirty to fifty feet, at San Antonio fifty-one feet, and at Iquitos twenty-five feet; its giant tributaries are all interrupted by rapids or falls not far from their confluence with the master stream, and the region drained ranks among the less utilizable of South American lands. The Amazon system constitutes the only means of transportation for an area two-thirds the size of the United States.

The system flowing into the Río de la Plata is inferior in size to that of the Amazon, but in its lower stretches it has acquired an importance which the northern river probably will never attain. Though sand bars, shifting channels, and floating islands hamper shipping, the various rivers have considerable value, particularly the lower Paraná and the Uruguay.

Few in number and small in size, the rivers of the west coast have only a minor importance. The Guayaquil River surpasses all in navigability, offering some one hundred and sixty miles of water negotiable to river craft.

The north coast, like the east, has three systems, but of lesser importance. The Magdalena has long been the vital artery of movement for Colombia, despite its numerous disadvantages of shallowness, shifting channels, fluctuating levels, and rapids. Although closed at the mouth by sand bars, it is navigable from Barranquilla for a total distance of 900 miles, but with breaks in transit and great loss of time. Farther to the east, the Catatumbo and Lake Maracaibo afford a significant outlet for a portion of Colombia and western Venezuela. The Orinoco, though carrying little traffic compared to other rivers, gives the only means of access to an extensive area in the *llanos* with more ease than possible on the Magdalena.

II. THE CHIEF PHYSICAL FEATURES OF THE CONTINENT

The great triangular continental mass, with its base on the northeast and its sides of nearly equal length converging to the south, presents conspicuous physical features. In the western portion the high, young, rugged cordilleras stretch from the placid blue waters of the Caribbean in Venezuela and Colombia to the cold turbulent Antarctic waters in fifty-five degrees south latitude (Fig. 1). To the east of this lie the vast interior lowlands. Farther east are two old worn-down mountain systems separated by the lower Amazon. South America lies chiefly in the tropics; one-half of the continent has undiluted tropical conditions. Were it not for the highland areas within the tropical portion, a larger part of the continent would feel the effects of enervating heat and humidity. Most of the tropical plains of South America support a dense growth of tropical hardwoods or tall coarse savanna grasses that do not favor a marked material advance. The very luxuriance of the vegetation and the enervating heat and humidity of those areas make the people exceedingly inefficient. Throughout the forests, communication, except on river highways, is far more difficult than on the rugged Andes.

With only a few animals that could be domesticated, the luscious grasses of the temperate grasslands of the southeastern part of the continent, the Chilean valley, and the high Andes could not express fully for the native Indians their full utility. Even under the colonial régime, and with introduced domesticated animals, the temperate grasslands did not assume a dominant economic and political rôle in Hispanic America.

Where the climate is dry or where there is a marked wet and dry season, the soil usually is fertile in mineral constituents, but in the very rainy regions the soils cleared of the heavy forest growth are subject to excessive leaching and soon become deficient in available plant food.

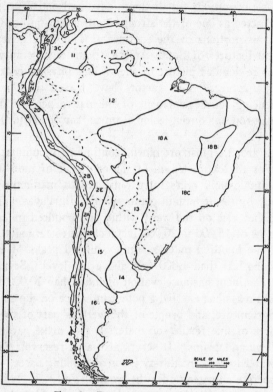

FIG. 1. PHYSIOGRAPHIC REGIONS

I. THE ANDES
  1. Southern Andes
  2. Central Andes
     2A. Western Ranges
     2B. Altiplano and Puna de Atacama
     2C. High Pampas of Peru and Ecuador
     2D. Central Ranges of Peru
     2E. Eastern Ranges
  3. Northern Andes
     3A. Western Range
     3B. Central Range
     3C. Eastern Ranges

II. PACIFIC VALLEYS AND RANGES
  4. Chilean Coastal Range and Chilean Archipelago

  5. Central Valley of Chile
  6. Nitrate and Peruvian Piedmont Pampas
  7. Pacific Plains of Ecuador and Colombia
  8. Colombia Coastal Range

III. THE CARIBBEAN LOWLANDS
  9. Magdalena-Cauca Plains
  10. Maracaibo Lowland

IV. CENTRAL INTERIOR PLAINS
  11. Llanos and Orinoco Delta
  12. Amazon Basin
  13. Paraguay-Paraná Plains
  14. The Pampa

V. INTERIOR BASINS AND RANGES AND THE PATAGONIAN TABLELAND
  15. Interior Basin and Range Lands
  16. Patagonian Tableland

VI. EASTERN HIGHLANDS
  17. Guiana Highlands and Coastal Plain
  18. Brazilian Highlands
     18A. Interior Plateaus
     18B. São Francisco Basin
     18C. Eastern Plateaus and Ranges

It is a question whether the hot, humid lowland soils can become permanently valuable farm lands without constant fertilization or rehabilitation. The minerals, especially gold, silver, tin, and copper, served as one of the basic conditions for the more advanced native peoples of the continent and acted as one of the strongest attractions in bringing Europeans to various portions of the continent. This very general picture of the physical features of South America point out the advisability of obtaining a more detailed picture of the various physical characteristics.

The Relief Features. Few factors have played a more important part in influencing the development of the native peoples and the advance of the Europeans during colonial times than the relief of the continent.

The Andes are the most prominent continuous mountain system on the globe. For the entire length of the continent of more than 4,000 miles, their titanic bulk rears lofty pinnacles to maximum elevations surpassed only by the mountain giants of the Himalayas. In much of their extent, they rise on the west, within one hundred miles from the coast, to heights of 15,000 to 20,000 feet; on the eastern side, a distance of less than one hundred miles separates rugged peaks of 20,000 feet from low plains less than 1,000 feet above sea level. Seven per cent of the entire continent has an elevation of more than 10,000 feet. This huge mountain mass has exerted a potent influence on the soils, climate, vegetation, agriculture, and people of the western part of the continent. It is the source of fine fertile soil materials that make garden spots of adjacent valleys and plains. It serves also as a reservoir for constant supplies of water to feed the thirsty crops of flanking oases. Its heights produce temperate climates under the tropical sun.

In its major outlines, the system shows three chief divisions, the Southern, Central, and Northern Andes (Fig. 2). These differ considerably in relief, elevation, and extent, as well as in relation to human activities.

The comparatively narrow zone of the Andes, which stretches from the southern border of the Puna de Atacama, in latitude twenty-eight degrees south, to the southern extremity of the continent, is the most compact part of the system.[4] It consists essentially of one main range in which lie both the greatest and least heights of the Andes; in latitude about thirty-six degrees south occurs a distinct break in structure and

---

[4] W. S. Tower, "The Andes as a factor in South American geography," in *Journal of Geography*, XV (1916), 1-8.

FIG. 2. DIAGRAM
OF THE ANDES

This diagram of
the Andes empha-
sizes some of the
more important fea-
tures and subdivi-
sions of the Andes.

also a transition between the arid Andes of Argentina and the more moist Patagonian Andes. In the north, the region reaches its greatest elevation, serves as the greatest barrier, and is least habitable. A good part of the land lies well above 10,000 feet, culminating in volcanic peaks like Mount Aconcagua at 22,812 feet, the highest point in the Western Hemisphere. The slopes are steep and long. Numerous structural basins exist. Everywhere enormous piles of talus have accumulated, and, owing to aridity, are removed slowly. In the southern portion, the region becomes lower and less continuous and has many lakes and low passes. The southern Andes did not harbor any important groups of natives, nor did they foster any significant development throughout colonial times. Even today they remain one of the most sparsely populated and most isolated portions of the entire continent.

In structure, relief, and human relations, the part of the Andes between northern Argentina and southern Colombia is the most complex portion of the great western cordillera. Its chief uniformity lies in its considerable width and elevation; much of the region exceeds 10,000 feet. In the south, two main ranges inclose elevated plateaus and basins which average between 11,000 and 13,500 feet above sea level. These converge north of Lake Titicaca in the Nudo (knot) de Vilcanota; and northward the region comprises three major mountain ranges, interrupted again by the Nudo de Cerro de Pasco in central Peru and the Nudo de Loja in southern Ecuador, and separated by parts of the Marañón, Huallaga, and Ucayali valleys. To the north of the last-named knot is the plateau of Ecuador which lies between two gigantic ranges that merge in southern Colombia in the Nudo de Pasto before splitting into the three main ranges of the northern Andes.

In the southern portion of this highland area between the western and eastern cordillera, lie the elevated Puna de Atacama and the Altiplano of Bolivia. The Puna de Atacama embraces a broad area of arid ridges and salt basins about 12,000 feet above sea level. Rugged, cold, arid, and isolated,[5] this region fostered some small interesting cultural and historical developments,[6] but it witnessed neither great native cultures nor marked activities during colonial times. On the other hand, the Altiplano of Bolivia with its high rugged bordering ranges was the scene of remarkable native cultures and a theater of great activity in

---

[5] I. Bowman, *Desert trails of Atacama*, 252-342.

[6] P. A. Means, *Ancient civilizations of the Andes*, 18-19.

colonial days. The Altiplano is a broad rolling plain. In the northern end lies the famous Lake Titicaca, forty miles wide and one hundred and twenty miles long, at an elevation of 12,508 feet above the sea; it has only one outlet, the Desaguadero River which drains southward at the southern end to Lake Poopo. Lake Poopo has no outlet except seepage and an excessive amount of evaporation. The tremendous accumulations of unconsolidated materials of the plain are capped with a moderately fertile soil. Around Lake Titicaca the land for some distance back from the shore is below 14,000 feet, the upper limit of potato cultivation.[7] Agriculture was possible under rather difficult circumstances, and raw materials for culture were present. With these and human energy, enterprise, and perseverance, this region afforded the bases for significant cultural advance.

On the north the Altiplano is bordered by the Nudo de Vilcanota across which communication is fairly easy to the high *pampas* and the three historically important deep intermontane valleys of Peru: the Mantaro, the Apurimac, and the Urubamba.[8]

The three valleys from about 9,500 to 13,000 feet above the sea are separated from each other by high ranges and cut off from the low, hot, forested country beyond. The area included in these three drainage basins, the adjacent high ranges, and the *pampas,* extends about four hundred miles from north to south and about one hundred and fifty miles from east to west. All of this area drains into the Amazon River system.

These valleys, at an average of about 11,000 feet above sea level, are temperate and capable of sustaining intensive agriculture. They contain raw materials for pottery, for textiles, for metal-working, and stone for architecture. The mere physical presence of these advantageous circumstances is not enough, however, to explain the flowering of advanced culture in that region. These elements were supplemented by a definite amount of human energy, ingenuity, and application. In such a climate as that of the Cuzco Valley, man engendered culture by combining these qualities with those factors so bountifully supplied by nature. In a climate more enervating, man's energies would have been sapped by lassitude; in a colder climate, they would have been exhausted by the unremitting struggle to keep his body above the freezing point

---

[7] Clarence F. Jones, *South America,* 209-210, 530.

[8] I. Bowman, "The canyon of Urubamba," in *Bulletin of the American Geographical Society,* XLIV (1912), 881-897.

and by anxiously hunting for food. Here there was a felicitous balance of factors and, as a result, a great civilization was born.[9]

In the Andes of Ecuador the drainage basins of the intermontane plateau are relatively small and, for the Andes, comparatively low. The western limit of the Ecuadorian *sierra* is an arbitrary north-south line on the western slope of the maritime cordillera at an altitude of about 4,000 feet above sea level. The eastern limit is a similar north-south line at an altitude of about 3,000 to 4,000 feet on the face of the eastern cordillera that overlooks the vast forests of Amazonia. On the eastern and western sides rise two titanic ranges in which Chimborazo towers to an elevation of 20,500 feet and Cotopaxi to 19,600 feet. This double row of snow-clad volcanic peaks—some of them still smoking—inclose the elevated plateaus or *pampas* at 7,000 to 14,000 feet above the sea. The intermontane surface is by no means flat. Various transverse spurs subdivide the area into many basins, each supporting its own concentration of people. On the whole, the valleys and *pampas* are well suited to tillage; their undulating surfaces have supported for centuries an intensive agriculture. These valleys and *pampas* embrace an area of approximately 2,500 square miles that was available to societies of the pastoral and agricultural type.

To Colombia and Venezuela, which otherwise have only the hot pestiferous lowlands, the northern Andes represent a boon of incalculable value. As a whole, they least hinder communication, since they extend parallel to the main direction of commerce in Colombia and lie near the coast in Venezuela. In general, they include three major subdivisions and their neighboring features: the *cordilleras occidental, central,* and *oriental* (or the western, the central, and the eastern ranges). Of these, the western and central ranges are well-defined in makeup, but the eastern ranges have a complicated nature and in reality embrace several distinct parts.

In the south, the *cordillera oriental* extends from Ecuador almost to Bogotá in one main range standing out in striking contrast to the Magdalena Valley and the eastern lowlands. North of Bogotá, the highland broadens and extends northeast as a number of parallel ranges, between which are high savannas, level basin areas, between 8,200 and 8,600 feet above sea level. Near the international border, the *cordillera oriental* divides, the Sierra de Perija extending northward in a series of parallel ranges and the Sierra Nevada de Mérida eastward. Succeeding the

---

[9] P. A. Means, *Ancient civilizations of the Andes,* 17-18.

Sierra de Perija at the north are the high Sierra Nevada de Santa Marta and the low ridges of the Goajira Peninsula. In Venezuela the towering peaks and ranges of the Sierra Nevada de Mérida give way to the subdued Segovia Highlands, the northern ranges of Venezuela and Trinidad, and to the fertile Lake Valencia Basin. The northern Andes in places provided the bases for significant native cultures. They were brought early under the influence of the Spaniards, and played a significant rôle throughout colonial times.[10]

In contrast to the central Andes and the northern Andes, the Guiana Highland and the Brazilian Highlands did not foster a high degree of native cultures. However, the natives of portions of the Brazilian Highlands were far in advance of those on any of the low plains of the continent at the time of the advent of the Portuguese and Spaniards. Though much of the lack of development may be a result of the human element, it is safe to assume that had conditions been as favorable here as in the central Andes, more marked native culture would have evolved. Presumably, if the natives there had been given more time, they might have evolved a high degree of culture. In the case of the Guiana Highlands, they are even more inaccessible than the fertile valleys of the central Andes. The low coastal plain to the north is bordered by broad swamps, infected with insects and diseases, and clothed with a dense tropical rain forest. The northern flanks of the highlands are covered with a dense forest and the streams are interrupted by a long series of rapids difficult to negotiate even with a canoe. The highland portion proper contains the remnants of ancient mountains as well as more recent plateaus, the highest lands lying in the northwest where Mount Icutu reaches 11,000 feet and on the southern borders where the Serra Parima and the Serra Pacaraima overlook the Amazon Basin. Deeply incised valleys have broken most of the region into a confusion of features.

In the case of the Brazilian Highlands, the long, high Serra do Mar rises almost directly from the sea and hinders access to the interior. Towards the Amazon Basin the highlands embrace the level-topped, though deeply stream-cut, plateaus of Matto Grosso, bordered on the east by several ridges in some places reaching an elevation of 5,000 feet. To the east lies the extensive basin of the São Francisco River, an area

---

[10] The Spaniards early entered the highlands of Venezuela; Valencia was founded as early as 1555. To the east of Valencia lay valuable gold washings first exploited in 1560. In this region the Aragua and Caracas valleys are garden spots. T. C. Dawson, *The South American republics,* II, 350-351.

comprising broad level platforms, and almost entirely surrounded by mountain ridges. North of this is the peneplained crystalline area of northeast Brazil, above which rise a number of low mountainous areas of limited extent. In the southeast lie the eastern plateaus and ranges, a region of mountain and plateau of great agricultural, forestal, and mineral wealth. In Minas Geraes, São Paulo, and Rio de Janeiro, the region consists of a complicated zone showing broad peneplained plateau-like areas as well as the lofty Serras do Espinhaço and do Matta da Corda. Consisting of broad rolling plateau surfaces and more subdued mountain ranges, the highland lacked the small isolated and well-protected fertile areas characteristic of the central Andes that fostered the development of agriculture and other industries of an early sedentary population.

Though fertile river valleys became the seat of many great civilizations in other continents, the low humid plains of South America did not witness the development of any great native cultures. On the other hand, small, isolated, arid valleys became the seat of high material and cultural development. Most of the plains of South America lacked some of the conditions necessary for the advance of a primitive people. Hot, humid, densely forested, swampy, and insect infested, they harbored some of the more primitive tribes of the continent. Because of these same conditions, they held little attraction for the colonist. Among the areas of this character may be included all of the wet tropical lowlands, such as the Guayas, San Juan, Atrato, lower Magdalena-Cauca River plains, and the Maracaibo, Orinoco, and the Amazon lowlands. Though the lowlands in general were avoided by the Spaniards, a few of their rivers became important highways as transient routes. The Spaniards soon recognized the value of the north-south extent of the Atrato Valley; in colonial times that district held distinctive importance, for despite its unpleasant climate it afforded an easy route for reaching the Pacific from the Caribbean, only a low divide separating the headwaters of the Atrato and the San Juan. For traffic to and from western South America this route at times rivaled the Old Gold Road across Panama. The Magdalena led the Spaniards from the Caribbean coast to the highlands of Colombia. Lake Maracaibo and the Catatumbo River carried them to the highlands of eastern Colombia and western Venezuela. But the other great rivers, the Orinoco, the Amazon, and the Paraguay-Paraná, did not become significant routes early because of the vast extent of the lowlands drained by them and the absence in these plains of products in active demand by the Spaniards and Portuguese.

The temperate plains of southeastern South America present a different physical picture. Separated from the Amazon Basin by a low divide with elevation less than 1,000 feet in Matto Grosso, the plains of the Paraguay and Paraná rivers encompass an extent of 1,500 miles from the watershed to the Río de la Plata. Though in respect to degree of relief they resemble the Amazon region, they exhibit broad differences. While the Paraguay and Paraná are among the great rivers of the world, there exists no system at all comparable to that of the Amazon. Indeed, great areas to the west of the Paraguay River have no visible drainage courses and are simply extensive featureless plains with broad swamps for part of the year.

Among the physical regions of South America, the *pampa* is distinctive in mode of origin, relief, and drainage, as well as in its unmatched agricultural possibilities. Its hundreds of feet of fine unconsolidated sediments covered with a deep mantle of loess are unique in South America. So uniformly has the thick mantle of materials been spread that only the gentlest swells disturb the surface of most of the far-reaching plain. The region is remarkably deficient in stream drainage, only one stream crossing the *pampa* from the west in its whole north-south extent of nearly 1,000 miles; hundreds of small ponds dot the landscape. Except in the small patches about the Sierras de Tandil and de la Vantana, none of the *pampa* has an altitude of 1,000 feet above the sea.

Though level, fertile, carpeted with luscious grasses, and salubrious, these extensive plains lacked small isolated and protected units that would foster the material and cultural advance of small primitive groups. They were inhabited by wandering tribes of hunters even though they were devoid of animal life that could support large numbers. Even after the Spaniards introduced cattle, horses, and sheep, they failed to initiate striking developments until late in the colonial period. The world at that time did not need or demand the products that these plains were so well adapted to produce.

Climatic Conditions. Perhaps no other factors played a more important part in the rise of native cultures and in the developments of the colonial period than climatic conditions.

The continent of South America has the unenviable distinction of having the greatest expanse with a rainy tropical climate. Those lands favoring human settlement, on the other hand, taper rapidly south of the Tropic of Capricorn. Though it does have most of its area north of latitude twenty-three and one-half degrees south, at the same time the lands south of that parallel have considerable extent. The mountains further modify the climatic situation in South America. The presence of the lofty Andes in tropical latitudes is a paramount consideration in the geography of most countries.[11] The mountains played a significant part in the early advance of the highland peoples in South America. There, men found relief from the heat of a high sun despite low latitude. The plateaus and mountains of Brazil have exercised a similar beneficial influence.

In contrast to the great height of the mountains is the uniformly low elevation of the vast interior plains. Lying at an altitude of less than 500 feet above the sea at a distance 2,000 miles inland, the great Amazonian plains give full reign to the play of a burning sun and an elevated relative humidity.

Stretching across the continent from northern Peru to southern Patagonia is a broad area of mountains, plateaus, and plains that receives annually less than ten inches of rain (Fig. 3). Throughout all of this area, crops can be grown only by the aid of irrigation, and the sparse bush and grass vegetation afford grazing for an extremely limited number of animals that have to wander far and wide to sustain life. To the east of this area and stretching from the northern Andes to the Atlantic in Argentina, is a broad belt that receives from ten to thirty inches annually. This belt embraces the areas of greatest native culture and the greatest colonial activity. Middle Chile has a similar amount of rainfall. In contrast to these areas several large expanses receive from sixty to more than eighty inches of rain per year. They embrace southern Chile, the Pacific margin of Colombia and Ecuador, and the vast Amazonian lowlands with adjacent parts of the northeast coast of the continent and the coast of Bahia. Truly these areas are too rainy for human comfort and progress.[12] In the major portion of these areas twenty inches or more falls in each three-month period; though some months are less rainy than others, no month can be considered as dry.[13] Thus everything is drenched with rain throughout the year. There is no distinct dry ripening and harvesting period, so necessary for most of the tropical crops like sugar, cacao, coffee, rice, and others. Further-

---

[11] J. R. Smith, "The economic importance of the plateaus of tropic America," in *Bulletin of the American Geographical Society*, XLIII (1911), 36-45.

[12] H. J. Spinden, "Civilization in the wet tropics," in *World's Work*, XLV (1922-23), 438-448.

[13] Charles Gooze and Clarence F. Jones, "The seasonal distribution of rainfall in South America," in *Bulletin of the Geographical Society of Philadelphia*, XXVI (1928), 93-115.

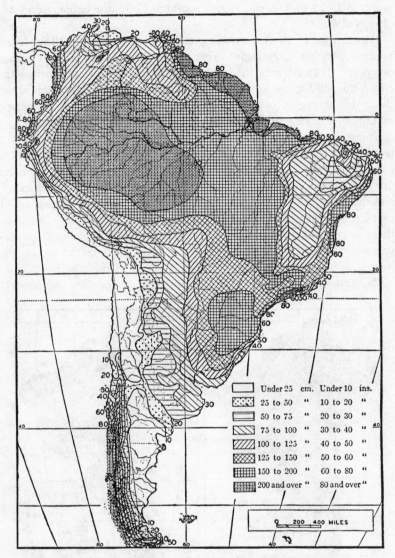

FIG. 3. ANNUAL PRECIPITATION

The rise of the Indians to advanced stages of culture in South America took place in arid and semi-arid regions. The great activities of colonial times also took place in regions of relatively low rainfall. The areas with more than 80 inches annual precipitation and without any marked dry season are too rainy for human comfort and advance. (From C. F. Jones, *South America*, Henry Holt & Company.)

more, in all of these areas, except southern Chile, the temperatures are always high.

Between the areas of excessive precipitation and those with moderate precipitation, are large regions that receive from forty to sixty inches per year. They embrace the great savannas of the continent such as the *chaco,* the *campos,* the *llanos,* and the Bolívar savannas, and much of the thorn forest region of northeast Brazil (Figs. 4 and 5). For nine months of the year these receive ample rain, but for three months vast districts get less than two inches (Figs. 6 and 7). Any place in the tropics that receives less than two inches in three months takes on desert characteristics at that period. All the small streams and the water holes dry up, vegetation adopts all xerophytic characteristics at its command, and man and beast suffer for water and food. With the cessation of rains, the whole area becomes a parched and desolate realm. None of these areas witnessed marked precolonial or colonial cultures or development. As a matter of fact, even today, they remain among the least known and the most undeveloped portions of the entire continent.

Vegetation and Animals. In South America, as elsewhere, nearly

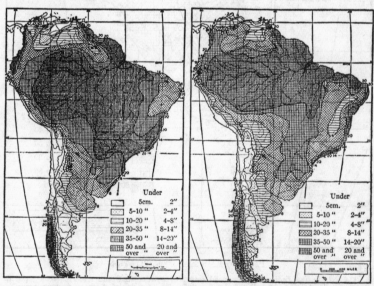

FIGS. 4 AND 5. AVERAGE PRECIPITATION, DEC.-JAN.-FEB.
AND MARCH-APRIL-MAY

Of great significance in understanding the life of the people is the seasonal fluctuation of precipitation. These maps, based on original statistics from some 320 stations, give a fairly accurate picture of the rainfall régime. (From C. F. Jones. *South America,* Henry Holt & Company.)

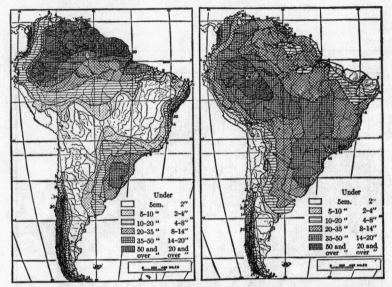

FIGS. 6 AND 7. AVERAGE PRECIPITATION, JUNE-JULY-AUGUST AND
SEPT.-OCT.-NOV.

The maps for December-January-February and June-July-August show the profound
influence of the migration of the vertical rays of the sun on the precipitation over a
large share of the continent. (From C. F. Jones. *South America*, Henry Holt & Company.)

every important human adjustment has shown certain intimate relations
to the natural vegetation. Often the adjustments have been more intimate and interesting in regions of sparse vegetation than in the dense
tropical forests. It is certain that products can be too abundant; where
the products of food and shelter may be gathered with little effort, as
in some rain forest regions, the incentive to advance beyond the mere
subsistence level of existence is lacking.

About one-third of South America supports a dense tropical rain
forest which has represented a major obstacle to settlement and cultural evolution (Fig. 8). Such forests embrace the Amazon Basin, the
upper portion of the Orinoco Basin, much of the Guianas, the middle
portion of the Maracaibo Lowlands, the middle lower Magdalena Valley, and the Pacific margin of Colombia and Ecuador. The variety of
plant life and its rapid growth in these forests are astonishing. So
completely do the forest growth, the swampy nature of the lands bordering the streams, the enervating climate, and insect pests impede overland travel that the wealth of the forests remains to a large extent unavailable.

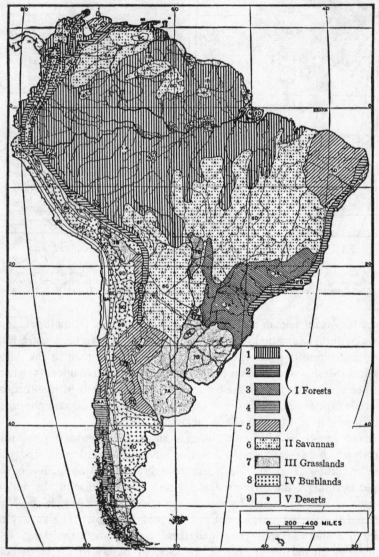

FIG. 8.   NATURAL VEGETATION

Natural Vegetation

I. FORESTS
1. Tropical rain forest
   1A. Amazon
   1B. Guiana
   1C. Pacific
   1D. Caribbean
2. Mountain tropical rain forest
   2A. Andes
   2B. East Brazil
3. Subtropical rain forest
   3A. South Brazil
   3B. Central Plateau of Eastern Brazil
4. Temperate rain forest
   4A. Middle Chile
   4B. South Chile
5. Dry forest
   5A. Mediterranean
   5B. *Monte*
5C. Northeast Brazil
5D. Caatinga
5E. Venezuelan *chaparral*
5F. Caribbean *espinar*

II. SAVANNAS
6A. Llanos
6B. Bolívar
6C. Guiana
6D. Campos
6E. Amazon
6F. Mojos
6G. Chaco

III. GRASSLANDS
7A. Pampa
7B. Paraná-Uruguay
7C. Patagonia
7D. Mountain
7E. Marsh

IV. BUSHLANDS
8A. Humid Mountains
8B. Arid Mountains
8C. Intermontane Valley
8D. Patagonia
8E. Inner Coastal Desert

V. DESERTS
9A. Peruvian-Chilean
9B. *Lomas*
9C. Venezuelan sand-dunes
9D. Salt plains
9E. South Andean glaciers

A large part of the continent of South America is in forests and savannas. Neither the tropical rain forests nor the savannas of the continent afforded conditions auspicious either to the advance of the Indians beyond the archaic stage of culture or to significant activities of Europeans during colonial times. (From C. F. Jones. *South America*, Henry Holt & Company.)

The several broad savannas of South America embrace approximately one-fourth of the continental expanse. Among the larger ones are the *chaco, campos, llanos,* and Bolívar savannas. They are in general far-flung expanses of tall coarse grasses interspersed here and there with strips of trees along water courses or clumps of thorn forests on sandy areas and individual solitary palms. Regions of rather heavy precipitation, they are rainy for nearly nine months of the year. During the rainy season the vegetation grows rapidly, but during the dessicating drought of the three month dry season, the vegetation withers and becomes dry and hard, the grasses losing succulence quickly and becoming harsh and unpalatable to livestock. In contrast to the savannas of Africa, these savannas did not support great herds of large herbivorous animals which could be hunted or domesticated.

However, even with land game scarce and other major handicaps, many of the Indians of these areas reached a stage of culture well above that of those of the tropical forest Indians. Some of them crudely cultivated corn, manioc, and beans, made useful dug-outs, built fair houses, ground manioc flower, spun cotton, and made pottery.[14] Nevertheless, by the time the Portuguese and Spaniards arrived, the stage of culture of these Indians was far below that of the civilized Indians of the Andes. Though supplying many of the necessary elements for cultural advance, the savannas did not favor continuous and hard labor, and the broad physical features did not provide small isolated areas that gave protection and stimulated material and intellectual advance of primitive groups.

Reference has already been made to the fact that the temperate grassland of southeastern South America, though large in extent and having wonderful conditions for grazing and farming, did not witness any marked advance of the natives inhabiting the plains. Like the savannas of the continent, these grasslands had no large animals. However, the *guanaco,* found in abundance, provided the chief means of subsistence for the nomadic tribes of the *pampa* and even of Patagonia. But the *guanaco* was not domesticated. For hundreds of miles the level surface of this area had almost no wood and practically no stones near the surface to serve for making tools, implements, or buildings.[15] Over most of the *pampa* a boy would have to look long and hard to find a stone

---

[14] T. C. Dawson, *The South American republics,* I, 298-300.

[15] Aleš Hrdlička, "Early man in South America," Bureau of American Ethnology, *Bulletin 52,* Washington, 1912. This gives detailed descriptions of the stone implements and artifacts of early man in eastern Argentina.

to throw at a dog, a *guanaco,* or a bird. This area, with a stimulating and otherwise favorable climate in its changes from season to season, favored the annual migrations of the *guanaco* and the nomadic Indians. Also the broad level expanses provided no isolated protected spots to encourage sedentary agriculture among small groups of the natives. In addition, the tough sod of the *pampa* could not be broken with the tools possessed by the Indians or the early colonists.[16]

In contrast, the temperate grasses and the bush vegetation of the Andes presented a different problem. Throughout the high Andes, from the Caribbean to Argentina, are numerous small valleys and high *pampas* that have excellent grasses and a sparse bush vegetation. In more ways than one the sparse vegetation was an advantage. The gnarled length of tough *algarroba,* the crooked trunk of the *quishuar,* or the outer shell of a cactus, held infinitely more utility for the highland Indian than a long clean bole of precious cabinet wood for a forest Indian of the Amazon. The thin sod and loose sandy soil could be broken with a stick.[17] The pastures provided forage for the numerous llamas and alpacas, the only animals with the exception of the dog that were domesticated by the Indians in the Americas.

III. CONDITIONS FOR CULTURAL DEVELOPMENT IN SELECTED AREAS

At this point it is desirable to change the point of view from the factors of the environment of the continent as a whole to the combination of the environmental conditions as a group in relation to the material and cultural advance of the natives and to the activities of the colonial period in selected areas. For this purpose many areas might be selected, but only two types of areas will be discussed: the tropical rain forests, and the highlands and valleys of the central Andes. ✓

Tropical Rain Forest Regions. From the standpoint of all the factors that favored the advance of primitive peoples and of settlement in colonial and modern times, the tropical rain forests of South America do not possess a single one. They do not have favorable relief,[18] a climatic

---

[16] O. Schmieder, "Alteration of the Argentine pampa in the colonial period," in *University of California Publications in Geography,* Vol. II (1927), 303-321.

[17] O. F. Cook, "Foot-plow agriculture in Peru," in *Bulletin of the Pan American Union,* LII (1921), 160-166.

[18] C. F. Marbut and C. B. Manifold, "The topography of the Amazon valley," in *Geographical Review,* XV (1925), 617-642.

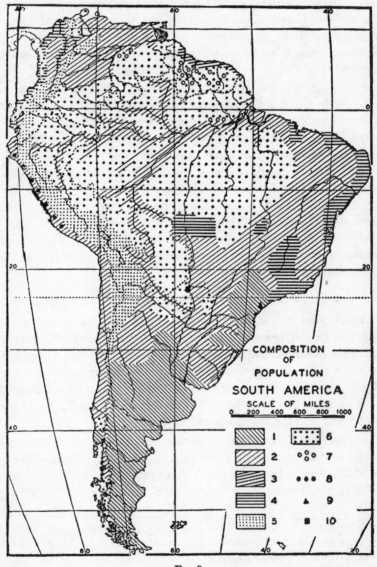

COMPOSITION
OF
POPULATION
SOUTH AMERICA
SCALE OF MILES
0   200   400   600   800   1000

⟍⟍	1	∴∴	6
⟋⟋	2	o°o	7
≡	3	•••	8
▤	4	▲	9
⋮⋮	5	■	10

Fɪɢ. 9

Composition of Population

(1) A population largely of European extraction—Indian and mestizo being replaced primarily by European immigrants during the last fifty years. (2) Spanish-Portuguese-Indian mestizo. The proportion of European blood varies greatly from a large fraction in the Central Valley of Chile and Antioquía, to only a sprinkling in the upper Amazon, eastern Paraguay, and the inner *llanos*. (3) British, Dutch, French—mestizo with a strong proportion of negro blood; many Hindoo and Chinese immigrants. (4) Mixed population of Indians, Europeans, and negroes. The proportion of European blood varies from a significant fraction in east central Brazil to almost nil in the Pacific Margin of Colombia. (5) Population dominantly Highland Indian and mestizo with a small fraction of European blood. (6) Pure Indians, or almost pure Indians, living in primitive conditions and largely apart from the influences of the republics. (7) Bush negroes little mixed with Indians living under primitive conditions. (8) Negro and Oriental blood introduced during the guano period. (9) Recent Japanese immigrants. (10) Mennonites in Paraguay. (From C. F. Jones. *South America*, Henry Holt & Company, New York.)

rhythm,[19] an easily utilizable natural vegetation, a fertile easily tilled soil, and any mineral resources.

Here certain conditions fostered native life at a low stage of culture. Though some of the Indians of tropical rain forests had reached the archaic stage of culture, many tribes had not advanced beyond the hunter-and-fisher stage of life. All the numerous streams are full of fish. Small short-pronged deer, fleeting in and out among the trees, droves of wild pigs (peccaries of the tropics) foraging on succulent root or stem, small and large monkeys of many colors chattering and swinging from branch to branch, glossy black and crimson-comb turkeys hid in the underbrush or perched high on swinging bough—all succumb to the deftly aimed arrow of the Indian archer and thus appease the pangs of hunger. Fruits and succulent roots can be gathered from the forest. Patches of corn, beans, and manioc also supply food without much skill or work.[20] In the humid, hot climate little or no clothing is necessary, and an easily constructed brush hut gives shelter from the scorching rays of the sun and pelting rains. But the sustaining of life at a low level does not give an incentive for man to advance in a material or cultural way (Fig. 9).

In contrast to these conditions which made life easy, primitive man faced many difficulties in the tropical rain forest. For thousands of miles, the low, flat terrain, crossed by numerous sluggish brown streams that reflect perfectly the bordering walls of rain-drenched forest, is exceedingly difficult to traverse. Only on the streams is travel fairly easy. A traveller on entering the lowland forest if bent on overland travel, leaves the pack animal behind and takes to foot with human porters, or, if desiring to traverse the region more hastily, takes to a canoe and glides or paddles swiftly down the meandering streams, stopping on some sand bar or sandy bank when night overtakes him.

In addition to being debilitating and enervating, the climate constitutes a marked disadvantage in other ways; food cannot be kept any length of time so that man is almost constantly employed in obtaining food for himself and family. No dry season favors the ripening and harvesting of crops; the hot sun and drenching rains burn the humus

---

[19] C. Eijkman, "Some questions concerning the influence of tropical climate on man," in *The Lancet*, CCVI (1924), 887-893, and G. T. Trewartha, "Recent thoughts on the problems of white acclimatization in the wet tropics," in *Geographical Review*, XVI (1926), 467-478.

[20] Herbert J. Spinden, "The origin and distribution of agriculture in America," in *International Congress of Americanists*, XIX (1917), 269-276, and reference on pages 274-275.

out of the soil and leach them so rapidly that burned-over patches produce only a few crops before being allowed to revert to bush and forest.[21] The high temperatures and heavy rainfall favor a rapid and rank growth of vegetation, difficult to cope with even in modern times. Diseases and insect pests are a constant menace. Malaria, yellow fever, dysentery, hook-worm, bubonic plague, and many other diseases sap the vitality and shorten the lives of the backward people dwelling there. Furthermore, the environment does not offer materials out of which can be fashioned necessary artifacts. It is true that the forests provide the bows, arrows, and the blowpipe (the *pucuna*) essential in shooting animals, fowl, and fish, and in waging tribal warfare. Also, the bark-woven shirt and trousers worn by many of the inhabitants are well adapted to the enervating heat of the day, but afford no protection at night from the voracious swarms of insects that suck and sting, making peaceful sleep impossible. But minerals are entirely lacking. In the early history of mankind, stone has been one of the most important and indispensable raw materials. Stone is lacking in the vast tropical lowlands of South America, so that the aborigines had to be contented with wood, shell, and bone for the manufacture of their implements. Consequently, none of the natives advanced beyond the archaic stage of culture.[22]

The same conditions that handicapped the native peoples in the tropical rain forests and the low stage of civilization of the scattered forest Indians made these forests unattractive to the Europeans throughout colonial times. Even in modern times, with all our science and medicine, these lands are avoided.[23] It is a question whether these hot, humid, and insect infested lands can ever become over large areas healthful and pleasant places in which to dwell.

The Central Andes. In striking contrast to the tropical rain forests are the deep valleys and high *pampas* of the central Andes. Here a combination of environmental conditions fostered the rise of several very advanced native cultures.[24] Here the Spaniards found conditions which made the central Andes one of the most prized of all Spanish colonial possessions (Fig. 10).

---

[21] C. F. Marbut and C. B. Manifold, "The Soils of the Amazon basin in relation to agricultural possibilties," in *Geographical Review*, XVI (1926), 414-442.

[22] Spinden, 269-276, and maps opposite pages 272 and 274.

[23] R. P. Strong and others, "Medical report of the Hamilton Rice Seventh Expedition to the Amazon," in *Contributions of the Harvard Institute for Tropical Biology and Medicine, No. 4* (Cambridge, 1926).

[24] P. A. Means, *Ancient civilizations of the Andes,* 48-49, 50 ff.

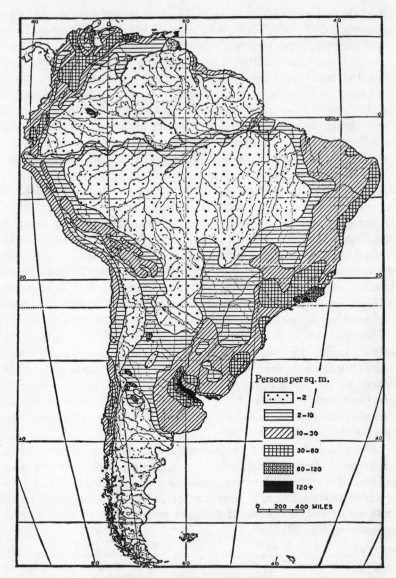

FIG. 10. POPULATION DENSITY

Most of the people of South America have concentrated in areas near the sea or in the highland sections in the tropics. (From C. F. Jones. *South America*, Henry Holt & Company.)

As previously stated, the Altiplano and the deep intermontane valleys of Peru, like the Mantaro, the Apurimac, and the Urubamba, afford relatively small isolated places effectively separated by topographical and climatic barriers from the Indians in other parts of the continent, especially the fiercer warlike tribes of the eastern lowlands.[25] Though these valleys drain into the Amazon system, they cut through the eastern cordillera in deep gorges that were easily defended portals. This isolation and protection induced early permanent settlement in certain areas.

The valley bottoms around 10,000 to 11,000 feet afford flat alluvial plains and adjacent piedmont slopes in close proximity to perennially flowing waters. These valleys have rather fertile soils capable of supporting the most intensive tillage. Above such lands, and adjacent to them, are steep mountain sides capable of producing crops with painstaking terracing and irrigation.[26] High above these, the natural grass and low shrubs grow abundantly and provide pasturage all the year. The great diversity of relief provides a variety of climatic conditions, vegetation, and minerals, all of which played a vital part in the evolution of culture.

Though lying within the tropics, these valleys and *pampas* are temperate in character. Here work is not so disagreeable as in the hot humid rain forests. The rather low rainfall of from ten to thirty inches makes irrigation necessary for the production of crops in some sections. Most of the rain comes during the warmer months when the crops can use it. Temperatures, though mild enough to give rather large yields under irrigation, require the preservation of food during the short winter period and during seasons of poor crops when an unsuspected frost in the middle of summer destroys what promises to be a major yield. Thus, to live here, the early peoples had to produce and save. The disagreeably cold climate makes warm clothing necessary and the seasonal and daily changes stimulate the people to activity.

The region has a variety of plants which were utilized by the Indians. Corn does not grow well above 10,000 feet. But potatoes,[27] *oca* and *olluca,* which are native tubers, and *quinoa,* a native cereal, grow up to 14,000

---

[25] Although the Incas never established themselves in the tropical rain forests, they obtained various products from the *montaña,* including coca, bamboo, *chonta* palm wood for weapons, some timbers for building, plumes for headdresses, and gold. See C. R. Markham, *The Incas of Peru,* 192-199.

[26] O. F. Cook, "Staircase farms of the ancients," in *National Geographic Magazine,* XXIX (1916), 474-534.

[27] C. F. Jones, *South America.* For potatoes and other crops, see pages 206-211, 247-248, 529-531.

feet and in sheltered places a little higher.[28] *Ichu* grass, grazed by llamas, alpacas, and vicuñas, is also useful for thatch, matting, and containers. The *totora* reed, growing among the margins of lakes and along the edges of swamps and the banks of streams, is employed in basketry and in making the *balsas,* the only boat used in the highland. The *tola* bush, the *llareta* bush, and the *queñua* tree provide valuable fuel in this almost treeless land. The *quishuar* tree supplies crooked tough wood for "foot-plows" and other plows which have been used for centuries.[29] The sparse vegetation, in addition to having a high degree of utility for the highland Indian, made easy the bringing of the valley floors and hill-sides under cultivation.[30]

As significant as the plants are the animals of this region.[31] The llama, in addition to being a very valuable pack animal, clothes the In-dian with its wool, furnishes fuel from manure carefully gathered and dried, and provides meat, fat, bone, and leather when it is no longer useful as a pack animal.[32] The alpaca yields fine wool, meat, bone, and leather. Other useful animals of this region embrace the vicuña, which grows a fine wool; the *viscacha,* a large edible rodent;[33] the *cui,* an edible guinea pig that abounds in the homes of the Indians;[34] and the *yutu,* a sort of partridge. In addition, other fowl and a variety of fish supplement the diet of the Indian.[35]

The abundant stone supplied materials for buildings, granaries, roads, bridges, irrigation works, and some artifacts.[36] Abundant clay furnished materials for building and pottery. The metals of the highlands gave these people a great advantage over the people in any other part of the

---

[28] Father Bernabé Cobo, *Historia del nuevo mundo* (Edited by Marcos Jiménez de la Espada, 4 vols., Seville). Potatoes, book 4, chapter xiii; *Oca,* book 4, chapter xiv; *Quinoa,* book 4, chapter v; *Ichu,* book 4, chapter cvi; *Tola,* book 5, chapter xliii; *Llareta,* book 4, chapter lxxii; *Queñua,* book 6, chapter cxxviii.

[29] Cobo: *Quishuar,* book 6, chapter xlix.

[30] Spinden, H. J., "The invention and, spread of agriculture in America," in *American Museum Journal,* XVII (1917), 181-188. Reference here is to page 186.

[31] Jones, 211-214, 248-249.

[32] P. A. Means, "The domestication of the llama," in *Science* XLVII (1918), 268-269.

[33] George F. Eaton, "Food animals of the Peruvian highlands," in *International Congress of Americanists,* XXI (1925), part ii, 61-66; and Cobo, *Viscacha,* book 9, chapter xlviii.

[34] Cobo: *Cui,* book 9, chapter xlvi.

[35] R. C. Murphy, "Bird life in the Urubamba Valley," in *Natural History,* xxi (1921), 507-512.

[36] Cobo, building stone and quarrying, book 3, chapters xiii-xviii; Jones, 170, 172; Markham, 21-39.

continent.[37] They furnished materials for utensils, implements, artifacts, and ornaments. In smelting, casting, hammering, welding, soldering, and plating metals the Incas had developed remarkable skill. Used from the earliest times, placer gold was produced from numerous mountain streams throughout the region;[38] these facts are also true of silver.[39] Copper came into use somewhat later, as did tin and lead.[40]

Thus the central Andes offered the Indians an amazing variety of √ environmental conditions and of raw materials that were basic to the rise in material and intellectual culture. This favorable combination of conditions was not found to quite the same degree in any other part of the continent. However, environmental conditions alone are not sufficient to cause great cultural advance even though they may be the most important element. In this region for thousands of years the Indians by slow steady steps rose from the archaic stage of culture to high ancient civilizations. Thus the ability and readiness of the Indians to utilize these resources played an important part in their cultural advance.

The same conditions that favored the rise of native cultures in this region attracted the Spaniards. The Spaniards were acquainted with the conditions of life in semiarid and arid areas. To them the civilized groups of Indians were prizes to be conquered. Consequently, their accumulated wealth, their buildings, lands, and mines, and even the Indians themselves, became the property of the Spaniards. With all these attractions the central Andes, the northern Andes, the coastal valleys of Peru, and the irrigated oases of western Argentina became the chief centers of Spanish colonial activity of the continent.

SELECTED BIBLIOGRAPHY

I. GENERAL

References 1 to 7 discuss general geographic conditions and the relation of the historical background in different portions of Hispanic America.

1. Enock, C. R., *Mexico* (London, 1910), pages 1-55.
2. Hrdlička, Aleš, "Early man in South America," Bureau of American Ethnology, *Bulletin 52* (Washington, 1912).

---

[37] P. A. Means, *Ancient civilizations of the Andes,* 21-22, 24-25, 117 ff., 524 ff.

[38] Cobo, gold, book 3, chapter xxxvi; W. H. Prescott, *History of the conquest of Peru* (Philadelphia, 1902), II and Index; Dawson, II and Index; W. C. Farabee, "Ancient American gold," in *Museum Journal,* Museum of the University of Pennsylvania, XI (1920), 93-129.

[39] Cobo, silver, book 3, chapter xxxvii; Prescott, Index; Dawson, II and Index; H. Bingham, "Potosí," in *Bulletin of the American Geographical Society,* XLIII (1911), 1-13.

[40] Baron E. Nordenskiöld, *The copper and bronze ages in South America;* Cobo, copper, book 3, chapter xlii; tin, book 3, chapter xliv; lead, book 3, chapter xlv.

3. Kroeber, A. L., "Coast and highland in prehistoric Peru," *American Anthropologist,* n.s., Vol. XXIX (1927), pages 625-653.

4. Prescott, W. H., *History of the conquest of Mexico* (Philadelphia, 1873), Vol I, pages 1-25.

5. Prescott, W. H., *History of the conquest of Peru* (Philadelphia, 1874), Vol. I, pages 3-40.

6. Means, P. A., *Ancient civilizations of the Andes* (New York, 1931), pages 3-27.

7. Smith, J. R., "The economic importance of the plateaus of tropic America," *Bulletin of the American Geographic Society,* Vol. XLIII (1911), pages 36-45.

II. Relief

References 8-12 are chiefly discussions of relief and the influence of relief and altitude.

8. Jones, Clarence F., *South America* (New York, 1930), pages 4-6, 14-29.

9. Marbut, C. F. and Manifold, C. B., "The topography of the Amazon valley," *Geographical Review,* Vol. XV (1925), pages 617-642.

10. Bowman, Isaiah, *Desert trails of Atacama* (American Geographical Society, Special Publication No. 5, New York, 1924), pages 11-39, 252-293.

11. Church, G. E., "South America: an outline of its physical geography," *Geographical Journal,* Vol. XVII (1901), pages 333-409, and maps op. p. 360.

12. Tower, W. S., "The Andes as a factor in South American geography," *Journal of Geography,* Vol. XV (1916), pages 1-8.

III. Climate and Man's Adjustment to Climatic Conditions

References 13 to 18 treat climatic conditions in South America and portions of Caribbean America. References 19 to 26 take up the problems of man's adjustment to climatic conditions in the high mountains of Peru and Bolivia and in the humid, hot lowlands of the Caribbean region and South America.

13. Jones, Clarence F., *South America* (New York, 1930), pages 30-49.

14. Gooze, Charles and Jones, Clarence F., "The seasonal distribution of rainfall in South America," *Bulletin of the Geographical Society of Philadelphia,* Vol. XXVI (1928), pages 93-115.

15. Kendrew, W. G., *Climates of the continents* (Oxford, 1927), selected portions.

16. Jefferson, M., "Actual temperatures of South America," *Geographical Review,* Vol. XVI (1926), pages 443-466.

17. Foscue, E. J., "Rainfall maps of Cuba," *Monthly Weather Review,* Vol. LVI (1928), pages 170-173.

18. Black, W. S., "Problem of life at high altitudes," *Engineering and Mining Journal-Press,* Vol. CXIV (1922), pages 800-804.

19. Bowman, I., "Man and climatic change in South America," *Geographical Journal,* Vol. XXXIII (1909), pages 267-278.

20. Eijkman, C., "Some questions concerning the influence of tropical climate on man," *The Lancet,* Vol. CCVI (1924), pages 887-893.

21. Gregory, J. W., "Inter-racial problems and white colonization in the tropics," *Scottish Geographical Magazine,* Vol. XL (1924), pages 257-282.

22. Huntington, E., "The white man and tropical America," *Journal of Race Development,* Vol. V (1914), pages 185-211.

23. Huntington, E., "Maya civilization and climatic changes," *International Congress of Americanists,* Vol. XIX (1917), pages 150-164.

24. Spinden, H. J., "Civilization in the wet tropics," *World's Work,* Vol. XLV (1922-23), pages 438-448.

25. Trewartha, G. T., "Recent thought on the problem of white acclimatization in the wet tropics," *Geographical Review,* Vol. XVI (1926), pages 467-478.

26. Strong, R. P. and others, "Medical report of the Hamilton Rice Seventh Expedition to the Amazon," *Contributions of the Harvard Institute for Tropical Biology and Medicine, No. 4* (Harvard University Press, Cambridge, 1926).

IV. Vegetation, Crops, and Animals

27. Jones, Clarence F., *South America* (New York, 1930), pages 50-73.

28. Denis, P., *Amérique du Sud,* in *Geographie Universelle,* Vol. XV (Librairie Armand Colin, Paris, 1927), selected portions.

29. Zon, R. and Sparhawk, W. N., *Forest resources of the world* (New York, 1923), Vol. II, selected portions.

30. Bowman, I. *The Andes of southern Peru* (Published for the American Geographical Society, New York, 1916), selected portions.

31. Schmieder, O., "Alteration of the Argentine pampa in the colonial period," *University of California Publications in Geography,* Vol. II (1927), pages 303-321.

32. Schmieder, O., "The pampa: a natural or culturally induced grassland," *University of California Publications in Geography,* Vol. II (1927), pages 255-270.

33. Cook, O. F., "Foot-plow agriculture in Peru," *Bulletin of the Pan American Union,* Vol. LII (1921), pages 160-166.

34. Cook, O. F., "Staircase farms of the ancients," *National Geographic Magazine,* Vol. XXIX (1916), pages 474-534.

35. Spinden, Herbert J., "The invention and spread of agriculture in America," *American Museum of Natural History Journal,* Vol. XVII (1917), pages 181-189.

36. Spinden, Herbert J., "The origin and distribution of agriculture in America," *International Congress of Americanists,* Vol. XIX (1917), pages 269-276.

37. Prescott, W. H., *History of the conquest of Peru* (Philadelphia, 1874), pages 134 ff.

38. Prescott, W. H., *History of the conquest of Mexico* (Philadelphia, 1873), Vol. I, pages 134 ff.

39. Mortimer, W. G., *Coca, the divine plant of the Incas* (New York, 1901).

40. Cobo, Father Bernabé, *Historia del nuevo mundo.* Edited by Don Marcos Jiménez de la Espada (4 vols., Seville, 1890-1893). Potatoes, book 4, chapter xiii; *Oca,* book 4, chapter xiv; *Quinoa,* book 5, chapter v; *Ichu,* book 4, chapter cvi; *Tola,* book 4, chapter xliii; *Llareta,* book 4, chapter lxxii.

41. Eaton, George F., "Food animals of the Peruvian highlands," *International Congress of Americanists,* Vol. XXI, part 2, (1925), pages 61-66.

42. Means, P. A., "The domestication of the llama," *Science,* Vol. XLVII (1918), pages 268-269.

43. Prescott, W. H., *History of the conquest of Peru* (Philadelphia, 1874), pages 146 ff.

44. Chapman, F. M., "The distribution of bird life in Colombia," *Bulletin of the American Museum of Natural History,* Vol. XXXVI (1917).

V. Minerals

45. Bingham, H., "Potosí," *Bulletin of the American Geographical Society,* Vol. XLIII (1911), pages 1-13.

46. Dawson, T. C., *The South American republics* (2 vols., New York 1903-04), Vol. I, pages 3-19, 21-40, 235 ff., 285 ff., 347 ff., 403 ff.; Vol. II, pages 13 ff.

47. Fiske, John, *The discovery of America* (2 vols., Boston, 1892), Vol. I, pages 29 ff., 483 ff.; Vol. II, pages 294 ff.

48. Markham, C. R., *History of Peru* (Chicago, 1892), pages 11 ff., 65 ff.

49. Bowman, Isaiah, *Desert trails of Atacama.* American Geographical Society, *Special Publication No. 5* (New York, 1924), pages 162-185.

50. Prescott, W. H., *History of the conquest of Mexico* (Philadelphia, 1873), Vol. I, pages 140 ff.; Vol. II, pages 194 ff.

51. Enock, C. R., *Mexico* (London, 1910), pages 255 ff.

52. Farabee, W. C., "The use of metals in prehistoric America," *Museum Journal,* Museum of the University of Pennsylvania, Vol. XII (1921), pages 35-42.

53. Farabee, W. C., "Ancient American gold," *Museum Journal,* Museum of the University of Pennsylvania, Vol. XXI (1920), pages 93-129.

54. Cobo, Father Bernabé, *Historia del nuevo mundo.* Edited by Don Marcos Jiménez de la Espada (4 vols., Seville, 1890-1893). Gold, book 3, chapter xxxvi; silver, book 3, chapter xxxvii; copper, book 3, chapter xlii; tin, book 3, chapter lxiv; lead, book 3, chapter lxv; building stones, book 3, chapters xiii to xviii.

CHAPTER FOUR

THE NATIVE BACKGROUND IN LATIN AMERICAN HISTORY

By PHILIP AINSWORTH MEANS

I. INTRODUCTORY REMARKS

TO THAT part of the Western Hemisphere which lies between the Río Grande on the north and the southern tip of Tierra del Fuego on the south we are wont to apply the name Latin America, doing so because European nations, Spain and Portugal, which are two among many "Latin" nations, were the instruments whereby European civilization was brought into that part of our continent. It would, however, be equally just to call the vast territory indicated by the name of Indo-America, for here, more than in the more northerly section of the continent where we ourselves dwell, the native race of America, the American Indian, still retains its numerical importance and likewise its cultural, social, and political importance. Ever since the epochal discovery made by Christopher Columbus, the American Indian has been a preponderating factor in the history (cultural, social, and political) of Latin America to an extent unknown in the parts of America settled by the English. It is because of this fact that any study of Latin American history must take into constant consideration the native background of the subject.

II. THE ORIGIN OF THE AMERICAN INDIANS

Ever since the time of Columbus there have been two schools of thought concerning the origin of the native race of America, the American Indian race. The so-called Diffusionist School, to which many European anthropologists adhere, but practically no American scientists of weight, has for its major tenet that the native cultures of America—as well as the race possessing them—came into the Western Hemisphere, partly or fully grown, from some other quarter of the earth. The major premise which underlies all varieties of the Diffusionist School of opinion is that any given discovery leading to any given cultural element can be made only once and that consequently all manifestations of its working, no matter how widely separated in space and in time, are invariably to be traced to a single source. Holding this view, the Diffusionists portray the American cultures as resulting from immensely long folk-movements across thousands of miles of deserts, mountains, forests, and across other thousands of miles of uncharted seas, all this moving being done by ancient hordes of people carrying with them well-developed culture from their old homes to their new habitats.[1]

Superficial resemblances between remote and unconnected cultures of similar rank are often so striking that one cannot wonder that the unwary often jump at the conclusion that they were directly connected with one another. A case in point is a publication of over twenty years ago in which three superb Maya sculptures are brought, by chance, into juxtaposition with three superb Chinese sculptures of the T'ang Dynasty (A. D. 618-907). The superficial similarities are indeed amazing, so much so that anyone not versed in the underlying factors and elements involved would inevitably assume that there had been a close and direct contact between the two groups of sculptures. In truth, however, each group was merely the result of similar environmental stimuli, and there was no connection between them.[2]

The other school is that of the Independent Creationists. It is as old as the other. It holds that the discoveries and inventions giving rise to the more or less advanced forms of culture have been made many times and in many regions, each occasion of the kind being unconnected with the others. Independent Creationists pay far more attention to environmental factors than do their opponents, exploring cultural similarities in unlinked localities largely in terms of similar environmental shaping. They do not lose sight, however, of the importance of diffusion within relatively restricted areas; they show, on the contrary, that inventions spread radially in their own regions, whether these be large or small. Each vicinity is a more or less continuous environmental region within which each given invention is both practicable and advantageous.[3]

As Dr. Dixon has pointed out, environment exerts its influence on humankind through three main channels: 1. Opportunity, or the pres-

---

[1] Modern writings of the Diffusionist sort include: Christian, 1932; Graebner, 1905, 1909, 1911, 1927; Rivers, 1914; Rivet, 1926, 1928, 1928a; P. W. Schmidt, 1913; G. E. Smith, 1916, 1917, 1924. (These are all works by scientists of good standing. It is not necessary to cite the numerous fantastic and ignorant writers who are also Diffusionists). Works cited in this "short form" in the footnotes will be found cited in full in the bibliography.

[2] See Tozzer, 1912, and two pages immediately following that article.

[3] Modern writings representative of the Independent Creationist School include: Dixon, 1928; Goldenweiser, 1916; Kroeber and Holt, 1920; Kroeber, 1927, 1928; Means, 1916; Wallis, 1930. See also Smith, Malinowski, Spinden, and Goldenweiser, 1927, the conclusion of this symposium being anti-Diffusionist.

ence of raw materials; 2. Observation, or the perception by man of the raw materials; and 3. Genius, or the ability of individuals to reason out the application of the raw materials perceived.[4]

If, now, one turns from man's culture to man himself, as an animal, to men as a race in America, one finds that the Independent Creationists are in nearly complete agreement with the Diffusionists. Both schools believe that the American race is of Asiatic origin, the only important divergence between them being that the Diffusionists hold that the migrating race brought well advanced culture with it from Asia and that the Independent Creationists hold that no such *advanced* culture was brought.[5]

To sum up, it may be said that the leading American anthropologists currently believe that man entered the Western Hemisphere much as did various animal races, by a long, slow, jerky, irregular process of movement from northeasternmost Asia over into northwesternmost America, and thence, still gradually and irregularly, down through the continental land-mass of the Americas. The process may have begun as much as 40,000 years ago, and it continued by fits and waves almost into the historical period. In point of culture the migrants were, at any rate at first, on a primitive plane not unlike that of the Stone Age folk in Europe. Later waves may have been somewhat less primitive. None of them, however, bore with them any full-fledged civilization even of the more modest types known in Asia.[6]

III. TYPES OF ENVIRONMENT AND TYPES OF CULTURE IN AMERICA

Dr. Clarence F. Jones has given in previous chapters an admirable description and analysis of the geographical background. One may now apply what he has said to the question of American cultures in general.

If, to begin with, there can be defined three major types of environment—sub-Arctic, temperate, and tropical—in America, so also there can be distinguished three major categories of culture. There are, then, at the northern and southern extremes of our hemisphere conditions so rigorous and so taxing to human energies that all that men could do was to continue to live in a nomadic or semi-nomadic manner upon the primitive hunter-and-fisher plane of culture which he brought with him

---

[4] Pertinent citations include: Dixon, 1928, chapter 2; Harrison, 1926, 1926a, 1927; Nordenskiöld, 1929; Wissler, 1926, pages 16-18 and chapter 5.

[5] Dixon, 1928, especially chapters 6-8; Hrdlička, 1912, 1912a, 1917, 1917a, 1930, especially pp. 355-366, 1932; Means, 1931, chapter 2; Wissler, 1922, chapter 21.

[6] Dixon, 1928, pp. 266-271; Wallis, 1930, pp. 410-415. As long ago as 1588 Father Acosta, a learned Jesuit, held views not unlike these. See Acosta, 1880, book one, chapter 24, pp. 69-70.

from northeasternmost Asia. One area where this sort of culture was the only one, until alien influences from Europe were brought into play in modern times, was the vast realm now occupied by Canada and Alaska, with certain small exceptional areas in the more southern part thereof. The other area of sub-Arctic environment and of purely primitive culture was the southernmost region of South America, notably Tierra del Fuego and the mainland adjacent to the north thereof. In those areas are found the only truly primitive cultures, based on hunting-and-fishing alone, and nomadic or semi-nomadic in kind, in all America. If, as may be safely done, one assumes that the general primordial drift of mankind in the Western Hemisphere was from north to south, one must assume also that the ancestors of the folk in the far south had been on a higher plane of culture than their descendants in that sub-Antarctic region, and that it was their being pushed into that region which caused those descendants to relapse into the primitive plane.

Temperate areas in America occur not only in the regions between the central tropical belt and the sub-Arctic or sub-Antarctic belts but also within the tropical belt itself, being there caused to exist either by elevation, as in our southwest, in the highlands of Mexico and of Guatemala, in the highlands of Colombia, and in the great Andean highlands of Ecuador, Peru, Bolivia, and northern Chile and Argentina. Modern civilization, constantly stimulated from outside by a multitude of influences, flourishes best in that part of the temperate area which lies between the sub-Arctic or sub-Antarctic belt and the tropical belt. Ancient native civilization, on the other hand, had no such stimuli from outside, and consequently it had to depend entirely upon the resources inherent in the environment and upon the ability of men to make use of them. The optimum of surroundings, so far as the native race of America was concerned, was in the temperate areas within the tropical belt, that is, in the mountain regions already indicated. In those temperate areas men who arrived there while still on a hunter-and-fisher or primitive plane of culture found that progress was easy for them. Materials for agriculture, for basketry, for pottery making, for weaving, for permanent house building either in wood or in stone, for the making of implements or of weapons from wood, stone, bone, shell, and perhaps also for the use of gold, silver, or even copper, existed and were made an important addition to the older and more simple ways which, incidentally, were continued in so far as they were still useful. Thus, in the highland temperate regions indicated, and also in the abnormal western coast of South America, there came into being a plane of culture which may best be termed "Intermediate." [7] It contained the germs, the initial forms, of many elements in material culture from which, under favorable conditions, more advanced forms could be evolved. The same thing may be said of intangible culture, of religion, of social organization, and of government. Intermediate American native cultures can be divided into two grand types, the static and the dynamic. The first is found, not in the temperate elevated tropical regions of which mention has been made, nor yet in the river-veined abnormally cool coastal desert of western South America where the Humboldt Current flowing northwards from the Antarctic to the Equator cools the shore country in much the same way that the Gulf Stream warms northern Europe; on the contrary, static Intermediate cultures, that is Intermediate cultures destined never to progress (without help from outside) beyond the Intermediate plane, are found along the tropical coasts of Mexico and Central America, in all parts of the Caribbean Islands, all along the northern and eastern coasts of South America down to the Plata River, and, finally, all through the great interior river basins of South America, namely, the drainages of the Orinoco, the Amazon, and the Paraguay-Paraná-Plata system. These are regions where simon-pure and unrelieved tropical conditions exist, their general character being far lower, as regards general advantageousness, than that of the highland temperate regions where the environmental optimum is found. Even in those tropical regions, however, it was possible for men to develop or to maintain (if they had it on their arrival) the Intermediate stage of culture, with agriculture as its economic basis, and with simple forms of the arts and industries, as well as of religion, social structure, and government. There were lacking, nevertheless, environmental opportunities and stimuli of sorts destined to produce further advancement. Therefore, the Intermediate cultures in these purely tropical parts were of the static type of Intermediate culture.

In the highland areas already mentioned, on the other hand, and also where the Humboldt Current cooled the west coast of South America, there was a wealth of stimuli and of opportunities which, working upon dynamic Intermediate culture, enabled it to rise into the plane of civili-

---

[7] This cultural plane is also termed "Archaic" or "Secondary." The first of these terms is misleading in that it seems to imply a place in time rather than a stage of development. "Secondary" is also unsatisfactory because in many areas there is no trace of an antecedent "Primary" (or primitive) phase of culture. "Archaic" culture may exist in any period. Therefore, the term "Intermediate" signifying a level midway between the lowest and the highest stages of culture, regardless of time, is here adopted.

zation. The most advanced native societies in the Western Hemisphere nearly all had their habitat in the temperate highland areas within the tropics, the only exceptions being those in Yucatan and on the west coast of South America. These matters will be treated presently in greater detail.[8]

IV. The Processes of Cultural Growth in Native America

A little reflection shows why the folk in the northern regions of the continent never made substantial advancement beyond the primitive stage and why folk forced into the corresponding regions far to the south fell back into that stage (assuming that their ancestors had once enjoyed a higher state). They were obliged, in both cases, to scour an inimical terrain in ceaseless quest for food, and so had neither time nor strength to ponder upon the potential raw materials for better living that may have lurked in the ground beneath their feet or in the natural world around them. Grim necessity compelled them always to struggle for a bare existence; leisure for original thought and vitality allowing play of the imagination were alike wanting. Consequently, culture either stood still or else advanced but little and with glacier slowness so long as they remained under the conditions indicated.

Those, however, who gradually wandered into regions of more benign sort became able to study their environment in the leisure which became theirs. With bodies better fed and with less tax upon physical energies, minds became reflective and analytical, and genius had opportunity to assert itself. A greater variety of edible animals and usable plants was perceived. Houses were improved. Wild seeds were dropped, either by accident or, later, by design near the houses; they were watered when drought was on, and tended otherwise if need arose. The initial forms of agriculture were born. Husbandry, even of the most rudimentary sort, obliges those who cultivate it to abide patiently in one place while waiting for germination and growth to culminate in ripeness. And, while the husbandman waits, he, whether tyro or adept, has long days in which to contemplate his surroundings. So, concurrently, he perceives raw materials lying to hand and his genius teaches him how to use them in new ways. Thus are born the early forms of basketry,

---

[8] Although the classification here offered of native American cultures rests chiefly upon such works as Spinden, 1928, p. 68, Toynbee, 1935, Vaillant, 1930 and 1930b, and Wissler, 1926, pp. 203-222, it has its roots in such works of long ago as: Acosta, (1588), 1880, book one, chapters 13 and 22-24; Cobo (1653), 1890-1893, book 9, chapter 10.

of pottery, of weaving, of permanent architecture in tree-products, or else in turf, baked earth *(adobe)*, or in uncut stones laid in mud or clay. A sedentary, or at least semi-sedentary, mode of life results. At the same time the population is increasing, and mankind learns to regard with awe the imperfectly understood majesty of the natural world around him, so replete with things that help him and with others which threaten his safety. Religion, both of the grateful and of the fearing, propitiatory sort, comes into being. Also, a need arises for social control, and clans, tribes, or other groupings of households are evolved to meet the need.

By processes here only hinted at, cultures of the Intermediate grade were developed in America (and in many another part of the world as well). Let it not be thought, however, that the Intermediate stage of cultural growth was either small or uniform; on the contrary, it contained—and contains—a tremendous range of variations both as to degree and as to kind. If, at its lower margin, it is hardly distinguishable from the most developed primitive culture, at its upper margin it is represented by peoples who, having made considerable progress in agriculture, in the arts, and in craftsmanship generally, stand on the brink of civilization. Peoples who thus stand are of the dynamic sub-type of the Intermediate in most cases, and they proceed to perfect all their methods and institutions into civilized forms. Others of them, who have been dynamic up to that point, become static and advance no further without alien help. The explanation, in all cases, of what takes place lies in the environment or in the use which men make of it.

Here one may make two special points, the one scientific, the other philosophic. The first is that, as culture progresses from stage to stage, it carries with it all that is most useful in the earlier stages. In other words, all higher cultures derive something from the lower; man, whether he like it or not, is the heir of bygone ages. The second point concerns the rôle played by art in culture. Among peoples of primitive culture utilitarian considerations are dominant in the handicrafts to such a degree that whatever decoration there may be is purely incidental. The impulse towards embellishment becomes intensive, systematic, and effective only in the Intermediate stage of culture, being there predominantly a matter of gratifying or of propitiating gods or spirits representative of awful nature by means of ritualistic symbols not primarily æsthetic in motive.[9] True æsthetics, that is, the creation and application of beauty

[9] See Karsten, 1926, chs. 7-11; Means, 1931, pp. 41-49; Murdock, 1934, (under "Arts" and "Fine Arts," in Index); Wallis, 1930, pp. 177-186.

for its own sake, for the joy which it gives to the eye and through the
eye to the mind, rises into a dominant position only in civilization. One
soon learns to distinguish between the inner purpose of Intermediate art
and the æsthetic purpose of civilized art. Here lies the philosophic character of this second point.

Intermediate culture, because it is a stage in development, not a point
in time, often displays extraordinary similarities in far separated and
unconnected regions having roughly the same environmental character.
To cite a specific case, one may mention that in regions so far apart as
the San Juan Valley, Utah, and the Province of Córdoba, northwestern
Argentina, there existed a process of making pots by smearing clay
within a basket to the desired thickness and then, after the clay had
dried, stripping away the basket so that a pot was left, decorated with
the pattern of the basketry. In both places the same process existed;
moreover, there were other cultural resemblances between them, particularly in the matter of house-types. The environments producing
these similarities are practically the same.[10]

Here the question arises: How was the Intermediate culture in all
its variations so widely dispersed in America? The answer to this
question, as to so many others, lies in the environment. Wherever the
surroundings of man provided the raw materials for advancement along
the lines already indicated and, at the same time, provided him with
vigor, health, and zest of mind sufficient to enable him to perceive both
the raw materials and the ways in which to use them, man advanced;
and his advance continued so long as the nice balance between the environmental offer and the ability to accept it was maintained. When
one or the other of these two factors ceased, advancement ceased also,
and the status reached became permanent. In general it may be said
that parallel cultural growths are products of similar environments which
enlarge and enrich human life from the primitive stage onwards to the
point where the nice balance referred to is lost.[11]

---

[10] I owe my knowledge of the Utah end of this cultural equation to Mr. J. O.
Brew, of the Peabody Museum, Harvard, who kindly showed me pots of the sort
referred to which he had dug up in Utah; the Argentine end of the equation will
be found in Gardner, 1919. For the house-type matter see: Debenedetti, 1930, and
also Bemis and Burchard, 1933, pp. 61-90; Murdock, 1934, (under "Dwelling"
and "House-building" in Index); and Wissler, 1922 and 1926, passim.

[11] Dixon, 1928, chapter 8; Wissler, 1926, chapter 5; Toynbee, 1935; Wallis,
1930.

V. Native American Civilizations

In every case the celebrated native American civilizations arose from an Intermediate culture of the dynamic sort. They did so only in regions where the optimum of environment, or some close approximation thereto, existed. Those regions have already been mentioned in general terms. We shall now deal with them in greater detail.

The Highlands of Mexico

In this region there was the optimum of environment, that is, the best air, the best soil, the best offering of nature, and the best ability of man. As long ago as 3,000 to 2,000 B. C., as shown by the excavations of Professor Byron Cummings at Cuicuilco, a little to the south of Mexico City, there was a town whose culture was on the border line between high Intermediate and modest civilized culture. There was a circular pyramid of somewhat rough masonry, and there were artifacts such as pottery and clay figurines. The whole was covered by a lava flow from a neighboring volcano some 4,000 to 5,000 years ago.[12]

Elsewhere in highland Mexico, and especially at such sites as Teotihuacán, Tenochtitlán (Mexico City), Cholula, Mitla, Monte Albán, and many others, civilization flourished for many centuries. Its base was in all cases an Intermediate culture, either evolved on the place or else imported from some region further north such as our southwest or some other southerly part of our country, or again from what is now northern Mexico. In broad terms it may be said that the civilization which existed, with phases, vicissitudes, and transitions, throughout south central Mexico was distinguished by pyramid temples, by markets for barter-commerce, by strict control through chiefs supported by a tribute-giving people, and by a military class. The economic structure rested upon highly developed agriculture. Life wore an aspect of regulated order and of amenity exemplified by a well-rounded art and technology, being in these respects comparable to many of the ancient civilizations of the Old World. Furthermore, there was a priestly class which shared with the chiefs and the soldier class the control of the masses and which, most likely, had a monopoly of scientific knowledge, including such things as medicine, hieroglyphic writing, astronomy, and calendric lore. Religion was formidable in its fierceness and goryness at times, especially in the Aztec period just prior to the Spanish conquest; but it was not the religion of savages. Like the Nahuatl language it was highly

---

[12] Cummings, 1922, 1923, 1926.

evolved and extremely intricate, being by no means without strange subtleties of its own. From the standpoint of post-conquest history, the chief fact about ancient Mexican civilization was that it drilled the people into a mute discipline which prepared the way for Spanish dominance and rule.[13]

Yucatan and Guatemala

Only in parts of this area did civilization flourish. The rest of Central America contained Intermediate cultures of the static sort. In northern and central Guatemala, in British Honduras, in northern Honduras, and, later, in Yucatan, there rose and fell the greatest of all native American civilizations, that of the Mayas. Highly important is the fact that by 613 B. C., having already passed through long and intricate preliminary processes, the Mayas evolved hieroglyphic and calendric systems of unique intellectual achievement. Only with the Maya do we have, in ancient America, a more or less accurately dated history which, in barest outline, is as follows.

Between about 613 B. C. (the date assigned by Dr. Spinden to the perfecting of the hieroglyphic and calendric systems) and 98 B. C. (the date inscribed on the Tuxtla statuette, found about 80 miles southeast from Vera Cruz and now in the National Museum, Washington) there was a period in which the Mayas were already civilized but not yet on the highest plane of civilization that they were destined to reach. They had already left their oldest known habitat in the Huasteca country (on the coast, north of Vera Cruz) where they had probably gone through the Intermediate state of culture, and were moving towards the Lake Peten district of northern Guatemala. They are known to have been in that district during the first century after Christ, having left dated monuments there. It was in the south, however, in the highlands of central Guatemala, that they attained to their first great florescence of very high civilization. But one must examine the environmental background of these earlier stages. The Huasteca country is coastal and

---

[13] Many works on ancient Mexico will be found cited in the bibliography. A few of the most important are: Beuchat, 1912, pp. 257-403; Brasseur de Bourbourg, 1857-59; Caso, 1932; Clavijero, 1780-81, 1787; Díaz del Castillo, 1908-1916; Gamio, 1920, 1922; Haeberlin, 1919; Holmes, 1885, 1895, 1914; Joyce, 1914; Krickeberg, 1925; Kroeber, 1925b; Linné, 1934; Nuttall, 1886, 1888, 1891, 1892, 1894, 1903, 1906, 1906a, 1925, 1927, 1930; Prescott, 1844; Saville, 1898, 1916, 1920, 1922, 1925, 1929, 1930; Reygadas Vertiz, 1930; Toro, 1930; Vaillant, 1928, 1930, 1930a, 1930b, 1931; Wissler, 1922. For sociology see Bandelier, 1878 and 1879; for folklore see Alexander, 1920.

tropical, but is sufficiently moderate therein to enable a dynamic Intermediate culture to develop and to progress into civilization. Some of the original Huasteca-Maya folk proceeded, as already said, southeastwardly into the Tuxtla district where tropical conditions are conspicuously more intense than they are in the Huasteca country. By that time (roughly the beginning of our era), however, the migrant Maya were culturally strong enough to resist adverse conditions for a time at least. They seem, nevertheless, to have moved onwards fairly soon, and to have arrived in the Guatemala highlands by the year 100 A. D., or a little before it.

During the first seven centuries A. D. the "Old Empire" of the Mayas flourished in central and northern Guatemala and in adjacent parts of British Honduras and of Honduras. Some of these regions are today intensely tropical and densely forested, but it is likely that in ancient times they were considerably less so. The "Old Empire" had more than twenty-five great cities, each one the nucleus of a well-organized city-state, each one rich in imposing pyramidal temples, lordly palaces, elaborately adorned and inscribed public monuments, each one, in short, a focus of highly developed polity manifesting itself in many media. Splendid roads which never knew the touch of a wheel, all commerce and all traffic being carried on men's backs, bound the many cities together. Towards the end of the period a transitional shift northwards began, largely because the peculiarly wasteful agricultural methods of the Mayas (such as the frequent burning-over of fields) were making the livelihood of a dense and chiefly urban population increasingly precarious.

The "New Empire" of the Mayas began with the transitional shift, already noted, which lasted from about 450 to about 990, in which period there was, together with an expansion into the more northern part of Yucatan, a marked recession of civilization, one may suppose, due to hostile climatic conditions, to wars, or to pestilence. From 990 to about 1200, however, the "New Empire" proper constituted a brilliant recrudescence of Maya civilization during which northern Yucatan was starred with glorious cities whose ruling dynasties were increasingly often at war with one another. As a result of the calling in of military aid from Mexico, about 1200, the Mayas found themselves under the domination of powerful aliens. The new rulers maintained the high level of civilization, however, and enriched it with cultural elements peculiar to themselves. About 1450 a new series of wars finally disrupted the Mexican hegemony in Yucatan and brought about a new decline which lasted until the Spaniards came.[14]

Colombia

Here, more than in any other part of native America, we see the effects of environment upon human culture. Along both the Pacific and the Atlantic (Caribbean) coasts of Colombia normal tropical conditions prevail under which Intermediate culture of varying grades existed. Some tribes had special abilities, such as that of the Quimbaya, for working gold with a skilfulness rarely equalled anywhere in the world. But, in general, the culture of the coast dwellers in what is now Colombia was medium to high Intermediate. In the interior of the country, particularly in the deep, hot, jungle valley of the Cauca-Magdalena river system, lower Intermediate culture prevailed among such tribes as the Panches and Colimas who thus perfectly reflect the peculiar disadvantageousness of their surroundings. On the other hand, in the highlands to the east of the Magdalena River, which flows northwards from southern Colombia to the Caribbean, the much higher culture of the Chibchas throve under salubrious conditions at 8,000 or more feet above sea level. Here we have a perfect example of how excellent natural surroundings engender civilization. The Chibchas, at the time of the Spanish conquest, were divided between two powerful chiefs, the Zaque of Tunja in the northern half of the Chibcha territory and the Zipa of Bogotá in the southern half. Both these potentates were absolute rulers over their respective realms, and both had under them hierarchies of lesser chiefs whose ancestors had been independent rulers of petty states. Very little is known of Chibcha history prior to about 1450, but from then onwards to the Spanish conquest there was a great struggle between the Zaque of Tunja and the Zipa of Bogotá in which the latter was gradually winning paramount position. In other words, the Chibchas were in a stage of modest civilization, at the time of the Spaniards' coming. It is likely

---

[14] In addition to several of the works cited in Note 13, the following are important: Blom, 1930; Blom and La Farge, 1925; Carrillo y Ancona, 1883; Charnay, 1885, 1887; Gann and Thompson, 1931; Holmes, 1888; Huntington, 1914, 1915, 1917; Lothrop, 1924, 1925; Maudslay, 1889-1902; Morley, 1915, 1917, 1920, 1922, 1927; A. A. Morris, 1931; E. H. Morris, 1931; E. H. Morris, Charlot, and A. A. Morris, 1931; Ricketson, 1927, 1928, 1928a, 1930; Saville, 1920, 1921, 1930, 1930a, 1935; E. S. Spinden, 1933; H. J. Spinden, 1913, 1917, 1917a, 1924, 1924a, 1928a, 1930; Stephens, 1841, 1843; E. H. Thompson, 1904, 1932; J. E. Thompson, 1930; Tozzer, 1907, 1911, 1911a, 1912, 1916, 1927, 1930; Totten, 1926.

that they were slow in arriving at that point and that, for many centuries previous thereto, they had been high Intermediate rather than low civilized. This is indicated by certain remarkable archæological finds in southern Colombia near the headwaters of the Magdalena at San Agustín, where large monolithic statues bearing what is unquestionably high Intermediate art, and where pottery, not of the fine sorts produced by civilizations, are found, these remains being of an age which cannot be determined as yet and of an ethnic affiliation not yet understood.

The Chibchas had a well-marked priestly class and worshipped the Sun as well as a great array of other deities. They had no notable architecture in stone, and no great use of the mound or pyramid. Nevertheless, their chiefs lived with a considerable degree of barbaric pomp in large dwellings built cleverly of wood and well-made thatch and surrounded by gardens and water. They used gold with great lavishness for decorative and ceremonial purposes. One of the minor chiefs, he of Guatavitá, was wont to have his naked body anointed with oil and then covered thickly with powdered gold which he proceeded to wash from him with lustral rites in a little tarn within his realm. He became the origin of the El Dorado (the Gilded Man) myth which later so greatly exercised the imaginations of Spaniards.[15]

It is noteworthy that nowhere in Colombia was civilization of a texture sufficiently sturdy to permit of its being taken over entire and woven into the fabric of colonial society. It is, in this respect, much lower than the civilizations of Mexico and of the Andean area. In Colombia the native masses became the peasantry of colonial times, but they did not preserve, as did the Mexicans and the Andeans, any considerable part of their own social institutions or of their peculiar culture.[16]

The Andean Area—Ecuador, Peru, and Bolivia

As already said, this region of South America affords highly favorable environment both along the coast, cooled by the northward flowing Humboldt Current, and in the highlands where elevation makes for temperate

---

[15] On this see Means, 1935, chapter 5.

[16] Works important for Colombia in pre-Spanish times include: J. Acosta, 1848, 1901; Acosta de Samper, 1894; Alexander, 1920, chapter vi; Bandelier, 1893; Beuchat, 1912, pp. 531-562; Bollaert, 1860; Castellanos, 1886; Cuervo Marquez, 1920; Fernández de Piedrahita, 1688; Hébert, 1896; Joyce, 1912, chapters 1 and 2; Markham, 1912, chapters 2-5; J. A. Mason, 1925, 1926, 1928, 1931; Preuss, 1921, 1922, 1929, 1930; Restrepo, 1895; Restrepo Tirado, 1912, 1917; Saville, 1927, 1928; Simón, 1627; Stübel and Uhle, 1889-1890; Wissler, 1922, pp. 245-248; Zahm, 1909, 1917; Zerda, 1883.

conditions in many parts. In both the zones thus indicated in general terms there were early established people of high Intermediate culture who, about the time of Christ, evolved into the first of a long series of civilizations which subsequently went through various vicissitudes and phases too intricate to trace here.

From the standpoint of post-Spanish history the most important phase of native Andean civilization was that represented by the justly celebrated Inca Empire.

The career and the achievements of the Inca dynasty were alike extraordinary. Beginning about 1100 as a humble little tribe of llama herders and tillers of the soil near Cuzco in southern Peru, they had at first a culture of high Intermediate sort, their ancestors having relapsed from an earlier stage of civilization. Little by little and reign by reign they steadily rose in a few generations to be the greatest imperial dynasty ever seen in native America, and one of the greatest ever seen anywhere. Under the Emperor Pachacutec, who ruled from about 1400 to about 1448, they reached their true apogee. He left a magnificently organized realm which stretched from what is now northern Peru down into Bolivia and into northern Chile and Argentina, including both highland and coastland country. The Inca Pachacutec was a great conqueror who knew how to bring states of varying greatness and power under his rule and how to weld them to the solid fabric of his empire. It was done by tact, organization, and good sense as much as by warfare. After his time the empire was almost doubled in size by expansion to the north in what is now Ecuador and to the south in what is now the northern two-thirds of Chile. Thus, by the end of the reign of the Emperor Huayna Capac, in 1527, the Inca Empire had a territory equal to that of all our Atlantic seaboard states added together. This great extent, however, was a source of weakness rather than of strength, as Huayna Capac seems to have realized dimly; for, at his death, he divided the empire into the Kingdom of Quitu (roughly equal to Ecuador) which he gave to a favorite illegitimate son, Atahualpa, and the remainder which he left to his legitimate heir, Huáscar. Naturally enough strife broke out between the brothers, and it was going on when the Spaniards arrived under the leadership of Pizarro and Almagro, a fact which in large measure facilitated the Spanish conquest of the empire of the Incas.

All the native civilizations of the Andes, both those prior to the Incaic and the Incaic itself, are intensely interesting. In all cases there was an underlying period of Intermediate culture which represented the cultural plane of the earliest migrants into the Andean area. As not even the faintest trace of hieroglyphic writing has ever yet been discovered in that part of civilized native America (or elsewhere in South America) we can only suppose that the original Intermediate-cultured immigrants must have left the Maya area before the first steps toward writing were made. This would put the earliest migrations before about 1000 B. C. Subsequently, although they never learned a system of writing, the descendants of the first migrants built up, as already said, a long series of successive civilizations in all parts of the Andean area, culminating in that of the Inca dynasty.

From the standpoint of Hispanic American history the most important features of the Inca civilization are two. First, there existed a society of rigidly, but not harshly, disciplined under a government of the aristocratic state socialism variety with the Inca Emperor at the pinnacle and all-powerful therein. Under him was a carefully graded hierarchy of officials down to those who had charge over ten households. The *puric,* or head of a household, was the unit of society, not the individual. All tribute to the state was paid by *purics* either in the form of labor on public works or in that of the products of their fields and herds. Only *purics,* men between 25 and 50 years of age, were expected to pay tribute and to do heavy work; women, young people, and old people of both sexes were exempt from tribute and performed only light work around their homes. Both unemployment and overwork were unknown. The state maintained finely built roads, storehouses, messenger service, reservoirs, irrigation canals, and fortresses which in their several ways combined to make life both pleasant and safe for everyone. There were periodical fairs of various grades at which goods were traded in on a basis of barter (money, happily, being unknown as it was in all ancient America). Thus, although the Inca was both omnipotent and divine, being the head of the state and of the official Sun-cult, his rule was beneficial to all classes. Many of these features, particularly the official hierarchy, were taken over by the Spaniards in modified form after the conquest.

Second, there existed a material culture and an artistic tradition which were both rich and practical. Houses, palaces, and temples were built of stone beautifully wrought and fitted, or, on the coast, of adobe equally well manipulated. The best Incaic pottery cannot be outmatched for charm of shape and of painted or modelled decoration. In the textile arts, although the looms used were very simple from a mechanical standpoint, the Incas' subjects (and the earlier peoples of the country) were unsurpassed. Their fabrics of innumerable kinds and richest coloring fill us with wonder to this day. In woodwork, stone-carving, bone-carving, and metalwork in copper, bronze, silver, and gold, the ancient Andeans were great masters. All these things were elements of culture which the Spaniards wove into the colonial culture of Peru after the conquest.

In short, when the Spaniards became rulers of Peru they found there so many things which they could sincerely admire and which they could adapt to their own needs, as, for example, the road and messenger systems, the irrigation and agricultural terrace systems, and the textile and ceramic arts, that they shaped the colonial civilization by means of a judicious combination of native with Spanish contributions. The result is that today the Andean countries, like Mexico, are partly Indian and partly Spanish in civilization.[17]

VI. THE STATIC INTERMEDIATE CULTURES OF NATIVE AMERICA

In the preceding section have been studied native American civilizations which all grew out of Intermediate cultures of the dynamic sort. There remains to be discussed the static sort of Intermediate cultures, that is, those whose environments were not sufficiently favorable to stimulate growth beyond the Intermediate plane into the civilized plane of culture. Sometimes, as in the case of the Greater Antilles and in the Lesser Antilles, the disadvantageous situation was no more than a question of too much moisture in the air and of too great ease in the obtaining of food so that men lacked both the energy and the incentive to seek

---

[17] The most important and accessible works on the Andean area, most of them having good bibliographies for further study, are: Baessler, 1902-1903, 1906; Bandelier, 1910, 1911; Barrett, 1925; Baudin, 1927, 1928, 1929; Bennett, 1934; Beuchat, 1912, pp. 563-692; Bingham, 1922, 1930; González Suárez, 1890-1903, 1908-1910, 1915, 1922; Hague, 1934; Harcourt, 1924, 1924a, 1934; Holstein, 1927; Jijón y Caamaño, 1914, 1918, 1918a, 1919, 1920, 1922, 1927, 1930; Jijón and Larrea, 1918; Joyce, 1912; Kroeber, 1926-1930, 1926, 1926a, 1927; Kroeber and Strong, 1924, 1924a; Larrea and Jijón, 1919; Latcham, 1922, 1923, 1927, 1927-1928; Lavachery, 1933; Lehmann and Doering, 1924; Lehmann-Nitsche, 1928; J. Levillier, 1928; R. Levillier, 1926; Markham, 1906, 1908, 1910; Mead, 1915, 1916, 1932; Means, 1931, 1932, 1932a; Minnaert, 1928, 1931a, 1932; Montell, 1929; Murdock, 1934; Murphy, 1925; Nordenskiöld, 1915, 1921, 1925, 1925a, 1931; Olson, 1931; Orchard, 1927, 1930; Prescott, 1847; Reiss and Stübel, 1880-1887; Sáenz, 1933, 1933a; Saville, 1907-1910, 1909, 1921a, 1924, 1927; M. Schmidt, 1929; Strong, 1925; Stübel and Uhle, 1892; Tello, 1929, 1930, 1931; Tessmann, 1930; Uhle, 1903, 1908, 1909, 1910, 1910a, 1910b, 1912, 1913, 1913a, 1920a, 1920b; Urteaga, 1921; Valcárcel, 1925, 1925a 1933, 1933a; Valdez de la Torre, 1921; Yacovleff, 1933a; Yacovleff, Muelle, O'Neale, and Weiss, 1932; Zurkalowski, 1919.

out improved ways of life. It was more reasonable for them to continue living by means of a little hunting, a little fishing, a little agriculture, wearing very little clothing, and building houses out of wood or
palm leaves, rather than take what seemed to them pointless trouble of
seeking to use more fully the latent possibilities of their habitat. In
other words, the peoples of the Antilles probably arrived in those islands
in a more or less developed Intermediate stage of culture, and they simply stayed in it instead of progressing as any of them would have done
if they had moved on to a more bracing climate.

In other localities as, for instance, the vast forest areas east of the
Andes in which the highland Incas and their subjects never succeeded
in establishing themselves with any degree of intensiveness, dense forests made a green roof over the heads of men and so confined their
range of vision to the earth, dwarfing their imaginations and concentrating their attention upon the things of nature closest to them. Their
whole field of vision and of thought was confined and limited. Consequently, they remained in a sphere of being where only rudimentary
forms of cultural elements—agriculture, pottery, weaving, and architecture chief among them—were known and practiced by them.

In still other localities, such as some of the higher-lying parts of
Brazil and of Guiana, or such as the plains sloping down from the
Andes in what is now nothwestern Argentina, there was some lack in
the environmental offering upon which man could draw, and as a result
of that lack culture remained Intermediate. Materials for the making
of good tools, stone capable of being finely carved and fitted, clay suitable for the best type of pottery—any or all of these may have been
wanting so that general advancement became impossible. Or a too great
variation as between rainy and dry seasons may have had a stunting
effect upon culture in those parts.

Whatever the causes may have been—and only a few of them are
here suggested—large areas in what is now Latin America never had
native culture of a sort higher than the Intermediate stage. All Central
America south of Guatemala, the Caribbean islands, and all South America except the Colombian highlands and the Andean area, and except
also the southern tip of the continent (where primitive culture was the
rule, as already stated), were the seats of Intermediate cultures more
or less developed. They were, however, Intermediate of the static variety because the quality of their natural surroundings obliged them to
be so. Had their surroundings changed, or had they moved into regions where natural conditions were better, any of these people would

have become, from being static, dynamic, and they would have progressed accordingly. Even as it was, many of them achieved high development in certain ways, such as the art of building dug-out canoes capable of filling even Europeans with admiration. Again, some Intermediate peoples were peculiarly skillful in the working of gold, others in the making of basketry or of beadwork, or in their manner of ridding certain plants of poisonous juices and so converting the plants into a valuable source of nourishment. In spite of these special skills, however, the general level of culture remained Intermediate in all environments which were not either the optimum or something close to it.[18]

VII. The Coming of the Spaniards and of the Portuguese

As it happened, the first contact between Europeans and native Americans took place in the Caribbean area where Intermediate culture prevailed. To the Spaniards, who were expecting and hoping to find the grandeurs of the Far East, the simple culture of the Antillean folk was something of a shock, as was also the kind of country in which they lived. Never before had Spaniards or other Europeans encountered markedly backward people who lived in tropical islands and belonged to a mysterious race which was neither white nor black, nor yet yellow. Consequently, there arose at once the question of how to administer these new folk if a Spanish colony were to be established in this New World.

For the Antillean natives the coming of the Spaniards was an equal shock. They knew naught of the civilizations on the mainland and

---

[18] Among the works descriptive of one phase or another of the Intermediate cultures the following are important: Abbad y Lasierra, 1866; Ambrosetti, 1902, 1902a, 1906; Bachiller y Morales, 1883; Beals, 1932; Boman, 1908; Booy, 1912, 1913, 1915, 1916, 1919; Bovallius, 1886; Branch, 1907; Buchwald, 1918a, 1918b, 1920; Debenedetti, 1931; Ernst, 1878; Farabee, 1918, 1922; Fewkes, 1904, 1907, 1908, 1922; Gardner, 1930, 1930a; Gardner and Gardner, 1931; Gower, 1927; Guevara, 1929; Haeberlin, 1919; Harrington, 1921; Hartman, 1901; Holmes, 1887, 1888; Hornell, 1925; Ihering, 1906; Jahn, 1927; Joyce, 1916; Karsten, 1926; Koch-Grünberg, 1906, 1908-1910; Krieger, 1931; Lafone Quevedo, 1904, 1905, 1908; Lavachery, 1932, 1933; Linné, 1929; Lothrop, 1919, 1921, 1926, 1926b, 1927, 1932a; Lumholtz, 1898; MacCurdy, 1911; Marcano, 1889-1890, 1889; Means, 1917, 1917d, 1918; Medina, 1882; Merwin and Vaillant, 1932; Métraux, 1928, 1930, 1930a, 1931a; Milla, 1879-1905; Netto, 1885, 1890; Nicholas, 1901; Nimuendajú, 1925; Nomland, 1933; Nordenskiöld, 1930a; Nuttall, 1910a, 1925; Ploetz and Métraux, 1930; Posnansky, 1914, 1918; Preuss, 1929; Rojas, 1878; Rosen, 1924, 1924a; Serrano, 1930, 1933, 1933a; Spinden, 1917, 1917a, 1917b; Steinen, 1897; Tessmann, 1930; Tozzer, 1907; Uhle, 1906; Vaillant, 1930, 1930b, 1931a, 1932b, 1934a; Verrill, 1927; Vignati, 1925, 1929, 1931, 1931c; Zerda, 1883.

so were utterly unprepared for collision with the still more complex civilization of Spain. In many cases the natives assumed that the strangers were gods and they sought to propitiate them with gifts; in other cases they tried to fight off the invaders but were soon overwhelmed by firearms, steel armor, and, above all, cavalry. In other words, in a clash between two such unequal cultures, the weaker inevitably was beaten or else forced to retreat to inaccessible places.

As time wore on, therefore, wherever Europeans (Spaniards and Portuguese) came into contact with Intermediate native cultures the latter were either extinguished or else forced to recede before an advancing front of European occupation. This does not mean that the Spanish government made no effort to protect the Indians' interests; rather, it means that in spite of all merciful intentions the only things of the Antilleans and of similar folk that the Spaniards could use were their gold and their physical labor, and it was precisely the combination of these that brought about the extermination of some peoples of Intermediate culture and the pushing back of others. Therefore, in colonial and modern times, the civilization which grew up in regions where those processes took place was and is predominantly Spanish in character with only a few minor contributions from the native culture, and those chiefly in the shape of food plants and methods of preparing them.

A quite different situation arose, however, when the Spaniards encountered the native civilizations. In Mexico, Yucatan, and the Andean area the native culture was so solid and so admirable that the invaders inevitably respected it and adapted many parts of it to their own needs and purposes. Thus was created a colonial civilization blended of elements drawn from both races and their cultures.

As native culture had achieved its greatest heights in regions where the best environmental conditions existed, that is, in the highlands of Mexico and of Guatemala and in the Andean area, so also did Spanish power and civilization, in colonial times, reach their highest development in those same favored regions. Even today it is true that several of the "Latin" American republics—Mexico, Guatemala, Ecuador, Peru, Bolivia—are direct representatives of ancient native civilization and so have both Indian and Spanish contributions in their contemporary culture. Indeed, most of the problems in those countries touch upon one or another aspect of the adjustment between the two contributing races.

SELECTED BIBLIOGRAPHY

NOTE: All the works cited in the footnotes in brief form will be found fully cited here. Many other works, also, are likewise listed in the bibliography here offered. Although it makes no claim to completeness, this bibliography will, it is hoped, aid the student to find his way into and through the vast literature of the subject.

Abbreviations used to designate periodicals and series.

AA—American Anthropologist.
A&A—Art and Archæology, Washington, D. C.
AASP—American Antiquarian Society Proceedings, Worcester, Mass.
AJA—American Journal of Archæology.
AMJ—American Museum Journal, New York.
AMNBA—Anales del Museo Nacional de Buenos Aires.
AMNRJ—Archivos do Museu Nacional do Rio de Janeiro.
APAMNH—Anthropological Papers of the American Museum of Natural History, New York.
APSP—American Philosophical Society Proceedings, Philadelphia.
ARBAE—Annual Report of the Bureau of American Ethnology, Washington, D. C.
AUC—Anales de la Universidad Central, Quito, Ecuador.
BAE, Bull.—Bureau of American Ethnology, Bulletin, Washington, D. C.
BANH—Boletín de la Academia Nacional de Historia, Quito.
BSAB—Bulletin de la Société des Américanistes de Belgique.
BSEEHA—Boletín de la Sociedad Ecuatoriana de Estudios Históricos Americanos, Quito.
BSGL—Boletín de la Sociedad Geográfica de Lima.
BSGLP—Boletín de la Sociedad Geográfica de La Paz.
CIAAP—Congrès International d'Anthropologie et d'Archéologie Préhistoriques.
FFLA—Facultad de Filosofía y Letras. Sección de Antropología. Buenos Aires.
GR—Geographical Review. American Geographical Society, N. Y.
HAHR—Hispanic American Historical Review.
HS—Hakluyt Society, London.
ICA—International Congress of Americanists, Report.
IN—Indian Notes. Museum of the American Indian, N. Y.
INM—Indian Notes and Monographs. Museum of the American Indian.
JAP—Journal de la Société des Américanistes de Paris.
JRAI—Journal of the Royal Anthropological Institute, London.
MCAAS—Memoirs of the Conn. Academy of Arts and Sciences, New Haven, Conn.
NGM—National Geographic Magazine, Washington, D. C.
NH—Natural History, American Museum of Natural History, N. Y.
NPMLP—Noticias Preliminares del Museo de La Plata, Argentina.
PASC—(Second) Pan American Scientific Congress.
PMAR—Peabody Museum Annual Reports, Cambridge, Mass.
PMEAC—Publicaciones del Museo de Etnología y Antropología de Chile. Santiago.
PMM—Peabody Museum Memoirs, Cambridge, Mass.
PMP—Peabody Museum Papers, Cambridge, Mass.
PPPSC—Proceedings of the Pan-Pacific Scientific Congress.
PWS—Festschrift Publication d'hommage offerte au P. W. Schmidt, Vienna, 1928.
RCHG—Revista Chilena de Historia y Geografía, Santiago.
RH—Revista Histórica, Lima.
RMLP—Revista del Museo de La Plata, Argentina.
RMNL—Revista del Museo Nacional, Lima.
RUBA—Revista de la Universidad de Buenos Aires.

SM—Scientific Monthly.
SMP—Smithsonian Miscellaneous Publications, Washington, D. C.
TCAAS—Transactions of the Conn. Academy of Arts & Sciences, New Haven, Conn.
UNBANME—Universidad Nacional de Buenos Aires, Notas del Museo Etnográfico.
UNTRIE—Universidad Nacional de Tucumán, Revista del Instituto de Etnografía.
WK—Wira Kocha, Lima.
YBCIW—Year Book of the Carnegie Institution of Washington.
ZE—Zeitschrift für Ethnologie, Berlin.

Abbad y Lasierra, Friar Iñigo:
  1866 Historia geográfica, civil y natural de la isla de San Juan Bautista de Puerto Rico. Puerto Rico.
Acosta, Joaquín:
  1848 Compendio histórico del descubrimiento y colonización de la Nueva Granada . . . en el siglo décimo sexto. Paris.
  1901 Compendio histórico, etc. Bogotá.
Acosta, Father José de (writing in 1588-1590):
  1880 The natural and moral history of the indies. Translated by E(dward) G(rimston), and edited by Clements R. Markham, London, HS, 2 vols.
Acosta de Samper, Soledad:
  1894 Los aborígenes que problaban los territorios que hoy forman la república de Colombia. ICA, IX, 373-437. Madrid.
Alexander, Hartley Burr:
  1920 The mythology of all races, Latin American. (Series edited by L. H. Gray, vol. xi), Boston.
Alva Ixtlilxochitl, Fernando de:
  1892 Historia chichimeca. Mexico.
Ambrosetti, Juan Bautista:
  1902 La civilisation Calchaquí. Région préandine des provinces de Rioja, Catamarca, Tucumán, Salta y Jujuy (République Argentine). ICA, XII, 293-297. Paris.
  1902a El sepulcro de "La Paya" últimamente descubierto en los valles calchaquíes (provincia de Salta). AMNBA, ser. 3, I, 119-148.
  1905 El bronce en la región Calchaquí. AMNBA, ser. 3, IV, 163-314.
  1906 Exploraciones arqueológicas en la Pampa Grande (Provincia de Salta). Buenos Aires.
  1907 Exploraciones arqueológicas en la ciudad prehistórica de "La Paya" (Valle Calchaquí—Provincia de Salta). RUBA, VIII, 15-97.
  1908 La question calchaquie. . . . ICA, XVI, 429-432. Vienna.
  1910 Resultado de las exploraciones arqueológicas en el Pukará de Tilcara. ICA, XVII, 497-499. Buenos Aires.
  1911 Idolo zoomorfo del Alto Paraná. AMNBA, ser. 3, XIV, 385-393.
  1917 Los vasos del Pukará de Tilcara del tipo pelike comparados con los de Machu Pichu. PASC, I, 38-39. Washington.
Ameghino, Florentino:
  1912 L'age des formations sédimentaires tertiaires de l'Argentine en relation avec l'antiquité de l'homme. AMNBA, XXII, 45-75, 169-179.
  1918 La antigüedad del hombre en el Plata. Buenos Aires, 2 vols. (First edition, Paris and Buenos Aires, 1880-1881, 2 vols.)
Anonymous Conquerer (Sixteenth Century):
  1917 Narrative of some things of New Spain. (Translated and edited by Marshall H. Saville, New York. Cortes Society).

Aparicio, Francisco de:
1922   Nuevos hallazgos de representaciones plásticas en el norte de la provincia de Santa Fé. RUBA, XLIX, 5-30.
1925   Les habitations troglodytiques des aborigènes de la région montagneuse de la province de Cordoba. ICA, XXI, Pt. II, 643-654. Gothenburg.
1925a Los aborígenes del Tucumán. RH, VIII, 61-85.
1928   Investigaciones arqueológicas en la región serrana de la provincia de San Luís. ˙ (República Argentina). ICA, XXII, Pt. I, 453-466. Rome.
1928a Apuntes para el estudio de la habitación serrana en la provincia de Córdoba. (República Argentina). ICA, XXII, Pt. II, 7-13. Rome.

Archeological Monuments of Mexico.
       Publications of the Department of Education of the Republic of Mexico. New York and London.

Bachiller y Morales, Antonio:
1883   Cuba Primitiva. Havana. (2nd edition).

Baessler, Arthur:
1902-1903 Ancient peruvian art. Berlin and New York. 4 vols.
1906   Altperuanische metallgeräte. Berlin.

Bancroft, Hubert Howe:
1883   The native races. San Francisco. 5 vols.

Bandelier, Adolph Francis:
1877   On the art of war and mode of warfare of the ancient Mexicans. PMAR, X, vol. 2, 95-162.
1878   On the distribution and tenure of lands and the customs with respect to inheritance, among the ancient Mexicans. PMAR, XI, vol. 2, 385-448.
1879   On the social organization and mode of government of the ancient Mexicans. PMAR, XII, vol. 2, 557-699.
1893   The Gilded Man: El Dorado. New York.
1910   The Islands of Titicaca and Koati. New York.
1911   The ruins at Tiahuanaco. AASP, n.s., XXI, 218-265. Worcester, Mass.

Barrett, Samuel Alfred:
1925   The Cayapa Indian of Ecuador. New York. (Museum of the American Indian). 2 vols.

Barrot, Frédéric:
1874   Sur quelques bijoux d'or péruviens. Archives de la Société Américaine de France, n.s., I, 257-258. Paris.

Basler, Adolphe, and Brummer, Ernest:
1928   L'art précolombien. Paris.

Bastian, Adolf:
1878-1889 Die culturländer des alten America. Berlin. 3 vols.

Batres, Leopoldo:
1906   Teotihuacan. Mexico.
1908   Civiliación prehistórica de las Riberas de Papaloapam. Mexico.
1909   Las ruinas de Palenque. Mexico.

Baudin, Louis:
1927   La formation de l'élite et l'enseignement de l'histoire dans l'Empire des Inka. Revue des Etudes Historiques, XCIII, 107-114. Paris.
1927a La statistique au temps des Inka. Revue politique et parlementaire, CXXXII, 460-464. Paris.
1928   L'Empire socialiste des Inka. Paris. (Institut d'Ethnologie).
1929   L'organisation économique de l'Empire des Incas. Revue de l'Amérique Latine, XVII, 385-393. Paris.

Beals, Ralph L.:
1932 The comparative ethnology of northern Mexico before 1750. Ibero-Americana II. Berkeley, California. (University of California.)
Bemis, Albert Farwell, and Burchard 2nd, John:
1933 The evolving house. Vol. I, A history of the home. Cambridge, Mass.
Bennett, Wendell C.:
1933 Archæological hikes in the Andes. NH, XXXIII, 163-174. New York.
1934 Excavations at Tiahuanaco. APAMNH, XXXIV, Pt. III, New York.
Berthon, Paul:
1911 Étude sur le précolombien du Bas-Pérou. Paris.
Beuchat, Henri:
1912 Manuel d'archéologie américaine. Paris.
Beyer, Hermann:
1921 El llamado "Calendario Azteca." Mexico.
Bingham, Hiram:
1912 Vítcos, the last Inca capital. AASP, n.s., XXII, 135-196. Worcester, Mass.
1913 In the wonderland of Peru. NGM, XXIV, 387-574. Washington.
1915 The story of Machu Picchu. NGM, XXVII, 171-217. Washington.
1915a Types of Machu Picchu pottery. AA, n.s., XVII, 257-271.
1916 Further explorations in the land of the Incas. NGM, XXIX, 431-473. Washington.
1917 The Inca peoples and their culture. ICA, XIX, 253-260. Washington.
1917a Inca land. Boston and New York.
1930 Machu Picchu, a citadel of the Incas. New Haven.
Blom, Frans:
1928 San Clemente ruins, Peten, Guatemala. JAP, n.s., XX, 95-101.
1930 Preliminary notes on two important Maya finds. ICA, XXIII, 165-171. New York.
Blom, Frans, and La Farge, Oliver:
1926-1927 Tribes and temples. New Orleans. (Tulane University). 2 vols.
Boas, Franz:
1911-1912 Album de colecciones arqueológicas. Mexico.
Bollaert, William:
1860 Antiquarian, ethnological and other researches in New Granada, Equador, Peru and Chile. London.
Boman, Eric:
1905 Migrations précolombiennes dans le nord-ouest de l'Argentine. JAP, n.s., II, 91-108.
1908 Antiquités de la région andine de la République Argentine et du désert d'Atacama. Paris. 2 vols.
1916 El pucará de los sauces. Physis, II, 136-145. Buenos Aires.
1923 Los ensayos de establecer una cronología prehispánica en la región Diaguita. BANH, VI, 1-31. Quito.
Boman, Eric, and Greslebin, Héctor:
1923 Alfarería del estilo draconiano de la región Diaguita. Buenos Aires.
Booy, Theodoor de:
1912 Lucayan remains on the Caicos Islands. AA, n.s., XIV, 81-105.
1913 Lucayan artifacts from the Bahamas. AA, n.s., XV, 1-7.
1915 Pottery from certain caves in eastern Santo Domingo, West Indies. AA, n.s., XVII, 69-97.
1916 Notes on the archæology of Margarita Island, Venezuela. New York. (Museum of the American Indian, Contributions, II, No. 5.)

1919   Archæology of the Virgin Islands. New York. (Indian Notes and Mono-
        graphs, I).

Bovallius, Carl:
1886   Nicaraguan antiquities. Stockholm. (Swedish Society of Anthropology
        and Geography).

Bowditch, Charles P.:
1910   The numeration, calendar systems and astronomical knowledge of the
        Mayas. Cambridge, Mass. (University Press).

Branch, C. W.:
1907   Aboriginal antiquities in St. Kitts and Nevis. AA, n.s., IX, 315-333.

Brasseur de Bourbourg, Abbé C. E.:
1857-1859 Histoire des nations civilisées du Mexique et de l'Amérique Centrale.
        Paris. 4 vols.

Bregante, Odilla:
1926   Ensayo de clasificación de la cerámica del noroeste argentina. Buenos
        Aires.

Brinton, Daniel Garrison:
1882   The Maya chronicles. Philadelphia.
1885   The annals of the Cakchiquels. Philadelphia.
1890   Essays of an Americanist. Philadelphia.

Buchwald, Otto von:
1908   Die Kara. Globus, XCIV, 123-125. Brunswick, Germany.
1908a Altes und neues vom Guayas. Globus, XCIV, 181-183.
1909   Das Reich der Chimus. Globus, XCV, 149-151.
1909a Zur wandersage der Kara. Globus, XCV, 316-319.
1909b Ecuatorianische grabhügel. Globus, XCVI, 154-157.
1909-1910 Zur völkerkunde südamerikas. Globus, XCVI, 317-320, XCVII,
        74-76.
1918   Tiahuanaco y Cuzco. BSEEHA, I, 105-108. Quito.
1918a Migraciones sud-americanas. BSEEHA, I, 227-236.
1918b Notas acerca de la arqueología del Guayas. BSEEHA, I, 237-252.
1920   Notas etnológicas del Ecuador occidental. BSEEHA, IV, 285-293.

Bunker, Frank F.
1929   The distinctively American art of the Maya. A&A, XXVII, 99-107.
        Washington.

Burgos, Fausto, and Catullo, María Elena:
1927   Tejidos incaicos y criollos. Buenos Aires. (Ministerio de Justicia é
        Instrucción Pública).

Burkitt, Robert:
1924   A journey in northern Guatemala. MJ, XV, 115-137. Philadelphia.
1930   Excavations at Chocalá. MJ, XXI, 5-40.

Cabello de Balboa, Father Miguel:
1576-1586 Miscelánea antártica. (Original Manuscript lost; a good 18th cen-
        tury copy in the New York Public Library).

Cabral, Jorge:
1913   Los cronistas é historiadores de indias y el problema de las dinastías de
        la monarquía peruana. Buenos Aires.

Calancha, Father Antonio de la:
1638   Coronica moralizada . . . Barcelona. (Pedro Lacavallería).

Capdeville, Augusto:
1921-1922 Notas acerca de la arqueología de Taltal. BANH, II, 1-16, 256-261,
        III, 229-233, IV, 115-118. Quito.

1923 Un cementerio chincha-atacameño de Punta Grande, Talta. BANH, VII, 34-49.
Carli, Count Gianrinaldo:
1780 Delle lettere americane. Cosmopolis (Florence). 2 vols.
1788 Lettres américaines. (Translated by J. B. Lefebvre de Villebrune). Paris. 2 vols.
1822 Las cartas americanas. Mexico. 3 vols.
Carrillo y Ancona, Bishop Crescencio:
1883 Historia antigua de Yucatan. Mérida, Yucatan. 2nd edition.
Carrión Cachot, Rebecca:
1923 La mujer y el niño en el antiguo Perú. Inca, I, 329-354. Lima.
1931 La indumentaria en la antigua cultura de Paracas. WK, I, 37-86. Lima.
Carrión Matos, Fermín:
1933 La prehistoria de Ancash ante la crítica moderna. El Comercio, Mon. 16 October, 1933. Lima.
Caso, Alfonso:
1927 El Teocalli de la Guerra Sagrada. Mexico. (Secretaría de Educación Pública).
1928 Las estelas zapotecas. Mexico. (Talleres gráficos de la Nación).
1932 Reading the riddle of ancient jewels. NH, XXXII, 464-480. New York.
Castellanos, Juan de (Sixteenth Century):
1886 Historia del Nuevo Reino de Granada. Madrid. 2 vols.
Castro Pozo, Hildebrando:
1924 Nuestra comunidad indígena. Lima.
Chamberlain, Alexander F.:
1910 The Uran, a new South American linguistic stock. AA, n.s., XII, 417-424.
1910a Sur quelques familles linguistiques . . . de l'Amérique du Sud. JAP, n.s., VII, 179-202.
1911 On the Puelchean and . . . Atacameñan . . . linguistic stocks. AA, n.s., XIII, 458-471.
1913 Linguistic stocks of South American Indians, with distribution map. AA, n.s., XV, 236-247.
1913a Nomenclature and distribution of the principal tribes and subtribes of the Arawakan linguistic stocks of South America. JAP, n.s., X, 473-496.
Charlevoix, Pierre François Xavier de:
1730-1731 Histoire de l'Isle Espagnole ou de S. Domingue. Paris. (J. Guerin). 2 vols.
1756 Histoire du Paraguay. Paris. (Didot). 3 vols.
Charnay, Désiré:
1885 Les anciennes villes du nouveau monde. Paris.
1888 The ancient cities of the new world. New York and London.
Christian, F. W.
1932 Polynesian and oceanic elements in the Chimu and Inca languages. Journal of the Polynesian Society, XLI, 144-156. New Plymouth, N. Z.
Cieza de León, Pedro de:
1553 Parte primera de la crónica del Perú. Seville. (Martín de Montesdoca).
1864 The travels of Pedro de Cieza de León, A. D. 1532-1550, contained in the first part of his chronicle of Peru. Translated and edited by Clements R. Markham. London. HS.
1880 Segunda parte de la crónica del Perú. Edited by Marcos Jiménez de la Espada. Madrid.
1883 The second part of the chonicle of Peru. Translated and edited by Clements R. Markham. London. HS.

Clavijero, Abbé Francesco Saverio:
1780-1781 Storia antica del Messico. Cesena, Italy. 4 vols.
1787 The history of Mexico. Translated by Charles Cullen. London. 2 vols.
Cobo, Father Bernabé (writing in 1653):
1890-1893 Historia del nuevo mundo. Edited by Marcos Jiménez de la Espada.
    Seville. (Sociedad de Bibliófilos Andaluces). 4 vols.
Cook, O. F.:
1916 Staircase farms of the ancients. NGM, XXIX, 474-534. Washington.
1920 Foot-plow agriculture in Peru. Smithsonian Report for 1918, 487-491.
    Washington.
Cooper, John M.:
1917 Analytical and critical bibliography of the tribes of Tierra del Fuego and
    adjacent territory. BAE, Bull. 63. Washington.
Créqui-Montfort; Count G. de, and Rivet, P.:
1925-1927 La langue Uru ou Pukina. JAP, n.s., XVII, 211-244, XVIII, 111-
    139, XIX, 57-116.
Cuervo Marquez, Carlos:
1920 Prehistoria y viajes; estudios arqueológicos y etnográficos. Madrid.
    2 vols.
Cummings, Byron:
1922 Cuicuilco. Ethnos, 2nd época, I, 90-94. Mexico.
1923 Cuicuilco, the oldest temple discovered in North America. A&A, XVI,
    51-58. Washington.
1926 Cuicuilco and the archaic culture of Mexico. SM, XXIII, 289-304.
Davis, Emily C.:
1931 Ancient Americans. New York.
Debenedetti, Salvador:
1908 Excursión arqueológica á las ruinas de Kipón. FFLA, No. 4. Buenos
    Aires.
1910 Exploración arqueológica en los cementerios prehistóricos de la Isla de
    Tilcara (Quebrada de Humahuaca, Provincia de Jujuy). FFLA, No. 6.
1910a Noticia sobre un cementerio indígena de Baradero. RUBA, XIII, 435-
    448.
1912 Influencias de la cultura de Tiahuanaco en la región del noroeste Argentino.
    RUBA, XVII, 326-348.
1917 Investigaciones arqueológicas en los valles preandinos de la provincia de
    San Juan. FFLA, No. 15.
1928 Relaciones culturales prehispánicas en el noroeste Argentino. Physis, IX,
    113-117. Buenos Aires.
1930 Chulpas en las cavernas del Río San Juan Mayo. UNBANME, No. 1.
1931 L'ancienne civilisation des Barreales du nord-ouest Argentine. Paris.
    (G. van Oest).
Diaz del Castillo, Bernal (In Mexico with Cortés):
1908-1916 A true history of the conquest of New Spain. Translated and edited
    by Alfred Percival Maudslay. London. HS. 5 vols.
Dieseldorf, E. P.:
1926-1933 Kunst und religion der Mayavölker. Berlin and Hamburg. 3 vols.
Dixon, Roland Burrage:
1912 The independence of the culture of the American Indian. Science, n.s.,
    XXXV, 46-55.
1928 The building of cultures. New York and London.
1932 The problem of the sweet potato in Polynesia. AA, n.s., XXXIV, 40-66.

Dorsey, George A.:
1901 Archæological investigations on the Island of La Plata, Ecuador. Chicago. (Field Museum).

Duran, Friar Diego:
1867-1880 Historia de las Indios de Nueva España. Edited by José F. Ramírez. Mexico. 2 vols. and Atlas.

Du Tertre, Father Jean-Baptiste:
1654 Histoire générale des iles de S. Christophe, de la Guadeloupe, de la Martinique et autres dans l'Amérique. Paris. (J. Langlois).
1667-1671 Histoire générale des Antilles habitées par les François. . . . Paris. (T. Jolly). 4 vols.

Eaton, George F.:
1916 The collection of osteological material from Machu Picchu. MCAAS, V. New Haven.
1925 Food animals of the Peruvian highlands. ICA, XXI, Pt. II, 61-66. Gothenburg.

Ehrenreich, Paul:
1897 Die Völkerstämme Brasiliens. Anthropologische studien über die urbewohner Brasiliens. Brunswick, Germany.

Ernst, A.:
1878 Indianische alterthumer aus Venezuela. Globus, 1878, 190-197.

Farabee, William Curtis:
1918 The central Arawaks. Philadelphia. (University Museum).
1922 Indian tribes of eastern Peru. PMP, X. Cambridge, Mass.

Febres Cordero, Tulio:
1920 Decadas de la historia de Mérida. Mérida, Venezuela.

Feldthäusser, Kurt.
1933 Schlangen-Darstellungen in der textilen und keramischen Kunst der Südküste Alt-Perus (Paracas und Nazca). Ohlau, Germany.

Fernández de Piedrahita, Lucás:
1688 Historia general de las conquistas del Nuevo Reyno de Granada. Antwerp.

Fewkes, Jesse Walter:
1904 Prehistoric culture in Cuba. AA, n.s., VI, 585-598.
1907 The aborigines of Porto Rico . . . and neighboring islands. ARBAE, XXV, 3-220. Washington.
1907a Certain antiquities of eastern Mexico. ARBAE, XXV, 221-284.
1908 Further notes on the archaeology of Porto Rico. AA, n.s., X, 624-633.
1922 A prehistoric island culture area of America. ARBAE, XXXIV, 35-271.

Förstemann, Ernst:
1880 Die Maya-handschrift der königlichen öffentlichen Bibliothek zu Dresden. Leipzig.
1906 Commentary of the Maya manuscript in the Royal Public Library of Dresden. PMP, IV, 48-266. Cambridge, Mass.

Gamio, Manuel:
1920 Las excavaciones del pedregal de San Angel y la cultura arcaica del Valle de México. AA, n.s., XXII, 127-143.
1922 La población del valle de Teotihuacán. Mexico. 3 vols.

Gann, Thomas, and Thompson, J. Eric:
1931 The history of the Maya. New York.

García Icazbalceta, Joaquín:
1858 Colección de documentos para la historia de Mexico. Mexico. 2 vols.

Garcilaso de la Vega, el Inca:
1869-1871 The first part of the royal commentaries of the Yncas. Translated and edited by Clements R. Markham. London. HS. 2 vols.

Gardner, G. A.:
1919 El uso de los tejidos en la fabricación de la alfarería prehispánica en la provincia de Córdoba (República Argentina). RMLP, XXIV, Pt. q, 128-168.
1925 On some Argentine rock-paintings. ICA, XXI, Pt. II, 584-595. Gothenburg.
1930 Comechingon pottery. ICA, XXIII, 313-346. New York.
1930a The rock-paintings of La Quebrada. Ipek for 1930, 80-92.

Gardner, G. A., and Gardner, S. E.:
1931 Rock-paintings of north-west Córdoba. Oxford. (Clarendon Press).

Gayton, A. H.:
1927 The Uhle collections from Nievería. UCPAAE, XXI, 305-329. Berkeley, California.

Gayton, A. H., and Kroeber, A. L.:
1927 The Uhle pottery collections from Nazca. UCPAAE, XXIV, 1-46.

Goldenweiser, A. A.:
1916 Diffusion vs. independent origin: a rejoinder to Professor G. Elliott Smith. Science, n.s., XLIV, 531-533.

González de la Rosa, Manuel:
1908 Les Caras de l'Equateur et les premiers résultats de l'expédition G. Heye sous la direction de M. Saville. JAP, n.s., V, 85-93.
1909 Ensayo de cronología incana. RH, IV, 41-54. Lima.
1910 Les deux Tiahuanaco, leurs problèmes et leur solution. ICA, XVI, 405-428.

González Suárez, Archbishop Federico:
1878 Estudio histórico sobre los Cañaris, antiguos habitantes de la provincia del Azuay, en la República del Ecuador. Quito.
1890-1903 Historia general de la República del Ecuador. Quito. 7 vols. and Atlas.
1904 Prehistoria ecuatoriana. Quito.
1908-1910 Los aborígenes de Imbabura y del Carchi. Quito. 2 vols.
1915 Notas arqueológicas. Quito.
1922 Estudio histórico sobre los Cañaris, pobladores de la antigua provincia del Azuay. Cuenca, Ecuador.

Gordon, George Byron:
1896 Prehistoric ruins of Copan. PMM, I, No. 1. Cambridge, Mass.
1898 Researches in the Uloa Valley, Honduras. PMM, I, No. 4.
1898a Caverns of Copan, Honduras. PMM, I, No. 5.
1902 The hieroglyphic stairway. Ruins of Copan. PMM, I, No. 6.

Gower, Charlotte:
1927 The northern and southern affiliations of antillean culture. Memoirs of the American Anthropological Association, No. 35.

Graebner, F.:
1905 Kulturkreise und kulturschichten in ozeanien. ZE, XXXVII, 28-53. Berlin.
1909 Die malanesische bogenkultur und ihre verwandten. Anthropos, IV, 726-780, 998-1032. Vienna.
1911 Methode der ethnologie. Heidelburg.
1926 Amerika und die südseekulturen. Ethnologica, II, 43-66. Leipzig.
1927 Betel und koka. Ethnologica, III, 295-296.

Greslebin, Héctor:
1926 El arte prehistórico peruano. Buenos Aires.
Guevara, Tomás:
1898-1913 Historia de la civilización de Araucanía. Santiago de Chile. 7 vols.
1928-1930 Sobre el orígen de los Araucanos. RCHG, LIX, 128-168, LXIV, 322-331. Santiago.
1929 Historia de Chile. Chile prehispano. Santiago. 2 vols. 2nd edition.
Habel, S.:
1878 Sculptures of Santa Lucia Cosumalwhuapa. Smithsonian Contributions to Knowledge, No. 269. Washington.
Haeberlin, Herman K.:
1919 Types of ceramic art in the Valley of Mexico. AA, n.s., XXI, 61-70.
Hague, Eleanor:
1934 Latin American music past and present. Santa Ana, California. (The Fine Arts Press).
Hamy, E. T.:
1888-1902 Decades americanae. Paris. 3 parts.
1897 Galérie américaine du Musée d'Ethnographie du Trocadéro. Paris. 2 parts.
Harcourt, Raoul and Marie d':
1924 La céramique ancienne du Pérou. Paris.
1924a Les tissus indiens du vieux Pérou. Paris.
1925 La musique des Incas et ses survivances. Paris.
Harcourt, Raoul d':
1934 Les textiles anciens du Péron. Paris.
Haring, C. H.·
1915 American gold and silver production in the first half of the sixteenth century. Quarterly Journal of Economics, XXIX, 433-479. Cambridge, Mass.
Harrington, M. R.:
1921 Cuba before Columbus. New York. (Museum of the American Indian). 2 vols.
Harrison, H. S.:
1926 Inventions: obtrusive, directional, and independent. Man, XXVI, 117-121. London.
1926a Variations and mutations in invention. Man, XXVI, 154-158.
1927 Analysis and factors of invention. Man, XXVII, 43-47.
Harth-Terré, Emilio:
1923 La fortaleza de Chuquimancu. Revista Arqueológica del Museo Larco-Herrera, No. 2. Lima.
Hartman, C. V.:
1901 Archæological researches in Costa Rica. Stockholm. (Royal Ethnographical Museum).
Hay, Clarence:
1923 The buried past of Mexico. NH, XXIII, 259-271. New York.
Hébert, J.:
1896 Particularités de l'exécution du décor sur terre cuite en Colombie. JAP, I, 175-178.
Heuzey, L.:
1870 Le trésor de Cuenca. Gazette des Beaux-Arts, 2nd period, IV, 113-127. Paris.
Holmes, William H.:
1885 The monoliths of San Juan Teotihuacan, Mexico. AJA, I, 361-371.

1887 The use of gold and other metals among the ancient inhabitants of Chiriquí, Isthmus of Darien. BAE, Bull. 3. Washington.

1888 Ancient art of the Province of Chiriquí. ARBAE, VI, 13-187. Washington.

1888a A study of textile art in its relation to the development of form and ornament. ARBAE, VI, 189-252. Washington.

1889 Textile fabrics of ancient Peru. BAE, Bull. 7. Washington.

1895-1897 Archæological studies among the ancient cities of Mexico. Chicago. (Field Museum.) 2 parts.

1907 On a nephrite statuette from San Andrés Tuxtla, Vera Cruz, Mexico. AA, n.s., IX, 691-701.

1914 Areas of American culture characterization tentatively outlined as an aid in the study of antiquities. AA, n.s., XVI, 413-446.

1916 The oldest dated American monument, a nephrite figurine from Mexico. A&A, III, 275-278. Washington.

Holstein, Otto:

1927 Chan-Chan: capital of the Great Chimu. GR, XVII, 36-61. New York.

Hornell, James:

1925 The archaic sculptured rocks and stone implements of Gorgona Island, South America. Man, XXV, 81-84, 104-107. London.

Hrdlička, Aleš:

1903 The region of the ancient "Chichimecs". . . . AA, n.s., V, 385-440.

1907 Skeletal remains suggesting . . . early man in North America. BAE, Bull. 33. Washington.

1911 Some results of recent anthropoligical exploration in Peru. SMP, LVI, No. 16. Washington.

1912 Restes, dans l'Asie orientale, de la race qui a peuplé l'Amérique. CIAAP, XIV, 409, 414. Geneva.

1912a The derivation and probable place of origin of the North American Indian. ICA, XVIII, 57-62. London.

1912b Early man in South America. BAE, Bull. 52. Washington. (In collaboration with Bailey Willis, W. H. Holmes, F. E. Wright, and C. N. Fennert).

1912c Early man in America. AJS, 4th series, XXXIV, 543-554. New Haven.

1914 Anthropological work in Peru in 1913. SMP, LXI, No. 18.

1917 Transpacific migrations. Man, XVII, 29-30. London.

1917a The genesis of the American Indian. ICA, XIX, 559-568. Washington.

1930 Anthropological survey in Alaska. ARBAE, XLVI, 19-374. Washington.

1932 The coming of man from Asia in the light of recent discoveries. APSP, LXXI, 393-402. Philadelphia.

Huntington, Ellsworth:

1914 The climatic factor. Washington. (The Carnegie Institution).

1915 Civilization and climate. New Haven.

1917 Maya civilization and climatic changes. ICA, XIX, 150-164. Washington.

Ihering, Hermann von:

1891 Versuch einer geschichte von Rio Grande do Sul. Globus, LX, 177-181. Brunswick, Germany.

1895 A civilisacão prehistorica do Brasil meridional. Revista do Museu Paulista, I, 34-159. S. Paulo.

1906 The anthropology of the State of S. Paulo, Brazil. São Paulo. 2nd edition.

1911 Os Botocudos do Rio Doce. Revista do Museu Paulista, VIII, 38-51.

Iklé, Fritz:
1930 Uber altperuanische stickereien des Trocadéro, Paris. St. Gallen, Switzerland.

Izcue, Elena:
1927 El arte peruano en la escuela. Paris. 2 vols.

Jahn, Alfredo:
1927 Los aborígenes del occidente de Venezuela. Su historia, etnografía y afinidades lingüísticas. Caracas.

Jaramillo Alvarado, Pío:
1925 El indio ecuatoriano. Quito. 2nd edition.

Jijón y Caamaño, Jacinto:
1912 El tesoro de Itschimbia (Quito-Ecuador). London.
1914 Contribución al conocimiento de los aborígenes de la provincia de Imbabura en la República del Ecuador. Madrid.
1918 Exámen crítico de la veracidad de la historia del Reino de Quito del P. Juan de Velasco, de la Compañía de Jesús. BSEEHA, I, 33-63. Quito.
1918a Artefactos prehistóricos del Guayas. BSEEHA, I, 253-275.
1919 La religión del imperio de los Incas. Quito.
1920 Nueva contribución al conocimiento de los aborígenes de la provincia de Imbabura. Quito.
1920a Los Tincullpas y notas acerca de la metalurgía de los aborígenes del Ecuador. BANH, I, 4-43.
1922 La edad del bronce en la América del Sur. BANH, IV, 119-126.
1927 Puruhá: contribución al conocimiento de los aborígenes de la provincia del Chimborazo. . . . Quito. 2 vols.
1929 Notas de arqueología Cuzqueña. Riobamba.
1930 Una gran marca cultural en el N.O. de Sud América. JAP, n.s. XXII, 107-197.

Jipón y Caamaño, Jacinto, and Larrea, Carlos M.:
1918 Un cementerio incásico en Quito y notas acerca de los Incas en el Ecuador. Quito.

Johnson, George R., and Platt, Raye R.:
1930 Peru from the air. New York. (American Geographical Society).

Joyce, Thomas Athol:
1912 South American archæology. London and New York.
1913 Note on a gold beaker from Lambayeque, Peru. Man, XIII, 65-66. London.
1913a The clan ancestor in animal form as depicted on ancient pottery of the Peruvian coast. Man, XIII, 113-117.
1914 Mexican archæology. London.
1916 Central American and West Indian archæology. London and New York.
1921 The Peruvian loom in the proto-Chimu period. Man, XXI, 177-180.
1922 Note on a Peruvian loom of the Chimu period. Man, XXII, 1-2.
1927 Maya and Mexican Art. London.

Karsten, Rafael:
1926 The civilization of the South American Indians. New York.

Kidder, Alfred Vincent:
1931 The archæological problem of the Maya. A&A, XXXI, 291-297. Washington.

Kingsborough, Lord:
1829-1848 Antiquities of Mexico. London. 9 vols. large folio.

Koch-Grünberg, Theodor:
1906 Les indiens Ouitotos. JAP, n.s., III, 157-189.
1908-1910 Zwei jahre unter den Indianern—reisen in nordwest-Brazilien, 1903-1905. Berlin. 2 vols.
1917-1928 Vom Roroima zum Orinoco. Berlin. 5 vols.
Krickeberg, Walter:
1925 Die Totonaken. BA, IX. Berlin.
1928 Mexicanisch-peruanische paralleln. PWS, 378-394. Vienna.
Krieger, Herbert W.:
1931 Aboriginal Indian pottery of the Dominican Republic. U. S. National Museum, Bull. 156. Washington.
Kroeber, Alfred Louis:
1925 The Uhle pottery collections from Moche. UCPAAE, XXI, 191-234. Berkeley, California.
1925a The Uhle pottery collections from Supe. UCPAAE, XXI, 235-264.
1925b Archaic culture horizons in the Valley of Mexico. UCPAAE, XVII, 373-408.
1926-1930 Archæological explorations in Peru. Chicago. (Field Museum). 2 vols.
1926 The Uhle pottery collections from Chancay. UCPAAE, XXI, 265-304.
1926a Culture stratification in Peru. AA, n.s., XXVIII, 331-351.
1927 Coast and highland in prehistoric Peru. AA, n.s., XXIX, 625-653.
1928 Cultural relations between North and South America ICA, XXIII, 5-22. New York.
Kroeber, A. L., and Holt, C.:
1920 Masks and moieties as a culture complex. JRAI, L, 542-460. London.
Kroeber, A. L., and Strong, William Duncan:
1924 The Uhle collections from Chincha. UCPAAE, XXI, 1-54.
1924a The Uhle collections from Ica. UCPAAE, XXI, 95-133.
Labat, Father Jean-Baptiste:
1931 Voyages aux iles de l'Amérique (Antilles) 1693-1705. Paris. 2 vols.
La Borde, le Sieur de:
1704 Voyage qui contient une rélation exacte de l'origine, moeurs, coûtumes, réligion, guerres et voyages des Caraibes. Amsterdam.
Lafone Quevedo, Samuel A.:
1892 Las huacas de Chañar-Yaco. RMLP, III, 35-62.
1892a El culto de Tonapa. RMLP, III, 323-379.
1904 Viaje á los menhires é intihuatana de Tafí y Santa Maria, RMLP, XI, 123-128.
1905 Viaje arqueológico en la región de Andalgalá. RMLP, XII, 73-110.
1908 Tipos de alfarería en la región Diaguito-Calchaquí. RMLP, XV, 295-396.
1912 Pronominal classification of certain South American linguistic stocks. . . . ICA, XVIII, 111-114. London.
1912a The Great Chanca Confederacy. . . . ICA, XVIII, 115-125.
Laguna, Frederica de:
1932-1933 A comparison of Eskimo and palæolithic art. AJA, XXXVI, 477-511, XXXVII, 77-107.
Landa, Bishop Diego de (Sixteenth Century):
1928 Relation des choses de Yucatan. Translated by Jean Genet. Paris.
Larco Herrera, Rafael:
1928 La civiltà Yunga. ICA, XXII, Pt. I, 565-581. Rome.
1930 Some exponents of Chimu ceramics. A&A, XXX, 121-127. Washington.

Larrea, Carlos M., and Jijón y Caamaño, Jacinto:
1919 Notas acerca de la arqueología de la provincia de Esmeraldas. BSEEHA, III, 85-109. Quito.
Latcham, Ricardo Eduardo:
1903 Notes on Chilean anthropology. JRAI, XXXIII, 167-178. London.
1909 El comercio precolombino en Chile i otros paises de América. Santiago de Chile.
1915 Costumbres mortuorias de los indios de Chile y otras partes de América. Valparaiso.
1922 Los animales domésticos de la América precolombina. PMEAC, III, 1-199. Santiago.
1923 La existencia de la propiedad en el antiguo imperio de los Incas. Santiago.
1924 La organización social y las creencias religiosas de los antiguos Araucanos. Santiago.
1927 The Totemism of the ancient Andean peoples. JRAI, LVII, 55-87. London.
1927a El dominio de la tierra y el sistema tributario en el antiguo imperio de los Incas. RCHG, LII, 201-257.
1927-1928 Los Incas, sus orígenes y sus ayllus. Anales de la Universidad de Chile, n.s., V, 1017-1154, VI, 159-233. Santiago.
1928 La alfarería indígena chilena. Santiago.
1928a Chile prehispano. RCHG, LVII, 44-91.
1928b Las influencias chinchas en la alfarería indígena de Chile y la Argentina. Anales de la Sociedad Científica Argentina, CIV, 159-196. Buenos Aires.
1929 Las creencias religiosas de los antiguos Peruanos. Santiago de Chile.
Lavachery, Henri:
1929 Les arts anciens d'Amérique. Antwerp.
1932 Un classement de la petite plastique mexicaine en terre cuite. BSAB, Dec. 1932, 95-110. Brussels.
1933 Préliminaires à une étude des arts archaïques de l'Amérique. BSAB, Aug. 1933, 59-73.
Lehmann, Walter:
1909 Methods and results in Mexican research. Translated by Seymour de Ricci. Paris.
1920 Zentral-Amerika. Berlin. 2 vols.
1933 Aus den pyramidenstädten in alt-Mexiko. Berlin.
Lehmann, Walter, and Doering, Heinrich:
1924 The art of Old Peru. London.
Lehmann-Nitsche, Robert:
1928 Coricancha, el Templo del Sol en el Cuzco. . . . RMLP, XXXI, 1-260.
León, Nicolás:
1904 Los Tarascos. Mexico. (Museo Nacional de México).
Levillier, Jean (Mme. Robert Levillier):
1928 Paracas, a contribution to the study of pre-Incaic textiles in ancient Peru. Paris.
Levillier, Robert:
1926 El Perú y el Tucumán en los tiempos prehispánicos. Lima.
1927 Nueva crónica de la conquista de Tucumán. Buenos Aires. 3rd edition.
Linné, Sigvald:
1925 The technique of South American ceramics. Gothenburg.
1929 Darien in the past. Gothenburg.
1934 Archæological researches at Teotihuacan, Mexico. London.

Locke, L. Leland:
1923 The ancient quipu or Peruvian knot-record. New York. (American Museum of Natural History).

López de Cogolludo, Diego:
1688 Historia de Yucathan. Madrid.

Lothrop, Samuel Kirkland:
1919 The discovery of gold in the graves of Chiriquí, Panama. INM, VI, 27-36.
1921 The stone statues of Nicaragua. AA, n.s., XXIII, 311-319.
1924 Tulum, an archæological study of the east coast of Yucatan. Washington. (Carnegie Institution).
1925 The architecture of the ancient Mayas. Architectural Record, LVII, 491-501. New York.
1926 Pottery of Costa Rica and Nicaragua. New York. (Museum of the American Indian). 2 vols.
1926a Nicoyan incense burner. IN, III, 79-81.
1926b Stone sculptures from Finca Arevalo, Guatemala. IN, III, 147-171.
1927 Pottery types and their sequence in El Salvador. INM, I, 165-220.
1928 Santiago Atitlan, Guatemala. IN, V, 370-395.
1928a The Indians of Tierra del Fuego. New York. (Museum of the American Indian).
1932 Aboriginal navigation off the west coast of South America. JRAI, LXII, 229-256.
1932a Indians of the Paraná Delta, Argentina. Annals of the N. Y. Academy of Sciences, XXXIII, 77-232.
1933 Atitlan. Washington. (Carnegie Institution).

Lovera, Mariño de (Flourished about 1540) :
1865 Crónica del reino de Chile. Edited by Diego Barros Arana. Colección de Historiadores de Chile, VI. Santiago.

Lumholtz, Carl:
1898 The Huichol Indians of Mexico. American Museum of Natural History, Bull. X, 1-14.
1902 Unknown Mexico. New York.

MacCurdy, George Grant:
1911 A study of Chiriquian antiquities. MCAAS, III. New Haven.

Magallanes, Manuel M.:
1912 El camino del Inca. RCHG, III, 44-75.

Maler, Teobert:
1901-1903 Researches in the Usumatsintla Valley. PMM, II. Cambridge, Mass.
1908 Explorations of the upper Usumatsintla and adjacent region. PMM, IV.

Marcano, G.:
1889-1890 Ethnographie ancienne de Venezuela. Mémoirs de la Société d'Anthropologie de Paris, 2nd. sr., IV, 1-218.
1889 Ethnologie précolombienne de Venezuela. Paris.

Mariscal, Federico E.:
1928 Estudio arquitectónico de las ruinas Mayas, Yucatan y Campeche. Mexico. (Talleres Gráficos de la Nación).

Markham, Sir Clements Robert:
1892 A history of Peru. Chicago.
1906 The Megalithic Age in Peru. ICA, XIV, 521-529. Stuttgart.
1908 A comparison of the ancient Peruvian carvings and the stones of Tiahuanacu and Chavín. ICA, XVI, 389-395. Vienna.

1910 The Incas of Peru. London and New York.
1912 The conquest of New Granada. London.

Marquez Miranda, Fernando:
1930 El sentimiento religioso en el arte prehistórico. La Plata, Argentina.

Marquina, Ignacio:
1928 Estudio arquitectónico comparativo de los monumentos arqueológicos de México. Mexico. (Secretaría de Educación Pública).

Martínez Hernández, Juan:
1928 The Mayan lunar table. ICA, XXXIII, 149-155. New York.
1928a Significación cronológica de los ciclos Mayas. Mérida, Yucatan.
1932 Correlation of the Maya venus calendar. New Orleans. (Tulane University).

Mason, Gregory:
1931 Columbus came late. New York.

Mason, John Alden:
1917 Excavation of a new archæological site in Porto Rico. ICA, XIX, 220-223. Washington.
1925 Archæological researches in the region of Santa Marta, Colombia. ICA, XXI, Pt. II, 159-166. Gothenburg.
1926 Coast and crest in Colombia. NH, XXVI, 31-43. New York.
1926a A puma stone cup. MJ, XVII, 278-283. Philadelphia.
1927 Native American jades. MJ, XVIII, 47-73.
1927a Mirrors of ancient America. MJ, XVIII, 201-209.
1928 The Egypt of America. NH, XXVIII, 394-406.
1928a Some unusual spearthrowers of ancient America. MJ, XIX, 290-324.
1929 Zapotec funerary urns from Mexico. MJ, XX, 176-200.
1931 Archæology of Santa Marta, Colombia. Chicago. (Field Museum).

Mathewson, C. H.:
1915 A metallographic description of some ancient Peruvian bronzes from Machu Picchu. AJS, 4th ser., XL, 525-602. New Haven.

Maudslay, Alfred Percival:
1889-1902 Biologia centrali-americana. Archæology. London. 4 vols.

Mayer, Brantz:
1854 Mexico; Aztec, Spanish and Republican. Hartford, Conn. 2 vols.

Mead, Charles W.:
1903 The musical instruments of the Incas. Guide Leaflet No. 11, American Museum of Natural History. New York.
1907 Technique of some South American featherwork. APAMNH, I, 1-17. New York.
1915 Prehistoric bronze in South America. APAMNH, XII, 15-104.
1916 Ancient Peruvian cloths. AMJ, 389-393. New York.
1917 Peruvian art. Guide Leaflet No. 46, American Museum of Natural History. New York.
1921 Prehistoric mining in western South America. NH, XXI, 453-456.
1932 Old civilizations of Inca Land. Edited by R. L. Olson. New York. (American Museum of Natural History).

Means, Philip Ainsworth:
1916 Some objections to Mr. Elliot Smith's theory. Science, n.s., XLIV, 533-534.
1917 History of the Spanish conquest of Yucatan and of the Itzas. PMP, VII. Cambridge, Mass.
1917a A survey of ancient Peruvian art. TCAAS, XXI, 315-442. New Haven.
1917b Realism in the art of ancient Peru. A&A, VI, 235-246. Washington.

1917c A note on the Guaraní invasions of the Inca Empire. GR, IV, 482-484. New York.
1917d Las relaciones entre Centro-América y Sud-América en la época prehistórica. BSGL, XXXIII, 152-170. Lima.
1918 A note on two stone objects from southern Bolivia. AA, n.s., XX, 254-256.
1919 La civilización precolombina de los Andes. BSEEHA, III, 213-242. Quito.
1919a Una nota sobre la prehistoria peruana. Lima.
1919b Distribution and use of slings in pre-Columbian America. . . . Proceedings of the U. S. National Museum, vol. 55, 317-349. Washington.
1920 Aspectos estético-cronológicos de las civilizaciones andinas. BANH, I, 195-226. Quito.
1923 Some comments on the inedited manuscript of Poma de Ayala. AA, n.s., XXV, 397-405.
1925 A study of ancient Andean social institutions. TCAAS, XXVII, 407-469. New Haven.
1928 Biblioteca andina, Part One. TCAAS, XXIX, 271-525.
1930 Peruvian textiles. With an Introduction by Joseph Breck. New York. (Metropolitan Museum of Art).
1930a The origin of tapestry technique in pre-Spanish Peru. Metropolitan Museum Studies, III, 22-37. New York.
1931 Ancient civilizations of the Andes. New York and London.
1932 A study of Peruvian textiles. Boston. (Museum of Fine Arts).
1932a Fall of the Inca Empire and the Spanish rule in Peru: 1530-1780. New York and London.
1934 Des commentaires sur l'architecture ancienne de la côte Péruvienne. Brussels.
1935 The Spanish Main. New York and London.

Medina, José Toribio:
1882 Los aboríjenes de Chile. Santiago.

Mejía Xesspe, Toribio:
1923 Costumbres indígenas. Región andina. Inca, I, 884-903. Lima.
1931 Kausay. Alimentación de los Indios. WK, I, 9-24. Lima.

Mercer, Henry C.:
1896 The hill-caves of Yucatan. Philadelphia.

Merwin, Raymond E., and Vaillant, George C.:
1932 The ruins of Homul, Guatemala. PMM, III, No. 2. Cambridge, Mass.

Métraux, Alfred:
1927 Migrations historiqués des Tupi-Guaraní. JAP, n.s., XIX, 1-45.
1928 La civilisation matérielle des tribus Tupi-Guaraní. Paris.
1929 Contribution à l'archéologie de la province de Mendoza (República Argentine). UNTRIE, I, 5-73. Tucumán.
1930 Contribution à l'étude de l'archéologie du cours supérieur de l'Amazone. RMLP, XXXII, 145-185.
1930a Études sur la civilisation des Indiens Chiriguano. UNTRIE, I, 295-493.
1931 Les hommes-dieux chez les Chiriguano et dans l'Amérique du Sud. UNTRIE, II, 61-91.
1931a Un mundo perdido, la tribu de los Chipayas de Carangas. Sur, I, 98-131. Buenos Aires.

Middendorf, E. W.:
1893-1895 Peru. Berlin. 3 vols.

Milla, José:
1879-1905 Historia de la América Central desde el descubrimiento del país por los Españoles (1502) hasta su independencia de la España (1821). Precedida de una "Noticia Histórica" relativa á las naciones que habitaban la América Central á la llegada de los Españoles. Guatemala. 5 vols. (Vols. 3-5 were produced under the direction of Agustín Gómez Carrillo after Milla's death in 1882).

Minnaert, Paul:
1928 Les institutions et le droit de l'Empire des Incas. Ostende, Belgium, and Paris.
1931 Polynésians et Andéens. BSAB, March, 1931, 3-28. Brussels.
1931a L'adoration dans la réligion péruvienne. BSAB, Dec., 1931, 40-65.
1932 La symbolique des vases Nazca. BSAB, Aug., 1932, 53-68.
1932a Un ornement d'or péruvien des Musées d'Art et d'Histoire. BSAB, Dec., 1932, 111-113.

Montell, Gösta:
1925 Le vrai poncho, son origine postcolombienne. JAP, n.s., XVII, 173-183.
1929 Dress and ornaments in ancient Peru. Gothenburg and London.

Montesinos, Father Fernando (Seventeenth Century):
1920 Memorias antiguas historiales del Perú. Translated and edited by P. A. Means, with an Introduction by the late Sir Clements R. Markham. London. HS.

Morley, Sylvanus Griswold:
1915 An introduction to the study of Maya hieroglyphs. BAE, Bull. 57. Washington.
1917 The rise and fall of the Maya civilization in the light of the monuments and the native chronicles. PASC, Sec. I, vol. I, 192-208. Washington.
1920 The inscriptions at Copan. Washington. (Carnegie Institution).
1922 The foremost intellectual achievement of ancient America. NGM, XLI, 109-130. Washington.
1927 New light on the discovery of Yucatan, and the foundation of the New Maya Empire. AJA, XXXI, 51-69.

Morris, Ann Axtell:
1931 The Temple of the Warriors, murals. A&A, XXXI, 316-322. Washington.

Morris, Earl H.:
1931 The Temple of the Warriors. New York and London.

Morris, Earl H., Charlot, Jean, and Morris, Ann Axtell:
1931 The Temple of the Warriors at Chichen Itzá, Yucatan. Washington. (Carnegie Institution).

Mortier, Florent:
1932 Les populations indigénes du Pérou et l'or. BSAB, Aug., 1932, 69-85.

Mortimer, W. Golden:
1901 Coca, the divine plant of the Incas. New York.

Motolinia, Toribio de (Sixteenth Century):
1914 Historia de los indios de la Nueva España. Edited by Daniel Sánchez García. Barcelona.

Mozans, H. J. See Zahm, J. A.

Muñiz, Manuel Antonio, and McGee, W. J.:
1895 Primitive trephining in Peru. ARBAE, XVI, 1-72. Washington.

Murdock, George Peter:
1934 Our primitive contemporaries. New York.

Murphy, Robert Cushman:
1923   Fisheries resources in Peru. SM, XVI, 594-607.
1925   Bird islands of Peru. New York and London.
Nestler, Julius:
1910   Die bedeutung der ruinenstätte von Tiahuanaco nach den publikationen von Dr. Max Uhle und Sir Clements Markham. ICA, XVI, 395-403. Vienna.
1913   Beitrage zur kenntnis der ruinenstätte von Tiahuanaco. Vienna.
Netto, Ladislau:
1885   Investigações sobre a archæologia brasileira. AMNRJ, VI, 257-555.
1890   Sur les antiquités céramiques de l'ile de Marajo. ICA, VII, 201-206. Berlin.
Nicholas, Francis G.:
1901   The aborigines of the Province of Santa Marta, Colombia. AA, n.s., III, 606-649.
Nichols, H. W.:
1929   Inca relics in the Atacama Desert, Chile. AA, n.s., XXXI, 130-135.
Nimuendajú, Curt:
1924   Os indios parintintin do Rio Madeira. JAP, n.s., XVI, 201-278.
1925   As tribus do alto Madeira. JAP, n.s., XVII, 137-172.
1926   Die palikur-indianer und ihre nachbarn. Gothenburg.
Noble, G. K.
1921   Pages from the photographic journal of the Harvard Peruvian Expedition. NH, XXI, 486-493.
Noguera, Eduardo:
1930   Decorative aspects of certain types of Mexican pottery. ICA, XXIII, 85-92. New York.
1930a Algunas características de la cerámica de México. JAP, n.s., XXII, 249-310.
1930b Ruinas arqueológicas del norte de México. Mexico. (Secretaría de Educación Pública).
Nomland, Gladys Ayer:
1933   Archæological site of Hato Viejo, Venezuela. AA, n.s., XXXV, 718-741.
Nordenskiöld, Baron Erland:
1906   Ethnographische und archæologische forschungen im grenzgebiet zwischen Peru und Bolivia. . . . 1904-1905. ZE, XXXVIII, 80-99. Berlin.
1913   Urnengräber und mounds in Bolivianischen flachlande. BA, III, 205-255. Berlin.
1915   Incallacta, eine befestigte und von Inca Tupac Yupanqui angelegte stadt. Ymer, XXXV, 169-185. Stockholm.
1917   Die östliche ausbreitung der Tiahuanacokultur in Bolivien und ihr verhältnis zur Aruakkultur in Mojos. ZE, XLIX, 10-20. Berlin.
1921   The copper and bronze ages in South America. Gothenburg.
1925   The secret of the Peruvian quipus. Gothenburg.
1925a Calculations with years and months in the Peruvian quipus. Gothenburg.
1929   The American Indian as an inventor. JRAI, LIX, 273-309. London.
1930   Modifications in Indian culture through inventions and loans. Gothenburg.
1930a L'archéologie du Bassin de l'Amazone. Paris.
1931   Origin of the Indian civilizations in South America. Gothenburg.
Nuttall, Zelia:
1886   The terra cotta heads of Teotihuacan. AJA, II, 157-178, 318-330.
1888   Standard or head-dress? PMP, I, No. 1. Cambridge, Mass.

1891 The atlatl or spear-thrower of the ancient Mexicans. PMP, I, No. 3.

1892 On ancient Mexican shields. Leiden.

1901 The fundamental principles of old and new world civilizations. PMP, II.

1901a Chalchihuitl in ancient Mexico. AA, n.s., III, 227-238.

1902 Codex Nuttall; facsimile of an ancient Mexican codex. Cambridge, Mass. (Peabody Museum.)

1903 The Book of the Life of the Ancient Mexicans. Berkeley, California.

1903a A suggestion to Maya scholars. AA, n.s., V, 667, 678.

1904 The periodical adjustments of the ancient Mexican calendar. AA, n.s., VI, 486-500.

1906 The astronomical methods of the ancient Mexicans. Boas Anniversary Volume, 290-298. New York.

1906a The earliest historical relations between Mexico and Japan. UCPAAE, IV, 1-47.

1906b Some unsolved problems in Mexican archæology. AA, n.s., VIII, 133-149.

1910 L'évêque Zumarraga et les idoles principales du grand temple du Mexique. JAP, n.s., VIII, 153-171.

1910a The Island of Sacrificios. AA, n.s., XII, 257-295.

1918 Ancient Mexican gardeners and flower lovers. International Garden Club Journal, III, No. 3. New York.

1922 Recent archæological discoveries in Mexico. Man, XXII, 4-6. London.

1925 La cerámica descubierta en Coyoacán, D. F. Ethnos, 3rd época, I, 82-86. Mexico.

1926 The Aztecs and their predecessors in the Valley of Mexico. Proceedings of the American Philosophical Society, LXV, 245-255. Philadelphia.

1927 Fresh light on ancient civilizations and calendars. Man, XXVII, 10-12.

1927a The ancient American civilizations and calendars. Science, n.s., LXVI, 194-195.

1930 The round temples of Mexico and Yucatan. A&A, XXX, 229-233. Washington.

1932 Sobre un monumento en Monte Albán de gran importancia. Mexico. (Sociedad Mexicana de Geografía y Estadística).

Olson, Ronald L.:

1931 Old empires of the Andes. NH, XXXI, 3-22. New York.

O'Neale, Lila M., and Kroeber, A. L.:

1930 Textile periods in ancient Peru. UCPAAE, XXVIII, 23-56.

Orchard, William C.:

1925 Minute gold beads from La Tolita, Ecuador. IN, II, 48-56.

1927 Nose-ornaments of gold. IN, IV, 118-124.

1930 Peruvian gold and gold plating. IN, VII, 466-474.

Orozco y Berra, Manuel:

1880 Historia antigua y de la conquista de México. Mexico. 4 vols. and Atlas.

Outes, Félix F.:

1907 Alfarerías del noroeste Argentino. Buenos Aires.

Oyarzún, Aureliano:

1910 Contribución al estudio de la influencia de la civilización peruana sobre los aborígenes de Chile. ICA, XVII, 354-397. Buenos Aires.

Oyarzún, Aureliano, and Latcham, R. E.:

1928 Album de tejidos y alfarería araucana. Santiago.

Palacios, Enrique Juan:

1924 Interpretación de la piedra del calendario. Mexico. (Museo Nacional).

1928 En los confines de la selva Lacandona. Mexico. (Secretaría de Educación Pública).
1932 La orientación de la pirámide de Tenayuca. . . . Mexico. (Universidad de México).
1932b Maya and Christian synchronology. New Orleans. (Tulane University).

Peñafiel, Antonio:
1890 Monumentos del arte Mexicano antiguo. Berlin. 3 vols.
1897 Nomenclatura geográfica de México. Mexico.
1900 Teotihuacan. Mexico.

Perrone di San Martino, Count Giuseppe:
1922 Il Perù. Rome.

Pi y Margall, Francisco:
1888 Historia general de América. Barcelona. 2 vols.
1892 Historia de la América antecolombiana. Barcelona. 2 vols.

Pietschmann, Richard:
1912 Some account of the illustrated chronicle by the Peruvian Indian, D. Felipe Huaman Poma de Ayala. ICA, XVIII, Pt. 1, 510-521. London.

Plancarte y Navarrete, Bishop and Archbishop Francisco:
1911 Tamoanchan. El estado de Morelos y el principio de la civilización en México. Mexico.
1923 Prehistoria de México. Tlalpam, D. F., Mexico.

Ploetz, Hermann and Métraux, Alfred:
1930 La civilisation matérielle et la vie sociale et religieuse des Indiens du Brésil meridional et oriental. UNTRIE, I, 107-238. Tucumán.

Polo, José Toribio:
1899 La piedra de Chavín. BSGL, IX, 192-231, 262-290.
1901 Indios uros del Perú y Bolivia. BSGL, X, 445-482.

Posnansky, A.:
1914 Una metropolí prehistórica en la América del Sud. Berlin.
1918 Los Chipayas de Carangas. BSGLP, XVI, 137-145.
1930 La remoción del cíngulo climatérico como factor del despueble del altiplano y decadencia de su alta cultura. ICA, XXIII, 235-246. New York.
1931 Leyendas prehispánicas sobre dos kerus. UNTRIE, II, 93-100. Tucumán.

Prescott, William Hickling:
1843 History of the conquest of Mexico. New York. 3 vols.
1847 History of the conquest of Peru. New York. 2 vols.

Preuss, Konrad Th.:
1921 Sänfte aus goldraht, Chibcha. ZE, LII, 460-461. Berlin.
1922 Die statuen von San Agustin am oberen Magdalena in Kolombien. Berlin Museen, XLIII, 126-130.
1929 Monumentale vorgeschichtliche kunst. Göttingen, Germany. 2 vols.
1930 Die ausstrahlung der San Agustin-kultur (Kolumbien) in Amerika. ICA, XXIII, 233-234. New York.

Putnam, E. K.:
1914 The Davenport collection of Nazca and other Peruvian pottery. Davenport, Iowa. (Davenport Academy of Science).

Radin, Paul:
1920 Sources and authenticity of the history of the ancient Mexicans. UCPAAE, XVII, 1-150.

Réal, Daniel:
1925 La décoration primitive de l'Amérique précolombienne. Paris.

Reichard, Gladys A.:
1930 Form and interpretation in American art. ICA, XXIII, 459-462. New York.

Reiss, Wilhelm, and Stübel, Alphons:
1880-1887 The Necropolis of Ancon in Peru. Berlin. 3 vols.

Restrepo Tirado, Ernesto:
1912 Los Quimbayas. Bogotá.
1917 Descubrimiento y conquista de Colombia. Begotá.

Restrepo, Vicente:
1895 Los Chibchas antes de la conquista española. Bogotá.

Reygadas Vertiz, José:
1929 The ruins of Labna, Yucatan. A&A, XXVIII, Washington.
1930 Exploración en la pirámide de Tenayuca por la dirección de Arqueología de México. ICA, XXIII, 172-180. New York.

Rice, A. Hamilton:
1928 The Rio Branco, Uraricuera and Parima. London. (Royal Geographical Society).

Ricketson Jr., Oliver:
1925 Burials in the Maya area. AA, n.s., XXVII.
1927 Report . . . on the Uaxactun project. YBCIW, XXVI, 256-263.
1928 Astronomical observatories in the Maya area. GR, XVIII, 215-225. New York.
1928a Notes on two Maya astronomical observatories. AA, n.s., XXX, 434-444.
1929 Excavations at Baking Pot, British Honduras. Washington. (Carnegie Institution).
1930 The excavations at Uaxactun. ICA, XXIII, 185-187. New York.

Ricketson Jr., Oliver, and Kidder, A. V.:
1930 An archæological reconnaissance by air in Central America. GR, XX, 117-206.

Riva-Agüero y Osma, José de la:
1910 La historia en el Perú. Lima.
1921 El Perú histórico y artístico. Santander, Spain.
1931 Raza y lenguaje de la civilización del Tiahuanaco. Mercurio Peruano, XX, 351-380. Lima.

Rivero, Mariano Eduardo de, and Tschudi, Juan Diego de:
1851 Antigüedades peruanas. Vienna. 2 vols.

Rivers, W. H. R.:
1914 The history of Melanesian society. Cambridge, England. 2 vols.

Rivet, Paul:
1924 L'orfèvrerie colombienne. ICA, XXI, Pt. I, 15-28. The Hague.
1926 Les Malayo-Polynésiens en Amérique. JAP, n.s., XVIII, 141-278.
1926a Le travail de l'or en Colombie. Ipek for 1926, 128-141. Leipzig.
1928 Migration australienne en Amérique. PPPSC, II, 2354-2356. Tokyo.
1928a Relations commerciales précolombiennes entre l'océanie et l'Amérique. PWS, 583-609. Vienna.

Rochefort, H. de:
1658 Histoire naturelle et morale des iles Antilles de l'Amérique. Rotterdam.
1667 Histoire naturelle et morale des iles Antilles de l'Amérique. Lyons. (Christophe Fourney). 2 vols.

Rojas, Arístides:
1878 Estudios indígenas. Contribuciones á la historia antigua de Venezuela. Caracas.

Rosen, Count Eric von:
   1924 Popular account of Archæological research during the Swedish Chaco-Cordillera Expedition, 1901-1902. Stockholm.
   1924a Ethnographical research work during the Swedish Chaco-Cordillera Expedition, 1901-1902. Stockholm.

Sáenz, Moisés:
   1933 Sobre el indio ecuatoriano y su incorporación al medio nacional. Mexico. (Secretaría de Educación Pública).
   1933a Sobre el indio peruano y su incorporación al medio nacional. Mexico. (Secretaría de Educación Pública).

Sahagún, Friar Bernardino de (Sixteenth Century):
   1829-1929 Historia general de las cosas de la Nueva España. Edited by Carlos María de Bustamente. Mexico. 3 vols. (Book 12 published by Extensión Universitaria. Mexico, 1929).
   1932 A history of ancient Mexico. Translated from the Spanish version of Carlos María de Bustamente by Fannie R. Bandelier. Nashville, Tennessee. (Fiske University). Vol. I, only.

Sarmiento de Gamboa, Pedro (Sixteenth Century):
   1906 Geschichte des Inkareiches. Edited and translated by Richard Pietschmann. Berlin.
   1907 History of the Incas. Translated and edited by Sir Clements R. Markham. London. H.S.

Saville, Marshall Howard:
   1899 Exploration of Zapotecan tombs in southern Mexico. AA, n.s., I, 350-362.
   1907-1910 The antiquities of Manabí, Ecuador. New York. (Museum of the American Indian). 2 vols.
   1909 Archæological researches on the coast of Esmeraldas. (Ecuador) ICA, XVI, 331-345. Vienna.
   1909a The cruciform structures of Mitla and vicinity. Putnam Anniversary Volume, 151-190. New York.
   1916 Monolithic axes and their distribution in ancient America. New York. (Museum of the American Indian).
   1920 Goldsmiths' art in ancient Mexico. New York. (Museum of the American Indian).
   1921 A sculptured vase from Guatemala. A&A, XI, 66-67. Washington.
   1921a A golden breastplate from Cuzco, Peru. New York. (Museum of the American Indian).
   1922 Turquois mosaic art in ancient Mexico. New York. (Museum of the American Indian).
   1924 The gold treasure of Sigsig, Ecuador. New York. (Museum of the American Indian).
   1924a A wooden ceremonial spade from Ica, Peru. IN, I, 189-194. New York.
   1925 The wood carvers' art in ancient Mexico. New York. (Museum of the American Indian).
   1925a Ancient mosaic ear-plugs from Peru. IN, II, 145-151.
   1925b Balance-beam scales in ancient Peru. IN, II, 266-283.
   1926 The pottery arybal of the Incas. IN, III, 111-119.
   1927 Some gold ornaments from South America. IN, IV, 209-214.
   1928 Fraudulent black-ware pottery of Colombia. IN, V, 144-154.
   1928a Shell carvings from Colombia. IN, V, 357-364.
   1929 The Aztecan God Xipe Totec. IN, VI, 151-174.
   1929a The wooden Kero of the Incas. IN, VI, 221-225.
   1929b Votive axes from ancient Mexico. IN, VI, 266-299, 335-342.

1930 Ancient causeways of Yucatan. IN, VII, 89-99.
1930a Toltec or Teotihuacan types of artifacts from Guatemala. IN, VII, 195-206.
1935 The ancient Maya causeways of Yucatan. Antiquity. IX, 67-73.
Schellhas, Paul:
1904 Representations of deities of the Maya manuscripts. PMP, IV, 1-47. Cambridge, Mass.
Schmidt, Max:
1909 Über altperuanische ornamentik. Archiv für Anthropologie, n.f., VII, 22-36. Brunswick, Ger.
1910 Szenenhafte darstellungen auf altperuanischen geweben. ZE, XLII, 154-164. Berlin.
1910a Über altperuanische gewebe mit szenenhaften darstellungen. BA, I, 1-61. Berlin and Leipzig.
1929 Kunst und kultur von Peru. Berlin.
Schmidt, P. Wilhelm:
1913 Kulturkreise und kulturschichten in Südamerika. ZE, XLV, 1014-1124. Berlin.
Seler, Eduard:
1893 Peruanische alterthumer. Berlin.
1902-1915 Gesammelte abhandlungen zur Amerikanischen sprach und alter-thumskunde. Berlin. 5 vols.
Seler-Sachs, Caecilie:
1915 Die Huaxteca sammlung des Kgl. Museums für Völkerkunde zu Berlin. BA, V, 98-135. Berlin and Leipzig.
Serrano, Antonio:
1930 Los primitivos habitantes del territorio argentino. Buenos Aires.
1930a La área de dispersión de las llamadas alfarerías gruesas del territorio argentino. Physis, X, 181-187. Buenos Aires.
1931 Arqueología del litoral, MMP, No. 4. Paraná, Argentina.
1932 Exploraciones arqueológicas en el Río Uruguay medio. MMP, No. 2.
1933 Observaciones sobre la alfarería de los médanos de Colón (Entre Ríos). MMP, No. 6.
1933a Las culturas protohistóricas del este Argentino y Uruguay. MMP, No. 7.
Shippee, Robert:
1932 The "Great Wall of Peru" and other aerial photographic studies by the Shippee-Johnson Peruvian Expedition. GR, XXII, 1-29.
1932a Lost valleys of Peru. GR, XXII, 562-681.
Simoens da Silva, A. C.:
1912 Points of contact of the prehistoric civilizations of Brazil and Argentina with those of the Pacific coast countries. ICA, XVIII, 302-310. London.
Simón, Pedro:
1627 Primera parte de las noticias historiales de las conquistas de tierra firme en las indias occidentales. Cuenca, Spain. (Domingo de la Iglesia).
Sivirichi, Atilio:
1930 Pre-historia peruana. Lima.
Smith, G. E.:
1916 The origin of the pre-Columbian civilization of America. Science, n.s., XLIV, 190-195.
1917 The origin of pre-Columbian civilization in America. Science, n.s., XLV, 241-246.
1924 Elephants and ethnologists. London.

Smith, G. E., Malinowski, B., Spinden, H. J., and Goldeweiser, A. A.:
1927   Culture. The diffusion controversy. New York.

Smith, Howell:
1926   Brief guide to the Peruvian textiles. London. (Victoria and Albert Museum).

Smith, Ledyard:
1932   Two recent ceramic finds at Uaxactun. Washington. (Carnegie Institution, publication 436).

Spinden, Ellen S.:
1933   The place of Tajin in Totonac archæology. AA, n.s., XXXV, 227-270.

Spinden, Herbert J.:
1913   A study of Maya art. PMM, VI. Cambridge, Mass.
1916   New data on the archæology of Venezuela. Proceedings of the National Academy of Sciences, II, 325-328. Washington.
1917   The origin and distribution of agriculture in America. ICA, XIX, 269-276. Washington.
1917a The invention and spread of agriculture in America. AMJ, XVII, 181-189.
1917b The archaic type. In Means, 1917a, 390-393.
1924   The reduction of Maya dates. PMP, VI, No. 4.
1924a New World correlations. ICA, XXI, Pt. I, 76-86. The Hague.
1928   Ancient civilizations of Mexico and Central America. New York. (American Museum of Natural History.) 3rd edition.
1928a The population of ancient America. GR, XVIII, 641-660.
1930   Maya dates and what they reveal. Science Bulletin, Brooklyn Institute of Arts and Sciences, IV, 1-111.

Squier, E. George:
1855   Notes on Central America. New York.
1877   Peru, incidents of travel and exploration in the land of the Incas. New York.

Starr, Frederick:
1894   Notes on Mexican archæology. Chicago.
1897   The little pottery objects of Lake Chapala, Mexico. Chicago.
1908   In Indian Mexico. Chicago.

Steinen, Karl von den:
1886   Durch Central-Brasilien. Leipzig.
1897   Unter den naturvölker Zentral-Brasiliens. Berlin.

Steinmayer, R. A.:
1932   A reconnaissance of certain mounds and relics in Spanish Honduras. New Orleans. (Tulane University).

Stephens, John L.:
1841   Incidents of travel in Central America, Chiapas and Yucatan. New York. 2 vols.
1843   Incidents of travel in Yucatan. New York. 2 vols.

Stolpe, Hjalmar:
1896   Studier i Amerikansk ornamentik. Stockholm.

Strebel, Hermann:
1885-1889   Alt Mexiko. Hamburg and Leipzig. 2 vols.
1899   The sculptures of Santa Lucia Cozumahualpa, Guatemala. Washington.

Strong, William Duncan:
1925   The Uhle pottery collections from Ancón. UCPAAE, XXI, 135-190.

Stübel, Alphons, and Uhle, Max:
1889-1890 Kultur und industrie der Süd-amerikaische völker. Berlin. 3 vols.
1892 Die ruinenstätte von Tiahuanaco. Leipzig.

Stucken, Eduard:
1927 Polynesisches sprachgut in Amerika und in Sumer. Leipzig. (Vorder-asiatisch-Aegyptischen Gesellschaft).

Tello, Julio C.:
1912 Prehistoric trephining among the Yauyos of Peru. ICA, XVIII, 75-83. London.
1917 Los antiguos cementerios del Valle de Nasca. PASC, I, 283-291. Washington.
1918 El uso de las cabezas artificialmente momificadas, y su representación en el antiguo arte peruano. Lima.
1922 Introducción á la historia antigua del Perú. Lima.
1923 Wira Kocha. Inca, I, 93-320, 583-606. Lima.
1928 Los descubrimientos del Museo de Arqueología peruana en la península de Paracas. ICA, XXII, Pt. I, 679-690. Rome.
1929 Antiguo Perú. Lima.
1930 Andean civilization: some problems of Peruvian archæology. ICA, XXIII, 259-290. New York.
1931 Un modelo de escenografía plástica en el arte antiguo peruanao. WK, I, 87-112. Lima.

Tello, Julio C., and Miranda, Próspero:
1923 Wallallo. Inca, I, 475-549. Lima.

Teeple, John E.:
1925-1928 Maya inscriptions. AA, n.s., XXVII, 108-115, 544-549, XXVIII, 402-408, XXIX, 278-291, XXX, 391-407.
1928 Factors which may lead to a correlation of Maya and Christian dates. ICA, XXIII, 136-139. New York.
1930 Maya astronomy. Washington. (Carnegie Institution, publication No. 403).

Termer, Franz:
1931 Zur archäologie von Guatemala. BA, XIV. Berlin.

Tessmann, Günter:
1930 Die Indianer nordost-Perus. . . . Hamburg.

Thomas, Cyrus:
1904 Maya calendar systems. ARBAE, XXII, 197-305.

Thomas, Cyrus, and Swanton, Jon R.:
1911 Indian languages of Mexico and Central America. BAE, Bull. 44. Washington.

Thompson, Edward H.:
1904 Archæological researches in Yucatan. PMM, III, No. 1. Cambridge, Mass.
1932 People of the Serpent. Boston and New York.

Thompson, J. Eric:
1930 The causeways of the Coba district, eastern Yucatan. ICA, XXIII, 181-187. New York.
1933 Mexico before Cortez. New York and London.

Toro, Alfonso:
1930 Las plantas sagradas de los Aztecas y su influencia sobre el arte pre-cortesiano. ICA, XXIII, 101-121. New York.

Torres, Luís M.:
1931   Hallazgos de ganchos de propulsor en un cementerio indígena de la cuenca del Río de Luján (Delta del Paraná). NPMLP, I, 101-105.

Totten, George Oakley:
1926   Maya architecture. Washington.

Toynbee, Arnold J.:
1935   A study of history. Oxford. 3 vols.

Tozzer, Alfred Marston:
1907   A comparative study of the Mayas and Lacandones. New York.
1911   The value of ancient Mexican manuscripts in the study of the general development of writing. AASP, n.s., XXI, 80-101. Worcester, Mass.
1911a   Preliminary study of the ruins of Tikal. PMM, V, No. 2. Cambridge, Mass.
1912   Exhibition of Maya art. Museum of Fine Arts Bulletin, X, 13-14. Boston.
1916   The domain of the Aztecs and their relation to the prehistoric cultures of Mexico. Holmes Anniversary Volume, 464-468. Washington.
1921   A Maya grammar. PMP, IX. Cambridge, Mass.
1927   Time and American archæology. NH, XXVII, 210-221.
1930   Maya and Toltec figures at Chichen Itzá. ICA, XXIII, 155-164. New York.

Tozzer, Alfred Marston, and Allen, Glover:
1910   Animal figures in the Maya codices. PMP, IV, 276-372. Cambridge, Mass.

Tschudi, Johann Jakob von, (see also Rivero and Tschudi):
1847   Travels in Peru, during the Years 1838-1842. Translated by Thomasina Ross. New York. (Also, London).
1853   Die Kechua-sprache. Vienna. 3 vols.
1868   Reisen durch Sudamerika. Leipzig. 5 vols.
1891   Culturhistorische und sprachliche beiträge zur kenntnis des Alten Peru. Vienna.

Tudela y Varela, Francisco:
1905   Socialismo peruano. Lima.

Ugarte, César Antonio:
1918   Los antecedentes históricos del régimen agrario peruano. Lima.

Uhle, Max:
1903   Pachacamac. Philadelphia. (University Museum).
1906   Los "Kjoekkenmoedings" del Perú. RH, I, 3-23. Lima.
1906a   Las llamitas de piedra del Cuzco. RH, I, 388-392.
1907   La estólica en el Perú. RH, II, 118-128.
1907a   La masca paicha del Inca. RH, II, 227-232.
1908   Uber die frühkulturen in der umgebung von Lima. ICA, XVI, 347-370. Vienna.
1908a   Zur deutung der intihuatana. ICA, XVI, 371-388. Vienna.
1909   La esfera de influencia del país de los Incas. RH, IV, 5-40. Lima.
1909a   Peruvian throwing-sticks. AA, n.s., XI, 624-627.
1910   Tipos de civilización en el Perú. BSGL, XXV, 289-294.
1910a   Las relaciones pre-históricas entre el Perú y la Argentina. ICA, XVII, 509-540. Buenos Aires.
1910b   Los orígenes de los Incas. ICA, XVII, 302-353. Buenos Aires.
1911   El aillu peruano. BSGL, XXVII, 81-94.
1912   Die muschelhügel von Ancon, Peru. ICA, XVIII, 22-45. London.
1913   Die ruinen von Moche. JAP, n.s., X, 95-117.

1913a Zur chronologie der alten culturen von Ica. JAP, n.s., X, 341-367.
1917 Fortalezas incaicas. . . . RCHG, XXI, 154-170. Santiago de Chile.
1917b Los aborígenes de Arica. Santiago de Chile.
1919 Fundamentos étnicos de la región de Arica y Tacna. BSEEHA, II, 1-37. Quito.
1919a La arqueología de Arica y Tacna. BSEEHA, III, 1-48.
1920 Apuntes sobre la prehistoria de la región de Piura. BSEEHA, IV, 165-167.
1920a Los principios de las antiguas civilizaciones peruanas. BSEEHA, IV, 448-458.
1920b Los principios de la civilización en la sierra peruana. BANH, I, 44-56. Quito.
1922 Orígenes centroamericanas. BANH, IV, 1-6.
1922a Sepulturas ricas de oro en la provincia del Azuay. BANH, IV, 108-114.
1922b Influencias Mayas en el alto Ecuador. BANH, IV, 205-240.
1923 Civilizaciones mayoides de la costa pacífica de Sudamérica. BANH, VI, 87-92.
1923a Toltecas, Mayas y civilizaciones sudamericanas. BANH, VII, 1-33.
1923b Las ruinas de Tomebamba. Quito. 2 vols.
1923c Cronología y orígen de las antiguas civilizaciones argentinas. BANH, VII, 123-130.
1924 Cronología y relaciones de las antiguas civilizaciones panameñas. BANH, IX, 190-207.
1924a Explorations at Chincha. UCPAAE, XXI, 55-94.
1926 Excavaciones arqueológicas en la región de Cumbayá. AUC, XXXVII, 1-33. Quito.
1928 Las ruinas de Cuasmal. AUC, XL, 183-234. Quito.
1930 El reino de Quito. BANH, X, 1-17.
1930a Desarrollo y orígen de las civilizaciones americanas. ICA, XXIII, 31-43. New York.
1930b El Templo del Sol de los Incas en Cuzco. ICA, XXIII, 291-295.
1931 Las antiguas civilizaciones de Manta. BANH, XII, 1-67. Quito.
1933 Estudio sobre las civilizaciones del Carchi é Imbabura. AUC, L, 351-412. Quito.

Urteaga, Horacio H.:
1909 El antiguo Perú á la luz de la arqueología y de la crítica. RH, IV, 200-223. Lima.
1917 El fetichismo de los Yungas. BSGL, XXXII, 165-183.
1920 El ejército incaico. BSGL, XXXVI, 283-331.
1921 La organización judicial en el imperio de los Incas. RH, IX, 1-50. Lima.

Vaillant, George C.:
1928 The native art of Middle America. NH, XXVIII, 563-576. New York.
1930 The archaic cultures of Mexico. El Palacio, XXVIII, 17-19. Santa Fe, N. M.
1930a Excavations at Zacatenco. APAMNH, XXXII, 1-197. New York.
1930b Notes on the middle cultures of Middle America. ICA, XXIII, 74-81. New York.
1930c Some resemblances in the ceramics of Central and North America. Globe, Arizona. (The Medallion).
1931 Excavations at Ticoman. APAMNH, XXXII, 199-439.
1931a Las antiguas culturas del valle de México. Quetzalcoatl, I, 2-4. Mexico.
1931b Enlivening the past. NH, XXXI, 530-538.

1932　A pre-Columbian jade. NH, XXXII, 512-520.
1932a Where the jade tiger was discovered. NH, XXXII, 556-558.
1932b Stratigraphical researches in Central Mexico. Proceedings of the National Academy of Sciences, XVIII, 487-490.
1934　The architecture of pre-Columbian Central America. NH, XXXIV, 117-132.
1934a Excavations at Gualupita. APAMNH, XXXV, 1-135.

Valcárcel, Luís·E.:
1923　Tampu. Inca, I, 79-82. Lima.
1924　El Cuzco precolombiano. Revista Universitaria del Cuzco, No. 44.
1925　De la vida inkaika. Lima.
1925a Del ayllu al imperio. Lima.
1926　Estudios arqueológicos. Revista Universitaria del Cuzco, No. 51.
1927　Tempestad en los Andes. Lima.
1932　Vasos de madera del Cusco. RMNL, I, No. 1, 7-18. Lima.
1932a El personaje mítico de Pucara. RMNL, I, No. 1, 18-32.
1932b El gato de agua. RMNL, I, No. 2, 3-27.
1932c Arquitectura incaica. RMNL, I, No. 2, 28-30.
1933　Esculturas de Pikillajta. RMNL, II, No. 1, 19-48.
1933a Final del Tawantisuyu. RMNL, II, No. 2, 79-97.

Valdez de la Torre, Carlos:
1921　Evolución de las comunidades de indígenas. Lima.

Vega Toral, Tomás:
1921　La Tomebamba de los Incas. Cuenca, Ecuador.

Velasco, Father Juan de:
1841-1844 Historia del reino de Quito. . . . Quito. 3 vols.

Verneau, R., and Rivet, P.:
1912-1922 Ethnographie ancienne de l'Equateur. Paris. 2 vols.

Verrill, A. Hyatt:
1927　Excavations in Coclé province. IN, IV, 47-61.
1929　Old civilizations of the new world. Indianapolis, Indiana.

Veytia, Mariano:
1836　Historia antigua de Mexico. Edited by C. F. Ortega. Mexico. 3 vols.

Vignati, Milcíades Alejo:
1925　Las antiguas industrias del piso ensenadense de punta hermengo. Physis, VIII, 23-58. Buenos Aires.
1929　Los túmulos del campo de Pucará en el valle de Lerma. (Provincia de Salta). Physis, IX, 421-435.
1930　Los cráneos trofeos de las sepulturas indígenas de la quebrada de Humahuaca (provincia de Jujuy). Archivos del Museo Etnográfico, No. 1. Buenos Aires.
1931　Investigaciones antropológicas en el litoral marítimo sudatlántico bonaerense. NPMLP, I, 19-31.
1931a Los elementos étnicos del noroeste Argentino. NPMLP, I, 115-157.
1931b Interpretación de algunos instrumentos líticos considerados como hachas insignias ó "Pillan-Toki." NPMLP, I, 173-187.
1931c Datos referentes á la arqueología de Punta Piedras (Provincia de Buenos Aires). NPMLP, I, 205-224.

Villar Córdova, Pedro E.:
1923　Las ruinas de la provincia de Canta. Inca, I, 1-24. Lima.

Virchow, Hans:
1930　Ein schrumpfköpfchen der tschibtscha. ZE, LXI, 213-222. Berlin.

Viteri Lafronte, Homero:
1917 La historia del reino de Quito. Revista de la Sociedad Jurídico-Literaria, XIX, 162-181. Quito.
Wallis, Wilson D.:
1930 Culture and progress. New York.
Warner, W. Lloyd:
1932 Malay influences on aboriginal cultures of north-eastern Arnhem Land. Oceania, II, 476-495. London and Sydney.
Waterman, T. T.:
1917 Bandelier's contribution to the study of ancient Mexican social organization. UCPAAE, XII, 249-282.
1924 On certain antiquities in western Guatemala. Pan American Union Bulletin, April, 1924, 1-21. Washington.
Whorf, B. L.:
1932 A Central American inscription combining Mexican and Maya day-signs. AA, n.s., XXXIV, 296-302.
1933 The phonetic value of certain characters in Maya writing. PMP, XIII, No. 2. Cambridge, Mass.
Wiesse, Carlos:
1913 Las civilizaciones primitivas del Perú. Lima.
Wissler, Clark:
1922 The American Indian. New York. (2nd edition).
1926 The relation of nature to man in aboriginal America. New York and London.
Yacovleff, Eugenio:
1931 El vencejo (cypselus) en el arte decorativo de Nasca. WK, I, 25-35. Lima.
1932 Las falcónidas en el arte y en las creencias de los antiguos Peruanos. RMNL, I, No. 1, 33-111.
1932a La deidad primitiva de los Nasca. RMNL, I, No. 2, 103-160.
1933 La jíquima, raiz comestible extinguida en el Perú. Un testimonio de la alfarería nasca. RMNL, II, No. 1, 49-66.
1933a Arte plumaria entre los antiguos Peruanos. RMNL, II, No. 2, 137-158.
Yacovleff, E., Muelle, J. C., O'Neale, Lila M., and Weiss, P.:
1932 Una exploración en Cerro Colorado. RMNL, I, No. 2, 31-102.
Zahm, J. A.:
1910 Up the Orinoco and down the Magdalena. New York.
1917 The quest of El Dorado. New York.
Zerda, Liborio:
1883 El Dorado: estudio histórico, etnográfico y arqueológico de los Chibchas. Bogotá.
Zurkalowski, Erich:
1919 Observaciones sobre la organización social del Perú antiguo. Mercurio Peruano, II, 337-352, 480-495. Lima.

CHAPTER FIVE

THE EUROPEAN BACKGROUND

By Marie R. Madden

THE choice of the term European background in connection with
Hispanic America, though its use has become conventional in
United States textbooks, is not very happy. In a certain sense
the background of Hispanic America is European, for the civilization
of the *Conquistadores* was European, that is, it was the product of the
common heritage of ideas, principles of action, and institutions of western Christian Europe; but in a more important and specific sense the
Conquistadores brought this heritage in its distinctive Spanish form to
the New World. In this, the general European element is of less import. Therefore, this chapter will outline only those distinctively Spanish elements in ideas and institutions which gave color and form to Hispanic American society and of which an explanation is necessary if the
conditions and problems of that society are to be understood by Americans of the United States.

I. The Spanish Character

In the introduction to his *Historia de América español*[1] Carlos Pereyra
has a significant sentence which is worth pondering by all students of
Hispanic American civilization. He says: "La historia es presencia de
almas, no simple rememoración externa de hechos materiales." Hispanic American history well substantiates this remark. Man indeed does
not so much live in history as in a stream of events or processes, which
when recorded are called history, as history lives in him; but not in the
sense, however, in which Benedetto Croce holds this to be true.[2] Only
as a man thinks and is, do his actions and their effects pass into the record of history. But Carlos Pereyra goes further. He does not say that
history is the presence of men, that is mankind, but history is the presence of souls.[3] In this distinction lies the key to the interpretation of

---

[1] 8 vols., Madrid, 1920.

[2] *On history,* translated by D. Ainslee (London, 1921).

[3] In the Dictionary of the Royal Spanish Academy (Madrid, 1925), *alma* is
defined as a spiritual and immortal substance, capable of understanding, desiring,
and feeling, which informs the human body and with it constitutes the essence of
man.

the whole of Spanish civilization and its extension into Hispanic America. It is the first fact in the background of that century which saw the beginning of the Spanish action in the New World.

Unless we grasp how the Spaniard defined man and the soul and interpreted its significance for the nature of man, we shall not comprehend how he viewed man himself and his place in the world. Lacking this knowledge, we shall not be able to understand why he set up the institutions he did set up and what he was attempting to accomplish in the New World.

These definitions and interpretations are set forth at length in the treatises of Scholastic philosophy. Briefly stated, man is considered a being with a threefold nature: spiritual, intellectual, and physical, the development of which integrates his whole personality into an individual character. He has an individual as well as a general destiny. He comes from God and will return to God along a path for which God has given him directions through His Church. These he is expected to follow and, in proportion to the fidelity of his obedience, his individual and final destiny will be assigned. From these accepted principles the Spaniards drew the norms for their conduct, both individual and social, and whether they lived up to them or not they considered themselves responsible. Also, as can readily be seen, it was not possible for the Spaniards to pursue their individual path without creating, through their institutions, a path, a way, for their society for which in turn they were responsible. This path, this way, gave to their society its special character, for, although in general the principles forming it were those of their Catholic theology and philosophy common to all Catholics, the national genius expressed these in characteristic forms.

To sum up: in the Spanish concept, history is the presence of men (souls), who direct their corporate and social action in response to a stimulus it is true, but not, however, a stimulus of blind force, of nature, or of mere will. It is one arising from a "directive" idea[4] transcending man himself and his social action.

As far as the action of the Spaniard in the New World is concerned, it was the product of a matured character steeled in a thousand years of struggle to maintain itself and its society against the forces of an alien foe. That the Spaniard did not succumb in this desperate warfare was due in very great part to the superiority and strength of the

---

[4] Cf. M.F.X. Millar, Hauriou, Suárez, and Chief Justice Marshall in *Thought*, VI, no. 4, particularly 594 ff.

idea to which he was devoted. This idea, as has been said, was the theory of life, both individual and social, presented by the doctrines of the Catholic Church. Not that it can be asserted that Spanish action always completely and adequately expressed this theory, for failures are as conspicuous as successes; but neither the success nor the failure can be estimated without the knowledge of the theory. Lacking this knowledge, is to find, indeed, the Spaniard a man of mystery and his actions without pattern and without form.[5] It is to be noted, however, that those who most complain of this are those who see in Seneca and Martial rather than in Isabella and Cisneros the typical Spaniards and in Stoicism rather than in Catholicism the true cast of Spanish thought.[6]

There are, of course, explanations of why these two schools of interpretation exist. Spanish character, while nourished and developed under the influence of the Catholic theory of life, received also cross currents from Stoicism, the great Roman theory with which Catholicism has so long been in struggle. It remains true, nevertheless, that Spanish civilization is dominantly Catholic. That the institutional forms of this civilization are frequently Roman is equally true and, given the facts of Spanish history, not surprising. This does not imply that Spanish genius is in its essence Stoic. There is a distinction between the form or organization of an institution and its idea as well as between these and the functions. This the Spaniards appreciated as may be noted in comparing the Justinian Code with the *Forum Iudiciorum* or *Las Siete Partidas* and the various municipal *fueros* of the ninth to the thirteenth centuries.

Discussion on the Spanish character began with the first challenge to the Spanish effort in the New World when Las Casas presented his criticism of the Spaniards whom he had observed in the Indies and raised the question of their fitness to remain there. Sepúlveda was ready with his answer. He presented not only a defense of the Spanish titles but an analysis of the character and personality which has remained the classic description. The storm of criticism on Spain and

---

[5] An interesting support for this view is to be found in Allison Peer's discussion of the Spanish character in his book, *Spain*. He considers that Europe has ever found the Spaniard a man apart, "one whose outlook on life refuses to conform to accepted criteria of logical behaviour, whose scale of values seems curiously remote from a modern age"; and he asks "where is the continuity, what the thread that winding through the mazes of time will give the clue to the pattern?" (See pages 1 and 2 and the greater part of chapter 1).

[6] For typical modern discussions on the Spanish character see the works of Ortega y Gasset, Ángel Ganivet, Unamuno, Madariaga, and others.

the Spaniards radiating out from this debate and fed by the increasing attacks of France and England during the next two centuries to dislodge Spain from her high position, together with the anthropological theories of the eighteenth and nineteenth centuries, gives the origin of all the discussion on the national character.

If critics in the sixteenth century found the Spaniard prudent, intelligent, humane, but inflexible, just, religious, sober, and courageous; if in the seventeenth century a more exhaustive analysis considers him also a thinker, contemplative, a master of asceticism, serious, taciturn, demanding respect but also respecting, in love with glory but also proud and envious; if in the eighteenth century he is described as apathetic in daily life, content with his fate, serene but superstitious and ignorant; if in the nineteenth century his laziness, impracticability, generosity impress while he is considered as revengeful but forgetful of injustices and inequalities, high minded but fatalistic; and if in the twentieth century his mysticism was to be hailed as poetic exaltation derived from African influences and his persistent idealism to be labelled fanaticism, the mere exaltation of action—then all this reveals much more the changing standards of the critics than it throws light on the Spanish character. It is the critics who are confused and contradictory and not the Spanish character.

The Protestant party criticism of the policies of Charles V and Philip II, the foreign policies of Cromwell, the French Encyclopedists, the materialistic and positivistic philosophy of the nineteenth century, the imperial ideas of the Habsburgs, the French liberalism of the Bourbons, the instinctive resistance of the Spaniards to the philosophy of the industrial revolution, are all elements in the criticism and all influences in moulding the Spanish character in each generation. So that, as each one of the various philosophies was uppermost, we find the criticism and the typical Spaniard.

In endeavoring to picture to ourselves a national character, it is well to keep in mind Altamira's wise remark that it is easy to confuse national with human characteristics. Many things said of the Spaniards can also be said of human beings almost anywhere. Nevertheless, it remains true that various societies do produce certain well-marked features, the product of the people themselves in these groups, as even the most superficial observation of travellers will attest. There is such a thing as a national ideal, and in this ideal can be observed a national character which will be well-understood by the society, although not each individual will be found to reflect it a hundred per cent. This national ideal may be considered the national character.

To return to the Spanish character. Aside from individual criticisms arising from the violent dislike and equally violent admiration which the Spaniard had the faculty of inspiring even in medieval days, a well-nigh unanimous verdict is passed upon the character by competent natives and foreigners alike. All find in it a sense of human dignity; a broad humanity; a detachment from the demands of time, money, and mere human comforts; an essential kindness and comprehension of the conditions of human nature; and a realization of the setting of the events of time in eternity and hence that patience which makes of tomorrow another day.[7] All this is truly characteristic of the typical Spaniard. In addition, there is above all that tendency to penetrate to the supernatural, to pierce through to an easy friendliness with God, to lose one's self in the contemplation of the Infinite Perfection only to return to the most severely practical concerns of daily life with an effortless adjustment which some call mysticism. In addition, we find in the Spaniards a certain hard realism, a cold severity, and a ruthless practicality which enables them to isolate events in the immediate exigencies of the moment and judge them accordingly. This in turn often engenders a haughty and inflexible pride, the mother of many vices. Often, too, we meet with characters seemingly bent on a cynical ambition to outrage to the utmost the national ideal.

Numerous are the misconceptions as to the influences in which these varied characteristics originated. Modern interpreters seek their origin in almost anything from the nature of peninsulas to the nature of the Moors, from Stoicism to chivalry, and from orientalism to nationalism. But if the foreigner attentively studies the native literature in which the Spaniard has been pleased to mirror his soul and to record his settled convictions and ideas, and is at the same time acquainted with the tenets of the Catholic religion which the Spaniard adopted from early days, the explanation of the ideal is not far to seek.

Whether one studies the great cycles of the ballads (Rodrigo, Bernardo del Carpio, Fernán Gonzales, Infantes de Lara, and the Cid) or the works of Ramón Lull, Eximeniç, Fray Luís de León, Francisco de Quevedo, or Cervantes, to mention a few at random, the Spanish criticism on human character, whether in its low failings or high achievements, sees reflected these two poles of Catholic thought as expounded

---

[7] *Manaña será otro día* as the proverb has it.

in Ecclesiastes and the Psalms.   But one is still more impressed by how
closely the ideal follows the outline of the Christian man as portrayed
in the works of St. Augustine,[8] and how this ideal was preserved for
the imitation of the people in the description of the king's character in
Las Siete Partidas.[9]

The qualities there admired—reverence for the things of God, a sensitive devotion to justice, courtesy, temperance, self-control, a love for
order, form, and discipline—are the characteristics of those men of
steel and determination who won for Spain her possessions beyond the
seas.   If a Jiménez de Quesada ranks among the first for nobility of
character and a Pedrárias Dávila at the other end of the scale for shame-
ful actions, in between were the hosts of *Conquistadores,* often lost to
history.   Many of these are of the type of Lorenzo de Cepeda, brother
of St. Teresa, who by the sheer strength of Christian character stamped
the wilderness of the Americas with the marks of Spanish civilization
and preserved it from the errors and vices of lesser men whose names
are more frequently remembered, since to fallen man evil is so much
more picturesque than virtue.   As for the excesses and peculiar vices,
departures from the ideal, these were often developed under the psychological strain produced by the close juxtaposition of two such opposite
cultures as the Hebrew and the Moorish and the terrific effort to maintain the integrity of the Spanish civilization against the influences of
these.

II. SOCIAL THEORY

The discoveries of the Spaniards in the New World fell towards the
close of the reign of the Catholic Kings, Ferdinand and Isabella, one of
the great reconstructive eras in Spanish history.   The work of these
sovereigns lies in the field of technical organization of institutions which
had long been in process of development.   The rulers did not aim to
change the character of Spanish society but rather to order it more com-
pactly and more decisively than the vicissitudes of previous reigns since
the publication of *Las Siete Partidas* had permitted.   If, in doing this,
they and their advisors created dangerous precedents in applying Roman
law principles with their underlying assumptions of Stoic thought, effects of this on the character of society were not apparent until reigns

---

[8] *De Civitate Dei,* v, 24. Latin text and French translation by L. Moreau,
Paris, s. d.

[9] *Partida segunda, Tít.* ii-ix.

very much later[10] and until the character of the new Hispanic American society was fairly well-established on the old basis.

Sociologically speaking, the organization of the social classes and institutions determine the character of a society,[11] and an analysis of these is essential to the understanding of that society. A comparative study of the two sets of institutions in Spain and Spanish America reveals the fact that the Spaniards did not transport *in toto* their own institutions to the colonies.[12] The very nature and flexibility of the theory forbade that. What they did transfer was their theory of social organization. Naturally, when the circumstances were such that a similar expression of it to that in Spain was advisable, the similar institution was set up in America. When the conditions were peculiar to the New World, either modifications appeared in the old institutions or new institutions were created. This adoption of means to an end, while preserving unchanged essential principles, is characteristic of Spanish action at this period and constitutes its title to colonizing and civilizing genius. A cursory examination, however, of the institutions, as is so often made without a survey of their underlying principles, leads to the misconceptions which criticize Spanish colonial effort as inept and insufficient. Hence, before taking up the fundamental institutions in Spain, that is, the background of the colonial society, a few words must be said in explanation of the underlying theories.

Society as viewed by the Spanish theorist was considered in the light of what may be called, to borrow a modern term, the sociological principles of St. Augustine. This great man, concerned with his personal problem of the search for happiness, was led to make a survey of what was man—of what was the nature of his life, his position in society, and his final end. In the course of this study, to which he devoted many volumes of profound thought expressed in his inimitable vivid and glowing style, he proposed and sometimes developed at length the various theories on which the society of the Christian middle ages was constructed. It was on these theories, through the agency of Isidore of Seville chiefly, that the Spaniards constructed their society, albeit slowly and painfully, after the fall of the Roman Empire and the successive invasions of the Visigoths and Moors.

---

[10] Marie R. Madden, *Political theory and law in medieval Spain* (New York, 1930), chapter iv.

[11] R. M. Maciver, *Society, its structure and changes* (New York, 1931).

[12] Marie R. Madden, "The Spanish plan of civilization" in *Thought*, vol. V, no. 1, 60-65.

According to these theories, man is considered a being composed of body and soul; and as the body is subordinated to the soul, so his soul in turn is subject to its Creator, God, in Whom man finds his final end, his Beatitude, as St. Augustine expresses it. His life then becomes a search for this Beatitude, or happiness, and his actions are nothing more than the selection of means to this end. He progresses when his means turn him towards God and produce the life of the City of God; he loses ground when he turns away from God and takes up the life of the terrestial city.[13] But this is characteristic of all men. All men seek happiness by their very nature, but incidentally find it nowhere except in that final end of God. All men, therefore, are bound together by this common interest which creates for them a series of social interests which in turn creates the life of society. Whether men see in this bond a mere practical necessity if the body politic is to be preserved at all as in pre-Christian times, or the expression of the precepts of Christ to love God with thy whole heart and thy neighbor as thyself, they inevitably, as a result of it, establish a social order, a society, that is a way of life. It is a Christian way, a Christian order in the latter case.

The discussion of this social order as it has developed in history and as it should develop, St. Augustine takes up in his great work *The City of God*. Many modern readers find this work confusing and difficult to read, because they miss the point of the contrast between the two social orders and because Augustine himself frequently shifts the stand from which he conducts the discussion. When he considers the social order from the point of view of a *way* of life (a manner, a method), he sees in his time, as coexisting side by side, the two social orders, the terrestial city and the city of God. When he considers the Christian life in relation to its end, he notes that it is a state essentially transitory.[14] It is a preparation for the life to come; then his city of God[15] is not a thing of this earth but a celestial city, Heaven.

Again, in surveying the social order of non-Christians, whether in past times or contemporary, he sometimes views the social order in its institutional aspects, as when for example he discusses the Roman Republic, the nature of peace, of war, the qualities of a ruler, and especially justice.[16] He does not describe the institutional organization, but

---

[13] *De Civitate Dei*, xi, 1; xii, 27; xv, 2-6. Cf. also E. Gilson, *Introduction à l'étude de Saint Augustin* (Paris, 1929).

[14] *De Civitate Dei*, x, 32.

[15] *Ibid.*, xi, 1, quoting from Psalm 86, etc.

[16] M. F. X. Millar, "St. Augustine and political theory" in *Thought*, vol. V, no. 2; also his "St. Augustine and Cicero's definition of the State," *Idem*. vol. IV, no. 2.

he outlines the principles upon which this can be established and was in fact established[17] when Rome had passed.

From another angle St. Augustine views the world and man's position in it from the point of view of Justice, that is the total order of creation as directed by Divine Providence. In the analysis of the content of this Divine Justice, St. Augustine finds the proper principles of relationships in the social order, a hierarchy of things and institutions all coördinated to serve the common end, the designs of Providence, and a hierarchy informed by the one common principle, the Eternal Law of God.[18]

Hence the social institutions of man must be regulated on the basis of this harmony and this law. In this standard, also, Augustine offers principles of social reform, for where these institutions depart from this social order, there is the point where retrogression sets in. Reform becomes a matter, then, of restoring the institution to its proper and due order in the total scheme of the Justice of God. It is to be noted here that it is on this point that the whole argument of the justification of the titles by which Spain held the Indies is developed.

This is why Spanish sociological thought is so concerned with justice and why all the codes, notably the *Forum Iudiciorum* and *Las Siete Partidas,* open with their beautiful tributes to this justice. This is also why justice is set down as the mark of kings, their justification and their purpose, why the Spaniards developed their legal way of handling things which has its dangers for the subtle intellect and the formal-minded, and why there was such great devotion to the *fueros.* These *fueros* represented the concrete expression of an important and necessary social order, and hence the Spaniard could not lightly view setting them aside in an arbitrary or conventional manner. The word *fuero* became the popular expression of, and the popular demand for, the more philosophical and transcendent term of the Justice of God. The demand for a *fuero* runs through all Spanish history, and even today when so much of its content has been erased from popular memory, it still has power to awaken the Spaniard.

These Augustinian distinctions passed into the warp and woof of the Spanish mind, and one who studies Spanish society will discover that they thread the whole institutional life of the people. At one time the Spaniard thinks of his institution as a *way* of life, at another he con-

---

[17] Cf. Dufourcq, *L'avenir du Christianisme, première partie,* vols. I-VII.

[18] St. Augustine's analysis of the eternal law was later supplemented by the analysis made by St. Thomas.

siders it under its technical aspect. The observer or student who fails to penetrate to the reason for this finds confusion, contradiction, and ineptitude in Spanish institutions. The popular view of the Inquisition is a notable example of this misconception.[19]

Characteristic of the thought of St. Augustine is the theory that the moral life is integrated into the social life. Many commentators are pleased to call this its theological aspect. The individual is never separated in his eyes from the city, that is, society.[20] The origin of the social life is to be found in the mainspring of the individual's life, that is, his love for God. By this fact all men are in relation to each other because of the common object of their love, and society itself (the city) is merely the expression of one part of the link (the other being the church) that binds them together. Society in turn becomes the object of their common coöperation; and their common objective is its welfare which he calls peace. Peace, however, demands order, and order demands arrangement on a principle. Hence, the development and furthering of institutions is the detailed business of society.

Of course, the explanation of society as linking the manifold relationships of men is not original with St. Augustine. This view is found in the practice of all ancient societies, the most civilized expression of it being the Greek and Roman city states. And religion, as the ultimate principle of it, was not unknown.[21] What is original with St. Augustine is that he brings things into focus with the true religion, deducing his explanation from the scriptures. By so much he presents a critical philosophy of society which may stand the tests of ethics, theology, and metaphysics. He did not, however, develop a complete and systematic sociology, nor has any Catholic since, though the great Scholastic philosophers have supplied the keystone to a sound scientific sociology.

The task of developing institutions requires unity, but not uniformity, and as men proceed to the practical details of this, they perceive the contradictions and difficulties presented by the presence of two cities, one the terrestrial (borrowing the word of Augustine) and the other the heavenly—the first expressing the unity based on an exclusive concern with the social relationships of man considered in themselves merely, and the other on these relationships viewed in their position in

---

[19] Cf. H. Nickerson, *The Inquisition, a political and military study* (London, 1923).

[20] E. Gilson, 220.

[21] C. Dawson, *Religion and progress,* and *The age of the gods* (London, 1928); Fustel de Coulange, *The ancient city* (Boston, 1874).

the Divine Will.[22] How may these distinctions and contradictions—
St. Augustine deduces these from the fall of man—be resolved into a
unity, a necessary condition of social peace?

The Spaniards in the course of their history found these elements a
very pressing problem, and in their dealings with the Visigoths and the
Moors they worked out in their *fueros* a *modus vivendi* whereby all
could live in harmony while leaving to time the establishment of customs and traditions. These are the social adjustments whereby the
terrestrial city is worked into the heavenly city, that is, into a Christian
society.[23] On principle, in the long run, the terrestrial city must yield
to the Christian society, but the development could not and should not
be forced. Hence, there is need of transitional institutions. It is of interest to note the contrast between this view and the modern attitude
towards the contradictions and problems of today. The problem of the
two cities is still with us. One group, such as the secularist and the
communist, holds that the terrestrial city is the only city to which all
else must be subordinate, while the Catholic view upholds the traditional
Christian theory and practice. It may now be clear why the Spaniards
were prepared to handle the problem of the savage and barbarian
societies of the New World where the two cities would directly and
completely come into juxtaposition.

So much for the social theory in general. Now as to the theory applied to the four great institutions developed in Spanish society: the
social classes, the monarchy, the *municipio,* and the *cortes.*

III. Social Classes

The social ideas of the classes were derived from the view of man
not only as a human being with interests directly arising out of his social
needs and by their nature demanding coöperation, but also as the Christian man redeemed by the merits of Christ and obligated to a coöperation which takes its direction from the Divine command to love one's
neighbor as one's self. From the first originated the interests of society
as represented in the various hierarchy of classes as found in all
societies; from the second resulted the interpretation of the functions
of these classes to the end that rights are seen to be correlative with
duties and privileges attendant upon obligations because of the final

---

[22] *De Civitate Dei,* xii, 27; xiv, 1, 28; xv, 1; xix, 12, 13, 24.

[23] Cf. A. González Palencia, *Los Mozárabes de Toledo en los siglos xii y xiii* (4
vols., Madrid, 1926-30) ; R. Menéndez Pidal, *La España del Cid* (2 vols. Madrid,
1929).

destiny of man as taught by Christ. In order to classify these functions and to arrange for the distinctions among them, each of the social classes had its *fuero;* but it was not intended to stratify them or to enclose them in a rigid framework enchaining alike flexibility and progress. These results did, indeed, develop in Spain later on as a result of the departure from the Christian-Augustinian idea of things in relation to God and the taking up of the pagan idea of things in relation to man. For a criticism of what this shift of viewpoint meant in Spanish society, Don Quixote may be studied with profit. But in the New World this danger was escaped owing to the decision taken in regard to the *encomiendas* and *repartimientos.*[24]

Basic to the ideas of the social classes was the principle of the essential equality of men from which all true democratic theories proceed. This did not preclude, as it does in some modern expressions of the democratic ideal, the Christian view of poverty, of suffering, and of the duties of one's state in life. There was no attempt to uphold the modern view that all could and should eventually rise to the top and the "standard of living" be thereby raised so that poverty would disappear and leisure would be the heritage of all. But there was a fluidity among the classes that left opportunity open where it was possible to take advantage of it, and the essential human dignity was respected by all. Snobs existed, of course, as did pride of place and position and the social corruption generally found when such things are striven for and valued exclusively.

The specific classes found in Spanish society at the time of the discoveries represented the social interests of property and the family. Many of the outward characteristics of the classes dated from the organization which imperial Rome had given to Spanish society, but the functions assigned to each class developed out of the wars of the Reconquest and the necessity of repopulating and resettling the lands so bitterly contested. In these conditions we find that the aristocracy took over the functions of military defense, organization, and direction of the newly-conquered territories.[25] It was composed of the various grades of *caballeros, ricos hombres* (men of power because of their wealth and position in the country), and *infanzones* later known as *hidalgos* (similar to the *ricos hombres* but in some cases lacking jurisdiction). All these together formed what moderns would call the as-

---

[24] Note the discussion on this point in Solórzano, *Política indiana* (Madrid, 1647, edition of 1930).

[25] Cf. Gama Barros.

cendant class. In general it gave the tone to Spanish society, and by
its cult of the noble sentiments of loyalty, devotion to duty, self-sacrifice,
and care for the unfortunate, exercised a beneficial influence. As a
leading class, the king could rely upon it for counsel, support, and administrative aid. The long minority of the kings had an unfortunate
influence upon this class, unbalancing as it did the mutual relations and
leaving the class without its natural check. Weak kings sought favorites
for personal satisfaction rather than advice from the experienced. The
rewards and favors dispensed by the kings tended to entrench this class
in wealth and privilege.[26] Already, in the time of the Catholic Kings,
the *caballeros* were appearing as a territorial nobility, many of whom,
enriched by the generous weakness of kings such as Juan II, formed
a court clique with all the evils this engenders. The *ricos hombres* by
the time of Enrique IV were a titled nobility, also, and had lost some
of their dignity and aloofness because of this. While the nobles were
not entirely exempt from taxation, they insisted upon their contributions
being considered a voluntary gift and not one of obligation.

As a consequence of this change of status and function, the ascendant
class began to lose the respect of the people and the confidence of the
monarch. When it was a question of ordering the new Hispanic
American society, a nobility was not established, but the old aristocratic
function of an ascendant and leading class was transferred to the holders
of the *encomiendas* and other estates. Thus the aristocratic tradition
was transferred to the New World, but not the nobility. This aristocratic tradition is nothing more than the recognition of the fact that
there must be a leading class in society, able and willing to take on the
burdens and responsibility of governing. From it must be chosen
those who are to fill the executive and administrative positions not only
in politics but wherever leadership is necessary. Therefore, this class
must have the support of sufficient wealth, either by their own efforts
or endowments, to give it the leisure necessary to prepare for and to
take up the responsibility involved.[27]

This view is not inconsistent with democracy (that is, the Christian
theory of equality), provided the class is left open and fluid with opportunity for all to compete and is sufficiently widespread. This demands,
of course, a lower standard of wealth and a wider distribution than is

---

[26] Marie R. Madden, chapters iii-iv.

[27] *De Civitate Dei*, v. 24; and Combès, *La doctrine politique de Saint Augustin*
(Paris, 1927), 113.

customary in capitalistic societies. But neither Spain nor Hispanic America were capitalistic societies.

This theory is thoroughly inconsistent, of course, with the eighteenth century Rousseauistic interpretations of the democratic theory demanding that the people govern and expecting government to be a matter of the will of the people. The influence of these ideas did eventually spread to Hispanic America and confused the aristocratic tradition into that of a nobility entrenched in place, position, and privilege, scornful of duties, and indifferent to responsibilities. It is in opposition to this corrupted tradition that the American of the United States finds himself. He rarely penetrates to the origin of the tradition and hence fails to see that the remedy does not lie in the doctrines of Rousseau. Thus he is not prepared to offer the proper coöperation with Hispanic America for the necessary reforms. Many Spanish Americans today are in agreement with the old aristocratic tradition but find it difficult to restore it in the face of the antagonistic attitude of the United States; and so on their part, also, coöperation becomes impossible.

The middle class in the Spain of the Catholic Kings was composed of the *caballeros* of the *municipios,* the townspeople, and *peones* and vassals of the countryside. The *caballeros* filled the administrative positions and were exempt from certain royal taxes. The professional and working classes of the towns had their own *fueros* and participated in the municipal life according to these. Their interests were represented directly before the king through their *procuradores* in the *cortes.* There was no sense of a nation being represented since the *cortes* was merely the body representing the interests of the social classes.

This class was also found in the New World which was essentially a society of *municipios* and landed estates as found in Spain. It had the same outlook and functions as in Spain. That it was small in number was due to the fact that the total population of Hispanic America was small in any one place, but it formed an important element in the society, for the main social functions were the same. This was the class in which the fusion of the diverse peoples and diverse cultures was proceeding into a homogeneous whole. In Hispanic America it occupied itself with the same work by gradually absorbing the *mestizo* population. The Indian group was treated as a separate class because of the barbarian and savage nature of its culture.

The background of this distinction lay in the Spanish-Christian social principle of the dignity of man because of his final end and the necessity of training him to attain this end. This training was not regarded as a passive thing to be imposed on man, but a dynamic thing in which man coöperated with his fellow man. Hence, institutions would have to be established which would regulate these relationships. The story of these does not belong to this chapter. It is sufficient to say here that for the Indian *repartimientos, encomiendas,* personal services, and *pueblos,* precedents in principle were found in the *fueros* for the *poblaciones, señorios,* and `behetrías` established in the regions conquered from the Moors.[28] The problem of the Indians was similar to the extent that in both cases the Spaniards aimed to raise the level of a lower culture, although the levels in Spain and in Hispanic America were not on an equality. The Moorish culture was essentially barbarian and hence lower than the Christian despite the superficial advantages that it had in the early days of the Reconquest of more education, refinement, and luxuries of living. But a culture is not judged essentially by its external achievements, but rather by its ultimate aim and principles of social organization.

It cannot be too often repeated that the unity which linked together these social classes and fused them into a society in Spain was not the political unity of a nation in the modern sense, but the social unity of a civilization. Expressed in the terms of the medieval vocabulary, it was their common *Christianitas* (or Catholicity) that bound them together, made them intelligible to one another, and gave them their common objectives. Hence, not only was nationalism unknown to them, but they were not even "unconsciously" striving towards it as so many modern observers think.[29] Nor was the unity associated with territory. Spain then was not Spain in the modern sense. Spain constituted a number of social units bound together and delimited in their relationships from other groups in the Catholic society by the fact of their submission to the authority of the Spanish monarch as representative of justice, that is, a justice participating in the Divine Justice, in regulating the relationships of these units to each other and to the final end of society.

IV. Political Institutions

Political relationships were thus seen to be a matter of authority over social interests, and jurisdiction, administration, or government a matter of directing or representing these interests. The institutions for

---

[28] Cf. E. Mayer, *Historia de las instituciones sociales y políticas de España y Portugal durante los siglos v-xiv* (Madrid, 1923).

[29] Cf. R. B. Merriman, *Rise of the Spanish empire* (3 vols., New York, 1918-25).

carrying out this idea were the monarchy and the *cortes*. The *municipio, señorio,* or *behetría,* political as well as social units, took charge of all those activities which we today frequently assign to the national government. Government as touching directly the interests of the people was a local thing and hence the only institution associated with territory was the local government. Hence, also, it was the only institution for government, together with the *repartimientos* and *encomiendas* to a certain extent, transmitted to the New World. It was the only one thought necessary. The principles of the authority of the monarch were unaffected by any discoveries in the New World, and his authority could operate from a center in Spain as well as from a center in America. The *cortes* as representative of the social interests was not transmitted, nor was representation in it granted the New World. For a society in process of formation it was considered that a viceroy could act as the link between the crown and the people. For matters of justice which needed to be decided on the spot, the *audiencias* were transmitted. Anything touching the local interests, the *municipios* managed. For matters requiring special consideration by all of the people a return was made to the local democratic assemblies of all the inhabitants so common in the society of the earlier middle ages in Spain. These had been found adequate for a nascent society and so were used again. Whether this situation would have developed an American *cortes* is only of academic interest. Certainly events in the New World and a change of ideas in the eighteenth century deflected any such development if it was due to form.

The Monarch

The position of the monarch in Spanish medieval society was so unlike the popular modern view of monarchy that a few words in explanation of it is essential to the understanding of the Hispanic American attitude towards the king and the devotion to him during the troubled days of the wars for independence.

In the first place, the king was not an administrator and hence did not govern or rule in the modern sense of these terms.[30] In the theory of St. Augustine expressed in the codes, the king was a leader of public opinion, a center of national—using national to describe a cohesive and coherent group—unity, a focus from which the combined energies of the people might radiate, a symbol of the collective mind of the people. On the positive side of his function, his first purpose was to see that

---

[30] Marie R. Madden, chapter v.

justice was carried out in conformity with the principles of the Eternal Law as well as of the positive law of the land, since he in common with his people was bound by the law and under the law. As the *Forum Iudiciorum* expressed it: Since God Who is the most powerful King over all things, the Creator and sole Providence over the safety and welfare of all, enjoins upon all on earth the obligation to guard justice as set forth in the holy law, it befits each one to submit himself to the commandments. And as the king wishes to guard the commandments, he gives laws (that is, rules of action and decisions of justice) for himself and his subjects who obey him.[31]

In other words, God has the supreme authority and to Him is due obedience, but the king in his function of deciding justice on earth, shares in that authority to that extent, and hence respect and obedience are due him from the people as a matter of obligation. The only share in this authority which they had was expressed in their choice of the one who was to be king. In his function of guarding the lives, safety, and welfare of his people the king had the necessary jurisdiction and no more. In exercising his functions the king was left to the guidance of his conscience and the direction of the church. He was expected also to ask the advice of the council and the *cortes*. He was the expression of justice, of authority, but not the administrative head of a state. The theory of the state was not sufficiently worked out at this time to allow of this view.

The Municipio

As was mentioned above, the administrative or governmental needs of the Spanish society was taken care of by the *municipio,* the true precursor of the modern state and its council, the *concejo.* The *municipio,* or *civitas* as it was known in Roman Spain, was the administrative unit. It consisted of a nucleus of the inhabitants of the city (the *oppidum)* and its territory, together with the surrounding rural regions in which the population lived either in towns *(aldeas)* or on scattered farms. The rural regions gathered together in assemblies at the nearest crossroads to conduct business and to administer justice, but these were subordinate to those of the towns. Gradually during the centuries the assemblies, particularly the urban, took on a wider administrative function as may be seen in a study of the development of the *fueros* from the eleventh to the fifteenth centuries.[32]

---

[31] *Lib.* ii, *tít.* i, *ley* 2 of the *Forum Iudiciorum.*
[32] Cf. Múñoz y Romero, *Colección de fueros municipales* (Madrid, 1847).

The degree of what today would be called democratic government which was practiced in the *municipios* was conditioned by the principles of liberty described in the *Forum Iudiciorum* and derived from the Augustinian definitions.

"It was not a liberty for the individual as an individual in the modern sense, but the liberty of an individual as an individual in his relationships with other individuals and their mutual relations to God. The individual was guaranteed his rights to the point where he had the necessary freedom to carry out the obligations arising out of this network of relationships." [33]

This liberty, then, was a series of particular liberties arising out of particular relationships. This principle was reflected in the *municipios*. Each *municipio* had its own *fuero* expressing its own peculiar privileges, constitutions, and physiognomy. If *fueros* reflected a common origin in particular instances, it is because the circumstances of each were similar.

At first all the inhabitants were eligible for office, although in the fourteenth century some municipal offices came to be the prerogatives of the *caballeros*. The class distinctions thus introduced led directly to the decay of the municipal organization which was already in process during the reigns of the Catholic Kings. Its old tradition as a place in which were resolved the various interests of the inhabitants became confused, and, in the attempt to reform the abuses thus created, the model of the bureaucratic Roman *municipium* was adopted to the ruin of the typical Spanish *municipio*.

The *municipio* was introduced into the New World just at this time of crisis, and its development there reflected the contradictions and confusions of the clash of these two traditions. The earlier tradition was the stronger at first, but it succumbed to the later Roman ideas in the eighteenth and nineteenth centuries.

The Cortes

In the *cortes* the Spaniards developed the institution which represented the interests of all classes of the people—the clergy, the aristocracy, and the *municipios*. Its function was to provide consultation and advice for the king. The *cortes* had the right of petition for redress of grievance, and thus it became frequently a kind of high tribunal where the greatest guarantees of justice could be received. It was in no sense a legislative body and never was considered to have any other function

[33] Marie R. Madden, 145.

than to represent the ideas and aspirations of the social classes interested in the duration and prolongation of political society. No one was called to sit in the *cortes* who was not a person or a corporation truly interested in social prosperity. Such juridicial entities properly constituted the state and supported the individual. Through them he found his opportunity for development and protection. They sum up the three great interests of all civilizations, the family, religion, and property; and hence the representation was crystallized in the three estates, ecclesiastical, military, and popular (the *municipio*). It was not necessary for all three estates to attend at the same time unless the interests of each were being discussed.

Thus it may be noted that the Spanish idea of representation was not class interest but social interest as conceived of in the light of the Augustinian concepts of civil society. In a society where all recognized the government to have the aim of securing justice so that each individual could realize his end here in order to attain his final end hereafter, there could be no real conflict of interests. Hence, there was no need of compromising or controlling these interests as is inevitable in our modern parliamentary systems which are too much informed by theories of class conflicts. This idea of conflicting class interests came in with the Roman law and ended by stultifying the institution of the *cortes*. This process was already far advanced by the sixteenth century and offers another explanation why no one considered it worth while to introduce the *cortes* into the New World. Besides, the *cortes* was not the only institution in which the needs of the social interests could be brought before the king.

V. Religious Institutions

What today we call the social institutions, that is, those directly serving educational, philanthropic, or charitable interests, were taken care of by religious institutions under the ægis of the church or by individuals in the course of their following of the Christian way. The reason for this lay in their principles of the Christian life, deriving from the great commandment of the New Law: Thou shalt love the Lord thy God with all thy heart and thy neighbor as thyself. The practical applications of this commandment were seen to be obligations upon individuals such as are detailed in the list of the spiritual and corporal works of mercy.[34] While for these purposes individuals might organize them-

---

[34] See *Catholic Encyclopedia*.

selves into groups or institutions, such as confraternities or religious orders, in order to accomplish them, no individual was considered exempt from the personal obligation in some form. Hence, it was entirely alien to the Spanish mentality to look upon any of these activities as functions of government, except by way of support, coöperation, or protection. Hospitals, orphanages, schools, homes for the aged, and institutions for the unfortunate were amply developed and well-supported by the people.

The only point to stress here is that this theory was carried to the New World. Such activities were not governmental. They might be royal, as the endowments and foundations of the various sovereigns testified, but only in the sense of obligations upon the king as an individual and not as king. This idea of personal responsibility in such matters and its necessary corollary that much of an individual's personal wealth should be devoted to these ends and not saved to reinvest in purely economic enterprises, acted as a check upon the advance of capitalistic ideas in Spain. This, also, was carried to the New World and became deeply ingrained in the Hispanic American character. It was responsible for what the moderns call indifference to exploitation of natural resources and the generally slower pace at which Hispanic American society developed industrially as compared with the English society in North America.

There were, however, two particular religious institutions of a special character which need to be noticed here since they had a great influence upon the social relationships. One was the *patronato real* and the other was the Inquisition.

The Patronato Real

Relations between church and state in Spain developed along the general ideas of medieval society summed up in the doctrines of St. Augustine and St. Thomas on the two swords. The popular saying went: There are two swords by which the world is maintained, the spiritual deals with the hidden evils (that is, in the interior life of man), the temporal with the open evils (that is, the external life of man). All authority comes from God, but there are two channels through which it may be exercised: the secular in the person of the monarch or the political institutions, and the ecclesiastical in the institution of the church. The medieval word "secular" was used in the modern sense of civil society and not in the modern sense of "lay" (nonreligious). These two channels, while each shares in the authority of God, are not coördinate, for the ecclesiastical dealing with the conscience and the relation of the individual soul to God is superior in judgment and decision since this is the higher part of man's nature; but each is distinct and has its own field of action into which the other does not step.[35] As both deal with the life of man which is a unit, there is need of coöperation, and society cannot expect to flourish when this coöperation fails.

In studying Spanish and Hispanic American society, it should be kept in mind that what the Spaniards erected, politically speaking, was a Catholic *respublica* in which the twin directing agencies were the ecclesiastical and the civil authorities, the first represented by the episcopate and the second by the king, the *municipio,* and other agencies.

"Each authority had its own special field of work but the complex nature of man frequently demanded that the ecclesiastical should advise the secular, and the secular support and defend the ecclesiastical. We see this concretely worked out in the mutual coöperation of each as specified in the codes and *fueros.* The important coöperation which the ecclesiastical authorities lent because of the special events in Spanish history gave a unique position to the Church in Spanish society. This is why we find individual ecclesiastics participating in the functions of government as members of the King's councils as *oidores* of *Audiencias* and as holders of *señorios.* This is why we have the recognition of canon law on a legal equality with that of the civil law and the interpretations of the latter with the principles borrowed from the canon. This is why Spain had ecclesiastical *fueros* and representation of the clergy in the Cortes derived directly from this situation but indirectly from the Catholic theory of social organization, which considers the spiritual interests as worthy of recognition and so important as to have this recognition publicly proclaimed in the proper institution— the Cortes—which represented the various necessary interests of man. This is why we also have the *diezmo* in Spain."[36]

These principles and distinctions were recognized as an integrating part of the whole social organization and adopted as principles of action from the day of the Third Council of Toledo. The coöperation of the church and the political institutions was quite generally harmonious. Disputes, however, did arise as to the exact delimitations of the fields of jurisdiction in the later middle ages as a result of the interpretations

---

[35] Cf. J. Maritain, *The things that are Cæsar's* (New York, 1931).

[36] *The Catholic Church in contemporary Europe, 1919-31,* vol. II of the *Papers* of the American Catholic Historical Association, New York, 1932, 295 ff.

of the *patronato* claimed by the Spanish monarchs beginning with Ferdinand of Aragon. Such disputes reached a serious crisis in the eighteenth century.

Under the influence of the Roman law, theories, and the secularist (lay) interpretation of authority, particularly of the civil authority in this century, the harmonious coöperation of the church and the government was definitely destroyed. The repercussions of this were felt in Hispanic American society. An understanding of this difficulty of the church and the consequent effect upon the religious life and ideals of the Hispanic American society, requires a knowledge of the *patronato* as it was in Spain.

The *patronato* was the name given to those privileges granted by the Holy See to various of the faithful from the fifth century on in order to encourage them to found churches and benefices. It consisted in the power to present a cleric for a vacant benefice, and it was gradually extended. As long as it was understood and practiced as a favor from the Holy See in coöperation with it, relations were harmonious. But when upon the advice of jurists addicted more to the study of the Roman law than to the canon law, the kings began to claim the *patronato* as a right and not as a favor. The next step was to call this "right" a natural right inherent in sovereignty, and the first step was taken in the long fight to secularize (laicize) all the social functions of the church. This led to restrictions on the social action of the church to the consequent disadvantage of the progress of Hispanic American society. The restrictions were especially evident in the exercise of the *pase regio,* a right claimed by the Spanish sovereigns to promulgate or to refuse to promulgate the papal bulls and pontifical decrees. Without this royal authorization they would not be legally binding in the Spanish possessions.

From these pretensions of the monarchs, especially in the eighteenth century, developed the long argument over regalism which finally caused the break with the Vatican. One result of this was to displace the clergy from its position in the ascendant class, and with the disappearance of their influence a new group took their place. This group, perforce, had broken with the old Augustinian definitions of the social interests and classes. Hispanic American society was not prepared for this change in the equilibrium of the society, and so gradually drifted into the confusion of the eighteenth century and the anarchy of the nineteenth.

The Inquisition

The Inquisition was familiar to medieval society before this period, and there were already in existence two schools of thought in regard to it as exemplified in the ideas of the popes in approving the papal Inquisition and in the ideas of the state as derived from the policies of the Emperor Frederick II. The divergence between these two finally reached the stage where the Inquisition became a purely secular institution and lost touch with Catholic principles.[37]

As far as Spain was concerned, the Inquisition had been introduced into Aragon during the thirteenth century when the Albigensian heresies were seeping into the Aragonese lands.[38] Isabella petitioned for its establishment in Castile where it was erected according to the bull of Sixtus IV in 1478. Cardinal Mendoza drew up a catechism for the use of the Inquisitors, and on September 14, 1480, the first statutes were drawn up. Popular suspicion was aroused against many of the converted Jews, and complaints of the severity of the tribunal were made to Rome. The Catholic Kings, convinced of its utility, requested the pope to establish the Supreme Council of the Inquisition, or the Holy Office, which was granted in February 11, 1482. Fray Tomás de Torquemada, Prior of Santa Cruz of Segovia, was the first president. His upright, severe, exacting character gave a tone to the organization of the Inquisition which aroused many complaints as a result of which he drew up in 1488 the famous instructions for the use of the Tribunal. Questions of heresy, apostasy, superstition, and books containing pernicious doctrines against the Catholic religion came before the Inquisition.

It was intended as an agency for inquiry, investigation, and reform and not as an agency of oppression.[39] The legal procedure and penalties followed the current practice of the times. The most objectionable feature of this, and the one most criticized, is the use of torture. This, however, was less cruel in Spain than in France of that period and more humanely managed in the Inquisition than elsewhere. It must also be remembered that torture in those days did not receive the popular disapproval it meets with today. Most of the popular modern views on this find their origin in the propaganda spread throughout the English-speaking world as part of that *leyenda negra* against Spain and all

---

[37] See *Catholic Encyclopedia.*

[38] Ballesteros y Beretta, *Historia de España,* III, 577.

[39] P. Jerónimo Montes, *El crimen del herejía* (Madrid, 1918), 76.

things Spanish which is criticized by reputable historians as part of the diplomatic game by which Spain was despoiled of her colonies in so far as this could be done by the action of European powers.[40]

The Inquisition had many defects. The judges were not always free from arbitrary action, and justice was not always tempered with mercy. It was accepted, however, by its contemporaries who were more impressed with the dangers and social evils attendant upon heresies than later ages.[41] It aimed to correct, to amend, and to stress the beneficent effects of penance, voluntary expiation, and reconciliation with God. A study of the treatises produced in Spain during the sixteenth century on the theory and practice of the Inquisition, such as those of Nicolás Eymeric, Juan de Torquemada, Gonzales de Villadiego, Alfonso de Castro, Diego Simancas, and Francisco Pena,[42] reveal that the intention behind the institution was the preservation of the order of Christian society.

Queen Isabella was much alarmed at the spread of the social evils consequent upon the practices of various relapsed converts among the Jews and Moors and the fascination which many of their tenets seemed to offer to certain of the Spaniards. This condition threatened to break up the social unity and hence to destroy the social peace. Heresy, apostasy, and crimes against religion as affecting social order as well as dangerous to the salvation of souls, came under the jurisdiction of the ecclesiastical and civil courts in the Roman Empire after Constantine and were dealt with in both the Theodosian and Justinian codes. These influenced similar legislation in the Spanish codes—the *Forum Iudiciorum,* the *Fuero Real,* and *Las Siete Partidas.*[43]

Nevertheless, the ideas on these questions suffered a deflection in Spanish society because of the influences from the study of the Roman law and affected the conduct and attitude towards the Inquisition. St. Augustine himself in his earlier views maintained a tolerant attitude towards disturbers of the public peace, as was consistent with his principles of social relations and his interpretations of the two cities. In his later days, after various experiences with the Donatists and other evildoers of the times and the increasing chaos in Roman society, he judged things more severely and advocated sterner measures. These

---

[40] Scelle, *La traité négrière aux indes de Castille* (Paris, 1906).

[41] Montes, 301.

[42] *Ibid.,* 31-33.

[43] *Forum Iudiciorum, lib.* xii, *tit.* ii, and *lib.* iv, *tit.* i; *Las Siete Partidas, Partida* vii, *tit.* xxvi.

are the passages which some in the later middle ages seized upon to justify their stand in regard to the Inquisition, not noticing that their principles were being steadily deflected from the Augustinian ideas because of the deep wedge which the formalism and emphasis upon the extrinsic norms of the Roman law had introduced into their thinking.

Pushed to their logical conclusions, this induced an exclusive, rigid attitude in the Spanish society which found no place for the Jew and the Moor, and led to various excesses. All this was quite contrary to the broad charity of the Augustinian teaching on the true meaning of the Christian life. In fact, it was also quite contrary to the actual practice of the Spaniards themselves in their earlier dealings with the barbarians. Then adjustments were sought and found. All this was frequently forgotten in the Spain of the Inquisition, so insidiously had the alien doctrines of the Roman law blinded their eyes to the change. By contrast it is interesting to note that the earlier tradition was preserved in the laws for the Indians, despite all the opposition raised by those versed in the Roman law.

VI. TITLE TO THE INDIES

As far as the laws for the Indies are concerned, the most important point in the background in Spain is found in the principles by which the title to the overseas possessions was held to be valid. A long debate in which the learned jurists and theologians were called into consultation was held on this subject. It opened with the reports which Columbus brought back from his first voyage, and it was considered to have been closed with the final hearing at Valladolid in 1550. It continued on among the jurists, however, for another hundred years. Having examined this question from every possible point of view, the Spanish Crown finally rested on the conviction that its title to the Indies was just. Therefore, its authority was adequate to deal with the situation in the New World and to decide the mooted points of jurisdiction, administration, and reform.

A false tradition has grown up in the English-speaking world that Spain justified her position in the Americas by the right of conquest, but the legal-minded Spaniards of the sixteenth century, product of the Augustinian tradition, held no such view. They approached the problem, for problem it was seen to be from the very beginning, from the view of authority and justice as they saw these in the light of the Augustinian definitions.

As has been made clear above, the Spaniard always envisaged political problems in their ethical setting. As the question was succinctly submitted to Vitoria for elucidation, it was phrased: Granted the existence of the New World and the conditions of the Indian life, could the Spaniards justly remain there and establish the necessary institutions? [44] Vitoria based his answer on the principles of authority as held in Spain.

The very terms which the Spaniards used to describe their possessions, *la dominación española en América,* reflect this. And it is the great merit of Vitoria (although he receives very little modern credit for it) that he called the attention of his generation to the misinterpretations which the Roman law trained jurists were then popularizing in Spain. He denied that the Spanish terms *potestad, autoridad,* and *dominación* (all synonyms) were translations of the Latin *dominium* or *imperium* which in the Roman law connotations expressed the ideas of command and rule. In his *De Indie et de Jure Belli*[45] he stressed the argument for the validity of the Spanish title on the principle of authority, reflecting St. Augustine's exposition of the text of St. Paul that all authority comes from God[46]: *La potesdad real proceda no de la república sino del mismo Dios, como sienten los doctores católicos.*[47] He viewed this principle in its setting of the Justice of God and the Eternal Law. His specific arguments, however, were drawn from the conditions of natural society, the practices of international custom and law, and the position of the pope in medieval society, and he justified the continued presence of the Spaniards in the New World. These were the arguments discussed by his generation, so concerned with legal problems.

In other words, the powers of the Spanish Crown as derived from the participation of the king's authority in the Divine authority were unaffected by conditions in the New World. It was merely extended into a new *milieu* as it had been extended in Spain from the Asturias to Granada during the wars of the Reconquest. The rules for its action laid down in the codes were still valid.

As the Spaniards became acquainted with the institutions of the Indians and began to appreciate the fact that they had their own society formed as men elsewhere form societies on the basis of fellowship and

---

[44] See Marie R. Madden, "The Spanish plan of civilization" in *Thought,* vol. V, no. 1, 53-60.

[45] Published by the Carnegie Institution, Washington, 1917.

[46] Epistle to the Romans, xiii, i.

[47] *"Relección de la potestad civil,"* page 14, in *Relecciones Teológicas* (Madrid, 1917).

social relationships, they questioned whether this society should remain independent of any connection with the society they themselves were forming. This was the view of men like Las Casas who imperfectly comprehended the traditional theory upon which the Spanish society had been erected. The vast majority of the learned men, however, comprehended very well that it would be impossible for the Spaniards and Indians to remain apart. By the peculiar needs of the Indians, due to their barbarian state, and by the efforts the Spaniards were bound to make to convert them and to raise their status not only by the laws of charity but also by the positive obligations induced from the bull of Alexander, contact between the two societies was inevitable.

The problem was merely to arrange the relations between the two; the principle for the solution was at hand in the Augustinian teaching on the nature of the two cities and the interpretations of justice to include both the spiritual and temporal interests of man. The link between the two societies was the authority of the crown, dispensing justice for each. In this function the king could set up the institutions necessary to manage the common relations and to guide all the relationships into that *pactum societatis,* the union of hearts, wills, and interests which should produce the Christian society of the City of God.

In his eighth title Vitoria discusses the argument by which the Spanish authority could justly modify the Indian institutions in the interests of the Christian way of life. He admits that in the true interests of the Indians, considering their great deficiencies both in principles and in institutions, the Spaniards would be bound to help them provided they kept clearly in mind the distinctions between the welfare of the Indians as children of God and the self-interests of individual Spaniards. He does not enter into details on this point nor on the practical basis for the regulation of all relations between barbarian and civilized cultures. The Spaniards of that century preferred the terms Christian and non-Christian societies, but the principles remain the same.

This is based on the teachings of St. Augustine on the obligations arising from the Eternal Law. As he pointed out: When God commands a thing to be done against the customs or compact of any people, though it was never done by them before, it is to be done; and if intermitted it is to be restored; and if never ordained, it is now to be ordained. This was the principle upon which the Spaniards proceeded in establishing their code for the Indies and in creating the social changes its institutions required.

From the *Política indiana* of Juan de Solórzano, the most famous commentator on the laws of the Indies, we may learn that in the seventeenth century the Augustinian tradition on these points was still maintained although the Roman law tradition was also being applied through its definitions of some of the terminology. Solórzano notes that although it was no longer necessary to justify the Spanish titles for the Indies, foreign criticism had been so unjust and unfavorable on the Spanish action[48] that he considered it necessary to review the question once more. He upholds the principle of St. Paul that all authority comes from God (Epistle to the Romans, xiii.1) and that there is nothing more conformable to justice than to follow what the Divine Majesty in His great wisdom and providence ordains as Augustine taught.[49] He reviews the titles upheld by Vitoria and the arguments for a just war as developed by Augustine[50] calling attention to the fact that in no sense could the Indians be forcibly converted as this was contrary to the Catholic teaching of St. Thomas and all the theologians.[51]

Nevertheless, the crossing of this tradition with the Roman law interpretations of the power of the king as an expression of his mere will and of the authority as supreme without relation to the authority of God, is quite evident in Solórzano. In the following passage, for example, the use of the term *dominio* for *potesdad* or *autoridad,* is the mark of the Roman jurist. In discussing the titles of the Spanish Crown, Solórzano remarks that although various Spaniards had made explorations and conquests independently on their own account it still remained true that the provinces, lands, towns, and property which they had won remained under the royal dominion (*queden en el dominio real*)[52] in acknowledgment of the supreme dominion (*supremo dominio*). The references to Bartolus and Baldo but strengthened this Roman interpretation. *Dominio* could be interpreted authority or jurisdiction, but the wedge to use the Roman meaning of ownership and command was easily introduced by the use of the Roman law term, and thus the departure from the Augustinian teaching was hastened.

In the bull of Alexander dated May 4, 1493, which Solórzano quotes,[53]

---

[48] I, 88. Grotius was an important critic who wished to justify invasions into Spanish territories. Other foreigners approved, *Ibid.,* 89.

[49] *Ibid.,* 89-90, quoting from *De libero arbitrio,* chapters v and vi, and Contra Faust, s. 74.

[50] *Ibid.,* 93, quoting *De Civitate Dei,* v, 12, 15, 17.

[51] *Ibid.,* 107.

[52] *Ibid.,* 90 and 92.

[53] *Ibid.,* 103-5.

it is of significance that the terms used in assigning jurisdiction to the Spanish kings are *poder* and *autoridad,* traditional terms. It is expressly stated that the right *(derecho)* so acquired was in virtue of the needs of converting the natives, and it was understood that such authority (that is, to further the work of conversion)[54] could only be conceded by the pope, *motu proprio,* and in the plentitude of his apostolic authority. The Spanish text used the word *poderio*[55] rather than *autoridad,* but there could be no confusion of the authority of the pope on this point with the Roman idea of dominion in that Catholic society.

It was not until later, partly under the stress of foreign attempts to dislodge the Spaniards from their position in the New World and partly from the pressure of the Roman trained jurists who were now considering the Spanish sovereign as a kind of second Roman emperor, that the argument began to deduce from the *poder* and *autoridad* of the bull a dominion foreign to the Augustinian philosophy of government. The point was then made that the dominion conceded was general and absolute by which the king remained master *(dueño)* of the province and persons discovered.[56] This point was also raised in the Assembly at Valladolid in 1550, but was not popular then and was carried to no conclusion. The discussion as to what kind of dominion was conceded reveals confusion among the theologians and jurists accordingly as the term was defined in the Augustinian or Roman law definitions. Again, some discussed the issue merely from the point of view of converting the natives, while others discussed it from the angle of the authority and jurisdiction of the king in all matters.

Thus no solution seemed possible, and as the interminable argument showed no sign of conclusion, the realistic Spaniards of the seventeenth century, with a Roman scorn of theorizing, rested on the facts of the case. As the great jurist Baldo expressed it: We have to consider what *is* now and make the adjustment accordingly. Of what avail would it be now to know whether the rule of Pompey or Cæsar were more just? We are living in this century in which the Spaniards give the customs and laws and these constitute our life, our nourishment, and our essence.[57] Time has its own prescriptions and it was now too late to withdraw from the Indies, even if the presence of the Spaniards there should

---

54 *Ibid.,* 114.

55 *Ibid.,* 104.

56 *Ibid.,* 108.

57 *Ibid.,* 110.

be proved to be unjust on this score. Too many other titles gave them justification to make this more than an academic question.

The long tradition of the authority and function of the king in Spanish society as the highest dispenser of justice and the arbiter of social conflicts, buttressed by the Augustinian tradition through the *Forum Iudiciorum* and *Las Siete Partidas* and the custom of nearly a thousand years, was sufficient to form public opinion. The people took little interest in the theories of the jurists and accepted the justice of their possession of the overseas territories.

The debate, nevertheless, was of capital importance in the background of the relations between the Spanish Crown and the Indies. The confusion in the use of the term *dominio* gradually accustomed the jurists to substitute for the idea of the Christian *auctoritas* the idea of the Roman *dominium* and so prepared the way for the acceptance of the assumptions of the Habsburgs and Bourbons of the eighteenth century. The centralizing, bureaucratic features introduced by these monarchs ruined the application of the original Spanish theory of social organization and removed the basis for the proper adjustment of the social relationships. To it may be attributed more than to any one single cause the loss of the Indies, the brightest jewel in the crown of Spain. To it also may be attributed the paralysis of social development from which the Hispanic American countries still suffer.

SELECTED BIBLIOGRAPHY

Works in English on the topics presented in this chapter are notably lacking, and of those few which do exist many are of such poor quality as to have little or no scholarly value. We mention in particular as belonging to this class, F. Meyrick, *The church in Spain* (1892), and C. H. Lea, *History of the inquisition in Spain* (1908). Neither of these works reveals the grasp of Catholic doctrine necessary to a scholarly interpretation.

Recent textbooks on Hispanic American history such as Mary A. Williams, *The people and politics of Latin America* (1930), A. Curtis Wilgus, *A history of Hispanic America* (1931), and J. Fred Rippy, *Historical evolution of Hispanic America* (1932), have combed the field for all available works in English. There seems no good reason to repeat here titles listed in these works. The bibliographies are not critical.

The Cambridge history, C. Chapman's *History of Spain* (New York, 1930), and R. B. Merriman, *Rise of the Spanish empire in the old world and the new*, (3 vols., New York, 1918-25), contain lengthy bibliographies, the latter being much the better of the two histories.

The excellent histories of Altamira, *Historia de España* (4 vols. Barcelona, 1900-11), and Ballesteros y Beretta, *Historia de España*, (7 vols., Barcelona, 1918-32), contain exhaustive bibliographies. Both of these discuss social classes and the institutional life of the middle ages.

In addition to works already quoted in the text of this chapter, the following may be listed:

A. On the Theories of St. Augustine see:
   De Civitate Dei (3 vols., Paris, n. d.). Latin text and French translation
   by L. Moreau. The Latin text also appears in the *Corpus scriptorum
   ecclesiasticorum latinorum*, Vienna, vol. XL, part 1 (1889), and part 2
   (1900).
   Combès, G., *La doctrine sociale de St. Augustin* (Paris, 1912).
   ————, *La doctrine politique de St. Augustin* (Paris, 1927).
   Gilson, E., *Introduction à l'étude de Saint Augustin* (Paris, 1929).
   Martin, J., *St. Augustine* (Paris, 1901, 2nd ed. 1923).
   O'Dowd, W. B., "The development of St. Augustine's opinions on religious
   toleration" in *The Irish Theological Quarterly*, October, 1919, 337-48.
   Vega, A. C., *Introducción á la filosofía de San Augustín* (El Escorial, 1928),
   English translation by D. J. Kavanagh.

B. On the Spanish Character see:
   Altamira, R., *Psicología del pueblo español* (Barcelona, 1902, 2nd ed. 1917),
   contains a bibliography.

C. On Political Institutions see:
   Altamira, R., *Cuestiones de historia del derecho y de la legislación com-
   parada* (Madrid, 1914).
   ————, *Historia del derecho español* (Madrid, 1903).
   Ballesteros, R., *Algunos fuentes de las partidas* (Madrid, 1919).
   Belloc, H., "Mr. Wells' Outline of History" in *The London Mercury*, 1920,
   III, n. 13, pp. 43-62.
   Fabié, A. M., *Ensayo histórico de la legislación española en sus estados de
   ultramar* (Madrid, 1896).
   Fernández y Gonzales, F., *Estado social y político de los mudéjares de Cas-
   tilla* (Madrid, 1866).
   Ferrar Penelas, F., *Estudio histórico acerca de las costumbres é institu-
   ciones principales que formaba la vida de los municipios en la edad media*
   (Valencia, 1905).
   Hinojosa, E. de, *Historia general del derecho español* (2nd ed., Madrid,
   1924).
   ————, *Estudios sobre la historia del derecho español* (Madrid,
   1903).
   Jiménez de Embún, *Origen de los fueros* (Zaragoza, 1887).
   Kurt, S., *Spaniens und Portugal als see und kolonialmachte* (Hamburg,
   1913).
   Levene, R., "El derecho consuetudinario y la doctrina de los jurídicos en la
   formación del derecho indiana," *Hispanic American Historical Review*,
   1920, III.
   Madden, Marie R., *Political theory and law in medieval Spain* (New York,
   1930).
   Mariéjol, J., *L'Espagne sous Ferdinande et Isabelle* (Paris, 1892).
   Matienzo, J., *Gobierno del Perú* (Buenos Aires, 1910).
   Mayer, E., *Historia de las instituciones sociales y políticas de España y
   Portugal durante los siglos v á xiv* (Madrid, 1925).
   Navarro, J. G., *El municipio en América durante la asistencia de España*,
   read in the Congreso Histórico Municipalista, Palma de Mallorca, Sep-
   tember 8-15, 1929, and published 1930.
   Pascual y Foncuberta, J. M., *Los repartimientos y las encomiendas según
   las leyes de indias y la política colonial de España* (Barcelona, 1913).
   Ruiz-Guiñazú, E., *La magistratura indiana* (Buenos Aires, 1916).

Sacristán y Martínez, A., *Municipalidades de Castilla y León* (Madrid, 1877).

Serrano y Serrano, R., *La representación política de España en las cortes del antiguo y del nuevo régimen* (Madrid, 1901).

Zimmermann, A., *Die kolonialpolitik Portugal und Spaniens* (Berlin, 1896).

D. On Social Conditions, see:

López Montenegro, F., *Apuntes para la historia de la formación social de los españoles* (Madrid, 1922).

Mauro Gamazo, G., *Rincones de la historia; apuntes para la historia social de España.* Siglos VIII to XIII, (Madrid, 1910).

Menéndez Pidal, R., *La España del Cid* (Madrid, 1929).

E. On the *Patronato Real* and relations of Church and State see:

Ballesteros y Beretta, *op. cit.* VI, pp. 373-4, and references listed.

Gams, P. B., *Die kirchengeschichte von Spaniens (3 vols. Regensburg, 1862-79)*.

García Villada, Z., *Historia eclesiástica de España* (Madrid, 1932), vol. II, part 1.

Gómez Zamora, *Regio patronato* (Madrid, 1897).

Gonzales Albern, J. Escobedo, *Las relaciones entre la iglesia y el estado en la historia, doctrina y los canones* (Madrid, 1927).

La Fuente, V. de, *Historia eclesiástica* (4 vols. Barcelona, 1855-59).

Ziegler, A. J., *Church and state in Visigothic Spain* (Washington, D. C., 1930).

F. On the Inquisition see:

Coulton, C. G., *The inquisition* (New York, 1929).

Guiraud, J., *The medieval inquisition* (London, 1929). Translated by A. Messenger.

Lea, C. H., *History of the inquisition in Spain* (New York, 1908).

Maycock, A. L., *The inquisition* (New York, 1929).

Montes, P. Jerónimo, *El crimen de herejía* (Madrid, 1919).

Nickerson, H. A., *The inquisition, a political and military study* (London, 1923).

Tuberville, A. S., *The Spanish inquisition* (London, 1932).

Vacandard, E., *The inquisition* (New York, 1908). Translated by B. Conway.

For a balanced interpretation of the institution and its principles, these works should be checked with Catholic doctrine and teaching.

G. On the Spanish title to the Indies see:

Levene, R., *Introducción á la historia del derecho indiano* (Buenos Aires, 1924).

Solórzano, J. de, *Política indiana* (5 vols., ed. of 1930, reprint of 1647 edition), I, 85-129.

H. For Studies on Sources and Collections of Documents, cf.

Sánchez Alonzo, B., *Fuentes de la historia española é Hispano-Americana* (Madrid, 1927), 217-29, and 267-88.

CHAPTER SIX

THE SPANISH CONQUEST AND SETTLEMENT OF THE INDIES

By Arthur S. Aiton

I. The Spanish Conquest

THE study of Spain's exploring and colonizing effort in America, merely as an introduction to the story of English colony planting on the Atlantic seaboard, has meant, until recently, that Americans were given an incomplete and erroneous picture of the extent, purpose, and nature of Spain's overseas venture. Actually the first century of Spanish endeavor in the Americas witnessed the most remarkable series of expeditions of exploration and conquest in the American continents that have in all probability been recorded in any other comparable period of written history. In addition, this brief space of time saw the establishment of permanent Spanish rule, through settlement and the transplantation of Spanish life and institutions to the vast areas of the Spanish American republics of today, below the borderland region of later English and American rivalry. The tremendous repercussion of the formation of this Spanish *Ultramar* on Europe in the form of wealth, new plant and animal life, extension of geographical ideas, trade, and emigration, makes it not only a story of surpassing interest but also an event an understanding of which is vital to a real knowledge of subsequent world history by reason of its far-reaching consequences. It is the purpose of this discussion to sketch the several movements that bear the general name of "the conquest," and then to present a summary view of Spanish achievement in settlement at the close of a century of effort.

After the discovery by Columbus, the conquest of the larger islands of the West Indies, Española, Puerto Rico (1508), Jamaica (1509), and Cuba (1511), absorbed local attention in the vicinity of first entry while, simultaneously, eager navigators explored the coast lines of the continents looking for new lands and for a waterway through to the fabled wealth of Cathay, Zipango, the Spice Islands, and India. Magellan, the famous Portuguese commander of the fleet that started on the first circumnavigation of the globe, of which the *Victoria* under El Cano was to reach the home port, found the straits which bear his name in

1519, and in 1526 Francisco de Hoces discovered Cape Horn. Northward, in 1525, another Portuguese, Esteban Gómez, a deserter from the Magellan enterprise, succeeded in completing the work of the numerous navigators by reaching the rugged cliffs of Labrador.

In the islands in the meantime, following the founding of Santo Domingo (1496), the first permanent Spanish town in America and for twenty-five years its seat of government, settlers poured in, mines were opened (the mines of Cibao, for example, yielded a considerable supply of the yellow metal before their early exhaustion), cotton and sugar were grown, and a cattle industry developed. The whole range of European plant life and animal life were introduced in short order, and prosperous settlements grew, there being thirteen chartered Spanish towns in 1513 on the Island of Española. The gentle Chemès, the natives of the larger island, were incapable of resisting the conquest imposed by Spanish horses, firearms, and dogs, and soon succumbed, over the protests of Father Bartolomé de las Casas and his fellow Dominicans, to the harsh enforced labor of the *repartimiento* and the later *encomienda* systems. This economic loss forced the importation of expensive African slaves as early as 1501 and raids on the surrounding areas in search of Indian slaves as replacements. These forays ranged as far as the north coast of South America, into the island and mainland area of the fierce, poisoned dart shooting Carib Indians; such an expedition in 1517, under Hernando de Córdoba, sailing from Cuba, discovered the Mayan civilization of Yucatan, and heard of the Nahua culture of the central valley of Mexico for the first time.

Prior to this, permanent lodgment on the continent had occurred at the Isthmus of Panama. Drawn to the shoulder of the continent by the lure of pearls and slaves along the Venezuelean shore, and the rich possibilities of grave robbing for gold ornaments on the Colombian littoral, two adventurers, the burly, headstrong Alonso de Ojeda, and the courtly but parsimonious Diego de Nicuesa, both planters on Española, secured grants of land named respectively Nueva Andalucía, running from Cape Vela to the Gulf of Urabá, and Castilla del Oro, including the Isthmus of Panama and the coast north to the eastern tip of Honduras.

Ojeda led three hundred adventurers to the site of later day Cartagena in 1509, among them being Juan de la Cosa, the first American geographer, Francisco Pizarro, later to conquer Peru, and Vasco Núñez de Balboa, a stowaway on the expedition, but destined to be its leader. Indian battles and disease reduced the force to sixty men who were left by Ojeda in a frail fortress named San Sebastián, near the western limits of his territory, when he returned to Santo Domingo to seek aid, only to die there from the hardships he had endured. Nicuesa's equally unfortunate venture came to grief in Veragua, and the survivors of both expeditions joined forces and formed a slender settlement at Darien. Balboa, who had suggested the move to Darien, succeeded to leadership after the enforced departure of Nicuesa, who put to sea in a leaky boat and disappeared from the narrative.

There followed the familiar story of the discovery of the South Sea in 1513 under the masterly leadership of Balboa. News of this great feat arrived too late in Spain to forestall the appointment of Pedrarias Dávila, the "Green-eyed Monster" and "Tiger" of Oviedo's narrative, to succeed Nicuesa. Balboa's skill and humane methods of treating with the Indians were thus lost to the Spanish conquest when he was beheaded in 1519, a victim of the new governor's suspicion and jealousy. Only the gloomy report of Andagoya concerning the possibilities of the west coast of South America prevented Pedrarias from capitalizing the preparation of Balboa for a conquest which might have anticipated Pizarro in Peru. Instead, angered by the appearance of Andrés Niño and Gil Gonzáles Dávila as interlopers in Central America, where they secured much treasure and reported the baptism of thousands of Indians, he turned to the conquest of the area for himself. As governor of Nicaragua, after 1527, to his death in 1531, he subdued the area of modern Costa Rica as well, and disputed Salvador, Honduras, and Guatemala with the earlier interlopers and the southward moving forces that spilled over from the conquest of Mexico by Hernando Cortés. The discovery of the Lake Nicaragua-San Juan River route from the west coast to the sea by Estete in 1529 was one of the few achievements of Pedrarias' otherwise tyrannical and ruthless career.

Over one hundred of the host of dandies and silken-clad gentlemen, who had come out to Darien with Pedrarias, left for Cuba in 1516, starved and disillusioned. Cuba appealed as a land of plenty where they might find food and useful employment. This latter was provided by a rich planter, Hernando de Córdoba, who chartered two vessels for a slave-hunting voyage and interested the governor, Diego de Velásquez, to venture one ship in the enterprise. The pilot advised a westerly course which brought them to the peninsula of Yucatan in 1517, and into contact with the declining civilization of the Mayas, a people who lived in substantial towns, wore cotton clothes, and were perhaps the most advanced of the aboriginal inhabitants of America. Landing at

various points, fighting several lively battles, and returning by way of
Florida, they brought back sufficient spoil in the form of gold vessels
and articles of superior workmanship to determine Governor Velásquez
to apply for the right to conquer the region and, in the meantime, to
launch a second expedition of reconnoissance character. Under the command of his nephew, Juan de Grijalva, in 1518, three vessels loaded
with "stores of salt-pork and cassava bread" followed the route of the
previous voyage and secured even more convincing evidence of civilization in the Mayan temples, towers, and towns. In addition, first news
of the Nahua civilization of Mexico was derived from the Indians of
the gulf shore, but the conquest was not entrusted to Grijalva, of whose
leadership his followers brought bad reports, but rather to Velásquez'
friend and companion-in-arms in the conquest of Cuba, Hernando
Cortés.

Cortés, the hero of W. H. Prescott's classic account of the conquest
of Mexico, was a native of Medellín in Estremadura. Scion of a poor
but proud country family, he had early evinced a taste for adventure,
and his studies at the University of Salamanca had been terminated by
faculty request. Excited by stories of New World adventure, he had
planned to go out with Ovando to Española in 1502, but had been prevented by an injury caused by a tumble while engaged in the dangerous
business of serenading a married lady. After flirting with the idea of
engaging in the Italian wars under Gonzalvo de Córdoba, "the Great
Captain," he had come to Española in 1504, and had played an important rôle in the subjugation of Cuba in 1511 under Velásquez. Indeed,
the two men had courted sisters and, after some unpleasantness, Cortés
had married Catalina Xaurez, the governor's sister-in-law, and had been
rewarded with the post of *alcalde ordinario* of Santiago.

Cortés was thirty-three years of age when he organized his expedition.
A vigorous, resourceful, crafty man of medium stature, well set-up,
with slightly bowed legs, and his clean-cut features partially obscured
by a beard, he saw his great opportunity in his appointment. By borrowing and by mortgaging his properties he acquired and equipped
eleven vessels and shipped five hundred and eight soldiers and one hundred and nine seamen, together with sixteen horses and a few small
cannon. Velásquez at the last moment became suspicious of his intentions and loyalty, but Cortés sailed nevertheless, after an off-shore
interview, February 10, 1519, while Velásquez, frustrated, "bellowed
like a bull in rage."

Limitations of space and an assumption of familiarity on the part of students with what followed, justify the briefest sketch of events. It should be pointed out, however, that the conquest of Tenochtitlán and the area controlled by the Nahua confederation in no sense was equivalent to the conquest of the vastly larger area which came to be known as New Spain. That remained as a further task for Cortés, his companions, and their successors. Cortés followed the path of his predecessors around Yucatan, successfully defeating the Indians at Champoton, Campeche, and Tabasco, although at times they "covered the plain" in seried ranks of warriors with quilted cotton armor, shields, and "great feathered crests," hurling javelins and stones, and filling the air with arrows. Gunpowder, steel, and horses, regarded as supernatural, were too powerful to be overcome. Fortune smiled in the form of two interpreters, a rescued Spanish castaway, Gerónimo de Aguilar, who knew the Mayan language, and the famous Nahua maiden captive, Doña Marina. At San Juan de Ulloa a landing was effected and emissaries of the fatalist war lord, Montezuma II, bringing rich gifts of a golden sun, silver moon, a helmet full of gold dust, accompanied by a request to depart, were given a red silk hat and assured that the Spaniards would not leave without visiting this ruler. There ensued the founding of the Villa Rica de la Vera Cruz, the surrender of his authority to the town council by Cortés, the return to him of authority as *alcalde* and captain-general, the scuttling of the ships, and the beginning of the march into the interior. Accompanied by forty native chiefs, as allies and guides, and a host of Indian auxiliaries and porters, the route led up through the luxuriant vegetation of the hot lands to the pine-clad slopes of the Sierra Madre, with snow-capped Orizaba gleaming on the left. Pitched battles with the Tlascalans won this valuable group to Spanish alliance. The Cholula massacre turned aside Montezuma's last desperate effort to stop the advance, thanks to Doña Marina overhearing the plot, and the Spaniards advanced down the road into the central valley with its clustered lakes and towns. Welcomed into the heart of Tenochtitlán in Lake Tezcoco and lodged in a god-house "the Tecpan of the Teules," Cortés and his men marvelled at the great temple, the floating gardens, and kindred wonders that met their eyes. Making a hostage of Montezuma, they were collecting treasure and destroying idols in the face of a sullen but paralyzed people, when Cortés was obliged to hasten to the coast to meet a formidable threat in the person of Pánfilo de Narváez and an armed force representing the interests of Governor Velásquez. Narváez was easily overcome by the smooth strategy of Cortés which won his men away from him, but behind Cortés the rash conduct of Pedro de Alvarado had provoked revolt in Tenochtitlán, so that on his return the entire force was obliged to fight its way out of the city on June 30, 1520, *la noche triste,* with terrific losses. Reorganized at Tlascala they recaptured Tenochtitlán in August 1521, after a desperate siege, and rebuilt it as Mexico City.

Recognized by the Emperor Charles V as governor and captain-general, Cortés and his followers spread their conquest in every direction. Sandoval subdued Vera Cruz, Orozco subjected Oaxaca, Alvarado swept from Tehuantepec to independent conquest in Guatemala and San Salvador, while Olid mastered Michoacán and, followed by Francisco de las Casas, subjugated Honduras. A little later Francisco de Montejos initiated the long conquest of Yucatan, and the area about Pánuco became the scene of the activities of Ganay and Nuño de Guzmán, operating independently of Cortés. The conqueror saw his authority gradually stripped from him and strove desperately to recoup his political fortunes by discoveries in the South Sea. The discovery of California by Jiménez in 1532, his short-lived colony there in 1535 at La Paz, and the Ulloa voyage to the head of the Gulf of Lower California were the disappointing fruits of this series of attempts. Nuño de Guzmán's conquest of Nueva Galicia (Jalisco and Sinaloa) in 1531, rounded out this group of *entradas* before the first viceroy, Antono de Mendoza, assumed control of New Spain in 1535. Concurrently with his administration, and in considerable part under his direction, came the great group of exploring expeditions into North America and to the Philippines which are an integral part of United States history. Preceded into the vast amorphous area of Spanish Florida by Ponce de León, were Ayllón, and Narváez; the De Soto expedition toured the southeast and the survivors under Moscoso succeeded in reaching Mexico. Fired by the glowing relation of Alvar Núñez Cabeza de Vaca and his companion wanderers, and the confirmation assumed to exist in Fray Marcos de Niza's report, the Coronado expedition pioneered through the southwest, probably to the plains of eastern Kansas, in search of the Seven Cities of Cíbola and Gran Quivira. At the same time Alarcón entered the lower Colorado River, Cabrillo and Ferrelo pushed their crazy craft to the Rogue River country of Oregon, and Villalobos crossed the Pacific to the Philippines and Moluccas.

The balance of the sixteenth century in North America witnessed a slower, but sounder, process of conquest whereby the frontiers of México moved north under the impetus of mining, cattle, and missionary

interest with the direction in the hands of proprietary governors
(adelantados), like Francisco de Ibarra, the founder of Nueva Vizcaya,
and Luís de Carabajal, the founder of Nuevo León. Westward, in the
Philippines, Legazpi founded Manila in 1572, while Urdaneta found a
return route across the north Pacific in 1565. Eastward, after failures
under De Luna and Villafane, Menéndez de Áviles planted the standard
of Castile quite firmly in Florida and along the Georgia coast after 1565,
while Juan de Oñate, in 1598, moved to the establishment of Spanish
New Mexico. The stir occasioned by the English voyages of Drake and
Cavendish was reflected in the Cerreño and Vizcaino voyages along the
California coast bridging the turn of the century.

In the meantime, the original impulse that brought settlers to Panama
had produced highly dramatic results in another direction. When
Pedrarias turned his back on the possibility of conquest down the west
coast of South America, two veterans of the Isthmus, whose dreams of
fortune were not yet realized, the illiterate ex-swineherd of Trujillo,
Francisco Pizarro, whose greatest gift was the power of dogged persistence, and his partner, Diego de Almagro, the more attractive personality of the two by reason of his generous, impulsive nature, undertook the difficult search that Balboa had initiated. After four years of
heartbreaking failure, they reached the northern part of the land where
the civilization of the Incas existed and returned with evidence of gold,
llamas, and vicuña shawls to justify royal permission to undertake a
conquest. The spectacle presented by the expedition of 1531, with a
tiny force of one hundred and eighty men and thirty-seven horses setting forth to overturn the Inca Empire with its sacred "God-king" commanding the services of thousands of warriors and with entry into the
land made difficult by the dizzy heights of the Andes, has attracted the
pens of many writers, notably W. H. Prescott, Sir Clements Markham,
and, more recently, Philip Ainsworth Means. Obviously, only the barest
outline of this story may be presented here.

Striking inland toward the great central plateau of Peru, where the
ancient "City of the Sun," Cuzco, seat of the empire, with its one hundred thousand houses, its mighty Temple of the Sun, and Cyclopean
walls and fortress built by an earlier people offered an unrivaled opportunity for spoil, the invaders met and seized Atahualpa, the Inca, at
Cajamarca. Fortune had smiled on them in that they had arrived at a
time of civil war at the very moment of Atahualpa's triumph over his
half-brother, the legitimate Inca, Huascar. He made the mistake of
underestimating his adversary and paid the price in royal ransom, a

dazzling roomful of gold and silver objects, only to be put to death on the excuse that he had murdered Huascar. Inca resistance which flared at this point came too late to be effective, and the land was Spain's save for the jealousies that plunged Peru into wars between rival factions for power and wealth. Lima, the City of the Kings, founded January 6, 1535, and the land beyond Cuzco, remained in the possession of Francisco Pizarro and his numerous brothers. Almagro and his men found themselves cheated of their due share in a land where at times even the horses were shod with silver because iron was scarce. Alternately frozen and blistered by heat in an attempt to find new wealth in Chile, Almagro declared war on the Pizarros in 1537. Defeated at Salinas in 1538, he was executed, and his son, in turn, assassinated Francisco Pizarro, only to be defeated and put to death by Gonzalo Pizarro. Vigorous royal intervention and the astute diplomacy of La Gasca ended the latter's separatist movement in 1548 and brought peace to the troubled land.

During the course of these events, side expeditions achieved new conquests and explored new regions. In 1533, Benalcázar, a lieutenant of Francisco Pizarro, invaded Quito, bought off the intruding Pedro de Alvarado, and went searching northward for the Gilded Man by way of the valley of Popayán. In pursuit of him, because of his desertion, came Gonzalo Pizarro to traverse the difficult hinterland of modern Ecuador in search of Omagua, the cinnamon country, to the upper reaches of the Amazon, while one of his followers, Orellana, made his escape twenty-five hundred miles down the Amazon to its mouth. Gonzalo's return journey was one of the finest feats of Spanish exploration in the age of the conquest. Southward, Pedro de Valdivia, an able soldier trained in the Italian wars, undeterred by Almagro's experience, led an expedition into the central valley of Chile in 1540 to found an agricultural colony in the face of great odds.

The first ten years of settlement, centered about the rock of Santa Lucía where Santiago was established, were comparatively peaceful, although marked by the usual hardships and privations that are common to pioneering. But when the energetic governor advanced into the Araucanian country south of the Bio Bio River, the story of town-planting yielded abruptly to fierce warfare, in the course of which Valdivia met his death. García Hurtado de Mendoza saved the situation by strenuous measures, and under his rule Chilean conquest was completed save for the Araucanians whose gallant resistance, lasting well down into the nineteenth century, is commemorated in Ercilla y Zúñiga's epic poem *La Araucana.* Between 1557 and 1561, expansion eastward across the Andes saw the founding of Mendoza, Tucumán, and Cuyo, in what is modern Argentina.

The area of the Río de la Plata, like Chile, lacked the inducement of mineral wealth and great native civilizations, and after early settlement was to develop slowly with the growth of its agricultural and stock-raising interests. The region, including roughly Paraguay, Uruguay, and Argentina, and extending into Bolivia of today, early excited attention as a possible route through to Asia by way of the Río de la Plata and, due to rivalry with Portugal, along the not too scrupulously observed line of demarcation. Juan de Solís, a celebrated sea captain from the north of Spain, sent out after news of Balboa's discovery reached Spain, entered the estuary in 1516 where he was killed by the natives. Alejo García and a group of castaways from this expedition wandered in the interior until 1524 looking for the White Chief *(El Rey Blanco).* Magellan wintered at the river's mouth in 1520 on his voyage to the East. Sebastián Cabot, pilot-major for Spain, was next to appear, and in 1526 and 1527 ascended the river to the forks of the Paraná, lured by distant rumors of Peru. Diego de García, a shipmate of Solís, joined forces with him in planting a settlement on the Paraná, called Sancti Spiritus, which met the sad fate of massacre when Lucía Miranda, wife of one of the settlers, spurned the love of powerful Chief Mangore. Permanent settlement followed with the arrival of Pedro de Mendoza, a gentleman of the king's court, as the first official *adelantado.* He brought with him an exceptionally large (two thousand five hundred men) and well-equipped force in a fleet of fourteen vessels. The unfavorable site selected for the settlement, Nuestra Señora de los Buenos Aires, in 1536, resultant sickness, and the retirement of Mendoza and his death en route to Spain, left the colony in the competent hands of two Basque lieutenants, Juan de Ayolas and Domingo de Irala, who moved the settlement upstream one thousand miles to lay the foundation there of Asunción in Paraguay among the Guaraní Indians.

After Ayolas perished while leading a group of expeditionaries across Bolivia, Irala, left in sole charge and even elected as governor, showed himself to be an excellent administrator. In the time down to his death in 1557, he ruled wisely, collected his settlers near Asunción, introduced the *encomienda* system, built towns, secured his frontiers, and provided for the future by encouraging interracial marriages. The appointment of Alvar Núñez Cabeza de Vaca as *adelantado* in 1540, and his arrival in 1541, marching overland from the coast of Brazil and then attempting to reach Peru by land, almost duplicating his earlier remarkable transcontinental walk from Texas to the west coast of Mexico, provided the only interruption. His deposal in 1544, left Irala supreme to work out his policies unmolested. Under the third governor, Juan Ortiz de Zárate (d. 1575), and his nephew, Juan de Garay, as *adelantado,* new towns were added to Ontiveras on the Portuguese frontier and Santa Cruz de la Sierra (1560) in later Bolivia, including Santa Fé, and, in 1580, Buenos Aires which was refounded. Cattle multiplied extraordinarily, typical *gaucho* life came into being, and in 1588 the first Jesuits arrived to start their remarkable work among the Guaraní Indians.

In the tracks of early explorers along the Venezuela and Colombian coasts (called *Tierra Firme*), *Conquistadores* came to add this additional geographical block to the Spanish Empire. On the coast, Rodrigo Bastidas settled at Santa Marta in 1525, and in 1533 Pedro Heredia, nicknamed "Slit-nose," established himself at Cartagena, from whence he led forays into the Atrato and Cauca valleys. Eastward in Venezuela, after the failure of an experimental Indian colony in 1521 under the control of Father Las Casas, Coro was permanently founded by Juan de Ampues in 1527, destined to be the seat of authority until the government moved in 1576 to Caracas. This area was alloted to the German banking house, the Welsers of Augsburg, in 1530, and became the base of German efforts to reach the land of the Chibchas under George of Spires and his lieutenant Federman.

From the interior plateau of Cundinamarca, stories of Chibcha wealth and civilization arrived at the coastal settlements. Legends of El Dorado (the Gilded Man), of Meta (the house of gold), of Omagua (the cinnamon country), and of the land of the Amazons, whetted the eagerness of explorers. Finally in 1536, a well-organized expedition under Jiménez de Quesada, the relatively unsung Cortés of this conquest, after a terrible journey up the Magdalena, discovered a pass through the mountains and won a new kingdom for the emperor. The conquest was barely consolidated when Benalcázar marched in overland from Peru and Federman arrived over the mountains from the east, to find the game in other hands. After founding Santa Fé de Bogotá in 1538, Quesada returned to Spain to secure royal confirmation of his right to rule, only to be despoiled of his hard won rights by the family of Don Pedro de Lugo, who had financed the original enterprise. Into the Orinoco River area, expedition followed expedition looking for the remaining marvels down to 1561, when the task was given up as a futile search. Sir Walter Raleigh and other English explorers came into the

Guianas to renew the hopeless search at the turn of the century, substituting new marvels, such as a hill of sapphires, for the earlier Spanish tales.

Such was, in broad sweep, the Spanish conquest of the Indies in its first tremendous rush in the sixteenth century, which for extent, for resolute elimination of well-nigh insuperable obstacles, for sum total of result, and for dramatic intensity, is unrivaled in all history, with the possible exception of the great conquests of Ghenis Khan and Tamurlane in Asia. The details in many instances are only now emerging from the vast documentary storehouses, the archives of Spain, and more especially the Archives of the Indies in Seville. There now remains for discussion the character of Spanish settlement that accompanied and came after the conquest.

II. THE SPANISH SETTLEMENT

Most cultivated Americans read W. H. Prescott's classic narrative of the conquest of Mexico and came away from its pages with a colorful picture of spectacular exploits on the part of Hernando Cortés and his *Conquistador* companions. What happened in Mexico, or elsewhere in Hispanic America, after the Indian civilizations were subdued, is seldom asked. They remain satisfied with the old fable that the Spaniards lured by gold merely explored and conquered but did not settle, and ignore the equally spectacular story of the subsequent transplantation of European culture to America. As Professor H. E. Bolton stated the matter in a recent book,

> "Few realize that, compared with their work of colonization, these epic explorations were but a minor part of what the two little nations of the Peninsula (Spain and Portugal) contributed to the making of the Western Hemisphere. Surely explorers did not build Mexico City and Lima. Surely, wild-eyed gold seekers did not found the Universities of Mexico and Córdoba. The old nursery tale of mere explorers must have been a myth along with Santa Claus. Spain and Portugal followed exploration by colonization. Only a small fraction of their pioneers in America spent their time running around the map. The vast majority were merchants, planters, ranchers, soldiers, priests, and miners. Settlement by them was so effective, that two-thirds of America are still Spanish and Portuguese today."

Before the first English settlement at Jamestown started its career, almost on the site of an earlier Spanish mission in Virginia, Spain had completed a full cycle of discovery, exploration, and settlement in

America. More important than that, Spanish civilization of the sixteenth century had been planted in America in all its details, and it must be remembered that Spain in that century possessed a civilization equal or superior to that of any other European power. By 1574 there were over one hundred and sixty thousand Spaniards in America, drawn from all walks of life, and over two hundred chartered towns. Before the advent of the English, the New World had been stocked with domestic animals, horses, sheep, cattle, goats, and pigs. The whole range of European plant life was likewise transplanted, even to roses and a wide variety of garden flowers. The vine and the olive, citrous fruits, sugar cane, and the precious cereals, on which European life was based, were introduced at an early date. On the cultural side her priority is equally impressive. The first American printing press arrived in Mexico City in 1536, and the first book printed in America came from it in 1539. Schools and universities were established shortly after the conquest. The first American universities opened their doors in Mexico City and Lima in 1553, long before Virginia had its "starving time" in 1610. A partial list of achievements reveals the minting of the first American money in 1536, pure food laws in 1537, price-fixing legislation before 1550, modern "city planning," and a sales tax of three per cent long before the *Mayflower* sailed. Of particular interest in connection with the University of Mexico is the establishment of the first American school of medicine and in it the first American chair of surgery. A somewhat detailed survey of this important branch of science as it developed at the University of Mexico, will serve to illustrate the nature and quality of the Spanish advance in America in the colonial period.

Cortés was succeeded in Mexico by builders and organizers, chief among whom is to be noted the famous first viceroy, Antonio de Mendoza (1535-1550), at whose suggestion the University of Mexico was ordered founded in 1551, simultaneously with the University of San Marcos in Lima, Peru. The University in Mexico started to instruct the first matriculants into an institution of higher learning in America in June 1553. It was patterned after the famous Spanish University of Salamanca and exchanged credits with the older university on a basis of equality. At the outset, it offered courses in the traditional fields of theology, the Bible, canon law, profane law, the arts, rhetoric, and grammar. Dr. Antonio Rodríguez, professor of grammar, was the first of the genus American University President. The Institutes and Code of Justinian were added to the law curriculum in 1569, and in 1580 courses of study in medicine were initiated under the first American professor of medicine, Dr. Juan de la Fuente. Medicine, requiring a higher degree, undoubtedly was added as a result of the royal permission to confer higher degrees granted in 1572. Prior to that time informal lectures in medicine had been offered at the secondary school in the suburb of Mexico City, Santa Cruz Tlaltelalco, by a surgeon barber, Francisco Soto. In 1575, two years prior to the opening of a regular course in medicine, courses in hygiene and physiology were offered as pre-medical work in the arts course. The first course in medicine was based on the works of Galen and Hippocrates. In the first year, *De elementis-De temperamentis-De humoribus-De anathomia-De facultatibus natibus-De pulsibus et urinis* were studied. In the second year *De diferentis februim-De arte curativa ad glauconem-De Sanguinis misione;* in the third year the *Aphorisms of Hippocrates,* the book *Ques et quando oportet purgard* and the ninth of *Rhazis ad almanzorem;* and in the fourth year the course was completed with a survey of *De crisibus-De diebus decretoriis* and a perusal of some of the books of Galen.

To this first course in medicine, in the year 1599, under the direction of Dr. Juan de Plasencia, an additional group of lectures was added dealing with matters of pathology and based on the works of Avicena. By 1621 the medical program had broadened to include additional courses in *metodo medendi,* anatomy and surgery, dissection, and astrology and botany. It is to be noted that astrology as a branch of medical study was required, even in the better French universities until the middle of the seventeenth century. The course entitled *metodo medendi* dealt with therapeutics, *materia medica,* and pharmacy, and made considerable use of Galen's *Morgis curandi.* Anatomy and surgery as a regular course was instituted in 1621 under the direction of Dr. Cristóbal Hidalgo Vandoval, both being taught in the Royal Hospital until an amphitheatre was provided. Prior to the introduction of these courses, the surgeons acquired their skill after graduation by serving an apprenticeship of two years under a practicing surgeon. Up to the establishment of a Royal College of Surgeons in 1768, this practice of acquiring skill in surgery outside the school continued as a regular procedure. After 1768 those still trained in the University were called "Latin Surgeons" to distinguish them from the graduates of the College of Surgeons who were known as externe or romantic surgeons. The establishment of the College of Surgeons forced these apprenticed surgeons to meet certain definite requirements, although bleeders, obstetricians, and pharmacists continued to go directly into practice from their apprenticeship.

The course in anatomy and surgery in the university was the only course not conducted in Latin due to the difficulty of explanations in that learned tongue. Lectures, textbooks, and demonstrations with skeletons constituted the work in anatomy, while the surgery was restricted to textbooks, chiefly Galen's *Usurpartium* and Hippocrates' *De arte curativa,* amplified by demonstrations of the use of surgical instruments. The dissection of cadavers was begun in 1804. Dr. Antonio Serrano of the Royal College of Surgeons at that time created a furore by dissecting the body of a hanged criminal. Thereafter, three dissections a year in the presence of the students became a fixed requirement. In the College of Surgeons the instructor need not be an M.D. nor a graduate of the university, but a competent surgeon who had acquired his skill by the apprenticeship method.

Students were faced with a long period of training when they sought the M.D. degree in colonial Mexico. To matriculate, they were required to pass preparatory courses, to show definite aptitude, to be legitimate, to be of pure blood, and lastly Catholic. As students they were not supposed to be armed, to smoke, or to wear colored socks. After three years of study and a comprehensive examination the A.B. degree could be secured with the payment of proper fees. There followed the medical course of four years for the bachelor of medicine degree. Then two additional years, under a competent doctor in practice, permitted one to set up for himself. Further study opened the way to the license and the M.D. degree. Public lectures and a severe examination ended the long road to the degree, if the examining board were favorable in their verdict. The degree entitled one to wear a ring, sword, spurs, and a velvet belt, and a mortar board with a yellow gold tassel.

It is interesting to note, in passing, that the highest paid professors in the colonial University of Mexico were the expounders of theology who received $700 a year while the professor of surgery and anatomy received less than half that princely sum!

Turning back from this special line of Spanish advance in America to the general theme of accomplishment in settlement, the question of numbers and kinds of settlers, as a measure for any appraisal of success or failure, is necessary. In the past our chief reliance has been the extensive work of Juan López de Velasco, royal cosmographer and geographer, whose *Geografía y descripción universal de las indias,* prepared in 1576, and first printed in 1894, offers a general census of Spanish America, prepared from official sources, in the year 1574. His accuracy is well attested by regional checks available in the census figures for New Spain of 1560,[1] the later census of Luís de Velasco of 1595, Francisco de Icaza's documented study of early Mexican settlers,[2] and, more recently, the extensive study by Luís Rubio y Moreno of the licenses issued to emigrants leaving Spain for the Indies.[3] Indeed, it is not too much to hope that we shall have a fairly complete picture of Spanish emigration overseas, something illustrative of the superiority of Spanish documentation which we shall never have for English colonization, when the record is thoroughly explored.

Velasco describes two hundred Spanish chartered towns in America in 1574, and additional mining settlements. One hundred and sixty thousand Spaniards are enumerated as living in these towns, at the mines, and on the ranches and plantations. Four thousand Spaniards are listed as *encomenderos,* the balance being scattered through the various trades, occupations, and professions. An Indian population of about five million souls, exclusive of wild Indians, is reported, and an additional group of forty thousand negro slaves and a considerable *mestizo* and mulatto element is noted. Velasco's description of areas shows clearly the superior attraction of the mineral area, with its sedentary tribes in Mexico, Central America, and Peru, over the original island settlements, which had been almost drained of population. In Española only ten Spanish settlements remained in which about a thousand settlers, owning over twelve thousand negro slaves, lived by stock-raising and the sugar industry. Santo Domingo, the oldest Spanish settlement, had less than two thousand settlers, while Cuba had only two hundred and forty Spaniards in its towns, Havana only being able to muster seventy inhabitants. Puerto Rico and Jamaica were threatened with extinction, and Venezuela stagnated in an economic backwater.

New Spain, on the other hand, bustled with activity. Mexico City boasted fifteen thousand Spaniards and close to one hundred and fifty thousand Indians. It was already a genuine metropolis, with the great fabric of its Cathedral slowly rising on the site of the great Aztec temple; its churches, monasteries, public buildings and town houses, with its shops and stores, where food, clothing, and luxuries from Spain were sold; and its narrow streets thronged with Indians, negroes, and Span-

---

[1] *Boletín del Centro de Estudias Americanistas,* Seville, VII, Nos. 36, 37, 45, 46.

[2] Francisco A. de Icaza, *Conquistadores y pobladores de Nueva España* (2 vols., Madrid, 1923).

[3] Luís Rubio y Moreno, *Catálogo metodológico de las informaciones y licencias de los que allí pasaron, existentes en el Archivo General de Indias,* vols. IX and XIII, in *Colección de documentos inéditos para la historia de Hispano-América* (Madrid, 1930 ff.).

iards. Horses, mules, great carts, and Indian carriers jostled there with friars, gentry of the viceroy's entourage, and stolid citizens. Apothecary shops, tailor shops, jewelers' shops, pastry shops, and taverns evidenced prosperity, while the university, schools, and hospitals showed cultural advance. Roundabout through the land a vast Indian population toiled on the ranches and in the mines under Spanish supervision, and even the unhealthy entry town of Vera Cruz had a population of two hundred merchant families. In remote Yucatan three hundred Spanish heads of families held sway over the Mayas on plantations and in four Spanish towns.

South America presents the same concentration in the Indian mining area, with a total of one hundred European settlements containing thirteen thousand five hundred families. The great bulk were farmers and traders, only two thousand controlling *encomiendas*. Mining, stock-raising, farming, and merchandizing were the chief occupations. Quito, in modern Ecuador, had four hundred Spanish families and boasted a hospital and three monasteries, one with an Indian school. Lima, the viceregal seat, was a great city with two thousand Spanish families, resting on a subject Indian group of twenty-five thousand Indians. The great wealth of the mines was reflected in buildings and churches, but the educational institutions lagged behind those of Mexico. Southward, the smaller settlements of the agricultural area of Chile and the Río de la Plata grew slowly, while the isolation of Nueva Granada impeded progress.

Were these colonists the adventurous and best from Spain's millions, or were they the undesirables and the misfits? Although we are still far from a complete answer to the question, some light has been thrown on it through the work of Luís Rubio y Moreno who has prepared the *Catálogo metodológico* referred to above. Rubio y Moreno secured his information from the licenses which were required from all of those who came to the New World. A review of the restrictions which the Spanish sovereigns placed upon emigration cannot fail to lead one to the conclusion that it was their intention to settle their overseas possessions with a desirable class of people. The licenses referred to were supposed to contain information sufficient to prevent any other class from emigrating. The information which was required to be given before a license would be issued by the *Casa de Contratación* included: a. the region or province in Spain from which they came; b. destination—place in the Indies to which they were going; c. *estado*—single, married, religious order to which they belonged; and d. class, rank, title, and profession to which they belonged.

Despite the rigid rules requiring them to do so, it appears that the officials of the *Casa de Contratación* did not secure the information which was supposed to be given by all those wishing a license or permit to come to the New World. Of the 26,619 *expedientes* issued during the period from 1534 to 1586 less than half give more than the names of the persons to whom they were issued, 10,820 give the point of destination, 7,897 give the region from which they came, 8,606 give their *estado,* and only 3,242 list their occupations.

Although all of the provinces of Spain furnished some colonists, the three leading provinces were Andalucía (1915), Castilla and León (1797), and Estremadura (601).

In the New World, 2,805 of the colonists went to North America, 5,726 went to South America, 1,025 to Central America, 1,217 to the islands, while the destination of 47 was unknown.

According to rank, 947—approximately one-tenth—belonged to the nobility. Not far removed from the nobility was another group comprising the high church, provincial, and municipal officers, numbering 698. Almost one-tenth of the total number listed a definite trade, which they were supposed to follow when they arrived in the Indies, while 141 indicated that they were members of the civil professions. Approximately one out of every fifty—262 out of 10,820—who came over in this early group held a license or degree from some institution of learning.

An examination of 1,018 licenses issued between the years 1534 and 1575 showed that 109 of them were issued to married men, and of this number 99 brought their families to the New World with them.

It is difficult to determine with any great degree of exactness the actual number which came to the Indies during a given period, due to the fact that the license was issued to the head of the family, and thus one license might care for several people—wives, children, and servants. Assuming that on the average one license would take care of three people, we would have approximately 80,000 people coming from Spain to the colonies during the period 1534 to 1586. This, taking into consideration the natural increase, and those who had come prior to this period, would give the New World a Spanish population of around 200,000 by the end of the sixteenth century. This figure agrees with the generally accepted estimate of Velasco.

The above data indicate, probably, that Spain used her colonies, not as a dumping ground for her undesirables or as a haven for her nobility, but as the home of a truly representative group of the Spanish people. The Spanish government made a sincere attempt to people the New World with a desirable class of people.[4] These people, a genuine cross section of Spanish life, undertook to lift the millions of Indians to their own mode of thought, life, and religion. It was a great, if hopeless, effort. If mistakes were made, if acts of cruelty occurred, as they did, nevertheless the conception was a noble one, and as one writer puts it, we should not ". . . appraise the Spaniards both by the modern standards and by the measure of their failure, rather than by the degree of their success." They were sixteenth century Europeans, the first moderns to attempt large scale imperialism, and, fresh from the long reconquest of the peninsula from the Moslems, employed the methods of the frontiers of Europe. They failed to appreciate, as they should have, the cultural attainments of certain Indian groups, but, granting all this, they did not exterminate the subject population, they did transplant their culture, and the government structure they built lasted for three hundred years, despite its imperfections.

SELECTED BIBLIOGRAPHY

The attempt to cover such an enormous field as Spanish conquest and settlement in America within the compass of two chapters, poses a well-nigh insuperable problem of citation. Indebtedness is obvious and too frequent to permit individual citation in the body of the text. In view of this, the following brief commentary on some of the leading sources of information may serve as an adequate substitute. E. G. Bourne, *Spain in America* (New York, 1904), is still a useful general survey and pioneered the way on many points. Bernard Moses, *The establishment of Spanish rule in America* (New York, 1898), a landmark in the field, may even today be consulted with profit. A useful work is H. I. Priestley, *The coming of the white man* (New York, 1929). The most recent general survey, based on a re-examination of a vast array of material, is the admirable work of R. B. Merriman, *The rise of the Spanish empire in the old world and the new* (4 vols., New York, 1918-1934). In Spanish, Barros Arana's *Historia de América* (2 vols., Santiago de Chile, 1908) is valuable for its inclusive treatment and frequent quotation from the documents. Carlos Navarro y Lamarca, *Compendio de la historia general de América* (2 vols., Buenos Aires, 1913) is undoubtedly the best brief treatment of American history through the wars of independence which has yet appeared. Carlos Pereyra, *Historia de la América española* (8 vols., Madrid, 1920-1926) is more interpretive, and shows a strong predisposition in favor of Spain. Rafael Altamira y Crevea, *Historia de España* (4 vols., Barcelona, 1928) contains a well-organized bibliography and relates the history of the colonies to that of the motherland at each stage of their development. An exceedingly useful annotated guide to the great body of historical literature is afforded by A. Ballesteros y Beretta, *Historia de España y de su influencia en la historia universal* (6 vols. to date, Barcelona, 1919ff). Illustrative of the printed chronicles of exploration and con-

---

[4] The writer is indebted to his student, H. C. Gregory, for this analysis of Rubio y Moreno's findings.

quest are Bernal Díaz del Castillo, *A true history of the conquest of New Spain* (5 vols., translated and edited by Alfred P. Maudslay, London, 1908-1916); Roberto Levillier (ed.) *Nueva crónica de la conquista del Tucumán* (3 vols., Buenos Aires, 1926); and J. A. Robertson (ed.) *True relation of the hardships suffered by governor Fernando de Soto . . . by a Gentleman of Elvas* (2 vols., DeLand, 1932-1933). An idea of the growing literature of the field may be obtained by a glance at J. Lloyd Mecham, "The northern expansion of New Spain 1522-1822: a selected descriptive bibliographical list," *Hispanic American Historical Review,* VII, 233-276.

CHAPTER SEVEN

COLONIAL GOVERNMENT

By Lillian Estelle Fisher

I. Portuguese Colonial Government

PORTUGAL, the great exploring nation, obtained its first experience in colonial administration in India. There was little machinery of government at the beginning, since the purpose of Portuguese colonization was not possession of the Indies themselves but their commerce. When the experiment of leaving a subordinate in charge of the factories during the interval between the departure of one fleet and the arrival of another proved unsatisfactory, a viceroy was appointed for three years. He was a civil and military chief, without whose consent no important affair of state could be concluded. His freedom of action was limited by the intervention of a council, the advice of which he had to take in all serious matters.[1] A few great viceroys like Almeida and Albuquerque planted the outposts of empire in India, but the government was never sound because Portugal chose the path of war rather than peace and alienated the native princes by vexations, greed, and religious intolerance.[2]

Governmental Authority of Portugal over the Colonies

The royal government of the mother country at first kept in contact with its remote dependencies without organizing a central power. Administrative organization never proceeded according to a uniform plan; it was determined by the march of events. Until the Spanish epoch there was not a council or minister in Portugal charged with the centralization of colonial affairs. The government of the colonies, as well as that of the home country, was concentrated entirely in the hands of a chancellor, a royal registrar, and a secretary of the king. The only special official of importance was the inspector of finance, who oversaw the finances of Portugal and the colonies. He also supervised the *Casa*

---

[1] Charles de Lannoy and Herman Vander Linden, *Histoire de l'expansion coloniale des peuples européens* (Bruxelles, 1907-1911), I. 106-108.

[2] *Ibid.*, I, 69; R. S. Whiteway, *The rise of Portuguese power in India 1497-1550* (Westminster, 1899), 104, 169-171, 175-176; Oliveira Martins, *Historia de Portugal* (Lisboa, 1893), 170-175; Paul Leroy-Beaulieu, *De la colonisation chez les peuples modernes* (Paris, 1902), I, 45.

da India which prepared the cargoes destined for the Indies and enlisted soldiers for colonial armies. His powers were those which ordinarily belonged to ministers of finance, treasury officials, and tribunals of accounts.

The religious administration of the colonies was under the control of an ecclesiastical council called the *Mesa da Consciencia e Ordens,* created in 1532, which exercised the rights belonging to the king as master of the military orders of the church. This body acted as a restraint upon all other officials, proposed candidates for benefices for the choice of the king, administered the resources of the Order of Christ, and judged the crimes committed by members of the military orders who served overseas. The numerous and indefinitely defined powers of the tribunal caused it to interfere frequently in colonial affairs.[3]

The Donatarios

From the beginning, the land in the colonies, which was considered crown land, was given to nobles under hereditary title as proprietors or *donatarios* and governors. This custom was practiced in the Madeira and the Azores islands as well as in Brazil and the East Indies. The *donatarios* were military chiefs in the colony. All the land belonged to them, but they were obliged to distribute it to the colonists for their use under conditions provided by law or specified in charters. The proprietors were almost absolute masters of their territories. The church only could restrain them when its members appealed to its jurisdiction, and there were many serious conflicts between the agents of the *donatarios* and the ecclesiastical judges.[4]

The Corregidor

The most important local officials in the colonies were the *corregidores* who represented the royal authority. At first they were inclined to defend the interests of the powerful *donatarios,* but gradually the sovereign brought them under his control by appointing trusted lawyers to the position. The chief functions of the *corregidor* were of a judicial and military nature, although they were often quite varied. When litigants complained, the *corregidor* revised the judgment rendered by the district judge; at regular intervals he reformed the decisions made by local

---

[3] Lannoy and Vander Linden, I, 82-84. Because of the preponderance of the commercial policy in the sixteenth century, finance was the most important branch of colonial administration.

[4] *Ibid.,* I, 88-89.

magistrates who were partial, supervised municipal administration, defended the people against the abuses of the proprietors, and until 1555 he was also the chief of the financial administration. In colonies inhabited entirely by Portuguese, as in the case of the Madeira and Azores islands, the *corregidor* filled his office as in Portugal and imposed his authority upon the *donatarios;* but in the slave colonies of Cape Verde, Saint Thomas, and Brazil his rôle of protector of the people against the privileged classes was not very important.[5]

Changes in Colonial Government under the Spanish Régime

When Spain and Portugal were united in 1580 the Spanish rulers considerably modified the inefficiently organized colonial government. Philip II abolished the inspectors of finance and replaced them, in 1591, by a Council of Finance with well-defined powers. The council was divided into four sections, three of which supervised a particular group of colonies. The reform did not have satisfactory results; therefore, in 1604 financial administration was confined to a special body, the Council of the Indies, which was granted jurisdiction over the civil, religious, and judicial affairs of the former Portuguese colonies. This council was divided into two parts: one was occupied with Brazil and Africa, and the other with the establishments in the Indian Ocean. Numerous were the conflicts between the divisions, but nevertheless the direction of colonial affairs was improved. The decision of all important matters was taken to Madrid, not to Lisbon. Philip IV interfered in all branches of administration and substituted his authority for that of the councils. Thus Portuguese administration was further assimilated to the Spanish model.

Colonial Government under the House of Braganza

The administration of the colonies did not return to its former condition when the subordination to Madrid ended. Perhaps through lack of energy John IV of the House of Braganza (1640-1657) kept the institutions created by the Spanish kings; he merely modified certain rules to make them function better. After his reign, until 1808, the appointment of viceroys and colonial governors belonged to the Council of State—the first council of the Portuguese kingdom. That body chose the members of the other councils and occupied itself with foreign affairs; it secretly played the rôle of a prime minister without the title. The Council of the Indies, which became the Overseas Council, admin-

---

[5] *Ibid.,* I, 90-91.

istered the American possessions. Its authority extended to civil, religious, and military affairs; it saw that the revenues were collected in the colonies and distributed what was necessary for military purposes and local needs; it sent the surplus to the royal treasury; and it supervised the colonial tribunals. There was a Privy Council which nominated candidates for judicial offices in the dependencies as well as in the metropolis. The power of the Overseas Council was insufficient. Since it did not appoint the governors and colonial judges it could not command respect; therefore, its functions were reduced to defense and to directing magazines and arsenals.

The Portuguese colonial government was very similar to that of the mother country, and it was not always adapted to conditions of the dependencies since it originated in rather a haphazard manner. The powers and duties of the functionaries were not fixed by law or general regulations. In the administration sometimes the usage and routine followed were in harmony with the intentions of the central government, while again they might be in opposition to them. The sovereigns had their lawyers who interpreted the laws of the kingdom for their interests, and the colonial governors also had theirs who gave to the laws and decrees the most favorable meaning for them. It was almost impossible to distinguish with certainty the laws which were applicable and those which were not. The *Ordenações philippinas,* which was confirmed by King John IV in 1643, remained the legal code of Brazil.[6]

Decrease of the Power of the Donatarios

When the centralizing tendencies began, the power of the *donatarios* steadily declined. The replacement of these functionaries by royal officials had commenced under John III and continued under the kings of the houses of Hapsburg and Braganza. By the end of the seventeenth century the centralized reform was virtually achieved and there was no captaincy of any importance left which was governed by a proprietor. After the administration of Pombal (1750-1777), where the *donatarios* were kept, as in the Azores, Cape Verde, or Porto Santo, their powers were decreased to those privileged proprietors, submissive to governors, but invested with control over local affairs. The government of the *donatarios* lost its force in captaincies inhabited by an energetic

---

[6] Lannoy and Vander Linden, I, 84-88; Wm. S. Robertson, *History of the Latin American nations* (New York, 1922), 140-141. The new code had replaced the *Ordenaçoes manuelinas,* published in 1521, for the internal administration of the colony.

people, as in Brazil where the powers of the proprietors were frequently reduced to complete incompetence.

Establishment of the Captaincies in Brazil

Brazil at first was considered practically worthless—a convenient place to stop on the route to India and in which to dump criminals for the relief of the mother country. Adventurous foreigners, especially Normans and Bretons, soon recognized the excellence of the country and its advantages for commerce. Portugal then decided to colonize and govern Brazil by the semifeudal system of proprietary grants or fiefs employed in the Madeira and Azores islands as a defense against the French aggressors. Although the feudal system was already abolished in Europe, Brazil was divided into hereditary captaincies, which were larger than the greatest kingdoms of Europe, and granted to proprietors who should defend and settle them at their own expense. In this way government resources could be used for the India enterprises. Although the inefficiency of such a colonial system was soon recognized, the fundamental principle remained more or less operative during the colonial period.[7]

From 1532 to 1539 twelve captaincies, following the contour of the coast and extending indefinitely into the interior, were mapped out.[8]

---

[7] Manoel de Oliveira Lima, *Formación histórica de la nacionalidad brasileña* (Madrid, 1918), 26-32; Albert Galloway Keller, *Colonization* (New York, 1908), 132-133; Manoel de Oliveira Lima, *The evolution of Brazil compared with that of Spanish and Anglo-Saxon America* (Palo Alto, 1914), 55.

[8] The twelve first captaincies were:

Captaincy	Size	Capital	Donatario
1. São Vicente	100 leagues	São Vicente	Martim Affonso de Souza
2. Santo Amaro	50 "	Santo Amaro	Pero Lopez de Souza
3. Parahyba do Sul	30 "	Villa da Rainha	Pero de Góes de Silveira
4. Espirito Santo	50 "	Victoria	Vasco Fernandes Coutinho
5. Porto Seguro	50 "	Porto Seguro	Pero de Campos Tourinho
6. Ilheos	50 "	São Jorge	Jorge de Figueiredo Corrêa
7. Bahia	50 "	Villa da Victoria	Francisco Pereira Coutinho
8. Pernambuco	60 "	Olinda	Duarte Coelho Pereira
9. Itamaracá	30 "	no capital	João de Barros and Ayres da Cunha
10. Rio Grande	100 "	" "	João de Barros and Ayres da Cunha
11. Ceará	40 "	" "	Antonio Cardoso de Barros
12. Maranhão	75 "	" "	Fernando Alvares de Andrade

The first eight captaincies formed the five provinces of São Paulo, Rio de Janeiro, Espirito Santo, Bahia, and Pernambuco. The remaining four, created later, varied in size and were indefinite in regard to boundaries. See María G. Andrade, *Resumo da historia do Brasil* (New York, 1920), 19-26; Herman G. James, *Brazil after a century of independence* (New York, 1925), 65-67.

These were distributed to favored persons and differed in size with the favor shown. The first man to take possession of one of the captaincies was Martim Affonso de Souza, well known in the history of Portuguese India, where he was afterwards governor, and in Catholic history for having taken Saint Francis Xavier to the east. He and his brother Pero Lopes de Souza went in person to explore Brazil and establish settlements. Martim surveyed the coast in the region of Rio de Janeiro, to which he gave that name because it was discovered on the first of January 1532. A settlement was made on one of the coast islands called Guiambé by the natives at twenty-four and one-half degrees of south latitude. At first the natives were hostile, but due to the influence of the shipwrecked Portuguese, João Ramalho, who lived there and had married the daughter of the chief, they became friendly. The place chosen for the new town was soon abandoned, and the colonists moved to the adjoining island of São Vicente from which the captaincy derived its name. The new settlement progressed rapidly, and sugar cane, which soon became the staple product for the captaincy, was planted.[9]

Success frowned upon some of the other proprietors in establishing colonies and developing their captaincies. Lopes de Souza was not as lucky as his brother. Nevertheless, the colony of Santo Amaro was established on a coast island and became the nucleus of the captaincy of that name. The new settlement did not prosper because of constant Indian attacks, and Lopes perished by shipwreck.[10] Pero de Góes, a friend of Lopes who loved Brazil very much, asked for a captaincy. Since he did not have influence at the court he obtained a grant of only thirty leagues. The town of Villa da Rainha was founded in his captaincy of Parahyba do Sul, but native hostilities caused the captaincy to be abandoned.[11] Francisco Coutinho had to retreat also with the colonists from his captaincy of Bahia since the warlike Indians were stronger than the Portuguese.[12] After he returned from India later he tried to occupy his captaincy again. He made an establishment at Villa Velha, but came into conflict with the natives and Caramurú, a shipwrecked Portuguese

[9] Alphonse de Beauchamp, *Histoire du Brésil* (Paris, 1815), I, 112-113, 116-119; Robert Southey, *History of Brazil* (London, 1822), I, 41-44.

[10] Andrade, 21; Beauchamp, I, 120-121.

[11] Andrade, 21-22; Southey, I, 45-46.

[12] Robert Grant Watson, *Spanish and Portuguese South America* (London, 1884), I, 156-157; Southey, I, 50-52.

sailor who became a patriarchal chief of considerable influence in that region.[13]

The four other captaincies of Espirito Santo, Porto Seguro, Ilheos, and Pernambuco were successful. Pero Tourinho was fortunate to make an alliance with the Tupiniquin Indians who lived in his grant of Porto Seguro, and his captaincy flourished. In the captaincy of Ilheos peace was also made with the natives who lived on friendly terms with the colonists. Pernambuco, toward the north of Brazil, with the beautiful Olinda as its capital, was particularly strong after the Cahetés were conquered inch by inch and an alliance made with the Tobayares.[14] Two attempts to colonize Maranhão, which had been given to the historian, João de Barros, failed absolutely.[15] Later in the eighteenth century Maranhão was split into the four captaincies of Maranhão, Pará, Piauhy, and Ceará, and six others were established in the south.[16]

Power of the Donatarios in Brazil

The charters granting the captaincies outlined the relations between the grantees and the crown. The agreements between the proprietors and the monarch were very simple and the powers of the feudatories very broad—somewhat more than viceregal. The *donatario* who administered a captaincy was frequently called captain-general; ten of the governors of the more important provinces could correspond directly with the home government, while the others were subordinate to the captains-general of first rank. In the seventeenth and eighteenth centuries at the head of the captaincy was a governor also called captain-

---

[13] Beauchamp, I, 140-161.
[14] Andrade, 22-26; Southey, I, 46-54.
[15] Beauchamp, I, 133-137.
[16] The later captaincies were:

Captaincy	Capital	Donatario
13. São Paulo	São Paulo	Antonio de Albuquerque Coelho de Carvalho
(Separated from Rio de Janeiro in 1710)		
14. Minas Geraes	Villa Rica (Ouro Preto)	Lourenço de Almeida
(Separated from São Paulo in 1720)		
15. Goyaz	Goyaz	Marcos de Noronha, Conde dos Arcos
(Separated from Minas Geraes in 1744)		
16. Matto Grosso		Antonio Rolim de Moura, Conde de Azambuja
(Separated from Goyaz in 1748)		
17. Rio Grande do Sul (1727)		Francisco de Brito Peixoto and João Magalhães
18. Santa Catharina (1737)		José da Silva Paes

See Andrade, 107; Herman G. James and Percy A. Martin, *The republics of Latin America* (New York, 1923), 72-73.

general and viceroy.[17] With the land granted to a *donatario* went perpetual power; he was to collect sailors to man his fleet and colonists to
take to America. The *donatarios* possessed an almost unlimited civil
and criminal jurisdiction; they had to see that justice was properly
administered and hear appeals from any part of the captaincy. They
could not, however, condemn persons to death or mutilation; the accused could appeal to the supreme court of Lisbon, the *Casa do Civil*
and later to the *Casa da Supplicação*. The seigniors oversaw all branches
of public administration within their districts: they were the commanders of the military forces; they could make concessions, found
cities, grant municipal privileges, appoint justices, governors, *alcaldes,*
and military commanders; they supervised finances and presided over
a tribunal of accounts; and they could dispose of the land which they
conquered. At first they were permitted to reduce the pagan Indians to
servitude and to sell a certain number of them in the market of Lisbon.
Proprietors could not have their rights and jurisdiction taken away from
them before the king heard the charges and investigated them. They
enjoyed all powers of taxation and collection of tribute, both ecclesiastical and temporal. Omitting the customs duties, from which the colonists in the captaincies, but not the people in Lisbon, were exempt, the
taxes consisted of the royal fifth *(quinto)* of precious metals and stones,
and one-tenth of all products for the church. From those contributions
the *donatario* received one-tenth of the fifth and another one-tenth from
the ecclesiastical *dizimo* or tithe.

The Portuguese government exercised over the captaincies a kind of
protectorate, with limited control, in return for the payment of a few
taxes, a monopoly over Brazilwood, the right of instatement when a
proprietor of a captaincy was changed, coinage, and diminishing the
territory in the grants. The intention was to keep each fief undivided
in the same family, but the heir always needed royal confirmation when
he succeeded to the estate. Because of such liberal concessions the greed
of the feudatories could not be prevented. Nevertheless, they might be
deprived of their fiefs if they neglected their development and defense,
if they committed a crime, or if their heirs were malignant. On account of the scant surveillance of the mother country Varnhagen said
that Portugal recognized the independence of Brazil before it was colonized.

---

[17] Lannoy and Vander Linden, I, 94; Robertson, 144. The governor or captain-
general residing at the capital city was ordinarily called the viceroy.

The colonists also had some rights—the protection of their lands and lives, freedom from all export duties to any Portuguese territory, free commerce among the captaincies if they did not associate with foreigners, and freedom from punishment because of the crimes of predecessors. These rights were put into ordinances and additions were made to them when necessary.[18] Only too frequently the Portuguese seigniors who were ambitious for higher elevation and fortune regarded their vast domains as lands for exploitation. They thought they could easily subject the ignorant natives without peril, but they were disappointed in this since the savage tribes resisted them in bloody combats.[19]

The Governor-General in Brazil

Many defects arose in the government of Brazil under the *donatarios;* the captaincies did not prosper as much as expected because of the lack of resources of the grantees, the original division of the land had been made on too large a scale for intercommunication, and each governor or captain-general exercised a separate authority which he often abused, thus encouraging local anarchy. It was impossible for the far-distant mother country to control the separate governments of the captaincies. The property, honor, and life of the colonists were at the mercy of the great seigniors, and the helpless people groaned under their tyranny. Even when they were honest the *donatarios* were pitiful failures; those in northern Brazil had almost all come to grief by 1550. The complaints of the colonists reached the ear of the monarch who deemed it necessary at last to establish a more centralized authority in Brazil in order to stop the disorder and anarchy which threatened utterly to destroy the newly acquired dependency. The advantage of sugar cultivation began to be realized, and the king wanted to prevent France from obtaining a hold on Brazil. It was known that French adventurers were trying to win over the natives of the coast.[20] In 1548 Luiz de Góes wrote from São Vicente to John III: "Come to our assistance: shortly this country will be lost to the French, who will then take Africa and will proceed to attack Portuguese Asia. . . ."[21] King John turned his

---

[18] Lannoy and Vander Linden, I, 88-89; Varnhagen, Visconde de Porto Seguro, *Historia geral do Brasil antes da sua separação e independencia de Portugal* (Rio de Janeiro, n. d.), I, 144-148; Oliveira Lima, *Formación histórica de la nacionalidad brasileña,* 59-60; Beauchamp, I, 113-115; Keller, 134.

[19] Beauchamp, I, 115.

[20] Beauchamp, I, 179-181.

[21] James, 71-72.

imperial glance upon the colony and came to its rescue, since he hoped
to increase the commerce between Brazil and his kingdom and he knew
that the concessions given in America did not benefit the crown. He,
therefore, decided in 1548 to revoke the powers of the *donatarios* and
appoint a governor-general with full civil and criminal authority.

Thomé de Souza, a noble of the royal house who had won his laurels
in Africa and India, was the fortunate candidate for that important
position. He was ordered to establish a new administration in Brazil
and to erect a city in the bay of Todos os Santos capable of braving the
fierce attacks of the natives and the aggression of Europeans. This city
was to be the seat of government and the capital of Portuguese America.
Souza, accompanied by the famous Jesuit Manuel da Nobrega, arrived
in the Captaincy of Bahia in 1549, where he was welcomed by Caramurú
and a treaty of peace was made with the natives. The new capital of
São Salvador was located in Bahia, which was called the Royal Captaincy. The governor-general did everything he could to regulate the
colonial government and to conciliate and civilize the Brazilians.[22] A
happy choice, indeed, was that of Souza, for his administration was a
landmark in Brazilian history.

The feudal *donatarios,* or their legal heirs, were left in possession of
their grants temporarily, but ultimately their estates reverted to the
crown and the captaincies were broken up. The captaincy system was,
like that of the chartered company, only a government makeshift. It
was too artificial and prevented natural development. Under it, settlement started in several distinct and disconnected centers; these feeble
centers were exposed to many perils and they prevented the formation
of a few strong populous nuclei in localities favorable for development.[23]

At the same time that Souza became governor-general of Brazil, a
commissioner-general of finances, a chief justice *(ouvidor geral),* and a
captain-major for coast patrol and defense were appointed.[24] Philip III
provided for final judicial authority in Brazil to be vested in two supreme courts *(relação).* One was established in 1609 at Bahia and the
other at Rio de Janeiro in 1751. In first instance justice was rendered
by municipal judges appointed by the local administrators or by the
royal judges.[25]

---

[22] Beauchamp, I, 181-188; Andrade, 31-32; James, 76. The captaincy of Bahia
had been purchased by the crown from the original *donatario.*

[23] Keller, 135.

[24] James, 73.

[25] Lannoy and Vander Linden, I, 94-96.

Brazilian municipal government was very similar to that of Portuguese towns. The towns were administered by a municipal council (*senado da camara*), the powers of which were determined by the charter which created the town. At first the municipal functionaries were elective, but, as in Portugal, the elections soon became a pure formality. In reality the town officials were designated by the royal functionary who presided over the elections and confirmed the magistrates chosen. Under those conditions the colonies had few electoral rights. In 1696 in Pernambuco and Rio de Janeiro, the two most important towns of Brazil, the town council consisted of the governor, the royal judge (*de fóra*), and the *ouvidor*. In spite of dependence upon royal officials, the municipal councils played an important part in colonial history and their power exceeded what was ordinarily given in municipal affairs. During the long maritime wars of the seventeenth century, when communication with the mother country was weak, those councils took complete charge of the local government of the colony. The council of a capital city might even temporarily fill a vacancy in the governorship. Pombal limited the powers of municipal councils because some of the members became too much interested in advancing their own affairs.

No rigid caste system existed in Brazil. In theory Creoles were admissible to the same offices as the Portuguese, but in practice only a few held high positions because the applicants had to be graduates of the University of Coimbra. The governorship was always reserved for a Portuguese, and, on account of the military functions of the governor-general, men of military experience were preferred. Governors and royal judges only served three years as in Portugal; however, the astute minister Pombal appointed them for an indefinite period. In three years they could not come to know their colony, or enter into the best relations with their subordinates, or learn the duties of their office.[26]

It is well known that the governors-general who succeeded the great Souza could never approach his standard of administration. Most of them were weak, and the man who immediately succeeded him, Duarte da Costa, probably did more harm than good in Brazil because of his violent and autocratic disposition. It took the energetic Mem de Sá to save Brazil after that critical period.[27] The system of government did not work very well in such a huge domain, therefore, in 1572 Brazil was divided into two captaincies-general, that of the north with Bahia

---

[26] Lannoy and Vander Linden, I, 96-99; James and Martin, 77.
[27] Andrade, 35 ff. and 41 ff.; James, 78, 80.

the capital and that of the south with Rio de Janeiro the capital. Antonio Salema was put at the head of the southern captaincy, while Luiz de Brito e Almeida, who had previously been appointed governor-general of Brazil, was permitted to govern the northern part beginning at Porto Seguro. Although the two governors worked in harmony and were worthy of their appointment, the divided forces caused inconveniences, it was difficult to defend the territory, more resources were required, and the administration was not energetic. In 1577 the king consequently united the whole country under Almeida as governor-general.[28] Under its Spanish rulers Brazil was again separated into two governments, but the experiment only lasted five years (1608-1613), after which the country was again administered by a governor-general or viceroy.[29]

The decadence of Portugal affected the dependencies; in the eighteenth century there was corruption from the highest official to the humblest subordinate. After 1750 the famous Pombal stopped most of the glaring corruption, but when he fell in 1777 the Portuguese government reverted to most of the old abuses. Brazil, however, had felt the good effects of his reforms. The commercial prosperity which he brought about especially benefited the Brazilian people, the impartial administration of law gave them some idea of civic pride, and the feeble encouragement of education helped to start an intellectual awakening which scattered in Brazil the seeds of the liberal movement fermenting in Europe at that time.[30]

One of the weaknesses of colonial government was due to the absence of morality in its agents. In 1779 the Marquis of Lavradio, viceroy of Brazil, said of Brazilian magistrates: "They do not come to fulfill their term of service [three years] but to acquire the title to a promotion in Portugal. During their sojourn their only thought is to accumulate as much as they can, so as to better the condition of their families on their return." [31] The low salaries of public officials no doubt caused much corruption. The salary of the governor-general was 3,000 *cruzados,* but that of other officials was so small that it compelled them to have

[28] Andrade, 48-50; Beauchamp, I, 333 ff; Watson, I, 250.

[29] James, 93; Andrade, 63-64, 84. Up to 1640 Brazil had been governed by seventeen governors-general. The last one, Jorge de Mascarenhas, appointed by Philip IV of Spain in that year received the title of viceroy, and succeeding governors-general frequently, but not always, were known officially by that title.

[30] Thomas C. Dawson, *The South American republics* (New York, 1910), I, 393-398; Andrade, 134-135.

[31] Lannoy and Vander Linden, I, 99.

recourse to questionable means of livelihood.[32] In spite of corruption and defects in the administrative system, the achievements of Portugal in Brazil can only challenge our respect. Within three centuries the exploring nation won a territory eighty times the size of the home country and colonized and governed large portions of it.

II. Spanish Colonial Government

Spain, the pioneer nation in America, was unprepared for the responsibility thrust upon it when Columbus and the other explorers won a new world. The success of Spain was remarkable, although there were many handicaps and the task of administration was more colossal than that of imperial Rome. The nation was equal to the task because of years of experience in dealing with similar problems in the Mediterranean and in the Canaries. The colonial policy constantly grew and changed to meet local needs and, in spite of its defects, was unusually wise for that epoch. Self-government could hardly be expected because the colonization of America occurred when Spain was developing a more centralized policy. Absolutism prevailed; the sovereign was the supreme governing authority as in Spain, since the Indies were considered personal possessions of the crown. It was thought that the political organization should be exactly like that in the mother country; consequently Spanish institutions were taken to America.[33] In the course of time the attempt to keep the government of the colonies separate from that of Spain, except in so far as the king was the political superior, necessitated the creation of new institutions and new laws for the American dependencies.

Organs of Government in Spain. The India House

Some of the organs of government for administering the American colonies were located in Spain and others were in the New World. A period of experimentation and adjustment followed the conquest. It was natural that when new problems arose the sovereigns should consult certain individuals of their court concerning matters of the Indies. One of the first persons in whom they confided and who obtained the right to intervene in such matters was Juan Rodríguez Fonseca, Bishop of Burgos and Palencia. Gaspar de Grisyo, the king's secretary, also helped with colonial affairs. Fonseca's duties and those of his subordinates

---

[32] Watson, II, 114.

[33] Jerónimo Bécker, *La política española en las indias* (Madrid, 1920), 24-25.

increased until he became a virtual colonial minister, who administered the colonies for about thirty years after his appointment in 1493 to help Columbus prepare for his second voyage.[34]

A shipping organization was first needed to aid the exploring expeditions bound for America, and in consequence the India House, or *Casa de Contratación,* was definitely established in 1503 and located in Seville to meet this need. It was a kind of commercial bureau, and in the beginning it played the part of a ministry. The *casa* had two aspects : one essentially scientific, since it was a true school of navigation and cartography which acquired great renown, and the other exclusively gubernatorial and mercantile. It exercised an active vigilance over all maritime commerce and regulated the conditions under which it was carried on.[35] Its officials were to meet twice a day to transact business and sign all dispatches. Delivering letters or dispatches to captains who undertook ocean expeditions, issuing licenses for everybody who went to America and keeping foreigners from going, seeing that all merchandise was registered, determining the quantity of products to be sent to the colonies, collecting and building vessels for exploration, providing for the payment of export and import duties, inspecting the registers and cargoes of returning vessels, taking care of the royal fifth from precious metals, preventing the sale of firearms to the Indians, receiving the goods of deceased persons and trying to find the legal heirs, making arrangement for the sale of all American products, seeing that the *alcabala* was paid on the first sale, and detecting frauds of every kind— these were some of the duties of the *Casa de Contratación.*[36]

As trade with the Indies increased, new duties were given to the *casa.* In 1510 its powers in judicial matters were augmented, and in 1512 the differences between merchants, owners of vessels, and mariners who went to America could be decided summarily by judges of trade *(jueces de contratación).* These judges even took cognizance of criminal cases and other acts of violence committed during the voyages to and from the Indies, but they could not inflict the death penalty. The *casa* had a judicial tribunal consisting of a treasurer, an accountant, and a factor or commercial agent. Every person who received any injury on the voyage could appeal freely to this tribunal or before an ordinary court

---

[34] *Ibid.,* 103.

[35] José de Veitia Linaje, *Norte de la contratación de las indias occidentales* (Seville, 1672), 3; Lannoy and Vander Linden, I, 339.

[36] Antonio María Fabié, *Ensayo histórico de la legislación española en sus estados de ultramar* (Madrid, 1896), 71-74; Bécker, 87; Veitia Linaje, 7, 19, 20, 98.

of Seville.[37] From its decisions appeal went only to the Council of the Indies. Ordinarily the officers of the India House consisted of a president, a treasurer, a secretary, an agent, three judges or commissioners, an attorney, and such other ministers and officials as might be provided by law. When the work of the *casa* grew the number of its officials also increased. In 1542 it had at least eight councilors, without counting the president, who was the grand chancellor of the Indies, the fiscal who was a lawyer, two secretaries, and the lieutenant of the chancellor.[38]

Under the scientific activity of the *casa* a vast amount of geographical knowledge was collected, since ship owners and pilots had to keep a daily record of their course and a description of all places visited; this information was deposited with the pilot-major *(piloto mayor)* at Seville. Other Spanish cities were consumed with jealousy on account of the prosperity of Seville, which was the only port from which ships might be sent to America and through which colonial products might enter on the return voyage. They desired to share some of its commercial advantages. In 1550 a fierce contest began between Cádiz and Seville for the trade of the Indies; Cádiz won, for in 1717 the king ordered the India House to be transferred to that seacoast city. By this time the functions of the *casa* were largely superseded by the Council of the Indies. Its administrative and judicial duties were greatly reduced and the remaining powers applied only to a few minor civil and economic matters. Up to the end of the seventeenth century the *casa* played a very important part in helping the king to maintain his policy of commercial monopoly. Its executive functions were extensive, it participated in the practical work of administration, acted as the agent of the king in carrying out the laws of the Indies, and its jurisdiction was without territorial limits, covering all matters included in the ordinances and reaching all persons who violated the laws. The work of the *casa* was finally finished and it was abolished in 1790.[39]

[37] Rafael Antúñez y Acevedo, *Memorias históricas sobre la legislación y gobierno del comercio de los Españoles con sus colonias en las indias occidentales* (Madrid, 1794), 4; Bécker, 88-92.

[38] Lannoy and Vander Linden, I, 340-341; Bernard Moses, *The Spanish dependencies in South America* (London, 1914), I, 235.

[39] Manuel Danvila y Collado, *Significación que tuvieron en el gobierno de América la Casa de Contratación de Sevilla y el Consejo Supremo de Indias* (Madrid, 1892), 23-34. This address appears in *España en América, el continente americano . . . conferencias dadas en el Ateneo . . . de Madrid* (Madrid, 1894), III, no. 12; Antúñez y Acevedo, 6 ff.; Moses, 235-236.

The Council of the Indies

The Council of the Indies was first in rank of the special agencies in Spain for governing the colonies. A permanent body was soon needed to advise the crown and act as a supreme governmental agency in America. Therefore, in 1511 Ferdinand created the *Consejo Real y Junta de Guerra de Indias.* This is believed to be the origin of the famous Council of the Indies. As the duties increased, the personnel of the council was expanded and changes occurred in its organization, as in 1524, the date usually given for its establishment. At that time García de Loaysa, the Dominican confessor of Charles V, became its president.[40] The organization was independent of the Council of Castile and the other provincial councils, deriving its authority directly from the king. It had supreme jurisdiction over the Spanish East and West Indies, the natives who resided in them, and over all affairs that might arise from the colonies.

The members of the council were chosen from among functionaries who had rendered important services to the dependencies or who had first-hand experience in America. It was very necessary that at least some of the councilors should have practical knowledge in colonial administration in order to give their colleagues the information required to enable them to act wisely. The council thus numbered among its members many returned officials from the Indies who had seen long years of service.[41] Their ripe experience was of great value in the decision of questions of colonial policy.

The council varied in size at different times and was subject to important modifications. After it was well-organized and had functioned for some time, the most important officials were: the president, the grand chancellor of the Indies who was also a councilor, eight councilors who were lawyers, a state attorney *(fiscal),* two secretaries, a lieutenant of the grand chancellor, three reporters *(relatores),* a clerk of the chamber of justice, four accountants, a treasurer-general, two attorney solicitors, a valuator of processes *(tasador),* a lawyer and solicitor of the poor, and a chaplain.[42] At first the council had only one state attorney, but in the reign of Charles III there were two. In 1776 under the influence of José de Gálvez the membership of the council was increased to fourteen ministers, who composed three chambers, one for Mexico, one

---

[40] Danvila y Collado, 25; Bécker, 104, 106.

[41] Lucas Alamán, *Historia de Méjico* (5 vols. Mexico, 1849-1852), I, 34-35.

[42] Bécker, 105-106.

for Peru, and one for hearing judicial cases. The latter chamber consisted of superior judges *(ministros togados)* who were trained legal advocates. The councilors in the administrative chambers were called ministers of the cap and sword and did not necessarily possess legal training.[43] When the council took over the functions of the India House it added a cosmographer, a chronicler, and a professor of mathematics.[44]

The Council of the Indies was always kept busy with its many colonial responsibilities. It was intrusted with governing the overseas provinces. As an executive body it proposed for royal confirmation the names of viceroys, captains-general, judges of *audiencias,* bishops, archbishops, and other important civil and ecclesiastical officials. It confirmed minor appointments made by colonial functionaries, removed officials when it saw fit, tried and punished persons accused of maladministration, regulated political and ecclesiastical territorial divisions, exercised a general supervision in the colonies, tried to provide for the good treatment of the Indians, endeavored to maintain harmony among the subjects of the king in the dependencies, carried on active correspondence with all colonial authorities and influential private individuals, supervised and spied on all the functionaries, and from time to time sent out investigators or visitors to the Indies, who examined the general conditions and made officials render account.

The council had the supreme direction of financial and commercial matters in America. One of its principal tasks was to make the colonies as profitable as possible to the mother country, and for that reason it closely watched financial administrators. It verified receipts and examined financial reports of viceroys and captains-general. By the eighteenth century this alone required a tremendous amount of work. Therefore, two financial departments were organized in the Council of the Indies, one for North America and the other for South America; each division was presided over by a minister of the council. For defense and war some members of the council formed a Council of War *(Junta de Guerra)* which dealt with colonial military matters.

The Council of the Indies was also a judicial court of final appeal for all cases sufficiently important to come before it. Colonial-born individuals living in Spain had to bring all their suits to it, and cases from the *Casa de Contratación,* certain ecclesiastical ones, and those from the highest colonial courts might be appealed to it. It exercised original

---

[43] Herbert I. Priestley, *José de Gálvez* (Berkeley, 1916), 17-18.
[44] Bécker, 108.

jurisdiction in matters relating to *encomiendas* of Indians, the annual income of which exceeded one thousand dollars. It also reviewed decisions in cases of *residencia* of officials who were subject to that form of judicial examination. The council was a legislative body which made the laws for Spanish America covering almost every phase of colonial activity. In all legislative matters no decision could be rendered except by a two-thirds vote.[45] The laws, decrees, ordinances, and pragmatics were later collected in the monumental *Recopilación de leyes de los reinos de las indias.* This constituted a code distinct from the laws of Spain which was one of the most remarkable pieces of colonial legislation ever compiled.

In 1714, under the Bourbons, the Council of the Indies was reorganized. Its duties were then restricted to hearing cases in litigation and other purely judicial affairs. It was not to issue decrees, dispatches, and other governmental orders, and its two secretaries (created in 1715, one for Peru and the other for Mexico) were not to send them to the colonies. The king himself took charge of everything that was executive or legislative in character, and created a ministry to which the council was subordinate. After this the sovereign sent out his orders to America through his ministers only, or *por la via reservada.* The influence of the council disappeared under the Bourbon policy of centralization, since the ministers regulated colonial affairs.[46] The council became one of the accessories of state, and in 1773 announcement was made that it was ended; but it still survived for some years longer. It was suppressed in 1809, then restored in 1814 by Ferdinand VII. When the Constitution of 1812 was reëstablished in 1820 this council and all the others were closed; it was revived in 1823 and lasted until 1834, when it fell for the third time.[47] It came into existence again in 1851 under the name of *Consejo de Ultramar,* was extinguished in 1854,[48] and revived in 1858 when two more ministers were added to it. However, it never functioned as before.[49]

---

[45] Lannoy and Vander Linden, I, 341-343; Moses, 234; Bécker, 106-107; Juan de Solórzano y Pereyra, *Política indiana* (Madrid, 1629-1639, 1930 ed.) vol. IV, *lib.* v, *cap.* xv-xviii; *Recopilación de leyes de los reinos de las indias* (Madrid, 1841), I, *lib.* ii, *tít.* ii; *lib.* v, *tít.* xiii.

[46] Priestley, 16-17; Lannoy and Vander Linden, I, 343-344; Alamán, I, 36; Danvila y Collado, 36-39.

[47] Danvila y Collado, 42, 45-46.

[48] José María Antequera, *Historia de la legislación española desde los tiempos más remotos hasta nuestros días* (2nd. ed., Madrid, 1884), 485. Antequera says the council was suppressed in 1812 instead of 1809 as Danvila y Collado states.

[49] Danvila y Collado, 46.

Spanish Organization in America

The machinery of government in America was very simple at first. Nevertheless, as new problems arose it became more complicated. Columbus, the first Spanish authority in the New World, was declared viceroy and captain-general of all lands which he might discover. He organized municipal governments and appointed local officials; with him were two treasury officials to regulate finances and guard the king's rights. In 1511 judges of appeal were created and thus the first *audiencia* or supreme court came into existence in Santo Domingo. Before the viceroyalties were inaugurated, its president was at the same time governor and captain-general. At the end of the colonial period there were twelve *audiencias* in Spanish America. When the exclusive administration of the *audiencia* proved to be a failure the first viceroyalty was established in Mexico in 1535. Three other viceroyalties were created later: that of Peru in 1542 because of the serious disturbances in that country; New Granada in 1718 owing to the quarrels among the judges of the *audiencia* and the rebellion of the governor of Cartagena, Diego de los Rios, against the supreme court; and that of Buenos Aires in 1776 as a barrier against Portuguese illicit commerce.[50] The more remote districts were organized as captaincies-general, of which there were six in the eighteenth century.[51] The *audiencia* districts were subdivided into *gobiernos* or governments, *corregimientos* or regions presided over by *corregidores,* and *alcaldías mayores* over which officials called *alcaldes mayores* were placed. The good results from the organization of the viceroyalties, which held for one nation such a vast extent of territory for almost three centuries, more than justified the venture.

The Viceroys

The viceroy was the highest representative of the absolute sovereign in the colony. One man, a powerful personage, was needed to govern kingdoms so far from Spain, one to whom the vassals in those remote provinces might go for assistance and from whom they might ask all which they hoped for from a king. The authority of the viceroy was

---

[50] Bécker, 51ff. According to Bécker, 45 and 48, and Antequera, 477, the twelve *audiencias* were Santo Domingo (1511) officially declared in 1526, New Spain (1527), Panama (1535), Lima (1542), Guatemala (1543), Guadalajara (1548), Santa Fé de Bogotá (1549), Charcas (1559), Quito (1563), Manila (1583), Chile (1609), and Buenos Aires (1661).

[51] The captaincies-general were Caracas or Venezuela (1773), Havana (1777), Puerto Rico, Guatemala, Santiago de Chile (1778), and the Philippines. See Lannoy and Vander Linden, I, 348.

almost supreme during the first half of the sixteenth century, but time and circumstances modified the extent of his power. He might do and order all that the monarch could do if he resided in America, and all the ceremonies provided for kings in the royal chapel were to be observed for the highest executive in the dependency.[52]

The viceroys were for the most part efficient men who tried to perform faithfully the trust placed in them, and some deserve to be ranked with the great administrators of all ages. In the sixteenth century they were carefully chosen, experienced men, who had already won distinction in the royal service; in the next century military viceroys were preferred; and in the following centuries the kings grew careless in the selection of these exalted authorities. The policy of advancing worthy governors or captains-general to the position of viceroy was followed in the later period. Promotion from one viceroyalty to another was frequent. Early viceroys had no fixed term, but served practically for life. Later the term was limited to six and then to three years, although it could be extended.[53] When a viceroy died in office the *audiencia* served until the next one arrived, but in the later seventeenth century the archbishop filled the office temporarily.[54] The viceroy's salary was 30,000 ducats for Peru and 20,000 for Mexico in the seventeenth century.[55] By the middle of the next century the salary was doubled and even trebled.[56] At the end of his term a viceroy was required to submit a detailed report to his successor for his guidance. These *instrucciones* and *memorias,* as they were called, provide some of the most valuable source material for the workings of the Spanish colonial system.

The power of early viceroys exceeded that of later ones, since they

---

[52] Charles François Croix, Instrucción que dejó . . . á su sucesor Don Antonio Bucarely y Ursua, Mexico, Sept. 1, 1771, *AGI* (Archivo General de Indias), 88-5-13; Montesclaros to his successor, 1615, *Colección de documentos inéditos, relativos al descubrimiento, conquista y organización de las antiguas posesiones españoles de América y Oceania* (Madrid, 1864-1884), VI, 189. This work will be cited hereafter as *Documentos inéditos . . . de indias.* See also Antequera, 484.

[53] Lillian Estelle Fisher, *Viceregal administration in the Spanish American colonies* (Berkeley, 1926), 4 ff.

[54] *Pliegos de mortaja* were letters sent by the king to a designate who should succeed a deceased viceroy. Antonio Xavier Pérez y López, *Teatro de la legislación universal de España é indias* . . . (Madrid, 1791-1798), XXVIII, 554-555.

[55] *Recopilación, lib.* iii, *tít.* iii, *ley* 72.

[56] Alamán, I, 44; Vicente Riva Palacio, *México á través de los siglos* (Barcelona, 1888-1889), II, 790; Manuel Rivera Cambas, *Los gobernantes de México* (Mexico, 1872-1873), I, 388; Niceto de Zamacois, *Historia de Méjico* . . . (Barcelona and Mexico, 1877-1882), V, 579; Gabriel Avilés, *Memoria del Virrey del Perú* (Lima, 1901, Carlos Romero ed.), appendix ix.

had to meet many new problems and emergencies in a country with a very indefinitely organized political system. It took several months before the king could be informed of a particular event and several more to receive an answer from him. In the meantime the viceroy had to decide what to do. The sovereign tried to legislate on every possible subject, but even then there were always many administrative details which the innumerable royal instructions could not cover. The widest latitude was permitted in the time taken by viceroys to obey their instructions and the royal decrees.[57] Kings themselves sometimes allowed measures to be ignored by the viceroys when they seemed contrary to the public welfare. Doubt often arose as to the interpretation of royal decrees and naturally executives did not enforce them until further information was obtained.[58]

A system of checks and balances was finally worked out, as was the case in the English colonies, to curtail the powers of the viceroys. Too much initiative on the part of colonial executives was always regarded by the king with suspicion and frequently he refused to approve their measures.[59] The ever-increasing volume of royal decrees deprived them of their initiative. The Spanish viceroys, not always scrupulous representatives of the royal power, were always conscious of the royal *audiencias* as a counterpart to their authority. These august bodies, in addition to their judicial functions, exercised a supervision over the behavior of the executive.[60] The *real acuerdo*, or viceregal council, likewise was a check upon the authority of the viceroy, but not in the same degree as the the governor's council in the English colonies.[61] A wise executive always submitted matters to the *acuerdo* and learned its opinions, but he might act as he thought best.[62] Various officials exer-

[57] Rivera Cambas, I, 487; Velasco to Monterey, *Documentos inéditos . . . de indias,* IV, 422-423.

[58] Montesclaros to his successor, *Documentos inéditos . . . de indias,* VI, 207; Rivera Cambas, I, 123; Palata to Monclova, 1689, *Memorias de los virreyes que han gobernado el Perú* (Lima, 1859), II, 40-41; El Conde de Revillagigedo, *Instrucción reservada . . .* (Mexico, 1831), articles 284-286.

[59] *Documentos inéditos . . . de indias,* XVIII, 20-21; Croix, Instrucción que . . . dejó, *AGI,* 88-5-13; Andrés Cavo, *Los tres siglos de Méjico . . .* (Jalapa, 1870), *Suplemento de Bustamante,* article 72, pages 357-358.

[60] *Documentos inéditos . . . de indias,* XI, 59-61, XVIII, 118, and XXV, 542-543; *Recopilación, lib.* ii, *tít.* xv, *ley* 36.

[61] Zamacois, V, 45-46; *Recopilación, lib.* iii, *tít.* iii, *ley* 45.

[62] *Documentos inéditos . . . de indias,* XXIII, 424; Palafox to his successor, 1642, *Documentos inéditos ó muy raros para la historia de México* (Mexico, 1905-1911), VII, 32, 69-70; *Memorias de los virreyes que han gobernado el Perú,* I, 288.

cised a restraining influence on the viceroy. The *fiscal* reported to the king everything relative to the treasury discussed or decided in the *acuerdo*.[63]

After 1776 the regent, a kind of chief justice of the *audiencia,* while he relieved the busy viceroy of some of his duties, at the same time decreased his powers and made him a mere honorary presiding officer of that tribunal.[64] The visitor-general, a direct representative of the king with unusual powers who was sent to investigate conditions in the colonies, was another effective check upon the actions of the viceroy. The most famous of these special officials was José de Gálvez. Careless executives always dreaded the coming of a visitor, and relations between the two officials were not always the best.[65] The *residencia* was the principal means employed by the king to keep viceroys and other officials under royal control. At the expiration of their term of service all functionaries had to undergo an official investigation of their conduct during incumbency. Even this rigid instrument for keeping officials in the straight and narrow path of duty lost much of its effectiveness because of the possibility of rich and powerful viceroys bribing the judges of *residencia* to overlook their misdeeds.[66]

The viceregal functions as they developed before the establishment of the intendancies in 1786 were generally grouped under four divisions. The first included the civil, political, and economic administration; the second the supervision of the royal treasury and its branches; the third the use and conservation of the royal patronage; and the fourth the duties of the office of captain-general.[67]

In the first department the executive was assisted by an assessor who gave him legal advice and by a secretariat which worked out all the cumbersome details of government; nevertheless his responsibilities were tremendous. Issuing instructions to governors and subordinates, making minor appointments, distributing lands and granting titles to them, overseeing the sale of public lands, promoting colonization, founding

---

[63] *Documentos inéditos . . . de indias,* XIX, 91-92.

[64] Bécker, 62-63. For a detailed account of the duties of regents see the royal instruction to those officials, June 20, 1776, in José María Zamora y Coronado, *Biblioteca legislación ultramarina* (Madrid, 1844-1846), V, 297-306.

[65] Solórzano y Pereyra, IV, *lib.* v, *cap.* x, *art.* 19; *Instrucciones que los virreyes de Nueva España dejaron á sus sucesores* (Mexico, 1867), 252.

[66] Revillagigedo, *Instrucción reservada,* article 140; Jorge Juan and Antonio de Ulloa, *Noticias secretas de América* (London, 1862), part II, pages 255 ff.

[67] Croix, Instrucción que . . . dejó, *AGI,* 88-5-13; *Instrucción que los virreyes de Nueva España dejaron á sus sucesores,* article 26, page 10.

new towns and cities, taking the census, superintending public works of all kinds, keeping order in the capital and elsewhere, settling disputes between municipal organizations, checking food profiteers, regulating prices, providing for public storage granaries, beautifying towns and cities, repairing damages from earthquakes, taking precautions against fires, regulating the department of public health, selling public offices to efficient persons, protecting the Indians, insuring the prompt delivery of mails, presiding over public functions, and improving the morals of the people—these were some of the numerous administrative duties of a viceroy.[68] The promotion of industries not prohibited in the New World—agriculture, mining, limited manufacture, and commerce—came under this department.[69] The viceroy also exercised some rather important judicial powers. Assisted by his assessor and an *auditor de guerra,* a kind of special military adviser, he took cognizance of Indian and military cases in first and second instances. As president of the *audiencia* until 1776 he was not a mere presiding officer. He enforced the laws, determined what affairs belonged strictly to civil administration and which matters were within the jurisdiction of the *audiencia,* saw that crimes were punished justly, decided questions of competency of jurisdiction between ecclesiastical and civil tribunals, and had a general vigilance over all courts.[70]

As superintendent of the treasury the executive exercised supervision over the whole financial system of his viceroyalty. In this second department his consuming ambition was to increase the revenues to the highest amount possible in order to win royal approval. In cases of emergency he made extraordinary expenditures with the advice of his council. He issued orders to the subtreasuries, protected precious metals coming from the mines to local depositories, dispatched the treasure to Spain, settled disputes among treasury officials, determined the amount of money to be coined, controlled the different monopolies and many divisions of finance, and collected forced loans when necessary.[71] Serious financial problems were always submitted to the *junta de real hacienda,* a special committee of finance, over which the viceroy presided.

The third department of the royal patronage was considered very

---

[68] For the details see Fisher, *Viceregal administration in the Spanish American colonies,* 51-93, 305-335. After 1590 Mexican viceroys also governed the Philippines. Lannoy and Vander Linden, I, 359 ff.

[69] Fisher, *Viceregal administration in the Spanish American colonies,* 108-129.

[70] *Ibid.,* 131-181.

[71] *Ibid.,* 94-108.

important since it was the chief agency for the promotion of the faith and the dissemination of civilization in America. As vice-patron of the church the viceroy aided the clergy in their missionary enterprises, supervised the building and repair of churches and convents, inspected ecclesiastical licenses, oversaw the collection of ecclesiastical revenues, settled religious disputes, attended provincial church councils, collected unauthorized papal bulls and sent them back to Spain, expelled the Jesuits, and exercised certain formalities in church elections. He was also the vice-patron of institutions of learning, institutions of charity, and hospitals. In this capacity he had the widest opportunity to encourage all the beneficent and gracious influences of colonial life.[72]

The viceroy as captain-general was the supreme military leader in his viceroyalty. Spain regarded the functions of this department as very essential. Therefore, many military men were chosen chief executive. As captain-general a viceroy acted on his own initiative more than under any of his other titles, since there were many emergencies to meet and strategic measures to be employed in Indian wars and foreign attacks. The preservation of peace in the country and the external defense of the viceroyalty were his principal duties. The captain-general was the commander-in-chief of the army which he supervised in a general way. He enlisted men for the army and armadas, supplied arms and munitions, provided barracks and military hospitals, made some military appointments, founded *presidios* to protect the distant frontiers, and carried on exploration.[73]

The Audiencia

The judges of the *audiencia* were the next highest functionaries to the viceroy, except when occasionally there was a visitor-general in the country. The *audiencia* was a powerful organ of the monarchy, since its jurisdiction was administrative as well as judicial. In the absence of the viceroy it also controlled military affairs. It had the privilege of corresponding directly with the king and the Council of the Indies to whom it was immediately responsible.[74] Very early the *audiencia* began to act as an advisory council of the viceroy who was bound to consult it on certain important matters. It issued *autos,* or court decisions, for local needs; this, with the ordinances and proclamations of

---

[72] *Ibid.,* 182-251.

[73] *Ibid.,* 251-304.

[74] *Documentos inéditos* . . . *de Indias,* VI, 266, and XI, 59; *Recopilación, lib.* ii, *tit.* xv, *ley* 40; Solórzano y Pereyra, IV, *lib.* v, *cap.* iii-viii.

the executive, constitutes the nearest approach to law making in colonial Spanish America.[75]

The *audiencia* was the highest judicial authority in the viceroyalty, for there was no appeal from it except in serious criminal matters and in civil suits involving large sums; such appeals went to the Council of the Indies.[76] It was primarily a court of appeal for deciding civil and criminal judicial matters. Cases in first instances were left to the proper local authorities and were not handled by the *audiencia*.[77] Individuals had recourse to the *audiencia* from the viceroy's decisions except in military matters which went to the *junta de guerra* of the Council of the Indies, and the executive could not prevent such appeals.[78]

The visitation of the provinces was another important duty of the *audiencia;* this was usually of an administrative nature and was to be made every three years throughout the entire district. The viceroy might require more frequent visitations, since the judges who went out on these trips of inspection were expected to help the busy executive in his administrative work and collect the information which he needed.[79] The visitation of treasury officials was also intrusted to these judges, but in that work they were sometimes subject to corruption.[80] Judges of commission (*pesquisidores*) were sent out by the *audiencia* or the viceroy to investigate special crimes or violations of laws.[81] The powers of the *audiencia* increased still more when a viceroy died; at that time the senior judge (*oidor*) performed all the duties of an executive until the next one arrived.[82] The members of the *audiencia* enjoyed great prestige and received large remunerations, but they were

---

[75] *Recopilación, lib.* ii, *tít.* i, *leyes* 33-34; *Memorias de los virreyes que han gobernado el Perú,* I, 17, 269.

[76] *Recopilación, lib.* v, *tít.* xiii, *ley* 1.

[77] *Ibid., lib.* ii; *tít.* xv, *leyes* 66-67, 70; *lib.* v, *tít.* iii, *ley* 1.

[78] *Ibid., lib.* ii, *tít.* xv, *leyes* 35, 43; *Instrucciones que los virreyes de Nueva España dejaron á sus sucesores,* article 35, page 70; Azanza, Instrucción sobre las provincias de la Nueva España . . . April 29, 1800, MS. num. 17, p. 18; Solórzano y Pereyra, IV, *lib.* v, *cap.* xiii, *art.* 41.

[79] *Documentos inéditos . . . de indias,* XI, 5-17; XVIII, 92-93, 192-193, 516-517; XXIII, 464, 526-530. See also *Recopilación, lib.* ii, *tít.* xxxi, *ley* 1; *lib.* ii, *tít.* xxxi, *leyes* 2-3, 20, 29.

[80] *Recopilación, lib.* ii, *tít.* xxxi, *ley* 22; *Instrucciones que los virreyes de Nueva España dejaron á sus sucesores,* 253.

[81] *Recopilación, lib.* ii, *tít.* xv, *leyes* 117, 176; *lib.* vii, *tít.* i, *leyes* 1-2, 11. See also *Documentos inéditos . . . de indias,* VI, 266.

[82] *Recopilación, lib.* ii, *tít.* xv, *leyes* 46-48.

required to keep aloof from all local interests.[83]   The *audiencias* varied in size, those of Mexico and Lima usually numbered fourteen members, including the fiscals, but the smaller tribunals had only four or five judges and one fiscal.   At the eve of independence the Mexican *audiencia* had seventeen members.[84]

Provincial Government

The provincial governments were headed by *adelantados,* captains-general, and governors.   Until the establishment of the intendancies they were the highest officials over divisions of territory which today correspond to states.   The title of *adelantado* was given only to a discoverer or pacifier of a new region not previously included under the jurisdiction of the viceroy or of an *audiencia.*   That official performed all the functions of a governor and was directly subject to the Council of the Indies.[85]   He disappeared quite early after the period of exploration ended.   Captains-general possessed both civil and military power and were usually placed over distant or frontier provinces.   When the chief administrative officer within one of the main political divisions possessed merely civil authority he was known as a president and the territory under his charge a presidency.   The later governors were general administrators of subdivisions of the presidencies and captaincies-general.   They were subordinate to the viceroy even when appointed by the king, yet in the distant provinces they had almost independent authority in purely local matters and occasionally refused to obey the executive.   The *corregidores* and *alcaldes mayores* were judicial and administrative officers of districts and municipalities, who took over many of the administrative duties of the governor.   Since their salary was low, their positions offered many temptations, and gross corruption became the rule.[86]

Municipal Government

Municipal government was more or less organized after the Spanish model.   At first there was a little freedom and opportunity for self-

[83] Fisher, *Viceregal administration in the Spanish American colonies,* 142 ff. For more details concerning the *audiencia* see Charles Henry Cunningham, *The audiencia in the Spanish colonies* (Berkeley, 1919).   This author is the chief authority on the colonial *audiencia.*

[84] Priestley, 61-62; Alamán, I, 49; *Recopilación, lib.* ii, *tít.* xv, *leyes* 3, 5.

[85] *Documentos inéditos . . . de indias,* VIII, articles 69, 87, pages 508, 513; *Recopilación, lib.* iv, *tít.* iii, *leyes* 14, 15, 25.

[86] Fisher, *Viceregal administration in the Spanish American colonies,* 81-86; Hipólito Villarroel, Enfermedades políticas, MS. i, pt. ii, p. 27 ff; *Memorias de los virreyes que han gobernado el Perú,* III, 365-78.

government through the *cabildos* or town councils. The *cabildo* usually consisted of from six to sixteen *regidores* or aldermen, at first appointed by the conqueror who laid out the town but later elected by the citizens, who in turn chose the *alcaldes* or justices. This was the only trace of self-government in colonial Spanish America; even this privilege was limited when the *cabildo* became a closed corporation and membership in it was purchased or inherited. The *cabildo* finally became entirely self-perpetuating and the election a mere farce. The functions of the *cabildo* and town officers were legislative, executive, and judicial. Everything they did depended upon the approval of the governor or the superior official over the province. Their powers were consequently limited, the development of democracy checked, and councilmen grew so careless in doing their work that viceroys and governors found it necessary to assume many of their duties.[87]

Frontier Institutions

The chief frontier institutions were missions and *presidios*. The missions served two purposes—to Christianize the natives and to hold the far-distant provinces for Spain. Along the northern frontier of Mexico the plan was adopted of erecting a chain of missions to keep out aggressive foreigners. The missions needed protection, consequently *presidios* were established for this purpose. *Presidios* also served to secure the routes of travel, protect communication with rich mines, and check invasions of hostile Indians. The *presidio* consisted of a fort and a number of soldiers and their families who lived there and developed farms in the district around the military post. In South America there was never any need for the establishment of a line of *presidios* to protect a frontier as in New Spain. Although less numerous in the southern hemisphere, the *presidios* were larger than in Mexico; sometimes they consisted of five hundred or nine hundred soldiers as in Callao and Buenos Aires. In North America along the northern frontiers there were many more *presidios*. However, they were smaller with from fifty to one hundred soldiers in them. Frequently important towns grew up around *presidios*.

The Intendant System

A revolutionary change occurred in the government of the Spanish colonies late in the eighteenth century on account of the rampant corrup-

---

[87] Fisher, *Viceregal administration in the Spanish American colonies*, 66-69; Villarroel, Enfermedades políticas, MS. ii, pt. iii, pp. 14-15; *Instrucciones que los virreyes de Nueva España dejaron á sus sucesores*, arts. 82, 87, pp. 21-22; *Memorias de los virreyes que han gobernado el Perú*, VI, 83.

tion, lax obedience to royal and viceregal orders, oppression of the Indians, the overworked viceroys, and the general administrative inefficiency. The viceroyalties were divided into intendancies of unequal size, twelve in Mexico and smaller numbers elsewhere. An intendant-general, who took charge of financial matters, resided in the capital of the viceroyalty. The old type of governors disappeared, intendant-governors were placed over each intendancy, and subdelegates replaced the *alcaldes mayores*. The total number of officials was greatly reduced, expenses were cut down, the revenues became more ample through more efficient collection, and the viceroy was relieved of some of his multitudinous duties.

The functions of intendants in the four departments of government—justice, general administration, finance, and war—were not only numerous, but detailed and exacting. In the first division, with the aid of their assessors, they took cognizance of cases relating to the royal treasury and the financial system of the viceroyalties. They exercised the administrative duties of the former governors, whom they superseded. In the fourth department they had charge of all military finances and the provisioning of the troops. Intendants communicated directly with the king, but they were still subordinate to the viceroy. The Ordinance of Intendants for New Spain, issued in 1786, was a remarkable piece of legislation; it was an attempt to recodify the laws of the Indies and make them work.

The intendant system on the whole caused improvement in colonial government, but it could not have permanent good results since the enactment did not provide for self-government or greater well-being through an evolutionary process of placing responsibility upon the colonial himself. In spite of defects, however, it removed some of the most noticeable abuses, infused new life and vigor into a corrupt and decadent colonial administration, and made it possible for Spain to hold its vast American possessions for another half century.[88] On the eve of independence, corruption had again crept into the administration, old abuses reappeared, Spain itself had pitifully declined and could no longer give the colonies an energetic government, and the colonies grew dissatisfied. It was only a matter of time until sparks of rebellion appeared and efforts were made to sever Spanish control.

---

[88] For more details see Lillian Estelle Fisher, *The intendant system in Spanish America* (Berkeley, 1929); *Real ordenanza para el establecimiento é instrucción de intendentes de ejército y provincia en el reino de la Nueva España* (Madrid, 1786).

III. Conclusions

In the foregoing discussion it has been seen that the Portuguese sovereigns did not spend much time on the study of the political administration of their colonies. The machinery of government for Brazil was never as complicated as that for Spanish America. Although equally corrupt and inefficient, it was not as rigid or harsh as the Spanish system. Local administration was never based on any well-thought out plan, but was transplanted from the mother country without regard to local conditions. Efforts were made by Spain to work out a centralized system for Brazil during the union of the Iberian kingdoms; nevertheless, they proved illusory because the captains-general were in fact independent of the governors-general, who were invested also with the title of viceroy. When Spanish rule ended in Portugal, the Lisbon authorities did not continue the centralizing policy. Each captaincy still remained an administrative unit, directly and individually subject to the orders of the metropolis; each one lived its own life more or less independent of its neighbors very much as did the English colonies of North America.

Spain, on the other hand, developed a very elaborately centralized governmental system—one of the most remarkable colonial systems ever in existence. Many checks and balances were applied to keep officials faithful to their trust. In the course of time the complications of administrative functions, the minute and multitudinous instructions of the mother country, and the endless red tape employed inevitably detracted from the vigor and progressiveness of the colonial system. Obedience to royal and viceregal orders consequently grew lax, and corruption increased. By the middle of the eighteenth century reforms were very much needed. Therefore, the intendant system was inaugurated. A gubernatorial system that had become corrupt and inefficient was thus regulated for a short time in the interest of efficiency and higher financial return, but the intendancies did not score the complete triumph expected. If the reform had provided for the elements of self-government, it might have served to establish a real and permanent union between Spain and Spanish America. To other hands and to other minds, unfortunately, the political evolution of Spanish America was to be intrusted.

SELECTED BIBLIOGRAPHY

I. Portuguese Colonial Government

This material may be found in the Bancroft Library and the University of California Library.

Andrade, María G., *Resumo da historia do Brasil* (New York, ed. of 1920).
  A good résumé of the history of Brazil, which is in the nature of a very much condensed textbook.

Beauchamp, M. Alphonse de, *Histoire du Brésil* (3 vols. Paris, 1815).

Book IV and part of Books V and VI of volume I treat the establishment of the captaincies and the first attempt at governmental organization in Brazil.

Dawson, Thomas C., *The South American republics* (2 vols. New York, 1910).

Vol. I, pp. 295-400, gives a brief and very readable account of the Portuguese colonial system as applied to Brazil.

James, Herman G., *Brazil after a century of independence* (New York, 1925).

Chapters II and III have very helpful sections on the organization of the government of Brazil.

James, Herman G. and Martin, Percy A., *The republics of Latin America* (New York, 1923).

Chapter II gives a very general account of colonial government in Brazil.

Keller, Albert Galloway, *Colonization* (New York, ed. of 1908).

Contains a brief account of Portuguese colonial government in the Orient and in Brazil.

Lannoy, Charles de and Vander Linden, Herman, *Histoire de l'expansion coloniale des peuples européens* (2 vols. Bruxelles, 1907-1911). Chapter III, pt. I, of vol. I, is especially good for colonial administration in the Portuguese colonies.

Leroy-Beaulieu, Paul. *De la colonisation chez les peuples modernes* (2 vols. Paris, 1902).

Chapter II, vol. I, treats the early attempt to organize a govermnental system in the Portuguese colonies.

Martins, Oliveira. *Historia de Portugal* (Lisboa, 1893).

A brief history of Portugal which has been translated into English by Henry Morse Stevens. One chapter deals with the Portuguese in the East and another with them in Brazil.

Oliveira Lima, Manoel de. *Formación histórica de la nacionalidad brasileña* (Madrid, 1918).

A very helpful book in which is given a good, brief, and concise account of the powers and duties of the *donatarios* of the captaincies.

Oliveira Lima, Manoel de. *The evolution of Brazil compared with that of Spanish and Anglo-Saxon America* (Edited by Percy A. Martin. Palo Alto, 1914).

A good comparative study of the governments of Brazil, Spanish America, and the English of North America.

Robertson, William S., *History of the Latin American nations* (New York, 1922).

This work contains a brief and very general account of Portuguese colonial government in Brazil.

Southey, Robert, *History of Brazil* (3 vols. London, 1822).

One of the older English accounts of the Portuguese in Brazil. Vol. I treats the early political organization.

Varnhagen, Visconde de Porto Seguro, *Historia geral do Brasil antes da sua separação e independência de Portugal* (2 vols. Rio de Janeiro, n. d.).

This is one of the older works which gives a complete account of the colonial history of Brazil. The formation, extent, and administration of the captaincies are discussed in detail.

Watson, Robert Grant, *Spanish and Portuguese South America* (2 vols. London, 1884).

In vol. I there is a brief old-time account of the organization of the government of Brazil.

Whiteway, R. S., *The rise of Portuguese power in India, 1497-1550* (Westminster, 1899).

A very complete account of Portuguese administration in India.

II. Spanish Colonial Government

A. *Documents and Manuscripts*

Avilés, Gabriel de Avilés y del Fiero, Marqués de, *Memoria del virrey del Perú* (Lima, 1901, Carlos Alberto Romero, ed.).

A description of the duties and work done by Viceroy Avilés of Peru.

Azanza José de, Instrucción sobre las provincias de la Nueva España; dada por el Exmo. Sr. D. José de Azanza á su sucesor . . . á 29 de Abril de 1800.

A manuscript account of the work done by Viceroy Azanza in Mexico.

Colección de documentos inéditos, relativos al descubrimiento, conquista y organización de las antiguas posesiones españolas de América y Oceanía (42 vols. Madrid, 1864-1884).

This collection contains many of the instructions of the viceroys to their successors.

Croix, Charles François, Marqués de, Instrucción que dejó . . . á su sucesor Don Antonio Bucarely y Ursua.

Mexico, Sept. 1, 1771, *AGI* (Archivo General de Indias), 88-5-13. A very helpful manuscript showing the powers and duties of a viceroy.

Documentos históricos del Perú en las épocas del coloniaje después de la conquista y de la independencia hasta la presente (10 vols. in 6, Lima, 1863-1877).

Some of these documents throw light upon colonial administration.

Documentos inéditos ó muy raros para la historia de México (35 vols. Mexico, 1905-1911).

This collection contains several of the instructions of the viceroys to their successors and much material concerning the duties of viceroys.

Documentos para la historia del virreinato del Río de la Plata (3 vols. Buenos Aires, 1912-1913).

In these documents may be found material on colonial government for the viceroyalty of Río de la Plata.

Instrucciones que los virreyes de Nueva España dejaron á sus sucesores (Mexico, 1867).

This volume contains ten of the instructions of the viceroys of Mexico to their successors, two royal instructions to the viceroys, and some of the correspondence of the viceroys.

Memorias de los virreyes del Perú (Lima, 1896, José Toribio Polo, ed.).

This volume contains the instructions of two viceroys to their successors.

Memorias de los virreyes que han gobernado el Perú (6 vols. Lima, 1859).

These volumes consist of long and very detailed instructions of ten viceroys to their successors. They contain very excellent material on viceregal administration.

Pérez y López, Antonio Xavier, *Teatró de la legislación universal de España é indias, por orden cronológico de sus cuerpos, y decisiones no recopiladas* (28 vols. Madrid, 1791-1798).

Helpful for ascertaining the functions of institutions.

Real ordenanza para el establecimiento é instrucción de intendentes de ejército y provincia en el reino de la Nueva España (Madrid, 1786).

In this document the power and duties of intendants are described.

Recopilación de leyes de los reinos de las indias (4 vols. 4th ed., Madrid, 1841).

The monumental code of laws for the Spanish American colonies.

Revillagigedo, Juan Vicente Güemes Pacheco de Padilla Horcasitas y Aguayo, Conde de, *Instrucción reservada que el conde de Revilla Gigedo, dió á su sucesor*

en el mando, Marqués de Brancifirte sobre el gobierno de este continente en el tiempo que fué su virrey (Mexico, 1831).
An excellent and detailed account of the work and duties of an eighteenth century viceroy.

Solórzano y Pereyra, Juan de, *Política indiana* (5 vols. Madrid, 1629-1639. Edition to 1930. Francisco Ramiro de Valenzuela, editor).
One of the chief authorities on Spanish colonial government.

Villarroel, Hipólito. *Enfermedades políticas que padece la capital de esta Nueva España en casi todos los cuerpos de que se compone; y remedios, que se la deben aplicar para su curación si se quiere que sea util al rey y al público. Tomos 4.*
A manuscript descriptive of political conditions late in the eighteenth century in Mexico.

B. *Secondary Works*

Alamán, Lucas, *Historia de Méjico desde los primeros movimientos que prepararon su independencia en el año de 1808 hasta la época presente* (5 vols. Mexico, 1849-1852).
Chapters II and III of vol. I deal with the Spanish colonial system in a general way.

Antequera, José María, *Historia de la legislación española* (2nd ed., Madrid, 1884).
Very helpful for tracing the legal phases of Spanish institutions.

Antúñez y Acevedo, Rafael, *Memorias históricas sobre la legislación y gobierno del comercio de los Españoles con sus colonias en las indias occidentales* (Madrid, 1797).
An authority on Spanish commerce and its regulation.

Bécker, Jerónimo, *La política española en las indias* (Madrid, 1920).
A helpful book on Spanish policies in the Indies.

Cavo, Andrés, *Los tres siglos de Méjico durante el gobierno español hasta la entrada del ejército trigarante; obra escrita en Roma por el padre D. Andrés Cavo de la Compañía de Jesús. Publicado con notas y suplemento en 1836 por el licenciado D. Carlos María de Bustamante* (Jalapa, 1870).
This book throws light on the working of the Spanish administrative system.

Cunningham, Charles Henry, *The audiencia in the Spanish colonies* (Berkeley, (1919).
The chief authority on the colonial *audiencia*.

Danvila y Collado, Manuel, *Significación que tuvieron en el gobierno de América la Casa de Contratación de Sevilla y el Consejo Supremo de Indias* (Madrid, 1892).
A good essay on the India House and the Council of the Indies.

Dawson, Thomas C., *The South American republics* (2 vols. New York, 1910).

Fabié, Antonio María, *Ensayo histórico de la legislación española en sus estados de ultramar* (Madrid, 1896).
The early laws governing the colonies are given in this work.

Fisher, Lillian Estelle, *The intendant system in Spanish America* (Berkeley, 1929).

Fisher, Lillian Estelle, *Viceregal administration in the Spanish American colonies* (Berkeley, 1926).

Groot, José Manuel, *Historia eclesiástica y civil de Nueva Granada* (5 vols. 2nd ed., Bogotá, 1889-1893).
In this work an account is given of Spanish administration in New Granada.

Jones, O. Garfield. "Local government in the Spanish colonies as provided by the Recopilación," in *The Southwestern Historical Quarterly*, XIX, 65-90.

Juan, Jorge and Ulloa, Antonio de, *Noticias secretas de América* (London, 1826).
    A good description of conditions in colonial Spanish America in the late eighteenth century.
Lannoy, Charles de and Vander Linden, Herman, *Histoire de l'expansion coloniale des peuples européens* (2 vols. Bruxelles, 1907-1911).
    Chapter III, pt. II, of vol. I treats Spanish colonial administration.
Leroy-Beaulieu, Paul, *De la colonization chez les peuples modernes* (2 vols. Paris, 1902).
    Chapter I of vol. I treats the Spanish colonial system.
Moses, Bernard, *The Spanish dependencies in South America* (2 vols. London, 1914).
    Chapters XIV and XV treat Spanish political administration in the colonies.
Priestley, Herbert Ingram, *José de Gálvez* (Berkeley, 1916).
    An excellent and authoritative account of Spanish colonial administration.
Quesada, Vicente G., *Historia colonial argentina* (Buenos Aires, 1915).
    This work treats colonial government in Argentina.
Riva Palacio, Vicente, editor, *México á través de los siglos* (5 vols. Barcelona, 1888-1889).
    A most useful work for all governmental agencies in Mexico.
Rivera Cambas, Manuel, *Los gobernantes de México* (2 vols. Mexico, 1872-1873).
    A good work for biographical sketches and the work of Mexican viceroys.
Roscher, Wilhelm George Freidrich, *The Spanish colonial system* (New York, 1904. E. G. Bourne, editor).
Veitia Linaje, José de, *Norte de la contratación de las indias occidentales* (Seville, 1672).
    Veitia Linaje is the author *par excellence* for the early work of the *Casa de Contratación*. The work was translated by Captain John Stevens, London, (1700?), under the title of *Spanish rule of trade to the West Indies*.
Zamacois, Niceto de, *Historia de Méjico desde sus tiempos más remotos hasta nuestros días* (18 vols. Mexico, 1877-1882).
    In this work a general account of colonial government in Mexico may be found.
Zamora y Coronado, José María, *Biblioteca legislación ultramarina* (6 vols. Madrid, 1844-1846).
    Very good for colonial legislation.
Zinny, Antonio, *Historia de los gobernantes de las provincias argentinas* (3 vols. Buenos Aires, 1872-1882).
    In this work a general account of colonial administration in Argentina is given.

CHAPTER EIGHT

THE CHURCH IN COLONIAL SPANISH AMERICA

By J. Lloyd Mecham

I. The Origins and Nature of the *Real Patronato de las Indias*

NEVER before or since did a sovereign with the consent of the pope so completely control the Catholic Church as did the Spanish kings in their American possessions. This union of altar and throne, known as the *real patronato de las Indias,* was unique and had no precedents in the history of church and state relations. For this reason an appreciation of the historic rôle played by the church in the Spanish Indies is impossible without a preliminary discussion of the origins and nature of *real patronato.*

Since the royal control over the church in the Indies was largely independent of that of Spain proper, although more complete, there is no need to introduce this discussion with a description of the *real patronato español.*[1] The patronage of the Indies was based largely, although not necessarily exclusively, on the following pontifical grants: (1) the bulls *inter cætera* and *eximæ devotionis* of May 4, 1493 by which Pope Alexander VI conceded to the Catholic Kings dominion of the Indies and the exclusive privilege of Christianizing the Indians; (2) the bull *eximæ devotionis* of November 16, 1501, published by Alexander VI, in which he granted to the Spanish crown the tithes in the Indies; and (3) the bull of Julius II, *universalis ecclesiæ,* July 28, 1508, which conceded to the kings of Spain the right of universal patronage over the Catholic Church in the Indies. The general nature of these grants will be examined.

Immediately after the return of Columbus from his first voyage of discovery, the Spanish rulers appealed to the pope to recognize their title to the newly discovered lands. Because of the zeal of the Catholic King to extend Holy Faith to the Indies, and the manifest impossibility of the pope assuming the task of proselytism, Alexander VI, an Aragonese by birth, was willing to oblige. By the bull *inter cætera,* May 4, 1493, he conceded to the Catholic Kings and their heirs, title to the new

---

[1] For the *real patronato español,* see Matías Gómez Zamora, *Regio patronato español é indiano* (Madrid, 1897), and for a short discussion, J. Lloyd Mecham, *Church and state in Latin America* (Chapel Hill, 1934), 1-12.

lands. The grant was conditioned by the obligation to Christianize the
natives.[2] This exclusive right of evangelization, it is held, conveyed to
the Spanish kings authority to exercise jurisdiction in all matters relating to ecclesiastical government in the Indies. Moreover, whatever
power over America the pope may have claimed, with or without valid
ground, was transferred to the Spanish Crown by the bull.[3]

By the bull *eximæ devotionis,* also published on May 4, 1493, Alexander VI conceded to the Spanish sovereigns whatever powers and
privileges had been given by other pontiffs to the kings of Portugal in
their new overseas dominions. The most notable of these earlier grants
to the Portuguese was that of Pope Calixtus III, in 1456, which conceded "complete spiritual jurisdiction" to the grandmaster of the Order
of Christ.[4] It does not appear that the Spanish kings actually enjoyed,
by virtue of this bull, the extravagant prerogatives which it seemed to
convey. Were that the case, subsequent grants of the patronage would
scarcely seem necessary.

The next pontifical concession which extended the jurisdiction of
the Spanish sovereigns over the church in the Indies was the bull *eximæ
devotionis,* published by Alexander VI on November 16, 1501. The
most significant feature of this bull was the grant to the crown of all
the tithes in the Indies. In return for this concession the king was
obligated to defray from the royal treasury all expenses of the church.[5]
This made the colonial church economically dependent on the crown, at
least in theory. It was a departure from the practice in Spain where
the clerical income was free of royal control.[6]

Although it would appear that the bulls of 1493 and 1501 conveyed
to the Spanish Crown full patronal rights over the church in the Indies,
Pope Julius II, successor to Alexander VI, seemed reluctant to recognize the concession of the very essence of patronage, that is, the right
of presentation or nomination to ecclesiastical benefices. When, in 1504,
Julius II published a bull providing for the erection of episcopal sees

---

[2] Francisco Javier Hernáez, *Colección de bulas, breves, y otros documentos relativos á la iglesia de América y Filipinas* (2 vols. Brussels, 1879), I, 12-14.

[3] Antonio Joaquín de Ribadeneyra, *Manuel compendio del regio patronato indiano* (Madrid, 1755), 58-60.

[4] Hernáez, I, 15-16. The grandmastership was later united with the Crown of
Portugal.

[5] Gómez Zamora, 299-301.

[6] J. Bécker, *La política española en las indias* (Madrid, 1920), 67; Rafael Altamira y Crevea, *Historia de España y de la civilización española* (4 vols. Barcelona,
1900-1914), II, 486.

in Española, he failed to mention either the royal right of presentation or the royal claims to the tithes.[7] King Ferdinand, who firmly believed in the patronal concession by the earlier bulls, would not allow the sees to be founded, and demanded that the pope make an unqualified grant of the right of patronage. Finally, Julius II acquiesced, and on July 28, 1508, in the famous bull *universalis ecclesiæ*, he conceded to the kings of Spain and their successors the patronage for all the ecclesiastical benefices in the New World.[8] "The bull of Julius II," writes an authority on the subject, "conceded to the kings of Castile, tacitly the right of universal patronage, perfect and complete." [9]

The bull of 1508 is generally regarded as the principal source of *real patronato de las Indias*. Whether it be true that it conveyed the original grant of patronage, whether it merely recognized and reconfirmed rights bestowed by earlier grants, or whether patronage was enjoyed exclusive of papal grant as a consequence of sovereignty, it matters not, for after 1508, and throughout the colonial period, the Spanish kings enjoyed uninterrupted exercise of the right of patronage.

So rapidly did the crown develop a policy of control and administration over the patronage that by the end of the reign of Philip II the civil control over the church was thoroughly consolidated. Subsequent history added nothing to its essential nature, except perhaps to strengthen and expand even more the royal control. In 1753 a concordat between Pope Benedict XIV and Ferdinand VI defined the exact nature of *real patronato español* concerning which there was much doubt and controversy. But because of the above-mentioned specific pontifical concessions there was no question regarding the nature of *real patronato de las Indias*. Consequently the concordat expressly excepted the church in America from the scope of its terms, "there having been no controversy concerning the nominations by the Catholic Kings of archbishops, bishops, and vacant benefices in the Indies." [10]

The legal source of *patronato de las Indias* has been the subject of controversy for several centuries. There are two schools of thought on the subject: the canonists and the regalists. The canonists hold that patronage, particularly the right of presentation, is a spiritual right and

---

[7] *Colección de documentos inéditos relativos al descubrimiento, conquista, y organización de las antiguas posesiones españolas de ultramar* (Madrid, 1894), II, 88-93.

[8] Hernáez, I, 24-26.

[9] Gómez Zamora, 292.

[10] Dalmacio Vélez Sarsfield, *Relaciones del estado con la iglesia en la antigua América española* (Buenos Aires, 1889), 42.

its original source can only be the will of the pope. The most extreme canonists contend that the sole title of *real patronato de las Indias* was the papal grant contained in the bull *universalis ecclesiæ* of 1508. A more moderate view is that the patronage in the Indies was conceded by various bulls, the most important being those of 1493, 1501, and 1508.[11] A simple statement of the canonists' theory is the following: "The pontificial concessions of the *patronato de las Indias* to the kings of Spain was a simple, juridic, unilateral act produced *motu proprio*. There were no concordats, contracts, or decrees, but only direct concession from the Holy See."[12] In support of the canonists' position it should be noted that the Catholic Kings recognized their privileges as having been derived from papal concessions. Indeed, they were accustomed to petition the pope for "concessions." The bull of 1508, for example, did not "recognize" patronage as already being existent, but the pope expressly "conceded" it.

The regalists hold patronage to be laical in source. They contend that the right proceeds from the acts of founding, constructing, and endowing churches. Philip II was the first king who held that patronage derived its validity from any other source than papal grant. In a letter of instruction to his viceroy in New Spain he wrote, June 1, 1574:

> "As you know, the right of ecclesiastical patronage belongs to us throughout the realm of the Indies—both because of having discovered and acquired that New World, and erected there and endowed the churches and monasteries at our cost, or at the cost of our ancestors, the Catholic Kings; and because it was conceded to us by bulls of the most holy pontiffs, conceded of their own accord."[13]

It is to be noted that even Philip based patronage, in part, on papal concessions.

The regalist position was defended by several notable writers af the colonial period. The great legal commentator, Solórzano y Pereyra, whose *Política indiana* was first published in 1647, defended regalism. During the Bourbon period of the eighteenth century when royal supremacy was reinvigorated, regalism was supported by several able writers, the greatest of these being Ribadeneyra. His *Manuel com-*

---

[11] Gómez Zamora, 292.

[12] Faustino J. Legón, *Doctrina y ejercicio del patronato nacional* (Buenos Aires, 1920), 186.

[13] N. A. N. Cleven, *Readings in Hispanic American history* (New York, 1927), 250.

pendio del patronato indiano is the outstanding work on the *patronato de las Indias*. Ribadeneyra held that the right of patronage inhered in the crown for the following reasons: (1) the acquisition of the Indies by the Spanish Crown; (2) the royal ownership of the lands in the Indies; (3) the construction, endowment, and foundation, at royal expense, of churches, monasteries, and benefices; (4) the redemption by the kings of Spain of lands held by infidels; and (5) the concession of privileges by the pope.[14] Ribadeneyra, like Philip II, recognized patronage as being based, in part, on papal grant.

This difference of opinion regarding the legal source of the patronage became a subject of far more than mere academic interest when the Spanish colonies asserted their independence. The new republics, desirous of maintaining control over the church such as had been exercised by the kings of Spain, regarded the patronage as being inherent in territorial sovereignty. Consequently, as the political successors of the Spanish rulers in America, they pretended to exercise the patronage, now on a national basis. Thus it was to the interest of the new states to support the regalistic theory. The pope and the church, on the other hand, contended that the patronage was a personal grant to the kings of Spain, was not a part of sovereignty, and was not transferrable. Conflict between the two theories strongly influenced the subsequent histories of the Latin American republics.

What was the nature, extent, and significance of the *real patronato de las Indias?* Most of this information can be secured by reference to the great compilation of laws for the Indies known as the *Recopilación de leyes de los reynos de las indias*. The incorporation in this collection of civil law of so many matters ordinarily a part of canon law illustrates not only the remarkable subordination of the spiritual to the temporal authority, but also the fusion of the two powers.

The most important feature of the patronage of the Indies was the right of presentation. To the king belonged the privilege of presenting candidates for all ecclesiastical offices, high and low. The nominations for prelates, like archbishops, bishops, and abbots, were presented to the pope for canonical installation. The candidates for lesser benefices were presented to the respective prelates to be installed in ecclesiastical office, and to be given canonical instruction.[15] Since it was impossible for the king to make all appointments in the Indies, Philip II, in 1574,

---

[14] Ribadeneyra, 70-72.
[15] *Recopilación de leyes de los reynos de las indias* (2 vols. 2nd ed., Madrid, 1756), *lib.* i, *tít.* vi, *leyes* 24, 36.

instituted the practice of vice-patronage. He reserved to himself the right to nominate archbishops, bishops, abbots, and dignitaries of cathedral chapters such as canons and *racioneros*. To the viceroys, captains-general, presidents, and governors, as vice-patrons, was delegated the power to make in the king's name nominations to lower ecclesiastical benefices. The practice of the vice-patronage, instituted by Philip II, remained substantially unaltered until the establishment of the intendancy system in the later eighteenth century. By the law of 1782 the intendants were made vice-patrons in the districts they administered, leaving the viceroy as the vice-patron in the metropolitan province alone. In 1795, when the intendancy system was modified, the intendants were allowed to retain the vice-patronage in their capacity as sub-delegates of the viceroys.[16]

One of the principal reasons for the creation of the vice-patrons was the desire to check the tendency of the prelates to violate the patronage by appointing priests *(curas)* and *doctrineros,* or those priests who ministered to the spiritual needs of the Indians.[17] A law of April 4, 1609, granted to the viceroys the power of appointing to parishes and *doctrinas;* but as for the higher ecclesiastical offices, the viceroy had to send the names of candidates to the king for his appointment. The prelates were required to present a list of three names *(terna)* to the viceroy from which he could select one. The viceroy's choice, however, was usually limited to the first name on this list. Viceroy Palafox of New Spain said it was dangerous not to select the first. Other viceroys also testified that, to avoid conflict, they selected the first name on the *terna*.[18] Throughout the colonial period the kings constantly cautioned their viceroys to see that the requirements for the provision of curacies were not violated. A method of evasion mentioned by a Peruvian viceroy was the presentation of three clerics for three places, each name being placed at the head of one of the lists, thus leaving the viceroy no choice.[19] The duties and authority of the vice-patrons extended, of course, beyond the right of presentation. Their other duties will be discussed in connection with other aspects of the patronage. Viceroy Marquina declared that the authority of the viceroy was made evident

---

[16] Lillian E. Fisher, *Viceregal administration in the Spanish American colonies* (Berkeley, 1926), 182-184.

[17] Vélez Sarsfield, 157.

[18] Fisher, 215-216; *Memorias de los virreyes que han gobernado el Perú en tiempo del colonaje español* (6 vols. Lima, 1859), IV, 27.

[19] *Memorias*, IV, 362.

by his functions as vice-patron, which caused him to be distinguished even by the ecclesiastics, who were always objects of veneration among the populace.[20]

The king insisted that ecclesiastical vacancies should be filled without delay. Due to the fact that there was necessary delay in receiving papal confirmation of appointments to prelacies, a period of one year was allowed. But the parochial benefices and *doctrinas* could not be vacant longer than four months.[21] It often happened that prelates presented by the king would assume the government of their sees before receiving papal bulls of institution. Although this practice was common, it was opposed by canon law and the popes never acquiesced in it. After presentation by the king or his vice-patron, the act of installation in ecclesiastical office and the bestowal of canonical instructions was a purely spiritual function; although before being consecrated the prelates had to swear an oath of allegiance to the king and promise to observe his patronal rights.[22]

Not only did the crown control the appointment of clerics but it also controlled their removal and resignation. Prelates were not allowed to remove lesser clergy from office without informing the viceroy of their reasons for so doing. The causes for all removals had to be sent to the king in order that he might know whether just measures had been taken. Resignations likewise were required to be reported to the viceroy so that he might be informed regarding the sufficiency of reasons for allowing them.[23]

Coincident with the royal right of controlling the presentation and removal of ecclesiastics, was that of controlling their movements. Only those licensed by the king could go to the New World. All names had to be approved first by the Council of the Indies. Foreign priests and monks were usually denied license. Before embarkation the officials of the *Casa de Contratación* carefully scrutinized the licenses. Expenses of transportation were paid from the royal treasury.[24] When the ecclesiastics arrived in America their movements were carefully controlled. They did not go where they pleased but where the viceroy or governor directed them. The vice-patrons were ordered to keep a careful check

---

[20] Fisher, 184.

[21] *Recopilación, lib.* i, *tít.* vi, *leyes* 19, 35, 48.

[22] *Ibid., lib.* i, *tít.* vii, *ley* 1.

[23] *Ibid., lib.* i, *tít.* vi, *leyes* 38, 51.

[24] *Ibid., lib.* i, *tít.* vi, *ley* 31; *lib.* i, *tít.* xiv, *ley* 19; *Doc. Inéd.,* xi, 63-64; J. Pérez Lugo, *La cuestión religiosa en México* (Mexico, 1927), 7-8.

on all religious, lay and regular, and to report their numbers and location. No priest was allowed to preach without a license from the viceroy. An attempt of the Jesuits in New Spain to preach without licenses precipitated a bitter quarrel with Viceroy Palafox.[25] When an ecclesiastic wished to return to Spain, the permission of the viceroy or even the pope did not suffice. No one could leave the Indies without special permission from the king.[26]

Not only did the crown control the movements of the clergy, but also their communications with the pope. A law of the patronage provided that all bulls, briefs, and rescripts of the Roman Curia which contained laws, rules, or general statements should be presented to the Council of the Indies before publication in America. Another law provided that no bull or brief which did not have the *pase* of the Council of the Indies was to be obeyed.[27] The reason for the royal exercise of the exequatur over papal documents was the desire of the king to prevent the pope from trespassing the limits of his divine office by legislating in purely temporal matters. It was a measure designed to maintain royal supremacy. The right of the *pase* was nothing unique in patronage, for it was based on ancient Spanish law. It was ineffectively enforced in America, for there were numerous instances of bulls and briefs being circulated without the permission of the Council of the Indies. According to Ribadeneyra only six bulls were retained by the council in over two centuries.[28] When the king refused to allow a bull to pass, the pope was never given reasons for its rejection. The king's attorney merely asked the pope to retain the document.[29] Thus, by the exercise of the right of exequatur, the king interposed himself between the pope and the church in America.

Next to the right of presentation, the control of the tithes was perhaps the most important feature of *real patronato*. The papal bull of 1501 conceded, as has been noted, all the tithes of the Indies to the Catholic Kings on condition that they endow churches and provide the clergy with proper support. This bull imposed on the Spanish kings the obligation of meeting all the expenses of the church in the New World. It made the church fiscally dependent on the royal control. Although the crown was free to devote to other purposes the income

[25] Fisher, 190.
[26] *Recopilación, lib.* i, *tít.* vii, *ley* 36; *lib.* ii, *tít.* xii, *leyes* 16, 18.
[27] *Ibid., lib.* i, *tít.* xiv, *ley* 41; *lib.* i, *tít.* vii, *ley* 50.
[28] Ribadeneyra, 226-229.
[29] Vélez Sarsfield, 86.

from the tithes, virtually all was devoted to religious purposes. The tithes of each diocese were ordinarily divided into four parts: one part went to the bishop, one part to the cathedral chapter, and the remaining two parts were divided into nine parts called *novenos*. Only two of the *novenos* were reserved to the crown for its own uses; the other seven *novenos* went to the lower clergy, the building fund, and charities.[30]

Whenever the tithes were not sufficient to meet clerical expenses the balance was always forthcoming from the royal treasury. The royal treasury officials had charge of collecting the tithes, and it was the duty of the viceroy to see that no one escaped. The Jesuits opposed payment of the tithes claiming exemption by virtue of pontifical privilege. This exception the Spanish kings refused to recognize, yet for many years this was a subject of controversy. By royal decree of 1735 the king ordered the payment of the tithes by the Order.[31]

The curates of parishes inhabited by Spaniards were not entirely dependent on their salaries paid by the crown. They supplemented whatever income was due them with charges for the services of baptisms, marriages, burials, and special masses. These were called *derechos parroquiales*. Because these special fees were excessive, Charles V ordered the *arancales,* or fee schedules, in New Spain reduced so as not to triple the fees charged in the Archbishopric of Seville.[32] Philip II reissued this regulation, and it was later incorporated in the laws of the Indies. It was constantly violated, however, for one encounters numerous references to excessive ecclesiastical fees. Moreover, although the Indians were supposed to be exempt, the priests often charged them for services.

Another feature of the *real patronato* was the royal control over the founding of churches and the delimitation of ecclesiastical districts. No church or other ecclesiastical establishment could be erected without the consent of the civil authorities. For the building of a cathedral it was necessary that the pope issue a special bull of erection, but only when solicited by the crown. For the erection of other churches the consent of the Council of the Indies had to be secured. Since the viceroys had been careless in granting permission too freely for the construction of monasteries and convents, the king ordered, in 1593, that

---

[30] *Recopilación, lib.* i, *tít.* vi, *ley* 23; *lib.* i, *tít.* xvi, *ley* 24.

[31] H. H. Bancroft, *History of Mexico* (5 vols., San Francisco, 1883-1887), III, 134-135, 428-431.

[32] Genaro García, ed., *El clero de México durante la dominación española* (Mexico, 1906), Doc. xxii.

all such construction must receive the royal approval. If construction were undertaken without royal permission, the buildings were to be demolished without delay.[33] In defraying the costs of building churches one-third was paid from the royal treasury, one-third by the *encomenderos,* and one-third by the Indians. In reality the Indians bore the entire burden, for they provided the manual labor, and by working for the *encomenderos* enabled them to pay their share. Also, they paid tribute to the king's treasury from which the royal third for church construction was drawn.

Closely connected with the royal control over the construction of churches was that of determining the limits of ecclesiastical districts. To the king belonged the right to determine the territorial limits of the various ecclesiastical jurisdictions. It followed naturally, therefore, that disputes concerning boundaries were settled by appeal to the civil authorities. In the laying out of parishes the crown delegated the authority to the prelates who had to act in concert with the vice-patrons. According to canon law the prelates enjoyed the exclusive control over the establishment of ecclesiastical districts. There were numerous exceptions to canon law in the actual operation of the *patronato de las Indias.*

Though otherwise much restricted by the civil power, the church in the Indies was permitted to have its own courts. In each bishopric there was an ecclesiastical court made up of the bishop, the *fiscal proctor,* and the *provisor.* All ordinary cases were tried and decided by the *provisor;* the more important cases were decided by the bishop. Appeals went to the archbishop. A bull of Gregory XIII, granted on petition of Philip II, provided that ecclesiastical cases should be concluded in the colonies. This was because of the great delay which would result from appeal to the Roman Curia.[34]

The church courts tried, according to canon law, all cases dealing with spiritual matters or with the clergy. If a civil or temporal case arose between priests, or in which a layman brought action against a priest, the case was tried in the ecclesiastical court. If a priest brought action against a layman it went to a civil court.[35] The privilege enjoyed by the clergy to be tried in their own courts was known as the *fuero eclesi-*

---

[33] *Recopilación, lib.* i, *tít.* vi, *leyes* 1, 2.

[34] *Ibid., lib.* i, *tít.* ix, *ley* 10.

[35] Bernard Moses, *The Spanish dependencies in South America* (2 vols., New York, 1914), II, 222.

ástico. The *fuero* was not a distinctive feature of the *patronato de las Indias* but was a customary practice dating back to the middle ages.

The line of division between the jurisdictions of the civil and ecclesiastical courts was poorly defined. Questions of jurisdiction were decided by the viceroy. All cases that in any manner touched on the *real patronato* were tried by the civil authorities, although they seemed to be matters attached to the spiritual sphere and involving persons who enjoyed privileges which would seem to exclude them from secular authority. According to canon law, cases involving patronage, *pleitos de patronato,* belonged to the spiritual authority, but in the Indies such cases came under the original jurisdiction of the civil courts and officials.[36]

The crown, also as a patronal right, intervened in the control of church councils and synods. As provided by papal decree, dated December 6, 1610, provincial councils were to be held in the Indies every twelve years. But as a matter of fact they were held very infrequently.[37] In the early colonial period no council could meet without the consent of the king; but later the approval of the vice-patron sufficed. The councils were presided over by the metropolitan, and were attended by the bishops, canons, presbyters, and superiors of religious orders. The viceroy attended in order to see that the right of patronage was not violated. Only the archbishop and bishops enjoyed a vote. The matters usually considered in the councils pertained to morality and good conduct of the clergy, enforcement of the decrees of the Council of Trent, the better treatment of the Indians, and purely spiritual subjects. Decisions of the councils could not be executed without royal approval. The acts of the provincial councils were authoritative only for the limits of the province or archdiocese.[38]

In compliance with the provisions of the Council of Trent the bishops each year held synods composed of the clerical members of their dioceses. The acts of the synods, having been approved by the bishop, were sent to the vice-patron in order that he might determine if they were in agreement with the royal patronage. All acts which appeared to be violative of the patronage were sent to the Council of the Indies.

---

[36] *Ibid.,* II, 221-222; Vélez Sarsfield, 51-52.

[37] Gómez Zamora, 404. Four were held in New Spain, six in Peru, and three in New Granada.

[38] Moses, II, 222-224; *Recopilación, lib.* i, *tit.* viii, *ley* 6.

No synodal measure could be published without the approval of the vice-patron or the king.[39]

The regular orders, like the secular clergy, were included within the scope of the *patronato de las Indias*. The provincials or custodians of the regulars in the Indies were named by their particular generals in Europe, but these appointments had to be approved by the Council of the Indies. The provincials were required to reside in the Indies. The consent of the council was also necessary for the creation or suppression of provinces and the founding of new convents. The viceroys were supposed to watch over the construction of new convents and allow none to be erected without the king's consent. Many convents were ordered demolished when erected without license. The viceroys and other vice-patrons were kept busy supervising the monks. They were instructed to keep close watch over the regulars and note the need and quality of their work. They were often required to intervene to settle disputes. When monastic elections occurred the viceroy was required by law to be present to preserve peace and cause the constitutions of the orders to be observed.[40] The extent of royal control over the regulars was quite as comprehensive as over the secular clergy.

Patronage was made up not only of privileges but also of obligations. The Spanish kings did not shirk their responsibilities to protect and extend the faith. The desire to spread the cult was an important feature of their ecclesiastical policy. The first article in the instructions to Columbus governing his second voyage commanded him to convert the natives of the Indies to the Catholic faith.[41] A clause in the will of Queen Isabella required her heirs to perform the duty of proselytism laid upon her by the papal bulls. Charles V commanded his subjects going to the New World to reveal the Catholic faith to the Indians, and Philip II charged his Council of the Indies with the special duty of taking all necessary measures to spread the faith and convert the Indians. He also ordered his viceroys to make it their constant care to secure the preaching of the faith for the benefit of the souls of the Indians.[42] Philip II declared in 1572 to his ambassador in Rome that it was the spiritual matters concerning America which preoccupied him

---

[39] Moses, II, 224-225; *Recopilación, lib.* i, *tít.* viii, *leyes* 3, 6; *lib.* ii, *tít.* xv, *ley* 147.

[40] Moses, II, 226.

[41] Antonio María Fabié, *Ensayo histórico de la legislación española* (Madrid, 1896), 16-18.

[42] *Recopilación, lib.* i, *tít.* i, *ley* 2; *lib.* iii, *tít.* iii, *ley* 2.

the most.[43]   Numerous decrees issued in the sixteenth and seventeenth centuries designed to propagate the faith were incorporated in 1690 in the laws of the Indies. That the rapid and extensive spread of Catholicism in the Spanish Indies was due almost entirely to royal support, encouragement, and protection was a self-evident fact. In this respect the crown fulfilled its patronal obligation.

Not only the extension of the cult, but the maintenance of purity of morals and dogma was another patronal obligation which the Spanish kings faithfully observed. Evidences of moral laxity among the clergy concerned the sovereigns greatly. The laws of the Indies are replete with provisions intended to prevent or remedy scandalous conduct by the clergy. The viceroys were ordered to punish irregularities and settle religious differences. They were to help prelates in their efforts to reform inferiors, and encourage those who were distinguished in virtue and learning. Also, they were empowered to expel rebellious ecclesiastics from their viceroyalties.[44] If, despite these laws, there was gross immorality among the clergy in America, and it must be confessed that it existed, it cannot be said that the crown was blind to the evil. The laws of the Indies prove its great concern over the problem.

To preserve purity of doctrine and faith, the royal patron adopted various expedients, the most notorious of these being the Inquisition. The organization and work of the dreaded Holy Office will be discussed later. Suffice it at this place to note that the Inquisition was an adjunct of the patronage, for with its aid and control the crown performed its patronal obligation to protect the cult.

The zeal of the Spanish rulers in protecting and propagating the faith was equaled only by their insistence that the patronage, as an exclusive and imprescriptible royal right, be cherished and observed. Many writers comment that the crown regarded the *patronato de las Indias* as the most valuable of its regal prerogatives. Ribadeneyra describes the *real patronato de las Indias* as "la piedra más rica, la más preciosa Margarita de su real diadema." [45] Ferdinand the Catholic and Charles V insisted on the maintenance of all those special powers and privileges over the church which had been conferred by the popes.[46]

---

[43] Lucas Ayarragaray, *La iglesia en América y la dominación española* (Buenos Aires, 1920), 19.

[44] Fisher, 184, 206, 213.

[45] Ribadeneyra, 3-4.

[46] Roger B. Merriman, *The rise of the Spanish empire*, (4 vols., New York, 1918-1934), III, 654.

Philip II, in a *cédula* of instructions to the viceroy of New Spain in 1574, ordered the protection of the patronage in the most vigorous language.[47]

The successors of Philip II were equally zealous defenders of the patronage. Philip III in 1639 wrote to the Bishop of Cuba: "As you know, or ought to know, the said patronage is a thing which I cherish greatly, and which I cannot and ought not permit to be injured." [48] There was need for the reiterated orders to guard the patronage, for Viceroy Velasco wrote in 1604 that the viceroy had to wage perpetual warfare in Peru to defend the royal patronage. Viceroy Palafox said that the rules of patronage were very lax among the religious orders who refused to present the viceroy with three names for appointments.[49] As has been noted above the bishops were required to swear oaths to protect the patronage.

The Bourbon kings, as was to be expected, were rigorous defenders of the patronage. "They laboured with decided firmness to emancipate the royal authority from the vassalage into which it was allowed to fall to the ecclesiastical power, due to the indolence of the last sovereigns of the House of Austria." [50] Charles III stated that since he was the Vicar and Delegate of the Apostolic See, the power belonged to him to "intervene in all matters concerning the spiritual government of the Indies to a great extent, for the Holy See had not only conceded in general its authority in the affairs of the dependencies and ecclesiastical matters, but also the jurisdiction over matters other than those for which a lay person is ineligible." [51] In 1783 Charles III wrote to the viceroy of Peru, Marquis of Loreto, urging him to conserve the patronage, and let no regular or secular infringe on it. The preservation of Spanish power in America depended largely on the vitality of Catholicism and on the organization of the cult. This explains the constant preoccupation of the Spanish kings in founding churches and protecting the patronage.[52]

Such was the nature of *real patronato de las Indias.* "Royal patronage could not be more complete, more singular, and private than that

---

[47] Cleven, 250-251.

[48] Sarsfield, 46.

[49] Fisher, 207.

[50] Frances Kellam Hendricks, *Church and state in Chile before 1891* (Ph. D. thesis, University of Illinois, 1931, unpublished), 26.

[51] *Ibid.,* 29.

[52] Lucas Ayarragaray, 37.

enjoyed by the Catholic Kings in the state of the Indies." [53]   It made
the Spanish kings more than ordinary patrons; by virtue of it they exercised quasi-pontifical authority. His Catholic Majesty was a king or
Caliph of the West. The pope could really do nothing in the Spanish
American colonies without the consent and coöperation of the crown.
It was a situation without precedent "either in law or ecclesiastical
usages or customs." [54]

II. The Organization and Activities of the Catholic Church in the Indies

The organization of the church in the Indies was the same as in
Spain, although naturally it was adapted in part to meet the needs of
the new country. The clergy consisted of (1) seculars of all grades
down to the priest or *cura,* and (2) the regulars, or monks and friars
of the religious orders. The seculars and the regulars maintained their
own separate and independent hierarchial organizations.

The secular clergy were made up of two classes: (1) the upper clergy,
or the archbishops, bishops, and dignitaries of the cathedral chapters,
and (2) the lower clergy, or curates, and *doctrineros.* The archbishops,
or metropolitans, presided over ecclesiastical provinces or archepiscopal
dioceses; the bishops presided over dioceses. In each cathedral church
was a chapter composed of canons, prebendaries, and other dignitaries.
When the archbishop or bishop died the chapter governed through a
vicar. The prelates of the province, with the archbishop presiding, were
supposed to meet in council at least once every twelve years. But as a
matter of fact very few provincial councils were convened in the Indies.
The first councils met in Mexico and Peru in 1555 and 1567 respectively.
They were occupied, like most of the councils, with matters of discipline
and the evangelization and instruction of the Indians. The viceroy was
privileged to attend the councils, but only the archbishops and bishops
could vote. Diocesan councils, or synods, composed of the clergy of the
diocese, were supposed to meet annually. They were concerned with
matters of cult, discipline, and treatment of the Indians.[55]

---

[53] P. J. Parras, *Gobierno de los regulares de la América* (2 vols., Madrid,
1783), I, 3.

[54] Sarsfield, 22.

[55] See above. Charles de Lannoy and Herman Vander Linden, *Histoire de
l'expansion coloniale des peuples européens: Portugal et Espagne* (Bruxelles,
1907), 408; Carlos Navarro y Lamarca, *Compendio de la historia general de
América* (2 vols., Buenos Aires, 1913), II, 372.

The parochial work in cities and towns inhabited by Spaniards was entrusted to ordained priests called rectoral curates or rectors. These clerics enjoyed, as a consequence of their ordination, the right to administer the sacraments; they were also privileged to preach. Religious instruction and administration of the sacraments in the villages of converted Indians were entrusted to another class of ordained priests called doctrinal curates or *doctrineros*. *Rectors* and *doctrineros* were secular, although it was common for regulars to be ordained to serve as *doctrineros*. It was provided by law that *doctrinas* might be entrusted to regulars, or to curates, but not to both together. Furthermore, no monastery could be established in a *pueblo* where the *doctrina* was in charge of a *cura*.[56] The law required that in every town, Indian as well as Spanish, there should be a church, a hospital, and a school for teaching the children.[57] Needless to say this law was largely disregarded with reference to the two last-named institutions.

Episcopal organization in America dates from 1511. Queen Isabella requested the pope to grant bulls for the erection of an archbishopric and two bishoprics in the island of Española. The bulls, dated November 15, 1504, failed to convey the expected rights of patronage over the new sees and so were withheld by the crown. In the famous bull of 1508, Pope Julius II gave in to the demands of Ferdinand and created, with full patronal rights vested in the crown, a metropolitan church in Ayguacen, and two cathedrals in Maguen and Bayunen; these being early settlements in Española. Due to the rapid decline of population in the island, the bishops for the three sees were never appointed. The king, instead, asked the pope to suppress the dioceses and create only one bishop for Española and another for Puerto Rico, both to be dependent on the Archbishop of Seville. This was done by the bull *Romanus Pontifex* in August 1511.[58]

The first bishopric in Cuba was that of Baracoa created by Leo X in 1518.[59] But before the decree creating the bishopric was carried out, Santiago became the chief city in the island, and in 1522 it was made the seat of the diocese. The first Bishop of Cuba, John De Witt, never

---

[56] *Recopilación, lib.* i, *tít.* xiii, *ley* 2; Navarro y Lamarca, II, 370-371; Moses, *Spanish dependencies*, II, 228.

[57] E. G. Bourne, *Spain in America* (New York, 1904), 304.

[58] Mecham, *Church and state*, 19-20. According to Lannoy and Vander Linden (p. 408) a third bishopric was created in Concepción de la Vega in Española, but there is no record that it was actually established.

[59] Moses (*Spanish dependencies*, II, 210) says that this was the first bishopric organized in America.

went to Cuba but undertook the administration of his office in Spain. In 1523 he issued instructions for the organization of the cathedral chapter of Santiago. In 1525 he retired and the see remained vacant until 1536.[60]

The episcopal organization of the church in New Spain had its beginnings in the creation, in 1519, of the Bishopric of Cozumel, a tiny island off the coast of Yucatan. Later the limits of the diocese were extended to include the mainland districts of Tabasco, Vera Cruz, and Tlascala. In 1526 Tlascala (later Puebla de los Angeles) became the official seat of the diocese. Father Julian Garcés, a Dominican friar, was the first bishop of Cozumel and Tlascala. In 1527 the Bishopric of Mexico was created with Fray Juan de Zumárraga as the first bishop. Zumárraga was also appointed "Protector of the Indians." In 1533 the cathedral chapter of Mexico was established. It was composed of a dean, archdean, precentor, chancellor, treasurer, and ten canons. In 1534 two new dioceses, Michoacán and Oaxaca, were created. By the middle of the sixteenth century the other dioceses created in New Spain were: Nueva Galicia, Yucatan, Guatemala, Chiapas, Honduras, and Nicaragua.[61]

The number of dioceses increased rapidly in other parts of Spanish America. Under Charles V there were twenty-two plus the three archbishoprics of Mexico, Lima, and Santo Domingo, which were created in 1546-1547. Prior to the creation of the archepiscopal sees in America, the bishops were suffragans of the Archbishop of Seville.[62]

The following figures will illustrate the development of the secular hierarchy in America during the colonial period. At the end of the sixteenth century there were five archbishops and twenty-seven bishops. By 1650 the number had increased to six archbishops and thirty-two bishops.[63] At the end of the eighteenth century there were seven archbishops and thirty-five bishops as follows: (1) Archbishopric of Santo Domingo composed of the folowing bishoprics: (a) Caracas, (b) Cuba, (c) Louisiana, (d) Puerto Rico, and (e) Cuayaba; (2) Archbishopric of Mexico including the following bishoprics: (a) Puebla (Tlaxala), (b) Valladolid, (c) Oaxaca (Antequera), (d) Guadalajara, (e) Yuca-

---

[60] Moses, *Spanish dependencies,* II, 210.

[61] *Ibid.,* II, 211-213; H. I. Priestley, *The Mexican nation* (New York, 1923), 105-106.

[62] Lannoy and Vander Linden, 408.

[63] Altamira, III, 345; Lannoy and Vander Linden, 408.

tan (Mérida), (f) Durango, (g) León (Linares), and (h) Sonora; (3) Archbishopric of Guatemala, and the dioceses of (a) Concuyagua (Honduras), (b) Nicaragua, and (c) Chiapas; (4) Archbishopric of Lima, and the dioceses of (a) Arequipa, (b) Trujillo, (c) Quito, (d) Cuzco, (e) Guamanga, (f) Panamá, (g) Santiago de Chile, (h) Concepción, (i) Nueva Cuenca, and (j) Mainas (created in 1802); (5) Archbishopric of Charcas, and the dioceses of (a) La Paz, (b) Tucumán, (c) Santa Cruz de la Sierra, (d) Paraguay (Asunción), and (e) Buenos Aires; (6) Archbishopric of Santa Fé de Bogotá, and the following dioceses: (a) Popayán, (b) Cartagena, (c) Santa Marta, and (d) Mérida. In 1803 the archepiscopal see of Caracas was created to include the dioceses within the captaincy-general of Venezuela (Caracas).[64]

Ecclesiastical provinces and dioceses did not always coincide with political divisions. For example the Bishopric of Mérida, created in 1777 under the Archbishop of Santa Fé de Bogotá, included territory in both the Captaincy-general of Caracas and the Viceroyalty of New Granada. Until 1795 the Bishop of Caracas was a suffragan of the Archbishop of Santo Domingo. Due to the occupation of Santo Domingo by the French in 1795, Caracas was for eight years without a metropolitan. In 1803 it was created an archbishopric and included the bishoprics of Guayana and Mérida. This act completed the ecclesiastical unification of Venezuela.[65]

Almost all of the secular prelates were *Gachupines,* that is, Spaniards born in the Peninsula. From 1492 to 1637, of 369 bishops, not a dozen were Creoles, that is, American-born of Spanish parents.[66] Although in the later colonial period more Creoles were admitted into the ranks of the higher clergy, the American-born were definitely discriminated against even as they were in political and military positions. This constituted one of the causes of Creole discontent with Spanish rule. The ranks of the lower clergy were recruited primarily from the Creoles; also to a limited degree from the *mestizos.* Since the prelates usually came from the families of highest rank, they were generally men of ability who were often called upon to occupy important governmental positions. No less than ten archbishops of Mexico became viceroys.

---

[64] W. S. Robertson, *History of the Latin American nations* (New York, 1932), 185.

[65] Mary Watters, *A history of the church in Venezuela, 1810-1930* (Chapel Hill, 1933), 31-34.

[66] Lannoy and Vander Linden, 408, note 1.

The regulars preceded the seculars to the Indies, for since the conquest was largely a crusading-missionary movement, this was the particular province of the orders. By special decrees based upon agreements with the generals of the orders, the regulars were authorized to undertake the all-important work of converting the natives. A large number of religious soon found their way to America. Twelve friars accompanied Columbus on his second voyage. Virtually every fleet bore its contingent of missionaries. The Franciscans came to the New World in the largest numbers. After them numerically came the Dominicans and the Augustinians. After the founding of the Company of Jesus the the Jesuits became important factors in the educational and missionary fields. A large number of orders were represented in the Indies. Fifteen different orders were established in New Spain alone. The most important were the Franciscans, Dominicans, Augustinians, Jesuits, and Mercedarians. Others of less importance were: La Caridad, San Hipólito, Carmelites, and Benedictines.[67]

The heads of regular orders were generals resident in Rome. They presided over hierarchial organizations entirely independent of the secular church. Each order maintained at Madrid a commissary-general to act as a sort of intermediary between the generals and the members in the Indies. Philip II attempted to secure control of the appointment of the commissary-general, but was unsuccessful with the exception of the Franciscans.[68] At the head of the orders in each of the viceroyalties were commissaries-general. The viceroyalties, or *comisarios generales,* were subdivided into provinces with provincials at the head. Within the provinces were *custodias* under custodians. The *custodias* were usually located in distant places on the frontiers and were called "incipient provinces." Groups of missions, also on the frontiers, were organized into *presidencias* under presidents and *partidos* under *procuradores.* The mission units were in charge of missionaries. The congregations of regulars were called monasteries, or convents, and were in charge of priors and abbots. The regulars, depending on the nature of their orders or rules, were friars and monks. The friars were by all odds the most active, numerous, and influential in Spanish America.

The following description[69] of the organization of the Franciscans in Mexico, although not applicable in all its details to the other orders,

---

[67] Priestley, 100-103.

[68] Ayarragaray, 57-60.

[69] Letter of Rev. Fr. Luís de Palacios to Señor Ingeniero Don Vito Alessio Robles, Zapopán (Santuario), Feb. 11, 1933.

should be helpful, for after all, the differences in regular organization were minor. The Franciscan Observants,[70] one of the three branches of the Order, were organized into five provinces: Santo Evangelio de México, San Pedro y San Pablo de Michoacán, San Francisco de Zacatecas, Santiago de Jalisco, and San Diego de México. There were also seven autonomous houses, or *colegios,* which were not dependent on the provincials. They were *colegios apostólicos de propaganda fide* of Santa Cruz de Querétaro, N. S. de Guadalupe de Zacatecas, S. Fernando de México, S. José de Gracia de Orizaba, N. Sa. de Zapopan, La Pma. Concepción de Cholula, and N. P. S. Francisco de Pachuca. The *custodias* of Nuevo México and Tampico were dependent on the province of Santo Evangelio; Santa Catalina del Río Verde on the province of San Pedro y San Pablo, and S. Antonio del Parral on the province of San Francisco de Zacatecas. Famous missions on the northern frontiers were dependent either on provinces or *colegios.* For example, the missions of Texas depended on the *colegios* of Querétaro and Zacatecas; the missions of Nuevo León on the province of Zacatecas; the missions of Sonora and Pimería Baja on the province of Jalisco; the missions of Baja California after the expulsion of the Jesuits, part to the province of Santiago de México, and part to the *colegio* of Guadalupe de Zacatecas; and the missions of Alta California on the *colegio* of San Fernando.

The regulars became active first and were more important than the seculars in the field of spiritual conquest in the Indies. They were the real founders of the church in the Indies. It is important to note that in the early sixteenth century most of the prelacies in the secular church were held by regulars. Their great work in the missionary field and as protectors of the Indians will be described later, as will also their work in education. The regulars, even more commonly than the seculars, held high governmental positions. The Dominicans were called upon most often to serve the king as viceroys, presidents, and *visitadores.*

Although canon law prohibited regulars from holding beneficial curacies, this ban was removed due to the scarcity of secular clergy. The popes by special dispensation permitted regulars to be ordained to serve as parish priests. Although the regulars holding curacies were placed under secular control, this practice caused great friction between the regular and secular organizations, for the seculars regarded this as an encroachment on their functions. The bishops usually resisted the ordi-

---

[70] The other two branches are the Capuchins and the Conventuals.

nation of regulars as priests.[71] In 1757 Ferdinand VI terminated the practice by ordering the secularization of the curacies and *doctrinas*.[72]

The prelacies in the regular orders, as in the secular organization, were monopolized by the Spanish-born. Perhaps a majority of the friars and monks were Spanish, the balance being Creoles. *Mestizos* were not numerous, and there were unsuccessful attempts to recruit Indians. However, many Indians served as *donados*. Convents for Indian women were no more successful.[73]

The church was first a great missionary organization. The Spanish sovereigns, as has been noted, regarded nothing as being more important than the conversion of the Indians. To fulfill the obligations imposed on them by agreements with the pope, the Catholic Kings turned first to the religious orders. The earliest and most active agents in missionary work were the contingents of friars who went to the Indies with every fresh party of settlers. The Dominicans, Franciscans, and Augustinians extended their missionary efforts over large areas before the regions were formally brought under the jurisdiction of the organized church. The missionaries accompanied and even preceded the *Conquistadores* in America. They were the first to fertilize the American soil with their blood.

Since it was represented to Queen Isabella that it was impossible to attract the Indians to the Faith unless they were forced to live in settled communities, the Queen sanctioned, primarily as a missionary measure, the iniquitous *encomienda* system. The Indians were forcibly subdued and divided, in *repartimientos,* among Spanish overlords who, in return for protecting and Christianizing them, were privileged to exploit their labor. Isabella's principal concern for the Indians was the fate of their souls. Provided their souls could be saved, the fate of their bodies was of little concern.[74]

The terrible abuses of the *repartimientos,* which imposed a condition of semi-servitude on the Indians, provoked the indignation of high-minded men like Bartolomé de las Casas who joined the Dominican Order for the specific purpose of devoting his life to the protection of the natives. The foremost champions of the rights of the Indians were the Dominicans, whose zeal for the welfare of the natives obtained "such root in that brotherhood as almost to become one of the tenets

---

71 Priestley, 110.
72 Watters, 36; Fisher, 194.
73 Lannoy and Vander Linden, 410.
74 Lesley Byrd Simpson, *The encomienda in New Spain* (Berkeley, 1929), 33.

of their faith."[75] It is to the credit of the church that, although it un-
wittingly contributed to the origins of the *repartimiento* system, it became the unremitting enemy of the institution and the most disinterested
aid of the Spanish Crown in its policy of protecting the Indians. The
church also protested vigorously against the illegal enslavement of Indians. Legally only cannibals and rebellious Indians could be enslaved,
but these prohibitions were grossly violated. Bishop Juan de Zumárraga,
in a letter to the king, protested the enslavement of Indians in the Province of Pánuco: "If it is true that your Majesty has granted permission,
you should, out of reverence to God, do humble penitence for it."[76] The
missionaries preferred to work alone with the Indians and keep them
isolated from all contaminating influences of the Spaniards. This was
the idea of Las Casas and the essence of the mission system. It was
practiced very slightly, however, until after the middle of the seventeenth
century.

The missions, located on the frontiers far removed from civilized
habitations, were recruited by inducing the wild Indians to join them.
It was the royal intention that reduction to the mission system should
be by peaceful persuasion—a substitute for the evils of the armed conquest. However, force was often necessary to recruit neophytes. Kid-
napping potential converts was a regular practice. The Capuchians of
Caracas, for example, often went out with armed forces to capture Indians and restrain them within the missions. From 1707 to 1720 the
missionaries, with the aid of 1,357 soldiers, captured 1,531 Indians.[77]
Once within the missions, the Indians were guarded like prisoners.
Those who escaped were hunted down, returned, and flogged.

The missions were entirely in charge of the regular orders. The missions of a district, or *partido,* were in the control of *presidentes* (Franciscan) or *procuradores* (Jesuit). At the head of each mission was a
missionary father superior. Although the fathers were in complete
control of the mission Indians, the neophytes were allowed to choose
certain local officials of their own; but they all functioned under the
absolute rule of the missionaries. Discipline was both gentle and strict.
The Indians were controlled with a military precision and strictness.

The main buildings of the mission grouped around an open square

---

[75] Sir Arthur Helps, *The Spanish conquest in America* (4 vols., London, 1900-
1904), I, 174.
[76] J. García Icazbalceta, *Don Fray Juan de Zumárraga* (Mexico, 1881), app.
24-25.
[77] Watters, 16-17.

were: church, school, residence of missionaries, and inn for travelers. Huts of the Indians bordered streets which ran at right angles to the square. Stretching away from the buildings were the mission lands— sometimes thousands of acres. The missions were administered on a communal basis. There were common lands and common mills and stores, all worked by Indian labor. The returns went into a common fund called the mission fund. Many of the missions became very wealthy. They possessed thousands of acres of fertile land and thousands of head of cattle. Some of them also engaged in industry and trade. The competition of their agriculture and industry with private enterprise often constituted a serious problem. For example, the lay settlers of Paraguay were seriously handicapped because of the unfair competition of the near-by Jesuit missions of the Paraná. The great economic success of the missions lead to charges that the missions were operated for the benefit of the missionaries alone, and that they exploited and isolated the Indians.[78]

The purpose of the mission was not only to convert and civilize the Indians. It was also intended to serve as an outpost of empire—a frontier defensive institution. The crown relied upon the missionaries with their small military guards to hold the frontiers—to substitute for garrisons and forts. This explains why the crown was willing to grant military and financial support to the missions. But as a frontier institution the mission was not permanent and stationary; it was supposed to move by progressive steps farther and farther into the interior extending the frontiers. When the mission Indians were deemed sufficiently civilized, the missions were converted into *doctrinas,* or secularized. The missionary gave way to the *corregidor* and the secular clergy. As a matter of history the regular and routine secularization of the missions occurred very infrequently. The mission fathers usually· claimed, with truth, that the Indians were unprepared for admission into civil life. Yet a more compelling reason for their opposition to secularization was their jealousy of the secular clergy and their unwillingness to release to them the fruits of their years of toil and hardship.[79]

The greatest missionary fields were northern New Spain, Venezuela, southern Chile, and Paraguay. Along the northern frontiers of New Spain from California to Florida groups of missions were established

---

[78] Roscher, 11-16; Navarro y Lamarca, II, 374.

[79] Herbert E. Bolton, "The mission as a frontier institution in the Spanish American colonies," in the *American Historical Review,* XXIII, 42-61.

by the Jesuits and the Franciscans. The most famous of these were the Franciscan missions of Alta California founded by Father Junípero Serra in 1769. In Venezuela the Capuchin missions of Cumaná and Caracas were the most numerous. The Franciscan Observants founded missions in Guayana. In the *llanos* of the Meta, Casanare, and Orinoco the Jesuit "missions of the plains" were located. The Jesuits also had missions among the Araucanians in Chile and the Guaraní in Paraguay. The most famous of all the American missions were the latter.[80]

Originally, thirteen Jesuit missions were founded along the upper Paraná, but due to the raids of slave-hunting *Paulistas* from Brazil (1630-1631) the missions were moved down the river to the south of the Iguassú Falls. Eventually there were thirty missions in the region between the Uruguay and Paraná rivers with an Indian population of over fifty thousand. Each mission, or reduction, was in charge of two fathers, a *cura* and a *"sotacura,"* who in turn were dependent on a father superior who resided in Candelaria. The authorities to whom the father superior was responsible were the provincial and the *colegio máximo* in Córdoba del Tucumán. Like other missions, but to a more accentuated degree, the economic management of the reductions was communistic. The fundamental note in the organization of the reductions was their uniformity and the regimentation of the lives of the Indians even to the smallest details. This was because of the general character of the Jesuit régime and because of the belief of the missionaries that the Indians were in need of rigorous and constant tutelage. So great was the authority of the Jesuits over the missions that they were called the "Jesuit Republic."

By the Treaty of 1750 with Portugal, Spain surrendered seven of the Guaraní reductions on the left bank of the Uruguay. The Indians, armed and drilled by the Jesuits, resisted the transfer; but after bitter fighting the revolt was crushed. Nevertheless, the treaty was annulled and the transfer did not take place. The War of the Seven Reductions cast a shadow of doubt on the loyalty of the Jesuits and was one of the reasons for their expulsion in 1767. After the expulsion the missions fell into decay, and the Indians relapsed into barbarism. Here was evidence that the Jesuit mission system which kept the Indians in servile

---

[80] For the missions of New Spain, see F. W. Blackmar, *Spanish institutions of the southwest;* C. A. Engelhardt, *The missions and missionaries of California;* H. H. Bancroft, *History of Mexico,* and *The north Mexican states and Texas;* H. E. Bolton, *Kino's historical memoir of Pimería Alta,* and *The Spanish border-lands.*

tutelage and robbed them of all initiative was a failure. The Indians were given, after a century and a half of endeavor, only a thin veneer of Christianity and civilization. The mission system in general was a failure because it forced nomadic Indians to a mode of life contrary to their nature. Moreover, the Indians were kept in a state of semi-servitude and exploited shamelessly.[81] This is not to ignore, of course, fine examples of self-sacrificing labours on the frontiers by missionaries in the service of God and king. The greatest contributions of the missions were perhaps to state rather than to church. They were a bulwark of the royal power; they helped to win and protect the frontiers of empire.

A general appraisal of the work of the church in the field of missionary endeavor is no easy task. Conversions were made by the thousands. Ruthless warfare was waged on ancient native idolatrous cults. In a short time there was hardly a community, Spanish or Indian, which did not have its church and clerics. It appeared to be one of the most rapid, extensive, and successful missionary movements in history. Yet what was the actual nature of these conversions? The mission Indians, as has been noted, soon relapsed into barbarism after the departure of the fathers. Those Indians who appeared to be permanently Christianized really entertained most remarkable notions concerning Christianity. Resulting from the manifest intention of the fathers to appeal to them by emphasizing the imagery and ceremonials of Catholicism, it happened that to the Indians the Faith meant just this. These trappings, the externals of the cult, became to the Indians the essence of Catholicism. They knew nothing, of course, about the philosophy and the moral ideas contained in Christianity. Moreover, there was a strange intermingling of Christianity and native paganism which has persisted to the present day among the Indians of Latin America. Christian saints have been identified as Indian gods. With clerical consent, but most generally without, native pagan rites have been engrafted on Christianity.[82] It was not Christianity but a hybrid cult which was developed among the Indians of America.

The clergy, the regulars and the seculars, became very numerous and

---

[81] For the Jesuits in Paraguay, see R. B. Cunningham Graham, *A vanished Arcadia;* B. Capdevielle, *Misiones jesuíticas en el Paraguay;* Blas Garay, *El comunismo de los misiones.*

[82] Father Sahagún condemned this countenancing of Indian rites. Alonso Toro, *Los judíos en la Nueva España* (Mexico, 1932), 10.

very wealthy in Spanish America. These two evils, so often selected for attack by the critics of the church, will be examined briefly.

Religious establishments and their clerical inmates multiplied very rapidly. According to Herrera there were at the end of the sixteenth century four hundred monasteries and convents, an infinite number of *cofradías,* or religious brotherhoods, and an innumerable quantity of curacies and *doctrinas.* By the middle of the seventeenth century the convents had increased to eight hundred and forty. In 1620 the viceroy of Peru told Philip III that the convents in Lima were so numerous that they occupied more territory than the civil population. In Mexico City the monasteries had become so numerous that the *cabildo,* in 1644, requested the king to stop the establishment of any more convents. Viceroy Barinas reported that the excessive number of the clergy was one of the greatest evils of the Indies.[83] In Chile in 1700, with a population of eighty thousand, there were forty-three regular establishments with four hundred friars and two hundred and fifty nuns. Also there were four hundred secular clergy. In 1800 the number of convents were as follows: Mexico, two hundred and fifty; Peru, one hundred and fifteen; Chile, forty-five; Buenos Aires, sixty-four; New Granada, sixty-six; and Caracas, twelve. Because of the excessive increase of friars, Ferdinand VI on July 20, 1754, in agreement with the Holy See, ordered that no more members of religious orders, "for any pretext," could be admitted for ten years. At the same time the age of entry into orders was restricted to youths over twenty-one years of age, "because of the continuous excesses of many individuals of the religious orders and the increase in the number of apostates."[84]

The mere number of convents, however, did not indicate an excessive number of inmates. For example, in 1570 the Franciscans had twenty-eight convents in the province of Neuva Galicia, but the personnel was no more than fifty. In Yucatan they had ten monasteries and twenty friars in all.[85] The superfluity of clerics, if such a condition existed, was of regulars, for certainly during the sixteenth century there was a great scarcity of seculars, and, as has been noted, the regulars were often called on to perform secular services. The apparent over-population of clergy was due to the fact that they were concentrated in the cities. Outside of the towns there was usually a scarcity of priests

---

[83] Altamira, III, 345-346; Lannoy and Vander Linden, 409; González Dávila, *Teatro eclesiástico* (2 vols., Madrid, 1649), I, 16-17; Toro, 34.

[84] Toro, 38; Hendricks, 63-64; Watters, 35.

[85] Lannoy and Vander Linden, 408-409.

and friars. The crown officers, under royal orders, constantly endeavored to disperse the ecclesiastics and force them to go where needed. But they were never successful in this. When it is remembered that the clergy, in addition to their spiritual duties, were virtually the only ones who conducted the schools and charitable institutions, their seeming excessive numbers should be discounted somewhat.

A decline in the number of ecclesiastics was noted in the eighteenth century. No longer was the church so attractive to those who sought a career. The army and civil service began to attract many away from the religious career. The expulsion of the Jesuits also contributed to a decline in members. A few years after the expulsion, a Bishop of Tucumán complained: "I do not know what we can do for the children and youths of these lands. Who are to instruct them? Who to man the missions? Where can one get so many clerics?" [86] In 1803 Humboldt estimated for New Spain 14,000 religious, or two per one thousand inhabitants.[87] The same ratio, certainly not excessive, could be applied to the rest of the Indies.

However improbable it may be that there was an excessive number of clergy in colonial Spanish America, it was true, nevertheless, that the wealth of the church was entirely disproportionate to the numbers of the clergy. This made it possible for a large fraction of the ecclesiastics to live in idleness. The subject of the actual wealth of the church has always been a controversial question and liable to extreme exaggeration, yet the testimony of competent authorities proves its possession of an excessive quantity of worldly goods.

The vast wealth of the colonial church was represented not only in ecclesiastical buildings and their ornate furnishings, but also in revenue-producing lands and capital loaned at interest on property of individuals. Most of this property was acquired by bequests of the faithful. This practice became so general and fixed that a French traveler, De Pons, wrote: "A will which contained no legacy in favor of the convents was considered an act so irreligious that it endangered the soul of the person who made it." Always zealous to accumulate property for themselves or the church, the clerics abused their spiritual office to induce the dying to will their estates to the church. The government, recognizing the evils of these deathbed donations, published a law in the eighteenth cen-

[86] Altamira, IV, 243.

[87] Alexander von Humboldt, *Political essay on the kingdom of New Spain* (4 vols., London, 1814), I, 229-232.

tury, after most of the harm had been done, forbidding notaries from passing any act or instrument of donation by which a sick person proposed to convey his property to his confessor or to an ecclesiastical organization. Unfortunately this law found no adequate support in public opinion.[88] What the church received it kept, for, because of the right of mortmain, a property acquired by the church was permanently lost to public and private uses. According to a decision of the Council of Trent, severe punishments were prescribed for usurpers of ecclesiastical property. This decision was subscribed to by the Spanish government.

The accumulation of land and other forms of wealth by the church was accomplished with as great expedition as its spiritual conquest. In 1556 Archbishop Montúfar of Mexico wrote:

> "Some check should be put upon the extravagant expenditures, excessive personal services, and sumptuous and superfluous works for which the monastic brotherhoods are responsible in the villages of these Indians, entirely at the cost of the latter. Some of the monasteries in places where there are not more than two or three monks would be inordinately superb even in Valladolid." [89]

In 1578 the *Cabildo* of Mexico complained that the Augustinians and Dominicans possessed in property the larger and best part of the city. It requested that the further acquisition of property by the church be prohibited. In 1644 the king was once more supplicated by the *Cabildo* of Mexico to refuse licenses for the founding of more convents.[90] In 1632 the Bishop of Santiago de Chile said that if the orders continued to acquire property at the same rate it would not be many years before they owned all. He said that the situation was the universal plague of the Indies.[91] Juan and Ulloa in their famous *Noticias secretas* (1748) comment on the wealth of the clergy in Peru. They reported that in Lima, out of 2,806 houses, 1,135 belonged to religious communities.[92] In Mexico City, in 1790, out of 3,387 houses, 1,935 belonged to the church. According to Lucas Alamán, who as a pro-clerical would not be expected to exaggerate, the property of the Mexican Church in the last days of the colonial period consisted of one-half of the total value of all productive real estate in New Spain.[93] Humboldt in 1800 esti-

---

[88] Moses, II, 230-231.

[89] *Col. Doc. Inéd.*, IV, 519.

[90] Toro, 34.

[91] Hendricks, 55.

[92] Jorge Juan and Antonio de Ulloa, *Noticias secretas de América* (London, 1826), 523-525.

[93] Lucas Alamán, *Historia de Méjico* (5 vols., Mexico, 1849-1850), I, 67.

mated the total property of the clergy in Mexico at 994,500,000 *reales*, or approximately $100,000,000. In the other viceroyalties the wealth of the church was excessive but not as great as in New Spain.

The crown did not view the accumulation of property by the church without alarm. In 1572 Philip II endeavored unsuccessfully to secure from the pope permission to restrict the right of religious orders to hold property. This problem always troubled the king who multiplied prohibitions, but unfortunately they were unsuccessful. The expulsion of the Jesuits in 1767 afforded the crown an excellent opportunity to recover vast estates held in mortmain. This was the most important action of the government affecting church property. In 1796 the king laid a tax of fifteen per cent on all property donated to the church for the support of *obras pías* (benevolent institutions). In 1804, real estate belonging to benevolent institutions was ordered sold. The united opposition of the clergy and the great landowners accomplished the defeat of this measure.[94]

As was to be expected, considering the wealth of the church, some of the prelates commanded princely incomes. According to Humboldt the Archbishop of Mexico received annually 130,000 *pesos*, the Bishop of Puebla 110,000, and so on down to the Bishop of Sonora, who received 6,000. The lower clergy, in glaring contrast, received one hundred to one hundred and twenty-five *pesos*.[95]

Next to its excessive wealth, the church in the Spanish Indies has been most severely criticized because of the moral laxity of the clergy. The riches of the church which conduced to idle living, the loosening of discipline because of the enforced isolation of so many clerics, the taking of orders not for pious reasons but for personal gain, and downright ignorance, were responsible for lax clerical morals. In general, it can be asserted with assurance, the morals and customs of the colonial clergy were not always as good as their sacerdotal state required.

Corruption and immorality were not slow in making their appearance among the clergy in America. Three years after the conquest Cortés urged the emperor to send to New Spain only clergy of exemplary and virtuous life. He said the propagation of the faith would be injured if

"the bishops and other prelates do not abandon the custom that on account of our sinfulness they pursue today of disposing of the goods of the church, spending them in pomp and other vices and

---

[94] *Ibid.*, I, 137.
[95] Humboldt, I, 229-232.

leaving inheritances to their sons and relatives; and this would be the worse because the natives' own priests versed in their rites and ceremonies were chosen both for their honesty and chastity, deviation from which was punished by death." [96]

Bishop Zumárraga complained that few of the clergy who came to America knew their religious office and fewer learned the Indian languages. He lamented their ignorance, corruption, and immorality. Viceroy Mendoza wrote to his successor, Luís de Velasco: "The clergy who come to these parts are malicious and selfish, and if it were not that His Majesty had ordered these Indians to be baptized they would be better without them." [97] The *informes* or instructions of the viceroys abound in cases of concubinage of clerics, malverism of funds, lavish living, disobedience to superiors, and violation of all the rules. The viceroys were kept busy settling disputes and quarrels among the clergy; sometimes there were noisy quarrels between Creole and *Gachupín* members of a convent. Often riots occurred between regulars and seculars. The nuns as well as the friars caused contentions. Often, when the civil authorities sought to correct abuses, conflicts of jurisdiction were precipitated.

Concubinage was very general among the friars and *curas* throughout the colonial period. The historian Oviedo alludes to concubinage in the early days of the conquest. In the middle eighteenth century concubinage was common in Peru according to Juan and Ulloa. The exceptional tolerance of irregular relations of the sexes in Spain, even including the clergy, was the heritage of age-long contact with Mohammedanism. Efforts to enforce celibacy attained only slight success, and although marriages of the clergy were not legal, yet a legal status was accorded their children. [98] It should be remembered that moral laxity of the clergy was merely a reflection of deplorable conditions in colonial society as a whole.

Although the clergy of the sixteenth and seventeenth centuries were sadly deficient in many respects, there was a further notable decline in the eighteenth century. The better classes began to send their sons into the army, the civil service, or the profession of the law. "The priesthood had come to be filled with men of no note and of obscure birth." In contrast with the zeal and enthusiasm of the early missionaries, De Pons reported that the clerics of Venezuela "fashioned their

---

[96] Gruening, 173 (fourth letter to Charles V, October 15, 1524).
[97] Toro, 19-20.
[98] Bourne, 306-307.

lives according to the spirit of man rather than the spirit of God." No longer was the martyrdom of a missionary attractive and glorious.[99]

Conceding the glaring examples, on a rather wide scale, of clerical worldliness, luxurious living, and loose morals, the critics of the colonial church have been too prone to emphasize these and disregard the examples, on an even larger scale, of devotion to vows, self-abnegation, and service. It was the regulars congregated in the convents who violated vows and cast a shadow of ill-repute over the clergy in general. The vast majority of the priests and friars, who labored for the faith in the parishes and among the neophytes in the missions, lived exemplary lives of pious service. The pages of the history of missionary endeavor in Spanish America are filled with the names of humble and fearless servitors of God like the more famous Kino, Garcés and Serra.

It was evident that, since the episcopate was distinguished on the whole by the secular aspirations of its incumbents and their ambition to secure the dominance of society, there should be conflict of jurisdictions and lack of harmony with the lay officials. This was quite in line with the crown policy of "divide and rule." One group was set against another for the purpose of more easily controlling both. The king would at one time uphold the secular arm against the claims of the spiritual, and again would reprimand some civil official for overstepping the limits of his jurisdiction and interfering in ecclesastical matters. Many of the disputes became so bitter and violent that it is conceivable they exceeded the royal intention.

Conflict between church and state in the Indies was one of the most common features of colonial history. A Chilean historian, Vicuña Mackenna, describes Chilean colonial history as follows: (1) Civil History—quarrels between the presidents and the dioceses; and (2) Ecclesiastical History—quarrels between the bishops and the presidents.[100] Ecclesiastical and lay officials, ambitious and jealous of their prerogatives, staged a perennial contest which often relieved an otherwise monotonous and drab existence. These contests were often accompanied by excommunications, interdicts, denunciations, riots, interminable litigation, and appeals to the king. The histories of the several viceroyalties are replete with cases of struggles between the two powers. A few examples, selected somewhat at random, will suffice.

Santa Fé de Bogotá was the scene of almost continuous conflict be-

---

[99] F. R. J. De Pons, *Voyage à Terre Ferme* (Paris, 1806), II, 136.
[100] Hendricks, 43.

tween the archbishop and the *audiencia*. One of the earliest contests originated in a decree of the archbishop, based on action of the Synod of Bogotá of 1556, to force the *encomenderos* to live up to their obligations, and instruct the Indians entrusted to them. The *encomenderos* resisted and found support in the *cabildo* and the *audiencia*. The latter body declared the action of the archbishop and the synod to be null and void.[101] Next there was a controversy over the right of asylum, a prolific cause of conflict. A priest, a fugitive from Lima, fled to Bogotá. He sought sanctuary in the cathedral, but by order of the *oidores* he was forcibly taken, over the protests of the archbishop. When the archbishop threatened to go to Spain to present the matter to the king, the *oidores* yielded and restored the priest to the sanctuary. On the request of the *oidores* the archbishop absolved them and imposed penance.[102]

Mexico was the scene of several most severe church-state conflicts. In 1624 Archbishop Serna excommunicated Viceroy Gelves and laid an interdict over the city in a quarrel growing out of the right of sanctuary. The viceroy retaliated by attempting to exile the prelate. The populace became aroused in favor of the archbishop, and in a general uprising burned the viceregal palace.[103]

Often the causes of conflict were trivial. The refusal of Archbishop Almansa of Bogotá, in 1630, to address the president of the *audiencia,* Sancho Girón, as "Señoría Ilustrísima," caused an open breach. Archbishop Liñán of Lima contended that he had the right to have six mules draw his carriage, but Viceroy Palata declared that he alone enjoyed that privilege. When the archbishop insisted on his right to use a parasol in the procession, this was objected to by the viceroy. The Council of the Indies was forced to decide this and other equally trivial questions of prestige and precedence.[104]

To protect the orthodoxy of the church against heretical contamination, the Inquisition was established in America. Although it is generally believed that the Holy Office was first introduced into the Spanish Indies in 1569, this was not the case. Prior to that date all its machinery was in active operation. Heretics were dealt with at first by inquisitorial agents sent from Spain, or by the bishops. The first to

---

[101] Moses, I, 283-284.

[102] *Ibid.,* I, 289-290.

[103] Vicente Riva Palacio, *México á través de los siglos* (5 vols., Barcelona, 1888-1889), II, 570-582.

[104] Fisher, 221-222; Moses, I, 88-91.

exercise inquisitorial functions in Mexico were the Franciscans who were given this authority by the will of Adrian VI in 1522. Using their powers, which were as ample in matters of faith as those possessed by the bishops, the Franciscans attacked idolatry, destroyed idols, and burned hieroglyphic pictures. Lic. Marcos de Aguilar, who with Luís Ponce de León was entrusted with the *residencia* of Hernán Cortés, bore the title of Inquisitor of New Spain. Fr. Domingo de Betanzos, considered the founder of the Dominican Order in Mexico, also bore the title of Inquisitor. He not only instituted various processes for crimes against the faith, but he condemned several accused to the flames. The visitor Francisco Tello de Sandoval bore the title of Inquisitor of New Spain.[105]

Bishop Zumárraga established the Tribunal of the Inquisition in Mexico with great solemnity on June 6, 1536. All the officials, including Viceroy Mendoza, swore to support and protect the Holy Office. Bishop Zumárraga seems to have preferred his inquisitorial functions to his episcopal ones. He discharged them with a zeal of a fanatic, as can be seen by the numerous processes in which he participated.[106] Jerónimo de Loaysa, first Archbishop of Lima, held *autos de fé* at Lima, Cuzco, and Charcas. In the first of these (1548), a Flemish Protestant, Jan Millar, was burned alive.[107] In the first half of the sixteenth century most of the processes were instituted by the Inquisition for the crimes of blasphemy and bigamy. Very few causes were instituted because of observance of the Law of Moses. This did not mean, however, that there were no Jews in the New World. In spite of numerous legal prohibitions a number of Jews went to the Indies.[108] Foreigners and "New Christians," that is, those who could not prove their Catholicism for several generations, also went to the colonies, thanks to lax enforcement of the exclusion laws.

Philip II, however, was determined to purge the colonies of all evil influences which might contaminate the orthodoxy of his subjects. In 1557 he prohibited foreigners from entering the colonies. In 1569 he decreed the establishment of separate tribunals of the Inquisition in the Indies. In 1570 the Tribunal of the Holy Office of the Inquisition was established in Lima, and in the next year another tribunal was estab-

---

[105] Toro, XXV-XXVI.
[106] *Ibid.,* 3-5, XXVIII.
[107] C. H. Lea, *The inquisition in the Spanish dependencies* (New York, 1908), 321.
[108] Toro, XXIII.

lished in Mexico City. Pedro de Moya y Contreras was appointed first Inquisitor-General of Mexico. Later he combined in his single person the offices of Archbishop of Mexico, Visitor-General, Inquisitor-General, and Viceroy of New Spain. A third tribunal was established in Cartagena in 1610 to have jurisdiction over the archbishoprics of Santo Domingo and Santa Fé de Bogotá.[109] Each tribunal was composed of two Inquisitors and a corps of aids, such as attorneys, secretaries, constable, treasurer, and warden. The Inquisitors acted through commissioners in different districts. Deputies, of whom there was a large number, were known as "familiars." Two important adjuncts of each tribunal were the strong-box and the jail.

The jurisdiction of the Inquisition extended over all the people in the Indies except the Indians. Protestant interlopers, priests, Jews, Spanish and Portuguese judaizers, and those accused of sorcery, black magic, blasphemy, and bigamy were the principal victims of the Holy Office. Indians, "because of their ignorance and their weak minds," were regarded as children and so were excused from inquisitorial control.

The proceedings of the Inquisition were secret. The accused often never knew the nature of his crime, the name of his accuser, or the names of the witnesses. Torture to gain confessions was resorted to, and even witnesses were tortured to produce the proper testimony. The closest family ties or ties of friendship did not excuse an individual from the obligation of denouncing a suspect of heresy. Thus, children were obliged to declare against parents, and friend against friend.[110] Espionage was favored, the secrets of the home were penetrated; nothing was safe from the terrorizing presence of the Holy Office. The accused were often arrested on anonymous information. The colonials at first were reluctant to approach the tribunal, but later they entered into the informing with enthusiasm. They showed a willingness to report the conduct of their neighbors, and they flooded the tribunals with complaints and charges. Thus the Inquisition presented to all persons a temptation and an opportunity which materially increased the hazards of life.

One accused by the Inquisition deserved no consideration. His liberty, honor, property and life were liable to forfeiture. Penalties imposed by the tribunal, and enforced by the lay officials, ranged from

---

[109] Moses, II, 338-339; Lannoy and Vander Linden, 405.
[110] Toro, 36-37.

light fines and penance, to flogging, imprisonment, work in the galleys, exile, and death. The most hardened heretics were burned at the stake, yet the penalty of death by fire was applied in only a few cases. In all the *autos de fé* celebrated in Lima (1573-1736) only thirty were burned alive. In Mexico (1570-1803) the tribunal placed on trial nine hundred and thirty-two persons, but only forty-one were put to death as unreconciled heretics.[111] As many were burned in a single *auto de fé* in Spain under Philip II. The Holy Office was not nearly so fearsome in America as in Spain. Invariably, when one was condemned by the Inquisition, his property was confiscated and turned over to the uses of the tribunal. This gave the inquisitors a source of income independent of the royal treasury. Needless to say this tempted them to condemn the accused who were wealthy.

The Inquisition was entirely under the control of the king in the *Consejo de la Suprema y General Inquisición*. The Inquisitors were appointed by the king and were responsible to him alone. In the colonies the viceroys took an oath to aid the Holy Office and to guard its privileges and immunities. They were likewise charged with reporting any invasion of the patronage. Frequently the Inquisitors tried to extend their power to the detriment of the prerogatives and patronage of the crown. Several decrees of the king reprimanded judges of the Holy Office for exceeding their authority. The Inquisitors manifested a desire to have their precedence recognized by the civil and ecclesiastical officers. They thus introduced a new element of discord into the community. Charles III gave the viceroy the final word in all matters of disputed jurisdiction with the Inquisition. He also commanded that no edict of the Holy Office could be published without viceregal approval.

The Inquisitors were also entrusted with the duty of censoring the reading material of the colonials. They prepared a lengthy list of prohibited books called the Index. Not only all Jewish, Mohammedan, and Protestant religious books were prohibited, but also, unfortunately for the intellectual development of the Indies, the writings of political and social philosophers like Addison, Defoe, Montesquieu, Rousseau, and Voltaire. Books which supported the principle of popular sovereignty were branded as heretical, for the church had endorsed the pretentions of the Spanish kings to rule by divine right. An edict of the Tribunal of Mexico, August 7, 1808, denounced the doctrine of sovereignty of the people as "manifest heresy." Bookshops were closely supervised and anyone who sold a prohibited book was suspended from business

---

[111] Navarro y Lamarca, II, 381; Fisher, 230.

for two years and sentenced to pay a fine of two hundred ducats. The commissioners of the Inquisition might enter private homes at any time of day or night to seek prohibited books.[112]

There is little doubt that the Index, notwithstanding widespread smuggling of prohibited books, was responsible for great retardation of intellectual development in the colonies. It was used, particularly in the last years of Spanish rule in America, not only to extirpate religious but also political heresy. Since church and state were so closely united it should be understandable why an ecclesiastical institution like the Inquisition was used for political objects.[113]

An event of great importance in the history of the church in Spanish America, which deserves at least passing mention in this survey, was the expulsion of the Jesuits from the Spanish Indies. The missionary activities of the Jesuits have been mentioned. They were also prominent in the field of education, particularly higher education. Their schools and colleges were undoubtedly the best in the Indies. They were also the spiritual directors of Spanish colonial society. Their wealth was excessive. They not only held vast areas of fertile lands, but they also engaged in industry and trade. In Peru, for example, they monopolized trade in wheat, wine, brandies, hides, and sugar. But it was not because of their position and activities in America that the Jesuits were expelled. The reasons were principally European, although the War of the Seven Reductions weakened still more the faith of the crown in the Order. There were 2,260 Jesuits in America at the time of the expulsion.

The expulsion order of Charles III was executed in America in June and July 1767. Suddenly and unexpectedly the Jesuits were ordered to depart. Despite precautions, disturbances occurred, particularly in Mexico. Viceroy Croix wrote: "All the inhabitants are zealous partisans of the Company. They [Jesuits] are the absolute masters of the hearts and consciences of the vast empire." Riots occurred in Guanajuato, San Luís Potosí, and other places despite the fact that the viceroy prohibited conversations and comments concerning the expulsion. "Subjects ought not to discuss or opinionate on high matters of state," he said.[114]

---

[112] Roscher, 31.
[113] The *Cortes* of Cádiz (1812) declared the Inquisition incompatible with the constitution. It was abolished in America, but shortly after was reëstablished with the restoration of Ferdinand VII. It was permanently abolished following the Revolution of 1820.
[114] Altamira, IV, 232-233.

The Jesuits were transported to Italy and paid small pensions. Their property was confiscated by the crown. This was the only instance of the confiscation of ecclesiastical property down to the end of the eighteenth century. Navarro y Lamarca (II, 418-419) holds that the expulsion of the Jesuits was a leading cause of the development of a revolutionary spirit in Spanish America. They had been one of the strongest supports of the crown in influencing the people to have respect for authority.

Unfortunately, the limits of this chapter do not allow for a discussion of the work of the church in colonial education. It must suffice to state that in so far as educational facilities existed in the colonies, and they were not inconsiderable, they were supported by the church. Of course, education was narrowly theological in content and scholastic in method. But this was a fault of the age, of a stage of European civilization, and not of Spain or of the church. The Franciscans were principally concerned with primary education, which was limited as a rule to religious doctrine, reading, writing, and arithmetic. The Dominicans and Jesuits were the most active in higher education. In 1551, by imperial decree, the royal and pontifical universities of Mexico and San Marcos in Lima were founded "to protect the inhabitants of our Indies from the darkness of ignorance." Instruction in the universities and colleges was by clericals and it was predominantly theological and scholastic in character. Through its supervision of education, the church performed one of its most important services, that is, the transmission of European culture and civilization to America.

SELECTED BIBLIOGRAPHY

I. *Real Patronato de Indias*

The principal collection of primary materials for the study of *real patronato* is *Recopilación de leyes de los reynos de las indias* (4 vols., Madrid, 1681). In this greatest collection of colonial legislation ever compiled can be seen the intimate relations which existed between church and state in the Spanish colonies. There are several commentaries on the laws of the Indies, the greatest of these being Juan de Solórzano y Pereyra, *Política indiana* (2 vols., Madrid, 1776, Valenzuela edition). *Patronato* was based in part on papal concessions; for the papal bulls see Francisco Javier Hernáez, *Colección de bulas, breves, y otros documentos relativos á la iglesia de América y Filipinas* (2 vols., Brussels, 1879). Valuable materials illustrative of the legal status of the church, as well as of its history, during the colonial period, can be found in *Colección de documentos inéditos relativos al descubrimiento, conquista y organización de las antiguas posesiones españolas de América y Oceanía* (42 vols., Madrid, 1864-1884). Also of great value for the history of the *real patronato* are: *Instrucciones que los virreyes de Nueva España dejaron á sus sucesores* (Mexico, 1867); *Memorias de los virreyes que han gobernado el Perú* (6 vols., Lima, 1859); and *Memorias de los virreyes del Perú* (Lima, 1896). These volumes consist of long and detailed reports and instructions of the viceroys to their successors.

The outstanding work written in defense of regalism during the colonial period was Antonio Joaquín de Ribadeneyra, *Manuel compendio del regio patronato indiano* (Madrid, 1755). Other colonial defenders of the regalistic position were: Pedro Frasso, *De regio patronato* (2 vols., Madrid, 1677), and Solórzano, just cited. More recent works written in defense of regalism are: Vicente G. Quesada, *Derecho de patronato* (Buenos Aires, 1910), and D. Vélez Sarsfield, *Derecho público eclesiástico, relaciones del estado con la iglesia en la antigua americana española* (Buenos Aires, 1889).

Perhaps the best work presenting the canonists' position is Matías Gómez Zamora, *Regio patronato español ê indiano* (Madrid, 1897). Other works in which the ultramontane doctrine is supported are: P. Leturia, "El origen histórico del patronato de indias" in *Razón y Fê* (vol. 78); Faustino J. Legón, *Doctrina y ejercicio del patronato nacional* (Buenos Aires, 1920); and Lucas Ayarragaray, *La iglesia en América y la dominación española* (Buenos Aires, 1920). The latter work is scholarly, being based on materials in the Vatican archives.

A general discussion of the origins and nature of *patronato* in Spain and in the Spanish Indies can be found in J. Lloyd Mecham, *Church and state in Latin America* (Chapel Hill, 1934).

II. *History of the Church in the Spanish Indies*

The materials, primary and secondary, for the history of the Catholic Church in colonial Spanish America are probably more complete than for any other phase of colonial activity. This arises not only from the fact that the church occupied a paramount position in colonial life, but also because the greatest and most numerous historians and chroniclers were ecclesiastics.

Primary references cited above (for *real patronato*), such as the *Recopilación de leyes, Colección de documentos inéditos,* and the instructions of the viceroys, are also most valuable for the history and activities of the colonial church. To these should be added: *Cartas de indias* (2 vols., Madrid, 1877), selected documents from the Archivo Histórico Nacional; *Documentos para la historia de Méjico* (21 vols., Mexico, 1853-1857), valuable diaries of missionary journeys; Genaro García, ed., *El clero de México durante la dominación española, según el archivo archiepiscopal metropolitano* (Mexico, 1907); A. B. Cuervo, *Colección de documentos inéditos sobre la geografía y la historia de Colombia* (4 vols., Bogotá, 1891-94); E. Lizana and P. Maulen, eds., *Colección de documentos recopilados del archivo del arzobispado de Santiago* (4 vols., Santiago de Chile, 1919-1921); and N. A. N. Cleven, *Readings in Hispanic American history* (Boston, 1927), which contains valuable selections bearing upon church history.

There is no general history of the church in Spanish America. There are short secondary accounts, and a large number of histories for geographical divisions, religious orders, and ecclesiastical institutions. The best short general accounts are: Rafael Altamira y Crevea, *Historia de España y de la civilización española* (4 vols., Barcelona, 1913-1914), and Carlos Navarro y Lamarca, *Compendio de la historia general de América* (2 vols., Buenos Aires, 1910-1913). In Bernard Moses' *The establishment of Spanish rule in America* (New York and London, 1898) and *The Spanish dependencies in South America* (2 vols., New York and London, 1914), are excellent chapters on various phases of church history. Short general histories of Latin America, such as W. S. Robertson, *History of the Latin American nations* (New York, 1925), and M. W. Williams, *The people and politics of Latin America* (Boston, 1930), contain helpful chapters on the subject.

Ecclesiastical histories more or less general in scope are: Gil González Dávila,

Teatro eclesiástico de la primitiva iglesia de las indias occidentales (Madrid, 1649-1655) ; Fr. José Amich, *Compendio histórico de los trabajos, fatigas y muertes de los ministros evangélicos de la seráfica religión* (Paris, 1854) ; and P. J. Parras, *Gobierno de los regulares de la América* (2 vols., Madrid, 1783).

There is an abundance of material, colonial and modern, on religious activities in New Spain. Of the colonial ecclesiastical histories the greatest are: Gerónimo de Mendieta, *Historia eclesiástica indiana* (Mexico, 1870. Written in 1596), and Juan de Torquemada, *Monarquía indiana* (3 vols., Madrid, 1723. First published in Seville in 1615). These are histories of Franciscan activities in New Spain in the sixteenth century. Augustín de Vetancurt, *Teatro mexicano, descripción breve de los sucesos exemplares, históricos, políticos, militares, y religiosos del nuevo mundo occidental de las indias* (Mexico, 1698), contains good surveys of the various religious provinces. Added to this work is the *Menologio franciscano,* really a separate work containing a list of notable Franciscans who worked in New Spain, together with an account of their activities. An authentic and objective account of Jesuit activities in New Spain from 1572 to 1763 is Francisco Javier Alegre, *Historia de la Compañía de Jesús en Nueva España* (3 vols., Mexico, 1841-1842). The standard history of the colleges of *Propaganda Fide* in New Spain is Isidro Félix de Espinosa, *Crónica apostólica y seráfica de todos los colegios de propaganda fide de esta Nueva-España* (Mexico, 1746). Juan Domingo Arricivita, *Crónica seráfica y apostólica de colegio de propaganda fide de la Santa Cruz de Querétaro en la Nueva España* (Mexico, 1792) is valuable for missionary activities in Coahuila and Texas in the eighteenth century. For the work of the missionary provinces in New Spain three outstanding works are: José Arlegui, *Crónica de la provincia de Zacatecas* (Mexico, 1737), a general history of the Zacatecan province from 1567 to 1733; Pablo de la Purísima Concepción Beaumont, *Crónica de la provincia de los santos apóstolos S. Pedro y S. Pablo de Michoacán* (5 vols., Mexico, 1873-1874. Written in 1780) ; and Fray Antonio Tello, *Libro segundo de la crónica miscelanea en que se trata de la conquista espiritual y temporal de la provincia de Xalisco en el Nuevo Reino de la Galicia y Nueva Vizcaya y descubrimiento del Nuevo México* (Guadalajara, 1891). The annals extend to 1650.

The most vitally important works on missionary activities in California, 1769-1784, are Francisco Palou, *Relación histórica de la vida y apostólicas tareas del venerable padre Fray Junípero Serra* (Mexico, 1787), and his *Noticias de la Nueva California* (4 vols., San Francisco, 1874). This has been translated and edited by H. E. Bolton (4 vols., 1926). For the remarkable missionary exploits of Fr. Kino see Herbert E. Bolton, ed., *Kino's historical memoir of Pimería Alta: a contemporary account of the beginnings of California, Sonora, and Arizona; 1683-1711* (2 vols., Cleveland, 1919) ; and R. K. Willys, *Pioneer Padre, the life and times of Eusebio Francisco Kino* (Dallas, 1935).

The best recent ecclesastical history of New Spain is Mariano Cuevas, *Historia de la iglesia en México* (5 vols., Mexico, El Paso, 1921-1928). The first four volumes are on the colonial period. John G. Shea, *The Catholic church in colonial days* (New York, 1886), traces to 1763 the work of the Catholic Church in the Spanish, French, and English colonies in that portion of North America which is now the United States. A monumental work on the California missions is Charles Anthony (in religion, Zephyrin) Engelhardt, *The missions and missionaries of California* (4 vols., San Francisco, 1908-1916). Of general histories which contain accounts, more or less extended, of colonial church history and missionary activities, the following are more useful: Lucas Alamán, *Historia de Méjico* (5 vols., Mexico, 1849-1852) ; H. H. Bancroft, *History of Mexico* (6 vols., San Francisco, 1883-1888), *History of California* (7 vols., San Francisco, 1884-1890), and *The north Mexican states and Texas* (2 vols., San Francisco, 1884-1889) ; Charles E. Chapman, *A history of California: the Spanish period* (New York, 1923) ; Herbert I. Priestley, *The Mexican nation: a history* (New York, 1923) ; and Vicente Riva Palacio, *México á través de los siglos* (5 vols., Mexico and Barcelona, 1887-1889).

There is a wealth of material on the famous "Jesuit Republic of Paraguay." From the extended list the following works have been selected: P. Nicolás Techo, *Historia de la provincia del Paraguay de la Compañía de Jesús* (Asunción, 1897) ; E. Gothein, *Der christlich sociale staat der Jesuiten in Paraguay* (Berlin, 1885) ; Francisco Xarque, *Ruiz Montoya en indias* (Madrid, 1900) ; R. B. Cunninghame Graham, *A vanished arcadia* (London, 1901) ; and Gregorio Funes, *Ensayo de la historia civil del Paraguay, Buenos Aires y Tucumán* (2 vols., Buenos Aires, 1910-1911).

The religious situation in Ecuador and Peru in the middle eighteenth century is frankly set forth in Jorge Juan y Santacilla and Antonio de Ulloa, *Noticias secretas de América* (2 vols., Madrid, 1918). For missionary activities in various sections of South America, the following works are useful: J. J. Borda, *Historia de la Compañía de Jesús en la Nueva Granada* (2 vols., Poissey, 1872) ; Fray Antonio de la Caluncha, *Crónica moralizada de la orden de San Agustín en el Perú* (Barcelona, 1638) ; P. Ceferino Mussani, *Noticias históricas sobre las misiones de Bolivia* (Paris, 1854) ; Juan Rivero, *Historia de las misiones de los llanos de Casanare y los ríos Orinoco y Meta* (2 vols., Bogotá, 1883) ; and Froilán de Rionegro, *Relaciones de las misiones de PP. Capuchinos en Venezuela, 1650-1817* (2 vols., Seville, 1918). An excellent account of Jesuit activities in the Indies can be found in Antonio Astrain, *Historia de la Compañía de Jesús en la asistencia de España* (7 vols., Madrid, 1920). Mary Watters, *A history of the church in Venezuela, 1810-1930* (Chapel Hill, 1933), contains an excellent chapter on the colonial background of the church in Venezuela.

An instructive interpretation of the mission system is to be found in H. E. Bolton, "The Mission as a frontier institution in the Spanish American colonies," *American Historical Review*, xxiii, 42-61. The mission is also discussed in F. W. Blackmar, *Spanish institutions of the southwest* (Baltimore, 1891). On the Inquisition the outstanding and most authoritative work on the subject is Henry Charles Lea, *The inquisition in the Spanish dependencies* (New York, 1908). Other works of exemplary scholarship on the Inquisition are: José Toribio Medina, *Historia del tribunal del santo oficio en Chile* (2 vols., Santiago de Chile, 1890), and his *Historia del tribunal del santo oficio de la inquisición en México* (Santiago de Chile, 1905).

Two biographies of great importance for the church history of the Spanish Indies are Joaquín García Icazbalceta, *Biografía de Don Fray Juan de Zumárraga* (Mexico, 1881) ; and Francis Augustus MacNutt, *Bartholomew de las Casas, his life, his apostolate and his writings* (New York, 1909).

CHAPTER NINE

COLONIAL SOCIETY

By IRVING A. LEONARD

A GENERATION ago it was the fashion to refer to the United States as the "melting pot." Politicians spoke movingly of this great experiment in human biology, boasting that a new race was springing up in that favored region. But, despite the multiplicity of elements entering the blood stream of a mighty nation, it is doubtful if the term used was ever as merited as in the case of Hispanic America. Broadly speaking, a gradual fusion of different representatives of the white race has taken place in North America; south of the Río Grande a vaster process of racial amalgamation has been in progress since the earliest colonial days. In the latter area there has been a coalescing of various divisions of Caucasians, but this is often less important quantitatively than the fusion with native Indian and negro blood. The descendants of these mixed races far outnumber the whites in modern Mexico, Peru, and Brazil, and entirely new variations of the human species have been developed; in other countries this is less true. This divergence, despite a common Spanish and Portuguese heritage, makes it difficult to generalize in a discussion of colonial society in Hispanic America, but limitations of space compel a broad treatment. To facilitate matters attention may be confined to a few common denominators such as the fundamental ethnic groups, that is, the Indian, European, and African, and the resultant hybridization, the occupations of the colonists and, finally, their amusements. In different degrees these aspects of society and social life were similar in all parts of Spanish and Portuguese America; still others which could be mentioned must be omitted from consideration.

I. PENINSULARS

Owing to the celebrity of Cortés, Alvarado, Pizarro, and a host of other *Conquistadores,* and also to certain similarities of the Spanish language spoken in America to that heard in Andalucía, the belief has been widely held that a large majority of the conquerors and later colonists came almost exclusively from southern Spain, though in Chile it was thought that the Basques predominated. Recent investigations, still incomplete, tend to prove that both of these theories are incorrect. While the men who accompanied Columbus on his first two voyages were probably all from Andalucía, as early as 1506 it was plainly evident that, politically at least, the Aragonese were dominant in Santo Domingo.[1] A careful study of the writings of the early historians and of the registers and lists of passengers embarking for the Indies clearly indicates that only forty-two and five-tenths per cent of the total recorded emigration was from the southern portion of the peninsula. Nearly an equal percentage came from the two provinces of Castile. The balance originated in other parts of Spain bordering on this central region and included representatives of Portugal, and the Balearic and the Canary Islands.[2] The preponderance of Castilians and southern Spaniards is explained by the complete monopoly which Castile exercised from the outset in the affairs of the Indies. It is unfortunate, perhaps, that this policy permitted the migration of a relatively small number of Basques, Galicians, and Catalans whose thrift and industry admirably adapted them to the task of developing the new colonies. The Basques did ultimately outnumber the Castilians in Chile, but not until the eighteenth century; in the early period of this region the sons of the high plateau of central Spain were most numerous.[3]

Immediately after the discovery, Spaniards began the process of colonizing the newly acquired possessions, and a steady stream of adventurers poured forth from the peninsula. The Portuguese, on the other hand, were at first too engrossed in their rich trade with the Far East to give much heed to the supposedly valueless portion of the western world that had fallen to their lot. Nearly a quarter of a century passed before Brazil entered seriously into the calculations of the authorities at Lisbon. Meanwhile, a few vessels had been coming from Portugal in quest of brazilwood and had left traders upon its shores who, joined by an occasional criminal fleeing from justice and Jews escaping the religious persecution of the peninsula, laid the foundation of the Portuguese colonies in the South American continent.[4]

The waning empire of Portugal in the Far East, the news of the

---

[1] Bartolomé de las Casas, *lib.* iii, *cap.* xxxv, cited in Pedro Henríquez Ureña, "Observaciones sobre el español en América," *Revista de Filología Española* (Madrid, 1931), XVIII, I, 122.

[2] *Ibid.,* 143.

[3] *Ibid.,* 127.

[4] Gonzalo Reparaz, "El Brazil, descubrimiento, colonización é influencia en la península," *El continente americano, conferencias dadas . . . con motivo del descubrimiento de América,* (Madrid, 1894), II, 11.

mines in the Spanish possessions, and the activities of corsairs along the Brazilian shore, moved the crown to bestir itself. In 1532 thirteen captaincies, feudal in nature, were created on the coast of Brazil and bestowed upon an equal number of court favorites. Since these colonies were agricultural, sugar cane was introduced and almost immediately negroes were imported from Guinea. Annual fleets brought fresh increments of white settlers, both male and female, from Portugal until, in 1580, the latter country fell under the sway of Philip II of Spain. And thus the seeds of the Brazilian nation were planted.

II. CREOLES

Unfortunately, the emigration of single women from Spain was never favored, though married men and higher officials were later required to bring their wives with them.[5] As a consequence, the proportion of white women was always exceedingly small. Despite this fact, however, a considerable element born of European parentage developed in the colonies. This group was called Creoles, and the discrimination against them fostered by the *Gachupines* and *Chapetones,* as the peninsular Spaniards were scornfully dubbed, continued to be a fruitful source of discord and jealousy throughout the whole colonial period. In general the American-born white was excluded from the higher and more remunerative offices, both ecclesiastical and secular, in his native land, and this distinction was naturally galling to one in whose veins flowed the undiluted blood of the proud *hidalgo.* This distrust of the Creole resulted in part from a belief widely held that the climate and environment of the New World were highly enervating and that, as a consequence, the children of Europeans born in America matured early in life and quickly entered upon a physical and mental decline. Moreover, the volatile nature of the Creole was thought little suited to the responsibilities of executive office. But it is probable that the pressing need of peninsular authorities to find a sufficient number of positions to appease the swarm of importunate individuals and greedy parasites which plagued the courts at Madrid and Lisbon was a factor in underestimating the abilities of the American-born Europeans. At any rate, few of the latter became viceroys or bishops, though later many lesser offices were open to them by purchase. In the Portuguese colonies the policy of the crown in this respect was less exclusive in theory, but the necessity of pursuing studies in the University of Coimbra to qualify for the

---

[5] *Recopilación de leyes, lib.* ix, *tít.* xxvi, *ley* 28.

more important posts[6] was a well-nigh insuperable difficulty for those born in Brazil.

Denied an outlet for their energies in administrative work and responsible participation in their own government, the overweening vanity and pride of the descendants of the *Conquistadores* did not permit them to devote themselves to commercial or industrial activities. The caste system of the peninsula and the prevailing distaste for manual labor or the technical crafts were perpetuated in an exaggerated form among the Creoles. As a class they were wealthy landowners preferring to live in the cities and larger towns where their lives were spent in indolence and, too often, in vice. The majority were temperamentally unsuited to persistent intellectual effort, and their ample leisure was rarely productive of more than a certain dilettanteism and an unrestrained flow of bombastic verse.

But if the Creole disliked the aristocratic peninsulars who obtained the higher and best paid offices in the government of his native land, he bitterly hated the humbler class of Spaniard who continued to pour into the Indies. Even though many of these immigrants were peasants possessing a scanty education and none of the graces, their European origin and white blood gave them a certain luster and importance that the Creole, tortured by an inferiority complex, secretly envied. These humble peninsulars often began life in the New World as small tradesmen and itinerant peddlars and frequently succeeded in building up a small fortune in a short time through industry and frugal habits of living. This circumstance permitted many of them to gain an entrée into the most exclusive Creole circles.

The American-born whites too often squandered their inheritance in idle or vicious amusements and were notoriously poor husbands. As a consequence, their womenkind displayed a marked preference for the sober and dependable immigrant who was thus able to marry into the most distinguished of colonial families. Some of these newcomers to the Indies, overwhelmed by the attentions showered upon them by aristocratic elements with whom they could have had no contact in Spain, abused their privileges and thus fanned the antagonism of the sensitive, lazy Creole into a passion of hatred. All over Hispanic America the towns and cities were divided into factions of Europeans and Creoles. Even within families in which there had been marriages with Peninsu-

---

[6] Charles de Lannoy and Herman Vander Linden, *Histoire de l'expansion coloniale des peuples européens: Portugal et Espagne* (Bruxelles and Paris, 1907), 97.

lars, much dissension existed. The children of an immigrant father and a Creole mother sometimes turned against their parents, and cousins despised each other profoundly. This hostility was occasionally manifested in local disturbances and open violence, although, considering the intensity and prevalence of this feeling, such incidents were exceedingly rare. Nor were the churches, convents, and monasteries exempt from the same sort of internal strife and jealousy.[7]

An adequate discussion of colonial society should include some account of the ecclesiastical element, ever a powerful influence in the community, which grew numerically larger in the course of the three centuries of Spanish and Portuguese domination. After the first flush of the period of militant proselytism, the easier life and wealth of the New World had a demoralizing effect upon many representatives of the church. Convents and monasteries multiplied, especially in Mexico and Peru, and became a heavy drain upon the resources of the community since they drew off a growing number of men and women from the upper classes of society and held them in a life of idleness which sometimes degenerated into one of outright vice. The rule of the monastic orders so far relaxed that many ecclesiastics, both regular and secular, lived outside the convent walls in private houses in which they maintained families and dependents. The two distinguished travelers of the eighteenth century, Juan and Ulloa, reported that the greater part of the religious body of Peru was living in this fashion; the convent buildings served only as a shelter for the poorer members and novitiates who were without means to lodge elsewhere.[8] As a consequence, these illegal families constituted no inconsiderable part of the society of the towns of the richer colonies.

III. FOREIGNERS IN COLONIAL HISPANIC AMERICA

The increment of European blood other than that of Spanish and Portuguese origin has never been adequately investigated. The extant legislation indicating a rigidly exclusive policy of the peninsular authorities has strongly colored the opinion of historians who have been prone to forget that the existence of prohibitory laws does not in itself imply a careful enforcement of them. Considering the individualistic character of the Spaniard especially, the remoteness of the colonies from the peninsula, and the lack of communication, it is not unlikely

---

[7] Concerning the rivalry of Spaniards and Creoles, see Jorge Juan and Antonio de Ulloa, *Noticias secretas de América* (Madrid, 1918), part ii, chapter vi.

[8] *Ibid.*, chapter viii.

that many of these laws quickly became a dead letter or were honored in the breach. There is much evidence, as yet unorganized, in the colonial records which suggests that foreigners in Hispanic America, though always forming a small minority, were more numerous than generally believed. The licenses and permits to embark for the Indies show clearly that Italians, Frenchmen, Flemings, Greeks, Germans, Irishmen, Scotchmen, and even a few Dutch and Englishmen were allowed to enter the colonies.[9] The archives of the branches of the Inquisition in the Indies afford indications of a considerable number of non-Spanish persons, particularly Jews and north Europeans, who were caught in the toils of the Holy Office.

All during the period of Spanish domination, the government at Madrid authorized the sending of skilled artisans, engineers, metallurgists, scientists, and others with a technical training, nearly all of whom were foreigners, to the Indies to stimulate certain industries and, in many cases, paid their salaries from the royal treasury. It is well known, also, that in the ranks of the missionaries some of the most active and learned were Italians, Flemings, Frenchmen, and other nationalities. Possibly the restrictive policy of the peninsula was, in actual fact, on a religious rather than an anti-foreign basis.

If the outsiders arriving with a legal sanction were numerous, those who entered the colonies without credentials of any sort probably exceeded them in numbers. The seaports invariably harbored subjects of other nations who had deserted or had been left by passing ships, and, when the necessity arose of fitting out a maritime expedition, the colonial authorities frequently resorted to impressing these individuals. Though by the sternest injunctions captains of vessels were forbidden to carry unauthorized passengers to the Indies, and port officials were cautioned to prevent illegal entries, there is little doubt that many foreigners, like forbidden books, found their way into the interior of Hispanic America.

In the Spanish colonies the Portuguese, who included many Jews exiled from the peninsula, were the largest single group of foreign origin. From 1580 to 1640 Portugal and its colonies formed an integral part of the Spanish empire and hence, for that period, were, strictly speaking, not outsiders. The proximity of Brazil also accounts for the large number of Portuguese in the Río de la Plata region. Even in

---

[9] Cf. Henríquez Ureña, 138, 139; also Edward Gaylord Bourne, *Spain in America* (New York and London, 1904), chapter xvi.

sixteenth century Chile, so sparsely inhabited by whites, it was easy to organize an expedition in which fifty-five of this nationality were included.[10] In 1646 an order was issued that all of these temporary subjects of Spain residing in Peru must leave the realm. Six thousand Portuguese presented themselves at this summons; this large number and the wealth that they represented were instrumental in bringing about the revocation of the edict of expulsion.[11]

Reference has been made to the presence of Jews in Hispanic America who had been driven from the peninsula. Pernambuco offered a place of refuge to many of these unfortunate people, especially during the Dutch occupation. When this region was restored to Portugal, however, the Jews were obliged to migrate to other parts of America.[12] The Island of Curaçao was an asylum for Semitic people who spread to the near-by coasts of Venezuela and Colombia.[13]

The union of Portugal and Castile in 1580 exposed Brazil to the attacks of the enemies of Philip II. As a result, the French, and especially the Dutch, gained temporary footholds in this new possession of the Spanish Crown. The Hollanders were established in the Pernambuco region for more than thirty years in the seventeenth century, and during this period probably left the largest single element of foreign blood in Hispanic America of any nation of Europe excepting, of course, the Spanish and Portuguese.

The French contingent was doubtless considerable, particularly after the accession of the Bourbons to the Spanish throne in 1700. As early as the first decade of the eighteenth century, French ships were numerous on the west coast of South America, bringing merchandise, fashions, and even literature which were popular in the wealthy centers such as Lima and Cuzco; the French court became the model of the gay life of the viceregal capital. Though officially the visits of these foreign vessels were frowned upon, regulations were not enforced, and both passengers and sailors readily disembarked and mingled with the population.[14]

---

[10] Henríquez Ureña, 124.

[11] *Ibid.*

[12] *Ibid.*, 125; also Argeu Guimarães, "Os judeus portugueses e brasileiros na America hespanhola," *Journal de la Société des Americanistes de Paris,* (Paris, 1926), XVIII, 297-312.

[13] Henríquez Ureña, *loc. cit.*

[14] The manuscript correspondence of the viceroys of Peru, preserved in the General Archive of the Indies at Seville, Spain, contains many letters and reports concerning the visits of French ships at Callao and other ports.

IV. Negroes

The conquerors and first settlers, both Spanish and Portuguese, were eager to gain wealth with the minimum effort. The unwillingness and inability of the Indians to perform efficiently the onerous tasks imposed upon them soon paved the way for the introduction of African slavery. In Spain and Portugal negroes were employed in the service of their masters, but the "peculiar institution," destined to bring much bloodshed and sorrow upon later generations in America, was already vanishing in the peninsula. The discovery of the New World was to delay the universal trend toward emancipation more than three and a half centuries. Within ten years of the first voyage of Columbus, slavery appeared in the Island of Santo Domingo.[15] The newly appointed governor, Nicolás de Ovando, was authorized to permit the importation of negroes, providing that the latter had been born among Christians. In 1503, the year following, Ovando asked that no more be sent for they were escaping to the hills and were joining the Indians.[16] Thus, almost coincident with the advent of the blackman in the colonies, came the problem of the *cimarrones,* escaped slaves who returned to their tribal ways, thus becoming a menace to their former masters. Seventeenth century Brazil witnessed the rise and fall in the Captaincy of Pernambuco of the well-ordered Republic of Palmares composed of fugitive negroes.[17]

Ovando's protest led to a momentary suspension of the slave traffic, but the extraordinary mortality of the Indians of Santo Domingo paralyzed the working of the mines and the plantations. Even ecclesiastics, the self-appointed guardians of the natives, recommended the use of African labor.[18] A direct slave trade between Guinea and America began and prospered as the Spaniards spread from the islands to the mainland. As early as 1514 the proportion of blacks to whites in Santo Domingo aroused the fears of the Spaniards for their own safety.[19] This anxiety proved well-founded, for in December 1522 the first insurrection of the negroes on that tragic island broke out. Twenty slaves of Diego Columbus, son of the discoverer, fled from his plantation and,

---

[15] Cf. Bourne, chap. xviii, "Negro Slaves."

[16] José Antonio Saco, *Historia de la esclavitud de la raza africana en el nuevo mundo* (Barcelona, 1879), 62.

[17] Cf. Charles Edward Chapman, "Palmares, the negro Numantia," *Journal of Negro History* (Lancaster, Pa., 1918), III, No. 1.

[18] Saco, 68, 93.

[19] *Ibid.*, 81.

joining others in revolt, killed several Spaniards.[20] Though the uprising was soon quelled, it was the first of many that fill the annals of the
colonial history of Hispanic America.

With the failure of the island mines to produce the expected gold,
slavery might soon have died out; but the introduction of sugar cane
prevented the early extinction of the institution. Columbus was the
first to bring this truer source of wealth to the Western Hemisphere[21]
where it quickly found suitable soil and climate, especially in the Antilles,
the Caribbean littoral, and in Brazil. For this industry, negro labor
was absolutely indispensable and the slave trade prospered.

It is unnecessary to dwell upon the subject of the *asientos* granted
for this traffic, nor are statistics desirable since the number of Africans
entering the colonies as contraband is impossible to estimate. Speaking
generally, the regions in which sugar cane flourished were those in which
negro slavery was most extensive and where, even today, the black population is densest. But these human chattels were by no means restricted
to the area indicated, and their economic and social significance was
great in more outlying parts of Hispanic America. A migration of
these enslaved people from the Antilles began almost with the conquest
of Peru. In April 1535, Charles I was advised that within five months
more than six hundred whites and four hundred negroes had passed
through Panama en route to the former empire of the Incas,[22] and the
restless Alvarado led an army to Quito which included two hundred
slaves.[23] In the centers of wealth and luxury that soon developed in
that vast region, the African and his descendants were more numerous
than in Mexico, although less so than in Venezuela and Cuba.[24] Even
before Pizarro's conquest, negroes had come into Guatemala and Nicaragua from New Spain and Panama, while about the same time Domingo
de Irala was authorized to take two hundred black servitors into the
Río de la Plata region.[25]

Throughout Hispanic America, then, African slavery had spread at
an early date. Without this help, particularly in the tropical lowlands,
the European masters would doubtless have been unable to convert so
much of a vast wilderness into a rich agricultural region, and thus create

---

[20] *Ibid.*, 130.
[21] *Ibid.*, 123-4.
[22] *Ibid.*, 164.
[23] *Ibid.*, 165.
[24] Bourne, chapter xviii.
[25] Saco, 166.

a permanent source of wealth. Hard as the lot of the negro undoubtedly was, the treatment that he received at the hands of his Spanish and Portuguese owners compares favorably with that of other Europeans. In Hispanic America the color line was less sharply drawn and there was less bitterness between master and slave than was the case in the French and English possessions. While the black man suffered everywhere, the ill-treatment that he received in Spanish and Portuguese America was more of neglect than of brutality.

Before turning to another section of colonial society, mention should be made of another source of enforced labor and foreign blood, although the contribution was relatively small. The merchant vessels that ploughed their slow and tortuous way across the Pacific from Manila to Acapulco carried alleged negroes from Malaca, the Moluca Islands, and from the Philippines, a traffic sufficiently large to move Spanish authorities to promulgate a prohibitory decree.[26] These slaves were probably Malays and may well have included a few Chinese. Thus a small contingent of Asiatics was added to the heterogenous population of Hispanic America.

V. INDIANS

In many countries south of the Río Grande the original inhabitants, the Indians, are still of fundamental sociological importance. In others they have disappeared so completely that they are of less significance than in the United States. These aboriginals scattered over the whole hemisphere differed greatly in character, and to these dissimilarities the Spanish and Portuguese were obliged to adapt themselves. The native stock was of a low order in the Caribbean islands and quickly succumbed to the new customs and diseases introduced by Europeans; thus the influence of these Indians on colonial society was negligible.

But the greatest differences in the native races were observed on the mainland. In the highlands the civilization notably of the Aztecs, Chibchas, and Incas was highly developed, and the populations were so vast that neither recurring plagues nor European exploitation prevented the indigenous elements from far outnumbering their white overlords. The relatively advanced culture and sedentary habits of the Indians in Mexico, Central America, the present republics of Colombia, Ecuador, Peru, and Bolivia engendered a certain passivity and fatalism which facilitated the control of the Spaniards after the first opposition to the conquest was overcome. The blood of the ruling and the subject peoples

---

[26] *Ibid.*, 246, 249, 272.

readily mixed in these regions, but the preponderance of the Indian made him, and to a large extent still makes him, the basis of society.

On the outermost fringes of Spanish and Portuguese possessions roamed the more nomad and warlike tribes that were little disposed to abandon their wild and free manner of living. The Europeans, foiled in their efforts to subjugate these barbarians by a swift, dramatic conquest, were compelled to wage almost constant guerrilla warfare during all of the colonial era. The untamed aborigines of northern New Spain were ever a thorn in the side of the crown and, added to geographical obstacles, greatly impeded the expansion of the Spaniards in that direction. But a more striking instance of the intransigence of the Indians is that of the Araucanians of Chile who continued to resist successfully the advances of the white invaders well into the nineteenth century. The obstinate defense of these Indians had an important social effect on their enemies, for it fostered a sturdy type of pioneering peasant in Chile not unlike the early settlers that created the United States out of a continental wilderness.

In parts of the Río de la Plata region, as in present Argentina and Uruguay, the fate of the natives was much the same as in North America; in Paraguay, the seat of the most striking social experiment of the Jesuits, the white element was never numerous and the population remained almost purely Indian. In Brazil, the Portuguese encountered a strong, warlike race called the *Tupis;* they were divided into sixteen tribes speaking a common language, were addicted to polygamy and cannibalism, and did not yield easily to the Portuguese who sought to enslave them.[27] The efforts of the Jesuits in their behalf met with the sullen opposition of the Portuguese colonists who needed enforced labor to work their plantations. Half-castes known as *mamelucos* became skillful horsemen and made a profession of hunting down Indians in the *sertão,* or wilderness, to serve on these vast estates, especially in the north of Brazil. Many of these half-breeds came from the southern part of the country where, in more stimulating climatic conditions, the whites worked harder and the fusion of ethnic elements was more equable.

That the sedentary tribes, numerically the largest group of Hispanic America, were exploited, often cruelly, cannot be denied. In theory the legislation governing the treatment of the aboriginals was enlightened. The fact that in actual practice it proved less humanitarian is not

---

[27] Reparaz, 17.

so much the fault of the Spanish and Portuguese as of the age in which they lived. The doctrine of human rights was scarcely embryonic in contemporary Europe. Moreover, the interposition of a wide ocean between the law-giving and the law-enforcing agencies made it inevitable that the protection of the Indians envisaged in the *encomienda* system, for example, should be subordinated to the material profit of selfish *encomenderos*. The Spanish policy was to reduce the natives to town or village life, convert them to Christianity, eradicate odious practices and vices, and train them in essential trades and occupations.[28] To this end the Indians were compelled to live in communities provided with the requisite number of municipal officials, a church, and a curate. Over them the *encomendero* exercised a sort of feudal sway. He was entitled to a certain tribute in return for the protection that he gave, and it was from this feature of the system that the gravest abuses arose.

The enforced labor at the mines, called the *mita,* was probably the cause of the greatest suffering and cruelty that the unfortunate Indians were obliged to bear, and many died from exhaustion induced by their inhuman tasks. In this respect the lot of the Peruvian natives was appreciably worse than those of New Spain, and the serious uprising of Tupac Amarú in the eighteenth century can be traced to this injustice under which the Incas grew desperate.[29] In judging the distress of the Indians during the colonial period, however, and in pointing out abuses such as the *mita,* it is important to recall the conditions which prevailed in contemporary Europe and institutions such as the *corvée* in France. Comparisons of this sort tend to indicate that, bitter and discouraging as was the situation of the Indian population, it was often better than that of the humble masses on the other side of the Atlantic Ocean.

VI. The Mixed Races

Having briefly discussed the three racial groups, the European, African, and native American, that came together in Hispanic America, there remains the large element resulting from the fusion of such disparate races. This kaleidoscopic miscegenation with its myriad shades and complexions and social castes requires a detailed study which can only be suggested here.

The laws of the Indies recognized the difference between mulattoes,

---

[28] Cf. Bourne, chapter xvii.
[29] Cf. Juan and Ulloa, part ii, chapters ii and iii.

mestizos (offspring of Indian and white mating), and *zambaigos*[30] (offspring of the union of an Indian and a negro, also called *zambos*); but these were but the rudimentary combinations. In the course of a few generations cross-breeding resulted in so many shades of color that an elaborate system of nomenclature was necessary to identify each gradation, and a complicated social hierarchy developed chiefly based on the amount of white blood in an individual's veins.

The names of these various classifications were often curious and of obscure origin. The progeny of a *mestizo* couple, for example, were commonly called *tente en el aire* (suspended in the air) because they frequently indicated no advance toward the white ancestry or no particular retrocession. If a *mestiza* woman married an Indian, their offspring bore the designation *salta atrás* (a throw-back) because the trend was toward the indigenous ancestor instead of the more highly esteemed white forbear. There were similar advances and retreats in the intermarriage of Indian and negro half-castes, and the union of these with *mestizos* and other elements created a bewildering mongrel population which cannot be further analyzed in this account.

The brief description of the component parts of colonial society set forth will indicate its heterogeneous character which furnishes an ethnic interpretation of the accepted political theory of the age summed up in the expression "divide and rule." The innumerable castes gave rise to a confusing array of social distinctions which were exaggerated and distorted by those imported from the mother countries. The mutual jealousy and lack of cohesion, even among those of undiluted white blood resulting from this situation, explain in large measure why the restiveness of the colonists, occasionally visible, was never translated into active opposition to either the Spanish or Portuguese governments; not until Napoleon had swept away momentarily the old order in the peninsula were the political ties broken at last with Spain and Portugal.

VII. Occupations

Social position, based largely on blood, determined to a considerable extent the occupation of the individual. The European-born whites constituted the aristocracy and the ruling class; the humbler type of peninsular formed the commercial element. The distaste of the wealthy Creoles for business or manual work made them a leisure class; from

---

[30] Saco, 225. This author gives a brief account of the various races and castes in Hispanic America in *ibid.,* 226-229.

their midst were drawn the students of the colonial universities who crowded the professions, namely, law, medicine, and the lesser offices of the church. Some became scholars or *literati* of merit.

The large hybrid population with its complex hierarchy had callings suited to its varying social distinctions. The upper strata were scarcely distinguishable from the Creoles; the lower were confused with the Indians and negroes and shared much the same fate. The *mestizo* class was conspicuous in the military service, and the term "Spaniards" used in official documents and reports of campaigns and battles invariably referred to persons of undiluted white blood. The trades and industries were also open to this group, though usually the more menial tasks. While the Indians were early taught some of the crafts and might engage in these activities, in the main they, like the negroes, were condemned to domestic service, hard agricultural pursuits, and the heavy work of the mines—slaves in fact if not in theory.

The more technical industries were organized into a series of *gremios,* or guilds, like those of medieval Europe, whose members, together with the shopkeepers and merchants, formed a sort of bourgeoisie. These corporate bodies were a legal classification of the various trades, and were created for the regulation of production and the collection of taxes; they were unions of artisans for self-protection and for improving the technique of their art. Carpenters, bakers, saddlers, tanners, smelterers, shoemakers, candlemakers, goldsmiths, silversmiths, ironsmiths, manufacturers of fireworks, and innumerable other occupations were thus organized. Within their own ranks they distinguished between the apprentice, craftsman, and master-craftsman, and only the latter, the *maestro* who had attained a high degree of mastery of his profession, could open a shop. Before authorization was given, however, his knowledge, both theoretical and practical, was tested by a competent board of peers from his own guild. When this tribunal, ever vigilant of the welfare of its calling, handed down a favorable decision, the city council issued a certificate, a species of license, permitting the candidate to establish his *taller,* and employ fellow-craftsmen and apprentices. At the beginning of every year the *maestros* of each trade assembled and appointed a *veedor,* or inspector, whose duty was to visit the shops and examine both the raw materials used and the finished product in order to guard against falsification or the manufacture of inferior goods. He must denounce any violations of the ethics or practices of his profession. These *gremios* flourished in the seventeenth and the early part of the eighteenth century, and, particularly in the wealthier colonies, exerted an important influence on economic and social life.[31]

Unfortunately, the proportion of the population thus usefully employed was relatively small. A far greater number of ignorant, superstitious, and vicious idlers congregated in the cities and towns and became the beggars, criminals, gamblers, and frequenters of *pulquerías*[32] or equivalent establishments with which all colonial communities were afflicted. Indians, negroes, mulattoes, *zambaigos,* etc., with a sprinkling of renegade Spaniards called *zaramullos,* constituted this unhappy sediment of society and were ever a potential cause of riots and public disturbances.[33] This idle riffraff seized every opportunity to rob or loot, and the public gallows continually displayed the lifeless corpse of some luckless vagrant. Not infrequently the tranquillity of colonial life was severely shattered by incipient outbreaks or street brawls when public vigilance was relaxed. The misery and utter ignorance of the multitude caused innumerable sorcerers and quacks, practicing magic rites inherited from African and Indian barbarism, to flourish; faith in witchcraft, illuminati, and other superstitions was general. The archives of the Inquisition are filled with records of arrests and prosecution as the Holy Office strove to stamp out these evils.

VIII. AMUSEMENTS

But life was not all dreariness and wretchedness in the colonies, for the masses possessed a vast capacity for enjoying simple pleasures; they loved spectacles, and the chronicles of the period teem with descriptions of glittering processions. *Fiestas* lasted for days, even weeks, with a full and varied round of activities. Only a few of these diversions, both

---

[31] This discussion of the colonial guilds is based chiefly on Manuel Romero de Terreros y Vinent, *Las artes industriales en la Nueva España* (Mexico, 1923), *Introducción;* see also, José Torre Revello, "El gremio de plateros en las indias occidentales," *Publicaciones del Instituto de Investigaciones Históricas* (Buenos Aires, 1932), núm. lxi.

[32] Taverns or saloons where an intoxicating beverage made from the maguey plant was sold.

[33] One of the most serious of these disturbances in Mexico was the so-called Corn Riot of 1692 of the Indians in which an effort was made to overthrow the viceregal government. See *Alboroto y motín de México del 8 de Junio de 1692, relación de Don Carlos de Sigüenza y Góngora* . . ., edited by Irving A. Leonard (Mexico, 1932). Hubert Howe Bancroft, *History of Mexico* (San Francisco, 1883), III, chapters xii and xiii gives a detailed account of this uprising.

public and private, which enlivened the daily life of all classes, can be mentioned.[34]

The many games of chance with cards and dice brought over by the *Conquistadores* became the common heritage of Hispanic American society and a besetting vice. Cock-fighting enjoyed a constant vogue among the poorer members and was ever associated with betting and gambling. These diversions sank deep roots into the habits of the colonists and retain much of their pristine vigor among the Latin Americans of today.

The hardy conquerors also brought a love of the more manly sports derived from war and the chase and calling for great skill in horsemanship and dexterity in the use of weapons. They delighted in tourneys and jousts in which men, armed with blunted lances and swords and protected by armor, attacked each other in groups or in single combat, striving to fell their opponents. As succeeding generations grew less inured to these violent and sometimes fatal encounters, shafts of light material were substituted for metal in the pastime called *jugar cañas.* With this was associated another exercise in skillful equestrianism termed *correr la sortija* which consisted of driving a lance or staff through a small ring while riding at full speed. These entertainments, recalling those of the Middle Ages, were attended by a pomp and ceremony which accounts for their popularity with all classes.

Bull-fighting was early introduced and quickly won a permanent place in the hearts of the Indian and African populace as well as their white masters. The *corridas* were often varied by novelties and theatrical effects. There were few or no professional *toreros,* and it was the custom of young hotspurs of the aristocracy to slip into the arena and display their dexterity and courage. The baiting of bulls and steers was a universal pastime, while extraordinary feats with the lariat were watched with fascination.

Probably the most popular and widespread of entertainments enjoyed by every class were the *cabalgatas* and *mascaradas.* The first were dignified parades of gaily caparisoned horses and riders resplendent in

---

[34] A brief description of games and sports popular in colonial days is that of Federico Gómez de Orozco, "Juegos y deportes en la Nueva España," *Anales del Museo Nacional de Arqueología, Historia y Etnografía,* (Mexico, 1932, although dated 1929), época 4a, vi, 10-16. Though referring to colonial Mexico, the pastimes described were universal in Hispanic America; see also, José Torre Revello, "Del Montevideo del siglo xviii: fiestas y costumbres," *Revista del Instituto Histórico y Geográfico del Uruguay,* VI, no. 2 (reprint separate).

bright uniforms, displaying decorated banners and emblems; the second were composed of groups of persons, either on horseback or on foot, wearing varied and peculiar costumes and masks, who marched in processions about the city streets by day or night. In the latter case torches were usually carried. The disguises might represent historical, mythological, and Biblical personages, the gods of primitive religions, and planets, or they might symbolize the Virtues, Vices, and other abstractions. The garbs of different nations were imitated, especially those of Turks and Indians; it was usual, also, to simulate the forms of birds and animals. Another familiar device was to represent the figures upside down with feet in the air and head toward the ground. Often *carros,* or floats, of an allegorical character accompanied these parades of masqueraders. Some *mascaradas* were given exclusively by students, or a particular guild, a racial group, and even by women and children.[35]

All of these diversions and many others formed the varied program of festivities in honor of a birth or marriage in the royal family, the reception of a viceroy, or some other joyous event or anniversary; and the *pièce de résistance* of these celebrations lasting for days was usually an elaborate display of fireworks.

Less boisterous pleasures were equally numerous. The open-air theater was exceedingly popular from the earliest days after the conquest, and the Indians themselves, under the tutelage of the missionaries, took part in the representation of *autos sacramentales.*[36] To a more select audience, conventional plays of the Spanish stage were given by white actors in closed theaters, though the proletariat was not excluded. The drama was ever dear to the heart of the Peninsulars, and this enthusiasm was fully shared by the colonists.[37]

The aristocracy took delight in ceremonious social functions affording opportunities for a rich display of jewels, wearing apparel, carriages, and uniformed lackeys. Besides the daily *paseo,* or stroll, to which everyone came to admire and be admired, there were the more formal *besamanos* and *saraos* on the birthday of kings, viceroys, and other high dignitaries. On these occasions the town or city was gaily bedecked

---

[35] A discussion of the *mascaradas* is given in Irving A. Leonard, "A Mexican 'Máscara' of the seventeenth century," *Revista de Estudios Hispánicos,* (New York, 1929), II, 156-167.

[36] Cf. F. A. de Icaza, "Cristóbal de Llerena y los orígenes del teatro en la América española," *Revista de Filología Española,* (Madrid, 1921), VIII, 121-130.

[37] Cf. J. R. Spell, "The theater in Mexico City, 1805-1806," *Hispanic Review* (Philadelphia, 1933), I, 55-65.

with banners and bunting. Toward evening, lighted by torches or lanterns, a procession of beautifully carved carriages, drawn by handsomely accoutered horses, and hand-chairs carried by liveried slaves or servants moved slowly down the avenue before the gaping populace and in the direction of the gate of the palace. The richly dressed and bejeweled ladies and gentlemen alighted at the door and marched majestically up the stairs to the reception chamber where the utmost ceremony was observed in the salutations, the dance, and at the sumptuous banquets.[38]

Many were the games proper to the *salón,* amusements designed to provoke the merriment of the assembled guests that seem infantile to a more sophisticated age. Social gatherings were enlivened by guessing contests, charades, forfeits, blind-man's buff, and innumerable other innocent pastimes enjoyed with the abandon of small children.[39] On the outer edges or in the corners older and more sober-minded men might sit and play checkers or chess, or merely smoke and chat.

Both young and old took keen delight in the pleasures of the swing, the seesaw, and dancing in the groves or public squares; children played marbles, spun tops, and played games whose equivalents are found in every land and age. The Spaniards, Portuguese, Africans, and Indians all possessed a great capacity for light-hearted enjoyment which made their lives far more happy than the environment, seemingly so harsh and unkind, would lead one to suspect. Indeed, it is an open question whether these childlike people of colonial Hispanic America did not enjoy as large a measure of contentment as has fallen to the lot of the masses of a later and, apparently, more fortunate age.

SELECTED BIBLIOGRAPHY

A truly descriptive account adequately portraying the colonial societies of Hispanic America in all their manifold aspects is yet to be written. The curious investigator must still content himself with fragmentary descriptions and the merest glimpses of the everyday life of the Portuguese and Spanish colonies which are widely dispersed in books and periodicals. No systematic effort has yet been made to utilize the immense amount of material of this nature found in scattered articles, old works which are generally bibliographical rarities, and old manuscripts whose existence is already known, as well as others yet to be ferreted out. Most of the general histories of Hispanic America in one volume or more suffer from the handbook method, particularly in their treatment of the society and culture of

---

[38] Romero de Terreros, *Ex-Antiquis, bocetos de la vida social en la Nueva España* (Guadalajara, 1919). See especially the sections entitled "Procesiones y Paseos" and "El Gran Mundo Social."

[39] A comprehensive list of games of this type popular in colonial days is given in Gómez de Orozco, 15, note 1.

the former possessions of Spain and Portugal. A few of the better representatives of this class giving a general idea of the subject may be cited.

F. García Calderón, *Latin America: its rise and progress* (London, 1913); Robert Grant Watson, *Spanish and Portuguese south America during the colonial period* (2 vols., London, 1884); Edward Gaylord Bourne, *Spain in America* (New York, London, 1904); A. Curtis Wilgus, *A history of Hispanic America* (Washington, D. C., 1931), especially useful for its bibliography; and J. Fred Rippy, *Historical evolution of Hispanic America* (New York, 1932), the most recent and an excellent survey, are all very useful to the student who reads only English. Charles de Lannoy and Herman Vander Linden, *Histoire de l'expansion coloniale des peuples européens* (Paris, 1907), is a valuable study; Carlos Navarro y Lamarca, *Compendio de la historia general de América* (2 vols., Buenos Aires, 1913) offers an excellent treatment of colonial society.

A few works emphasizing the sociological and ethnic aspects of colonial civilization are cited at random. A. Colmo, *Los paises de la América latina* (Madrid, 1915); A. G. Keller, *Colonization* (Boston, 1908); Jerónimo Bécker, *La política española en las indias* (Madrid, 1920); Gregorio Torres Quintero, *México hacia el fin del virreinato español; antecedentes sociológicos del pueblo mexicano* (Mexico City, 1921); Luís Thayer Ojeda, *Elementos étnicos que han intervenido en la población de Chile* (Santiago de Chile, 1919).

Much information can be gleaned from the contemporary accounts of travelers from Europe who visited the various colonies in America. Among the best of these are the writings of Jorge Juan and Ulloa whose *Noticias secretas de América* has been cited. The latter is, perhaps, the most informative, but Antonio de Ulloa, *A voyage to South America* (translated from the original Spanish by John Adams, in John Pinkerton, ed., *A general collection of the best and most interesting voyages and travels* . . ., London, 1808-1814) affords much descriptive material of great value. The writings of Alexander Humboldt, particularly the *Personal narrative of travels to the equinoctial regions of America, during the years 1799-1804* (3 vols., London, 1852-53), and the *Political essay on the kingdom of New Spain* (London, 1811), are, of course, exceedingly important. Also François Raymond Joseph De Pons, *Travels in South America during the years 1801, 1802, 1803, and 1804* (London, 1807), and his *A voyage to the eastern part of Terra Firma, or the Spanish Main* (New York, 1806). Earlier travelers giving intimate glimpses of society in New Spain are: Thomas Gage, *A new survey of the West Indies* (London, 1699, and many subsequent editions); and Giovanni Francesco Gemelli Careri, *Giro del mondo, parte sesta* (Napoles, 1721, with an English version in Awnship Churchill, *A collection of voyages and travels,* London, 1752, vol. iv). The various collections of *memorias* of the viceroys or instructions to their successors often contain much interesting information regarding colonial society. For Peru see especially Manuel Anastasio Fuentes, ed., *Memorias de los virreyes que han gobernado el Perú, durante el tiempo del coloniaje español* (6 vols., Lima, 1859), and José Toribio Polo, *Memorias de los virreyes del Perú, Marqués de Mancera y Conde de Salvatierra* (Lima, 1896). For New Spain, see *Instrucciones que los virreyes de Nueva España dejaron á sus sucesores* (Mexico, 1867).

Another class of source material of first importance is represented by a number of diaries which have subsequently been printed. These daily records were kept by individuals in the colonies who noted down public and private incidents of the life around them. Though often brief and sketchy they are valuable first-hand accounts not written deliberately for publication. Among these are: Joseph de Mugaburu and Francisco de Mugaburu, *Diario de Lima (1640-1694) crónica de la época colonial. Colección de libros y documentos referentes á la historia del Perú,*

Lima, 1917), tomos vii, viii; Antonio de Robles, "Diario de sucesos notables," in *Documentos para la historia de México* (Mexico, 1853), ser. i, vols. ii, iii; Juan Antonio Rivera, "Diario curioso de México," in *Documentos para la historia de México* (Mexico, 1854), ser. i, vol. vii. To these might be added José Toribio Medina, *Cosas de la colonia* [Chile], (Santiago de Chile, first ser., 1889, second ser. 1910).

Varying amounts of material will be found in the histories of special regions or areas. It is, of course, impossible to give a complete bibliography here, but the following are representative and contain considerable information. For Portuguese America, Robert Southey, *History of Brazil* (London, 1817-1822), and F. A. Varnhagen, *Historia geral do Brasil* (Rio de Janeiro, 1877), are still the most useful. Social conditions and the treatment of the Indians in Brazil can be studied in Affonso de E. Taunay, *Historia geral das bandeiras paulistas* (6 vols., São Paulo, 1924-1930). Some exceptionally good treatments of colonial society are found in the case of New Spain in English. Hubert Howe Bancroft, *History of Mexico* (6 vols., San Francisco, 1883-1888), contains what is still one of the best descriptions (vol. iii). Herbert Ingram Priestley, *The coming of the white man* (New York, 1929), is a recent and very readable treatment of the subject. The monumental work under the editorship of Vicente Riva Palacio, *México á través de los siglos* (5 vols., Mexico, 1887-1889), replete with illustrations, is the most ambitious survey of the colonial period particularly (see volume ii). Luis González Obregón, *Época colonial. México viejo* (Paris and Mexico, 1900), and his *México viejo y anecdótico* (Paris and Mexico, 1909), give much of the color and atmosphere of colonial life. Numerous other works of varying value such as Isaac Barrera, *Quito colonial, siglo xviii* (Quito, n. d.) could be cited, but they afford an incomplete picture of society itself.

With regard to works, usually articles, dealing with customs, amusements, and occupations, a systematic search would undoubtedly bring together a considerable literature from widely scattered sources. This task remains to be done, and here only a short suggestive list is offered. Nicholás Rangel, *Historia del toreo en México, época colonial, 1529-1821* (Mexico, 1924), is more comprehensive than its title indicates as it gives something of a survey of the society of the times. The studies of the representative of the *Boletín del Instituto de Investigaciones Históricas* of Buenos Aires in Seville, Spain at the Archive of the Indies, José Torre Revello, are largely related to the social and cultural history of the Spanish colonies. While many of his articles refer to Argentine history, they are of universal application to conditions elsewhere in colonial Spanish America. A few of these are: "Los bailes, las danzas, y las máscaras en la colonia," (*Bol. Inst. Inv. Hist.*, vol. X, no. 46, Oct.-Dec., 1930, 434-454); "Los orígenes de la danza, la canción y la música populares argentinas" (Seville, 1926), and the study of the guild of silversmiths in the Indies cited in the text. Also "Un pleito sobre bailes entre el cabildo y el obispo de Buenos Aires," (*Bol. Inst. Inv. Hist.* vol. V, 1926-1927, 285 ff.); José Antonio Pillado, *Buenos Aires colonial, edificios y costumbres, estudios históricos* (Buenos Aires, 1910); Juan Canter, "El teatro de la ranchería o casa de comedias, y los bailes de máscaras del coloniaje," *Revista Argentina de Ciencias Políticas*, vol. XX, nos. 115-117, p. 145-153 (Buenos Aires, 1920); and J. F. del Barrio Lorenzot, *El trabajo en México durante la época colonial. Ordenanzas de gremios de la Nueva España* (Mexico, 1920).

Lastly, the historian need not scorn, and the student will enjoy, those creative works in which certain historical writers have turned from the sometimes arid pursuits of research and given their bridled fancy free rein. Occasionally, in departing from recorded facts they have been able, by long association with the period, to bring to their narratives certain intangible qualities, an authentic atmosphere and understanding, which are quite as important as the cold facts from which history is written. The most celebrated, and justly so, are the *Tradiciones peruanas,* (4 vols., Madrid, 1924, and various other editions) of the distinguished historian and man of letters of Peru, Ricardo Palma. These tales are based on facts gleaned from the author's familiarity with colonial records and are not only essentially accurate history but literature of a high order. For an inspired description of colonial life in Peru these legends are warmly recommended.

CHAPTER TEN

THE TRANSMISSION AND DIFFUSION OF CULTURE IN THE SPANISH AMERICAN COLONIES

By Cecil Knight Jones

I T IS the writer's wish to discuss briefly the transmission and diffusion of Spanish culture in the Spanish American colonies and to indicate some of the characteristics and results of the colonial educational system which shaped intellectual life and activities.

In attempting to outline the essential factors that determined the cultural and intellectual life it seemed necessary to sketch briefly the Spanish background during the three centuries of colonial dominion, and to call attention to the origin and development of colonial society, and to significant aspects of colonial administrative policy.

The writer must disclaim in advance any attempt at originality. The statements made are drawn from secondary sources for the most part, and from sources that are interesting for the study of the colonial background of nineteenth century literature. From these the writer will quote fully and extensively, a procedure not devoid of purpose.

The three centuries of colonial dominion form a stage of infinite variety of settings, varying as to time and clime. On this stage is portrayed the vivid panorama of the birth and development of new national entities, and corresponding cultures. In this composite scene factors apparently trivial may, properly estimated, prove valuable in indicating the character and boundaries of human intelligence and psychology at a given moment. As today, when politics and economics are strangely blended, so during the colonial period economic and administrative policies exercised a strong influence in determining the ideas and preoccupations, the thought and actions of the people. Even in conventual disputes and scholastic discussions, as Barreda says, it is possible to glimpse an immense and unexplored region of human psychology. Thus it seems necessary to consider various factors as determinants of the colonial mind, of the intellectual and cultural life of Spanish America in its progress from the beginning of the sixteenth century to the period of emancipation.

I. The Spanish Cultural Background

The year 1492 was a memorable one in the historical annals of Spain. It marked the end of one cycle and the beginning of another of even greater significance. The capture of Granada and final defeat of the Moors ended the long and varied drama of the Wars of the Reconquest, of the secular crusade of the cross against the crescent, which had operated so powerfully in forming national character, in determining individual psychology, and in shaping Spain's historical destinies.

The discovery of America during the same year initiated the marvelous era of discovery, exploration, and settlement which was to bring to Spain colonial possessions of fabulous extent and opulence, an exotic empire that formed a vast theater for adventurous exploits, a virgin field for economic exploitation, and a new sphere for the exhibition of Spain's evangelizing fervor. Spain's colonial empire in the Western Hemisphere lasted some three hundred years, from the beginning of the sixteenth to the beginning of the nineteenth century. This period of settlement and of political organization is a period of gestation for the American colonies. It involved the creation of new racial types progressively developing a psychology and orientation distinct in many respects from those of the metropolis. During this period, with the evolution of new ethnic blends, new ideas were developed typical of the political, social, and physical environment. The civilization and culture pattern evolved under these unique conditions necessarily implied a new evaluation of Spanish tradition, a new political and spiritual orientation resulting finally in the birth of the present Hispanic American republics.

In examining the cultural elements, social, intellectual, and artistic, of the Spanish colonies, one is inevitably forced to a preliminary consideration of Spain's history during these three hundred years of dominion and direction. One must have some conception of Spain's administrative objectives and processes in its relations with its colonies. One must know something of educational methods and cultural conditions in the mother country. One must inquire into the policy and factors that determined the transmission of culture to the colonies. For it is only by an adequate acquaintance with Spain's history and with Spanish thought that one may hope to understand the processes and elements that operated in forming colonial culture. It is only by the aid of such a study of background that one may form an equitable conception of the value of Spain's contribution to the development of educational culture in its colonies.

The fifteenth century initiated the most brilliant period of Spanish history. Succeeding Ferdinand and Isabella came the Hapsburgs. Under the first two monarchs of that house, Charles I and Philip II, Spain advanced rapidly in all the orders of national life—political, economic, and cultural. It became the most powerful nation in the world, whose far-flung empire embraced large portions of both hemispheres. Nor was its primacy limited to the political field. The intense and remarkable intellectual productivity of the Golden Age was unparalleled. And one may add that the literary and artistic activity, due to the momentum acquired during the period of its rapid ascent, lasted well into the period of decline. Altamira gives an excellent picture of this period of national greatness.

"The sixteenth and seventeenth centuries represent the highest point in the history of Spanish intellectual achievement, in science, literature, and art. Two manifestations characterize the era: an abundant productivity which was as high in quality as it was great in amount; and the diffusion of Spanish learning in the other countries of the civilized world, so that for the first time (except for the transmission of Moslem culture) Christian Spain became a vital factor in European thought, whereas in former years she had merely received the instruction of others. The reasons for this intellectual outburst were various. For one thing, the natural evolution from the past seemed to render inevitable a high degree of attainment. For another, the general effects of the Renaissance in Europe made themselves felt in Spain. In the third place, this seems to have been the era of the ripe maturity of the Spanish people, when they were at the height of their capacity in every walk of life. Finally, as has happened so many times in the history of other nations, the very fact of the establishment of a great empire was bound to react both materially and psychologically to produce an unwonted expansion intellectually. These operated directly to make Spain an innovator in scientific thought, and provided the first noteworthy material for mental stimulus in the era." [1]

The discovery of America contributed to this result, providing a vast field for that marvelous burst of energy in national expansion and exercising a catalytic effect upon national, political and intellectual activities.

Education is a fundamental factor in the creation of culture. Its consideration, then, is vital in relation to intellectual life, to the foundation of that brilliant galaxy of authors, philosophers, theologians, scientists, and jurists that represented Spain during the Golden Age.

---

[1] Charles E. Chapman, *A history of Spain,* founded on the *Historia de España* by Rafael Altamira, 339.

And in examining the character and extent of the educational system of the period, one is amazed at the multiplicity of universities and collegiate schools of the religious orders, affording opportunities for advanced studies. Education was aristocratic in type. Primary education was neglected. An appreciation of the value of the education of the lower classes as a means of raising the general level of culture was not common at the time, either in Spain or elsewhere.

In 1516 there were eight universities in Spain, including the famous institutions, Salamanca and Alcalá. The former offered a fuller curriculum with about 60 chairs; it also attracted a greater number of students, 6,778 in 1584.

> "The medieval type of internal management remained as the essential basis of university administration, characterized by the close connection between the university and the civil authorities . . . by an intimate relationship with the cathedral or other local churches, and by the ecclesiastical origin of many of the university rents." [2]

During the sixteenth century twenty-one universities were founded, and five were established in the seventeenth century—a total of thirty-four. In addition to these, there were such special institutions of higher learning as the *Estudios Reales de San Isidro,* under Jesuit direction, and the renowned nautical school of the *Casa de Contratación,* besides various schools both religious and secular, principally for the study of Latin.

Of major interest to us in the character of studies carried on in the universities during the period of Spain's ascendancy, and some acquaintance with the outstanding characters produced by these institutions of higher learning. Such an inquiry involves an analysis of the reaction of Spanish intellectuals to the new ideas resulting from the Renaissance.

This significant movement, developed by a slow gestation in Italy, represents the transition from the Middle Ages to the modern era. It affected human life in all its varied aspects and orders, bringing a new orientation. The revival of learning brought an acquaintance with Greek language and thought which had been lost to western Europe.

> "The resurrection of classical antiquity, apart from the enrichment that all that lost culture supposed, produced a new spirit of individual liberty in the exercise of human reason and fancy. For this reason it has been said that with the Renaissance was born a

[2] Chapman, 340.

new historical factor: the individual man. During the Middle Ages the individual was under the guardianship of institutions and ideas of universal character: the dominant conception was that of a universal church and a universal empire. The supreme mental force was the scholastic philosophy, product of the effort to codify the whole of existing knowledge under certain laws and formulas which made this reconcilable with the sole truth, that which the church had sanctioned. But in the fourteenth and fifteenth centuries there was born and developed in Italy, from the warmth of the resurrection of classical antiquity, a new intellectual movement, Humanism, which from the beginning bore as characteristic notes the aspiration to the spiritual liberty of man and the full development of his being." [3]

The inspiration of the new truths of the Renaissance and of Humanism was soon felt in other countries of Europe, one of the most interesting manifestations being the influence upon the church, the Christian Renaissance. This itself developed two forms, the one orthodox, reconciling the new intellectual demands with dogma; the other heterodox, giving birth in Germany to the Reformation. Erasmus represents the first, Luther the second.

What was the reaction of Spain and the universities of Spain to this movement which was transforming life and thought throughout Europe? Spain was essentially a Catholic country. By historical antecedents, as seen in the centuries-long struggle against an infidel invader and by the convictions and directions of its two great Hapsburg sovereigns, Spain was cast for the rôle of the defender of the faith against the invasion of heresies and the encroachment of novel ideas. And the church with its fundamental dogmas and its necessary conservatism found itself challenged by much of the new thought. Christian faith, moreover, had been the one unifying influence under Ferdinand and Isabella in welding the integrating elements of the Spanish kingdom. Under such conditions the assumption of Spain's rulers and the Spanish church of the leadership of the Catholic reaction was logical, if not unavoidable.

In analyzing Spain's position—and this has a significant bearing upon its colonial administration—two fundamental state policies must be recognized: (1) the maintenance of the faith against heretical beliefs, and (2) the successful effort to secure political control of the church, the *patronato real*. With respect to the second, students have noted in Spaniards an astounding ability to harmonize absolutism in government with a stout individualism and in a somewhat comparable way to see no in-

---

[3] F. de Onís, *Ensayos sobre el sentido de la cultura española*, 66-67.

compatibility between defense of the faith and independence of papal authority. A clear distinction was recognized by the apologists between the Catholic faith and the church organization.

To turn again to the universities during this period of transition, one finds a dominant interest in theological and philosophic studies, especially during the sixteenth century, limited in originality by need of conforming to Catholic doctrine. One significant reaction to humanistic studies was the introduction in 1508 of the study of Greek in the University of Salamanca and the preparation, under the inspiration of Cisneros, of the Complutension Polyglot Bible, Spain's most notable contribution to Christian humanism. Later, Biblical studies based on critical methods and examination of sources fell under the condemnation of the reactionaries and the Inquisition—the latter, however, being less severe than the university corporations. This is seen in the proceedings against two of Spain's most distinguished humanists, Sánchez de Brozas, *El Brocense,* and Luís de León.

An interesting comment on the educational institutions is made by Altamira:

> "The extraordinary number of these centers finally alarmed the economists and statesmen who endeavored to put a brake upon the resulting evils. The matter was discussed in the Cortes of Madrid of 1619, and formed the material for various decrees. In general, the plethora of institutions of learning, including the universities, . . . was held to be an evil. . . . Navarrete, epitomizing the causes that were alleged, principally against the schools of grammar, says that they diverted many of the common people from the service of arms, from agricultural labor, from the exercise of trades, and, in fine, from the interests and occupations of their fathers without commendable result." [4]

The universities responded to the prevailing philosophy and spirit of Spain. They felt the influence of Spain's position under Charles I and Philip II as the head of the Catholic reaction against the spread of Protestantism and heretical beliefs, one of the results of the Renaissance, which threatened the purity of the faith. Onís quotes Chacón's appreciation of the accomplishments of the universities and of the ideals that inspired their instruction:

> ". . . Up to the present time it has not been found, either in history or the memory of men, that any one formed in the University [of Salamanca] has been disobedient to the pope, disloyal to the

---

[4] R. Altamira, *Historia de España,* iii, 543-544.

king, or convicted or suspected of heresy. They have, on the contrary, been loyal servants of their king, obedient to the Holy See, and eager to recognize its authority, dignity, and power." [5]

Onís concludes that except in the faculties of theology, canons, law, and medicine there was practically no response to the new forces by the University of Salamanca from the introduction of Greek in 1508 to the end of the eighteenth century.

Such an unprogressive, static university life may be regarded as the normal result of the increasing tension in European thought. It marks the beginning of Spain's isolation, of its separation from the current of continental thought. Spain's position due, as we have seen, to historical antecedents, as leader of the Catholic reaction against the Reformation, was becoming more accentuated. The policy of the Spanish monarchs promoted a struggle not only of ideas but of armies. This policy in religious matters involved two elements: (1) the persistent and successful effort to secure from the pope the control of the state church through the establishment of the *pase regio* and the right of appointment to ecclesiastical benefices, and (2) to maintain the purity of the faith. In the accomplishment of the latter of Inquisition and the Jesuit Order were the most effective instruments.

Thus, Spain's advancement from the Middle Ages was not so marked. It has been said and repeated that Spain has never emerged from the Middle Ages. This question is, however, beyond the scope of the present discussion. It is one that probably needs thorough study. Possibly Spain has suffered from the interpretation of its history by scholars of different orientation and unintentional bias. Intolerance was common at the time; it was not limited to Spain, nor for that matter to the sixteenth century. It would not be difficult to cite ample testimony today of man's great capacity to immolate the dissentient. *Homo homini lupus,* man's inhumanity to man is not of a special time or a special land.

With respect to the highly controversial question of the Inquisition, opinions are being modified by the studies of contemporary scholars. Menéndez y Pelayo, the great humanist and scholar, in discussing Spain's unity during the sixteenth century frankly recognizes and defends the Inquisition:

> "Intolerance is a necessary law of human understanding in a state of health. Tolerance is a facile virtue, a disease of periods of skepticism or lack of faith. The one who holds that heresy is a

[5] F. de Onís, 63.

grave crime and sin, threatening the existence of civil society, must accept the spiritual and temporal punishment of heretics. To the atheistic economist the smuggler will always be a greater criminal than the heretic. How can such minds be made to understand the spirit of life and fervor which animated inquisitorial Spain? How can they be made to comprehend that doctrine of St. Thomas: it is more serious to corrupt faith, the life of the soul, than to alter the value of money which provides for the needs of the body?" [6]

It is eminently necessary to understand the spirit of Spain in order to comprehend not only its domestic policy in supporting the Inquisition as the instrument of national unity, political as well as religious, but also its colonial policy, political and cultural.

Despite the repressive measures against the invasion of heretical thought, there were groups and individuals who represented Protestant doctrines, but only groups and individuals. Spain achieved spiritual unity during this age of political and intellectual grandeur. During the Golden Age it reached the full maturity of its genius. In the field of literature the inspiring influence of the Renaissance and humanism were felt in a more direct and untrammeled manner, and the incomparable achievement in the various fields of belles-lettres—the drama, the lyric, and the novel—needs no comment.

Nor was Spain distinguished only in literature. It made notable contributions in all fields of knowledge.

The Catholic Kings, Ferdinand and Isabella, were patrons of culture. The importation of books was encouraged by exempting them from duty. Many Spaniards studied abroad and returned with their acquired learning. Among these Antonio de Nebrija was the most notable for his encyclopedic knowledge and humanistic culture. At a somewhat later period there were distinguished Spaniards in various fields of thought. In philosophy Luís Vives, possibly of equal attainments with Erasmus, anticipated many ideas usually credited to later thinkers. In political science and jurisprudence Victoria, Martinez de la Mata, and Solórzano showed undoubted originality and made definite contributions to knowledge. In history Mariana, Zurita, Páez de Castro, Ocampo, the many well-known historians of the Indies, and others are distinguished for their development of historiographic methodology. In geographical knowledge, cosmography, nautical science, and even in the physical sciences Spaniards made notable contributions. To the encouragement of

---

[6] M. Menéndez y Pelayo, *Historia de España* (Madrid, 1934), 169.

such studies the exploration and settlement of the Indies was a powerful stimulant.

The Golden Age corresponds with the first half of Spain's colonial era. Note the contrast during the second half.

At the end of the seventeenth century Spain was in a state of utter prostration—politically, economically, and intellectually bankrupt. The magnificent efflorescence of national genius during the sixteenth and early seventeenth centuries was past. A galaxy of richly endowed authors had realized a great accomplishment in giving concrete expression to Spain's grandeur and culture in a great and distinctive national literature. Lope de Vega, Cervantes, Ruiz de Alarcón, Gabriel Téllez, to mention but a few of these illustrious names, had through their works erected a monument to national character and national genius that makes Spain's Golden Age the outstanding period of its secular history. It was the achievement of greatest significance in Spain's influence in foreign countries.

But in the realization of this splendid incarnation of national culture, Spanish genius had exhausted itself; its great creative energies were spent. At the death of Calderón in 1681, no one was left worthy to wear his mantle. There ensued an extended period of literary sterility and intellectual impoverishment which lasted well into the following century.

It is to be noted that Spain's most brilliant period of literary activity is not wholly contemporary with its political grandeur. The political and economic decay had begun even under Philip II, one of the greatest monarchs of the Austrian Hapsburgs, who ruled Spain for the two centuries of its greatness and decay. Under his successors, Philip III (1598-1621), Philip IV (1621-1665), and Charles II (1665-1700), lacking the ability of their predecessors, uninterested in the vital questions affecting the realm, and influenced by favorites rather than by capable and responsible ministers, the decadence was accelerated.

Under Charles II Spain reached its lowest depths of political impotence and intellectual barrenness. The king was practically an imbecile, endowed to an extreme degree, by the cumulative influences of consanguineous marriages in the Austrian house, with the physical and mental peculiarities of that family. His court became a center of political intrigue promoted by the dynastic ambitions of France and Austria. Charles died without issue October 29, 1700, but a short time before his death he was prevailed upon by those favoring French influence to execute a will designating Philip of Anjou, grandson of Louis XIV of

France, as his successor. With his death ended the line of Hapsburgs in Spain.

The accession to the throne of a scion of the house of Bourbon in the person of Philip V brought a new orientation into the internal and external affairs of Spain. Altamira points out that the four Bourbons who ruled Spain during the eighteenth century: Philip V (1700-1746), Ferdinand VI (1746-1759), Charles III (1759-1788), and Charles IV (1788-1808), possessed distinctive qualities in common. "They almost all showed great zeal for internal problems affecting the intimate life of the nation or of the state; the reconstruction of national wealth and of the public revenue; the increase of the population and of agriculture; the renaissance of traditional industries and of mercantile relations; and the spreading of culture."

Beneficent results in the fullest measure did not, as might have been expected, flow from these policies because of frequent wars, defensive, imperialistic, and political. The War of Spanish Succession in which Philip, assisted by Louis XIV, defended his succession against the conflicting claim of the Archduke of Austria lasted until the Treaty of Utrecht in 1713 and of Rastatt in 1714. During the later years of his reign there was a series of European wars caused by the dynastic ambitions of Philip's second wife, Elizabeth of Farnese. In later reigns, wars resulted from the defensive and offensive alliance with France, the *Pacto de familia.*

However, despite resulting serious losses of territory and financial exhaustion, capable administration, directed by competent ministers, Orry, Patiño, Somodevilla, Aranda, Floridablanca, Campomanes, and others, brought a distinct renovation in the political, economic, social, and intellectual conditions in Spain that was not arrested until the reign of Charles IV and the attempt of Napoleon to add Spain to his empire.

It is seen, then, that during the three hundred years of Spain's colonial empire in America, Spain itself passed through the period of its greatest power, political as well as intellectual and cultural, which was followed by an unparalleled degeneration under the later Hapsburgs and a partial regeneration under the Bourbons in the eighteenth century.

Menéndez Pidal analyzes the spirit of the Golden Age as follows:

"Almost all the intellectual activity of Spain in her Golden Age was devoted to the development of ideas that in the northern European countries had attained their zenith in the Middle Ages and a fresh and unexpected value when reshaped by Spain in a more modern atmosphere. From the conception of a universal empire allied to the church, from the Society of Jesus, the new mysticism of Santa Teresa and St. John of the Cross, and the new scholasticism of Victoria and Suárez that was the forerunner of modern international law, down to the chivalric novel, the ballad, the drama —all were instances of the reflorescence that was the more luxuriant in that it came at a later time." [7]

II. ELEMENTS OF COLONIAL SOCIETY

One may now briefly examine the type of culture developed in the American colonies of Spain, and to this end is imperative an acquaintance with the previous and contemporary history of Spain—to have in mind the increasing absolutism of its monarchs and its position as the militant defender of the integrity of the Catholic faith.

Menéndez Pidal has found in the Cid the typical representative of Spanish character and of its most notable trait, action. The long war of the Reconquest prepared Spain for the hardships of its great adventure in the exploration and settlement of its colonial empire.

It is to be noted, however, that at the end of the fifteenth and beginning of the sixteenth centuries the unity of Spain, political, social, and linguistic, was not an accomplished fact. Thus at this period, when Spanish civilization began to be transmitted to the New World, it was inevitable that the genius of medieval Spain should inform the nascent society of the colonies.

"The language," to cite Rojas,[8]

"began to assume the formation of a literary language distinct from the colloquial romance. . . . What passed to the New World with the soldiers of the conquest was the living language of illiterates who came for the most part from dialectal regions. It is, consequently, in the oral romance rather than in the literary language of the Golden Age that must be sought the origin of our own language."

In discussing the initiation of a colonial society as the result of the epic deeds of the conquest, special attention must rightly be devoted to the character of the conquerors and first settlers, the *Conquistadores* and *primeros pobladores*. Who were they? To what social classes in Spain did they belong? What influence did environmental conditions exercise upon them? It is appropriate to inquire whether the qualities exhibited by the conquerors may be explained by racial inheritance and the cultural traditions of the conquering country as the biologist and

---

[7] Menéndez Pidal, *The Cid and his Spain*, 472.
[8] Rojas, *Eurindia*, 61.

ethnologist might assert, or by physical environment, emphasized by the youth of the invaders, by remoteness from the colonizing country, and by the complete absence of any social fabric in the colonized countries.

Dr. Juan B. Terán, formerly rector of the University of Tucumán, has studied these problems in a most interesting and informative way in his *El nacimiento de la América española*. To his well-documented and suggestive discussion the writer must acknowledge his indebtedness.

The conquest and colonization of Spanish America was effected not by direct action of the Spanish government, but by individuals acting under definite agreements, or capitulations, with the Spanish Crown. These individual leaders organized their own expeditions, and in accord with the terms of their agreements were entitled to enjoy the advantages that resulted from their actions, subject to certain definite returns to the crown, such as the royal fifth, and subject also to certain obligations with respect to the care, instruction, and conversion of the natives. The term *adelantado* was frequently applied to such leaders, a term of common application in Spain during the Reconquest.

The organizers of these expeditions were generally young. "Cortés was nineteen when he embarked for America and Cieza de León scarcely thirteen, Gonzalo de Sandoval, a captain of Cortés, was twenty-two, and Andrés de Tapia twenty-four, Lope de Aguirre, dead at fifty, had passed half of his life in America" (Terán).

The *Conquistadores*, young, adventurous, far from the restraining influence of social relations of home, received the full impact of an exotic and marvellous physical environment.

Probably never before in history was there so extraordinary a social phenomenon as that presented by the Spanish conquest and settlement of America. On no other occasion of the contact of a conquering and a conquered race has there been so marked a difference between the one and the other, so extended a theater of operation, so astounding the character of the new habitat of the conquerors. Greece, captive, took its victor captive. The effects of high cultural development in the conquered has always exerted a marked influence upon the victors. The Goths in their invasion of western Europe yielded to the cultural influences of Roman civilization.

No similar condition existed in the contact of the Spaniards with the indigenous population of the New World. The conquest and settlement of America was not only a military achievement and economic exploitation, but the transmission and diffusion of the cultural elements of the colonizing race.

Columbus was deeply impressed with the exuberant nature of the New World. He writes in his diary, October 21, 1492:

"Here are great lagoons and over and about them a marvellous wood and here and throughout the island all is green and the vegetation is like April in Andalucía. And the songs of the birds such that man, it seems, would never wish to leave here. And the flocks of parrots obscure the sun, and birds of all kinds wonderfully different from ours. Then there are trees of a thousand varieties and and all manners of fruits of marvellous perfume and I am pained beyond expression not to know them." [9]

In considering the influence of the new habitat upon the *Conquistadores,* Terán says: "Probably never before has human nature been submitted to such a test."

Conditions, to be sure, varied in the different colonies. Mexico was in its physiographic features most similar to Spain, and colonial life there bore the closest resemblance to life in the mother country.

But it may be said in general that the conditions faced by the colonists were of a nature that relaxed the restraints imposed by the civilization of the homeland and released the primitive passions of man—cruelty, greed, and lust—that were so manifest in the conquest. It is, then, not to racial inheritance, not to the character of the colonizing country, that we must wholly impute the characteristics of nascent social life in America, but to the physical and social environment of the *Conquistadores.* The essential qualities of Spanish national character, chivalry, loyalty, and religious faith, were notably modified by such environmental factors.

Significant, too, in the period of the conquest and early settlement was the absence of white women. Terán quotes Bernal Díaz to the effect that in Cortés' expedition of some five hundred and fifty men only nine Spanish wives were found. In fact, the crown showed an early solicitude for the moral question involved in the abandonment of wives by those who had joined the expeditions to the New World.

Thus it was that, in absence of opportunities for the formation of families by marriages between members of the same race, unions of Spaniards and Indian women were common, either legal marriages or unions of temporary and incidental character.

Such marriages were recognized early in the colonial period. Indeed, it is a matter of history that the Spaniard has felt no repugnance to mixing his blood with that of other races, probably a result of ethnic

---

[9] Terán, 57-58.

background and historical antecedents. This attitude, considered from the point of view of racial psychology may, as Maeztu concludes, demonstrate the essential democracy of the Spanish people, the ability to regard all men as equals. In support of this he quotes Alonso de Ojeda's speech to the Indians on landing at the Antilles in 1509: "God, our Lord, who is unique and eternal, created the heavens and the earth and a man and a woman from whom descend you, I, and all men who have been, are, and shall be on earth."[10] We must add, however, that this humane dogma was not applied in relations with the natives.

This hybridization which began with the conquest is a factor of great significance in the cultural and political history of Spanish America, contributing as it did an important integrating factor in the formation of colonial society and determining in large degree the nature of family life. It marked the beginning of a new race. Juan and Ulloa, some two centuries after the conquest, found few families that did not show evidence of mixed blood, blends of Spaniard and Indian or negro, Indian and negro, and many other combinations. It is a confused ethnology. And the question of pureness of blood, *limpieza de sangre*, was a matter of moment in the colonies as it was in Spain where the infusion of Jewish or Arab blood was sedulously guarded against. Certificates testifying to uncontaminated blood were officially issued, but inasmuch as they rested upon personal testimony, they are not always to be taken at face value.

"Laws and customs," says Arcaya, "gave the classification of whites to all *mestizos* in which the white race was mixed only with the Indian." And again: "To be considered as a white of pure blood . . . it was sufficient to prove descent on one side from Europeans although the one in question confessed that through other branches he descended from Indian ancestry. The only thing necessary to prove was that he had no ancestor of African blood."[11] It was such conditions that justified the statement that the colonization of America brought the beginning of a new race, of a new social pattern.

And the society developed during the colonial period possessed distinctive features. The Spanish settlers changed, as has been said, by environmental conditions, and intermarried with Indian women, produced a type of family life lacking all wholesome elements. The gulf between the cultural standards of father and mother, the husband's con-

---

[10] Maeztu, *Defensa de la hispanidad.*
[11] Pedro M. Arcaya, *Estudios de sociología venezolana.*

sciousness of the inferiority of the wife and offspring, could not elicit the mutual respect and unselfish devotion that should characterize the normal family. "The absence of the white woman from the hearth and family deprived society of an abundant source of tranquillity and poisoned the arrows with which the youth, transformed into a man, sets out in pursuit of his ambitions. Man pays society in the same coin he received when a youth." [12] One sees, then, the development of a society of castes, of discordant elements, of incompatibles.

Vasconcelos expresses the following judgment:

"Notice the fact that the mestizo represents an entirely new element in history; for if it be true that in all times the conquered and the conqueror have mixed their bloods, it is also unquestionably true that never before had there come together and combined two races as wide apart as the Indian and the Spaniard, and never before had the fusing processes of two such different castes been made on such a large scale." [13]

The integrating elements of the society developed in the Spanish colonies is thus described by Humboldt who visited America toward the end of the colonial period:

"The Mexican population is composed of the same elements as the other Spanish colonies. They reckon seven races: 1. the individuals born in Europe, vulgarly called *Gachupines;* 2. the Spanish *Creoles,* or whites of European extraction born in America; 3. the *Mestizos,* descendants of whites and Indians; 4. the Mulattoes, descendants of whites and negroes; 5. the *Zambos,* descendants of negroes and Indians; 6. the Indians, or copper-colored indigenous race; and 7. the African negroes." [14]

A society thus formed constitutes a challenge to ethnological speculation. Does a *mestizo* race possess the stability and cohesiveness that condition and permit of progress? Does it inherit, as has been said, the vices of both parent races and the virtues of neither? Does it tend to a reversion to the lower level?

With respect to such questions there seems no sound basis, in the opinion of many modern scientists, for the assumption of inferiority of mixed races. In fact, which are the pure races? Environmental factors are as influential as inheritance. Probably the greatest obstacle to the cultural and economic progress of the *mestizos* is to be sought in

---

[12] Terán, 84.

[13] José Vasconcelos and Manuel Gamio, *Aspects of Mexican civilization,* 83.

[14] A. von Humboldt, *Political essay on the kingdom of New Spain* (Tr. by John Black), Chapter VII.

Spain's administrative system. Under the established organization Spaniards of European birth formed the privileged class, holding practically all important offices, the beneficiaries of the distribution of lands, agricultural and mining, and of *encomiendas* and *repartimientos*. The Creoles, equal in the letter of the law with the Spaniards, were excluded from extensive participation in the conduct of administrative affairs, and the *mestizos* were economically and socially inferior to both Spaniards and Creoles. "Without land grants or mines, commerce or positions of responsibility in church or state, they naturally became a deterrent to progress," says Priestley.[15] Much worse, however, was the fate of the indigenous population.

The primary objective of the *Conquistadores* and first settlers was the rapid acquisition of wealth that would enable them to repatriate themselves and live in luxury. The popular conception of the marvellous New World and of the opportunities for the easy attainment of riches exercised a powerful fascination over the minds of the adventurers.

"Rarely," says Terán, "has a collective hallucination exhibited such clear examples." But the reality faced by the conquerors differed materially from their anticipations. The precious metals were not readily obtainable. The land paid its rich tribute only as a result of the labor applied to its cultivation. The colonizers were far from being disposed to work. Under the circumstances the Indian was the readiest instrument for material aggrandizement; enforced labor was most easily transformed into wealth, either through land cultivation, mining, tribute, or personal service.

This end was accomplished by the institution of the *encomienda,* or the distribution of the natives among the settlers and their subjection to personal service for their *encomenderos*. This semi-feudal institution was borrowed from the Middle Ages. It differed from feudal serfdom in that such grants were not in perpetuity, but limited usually to two generations. They involved, moreover, distinct obligations regarding the conversion and instruction of the Indians. In fact, the Spanish Crown, in sedulous consideration for the welfare of the Indians, wards of the crown, looked upon the *encomienda* at the time of its establishment as a most effective means for the moral and physical improvement of the natives.

But disillusionment soon came as to the moral character of this insti-

---

[15] Priestley, *The Mexican nation.*

tution, and persistent efforts were made to abolish it or limit its deplorable effects. The selfish interests of the beneficiaries were, however, able to thwart the good intent of the monarchs. Many are the humanitarian laws found in that colonial code, the *Recopilación de las leyes de las indias,* but like many other provisions of similar spirit they were treated with callous disregard by most colonial administrators.

It is said that the *encomienda* was the economic backbone of colonial society as well as of public finance. It is a commonplace to say that it was causing the rapid destruction of the Indians. All know the nature of Las Casas' campaign in favor of the aborigines. In substantiation of the charges against the *encomienda,* Terán quotes some statistics from documentary sources of about the year 1582. In the city of Preto of 20,000 Indians, there remain only 8,000 distributed among twenty-eight citizens of a Spanish population of 250. In Almaguer in thirty years Indians were reduced from 15,000 to 2,000 divided among fourteen citizens. In Popayán 4,500 were left of 12,000, in Temana after forty years only 700 were left out of 20,000.

In addition to the devastating effect upon the Indians, the moral effect upon the Spanish settlers of a society with such an economic basis was deplorable, lowering their standards of conscience and their religious integrity.

The protectors of the Indians were the members of the clergy during the sixteenth and seventeenth centuries. They were the real frontiersmen, performing a civil as well as a religious function. Through the organization of missions, doctrines, or reductions, later to be turned over to the civil authorities, they instructed the Indians in religious matters and in trades. But when the period of conquest and settlement was past and some degree of social stabilization was attained, the church and the religious orders showed a marked lowering of moral stamina and religious zeal. This loss of fervor manifested itself clearly and unmistakably in the treatment of the Indians. Juan and Ulloa in their *Memorias secretas* found that modest Indian curacies were allocated for relatively exorbitant sums which seemed, however, proportionate to the income derived by the incumbents through extortion practiced upon the Indians under their charge. It was not unusual to find, for instance, that the property left by an Indian at death was wholly absorbed by the religious rites charged against the deceased.

Negroes formed another element that entered into the racial hybridization of the nascent society. Slaves were introduced into the colonies at an early date, and in large numbers. An interesting history lies back of such importations of human power. The status of the negroes was not, in theological dogma, so high as that of the Indians, although the latter were held to be animals rather than men by many authorities, including Solórzano Pereira in his *Política indiana*. However, theological discussions aside, the advent of the negro slave was determined mainly by economic reasons, among which were the disappearance or rather the destruction of the Caribs of the Antilles with the consequent necessity of supplying other labor, and on the greater adaptability of the negro to agricultural operations. The *Conquistadores* and early settlers were decidedly averse to physical labor, looking upon it as degrading, and thus stockraising, requiring fewer workers, was preferred to cultivation in regions such as the Río de la Plata provinces, while sugar growing, which was soon profitably developed in Cuba and Mexico, required a great deal of manual labor. It resulted that the regions where slaves were most numerous were Cuba, Venezuela, Brazil, and elsewhere, while in Mexico they were mostly used in the *tierras calientes,* or hot tropical sections, rather than in the city. They were, however, very numerous in Lima, where they were used as household servants. In fact, Juan and Ulloa describe the population of Lima as consisting of Spaniards, negroes, Indians, and *mestizos*. Of these the most numerous class was the negroes, mulattoes, *pardos,* and other colored blends.

Thus have been indicated the different classes that soon formed and integrated colonial society, forming social, political, and economic categories. And it is the emergence of these classes, with their clashing interests, their diverse opportunities, their racial varieties determined by different Indian types, and divergent physical environment, that ultimately frustrated Spain's efforts to develop a colonial society upon the pattern of that in the Peninsula.

Such results were of slow development. If one considers the period of Spain's colonial domination as divided into three eras, (1) discovery and exploration, (2) settlement, and (3) the eighteenth century when Creoles and *mestizos* began to cherish vague sentiments of a social and political life independent of Spain, the second may be seen as the time of Spain's most constructive work.

Bernard Moses remarks:

"The organization founded was a creation of the Spanish mind, the Spanish mind still true to its European conceptions. And the government of Spain was not less true to these conceptions in its remarkable efforts to carry Christian faith to the Indians. Spanish America was to be assimilated to the mother country, not merely with respect to religion but also with respect to the form of society; its life was expected to grow into conformity with the European type." [16]

And in his *Intellectual background* Moses expands his views of the factors in colonial society.

"The government in Spain aimed to establish and maintain in America such class distinctions as had existed in Europe. It created a nobility; it granted lands to certain Spaniards emigrating to its American possessions; it required from the grantee a feudal oath similar to that exacted from the king's vassals; to certain landholders it assigned Indians to be their dependents, serfs, or slaves; it created a class of officials almost entirely composed of men sent from Spain. Besides these classes based on the king's favor, there were other classes recognized by their racial peculiarities or the countries of their origin. The Spaniards' habit of regarding the Creoles as untrustworthy and inferior to themselves resulted in making the two groups assume the attitude towards one another which is ordinarily assumed by different peoples. The practice of ignoring the Creole's claim to public office was not so much the result of legal prohibition as the effect of social prejudice directed against him."

The constantly widening breach between Spaniards and Creoles was not wholly attributable to the Spaniards' feeling of superiority, but in large measure, as Juan and Ulloa noted, to the vanity and presumption of the latter toward the immigrants of a later period who were usually of humble extraction and of low economic status. The Creoles' aversion to work was in many cases the result of their training in childhood when parents were wont to entrust the care and upbringing of their children to negro nurses. Under such conditions there is little wonder that the children should develop an aversion to constructive activities involved in the management and improvement of their property, and to participation in trades. The opportunities afforded by such conditions were promptly seized by the ambitious immigrants to the economic prejudice of the Creoles who saw their ancestral acres slipping from their inefficient hands. This economic inefficiency of the Creole, and his envy and resentment against the prosperous European, did much to determine the political ideas and aspirations of the two classes, making of one the exponents of liberty and independence, and of the other representatives of conservatism and reactionism, the supporters of the *status quo*.

---

[16] B. Moses, "Social revolution of the 18th century in South America" in American Historical Association, *Annual Report,* 1915.

The aspirations for liberty were, however, of slow growth and the result of various causes that operated most obviously during the eighteenth century. In a society formed of more or less antagonistic factions, Spaniards, Creoles, *mestizos,* and other castes, the development of a sense of social and political solidarity, a civic consciousness, was conspicuously absent. The attempts of Spain to set up in the colonies a society formed upon the class distinctions that existed in the Peninsula and the general restriction of the colonial administrative system did not tend to create a colonial society conscious of its special interests.

In developing its colonial organization, Spain adopted as far as applicable the administrative system developed during the wars of the Reconquest. The sole authority was lodged in the Crown of Castile, to which was granted by papal bulls sovereignty over lands conquered and settled in the western world. The monarch received this cession under a certain contractual obligation with the Papal See to undertake and be responsible for the conversion and instruction of the infidels. The essential character, then, of government set up in the colonies was its absolutism, political and ecclesiastical, being in this similar to the government of Spain. The conquest was effected by the soldier and the priest, by the secular and the ecclesiastical arms. Promptly upon the coming of the soldier, came the missionaries, usually members of the religious orders, Franciscans, Dominicans, Augustinians, and others. It would be difficult to overemphasize the importance and effectiveness, the zeal and devotion, of the missionaries in the processes of conquest and settlement, and in the formation and organization of colonial society. As has been said, they were the real frontiersmen, moving forward with the military expeditions or promptly following them, drawing together the Indians in missions, *reducciones,* or *doctrinas,* converting and teaching them the Christian faith as well as practical arts and trades, and later turning over such centers to the civil arm. The missionaries were, indeed, the most effective agents of the conquest, performing both administrative as well as ecclesiastical functions. The control of education and the shaping of intellectual life was theirs. And their position in the colonial organization as agents of the crown was rendered possible by the thoroughgoing control exercised by the king over the church in America, the *patronato real,* even more effective than that granted him by the pope over the Spanish church.

Mecham, in fact, in speaking of the royal patronage says that the king was invested with quasi-pontifical authority by reason of privileges granted by Alexander VI and confirmed by Julius II in the papal bull, *universalis ecclesiæ*, July 28, 1508.[17]

The progress of settlement was marked by the founding of cities originally as military centers, the organization of administrative districts, viceroyalties, captaincies-general, *gobiernos, corregimientos,* and others, and the installation of colonial functionaries, viceroys, *audiencias,* and other necessary agents. In a similar manner were established the territorial divisions or provinces of the religious orders.

The cities and towns were naturally the social and cultural nuclei of this incipient society. The cities, unlike European cities which grew gradually and irregularly as social, commercial, and industrial centers, were founded upon a more or less uniform and conventional plan prescribed by law. There was a compulsory reservation of certain communal lands belonging to the municipality: (1) *ejidos,* reserved for recreation facilities of the population; (2) *dehesas,* for common pasturage; and (3) *propios,* for municipal use. These jointly formed the *tierras baldías* and as such were not subject to individual ownership. Outside of these limits, lands were allotted in perpetuity to individuals, forming in many cases the source of great wealth through appreciation in value owing to the growth of the town, the unearned increment.

Land distribution was in general a royal prerogative, though permission to exercise this privilege was usually granted to founders of cities. Landholding was a privilege of the wealthy classes, the conditions of assignment differing in different regions, and agriculture and stock-raising were, especially in La Plata provinces, the most important industries.

The history of agriculture, in fact, constitutes an interesting chapter in the cultural as well as the industrial history of the colonies. The introduction of the domestic animals and of European species of grains, vegetables, and fruits was a significant element in the transfer of Spanish civilization. And while it is common, and largely correct, to look upon the *Conquistadores* as gold seekers, *buscadores de oro,* as a means of rapid enrichment, the economic significance of agriculture is of greater import in considering the three centuries of colonial rule.

From the horses and cattle introduced in the early days of settlement grew the countless number of wild horses and cattle that roamed the plains of La Plata region and Venezuela. The hog, furthermore, was the source of a food supply that contributed in an important degree to

---

[17] J. L. Mecham, *Church and state in Latin America.*

the success of exploring expeditions. And the type of plainsmen, such as the *gauchos* of Argentina and the *llaneros* of Venezuela, was influenced by such conditions.

Cortés, as early as 1522, asked that sugar cane, mulberry trees for silk worms, and various other plants be sent from Spain, and the crown in issuing charters for new expeditions usually required that seeds and plants form a part of the equipment. Sugar growing soon became an important industry in the Antilles, and in suitable regions of the mainland. Pereyra[18] likens the conquered lands to experimental fields, and quotes the significant statement of Humboldt:[19]

> "In studying the history of the conquest, we admire the extraordinary rapidity with which the Spaniards of the sixteenth century spread the cultivation of the European vegetables along the ridge of the Cordilleras, from one extremity of the continent to the other. The ecclesiastics, and especially the religious missionaries, contributed greatly to the rapidity of this progress. The gardens of the convents and of the secular priests were so many nurseries, from which the recently imported vegetables were diffused over the country. The *Conquistadores* even, all of whom we ought by no means to regard as warlike barbarians, addicted themselves in their old age to a rural life. These simple men, surrounded by Indians, of whose language they were ignorant, cultivated in preference, as if to console them in their solitude, the plants which recalled to them the plains of Estramadura and the Castiles. The epoqua at which a European fruit ripened for the first time was distinguished by a family festival. It is impossible to read without being warmly affected what is related by the Inca Garcilasso as to the manner of living of these first colonists. He relates . . . 'How his father . . . collected together all his old companions in arms to share with him three asparaguses, the first which were grown on the tableland of Cuzco.' "

Variant accounts are found of the romance of the introduction of wheat, one being that this was due to the finding of a few grains in a barrel of rice by Inés Muñoz, who carefully planted them, and after repeated operations on a minor scale finally secured a sufficient amount for practical growing. Similar stories are told of the olive, *el olivo castellano,* in Lima and of the fabulous prices paid for the first fruit. To give six to a guest was a royal gesture. The vine was soon introduced and throve lustily in many regions such as Mendoza. Indeed, it

---

[18] C. Pereyra, *La obra de España en América.*

[19] A. von Humboldt, *Political essay on the kingdom of New Spain* (tr. by John Black).

seems no exaggeration to conclude that the introduction of plants and animals exercised a definite influence in the development of the culture pattern of the colonies, supporting and perpetuating the Spanish tradition.

A comprehensive study of the economic and social life of the rural classes would, in the writer's opinion, form an interesting and important contribution to the general study of colonial society, especially with relation to the political organization after the achievement of independence.

In certain regions, where the lack of mineral wealth even at an early period made agriculture and stockraising an important economic pursuit, such as Argentina and Venezuela, there is much evidence regarding the *gauchos* and *llaneros,* who formed, what may be called, a rural proletariate.

Juan Agustín García, in his interesting and penetrating study, *La ciudad indiana,* presents some interesting data on the origin and development of nonurban groups, especially the nomadic population of the broad Argentine *pampas.*

The rural population of the *pampas* developed with none of the elements that make for social and economic advancement. The character and stability based upon property and family were denied them. In the political and economic organization of society developed in the colonies in the seventeenth and eighteenth centuries, especially in the provinces of the Río de la Plata, land ownership was a privilege of the favored and influential families. In Buenos Aires, for instance, even in the original distribution of land, after the usual reservations of *ejidos, dehesas,* and *propios,* or *terrenos baldíos* held in commonalty, lands were assigned to Spaniards of influence, and consolidation of holdings by the acquirement through economic pressure and invasions of the rights of the poor was the tendency. With the growth of population, urban and rural, an expansion of occupied land was obligatory. But in this transformation the position of the landless class was precarious indeed. There was slight opportunity for employment by landowners, inasmuch as rural industry was definitely interested in stockraising which required little labor, this being supplied by negroes and Indians. In consequence, a large element of the population was forced toward the expanding frontiers, there to build their cabins and find maintenance without legal safeguards, division of lands, homesteading acts, or any provision for security of tenure. As such properties increased in value as a result of the squatters' efforts, they were absorbed by the privileged class who could make effective their interests before administrative authorities. In this process we see the origin of the *gauchos* of the *pampas,* a class so significant in Argentine history, with its scorn of law which was synonymous with the arbitrary action of some official. To quote García:[20]

> "The colonial proletariate is born in free love, is reared by hazard, with animals, without a home, without other material than that indispensable to sustaining life.
>
> "As early as his precocious physique permits he mounts his horse and sets out to find a living how and where he can. His property consists of mares, horses, silver spurs, some articles of clothing, arms, and beads to buy two, three, or four women from the Indians, which constitutes his marriage. . . . Such bonds, light and vicious in themselves, are broken at the first friction, and with them disappear moral duties, education, the formation of character, filial relations which develop in the heart the germs of sympathy, the habit of obedience to and respect for paternal authority, and prepares man for submission to the rule of civilized life."

If the King had equitably subdivided the land, thus insuring the formation of a stable society attached by interests and sentiments to the soil, the long period of internal disorganization and discord that followed the emancipation might have been avoided, and the antagonism of the unitarians in the landholding and conservative class and the federal proletariate might have been prevented.

The agrarian problem was not peculiar to Argentina; in Mexico, in Chile, and other regions it assumed preponderant importance.

Thus have been pointed out briefly the elements that formed the social structure of colonial society and the conditions that determined their development and shaped their destinies. A concluding general observation is necessary: one must bear in mind that in studying the objective factors of colonial culture and intellectual life reference is made to only a small group of educated men, but an articulate group. The great anonymous mass of illiterates, profoundly ignorant, is, for the purpose of this study and for the colonial period, almost wholly inarticulate. Under the democratic institutions set up after the emancipation, this mass, numerically far greater than the former, found itself possessed of the right of suffrage and presumptively possessed of a new economy and ideology, together with a new conception of social and political relations. Under such conditions the period of domestic turmoil, the régime

---

[20] Juan Agustín García, *La ciudad indiana* (2nd edition, Buenos Aires, 1909), 264-265.

of *caudillaje,* was not strange. Indeed, it was inevitable. The perplexities of the new citizens and their groping efforts to comprehend and evaluate the meaning of liberty is illustrated in the naïve *gaucho* dialogues of Bartolomé Hidalgo. It takes more than a revolutionary shifting of sovereignty to create an intelligent citizenry.

III. Colonial Culture

Having examined the social organization that developed during the course of Spain's domination, the formation of a society of castes, the city as the center of culture and educational opportunity, which to Sarmiento represented civilization as opposed to barbarism, it is now necessary to consider with similar brevity the more formal elements and aspects of culture that affected the colonial mind and its orientation toward life.

The most important instrumentality in the diffusion of formal intellectual culture was education. And few of Spain's colonial measures have occasioned more controversy. Many have been the charges leveled at Spain by Spanish American and foreign critics regarding the obscurantist character of its colonial educational system. The dominance of theology, and the inattention to natural and political sciences in the curricula of the universities have been the subject of bitter criticism as fundamental causes of the slow growth of liberal thought and of the administrative ineptitude of the early days of independence.

A fair examination of the history of colonial education throughout the three centuries of Spain's dominion does not seem to justify such criticism. And an analysis of the opinions of sound and authoritative contemporary students removed from the inflamed patriotism of the revolutionary period seems to vindicate the ideals and methods of the mother country. Reference may be made to such authors as Vasconcelos, Grisante, Angel César Rivas, Carlos Pereyra, and Ricardo Rojas.

To approach this subject with an unbiased frame of mind, it is necessary to consider with serious attention the ideas and educational processes current at the time not only in Spain but also in France, England, Germany, and Italy. It is necessary, furthermore, to have in mind the political and domestic history of Spain during the period and the increasing absolutism of the sovereigns, both Hapsburgs and Bourbons. After giving due consideration to the period and to comparative methods, one must conclude that Spain gave what it had. The opinion expressed by Rivas could easily be paralleled by many others of Spanish American scholars. He said:[21]

> "With respect to instruction, as with respect to beliefs, many are the charges made against the Spanish régime. Spain transmitted to the societies created in America all the wisdom her sons had accumulated. From the initial period and wherever conditions made it possible as in Lima and Mexico, she founded universities and promoted the progress of letters. And if the instruction given in the colonial institutions was continuously of strongly theological type, this was because officially and throughout the whole cultural world of that time, in Paris as in Heidelburg, in Oxford as in Salamanca, the post of honor was still held by the science of St. Augustine, Sánchez, Aquinas, and Suárez. To demand that the colonies should have been granted an educational system not found in the Peninsula is absurd to a degree. At all events, it will always be a matter worthy of praise that Spanish officials permitted the introduction of books that favored the exchange of ideas and facilitated an acquaintance with scientific progress. The historian Yanes certainly did not err through exaggeration when he wrote the following phrases which may be usefully held in mind: It has been believed by many that the years preceding the revolution were years of barbarity and cruelty. Speaking justly the Spaniards gave to America all that they had; if education in the colonies contained few branches in its curriculum, almost the same were cultivated in the mother country. By 1810 there had arisen a youth hungry for ideas, interested in letters, intelligent and thoughtful, with the stamp of good taste and elegance. The great men who gave luster to Colombia were formed under the colonial system."

The preceding quotation regarding the general character of the education afforded the colonists will assist in properly interpreting the estimate of Moses:[22]

> "There is no doubt that instruction by the clergy, and particularly by the Jesuits, gave efficiency in a predetermined direction, but it did not emphasize the idea of progress or provide for society that variety of intellectual equipment required to promote the many interests of a well-balanced and progressive commonwealth. . . . The predominance of historical, philosophical, and theological investigation and writing, and the comparatively limited amount of thought given to more practical subjects furnish evidence of the one-sidedness and conservatism of mental development in the Spanish colonies."

---

[21] Angel César Rivas, *Ensayos de historia política y diplomática.*

[22] B. Moses, *Intellectual background of the revolution in South America,* 4-5.

These general evaluations are cited by way of introduction. Turn now and consider a few factual historical data.

The famous historian Altamira says that wherever Spain established itself it set up a school, an observation fully applicable to the American colonies. In Mexico the first viceroy, Antonio de Mendoza, and the first bishop, Zumárraga, promptly set about making provision for education by establishing schools not only for the children of the *Conquistadores* but also for the Indians and the *mestizo* children. Nor was the education of girls overlooked. Teachers were found in the ecclesiastics, lay and regular. In addition, secular teachers were in many cases appointed by city councils *(ayuntamientos)*. Prominent among the educators of the time was Pedro de Gante, whose enthusiasm, competency, and pedagogical methods can scarcely be overemphasized. In his school were taught the trades—shoemaking, tailoring, carpentry, blacksmithing, painting, as well as music.

Bishop Zumárraga established his school for the Indians, Santa Cruz de Tlateloleo, where instruction in religion, good manners, reading, Latin grammar, rhetoric, music, philosophy, and native medicine was given. From this school came many natives who became teachers of their own people.

Mendoza established San Juan de Letrán, a sort of normal school, and later Alonzo de Veracruz founded the *Colegio de San Pablo,* equipping it with an extensive library, maps, and scientific instruments.

The work of these schools with the young aroused a consciousness of the need of an institution for higher studies, and Charles V by royal *cédula* of September 22, 1551, created the University of Mexico which was opened in 1553. The establishment of the university was confirmed by a papal bull in 1555, the full title becoming the *Real y pontificia universidad de México.* Theology, scripture, scholastic philosophy, grammar, and later medicine and Mexican languages comprised the curriculum. The University, as also the University of San Marcos in Lima, was granted the same privileges as those of Salamanca.

The Jesuits, whose devotion to education is demonstrated throughout colonial history, came to Mexico in 1572 and in 1576 founded the famous College of St. Peter and St. Paul which was reorganized in 1612 as the College of St. Ildefonso.

In the process of time, with the increase of population, more settled conditions, and the improvement in economic well-being, came parallel improvements in cultural status. Schools and colleges multiplied in response to cultural and practical needs. The *Real seminario de minería* was established in response to the demand for mining engineers and metallurgists. The university prospered notably, enlarging its curriculum by various additional chairs. In 1783 the *Academia de San Carlos* was founded devoted to painting, sculpture, and architecture.

These brief remarks will serve to indicate the progress of education in the Viceroyalty of New Spain and to show the zealous interest of the Spanish Crown in providing for its colonies the solid elements of culture.

Baron von Humboldt, who visited Mexico very early in the nineteenth century, expressed high praise of the conditions he observed:

> "No city of the new continent, without even excepting those of the United States, can display such great and solid scientific establishments as the capital of Mexico. I shall content myself here with naming the School of Mines, directed by the learned Elhuyar . . . and the Botanic Garden; and the Academy of Painting and Sculpture. This academy bears the title of Academia de las Nobles Artes de Mexico. We are astonished on seeing that the Apollo of Belvidere, the group of Laocoon, and still more colossal statues, have been conveyed through mountainous roads at least as narrow as those of St. Gothard; and we are surprised at finding these masterpieces of antiquity collected together under the torrid zone, in a tableland higher than the convent of the great St. Bernard. The collection of casts brought to Mexico cost the king 200,000 francs. . . .
>
> "Since the close of the reign of Charles III, and under that of Charles IV, the study of the physical sciences has made great progress, not only in Mexico, but in general in all the Spanish colonies. No European government has sacrificed greater sums to advance the knowledge of the vegetable kingdom than the Spanish government. Three botanical expeditions in Peru, New Granada, and New Spain, under the direction of Mm. Ruiz and Pavón, Don José Celestino Mutis, and Mm. Sesse and Mocino, have cost the state nearly two millions of francs." [23]

This long quotation—and it might have been much longer—is introduced here as the opinion of a highly trained observer. His remarks on the attention devoted to the study of chemistry, minerology, mathematics, and astronomy are illuminating as are his comments on the Mexican savants, Alzate, Velásquez, and Gama.

In the great viceroyalty of South America, Peru, is exhibited a similar history of educational organization and development, beginning with the conventual schools—and a school was attached to almost every

---

[23] A. von Humboldt, *Political essay on the kingdom of New Spain* (tr. by John Black), chapter vii.

monastic establishment—of the various religious orders, Benedictines, Franciscans, Augustinians, Mercedarians, and later, the Jesuits.

Lima, the City of the Kings, "was even in colonial times famous for its wealth, its aristocracy, and social culture." [24] Quesada quotes Burck to the effect that in 1715 there were in Lima 4,000 carriages, fifty-four churches, twenty monasteries, twelve convents, twelve hospitals, and many special foundations. And these with a population of approximately 30,000!

Its famous University of San Marcos was in keeping with its environment. It was created at the instance of the Dominicans by royal *cédula* of Charles V, in 1551, confirmed by bull of Pius V July 25, 1571. In 1576 it was placed under royal patronage, the Dominicans having been unable to realize their objectives in its maintenance. Like the University of Mexico, it was granted the same privileges as those of Salamanca, and its curriculum reflected the ideas and tendencies of the period.

In addition to the University of San Marcos and various other schools and colleges in Lima, a university was founded in Cuzco in 1578 and one in Trujillo in 1677, while in Alto Perú, now Bolivia, the University of Charcas was established in 1623 under the direction of the Jesuits until their expulsion in 1767.

The last institution named was of signal importance, and in its liberal atmosphere were trained several leaders of political thought in Argentina during the last quarter of the eighteenth century. Alto Perú, or the territory forming the *Audiencia* of Charcas, was added to the Viceroyalty of Buenos Aires by royal *cédula* of February 26, 1776, which created that viceroyalty. It is of interest to note that despite requests of the university, royal consent for the establishment of a printing press was not granted. Relatively little is known of the intellectual activities in Alto Perú during the colonial period.

It is interesting to note, also, that mulattoes, *mestizos,* negroes, and other castes were excluded by law from admission to the universities and the practice of professions and from public office, a clear indication of class hatred and of the aristocratic atmosphere of Lima. On the other hand, Indians, descendants of *caciques,* were declared of pure blood, *limpios de sangre,* and permitted to enjoy the privileges attached to that class. Such was the law; but as in many other provisions, it was more

[24] V. G. Quesada, *La vida intelectual en la América española durante los siglos 16, 17 y 18,* 213.

honored in the breach than in the observance. In fact, the enlightened and humanitarian colonial code has relatively little value as an indication of practice. Parallel with the meticulous administrative provisions of the code was a corresponding disregard of the law.

Other universities were founded during the seventeenth and eighteenth centuries, seventeen in all, among them Santa Fé de Bogotá, 1573; Córdoba, 1613; Guatemala, 1675; Caracas, 1738; Santiago, 1782; Havana, 1782; and Quito, 1791.

Thus, there was no lack of educational institutions in most cases equipped with libraries. And from these institutions, despite the restricted curricula and theological bias, emerged scholars respected in Spain: humanists, philologists, polygraphers, historians, and poets. Cervantes in his *Viaje del parnaso* mentions several colonial poets. Garcilasso de la Vega is known to all students through his *Comentarios reales;* Alarcón, born in Mexico is one of the glories of the Spanish drama of the Golden Age. Pedro Peralta Barnuevo, "monster of erudition," was like Feijóo in the versatility of his genius. José Eusebio de Llano Zapata, of notable scientific attainments; José Pardo de Figueroa; Carlos de Sigüenza y Góngora, an author of encyclopedic character; Santa Cruz y Espejo, whose *El nuevo Luciano o despertador de ingenios* was influential in Spain as well as the colonies. Opposed to the scholastics in some of his views, his work contains a certain Cartesian element.

It is evident from an examination of the work of colonial authors that during the last half of the eighteenth century, due in part to the Bourbon influence in relaxing the restrictions imposed upon the importation of books and in larger part to contacts with other Europeans, notably in Venezuela and Argentina, and to the clandestine importation of prohibited books, was a notable quickening and liberalization of thought. Dr. David Rubio, in the introduction to his *La universidad de San Marcos de Lima durante la colonización española,* has noted many relevant facts. Father Mangin in Quito taught cartesianism in 1736. The Jesuit Aguirre, of the same city, commented upon Leibnitz. Bacon was defended by Father Hospital. Domingo Muriel introduced into La Plata provinces "the exact knowledge of modern philosophy" from 1749 and in all probability even before that date. Dean Funes mentioned "the followers of Newton and Descartes who, crossing the ocean, introduced discord in the lecture halls, where Aristotle, banished from Europe, expected to dominate in peace." In 1735 anatomy was practiced freely in Lima, and its university professors encouraged by Viceroy Guirión gave vogue to contemporary European ideas. In 1774 the Mexican Benito Díaz de Gamarra published a work on modern philosophy, *Elementa recentioris philosophiae*. Felipe Barreda in his *Vida intelectual de la colonia* draws a dismal picture of educational trends in Lima, especially in the university. He finds an accentuated conflict between scholasticism and cartesianism, prostration of scientific studies, and almost utter abandonment of the study of medicine. Thus in 1752 there were, he says, only four graduates in medicine, but numerous *curanderos* or quacks. The most distinguished representative of scientific studies in Peru during the first half of the eighteenth century was Llano Zapata, of assured fame by reason of his *Memorias histórico-físicas, crítico-apologéticas de la América meridional*. In unequivocal terms he attacked the prevailing educational system, proposing in substitution therefor a system scientific in character, abandoning theology, and addressed to the conciliation of classical culture and scientific instruction.

Political ideas such as those that led up to the French revolution were not so current. The introduction of ideas that might imperil Spain's colonial dominion were naturally prohibited, but they were familiar to many leaders of political thought. Rousseau was probably the most important of the French ideologists. Of him J. R. Spell says in a recent article:[25]

> "The influence of Rousseau on Spanish America . . . was threefold—political, educational, and literary; and these different threads are sometimes strangely and inextricably interwoven. From the first definite trace of his political influence in the constitution that Berney drew up for Chile in 1780 until after the middle of the nineteenth century, the *Social contract* was the inspiration of most American leaders. . . . It is probably no exaggeration to say that Rousseau, for a century after his death, wielded more influence in shaping the thought of Spanish America than did any other single writer."

The presence of such currents of thought in centers of culture marks the profound changes that had been going on since the sixteenth century. The development of a better integrated social fabric and the improvement in economic status brought a demand from well-to-do Creoles for a better cultural atmosphere. Many sent their sons to European universities where they imbibed ideas that matured in the philosophy of independence.

Turning back to the early days of the colonial period one may see

---

[25] *The Hispanic American Historical Review*, May 1935.

what was Spain's policy with regard to the regulation of the press and the book trade. And here, as in considering colonial education, there is necessary a sound and historical perspective. Reading is a major instrument of culture. It conditions in large measure literary and intellectual activity. It is thus of interest to know what the colonists read. What books, supplementing formal instruction, formed the colonial mind?

It should be remembered that Spain was as zealous in the propagation and maintenance of the faith in the colonies as at home. José Gabriel Navarro well says:[26] "Spain developed in its Indies a type of colonization unique in history. With the cross on its standard and the propagation of the faith as an ideal, it broke all molds and differed essentially from the old conception of a colony; it is a new cultural category."

One is not surprised, therefore, that severe restrictions were imposed upon the printing and importation of books. The press was introduced into Mexico by Viceroy Mendoza and Bishop Zumárraga some twenty years after the conquest of Cortés. It was functioning in 1539, and there were published during the remaining years of the sixteenth century some 116 books. It was introduced in Lima about 1583, the first book printed in South America being the *Doctrina cristiana* printed in Lima by Antonio Ricardo, "the first printer in these kingdoms of Peru." Periodicals called *gacetas* appeared about the middle of the eighteenth century, and assumed a more or less definite and modern form in *El Diario erudito, económico y comercial de Lima* in 1790 and in the valuable *Mercurio peruano de historia, literatura y noticias públicas* in 1791.

Presses were set up in other administrative divisions, during the sixteenth, seventeenth, and eighteenth centuries, but the output of the colonial presses was sharply conditioned by the restrictions imposed by the colonial code.

Title 24 of Book I of the *Recopilación de leyes de los reinos de las indias* contains fifteen laws on the books that are printed and sent to the Indies. Of these, the first, promulgated by Philip II on September 21, 1556, provides that no book concerning the Indies shall be printed or sold without special permission of the Council of the Indies and that no printer or book dealer shall print, possess, or sell any such book under penalty of a fine of 200,000 *maravedís* and confiscation of his press.

---

[26] *Sociedad española de amigos del arte.   Aportación al estudio de la cultura española en las indias.*

The fourth law of Charles V, September 29, 1543, prohibited the print-ing, sale, or possession of romances which treat of *"materias profanas y fabulosas y historias fingidas,"* reading matter unsuitable for Spaniard or Indian.

The double censorship, civil and ecclesiastical, was strictly enforced, and the Inquisition was in large measure the effective agency in the enforcement of the laws. Thus, the residents in the New World could not, under the law, enjoy the relaxation in moments of leisure of read-ing a romance of chivalry, or under a strict interpretation of the law, even *El Quijote.*

And again, the provision requiring, as antecedent to printing, the examination and approval of the council, imposed an almost prohibitive burden upon the colonial author who might reasonably wish to write upon the history, description, or conditions of life in the land of his domicile. For it was incumbent upon the author either to make a long, hazardous, and expensive trip to Spain in order to submit his manu-script to the decision of the council, or else entrust his work to the negotiations of an agent or attorney, with the attendant risk of loss by shipwreck or to the chance of its being pigeonholed in the archives of the Council of the Indies.

Many interesting illustrations are available of the sad experiences of authors of valuable manuscripts. And many were the manuscripts unpublished during the colonial era, some of which have been brought out in recent years.

Printing, too, was a costly process in the Americas. Paper was fre-quently hard to get. Prices of books printed under such conditions were excessive. Under these difficulties and restrictions, it is easy to understand why in the notable product of the colonial presses there are so few books dealing with American affairs, and why most of such books were published in Spain. Quesada[27] points out that scientific works that could be imported from Europe were cheaper than they could be printed in America, which explains why so few works of this nature were represented in the colonial output. "The matter of prime importance," he says, "for the extension of instruction was the printing of primers, devotional works, and books on the Indian languages." For at the end of the sixteenth century there were books in Mexican, Otomí, Tarascan, Mixtec, Chuchón, Huastec, Zapotec, and Maya, without including those relating to the languages of Guatemala. And this refers to Mexico alone.

---

[27] V. G. Quesada, *La vida intelectual en la América española,* 18.

But despite all the restrictive measures directed to the maintenance of the purity of the faith and to preventing the development of any collective body of opinion threatening to Spain's dominion, there existed even during the sixteenth century very considerable literary activity and during the last half of the eighteenth century a notable diffusion of liberal ideas among the intellectuals.

The character of the liberal culture in Venezuela, for example, during the last half of the eighteenth century is described by De Pons, Segur, and others. And Bolívar himself indicates the nature of his education:

> "To be sure, I did not study the philosophy of Aristotle nor the codes of crime and error, but it may be that Mallien has not studied so deeply as I, Locke, Condillac, Buffon, d'Alembert, Helvetius, Montesquieu, Lalande, Rousseau, Voltaire, Rollin, Berthel and all the classics of antiquity, historians and poets and the modern classics of Spain, France, and Italy, together with a large part of the English." [28]

Such a course of reading certainly implies a most interesting adventure in the domain of liberal thought. It represented, however, a self-directed excursion. Bolívar, like other leaders in the pre-revolutionary school of thought, was largely self-taught. And where such liberal and advanced ideas were possible only through self-education, it is easy to understand the severe criticisms launched against the lay and ecclesiastical institutions of learning.

Again to quote Grisante:

> "It is incontestable then, that ideas of political, social, and educational reform were the order of the day. Attacks upon the universities were current topics. . . . Thanks to Olavide, Espejo, Forner, Llano Zapata, Marchena, Sanz, and other worthy agitators, Spain and America, now at the opening of the nineteenth century could count upon eminent scientists in all branches of human knowledge." [29]

One may dwell very briefly on the literature produced in the colonies during the three centuries of Spanish domination, using the word literature in its broad sense. And it is well, at the risk of seeming platitudinous, to emphasize the value of the study of this literature.

Contemporary literature is source material for the study of a given period. It presents not only factual matter, but points of view, matters

---

[28] A. Grisante, *La instrucción pública en Venezuela*, 90.
[29] *Ibid.*

of interest, and intellectual life—in short, the world as the people of the time saw it. As such it is of greater significance than the reconstructions of historians of today. And it is this consideration that makes so necessary recourse to the works of contemporary authors in various fields—literature proper, history, geography, philosophy, and theology—if one wishes to acquire a really vital acquaintance with the life, thought, feelings, and ambitions of colonial society. Moses[30] says most appropriately that

> "in order to know a nation's life as known at a given epoch, or to visualize the worldly show that passed before the thoughtful contemporary mind, one should refer, not to the artificial creation of the modern historian with its twentieth-century atmosphere, but to what men wrote of their own times or times near their own. Our ancestors' vision of the world and the reaction which the world produced in their minds are revealed in the various forms of their literature."

The viceregal cities, Mexico and Lima, were from their political importance, opulence, and society, the most important centers of literary activity, although Quito, Sucre, and Bogotá made notable contributions.

The books written during the sixteenth century were largely chronicles and relations of the different theaters of exploration, conquest, and settlement by Spanish officials and soldiers. Of similar interest were the regional chronicles of the churchmen. The lure of the New World also attracted various Spanish men of letters, either as office holders or visitors. Mexico was easier to reach and was visited by Gutierre de Cetina (who died there), Juan de la Cueva, and Eugenio Salazar de Alarcón. Bernardo de Balbuena wrote his *Grandeza mexicana* which has been called the first poem of genuine American inspiration. Mateo Alemán, author of the famous picaresque novel *Guzmán de Alfarache,* also visited Mexico about 1608.

Toward the end of the sixteenth century, native authors began to appear, poets especially, not of extraordinary merit, to be sure, but indicative of Creole culture. The next century, however, is marked by two authors of great distinction, Juan Ruiz de Alarcón, previously mentioned, and Sor Juana Inés de la Cruz, "the tenth muse," "a notable poetess who aroused the admiration of both continents." [31]

The last half of the seventeenth century and the whole of the eighteenth century were marked by the influence of gongorism and con-

---

[30] B. Moses, *Spanish colonial literature in South America,* page vi.
[31] M. Henríquez Ureña, *El retorno de los galeones,* 131.

ceptism, as in Spain, the blight of artificiality and obscurity. The development of periodical publications in the eighteenth century favored authorship, *La Gaceta de México, El Diario literario de México, La Gaceta literaria de México,* and others.

Poetical contests were popular. Balbuena participated in one in 1585, being awarded the prize over some three hundred contestants.

Luís G. Urbina speaks of the dawning influence of neoclassicism as a corrective of the artificiality and distortion of *culteranismo,* and of the effect of Luzán and Meléndez Valdés, but finds that "the literary forms of the seventeenth century refused to disappear, finding life and vigor not only in methods of instruction but also in our colonial mode of life, in our old and persistent habits which gave us at the beginning of the nineteenth century the appearance of an archaic Spain."[32] He concludes, however, that in a population of 150,000, comprised mostly of illiterates, the fact that some two hundred poets presented themselves as contestants in a *certamen* shows conclusively that there were groups essentially literary.

Verse was the preferred form of literary expression, a form not only sanctioned by the example of Spain and Italy but singularly appropriate to the exaltation of soul inspired by the spirit of adventure of the conquest. And in verse were written several of the important chronicles, historical or epic in character. Ercilla y Zúniga's *La araucana* illustrates this. It tells the story of the attempt to subdue the brave and warlike Araucanian Indians of Chile. Ercilla's work is considered by many critics the finest artificial epic in the Spanish language. Its popularity was great, and it was imitated by Pedro de Oña in his *Arauca domado,* which deals with the same subject but from a different point of view. Oña was born in Chile and was the first of his countrymen to achieve literary distinction. Alvarez de Toledo added to the historical poems treating of the Araucanians by composing his *El purén indómito.*

In speaking of chronicles in verse one can not omit mention of Martín del Barco Centeneras' *La Argentina y conquista del Río de la Plata, con otros acaecimientos de los reynos del Perú, Tucumán, y estado del Brasil,* and of Juan de Castellanos' *Elegías de varones ilustres de las indias.* The author calls this work his swan song:

> "A cantos elegíacos levanto
> Con débiles acentos voz anciana,
> Bien como blanco cisne que con canto
> Su muerte solemniza ya cercana."

---

[32] Luís G. Urbina, *La vida literaria de México,* 82.

"With feeble accents I lift my aged voice in elegiac songs, like the white swan which solemnizes with song his near approaching death."

It is an extraordinary and unique swan song, being recognized as the longest poem in the Spanish language, consisting of over 150,000 hendecasyllabic verses. Menéndez y Pelayo, the great Spanish humanist and critic, says of this poem:

> "His work, monstrous beyond comparison as regards plan, is not really a poem, nor even a chronicle, but a forest of rhymed chronicles in which may be distinguished as many as there are characters. But the one possessed of the time and courage to penetrate this wood will not find his effort in vain when he comes upon episodes such as that of the shipwreck of licentiate Zuazo or the tremendous story of Lope de Aguirre or the pleasing description of the island Margarita." [33]

Of later date and by a native author *Lima fundada e conquista del Perú* by Pedro José de Peralta Barnuevo really harks in subject and form to the earlier chronicles in verse. The author, professor of mathematics, rector of the University of San Marcos, scientist, cosmographer, engineer, and lawyer, was a man of formidable intellectual accomplishments.

Previous mention has been made of the numerous histories and religious chronicles as essential source material for the study of the colonies. These by Spaniards or Creole authors writing from about the time of the conquest to the end of the eighteenth century are numerous and cover many phases and regions of colonial life.

The religious chronicles are of great significance in secular as well as ecclesiastical matters. Each religious order had one or more chroniclers to record the activities of their respective orders in their various provinces. For example, the *Cronicón sacro imperial de Chile* by Francisco Javier Ramírez is Franciscan, the *Crónica de la provincia peruana* by Bernardo Torres is Augustinian, the *Estado de las misiones en Chile* is Jesuit, and the *Tesoros verdaderos de las indias* by Meléndez is Dominican.

With respect to literature proper, the spirit and movements in the colonies reflected in large measure the contemporary literature of the Peninsula. As Rojas says,

> "Without social personality and culture of our own, our country could not then have a literature in the true sense of the word. This we did not possess, either as a profound function of national life

---

[33] M. Menéndez y Pelayo, *Historia de la poesía hispano-americana.*

nor as lofty expression of esthetic sentiment. Nationality and beauty are flowers that open in history when a select race attains the fullness of its autonomy and ideals." [34]

But it would be an error to assert that the colonial literature was merely an extension or prolongation of that of Spain. While possibly no true American note was struck, while there was little or nothing to indicate civic and social consciousness and aspirations, the effects of the exotic nature of the New World and of the great drama of the conquest were sufficiently arresting to influence Spanish literature to a very considerable degree.

Belaúnde's statement seems basically sound:

> "The discovery of America enriches Spanish literature and inaugurates American literature. Thus as the political and military expansionist movement was original and creative, similarly and equally in the literature was expressed the reflection of this movement. The discovery of America produced three effects in Spanish letters: a more intense feeling for nature, the development of the epic, and the cultivation of a new historical *genre*. Literature, to be sure, remained Spanish in language, but it acquired a new color in reflecting the American scene and nature. Heroic literature, epic and history, cantos, in many cases rhymed chronicles or relations in which palpitates the epic, manifest the synthesis of the Spanish soul and American nature." [35]

Belaúnde recognizes, even in the initiation of colonial culture, a certain *mestizo* character arising from the relations between the *Conquistador* and Indian, and this character is emphasized by racial fusion.

The colonies suffered, of course, as did Spain, the sterilizing blight of *culturanismo* in the seventeenth and eighteenth centuries. But in the latter century was initiated a period of transition, the initiation and growth of a different intellectual pattern. There is unequivocal evidence of the birth of a self-conscious colonial mentality. Many factors contributed to this end. In the first place, the marked deterioration in the moral fibre of the priesthood, regular and lay. The church had grown wealthy; it held much valuable property; and the zeal in self-sacrificing, unselfish service in the work of evangelization even at the price of martyrdom that characterized the earlier period, was lost. Juan and Ulloa in their *Noticias secretas,* prepared especially for the instruction of the king and his ministers, paint a dismal picture of the "perverted,

---

[34] R. Rojas, *Obras,* X, 15.

[35] V. A. Belaúnde, *La realidad nacional,* 143.

disorderly, and scandalous life" of the clergy, with the notable exception of the Jesuits.

According to Mecham,[36] the wealth of the church was represented not only by church edifices but also by income-producing lands and interest from loans secured by property of individuals. "In Lima," he says, "out of 2,816 houses, 1,135 belonged to religious communities, secular ecclesiastics or pious endowments." But in considering the charges leveled at the church during the eighteenth century for its concentrated wealth, profligacy, and immorality, we should remember the history of the ecclesiastics, regular and secular, of the sixteenth and seventeenth centuries, their virtues and accomplishments. "So conspicuous," says Mecham, "was the work of the Catholic Church in the missionary field, in education, the charities, and the arts, that failure to recognize its constructive achievements would be most unjust." [37]

Another contributory cause was the expulsion of the Jesuits in 1767. This significant step must be considered a blow to educational progress and literary activity. "It closed the most efficient schools," says Moses, "and silenced those persons who might have continued to spread enlightenment through their writings." [38]

An event that stimulated thought, especially in scientific fields, was the organization in New Granada of the botanical expedition under the direction of José Celestino Mutis.

Indications of a new spirit in the Creoles caused by continuing administrative exclusion, a spirit that heralded the dawn of revolutionary ambitions, are seen in the organization of literary societies and the establishment of periodicals such as *El Mercurio peruano*. Again, to borrow Moses' words: "More men began to think in terms of worldly things; instead of exercising their imaginations in creating a heavenly state, they began to look forward to a new earthly state. The new idealism, imposed upon men by the rising spirit of revolution, contained a force competent to transform the world."

There was a widening breach between the ecclesiastics—with notable exceptions—representing medievalism, reactionism, the *status quo,* and the apostles of a new liberalism and of scientific investigation.

During the last quarter of the century a considerable body of verse, satirical, narrative, and lyric, was produced, but the intellectual interests were of political rather than poetic character. The drama, also, was

---

[36] J. L. Mecham, *Church and state in Latin America,* 45.
[37] *Ibid.* 49.
[38] B. Moses, *Spanish colonial literature,* 531.

cultivated by some, and it must in fairness be said that many viceroys encouraged the cultivation of letters when there was no intrusion of inflammable political material. Such were Vértiz of La Plata provinces and Taboada Lemos of Lima, to mention only two. The translation of Rousseau's *Les droits de l'homme* by Antonio Nariño, however, met with prompt punishment.

To the consideration of literature must be added that of art as an important element of culture. Material for the study of Hispanic American art is by no means abundant; it is, in fact, as yet quite inadequate and what exists is for the most part a recent product. This is regrettable from intrinsic as well as relative considerations. To the study of colonial culture an analysis of the origin and development of the fine arts would form an important and interesting contribution. In architecture, in sculpture, and in painting there is much that challenges interest, for in colonial art is reflected the contemporary art of Spain influenced by a changed environment and containing some elements of native art.

The existence, moreover, in cathedrals, convents, and private homes of canvasses of famous European masters—Murillo, Rubens, Titian, Zurbarán, and others—is in itself an interesting indication of the cultural standards that obtained in the capitals and large cities of the New World.

Among the representative contributions to this study are Guimaraes' *Historia das artes plasticas no Brasil,* José Gabriel Navarro's *Contribuciones a la historia del arte en el Ecuador,* Eduardo Schiaffino's *La pintura y la escultura en Argentina,* Roberto Pizano's *Gregorio Vázques y los Figueroa,* Cossío del Pomar's *La pintura en el Cuzco,* the Marqués de San Francisco's *El arte colonial en México,* and the interesting address of Dr. Enrique Finot, the minister from Bolivia, given before the Washington chapter of the *Instituto de las Españas* on "Spanish colonial culture in Upper Peru" and published in the April number of the *Bulletin* of the Pan American Union.

The aboriginal population in certain sections, such as Mexico and Peru, had made notable progress in architecture, sculpture, and gold- and silversmithing. This is demonstrated by the monuments of pre-Columbian art in Mexico, Tiahuanacu, and Cuzco, the product of Mayan, Aztec, and Inca civilizations. It is unfortunate that the proselyting zeal of the Spaniards destroyed many of the native art monuments.

During the colonial period the cultivation of the arts was notable in the larger and more important centers, Mexico, Lima, Cuzco, Potosí, and Quito, by artists, architects, and artisans from Spain.

Nor was it unusual to find Indian representatives in the artistic activities, especially in sculpture, as for instance Caspicara of Quito. In this connection an interesting comment is that of Aristide Sartorio, art commissioner of the Italian Government who visited several countries of South America in 1924. He said:[39] "This sculpture, in which converted Indians like Caspicara and José Díaz manifested aptitudes of true and great artists, had its center of expansion in Quito and it is incumbent upon American students to execute not only a long work of investigation and classification but also an examination of styles." And he continues:

"In the course of this journey, I have convinced myself of the existence of an American art and I have come upon unsuspected traditions of prehistoric and modern times, traditions which will in the future impress upon said art precise characteristics. And if at first view, observed here and there, this art appears confused and fabulous, after a visit to the monuments of Quito, it shows definiteness and logical development in all its features, even in the indigenous contribution."

It would be interesting to know something about the daily life of the people, their manners and customs, occupations and amusements, and thoughts. Such information is not to be gleaned from official chronicles or from the reports of viceroys and other officials. It is known that in Mexico, and to an even greater degree in Lima, the most important seats of viceregal courts, there was a degree of ostentation and display, of "pomp and circumstance" that vied in splendor and luxury with the royal court in Madrid.

But there is a curiously interesting book that gives in quaint language a picture of life in Lima as witnessed by a soldier chronicler. This is the *Diario de Lima (1640-1694) crónica de la época colonial* by José de Mugaburu and Francisco de Mugaburu, the son, edited by Horacio H. Arteaga and Carlos A. Romero. Dr. Arteaga tells us in the prologue that Lima is assuredly the only viceregal city possessing so valuable a jewel.

"More than a diary of Lima, this book is the *speculus majus* of the colonial society of America. That which political, courtly, polished, and hypocritical history has not said nor the relation addressed to the king or nobles, reports which disfigured facts from

[39] E. Schiaffino, *La pintura y la escultura en Argentina,* 28.

design or fear, is told in this diary without fear or reservations.
It avoids the known and scrutinizes the hidden and unknown; it
envisages the intimate social action rather than political life and
external events motivated in officialdom."

This interesting diary brings before our eyes the pageant of colonial
life, a life of glamor and ostentation, of bull fights, religious processions,
examinations for positions in the university faculty, receptions of viceroys, *avisos* from Spain, Chile, and Panama, executions, obituary no-
tices, murders, the earthquake of November 1665, *autos de fé,* processions of the guilds, elections of *alcaldes,* the execution and burning of
a counterfeiter, fireworks, bonfires, etc.

Some of the spectacles were of extraordinary elaborateness, worthy
of a Mardi Gras performance. In the celebration of the religious fes-
tival in Lima of the Immaculate Conception large and colorful floats
were commonly used, and are described with simple but graphic force.
The earthquake of November 13, 1665, is described in considerable detail: "All the inhabitants congregated in the plazas, streets, corrals, and
gardens, because for thirteen days there were over 100 shocks. . . . And
for fifteen days the churches were open day and night and the Host exhibited. In the plaza there were three pulpits where there was a ceaseless series of sermons."

Sargeant Mugaburu describes an *auto de fé,* October 8, 1667, with
characteristic naïvete. The heretic was Don César de Bandier, a physician brought to Peru by Viceroy Count de Santisteban. "He was physician of the Hospital Real de mi Señora Santa Ana of this city of the
Kings and during his incumbency he killed over 2,000 Indians. . . . He
denied the immortality of the soul and was worse in his errors than
Luther, Arius, or Mohamet." He was sentenced to life imprisonment
and banishment from Peru.

An order of December 10, 1667, prohibited any mulatto or negress,
free or slave, from wearing silk with gold or silver ornaments, a reflection upon the effort of the lower classes to imitate their superiors. There
are noted various provisions regulating the currency, trade, etc. The
baker who sold bread of short weight was finèd 200 *patacones.*

As the editor well says,

> "To uncover the life of past generations, to become acquainted
> with the intimate home life, to know the details of their customs,
> affections, devotional practices, and original thought, without be-
> ing filtered through official reports, was for contemporaries a work
> of exhausting and not always happy inductions. This book clears

the obstacle and is the ray of light that dissipates forever the obscurity."

It is interesting to consider the cultural and political training of Spanish America during the colonial period, especially with respect to its fitness for the inauguration of democratic government after the revolution. Some broad generalizations may be permissible. Spain transmitted its culture to the colonies, modified as has been indicated. Blanco Fombona cites certain apparent contradictions in the Spanish character that appear in Spanish Americans:[40]

"As a people they are essentially democratic and at the same time eminently despotic; they are proud and yet beg alms; they are of indomitable personal independence but as a nation submit to the most pronounced absolutism; they are very Catholic yet little religious. The Spaniard and the Spanish American do not tolerate abuses from servility, but from excess of individualism, through lack of social cohesion and through failure to exercise their rights."

It may be said at once that there was little in inherited qualities, education, or political training to equip the colonies for the operation of a democratic form of government which requires for successful practice the intelligent application of a selective function in order to prevent its control and direction by a special class, whether that class be priests, *caudillos*, entrenched wealth, or coercive minorities.

Despite the anathemas to which Spain's colonial régime has been subjected, it may be correctly assumed that dispassionate-minded scholars recognize that Spain gave what it had. More than this, it could not do. Núñez de Arce, the Spanish poet, expressed a historic fact in his apostrophe to Spanish America: "Spain oppressed you but do not blame her for when was barbarous conquest just and human? In clemency she gave you her blood, her noble language, her laws, and her God. To you she gave all except liberty. And how could she give that which she did not herself possess?"

There were positive elements in colonial administration opposed to the birth and growth of a democratic spirit. These have been previously mentioned—legal restrictions upon the colonies, the semi-feudal encomienda system, the creation of a titled nobility and privileged class, reservation of land grants to the influential class, and the failure to make provision for Creoles and *mestizos* that would encourage ambition, equalize political and economic opportunities, and develop a democratic feeling of social and political homogeneity.

---

[40] R. Blanco Fombona, *El conquistador español*, 169.

In conclusion, the writer wishes to present the reasoned judgment of a Spanish American critic of intellectual distinction, Max Henríquez Ureña:

> "During the colonial period Spanish America produced outstanding men in science, letters, and the fine arts; and in colonial culture the liberators tempered their spirits for the great campaign for emancipation. Despite the Inquisition which was established in America and exercised its lamentable mission with absurd sentences and *autos de fé* in Peru, New Granada, and Río de la Plata, although it was mild in other localities and never had the significance that it had in the Peninsula; despite the legal restrictions placed upon the introduction of profane books in America and the suspicions and limitations with which the founding of typographical establishments was authorized; despite many errors of political character and many defects of practical nature, Spain performed in America its colonizing mission and transmitted to it its culture and its civilization." [41]

---

[41] M. Henríquez Ureña, *El retorno de los galeones,* 234.

CHAPTER ELEVEN

COLONIAL ECONOMIC LIFE

By ROLAND DENNIS HUSSEY

A. SPANISH AMERICA[1]

I

SPANISH America's fertility, climate, plant and mineral resources, and aboriginal population offered large economic opportunities. The Spanish people who utilized these opportunities shared the common European theories and practices. They believed that bullion was wealth, that colonies existed only to benefit the mother country, and that foreigners should not share the national riches. Monopoly was a normal business method. The state, or trade gilds, regulated prices and qualities. The complicated, heavy taxes were frequently farmed.

Spain differed, however, in certain ways. For various reasons, her people, more than most Europeans, subordinated economic interests to those of warfare and religion, considered manual labor degrading, and were not notably seafarers. Solely the Crown of Castile possessed the Indies. Finally, Castile was first by a century to face the problems of distant colonies, tropical labor, and bullion inflation. Lacking experience, and with a medieval viewpoint, she formulated a system for a modern age.

This discussion treats the system and life largely in its stabilized form after the mid-sixteenth century. Important developments preceded that period. Colonization began as a rush of Spaniards to exploit American riches. With them, without much plan, went Spanish economic life. As population and profits expanded, distance from Spain and distinctive American elements produced new problems and, therefore, new devices and methods. That is, the Indies started as a royal plantation, in which settlers were hired servants of the crown, and all trade and profits went to their royal employer. There were few taxes

---

[1] Individual printed or manuscript documents, although much depended upon for this discussion, are not cited if more generally usable authorities are fairly satisfactory.

and little organization.² Exploitation on that basis proving impracticable, the crown opened mining and trade to private ventures, and in 1498 sent the last known salaried emigrants. It reserved a monopoly of salt and dyewood gathering, worked some mines, and carried on some trade for years, but in general thereafter America lived by private, although royally-controlled, enterprise. Charles V and Philip II largely organized the system. After Philip's death (1598) only minor changes occurred until the eighteenth century.

In accordance with prevailing economic theory—later called mercantilism—the crown intended³ the empire to be one self-contained economic unit. In it the colonies should specialize on raw products, and the peninsula on manufacturing and commodities such as wine and olive oil. Foreigners should be excluded. As the Crown of Castile owned the Indies, Castilians would enjoy a preference, and revenues and overseas trade would receive special attention. In reality, restrictive laws were fewer than might be supposed. Manufacturers were little hampered, vineyards and olive trees were frowned on rather than prohibited, and non-Castilian Spaniards ceased after Isabella's death to be required to have special licenses for emigration. Revenues and trade, however, were rigidly controlled.

Taxes⁴ were usually collected and administered by revenue officials, but were sometimes farmed, or compounded for on an estimated basis by individuals and the organized merchants. The earliest imposts included Indian tribute, a mining royalty, and customs duties (*almojarifazgos*). The latter were collected in America from 1497, but not until 1543 in Spain on American goods.⁵ Other taxes, added as the Spanish emergency grew, included the sale of indulgences under the bull of

---

² *Cf.* Navarrete, *Colección de viages* (Madrid, 1825-1837), I, 238, and II, 51-54, 162-164; Múñoz, *Historia del nuevo mundo* (Madrid, 1793), *lib.* v, *par.* 33, *lib.* vi, *par.* 53; Herrera, *Historia general* (Madrid, 1601-1615), *dec.* i, *lib.* ii, *cap.* 18; *Col. de doc. inéd. rel. al descubrimiento* (2a serie, Madrid, 1885 ff.), V, 9-18; Haring, "Early Spanish colonial exchequer."

³ Colmeiro, *Historia de la economía política*, II, 332-355, 376-396; Haring, *Trade and navigation, passim,* especially 96 ff., 108, 111 ff.; *Recopilación de las leyes de las indias,* especially *lib.* iv.

⁴ *Cf.* Bancroft, *History of Mexico,* III, 651-680; Haring, "Early Spanish colonial exchequer" and *Trade and Navigation; Recopilación, lib.* viii; De Pons, *Travels in South America,* Ch. ix; Humboldt, *Essai politique sur Nouvelle Espagne* (Paris, 1811), Bk. 6.

⁵ Haring, *Trade and navigation,* 6, 83.

crusade, the sale after 1557 of the lesser offices,[6] and the sales tax
(alcabala) after 1570. Clerical tithes were taken from 1501, and multitudinous local excise and license fees existed. All differed in amount
according to time and region. The *almojarifazgo* was usually seven and
one-half per cent on imports and on exports, but reached seventeen per
cent in the seventeenth century. It was figured on market values at
the destination. The *alcabala* rose from two to six per cent, and pyra-
mided because it was exacted on every transfer. All adult male Indians
owed tribute.[7] Free negroes supposedly did likewise, but somehow did
not pay. Indian obligations, set by local authorities, were often accepted
in produce. Originally they were equivalent to three silver dollars, but
usually they averaged one, and finally two. The *quinto,* or mining
royalty, as implied by its name, was commonly one-fifth. It called for
two-thirds, however, in 1495 and shortly thereafter, and was reduced
for poor deposits. One-tenth became general in New Spain in 1716,
and in Peru in 1735. Proclamation of the bull of crusade[8] began in
Spain with a medieval papal grant to finance war against the Moors.
Its indulgences, sold in America by 1532, were frankly authorized there
in 1573. Prices were graduated according to rank, time, and place. In
general, the lower class paid two silver reals and better class buyers contributed two to four *pesos,* but prices increased in the later period. As
benefits were extensive, purchase was nearly universal. Other levies
included the *averia* or tax on overseas cargoes to pay for a convoy,
ship-tonnage duties, inheritance fees, the half annates or half of the
first year's salary for appointment to office, the *lanzas* or tax on titles,
and stamp taxes on legal papers. Among lucrative business enterprises
monopolized by the crown were the exploitations of mercury, salt, tobacco, gunpowder, playing cards, stamped paper, *pulque,* lotteries, and
cockfights.

Rates were no heavier than in Spain[9] and they satisfied contemporary

---

[6] *Recopilación, lib.* viii, *tít.* xx. For lists and prices in North America, see Diez
de la Calle, *Memorial y noticias sacras y reales* (Madrid, 1646, or Mexico, 1932).

[7] *Recopilación, lib.* vi, *tít.* v, and *lib.* vii. *tít.* v; see also travellers' accounts and
relaciones.

[8] Besides the general references, see: *Catholic Encyclopedia,* article "Crusade,
Bull of"; Stevenson, *Historical and descriptive narrative,* I, 204-206; Robertson,
History of America (London, 1777), n. 80; and Solórzano Pereyra, *Política
indiana* (Madrid, 1648), II, 218-225.

[9] Haring, "Early Spanish colonial exchequer," 780.

standards. Also, exceptions were constantly made for impoverished regions like the Antilles and Venezuela. By 1696 the inhabitants of Santo Domingo City suffered no royal levies except the *alcabala* and the use of stamped paper.[10] Nevertheless, the system was onerous, complicated, and uneven in incidence. It handicapped trade and other economic activity, and bore heavily on the Indians and other poor. If the tribute was small, so were earnings, and though the Indian had immunities,[11] such as freedom from the *alcabala* and license fees on salt-gathering, these did not compensate for the excessive clerical exactions and numerous other imposts. Wealth in the form of land paid no tax.

Royal profit was smaller than is often supposed. The later imposts involved disproportionate costs of collection, and American outlays rose enormously. "There never came lesse for the King then now," reported the English ambassador from Madrid in 1670,[12] "and the reason given is, that near three millions were spent in paying the sallaryes of the Governors, Councells and souldiers in the Tierra Firme and chiefly in repaireing and building forts and castels." The ambassador wrote at a crucial moment, but defense had constituted an increasingly heavy drain. Until the eighteenth century or later, the Antilles, Florida, Venezuela, Chile, and the Philippines raised insufficient income for expenses. Their subsidy averaged, during the last years, nearly four million *pesos* annually from Mexico, and one million from Peru. Governmental costs, including the subsidy, took one-half of Peru's total revenue in 1614. New Spain suffered a deficit from 1644 to 1673. Expenses averaged four-fifths of all American revenue at the end of the colonial period.[13]

Net proceeds averaged annually about 140,000 *pesos* from 1503 to 1530. They rose to 700,000 from 1531 to 1550. During the next decade they jumped to 1,750,000, and then climbed to a long-time apogee (1590-1600) of seven million. By 1651-1660 they had declined to one

---

[10] Haring, *Trade and navigation,* 55n.; *Consulta* of the Council of the Indies, Sept. 1699, in Archive of the Indies (hereafter called *A. I.*), 55-1-10.

[11] De Pons, I, 232; H. I. Priestley, *Coming of the white man* (New York, 1929), 127; Humboldt, I, 431.

[12] Godolphin to Arlington, Madrid, July 8, 1670 in Public Record Office, S. P. 94 (Spain), v. 56.

[13] Haring, "Ledgers of the royal treasurers"; Bancroft, III, 675-676; Canga Argüelles, *Diccionario de hacienda* (London, 1826-1827), I; 85 and *passim,* III, 264-265, V, 58 ff.; Humboldt, V, 31-33, 37-41; Mata Linares manuscript (Academy of History, Madrid), v. 68.

million,[14] and made little recovery until the eighteenth century reforms.[15]

Spanish interests were guarded by the *Casa de Contratación* or House of Trade at Seville, and by revenue officials in America. When established (1503), the *casa*[16] was a royal trading corporation. From the first its officials also supervised private trade with America, the Canaries, and the Barbary Coast. The supervisory function soon became basic, and the *casa*, subject to the Council of the Indies, controlled all overseas economic affairs. It administered matters of trade, navigation, and emigration. It regulated the fleets, maintained warehouses through which imports and exports passed for registration and taxation, examined the quality of ships, trained pilots, prepared maps, and issued or refused licenses for ships, officers, seamen, and passengers. It had large judicial and advisory powers in the same fields. The revenue agents also were established early.[17] The chief functionaries, called "Royal Officials," included a treasurer, accountant, and, at first, an inspector and a factor, resident in each capital, with lieutenants in other important cities or seaports. They held high rank, salaries, and honors, and exercised complete administrative, advisory, and judicial powers over the American exchequers. Though expected to coöperate with other crown agents, they formed a separate hierarchy and disputes often arose.

II

Generalization is now possible on colonial economic life. Exceptions were numerous everywhere, frontiers departed widely from the norm, and neither life nor system were as static as may sometimes be implied.

The economic aspects of the population can be determined only in part. The Amerind element formed a vast majority in most regions. Whites and negroes made smaller but economically important groups.

---

[14] Hamilton, *American treasure*, 462-469. Like most others, Hamilton's figures are for bullion only. The crown received some produce. For other data, see: Haring, *Trade and navigation*, App. 4, and "Early Spanish colonial exchequer," 780; Razón del oro y plata (1523-1596), Rich manuscript (New York Pub. Library) v. 5; Altolaguirre, "Presupuestos de ingresos . . . 1594" in *Revista de Geografía Colonial y Mercantil*, XX, 54-63; *Col. de doc. inéd. para la hist. de España* (Madrid, 1842-1895), XXXVI, 549; Weiss, *España desde el reinado de Felipe II* (Madrid, 1845), II, 102.

[15] Canga Argüelles, I, 85, II, 55, 123, III, 158, V, 55; Anderson, *Historical deduction of commerce* (London, 1790), III, 473; "Memoria" by Ensenada, in [Valladares], *Semenario erudito*, XII; and *infra*, n. 90.

[16] Haring, *Trade and navigation*, 21 ff; *Recopilación, lib.* ix.

[17] Haring, "Early Spanish colonial exchequer," 792-796; *Recopilación, lib.* viii, *tít.* iii, iv.

Negroes entered as slaves.[18] Casual imports began in 1502,[19] but the large movement began in 1517, as the Indian laborers of the Antilles vanished. Thenceforth, they came in large, predominantly male groups, through the *asiento* or contract trade. An asientist paid the crown a lump sum plus a head tax for a monopoly limited as to numbers, places, time, and prices. Since foreigners controlled the only good sources of supply on the African coast, most asientists were foreign. The Portuguese, the Dutch, the French, and the English successively dominated the trade. Much illegal importation occurred. There was, probably, little natural increase in America. Las Casas wrote that climate in the Antilles was so favorable that at first, "unless one chanced to be hanged, none ever die." He added that work became arduous as sugar mills rose, and that negro addiction to homemade rum was deadly. Other writers agree.[20] But as negro blood might increase through racial intermixture without an increase in negro polls, the question is open.

The white group grew by natural increase as well as by immigration, but little is known about its vital statistics. Spain regulated immigration[21] in an effort to ensure a population of good character. The crown encouraged[22] farmers, laborers, and persons going to neglected regions by granting of land, tools, seed, animals, and transportation. Results were disappointing. The governor of Puerto Rico about 1552 wrote of a typical case:[23] "Useless are such settlers. . . . Brought under the name of laborers, they were barbers, tailors, and useless gentry, who very soon sold the twelve cows and a bull . . . for food, knew nothing of work, and peopled only the hospitals and graveyards. More than enough such settlers come without Your Majesty paying passage charges." Restrictions counterbalanced the encouragements. The prohibition of foreigners excluded even those Flemings and Italians ruled by Spain. Spaniards must prove ancestry untainted by the suspicion of heresy. Married men must take their families or, in special cases,

---

[18] *Infra*, n. 51; Scelle, *Traité négrière*.

[19] Herrera, *dec.* i, *lib.* iv, *cap.* 12; *Col. de doc. inéd.*, 2a. serie, V, 47; Saco, *Historia de la esclavitud africana*, I, 62-69.

[20] Bourne, *Spain in America* (New York, 1904), 275-276; Las Casas, *Historia general, lib.* iii, *cap.* 129; Herrera, *dec.* ii, *lib.* iii, *cap.* 14; De Pons, I, 496.

[21] Haring, *Trade and navigation*, 96 ff; *Recopilación, lib.* ix, *tít.* xxvi, xxvii.

[22] For early cases, see: Herrera, *dec.* iii, *lib.* ii, *cap.* 10, and *dec.* iv, *lib.* x, *cap.* 5; Saco, I, 147-149, 155; *Col. de doc. inéd. rel. al descubrimiento* (Madrid, 1864-1884), II, 204-208.

[23] *Col. de doc. inéd. rel. al descubrimiento* (Madrid, 1864-1884), XXVI, 204-205; Saco, I, 204.

post a thousand ducat bond.[24] Unmarried women might go only as members or servants of an emigrating family. Finally, the cost of passage and its rigors[25] must have deterred many, as would America's lessened attraction as the conquests and the chief mining discoveries ended.

These difficulties were partially offset by the economic decline of Spain, and Cervantes infers[26] that bankrupts or criminals looked for refuge in the Indies. Also, the restrictions were evaded. Unlicensed persons easily reached the New World as stowaways or seamen. Foreigners proved impossible to exclude. Shortages of mariners and shipmasters compelled legalization of foreign substitutes; foreign engineers supervised the mines of the Antilles and the drainage of Mexico City; foreigners came in the monastic orders; foreign slave ships had permits for many ports.[27] From them and from smugglers' craft men visited and sometimes stayed. Portuguese were especially numerous everywhere, and foreigners of all nationalities were more common in the Caribbean and the Plata than elsewhere, but all regions had their share.[28] Many of the interlopers held influential places. Hakluyt's accounts suggest that while Anglo-Spanish relations grew critical in the sixteenth century, English traders lived unmolested in Mexico or Peru if they were orthodox, unobtrusive, and sailed under the Spanish flag. Portuguese Jews monopolized Lima's trade in the early seventeenth century.

[24] Haring, *Trade and navigation*, 102 n.; *Recopilación, lib.* ix, *tít.* xxvi, *ley* 29.

[25] *Cf.* Bourne, 252; Haring, *Trade and navigation, passim;* Priestley, 5-6; Gage, *New survey of the west indies* (New York, 1929), 369, 377-378; Castro y Bravo, *Naos españoles,* 123 ff.

[26] "The jealous husband" in the *Exemplary novels* (Mabbe's translation, London, 1640).

[27] Haring, *Trade and navigation,* 258-261; Bancroft, III, 9-11; also printed and manuscript documents.

[28] *Cf.:* Riva Agüero (ed.), *Descripción anónima del Perú . . . por un judío portugués;* Lizárraga, *Descripción del Perú, lib.* i, *cap.* 67, 71, 74, 102, and *lib.* 2, *cap.* 75; *Relaciones históricas y geográficas de América Central,* 166, 177; Gage, 198; Bancroft, III, 223-224; Rubio Moreno, *Pasageros á indias,* I, 384-386; Lea, *Inquisition in the Spanish dependencies* (New York, 1908), 229, 419, 425 ff.; works of Medina on the Inquisition in various countries; *Correspondencia de la ciudad de Buenos Ayres con los reyes* (Madrid, 1918), II, 161; *Documentos para la historia argentina,* V, 105-106; Lafuente Machain, *Portugueses en Buenos Aires;* accounts by Tomson and Chilton in Hakluyt's *Principal navigations;* Cundall, *Jamaica under the Spaniards* (Kingston, 1919), 34; Relación de los estrangeros [en Venezuela] 1607 in *A. I.* 54-4-15; Descripción de beneçuela [1630?] in *A. I.,* 54-4-2; Autos y testimonios [on Hispaniola] 1606 in *A. I.,* 53-6-6; Junta de Guerra de Indias, July 11, 1661 in *A. I.,* 54-6-28; accounts of Puerto Rico (1645 and 1647) and of Santiago in Española, 1709 in *A. I.,* 54-3-7, 55-1-10.

The city's other residents included French, Italians, Germans, Flemings, Greeks, English, Moors, Chinese, and East Indians. The port of Arica had but forty Spaniards among its hundred and fifty men. The rest included known heretics, English and German. The *alcalde* of the important Apurimac bridge was Flemish. Panama, in 1607, numbered fifty foreigners among some thirteen hundred whites. Venezuela in the same year registered one hundred and twenty-four, including one Maltese and one Pole. Several were burghers and clergymen. Two were respectively a sheriff and an alderman. In Española (1606) among six hundred and forty-eight burghers, eight were Portuguese, and one each English, Greek, and Fleming. In 1661 the island's only artillerymen were Portuguese. The Englishman Gage traveled freely once he reached. Mexico, and reported that Guatemala's five wealthiest men included one Genoese and two Portuguese. The Inquisitors of Cartagena defended their foreign interpreter against the governor (1621) on the grounds that the interpreter was married, resident twenty years, and had indispensable knowledge of Flemish, German, and English. English and Irish were apparently resident near Buenos Aires early in the next century. By 1596 the crown began compounding with resident foreigners married to Spanish women.[29] Legitimization was permanent, but supposedly barred participation in overseas trade and required residence away from seaports.

Fifteen hundred Spanish immigrants a year, after the later sixteenth century, seems a reasonable estimate. Official figures of 1600 stated that two thousand, three hundred and sixty-two passengers had been licensed in the past two years, and that eight hundred probably went illegally. This accords well enough with the six hundred and thirty-seven passengers who sailed for New Spain and the Antilles (1573) and with Humboldt's belief that, about 1800, Spain annually sent fewer than eight hundred emigrants to Mexico.[30]

Most contemporary figures for total or regional populations are sheer guesswork. Others had more basis, usually in clerical counts which listed communicants and allowed for young, old, and backsliders. The best are contradictory, incomplete, and often give some figures for all inhabitants and others only for burghers *(vecinos)*. Indians listed

---

[29] Haring, *Trade and navigation,* 110-111.

[30] Consejo de Estado, Sept. 4, 1600 in Archive of Simancas, Estado 1022; Relación de las personas . . . (1573) in *A. I.,* 149-5-1; Humboldt, I, 365; Bourne, 250-252.

are usually only the tributaries. Careful interpretation justifies the following compilation for the early years:

About 1550 [31] Whites	Region	About 1570 [32] Whites	Indians (under White control)
2,000	Antilles and Margarita	2,000	1,000
	Forida including 150 troops	300	....
1,000(?)	Venezuela and Río de la Hacha	2,000	180,000
⎧	Mexico _(Audiencia of)_	24,000	750,000
16,000 ⎨	Guadalajara " "	10,000	60,000
⎩	Yucatan and Tabasco " "	2,600	180,000
4,000	Guatemala " "	17,000	360,000
1,000(?)	Panama " "	6,000	....
3,000(?)	Bogotá " "	13,500	510,000
⎧	Quito " "	10,000	570,000
8,000 ⎨	Lima " "	36,000	900,000
⎩	Charcas " "	13,000	300,000
500	Chile (Province of)	15,000	260,000
500(?)	Río de la Plata " "	3,000	40,000(?)
36,000		**153,400**	**4,110,000**

In 1550 the Antilles had few Indians but thousands of negroes. New Spain, besides many Indian tributaries, had perhaps twenty thousand negroes and mulattoes, mostly in the mines near Mexico City. South America had few negroes, but subdued Indians numbered 280,000. In 1570 negroes totalled forty thousand, of whom twelve or thirteen thousand lived in Española and unstated numbers in the other Antilles, New Spain, Panama, and Peru. The whites were concentrated in two hundred towns.

Growth was fairly steady in later years, but the economic importance of the population was less than its size might indicate. Most individuals were too poor to buy much from Spain or pay much tax. They served chiefly as instruments for exploiting American riches.

Usages and customs in that exploitation were those of Spain, modi-

---

[31] Herrera, _dec._ viii, _lib._ iii, _cap._ 1; Douglas-Irvine, "Landholding system," 483 and references there; Altolaguirre, _Relaciones de Venezuela,_ xvi; Saco, I, 185; Benzoni, _History of the new world_ (London, 1888), 96 and _passim; Biblioteca histórica de Puerto Rico_ (Puerto Rico, 1854), 333-334; Wright, _Early history of Cuba_ (New York, 1916), 260; Cundall, _passim;_ Tomson's account in Hakluyt; "Censos de la población del virreinato de Nueva España" in _Boletín del Centro de Estudios Americanistas de Sevilla,_ No. 36/37, pp. 44-66; Blanco Herrera, _Política de España en ultramar_ (Madrid, 1888), 72. Figures followed by a question mark are based only on the present writer's general impressions.

[32] López de Velasco, _Geografía y descripción universal de las indias. Cf._ Torre Revello (ed.) "Resumen aproximada de los habitantes del . . . Perú en la segunda mitad del siglo XVI" in _Boletín del Instituto de Investigaciones Históricas_ (Buenos Aires, April-June 1929), vii, 297-300.

fied by the presence of mines, free lands, a subjugated population, and other American conditions. Land grants[33] to the whites began in 1497.[34] Each town, also, had communal lands. Those of the Indians were inalienable. Private possessions were given in *caballerías,* or the portion of a horseman, and *peonías,* or that of a foot soldier. Full title passed after four or five years' residence. The *peonía* had a town lot *(solar)* fifty by one hundred feet, and farming and grazing lands suited to the owner of a few cattle. The *caballería* had a lot one hundred by two hundred feet, and five times the other lands. Actual size varied[35] according to water supply, fertility, and other factors. *Caballerías* granted in Guatemala (1528) averaged 174 acres, but about 1800 Humboldt supposed thirty-two acres to represent the unit in Mexico and Cuba, and the town council in San Juan de Puerto Rico calculated it at twenty, shortly before. Whatever the initial grant, the poor man had little chance after the conquests. Entails, the character of the soil, and the labor system, all tended to concentrate vast holdings in the hands of a few. This discouraged the rise of a small farmer class and efficient use of the land.

As for labor, American conditions revived the tendency to servitude which was declining in the old continent. The white population was weighted with fortune seekers and adventurers, soldiers and gentry. Forced labor by Indians and negroes offered competition socially disgraceful and economically impossible to meet, and their free labor was little better. The Indian artisans, said Henry Hawks to Hakluyt (1572) after five years in Mexico, "do worke so cheape that poore young men that go out of Spain to get their living are not set on worke . . . for the Indian will live al weeke with lesse than one groat, which the Spanyard cannot do, nor any man els." "The Spaniards in the Indies," explained Ordóñez de Ceballos (1614),

> "neither plow nor dig as in Spain, and even presume not to do service . . . holding themselves as caballeros or hidalgos. Hardly will one find a Spanish lackey or page, nor has any personage been able

---

[33] *Recopilación, lib.* iv, *tít.* xii; Ots Capdequi, *Derecho de propriedad,* 60-94; Viñas Mey, "Datos," 70-81, and *Régimen de la tierra;* Priestley, 96 ff. and 129 ff; Bancroft, *History of Mexico,* III, 605-607; Bancroft, *History of Central America,* I, 496 ff. and II, 98-99; De Pons, I, 380-384; McBride, *Land system, passim.*

[34] *Col. de doc. inéd. rel. al descubrimiento,* XXXVI, 174-177.

[35] Bancroft, *History of Central America,* II, 98 n.; McBride, 107-108; Humboldt, III, 181; Humboldt, *Essai politique sur Cuba* (Paris, 1826), I, 210 n.; Coll y Toste, "Propriedad territorial," 242, 264. *Cf.* definitions in large Spanish and Spanish-American dictionaries.

to maintain them except only the viceroy. . . . They attach themselves to merchants and traders and to keeping shops of eatables
and of Castillian or native clothing . . . and act as overseers. . . .
The reason is . . . that as their thought and inclination takes them
there to enrich themselves and return to Spain with an estate, they
apply themselves to the employs and activities which offer the
greatest chance to gain it." [36]

Whites, therefore, were largely landowners, officials, clergy, professional men, traders, or soldiers.

Free labor, however, was sometimes white. This was commonest in
the skilled crafts, organized in gilds[37] with fraternal and regulatory
functions. Gold, silver, and other smiths, carpenters, tailors, shoemakers, and hairdressers were fairly common. Even unskilled labor
existed.[38] The Portuguese in Venezuela in 1607 included several field
hands, and the small farmers who rallied to the defense of Santo Domingo (1654) apparently included some whites. The *Cabildo* of
Buenos Aires complained, as late as 1619, "the very burghers are compelled [by poverty] to work [the fields] with their hands," and the
Buenos Aires census for 1778 recorded a number of *labradores*. Gage
saw immigrants laboring in Mexico, and Ulloa records that fear of starvation often forced stowaways at Cartagena to the most menial tasks.
Both accounts add that such men were likely to marry colored women,
so that they would not have perpetuated a white laboring class.

Free labor, therefore, was mostly colored. Besides working their
communal lands, Indians served on hire or engaged in small industries
and trade. "The Indians," noted López de Velasco, "have much patience to learn and carry on mechanic arts, of which there are many
and good operators, although the works . . . always are recognized by
a certain imperfection." Later observers criticized nothing but their
sloth.[39] They were reinforced by growing numbers of *mestizos* and
free negroes and mulattoes.

---

[36] Ordóñez de Ceballos, *Historia y viage del mundo* (Madrid, 1691), *lib.* iii, *cap.*
22.

[37] *Cf.* Torre Revello, *El gremio de plateros;* Levene, *"Los gremios";* del Barrio Lorenzot, *Trabajo en México.*

[38] *Supra,* n. 28; *Documentos para la historia argentina,* XI, *passim; Correspondencia de la ciudad de Buenos Aires con los reyes* (Madrid, 1915 ff.), I, 38,
169 and II, 143; Juan and Ulloa, *Voyage to South America* (London, 1760), I,
35-37 and II, 55.

[39] López de Velasco, 185. *Cf. idem,* 481; Gage, 248; Juan and Ulloa, I, 31,
278. The mid-sixteenth century Sahagún *codex* depicts Indians practicing the

Enslaved "whites," mostly in the Antilles, are mentioned as late as 1550, but were female Berber domestics.[40] Criminals, white or colored, were sometimes sentenced to labor. Pirates went to the mines of Huanacavelica and of Margarita for life (1682), and whites implicated in the Mexican corn riots (1692) were ordered to labor under guard in the Antilles and the Philippines.[41] But these were unimportant additions to the régime of colored dependent labor.

Forced labor by an hereditary lower class was a commonplace. It was "necessary," moreover, if Spain was to occupy the Americas. The humanitarian Luís Sánchez expressed this (1560) with an unusual irony. Speaking of the decline of the Indians, he said,[42] "The cause . . . is that all who go to the Indies go with the intention of returning to Spain very rich, a thing that is impossible—since from here they take nothing and there they do nothing—except at the cost of the sweat and blood of the Indians."

Columbus contemplated complete enslavement for the aborigines. The crown promptly forbade this except for cannibals or Indians "rebellious" against the whites. These exceptions long cloaked slaving raids against groups like the Apaches, Araucans, and Caribs; but as a whole Indian slavery was unimportant.[43] Columbus also started a feudal serfdom which became the *encomienda* under his successors. In 1503, finding that the Indians withdrew from white neighborhoods, Queen Isabella ordered them settled "as free men" in villages with inalienable lands, and christianized, but permitted them to be put to work for wages on public needs. American officials interpreted this by allocating Indians to a permanent master. The master had the duty of christianizing them, and laws fixed other safeguards, but they were disregarded.[44]

handicrafts newly learned from the Spaniards. The illustrations are reproduced in M. Cuevas, *Historia de la iglesia en México* (Mexico, 1922 ff.), II, facing pages 268 and 278.

[40] Ayala, *Diccionario de gobierno,* II, 180-181; Rubio Moreno, I, 352; Saco, I, 62, 73, 80, 164; Torre Revello, "Esclavas blancas," and manuscript sources.

[41] *Recopilación, lib.* vii, *tít.* viii, *leyes* 11, 14; De Pons, I, 314, 319; Bancroft, *History of Mexico,* III, 257, n. 3; manuscript in *A. I.,* 152-4-22.

[42] *Col. de doc. inéd. rel. al descubrimiento,* XI, 163.

[43] Saco, *Historia de la esclavitud indiana;* Navarrete, I, 231-233; Múñoz, *lib.* v, *par.* 34; Las Casas, *lib.* i, *cap.* 155; *Col. de doc. inéd.,* 2a. serie, X, 38-43; *Recopilación, lib.* vi, *tít.* ii, *ley* 1; Benzoni, 11-12; Pereyra, *Historia de América española* (Madrid, 1920-1925), VIII, 112; Barber, "Indian labor," 328 ff.

[44] Las Casas, *lib.* i, *cap.* 105, 161, and *lib.* ii, *cap.* 12-14; Herrera, *dec.* i, *lib.* ii, *cap.* 13, 16, 17, *lib.* iv, *cap.* 12, 13, *lib.* v, *cap.* 11, 12; Múñoz, *lib.* v, *par.* 30; *Col. de doc. inéd.,* VIII, 9-10, XXXI, 13-25, 209-212; Navarrete, 299-300; *Recopilación, lib.* vi, *tít.* viii, *ley* 1.

The campaign for modification has often been related.[45] The Indians of the Antilles—partly because of new diseases like smallpox—practically vanished by 1548.[46] They declined everywhere, causing apprehension over the loss of labor among persons otherwise unconcerned. Ameliorating laws were numerous but ineffective until the "New Laws" (1542) substituted payment of tribute to the master for the former obligations.[47] The institution itself, although intended for early abolition lasted into the eighteenth century,[48] but retained no legal importance as a source of labor.

This did not end the "necessity" of Indian workers. "Without them," explained Judge Matienzo of Peru, about 1570, "[the commonweal] could not be conserved, because Spanish do not serve, nor is it fitting that they should. Negroes are few, and it were better were they fewer." Involuntary Indian servitude, therefore, arose in other forms. The Chilean *inquilino* or Peruvian *yanacona* was a serf attached to an estate, who owed his master some days' labor annually in field, house, or mine. In return he had the use of land, oxen, and tools, and received clothes and small wages.[49]

Most Indians served under the *mita*.[50] Viceroy Toledo created this régime in Peru. Modified by royal action, it extended to other parts. Under it adult males owed labor in the fields and mines, with the herds, or as pack train drivers or servants in the public inns. Service in factories was prohibited. Only one-seventh in Peru and one-twenty-fifth in Mexico might be called at once, pay was required, and other safeguards existed. In practice, abuses were common and the ban against factory assignments was forgotten. The number of Indians affected, however, soon declined even in Peru and Bolivia. The institution disappeared in Mexico before Humboldt's time, although debt peonage replaced it in factories.

---

[45] For instance, in works by Lea and Simpson mentioned in the bibliography. All accounts depend largely on Las Casas' writings.

[46] Oviedo y Valdes, *Historia general* (Madrid, 1856), *lib.* iii, *cap.* 6.

[47] Stevens (ed.), *New laws of the indies.*

[48] Priestley, 121; Barber, 249-250; De Pons, I, 35; Amunátegui Solar, *Encomiendas,* II, *passim.*

[49] Lorente, *Historia del Perú bajo la dinastía austriaca* (Paris, 1870), *passim;* Matienzo, *Gobierno de Perú,* chapter viii; Amunátegui Solar, I, 421.

[50] Matienzo, (Buenos Aires, 1910) 25-28; Solórzano Pereyra, *lib.* ii, *cap.* 5-7; *Recopilación, lib.* vi, *tít.* xii, xiii, xv. Cf. Barber, *passim;* Gage, 230-234; Juan and Ulloa, I, 440 and *passim,* and *Noticias secretas, passim;* Ulloa, *Noticias americanas,* 281; Viñas Mey, "Datos," 206 ff.; and Humboldt, *Essai politique sur Nouvelle Espagne* (Paris, 1811), I, 360 and IV, 45, 298.

Negro slavery[51] spread throughout the tropics. Legally, Spanish American slaves had a better status than most others. One could change masters by persuading someone to pay his market value. He could marry his choice, and had the right to buy himself, his wife, and his children at the lowest price. This was valuable, since slaves often toiled for hire and kept anything above a set sum. In Havana, reported Gemelli Careri, the masters "exacted four reals a day and six when the fleet was there, and at least three of the women." [52] Gemelli Careri thought the amount high, but many negroes acquired their freedom by some such method. Slaves often suffered neglect, and could not always enforce their legal rights, but an English traveller in Peru about 1800 believed "Spanish slaves . . . more fortunate and happy than the laboring classes at home." [53]

Standards of money, weights, and measures came from Castile.[54] Coins originally were sent from Spain, but after 1536 American mints commenced operations. Indians long continued to use cocoa, coca, textiles, and iron wedges for currency.[55] Gold was probably not minted until the seventeenth century. Copper appeared in subsidiary coinage, but the standard was the silver *peso* ($1.00 U. S., before 1933) containing eight silver *reales*. Ducats, doubloons, and other units complicated figuring, but the system was good judged by contemporary ideals. Though debased coins long circulated in the Antilles and Venezuela, paper was unknown. No banks existed. The church and others lent on mortgages, and large merchants granted one- to three-year credits.[56]

Transport and communications distressed even contemporaries. Despite royal aids, most highways were trails unfit for wheeled traffic. Travellers on major routes ferried or forded dangerous rivers, risked South American chasms on tremulous rope bridges, and used different roads in wet and dry weather. Gemelli Careri, after crossing Mexico from Acapulco to Vera Cruz, gasped, "I thought it a miracle that our

---

[51] Saco, *Esclavitud africana; Recopilación*, lib. vii, *tít.* v; Bourne, 268-281; De Pons, I, 155-168.

[52] Gemelli Careri, *Voyage*, in Churchill's *Voyages* (London, 1704), IV, 533.

[53] Stevenson, I, 430-439.

[54] For English equivalents, see Walton, *Present state of Spanish America*, I, 350; Bancroft, *History of Central America*, I, 192-193, n.; Haring, "American gold and silver production," 475-479.

[55] Acosta, *Historia natural*, lib. iv, *cap.* 3; Champlain, *Brief narrative* (Toronto, 1922), 44-45; Herrera, *dec.* viii, *lib.* v, *cap.* 8.

[56] Aiton and Wheeler, "First American mint"; Medina, "Primera casa de moneda"; Haring, "American gold and silver production," 475-479; De Pons, II, 40; and manuscripts and travel accounts.

beasts came off safe." Passage across the Isthmus, the jugular of America, was worse. "It is the moste filthiest way in all the worlde," said the engineer Antoneli (1590). Ulloa preferred the Chagres River to the "narrow crazy roads." In fact, everyone who could, utilized river and coastal traffic. Land travellers carried bedding and food for use in the wretched shelters found along the way. Freight moved by mule train.[57] Mail found frequent enough ocean passage in trading ships and in fast dispatch caravels, but outside the Peruvian areas a system for distribution on land hardly existed. The economist Bernardo Ulloa (1740) thought the pre-conquest Indians better off for postal service than his colonial contemporaries.[58]

III

Agrarian pursuits, throughout the world, afforded most persons subsistence. America was no exception.[59] Farming suffered from the semi-aridity of many parts and the Spanish preference for pastoral life, but crops were needed for domestic consumption, and some had markets abroad. The crown encouraged farming through tax remissions and gifts of seeds and tools. It emphasized semi-tropical produce, but European plants and animals thrived.[60] Irrigation and fertilization, with ordinary dung, were widely practiced. Various travellers noted the use of guano in Peru, raising of clover by the Arequipa Indians expressly to be turned under, and similar use of burned stubble in Guatemala. But working tools were primitive. Frezier described the plow as "a crooked branch of a tree," and Walton (1810) noted use of "the same

---

[57] Viñas Mey, "Derecho obrero," 52-54; Aiton, *Antonio de Mendoza* (Durham, 1927), 102; Gemelli Careri, 475-520 and *passim;* Antoneli, True relation (1594), manuscript in Huntington Library, EL 1682; Juan and Ulloa, *Voyage* (London, 1760), I, 106 and *passim;* Ordóñez de Ceballos, 391. *Cf.* Bancroft, *History of Mexico,* III, 303, 636-638, and Stevenson, II, 75-77, 112-113. A typical oxcart of the *pampas,* one of the few areas where they were commonly used, is pictured by Wilcocke, *History of the viceroyalty of Buenos Aires* (London, 1807), facing p. 481.

[58] Alcazar, *Historia del correo;* Cárcano, *Historia de los medios de comunicación;* Haring, *Trade and navigation,* 34-35, 230; *Recopilación, lib.* ix, *tit.* vii; Bancroft, *History of Mexico,* III, 639-640; Bernardo Ulloa, *Restablecimiento,* II, 247-251.

[59] Cappa, *Estudios críticos,* V, VI; De Pons, chapter viii; Bancroft, *History of Mexico,* III, 603-626; Priestley, 24-25, 96 ff.; Riva Palacio, *México á través de los siglos* (Barcelona, 1888-1889), II, 671-675; Humboldt, *Essai politique sur Nouvelle Espagne,* Bk. 4, chs. ix, x; works by Acosta, Camacho, Cobo, and López de Velasco; and manuscripts and travel accounts.

[60] Bourne, 215-218 and *passim;* Viñas Mey, "Datos," 60-68; James A. Robertson, "Some notes on the transfer . . . of plants and animals."

misshapen and uncouth plow as that described by Virgil . . . without any improvements, though so many have been made by other nations." The hoes and crowbar that Las Casas mentions remained the chief implements.[61] Maize, cassava, potatoes, and yams were joined by Spanish vegetables, fruit, and wheat as mainstays of local consumption. Mexico raised grapes and olives about 1531, and Peru a generation later. Sugar, the chief export product,[62] started overseas from Española in 1515, from Puerto Rico in 1533, and from Mexico in 1553. It was later important in Cuba and most of South America. Tobacco, grown as widely as sugar, was exported by 1600, and cocoa from Venezuela, Quito, and Guatemala shortly thereafter. Indigo, vanilla, ginger, cassia, and various drugs were other exports.

Vast herds of kine, sheep, goats, swine, horses, and mules grazed on open ranges. Owners of twenty cows or mares, or of three hundred small varieties, automatically became brothers of the *mesta,* or stockraisers' gild,[63] which regulated brands, quarrels over ownership, and like matters. The stock increased greatly. In New Spain, said González de Mendoza (1585),

> "there are bred and brought up more cattell then in any other parts known in all the world . . . because they have many fields in that countrie and much people that doo give themselves unto that kinde of gettings (as grasiers) . . . there is so great abundance, and solde for a smalle price, and manie times it happeneth that the bringers up of them doo kille tenne thousand head of them onely to profite themselves with the skinnes, in sending of them unto Spaine, and leave the flesh in the fieldes to feede the foules of the ayre." [64]

Others repeat his comments for many regions.

Cash values of agrarian produce are hard to calculate, but were large.[65] In 1502, while the miners of Española were in sore distress,

---

[61] Frezier, *Voyage to the South Sea* (London, 1717), 76, 147, 152 ff.; Lizárraga, *lib.* i, *cap.* 66; Gage, 220-221; Walton, II, 84; Las Casas, *lib.* ii, *cap.* 6; Stevenson, I, 40-41, 426.

[62] Oviedo y Valdes, *lib.* xxix, *cap.* 11; *Biblioteca histórica de Puerto Rico* (Puerto Rico, 1854), 333; Humboldt, *Essai politique sur Nouvelle Espagne* (Paris, 1811) III, 172; Valverde, "Estanco del tabaco"; Wright, "Industria azucarera," 32 ff.; and manuscripts.

[63] Klein, *Mesta,* 276; *Recopilación, lib.* v, *tít.* v; *Col. de doc. inéd.,* 2a serie, IX, 135-137; Bancroft, *History of Mexico,* III, 615.

[64] González de Mendoza, *Historie of . . . China . . . [with a] commentarie . . . of . . . thinges betwixt Spaine . . . [and] China* (London, 1588), 319.

[65] Canga Argüelles, I, 273-274; Las Casas, *lib.* ii, *cap.* 6; Humboldt, *Essai politique sur Nouvelle Espagne* (Paris, 1811), II, 25-28, III, 282 ff.; Viñas Mey,

says Las Casas, "those who had devoted themselves to cultivation . . . were rich according to the riches of the time." Three centuries later, the exported crops alone exceeded the exported bullion in value for all colonies except New Spain, and the total agricultural wealth of New Spain was believed greater than that of its mines.

Extractive industries seemed most important to contemporaries. Salt evaporating and fishing were important in many localities, and gathering of pearls, dyewood, and cochineal gave value to restricted areas. Mining requires more description.[66]

Though deposits of many ores occurred throughout the tropical latitudes, metals other than gold or silver received little attention. Copper was experimented with in Cuba and Chile. The crown permitted mercury to be worked only in Peru, although it was known in Quito and Mexico. Precious stones were sought in New Granada and Quito. Iron, tin, and lead were neglected.[67]

Mining of precious metals began in the placer gold workings of the Antilles. Between 1501 and 1519, these probably yielded eight million *pesos*. They declined rapidly thereafter, and were soon virtually abandoned. The mainland also had placers and gold, but its great era dates from the finding, after 1545, of silver ore mines such as Potosí, Zacatecas, and Guanajuato. Smelting was originally used for extraction, but a mercury amalgam method soon replaced it except for refractory ores. Germany used such a technique for gold in the fifteenth century. A German expert contracted to apply it in Española (1495), but broke his agreement.[68] A Mexican miner adapted it to silver (1556) and another man carried it to Peru in 1573.

Production[69] rose until about 1600, after which it fell until the eight-

"Datos," 82-91; *Relaciones históricas y geográficas de América Central,* 209; Lizárraga, *lib.* i, *cap.* 96.

[66] Besides books on mining listed in the bibliography, see: Gemelli Careri, 501-507; Acosta, *lib.* iv, *cap.* 4-13; Humboldt, *Essai politique sur Nouvelle Espagne* (Paris, 1811), especially Bk. 4; Frezier, 106-115, 155-168; Juan and Ulloa, *Voyage,* I, Bk. 6, chs. x and xi, *passim;* Stevenson, especially II, 31 ff.; Haring, *Trade and navigation,* chapter vii, and Bancroft, *History of Mexico,* III, 553-602. There are contemporary illustrations in Gemelli Careri, 491; Frezier, pl. xxii; Oviedo y Valdes, Bk. 6, ch. viii; Priestley, pl. 5.

[67] Wright, "Minas," and *Early History,* 308-311; Juan and Ulloa, *Voyage,* I, 477-478, II, 271; De Pons, I, 57-58; Bancroft, *History of Mexico,* III, 584.

[68] Múñoz, Bk. 5, par. 33; contemporary manuscripts.

[69] Haring, "American gold and silver production," and "Ledgers of the royal treasurers"; Hamilton, "Imports of American gold and silver"; Humboldt, *Essai politique sur Nouvelle Espagne* (Paris, 1811), especially III, 377, IV, 102, 174 ff., 212, 218, 259; Angelis, *Colección de obras y documentos* (Buenos Aires, 1910),

eenth century. In 1600 South America led, with Potosí alone averaging seven million *pesos* annually. By the end of the colonial era that mine had yielded some eight hundred million *pesos,* but its decline in the seventeenth century had not been sufficiently offset by discovery of other South American veins. New Spain averaged four million *pesos* at the beginning of the eighteenth century, eleven in the middle, and twenty-three at the end. At that time South America produced only sixteen million *pesos.*

Manufacturing industries[70] met handicaps in dependent labor and the emphasis on mining. But distance from Europe and the restricted trade protected home produce, and much of the population could not have bought European goods at European prices. A large amount of manufacturing appeared. Quito and Puebla de los Angeles were notable centers; Panama was the only area practically without industries. Food processing was universal. Wheat flour, butter, cheese, lard, dried fruits and those conserved with sugar, and snuff and cigars, were regularly made for sale. In 1520 Española had no less than twenty-eight water powered sugar mills,[71] and probably others run by mules. Few settlements lacked them by 1570. By that date south Peru produced wine. A generation later Chile and Tucumán acquired the art, although it was never common elsewhere. American olives were generally used only for eating, but Peru began making oil in the early seventeenth century. Both continents made soap and gunpowder. Woodworking, tanning, and fabricating of leather chests, beds, saddles, and shoes were widely important. Pottery, basketry, and hammock and textile making were notable wherever they had been before the conquests. North Peru produced lamp wicks for miners and matches for firelocks; Chile, Peru, and Central America provided ship rigging; Puebla made glass by 1625, and Ica in Peru later produced it "green, foul and ill wrought," from saltpeter.

Most of these things were made by those who raised the raw materials. Textiles, however, were commonly the output of real factories

---

II, ii; Bancroft, *History of Mexico,* III, 588-589. Hamilton's figures are the most trustworthy general figures. They represent only amounts sent to Spain, but America permanently retained very little.

[70] Cappa, VII-XII; Viñas Mey, "Datos," 84-85, 181-198; Bancroft, *History of Mexico,* III, 616-624; Humboldt, *Essai politique sur Nouvelle Espagne* (Paris, 1811), Bk. 5; Acosta, *lib.* iii, *cap.* 24, *lib.* iv, *cap.* 32, 33; and descriptions and travellers' accounts.

[71] Peter Martyr, *De orbe novo* (New York, 1912), II, 52.

(obrages),[72] organized by Indian communities or by individual whites. Peru had a Spanish *obrage* by 1544. New Spain, besides cotton and wool weaving, had forty establishments making velvet in 1543, and velvet or other silken stuffs long remained a distinctive product of that area. New Granada wove cotton by 1547. Two years later Tucumán already produced cotton and was building *obrages* for wool.

Acosta considered Chilean wine equal to Spanish, and others waxed enthusiastic over wine from Ica. Henry Hawks thought Mexican hats superior to Castilian; Gage reported that Puebla's cloths and felts matched the famed stuffs of Segovia in Spain, and hurt Spanish sales; Frezier found Cuzco's baize and cottons "some small prejudice to the Trade of Europe"; and Lizárraga said that La Paz made textiles "better than those brought from Castile." In De Pons' time foreign shoes must be of excellent quality to compete with Venezuelan, and Mérida wool and cotton was preferred to Spanish linen. But these witnesses agree with the generality that quality was usually inferior, suited only to colored people and poor whites. "Whether because the wool is less fine, or because the *obrages* do not work it well," admitted Acosta, "clothing brought from Spain has a great advantage over that made in the Indies." Ordóñez de Cabellos records that Spanish vintages in Quito brought half again as much as those of Lima. Frezier explained, "[Peruvian] wines are extraordinarily strong and not very wholesome . . . . Spaniards scarcely drink any of them, the sale being almost entirely among the Blacks, the Indians, the Mulattoes and such like people."

A few finer commodities competed with prized Spanish lines. Jewelry-making is one illustration. Cabinet-making with native woods and varnishes was good by the eighteenth century. Fine needles were made in Mexico City in Gage's time, and Española shipped artificial flowers to Spain in 1789. Several areas cast cannon[73] and bells. Cuba produced guns for its defenses (1596-1608) about the same time that Lima made others for the Peruvian fleet and Chilean forts. Mexico had a

---

[72] Viñas Mey, "Datos," 181-187; Juan and Ulloa, *Voyage,* I, 309, 318, 321, 421; Juan and Ulloa, *Noticias secretas, passim;* Frezier, II, 464-472; Humboldt, *Essai politique sur Nouvelle Espagne* (Paris, 1811), IV, 294-295; Lorente, 167-171; García Icazbalceta, *Industria de seda.*

[73] Pezuela, *Historia de Cuba* (Madrid, 1868-1878), I, 340-341; Champlain, 74; Junta de Guerra de Indias, Nov. 6, 1607 in *A. I.,* 147-5-16; Riva Agüero (ed.), 364; Frezier, 53; Bancroft, *History of Mexico,* III, 416, n.

foundry later. Shipbuilding[74] began during the conquests. Large construction on the Pacific later centered at Guayaquil, but the yards of Chile, Realjo in Nicaragua, and of San Blas after 1769, were famous. Those of Havana and Española built royal galleons in the seventeenth century, and Venezuela produced seventy-gun naval vessels in the eighteenth.

Commerce gave many a living. That with the Peninsula[75] was rigidly controlled, due to determination to monopolize all benefits for Spain and the crown, plus increasing danger from pirates and contrabandists. The trade was very vulnerable to foreign attack. Geographic factors practically compelled bullion and semitropical produce to leave for Spain from the Caribbean and through the Florida channel. Compulsory use of a convoyed fleet facilitated regulation, taxation, and defense.

The system was crystallized between 1561 and 1566. Thenceforth only Spanish traders, ships, and crews might participate. Permitted ports included only Seville, Cádiz, and San Lucar in Spain, and Vera Cruz, Cartagena, Puerto Bello, and certain minor ports in America. All trade was to pass between them in two annual convoys. These sailed together from Spain to the southern Antilles. Thence, while the "Galleons" continued to Cartagena and the Isthmus and Panama, the "*Flota*" proceeded to Vera Cruz and detached ships for the Antilles on the way. All returned to Spain via Havana, usually together. American distribution and collection followed set routes. From Vera Cruz goods went to Mexico City and on from there. Cartagena supplied New Granada and, at times, Quito. The isthmian road caused debate and canal projects from 1521, and goods took various land or water routes to Panama. The Peruvian fleet carried goods to Callao, from whence they reached Lima, Chile, the Plata, and sometimes Quito.

The Philippine system represents a curious compromise. Trade, necessary for continuance of the missions and colony, was really exchange with China and India. These countries would accept only silver, and offered textiles and other goods considered harmful to American

[74] Cappa, X-XII; Haring, *Trade and navigation*, 241, 266-267; Viñas Mey, "Datos," 197-198; Wright, "Maestre de campo . . . Texeda" in *Reforma Social* (Habana, 1910), XIII; De Pons, I, 64-65; Riva Agüero (ed.), 349; Lizárraga, *lib.* i, *cap.* 5; Stevenson, I, 126, II, 220-222; Manuscripts in British Museum, Egerton 320, f. 44, and in *A. I.*, 152-3-6, etc.

[75] Haring, *Trade and navigation; Recopilación, lib.* iv; and manuscripts. *Cf.* Bancroft, *History of Central America*, II, 391-392, 468-474, and *History of Mexico*, III, 627-650; and most travel accounts.

and Spanish markets. Other nations blocked Spain from rounding Africa. As return through the Straits of Magellan was unfeasible, America had to be crossed, involving a certainty of illegal trade. The solution finally settled upon[76] simply crossed America at the least objectionable place and restricted trade as much as possible. Permitted ports were Acapulco and Manila, and two ships totalling six hundred tons made the annual quota. Mexico could send only five hundred thousand silver *pesos* each year. Later, one large ship and a million *peso* limit were substituted. South America could not participate.

The artificial method of American trade required special control mechanisms. The *consulado* was one. This body, a gild of merchants trading to the Indies, was organized at Seville (1543) for usual gild purposes, and especially to settle business disputes under simple procedure. As need of a general control agency grew, the *consulado* became an advisory body for the *Casa de Contratación* and a coördinator for the traders, deciding the amount of goods and the number of ships required, apportioning cargo space, and handling other such duties. Similar bodies were created later in Mexico City and in Lima. The *feria*[77] was the other unique institution. The unhealthy American ports had little white population, but to them, once a year, came all the goods arriving from or going to Spain. The European fair *(feria)* suggested the needed method for prompt wholesale exchange. Ulloa described it at Puerto Bello. Representatives of the American and Spanish merchants drew up a price schedule. "All preliminaries being adjusted in three or four meetings," he said, "contracts are signed and made public that everyone may conform." Brokers then arranged individual transfers, and everyone removed his lading within two to six weeks from the start. Though accompanied by soaring prices for food and lodging and by terrific losses from illness, the *feria* served its end. It existed in the terminal ports, Mexico City, Bogotá, and Lima.

Forced exceptions early liberalized some phases of the system. Foreign ships and sailors were tolerated for lack of Spanish, and Seville and Cádiz traders notoriously were foreign agents. "Register ships" with special licenses often served Caribbean areas, and Buenos Aires occasionally could trade direct with Spain. The *consulado,* however, became a powerful combination in restraint of trade, and other evil

[76] Haring, *Trade and navigation,* 143-149; papers by Schurz listed in the bibliography.
[77] Besides references above, see: Bourne, 292 ff.; Juan and Ulloa, *Voyage,* Bk. 2, Ch. vi; Gage, 367-369.

aspects of the system are obvious. González de Mendoza remarked
(1585) of Española, "All . . . thinges of that countrie [are cheap]
. . . although that the marchandise of Spain is very deere." He could
have said the same of any other area.

Spain sent manufactures and some foods. Major articles were textiles, clothes, hats, shoes, hardware, glass, china, paper, mercury, flour,
dried fish, wine, *aguardiente,* olive oil, and olives. Lesser items included books, playing cards, ink, soap, wax, and thread, and fine grades
of cheeses, hams, almonds, spices, figs, and raisins. America returned
bullion, sugar, hides, and dyewoods, and lesser quantities of precious
stones, cocoa, drugs, spices, cochineal, and indigo. Trade declined in
the seventeenth century, however. As the colonies expanded and foreign nations prospered, Spain became unable to supply colonial needs
or repulse foreign encroachments. A Spanish and foreign contraband
trade began everywhere before 1600. Foreigners preferred the Platine
and Caribbean areas, in several parts of which they had more trade
than had Spain by 1700.

Domestic trade[78] was less restricted by law than by bad transportation
and similarity in regional produce. Spain forbade most exchange between Peru and Mexico after Asiatic imports began, and barred sales to
the interior through Buenos Aires to prevent diversion of Andean
bullion from the protected fleets. But trade was quite free in the Caribbean and Gulf of Mexico, and not unimportant in the Pacific. By the
eighteenth century Venezuela exported cocoa to New Spain and the
Antilles, Mexico and Lima used Havana tobacco, flour moved from
Mexico to Venezuela and the Antilles and from Chile to Peru; and
Peru sold wine to Panama and Central America. As areas which most
needed mules could not breed them, Chile and Tucumán annually furnished scores of thousands for the killing toil in Peru, and northern
South America had a smaller market in the Antilles. Domestic trade
was also extensive between city and country. Whites handled the
larger operations and owned most of the crude, ill-lighted shops maintained in private houses. *Mestizos* took an active part in the open-air
markets, or as pedlars with packs or mule trains.

Travellers[79] supposed trade was productive of wealth estimated as

---

[78] *Recopilación, lib.* ix; Haring, *Trade and navigation,* especially 149-150;
Wrigley, "Salta"; Bancroft, *History of Mexico,* III, 610-642; manuscripts and
travellers' accounts.

[79] Gage, 119, 198; Riva Agüero (ed.), 359; Juan and Ulloa, *Voyage,* I, 363,
II, 111; "Noticia de los vecinos más acaudalados de Buenos Aires" in *Boletín del
Instituto de Investigaciones Históricas,* VI January-March, 1928, 498-499.

high as a million *pesos* for some individuals in the seventeenth century. Ulloa, though less enthusiastic, admitted that in Lima, aside from some dozen wealthier merchants, many possessed one to three hundred thousand *pesos*. "These," he said, "are indeed the persons who compose the main body of the traders." A careful official rated the eleven richest men of Buenos Aires, in 1766, at figures between five hundred thousand and sixty thousand *pesos,* and averaging one hundred seventy-five thousand. Trade possibilities there were still very restricted.

IV

Certain late developments have so far been neglected.[80] They grew partly from general eighteenth century enlightenment, and partly from realization that the existing system injured Spanish revenues. Foreign expansion added a factor. Even the distant Pacific coasts saw one hundred and seventy-five French ships from 1695 to 1751, and Russia and England were menacing. Spanish thinkers saw painful contrasts between the foreign and Spanish Antilles, and pointed out that the best way to defend the colonies, help Spain, and avert revolt, was to make America prosperous, well-peopled, and contented.

Though drastic remedies were suggested in the seventeenth century, Spanish decadence minimized accomplishments. Advent of the Bourbon dynasty (1700) improved the situation. Immediately, the War of the Spanish Succession ruined commerce and revenue, and France exacted a slaving *asiento* as the price of supporting Philip V. England took this (1713) as a spoil of war, and maintained it until 1750 for its own sake and as a cloak for contraband.[81] But the Bourbons were enlightened, chose advisers wisely, and cared little for Spanish tradition. France, also, desiring a strong ally, worked for modernization. New ideas, therefore, received a favorable hearing.

At first reformers concentrated on Spanish needs or on parts of the

---

[80] This section depends almost entirely on manuscripts. *Cf.* works of the economists Uztariz, Campillo, Ulloa, and Ward; Priestley, Ch. vii, and *José de Gálvez, passim;* De Pons, Ch. viii; Pierre Muret, "Papiers de l'Abbé Beliardi" in *Revue d'Histoire Moderne et Contemporaine,* IV, 657-672; Aiton, "Spanish colonial reorganization under the Family Compact" in *Hispanic American Historical Review,* XII, 269-280; Colmeiro, II, 356-374, 412-413; Hussey, *The Caracas company;* Dahlgren, *Voyages français à . . . la mer du sud* in Nouvelles Archives des Missions Scientifiques et Littéraires, XIV (Paris, 1907).

[81] Scelle; Dahlgren, *Relations commerciales;* Bancroft, *History of Central America,* II, 586-587, and *History of Mexico,* III, 287-289; Saco, *Historia de la esclavitud africana,* I, 295-311; Nettels, "England and the Spanish American trade, 1680-1715" in *Journal of Modern History,* III, 1-32.

American system most under Spanish eyes. They fundamentally revised control agencies in Spain (1714-1717) by creating a Secretary of the Indies and provincial intendants. The Cádiz intendant assumed the *casa's* administrative functions and that body was removed to Cádiz,[82] whose harbor the fleets had long preferred. Better provision for postal ships was made.[83] One trading tax[84] replaced most of the old complexities. Monopolistic companies were tried, following foreign examples, in hopes of restoring trade in the Antilles and Venezuela. Spain's commerce there was so small that experiments could do no harm. The corporations included the Caracas Company (1728-1784) for Venezuela, and the Havana and Barcelona companies later organized for the Antilles. The first, aided by a virtual monopoly of the world's cocoa supply, was economically successful, but caused a revolt (1749-1751). The others never met Spanish hopes, and monopoly declined in favor.

Charles III (1759-1788) instituted fundamental changes. Previous accomplishments in Spain and a disastrous colonial war (1762-1763) focussed attention on American weakness. Much was done to foster roads, water supply, cattle-breeding, and land apportionment. Foreign aids were welcomed.[85] In 1778 the crown allowed immigration by certain foreign artisans and skilled farmers. In 1801, while loosening restrictions on Spanish immigration, it allowed that by others to be tolerated. Foreign experts and agricultural machines, including a cotton gin, were brought into Venezuela by 1777. Puerto Rico and Peru had gins before Spanish control ended. Sugar mill machinery from foreign colonies was frequently imported. Mining experts like Helms, and a Yankee shipwright for San Blas, were hired by the Spanish government. They were not always welcomed by colonial officials, but foreign residents were numerous in Mexico, the Caribbean, and the Platine areas by 1800. To encourage mining, the crown also organized (1777) the *cuerpo de minería* in Mexico.[86] This gild fostered a school of mines,

---

[82] *Cf.* Adolfo Castro, *Vida . . . de Pez* (Cadiz, 1879) ; Antonio Rodríguez-Villa, *Patiño y campillo* (Madrid, 1882), 60-61, 185-187.

[83] *Aprobación de la escritura en que el consulado . . . se encarga . . . de ocho navíos* (Madrid, 1738).

[84] *Documentos para la historia argentina,* V, 21-77 ; Antúñez y Acevedo, *Memorias históricas,* 247-248.

[85] *Cf.* Rydjord, "French revolution and Mexico" in *Hispanic American Historical Review,* IX, 60-98 ; *Documentos para la historia argentina,* XI ; Stevenson, I, 353, II, 107-108, 183 ; De Pons, I, 109-112 ; Helms, *Travels.*

[86] Mecham, "Real de minas" ; Bancroft, *History of Mexico,* III, 592-596 ; Helms, 87 ; Pereyra, VIII, 168 ; Humboldt, *Essai politique sur Nouvelle Espagne* (Paris, 1811), I, 363, IV, 17-19.

and improved the chaotic mining law by compiling the *ordenanzas reales de la minería*. Humboldt ascribed improvements to its work. Gild and ordinances were copied in South America.

Creation of American intendants, from 1764,[87] bettered economic administration. Postal benefits began that same year, by abolition of hereditary monopolies, organization of a royal service on land, and routing of new postal ships from Galicia to Havana.[88] Taxes, such as the *alcabala* in Havana, were imposed in places formerly exempt, but customs duties were generally lightened.

Monopoly was finally abandoned as a trade principle.[89] Minor departures from it had already occurred as desperate expedients. In 1735 fleets were suspended until the American markets disposed of surplus piled up by contrabandists. Meanwhile, register ships served special needs. The galleons, except for a small convoy in 1737, never sailed again. New Spain's *Flota* resumed in 1757. In 1748 the ministry, facing a war-ruined treasury, licensed ships to enter the Pacific around the Horn. The practise continued thereafter. Meantime, tolerance for war-time trade by allies and friendly neutrals became less grudging. Results of these early liberalizations encouraged proponents of freedom, and in 1765, against general opposition, the ministers tested free trade in the Antilles. Thenceforth any Spaniards with Spanish ships might trade at any time between numerous ports in Spain and the Antilles, very slightly restricted as to licenses, goods, or taxes. As trade revived astoundingly, the régime was extended. By October 1778, it embraced all America except Venezuela, New Spain, and the Philippines. It reached Venezuela in 1781 and New Spain in 1789. The Manila Galleon and a chartered company (1785-1833) continued the old principles in the Philippines, but even those regions traded with Spain around the Horn from 1765, and received concessions as to permitted goods. Bans on Pacific trade ceased (1774), and legal trade through Buenos Aires to the interior began. The *casa* was abolished (1790) as useless. *Con-*

---

[87] Pierson, W. W., "Institutional history of the intendencia," in *James Sprunt Historical Studies,* XIX, No. 2; Fisher, *Intendant system* (Berkeley, 1929).

[88] Alcazar, *Reglamento provisional del correo marítimo de España á sus indias* (Madrid, 1764).

[89] *Documentos para la historia argentina,* V, 115-123; Antúñez y Acevedo, XXIX, XXXIII-XXXV; Mitre, "Comprobaciones históricas" in *Nueva Revista de Buenos Aires,* II, 244-274; *Reglamento y aranceles reales para el comercio libre* (Madrid, 1778); Schurz, "Royal Philippine Company"; Hussey, *Caracas Company,* especially chapter vii.

sulados developed (1784-1803) into counterparts of present-day chambers of commerce, located in the major cities of Spain and America.

V

These reforms produced excellent results. Nearly constant war somewhat lessened their value for Spain by hampering Spanish merchantmen and encouraging colonial crafts. Humboldt noted, among industries recent in Mexico, steel and clock making, and production of harpsichords and pianos. The Viceroy of Peru exclaimed (1795) that lack of European supplies was the reason that Cuzco's manufactures supplied "a majority of its inhabitants and in part those of the Platine viceroyalty." Nevertheless, Spanish sales and revenues rose greatly after 1778.[90] Spanish exports to America climbed from seventy-five million to three hundred million *reales de vellón* in ten years after 1778. The Buenos Aires customs duties equalled only twenty-four thousand *pesos* annually in the quinquennium before 1778. In five years thereafter, despite a war, annual receipts averaged one hundred and fifty-two thousand *pesos,* and they reached nearly four hundred thousand from 1791 to 1795. Other formerly restricted areas showed like increases. By 1755-1763, omitting the war year of 1762, the crown's average revenue exceeded four million *pesos,* and reached six to eight million by the early nineteenth century.

The larger mining production was noted elsewhere. Agricultural statistics show the same thing. Allowing for exemptions and frauds, production might equal eleven times the tithe. If so, annual values in Mexico, 1770 to 1803, rose from fourteen to twenty-five million *pesos*. Peru, in the mid-eighteenth century, produced two million five hundred thousand *pesos'* worth, but over twice that in 1803. Cuban produce doubled between 1790 and 1804.[91] New crops such as coffee accounted for part of this. Most came from expanded cultivation as markets improved.

---

[90] For quoted figures, see: Humboldt, *Essai politique sur Nouvelle Espagne* (Paris, 1811), III, 294-295, IV, 290, 310 ff., 436, V, 37-38; Canga Argüelles, IV, 122-124; Ricardo Levene, "Aduana de Buenos Aires" in *Revista de Ciencias Económicas,* IV, 374-377; Tabla No. 9 prepared by Junta on Comercio Libre, 1765, in Archivo Histórico Nacional (Madrid), Estado 3214; papers in *A. I.,* 146-3-28, 151-5-15.

[91] Canga Argüelles, II, 332-333; Humboldt, *Essai politique sur Nouvelle Espagne* (Paris, 1811), III, 282 ff., *Essai politique sur Cuba,* I, 231; Pereyra, VII, 261.

Population data for the late years show :[92]

	1778		1792		1810	
	Whites	Total	Whites	Total	Whites	Total
New Spain	900,000	3,200,000	......	4,500,000	1,100,000	5,760,000
Guatemala	......	800,000	......	....	150,000	1,200,000
Cuba	95,000	170,000	155,000	275,000	275,000	600,000
Puerto Rico	37,000	80,000	......	120,000	80,000	180,000
Santo Domingo .	......	115,000	......	160,000	....	104,000
Peru (vice-royalty)	......	....	140,000	1,100,000	....	1,555,000
New Granada (viceroyalty) .	......	1,300,000	......	....	....	1,800,000
Plata (vice-royalty)	......	800,000	......	....	300,000	1,150,000
Chile	80,000	260,000	......	300,000	....	400,000
Venezuela	......	600,000	......	....	160,000	800,000

Negroes and mulattoes formed the entire colored population of the Antilles, two-thirds that of Venezuela, one-tenth that of the Platine viceroyalty and of Chile, and one-twelfth that of Peru. They were also numerous near Panama, Vera Cruz, and Acapulco.

Spanish American economic advancement by 1808 must not be over-estimated.[93] The antiquated agricultural methods have been referred to. Mining technique as a whole displeased foreign experts, in spite of the introduction of water powered stamping mills and some other advances. Roads continued bad, although short stretches were improved near Mexico City, Vera Cruz, Lima, and Caracas. Mexico's silk weaving and Puebla's fine pottery making had nearly vanished, killed by free trade. Mexico and Bogotá got their best coaches from London, and the United States undersold Mexican flour in Havana and supplied

[92] Calculated from contradictory, incomplete figures in: Canga Argüelles, III, 418, IV, 332, 359 ff.; Humboldt, *Essai politique sur Nouvelle Espagne* (Paris, 1811), II, 7, 38-39, 55, 91-101, 173, IV, 472-473, V, 132; Humboldt, *Essai politique sur Cuba*, I, 114, 126, 133, 134; De Pons, I, 106, 142; *Informe sobre el censo de Cuba* (Washington, 1900), 87; *Biblioteca histórica de Puerto Rico* (P. R., 1854), 516 ff.; García, *Compendio de la historia de Santo Domingo* (Santo Domingo, 1893-1900), I, 229; Priestley, *Gálvez*, 329, 353; Robertson, *History of America*, n. 54, ch. vii, par. 60; Pezuela, II, 431; Pereyra, VIII, 150, 161; Altolaguirre, *Relaciones de Venezuela*, XXI; Juarros, *Statistical and commercial history of Guatemala* (London, 1823), 11-12; *Relaciones históricas y geográficas de América Central*, 309; "Vista política de la América española," in *Boletín del Centro de Estudios Americanistas de Sevilla*, Año IX, No. 56-57 (1922), facing p. 92; other minor data from manuscript and printed sources.

[93] Cf. Bancroft, *History of Mexico*, III, 638; Humboldt, *Essai Politique sur Nouvelle Espagne* (Paris, 1811), II, 107 ff., IV, 274, 296, 300-301, 323-324, 330 ff.; De Pons, II, 84; Helms, *passim;* Stevenson, I, 120, 139, 360, III, 182; Fisher, "Commercial conditions in Mexico," in *New Mexico Historical Review*, VII, 159-161.

that city with furniture made from Cuban woods. Even soap, a promising field for home industry, was so exorbitantly priced throughout the Indies that much came from Spain. But assuredly conditions were less evil than is often supposed. They differed from what they might have been had the colonies grown freely, and, therefore, offered an unfortunate basis for independent days. They were not, however, unlike those of many other regions. Life was thriving, it was satisfactory to many of those who lived it, and it produced wealth unknown elsewhere in the Americas, however badly the wealth was distributed.

B. PORTUGUESE AMERICA[94]

I

Portugal, smaller and poorer than Spain in natural resources, found a sea route to Asia's wealth before she discovered Brazil. Brazil's mines were long unknown. Her adaptability for semi-tropical produce caused some interest, but for years neither Portuguese government nor people paid her much attention.

Portuguese colonial theory, therefore, though identical with Spain's, was more liberally applied.[95] Except for some effort to prevent competition with Asiatic goods and to encourage sugar planting, economic activity remained free. Foreign colonists, if orthodox, were admitted with slight handicaps. Administration was sketchy. Treasury inspectors in Portugal supervised the whole empire, the *Casa da India* handled Brazilian along with Eastern trade, and distinctively economic officials in Brazil were probably few. Royal revenues came chiefly from customs duties and from monopolies of dyewood, spices, salt, and whaling. A fifth on minerals, clerical tithes, sale of indulgences under the bulls of crusade, and other imposts augmented the list at various times. The annual income was estimated[96] about 1585 at one hundred fifty thousand ducats, mostly spent in Brazil.

Although at first, population grew slowly, by 1574 the sixteen towns had about three thousand burghers, perhaps equivalent to fifteen thousand whites. Two-thirds lived in present-day Bahia and Pernambuco,

---

[94] Generalizations based on the standard narrative histories are not backed by citations.

[95] Lannoy and Vander Linden, *Histoire de l'expansion coloniale . . . Portugal et Espagne, passim;* Oliveira Martins, *O Brasil* (Lisbon, 1877), *passim;* Pereira da Silva, *Historia da fundação do imperio brasileiro,* I, 228, 230.

[96] Rebello da Silva, *Historia de Portugal* (Lisboa, 1860-1871), III, 203, citing the Dutch voyager Linschoten.

and half the rest in São Paulo. A decade later there were twenty-five thousand whites, eighteen thousand five hundred subdued Indians, and fourteen thousand five hundred negroes. Foreigners were numerous in this century, and a Jewish synagogue existed in Bahia.[97]

Economic usages were essentially those of Portugal. Land was granted[98] in perpetuity after three years' occupation and improvement, although the crown exacted a quitrent after 1695. Great landholders early reduced the small farmers to tenantry. Money, weights, and measures were those of the home country.[99] Coins came from Portugal. Roads hardly existed; the Dutch built at Recife (1639) perhaps the first real bridge in Brazil; and postal service remained to the end a mismanaged private monopoly.

Free artisans or other town laborers were known, but whites were few and usually recent immigrants. Most labor was colored and involuntary. Colonists put the Indians to work without question of legality, purchased them as prisoners of war from other Indians, or even persuaded them to sell themselves. The crown forbade their slavery in 1570 and later, but as no one except the Jesuits desired to enforce the law, Indian servitude long continued. African slaves, first imported in 1525, became numerous in the north. "They are more certain than the Indians," explained Magalhães, ". . . because they never flee, as they have nowhere to go." They were well enough treated, and emancipation was easy, so that free negro laborers finally appeared.

Agrarian pursuits offered the chief mode of livelihood for nearly two centuries, though many fished, whaled, gathered ambergris, or cut dyewood.[100] The south bred many cattle. Crops used locally included cassava and maize, some cotton in the north, European vegetables and fruits, grapes for eating, and low-grade pepper. Southerners early tried wheat raising and practically abandoned it. Sugar was the mainstay.[101] The crown ordered a refinery set up in Brazil in 1516 as the price rose in Europe, and sugar was produced by 1526. Output increased enormously thereafter and for a time dominated the world market.

---

[97] Magalhães, *Tratado da terra do Brasil;* Soares da Souza, *Tratado descriptivo do Brasil em 1587;* Keller, *Colonization,* 142; Leite, *Judeus no Brasil.*

[98] Manchester, "Rise of the Brazilian aristocracy" in *Hispanic American Historical Review,* XI (1931), 149-152, and references there.

[99] Table in Southey, *History of Brazil* (London, 1810-1819), III, 900.

[100] *Cf.* Magalhães; Soares da Souza; Cardim, *Tratados da terra . . . do Brasil;* Pyrard, *Voyage.*

[101] Lippmann, *Geschicte des Zuckers,* especially 415 ff.; Rocha Pombo, *Historia do Brasil* (Rio de Janeiro, 1905-1906), III, 28, 74; and all descriptive accounts.

A constant search for mines resulted only in unimportant discoveries.[102] Manufacturing consisted largely of food processing. By 1574 some sixty water or mule driven sugar mills existed. Ten years later there were one hundred and twenty, over half in Pernambuco. Small shipbuilding was probably wide-spread. Soares da Souza noted that the inhabitants of São Vicente made wine and milled a little flour from local wheat, and that those of Porto Seguro sold locally manufactured toilet water in Bahia. By Pyrard's time (1610) rum was distilled.

Commerce, although slight within Brazil, bulked large with Portugal. The Portuguese system demanded a "caravan," or convoyed fleet, as in the Asia trade, but was liberal as to the number of ships and ports. The latter included Lisbon and Oporto in Portugal, and Rio de Janeiro, Parahyba, Olinda, and São Salvador in Brazil. Two ships annually sufficed before 1548. Forty years later they averaged forty-five, and a Portuguese eulogist set them at two hundred in 1620. These were mostly small, of one hundred fifty tons or less. They carried out practically everything used in Brazil and many went in ballast to bring back sugar.[103]

Even by the early seventeenth century, northern opulence impressed Pyrard, fresh from Asia. The Jesuit Cardim, a generation earlier, reported similarly. The southerners lived a simpler life, and nowhere did the lower class share the wealth.

II

Brazil's value rose rapidly in the seventeenth century. Spanish domination of Portugal (1580-1640) somewhat improved the amorphous colonial system. It was accompanied by foreign attacks on Brazil, including the Dutch conquest of the north.[104] Immediately, this hurt cattle and sugar production. But the Dutch introduced some new methods, crops, and public works, and acquainted Europe with Brazilian rum and tobacco. Furthermore, disaster in the north turned Portuguese efforts to the south, and the loss of Portugal's Asiatic empire increased Brazil's esteem. Discovery (1683-1730) of gold and dia-

---

[102] Magalhães, pt. 2, ch. ix; Southey, I, 260, 312-314, II, 669, and references there.

[103] Keller, 138 and references there; Oliveira, *Livro das grandezas* (Lisboa, 1620 or 1804), *trat.* vii, *cap.* 5.

[104] Best treatment for economic aspects is Hermann Watjen, *Das hollandische kolonialreich in Brasilien* (The Hague, 1921).

monds in Minas Geraes, Goyaz, and Matto Grosso finally rivetted attention on the colony.

European control tightened.[105] The governing mechanism benefited by substitution (1591) in Portugal of a Treasury Council for the Inspectors, and by a little more centralization and specialization in Brazil. Numerous regulatory ordinances were issued. Non-Portuguese were supposedly banned in 1591. After mining began, further restrictions were enacted and better enforced. Foreigners, except English and Dutch, even if naturalized, were ordered ejected from Minas Geraes (1711). Later laws permitted them to remain if they were married and were not traders, but extended the general provisions to other regions. Portuguese immigration was rigidly controlled. Utilization of important crops was restricted in an effort to retain benefits for Portugal. Thus, manufacture of rum and other products than sugar from the cane was forbidden (1647), and tobacco was partially reserved for Portuguese factories.

On the other hand, sugar production received aid from 1663 on, through partial exemption of planters from arrest for debt. About the same time the crown ended prohibitions on growth of Asia produce and fostered planting of tobacco, cotton, vanilla, spices, and other non-European crops. As inferred above, the English and the Dutch retained much freedom. The Netherlands, by the peace treaty, gained the right to trade with Brazil in all commodities except dyewood. England exacted the same privileges as part of a marriage alliance, and improved her status in 1703. Both countries could trade directly with the colony, but they worked mostly through Portugal, and the Dutch finally lost the legal right of direct access.

Brazil developed markedly. Mining[106] progress was spectacular. Stringent regulations supplemented the mining ordinances of 1618 shortly after the great era began. Gold fields and the diamond area formed separate governments under all-powerful intendants. Entry and exit was licensed, gold must pass through royal smelting houses, and bullion or diamonds might be shipped only on royal craft. Evasion of royalties forced experimentation with other collection methods. A capitation tax on slaves used in the gold workings was several times tried, but the generally favored method was payment of a flat yearly

---

[105] *Cf.* Lannoy, 77, 84 ff., 145; Pereira da Silva, I, 167 ff., 193 ff., 228 ff.; Southey, III, 133 ff.

[106] See especially Southey, III, chs. xxxii, xxxiii, xxxvi; Varnhagen, *Historia geral do Brasil* (Rio de Janeiro, 1854-1857), II; Pereira da Silva, I, 261 ff.

sum, apportioned by the miners among themselves. Diamond smuggling being harder to stop, the crown applied a capitation tax immediately (1730) and assumed a monopoly in 1734. Usually, thereafter, some private company bought a concession. As a seventy-five per cent drop in prices within two years after mining began was one reason for establishing the monopoly, the concessionaire had to agree to limit the number of workers.

Mining technique was primitive. Gold deposits occurred in alluvial soil, which was dug from open pits. The metal was washed out by cradling in running water. Extraction[107] reached its high point about 1750. The total to 1820 probably exceeded a half billion in United States dollars, two-thirds of which came from Minas Geraes. Diamonds averaged twenty-five thousand carats a year—valued at ten dollars each—although the figure reached nearly sixty-six thousand in 1778, and about thirty-six thousand from 1772 to 1790.

Agriculture grew steadily before mining eclipsed it.[108] Sugar required some six hundred mills by the early eighteenth century. Cotton production increased, especially in the interior where natural conditions, a tendency to small farming, and scarcity of slaves made sugar impossible. Cultivation of tobacco and cocoa, native to the north, began. The former was exported early in the seventeenth century. Cocoa, originally grown in the interior, was tried on the coast from 1746. Its competition with Venezuelan cocoa perturbed Spain by that time.

Trade proceeded on a changed basis.[109] Monopolistic companies were highly favored throughout Europe in the seventeenth century, and the Dutch examples most familiar to Portugal were conspicuously formed for fighting as well as trading. As Portugal needed such a combination to restore her overseas interests, several attempts (1623-1640) to form a corporation had been made during the Spanish domination. After freeing herself from Spain, Portugal created (1647) the Company of Privileged Navigation for Brazil. This body enjoyed a monopoly of trade in oil, wine, flour, codfish, and dyewood. In return, it armed ships against the Dutch and convoyed merchantmen between

---

[107] Keller, 165-167; Pereira da Silva, I, 268; Southey, III, 642, 824, n.; illustrations of mining methods, essentially those of the earlier days may be found in Mawe, *Travels* (London, 1812).

[108] Antonil, *Cultura e opulencia do Brasil;* Schmieder, *Brazilian culture hearth,* 191; manuscripts in Spanish archives.

[109] Lannoy, 146-149; Pereira da Silva, I, 302-305; Southey, II, 604 ff., III, 1 ff.; Varnhagen, II, 37 ff.; Rebello da Silva, III, 330-331; manuscript in Archive of Simancas, estados 804 and 1102, etc.

Portugal and Brazil. Trade was restricted to one annual fleet. The company's privileges aroused prompt opposition, and the Dutch treaty (1661) removed the military motive for its existence. It soon lost its monopoly, but lasted in attenuated form until 1720. Meantime (1682), another company replaced it in Pará and Maranhão in an effort to foster settlement of those frontier provinces. This body held a twenty year monopoly of all trade in its area, and promised to introduce five hundred slaves a year and to bring in experts to teach cultivation of new crops. A serious revolt (1684-1685) aided its quick abolition. As a result of danger from the Barbary pirates, however, overseas commerce continued to be limited to one fleet until 1765.

Trade expanded in spite of its new bonds. A large exchange began with Spanish La Plata. In 1586 an English ship captured two Portuguese craft on their way up the river. About the same time the town council of Santiago del Estero wrote, "There are in this city Portuguese merchants . . . selling the things they have brought [from Brazil]." [110] The practice increased from that time, and was little handicapped by the separation of Portugal and Spain. Portugal's trade with Brazil[111] equalled her trade with Europe by 1700. Frezier, while at Bahia, said that "every year about March there arrives a Fleet of about Twenty Ships from Lisbon, laden with Woolen Cloths and Stuffs . . . Stockings, Hats, Iron, Kitchen Furniture, but above all, Biskets, Meal, Wine, Oil, Butter, Cheese . . . . The same Ships . . . carry back Gold, Sugar, Tobacco . . . Brazil Wood, Balsam, Oil of Capayba . . . some rawhides, etc." England and the Netherlands took much of the benefit through their Portuguese agencies.

Population grew unevenly. Dutch conquests in the north caused thousands to emigrate to the south and encouraged direct movement to that area from Portugal. The population of all Brazil in 1640 may have been two hundred thousand.[112] Discovery of mines increased the total and the southern proportion. Ninety-seven ships, crowded with passengers, and eight warships composed the trading fleet of 1709. The crown, alarmed lest Portugal be depopulated, first restricted and then (1720) forbade ordinary emigration, though many evaded the law. White population in the north probably grew mainly by natural increase.

---

[110] Sarracoll's account of Withrington's voyage, in Hakluyt; *Gobernación del Tucumán. Correspondencia de los cabildos* (Madrid, 1918), 259.

[111] Keller, 138 and references found there; Frezier, 303.

[112] Rocha Pombo, III, 754.

Slave imports, however, were so large there that Frezier estimated that Bahia had twenty negroes for every white.

Changes in other fields accompanied this growth. The newly important mining royalties were reinforced by other novel taxes, and forced "gracious donations" became as common as in Spanish America. Brazil also acquired its own coinage[113] after discovery of the needed bullion. Early gold finds were informally and crudely minted, and the pieces were so clipped and mutilated that they were commonly used by weight. As it proved difficult, for other reasons, to keep a sufficient currency in Brazil, the crown decided to strike off a specially marked money, debased to prevent it leaving the colony. This was first done (1695-1699) by a transient mint, but permanent ones were later established. Gold *moidores,* equivalent to about $6.50 in United States currency before 1933, were the standard, with subsidiary pieces in various metals.

Roads improved slightly. The Jesuits early constructed a route from the coast to their mission of São Paulo on the plateau, and the gold rush brought two others into being from São Paulo and Rio de Janeiro to the mines. Weekly caravans plodded over them, and towns grew along their course. But they never accommodated wheeled traffic, and northerners used the São Francisco river for interior travel as generally as the Paulistas used the Tieté. The Jesuit "road" was a terrifying mountain trail. A priest wrote of it in 1663: "The greater part of the way one cannot so much travel as clamber with hands and feet by the roots of trees, and this among such crags and precipices that I confess that my flesh shivered . . . when I looked down." [114]

III

Eighteenth century enlightenment somewhat affected Brazil. The Marquis of Pombal, as Portuguese premier (1750-1777), reflected its ideas and recognized the importance of Brazil and of trade.[115] He increased restrictions when that seemed best for Portuguese interests. In 1755, for instance, he created a monopolistic company for the Gran Pará and Maranhão, and four years later another for Pernambuco and Parahyba. Both brought in many slaves before their abolition in 1778 and 1780.[116] In 1766 and later, he practically banned industries, and

---

[113] Motta, *Moeda do Brasil;* Southey, II, 669, III, 22-23, 150, 883 ff.

[114] Vasconcellos, *Chronica da companhia,* pt. 1, par. 148.

[115] Lucio d'Azevedo, *Politica de Pombal em relacção ao Brasil;* see also general studies of his career and of Brazil's history.

[116] Lannoy, 150-151; Southey, III, 549 ff., 655-656; Smith, *Memoirs of Pombal* (2 vol., London, 1843), I, 76-77, 305, II, 296.

in 1777 severely restricted diamond mining while trying to prevent frauds. Other actions, although not necessarily harmful, were not reflections of liberalism. In 1762, for instance, he abolished the capitation tax for mining and returned to collection of the fifth. Nine years later, discontinuing farming of the diamond fields, he took over their exploitation through royal agents.

In general, however, Pombal followed liberal ideas. He established unqualified freedom for the Indians (1755-1758). Trade benefited from lower taxes on sugar and tobacco, and by abolition of the convoyed fleet. Peace with the Barbary Powers made this unnecessary, and after 1765 the trade of Rio de Janeiro and Bahia lay open to single ships. Agriculture received aid through tax exemptions or decreases on coffee, indigo, and rice, and by encouragement for the slave trade and white immigration. The latter included some criminals from Portugal,[117] but also thousands of desirables from the Atlantic islands. Though some of Pombal's measures were reversed at his fall, a liberal trend continued. At the end of the century a tax replaced the obnoxious salt monopoly.[118]

Considerable growth resulted,[119] especially in agriculture. Sugar regained its importance in world markets as the Haitian revolution and the Napoleonic wars injured competitors. Rice became an export soon after it was planted in 1766. Coffee culture, tried by 1727, really dates from the tax remission of 1761. Small quantities were exported within twenty years. The southern outpost, Rio Grande do Sul, revived wheat growing and bred mules for the mines. Various men tested silk culture and a hemp substitute, and indigo and cochineal flourished until governmental stupidity ruined their growth. Manufacturing rose for a time. Pombal himself sent experts to aid cotton weaving in the north. Though he soon turned against the idea, it is evident that goldsmiths were active and that much cotton and wool and some silk and linen were woven during his régime. Viceroy Lavradio thought (1779) planters, as well as slaves in Minas Geraes, independent of European looms. The laws mentioned above ended the development. They made exceptions for weaving of coarse stuffs for slaves, for a tanyard at Rio, and for a sailcloth factory at Bahia. Some shipbuilding continued at that place, per-

---

[117] Southey, III, 590-591.

[118] *Ibid.*, 686. See argument against the salt monopoly in Cunha de Azevedo Coutinho, *Ensaio economico*.

[119] Besides references above and below see Pereira, I, 75, 229 ff., 246-249, 306-308; Lavradio, *Secret instructions*, 221, 224-231; Southey, III, 48 ff., 589, 655 n., 742, 854, 868; John Adams' notes to his edition of Juan and Ulloa's *Voyage* (London, 1806), II, 333-335.

haps largely for the royal navy. The Indians never ceased their hand-crafts, and northerners made rubber bottles, shoes, and hats for local use.

Population grew enormously.[120] A total of 1,900,000 is likely, for 1776. In 1798 a careful reckoning returned 2,852,000 souls. About 800,000 passed for white, Indians fell short of 300,000, and negroes perhaps numbered 1,000,000. The rest were half-castes. Nine-tenths of the negroes and one-third of the castes were slaves. Assuming an actual total of 3,000,000, the captaincies of Minas Geraes had 611,000, Bahia 530,000, Pernambuco 480,000, and Rio de Janeiro 380,000. Those of Maranhão, São Paulo, and Pará ranked next. In 1806 the biggest cities, including troops and transients, were: the capital, Rio de Janeiro (50,144), Bahia (45,600), Recife (30,000), São Luis de Maranhão (22,000), and São Paulo (18,000). In 1818 the total population numbered 3,617,000. Foreigners must have been few. Their welcome had so declined by 1800 that the crown, on hearing that "one Baron von Humboldt" proposed to visit Brazil, ordered the viceroy to examine him, though courteously, as a suspicious character.[121]

Brazil by the early nineteenth century was reverting toward an agra-rian status.[122] Mines produced four million dollars a year. Agriculture more than doubled that value. Toward the end of the eighteenth cen-tury one hundred ships annually carried overseas thirty thousand cases of sugar, sixty thousand hundredweight of tobacco, half that amount of dyewood, five thousand hundredweight of wool, and twenty thousand hides. This was valued at $9,700,000 in United States currency before 1933. The cargo also included nearly eight millions in gold and dia-monds. In 1806 the crops were worth about eight and one-half million dollars, and the rest, five and one-half. Of the total imports of four-teen million dollars, the captaincy of Rio de Janeiro took four million, seven hundred thousand, that of Pernambuco three million, eight hun-dred thousand, Bahia three million, three hundred thousand, and Maran-hão one million, five hundred thousand. Revenues, aside from the dia-

---

[120] Humboldt, *Essai politique sur Nouvelle Espagne* (Paris, 1811), V, 142-144, and *Essai politique sur Cuba*, II, 134-136; Pereira da Silva, I, 206-209, and refer-ences there; Perdigão Malheiro, *O escravidão*, part iii, pages 13-14.

[121] Royal orders, June 2 and October 12, 1800, printed verbatim in Pereira da Silva, I, 199, n. 4. Compare accounts by Mawe, Lindley, and Semple-Lisle of their experiences.

[122] See descriptions, illustrations, and figures in Mawe; Lindley, *Narrative of a voyage;* Semple-Lisle, *Life;* Balbi, *Essai statistique;* Southey, III, ch. xliv, etc.; Humboldt, *Essai politique sur Nouvelle Espagne* (Paris, 1811), IV, 218; Canga Argüelles, I, 389-390, IV, 194.

mond monopoly, netted the crown annually some two million Portuguese *milreis*.

There was some improvement in important roads from about 1790, but ferries, a royal monopoly, were the usual aid in crossing rivers. In one case[123] a private citizen's offer to build a bridge met with threat of imprisonment from the horrified officials. Mawe frequently criticized crude methods in mining and agriculture. "In no branch of husbandry," he exclaimed, "are the farmers so defective as in the management of cattle." Perhaps he was unreasonable in objecting to lack of fences and of regular milking, but he saw also oxen dragging a crooked stick for a plow, seed sown at random, and fields unweeded. Farmers stored no fodder against seasons of scarcity, produced butter and cheese only carelessly, and grew few grapes, apples, pears, and other fruits in areas well adapted to them.

Brazil certainly had not realized its full possibilities even by contemporary standards. But the distress incident to decline of the mines was over, and fair basis for the future existed.

SELECTED BIBLIOGRAPHY

I. SPANISH AMERICA

A. *General Secondary Accounts*

Several treatises have general value for Spanish American colonial economic history. Ricardo Levene, *Investigaciones acerca de la historia económica del virreinato del Plata* (2 vol., La Plata, 1927-1928), and Domingo Amunátegui Solar, *Historia social de Chile* (Santiago, 1932), authoritative for their areas, have extensive value for all the colonies. Ricardo Cappa, *Estudios críticos acerca de la dominación española en América* (Madrid, 1889 ff.) is less critical, but presents much factual material. Carmelo Viñas Mey, in his "Datos para la historia económica de la colonización española" in Revista Nacional de Economía, VIII (Madrid, 1923), 57-98, 181-209, as in his titles listed below, confuses royal law with American achievement, but utilizes sources not widely available. A. G. Keller, *Colonization* (Boston, 1908), and Charles de Lannoy and Herman Vander Linden, *Histoire de l'expansion coloniale des peuples européens. Portugal et Espagne* (Brussels and Paris, 1907), are good compilations. Four works useful, especially for phases of eighteenth century developments, include G. N. Desdevises du Dezert, *L'Espagne de l'ancien régime* (3 vol., Paris, 1897-1904) ; H. I. Priestley, *José de Gálvez* (Berkeley, 1916) ; William Robertson, *History of America* (2 vol., London, 1777, or later editions) ; *Abbé G. T. F. Raynal, Historie philosophique et poltique des établissements . . . dans les deux indes* (4 vol., Amsterdam, 1770, or later editions). The last is undependable for factual statements, but illustrates the enlightened French viewpoint which affected Spain.

B. *Spanish Theory and Control*

Spanish theory and control is discussed by Earl J. Hamilton, "Spanish mercantilism before 1700" in *Facts and factors in economic history* (Cambridge, Mass.,

---

[123] Southey, III, 872.

1932), and in Manuel Colmeiro, *Historia de la economía política en España* (2 vol., Madrid, 1863). The most important national theorist was Gerónimo Uztariz, whose *Teórica y práctica de comercio y marina* (Madrid, 1724) was several times reprinted and translated into English and other languages. Notable followers include Joseph del Campillo y Cosio, *Nueva sistema de gobierno económico para la América* (written about 1742 and printed at Madrid, 1789) ; Bernardo de Ulloa, *Restablecimiento de las fábricas y comercio española* (Madrid, 1740) ; and Bernardo Ward, *Proyecto económico . . . escrito en el año 1762* (Madrid, 1779). J. W. Horrocks, *Short 'history of mercantilism* (New York, before 1927), rather casually notes the Spanish part in European theory. Guillermo Subercaseaux, *Historia de las doctrinas económicas en América y en especial en Chile* (Santiago, 1924) is valueless for the colonial period.

Economic law as revealed by the *Recopilación de las leyes de las indias* (Madrid 1680, or later editions) must be supplemented by other compilations and interpretative treatises. The most useful supplement so far published is the *Disposiciones complementarias de las leyes de indias* (3 vol., Madrid, 1930). This is a selection from manuscripts now in process of extended publication as Manuel de Ayala, *Diccionario de gobierno y legislación de indias* (Madrid, 1929 ff.). Economic material occurs constantly throughout the series. Contemporary commentators include : Juan Matienzo, whose *Gobierno del Perú* was written about 1570 but first published at Buenos Aires in 1910; Antonio Rodríguez de León Pinelo, *Tratado de confirmaciones reales de encomiendas* (Madrid, 1630) ; and Juan Solórzano Pereyra, *Política indiana* (Madrid, 1648, or 1930). Modern writers include : Ricardo Levene, *Introducción á la historia del derecho indiano* (Buenos Aires, 1924) ; J. M. Ots Capdequi, *Derecho de familia y el derecho de sucesión en nuestra legislación de indias* (Madrid, 1921), and his "Derecho de propriedad en nuestra legislación de indias" in *Anuario de Historia del Derecho Español*, V (1928), 49-168.

The revenue system is treated in many of the books listed above and below, notably in Priestley's *Gálvez* and Haring's *Trade and navigation.* Fabian de Fonseca and Carlos de Irrutia, *Historia general de la real hacienda* (6 vol., Mexico, 1845-1853), is a careful study made by Mexican treasury officials about 1790. Francisco Gallardo Fernández, *Origen, progresos y estado de las rentas de . . . España* (3 vol., Madrid, 1805), discusses American revenues as group nine of his classification. The early formative period is treated by A. S. Aiton, "Real hacienda in New Spain under the first viceroy," in *Hispanic American Historical Review*, VI, 232-245, and in two papers by C. H. Haring, "Early Spanish colonial exchequer," in *American Historical Review*, XXIII, 779-796, and "Ledgers of the royal treasurers in Spanish America in the sixteenth century" in *Hispanic American Historical Review*, II, 173-187.

C. *Original Sources*

Much of Spanish American economic history can yet be understood only by a study of original sources. In print, these include general documentary collections, the *Relaciones de los virreyes,* geographical descriptions, and travellers' accounts. Several collections of documents bearing on economic affairs as such have appeared in Argentina. Though the Plata valley was a nontypical part of the Spanish colonial empire, the collections have excellent introductions, and some documents, of more than regional interest. Roberto Levillier edited *Antecedentes de política económica en el Río de la Plata. Documentos originales* (2 vols., Madrid, 1915), *Correspondencia de la ciudad de Buenos Aires con los reyes* (Madrid, 1915 ff.), and *Correspondencia de los oficiales reales de hacienda del Río de la Plata con los reyes* (Madrid, 1915 ff.). Various editors compiled the *Documentos para la historia argentina,* including : volumes I and II, *Real hacienda, 1774-1780* (Buenos Aires, 1913-1914) ; volumes V, VI and VII, *Comercio de indias, 1713-1809* (Buenos Aires, 1915-1916) ; volumes XI and XII in *Territorio y población . . . de Buenos Aires, 1778-1810* (Buenos Aires, 1919). Volume X of the series should cover *Territorio y población* (1726 to 1744), but does not seem to have been published.

José Canga Argüelles, *Diccionario de hacienda* (5 vol., London, 1826-1827; 2d ed., revised, 2 vol., Madrid, 1833-1834; supplement, 1840), offers statistical data on American as on Spanish taxes, trade, population, mines, and agriculture, chiefly for the later eighteenth century. Antonio de Alcedo, *Diccionario geográfico histórico de América* (5 vol., Madrid, 1786-1789), has no such value, but in translating it as *The geographical and historical dictionary of America* (5 vol., London, 1815), G. A. Thompson added information on economic affairs useful to British traders. Indispensable data on the population, mines, products, industries, trade, and revenues of Spanish North America appear in J. A. Villa-Señor y Sánchez, *Teatro americano* (2 vol., Mexico, 1746-1748) ; Alexandre von Humboldt, *Essai politique sur . . . Nouvelle Espagne* (5 vol., Paris, 1811), and the same author's *Essai politique sur l'Île de Cuba* (2 vol., Paris, 1826). The earlier work is less complete and dependable than are those of Humboldt, but is the only extensive work for its period. Humboldt's critical analysis of offcial data produced results for the later years more accurate than the data itself. His books were several times reprinted and translated, including John Black's edition, *Political essay on the kingdom of New Spain* (4 vol., London or New York, 1811-1812), and J. S. Thrasher's unsatisfactory edition, *Island of Cuba* (New York, 1856).

So called "geographical relations" discuss, among other things, population and produce. Printed examples include : Juan López de Velasco, *Geografía y descripción universal de las indias, 1571-1574* (Madrid, 1894) ; German Latorre (ed.), *Relaciones geográficas de indias . . . del siglo XVI* (Sevilla, 1919) ; Manuel Serrano y Sanz (ed.), *Relaciones históricas y geográficas de América Central* (Madrid, 1908) ; Marcos Jiménez de Espada (ed.) *Relaciones geográficas de indias. Perú* (2 vol., Madrid, 1881-1885) ; and Angel de Altolaguirre y Duvale (ed.), *Relaciones geográficas de la gobernación de Venezuela, 1767-1768* (Madrid, 1908). The same sort of information occurs in José Luís Cisneros, *Descripción exacta de la provincia de Venezuela* (Valencia, 1764, or Madrid, 1912).

Travellers were universally interested in economic conditions. Only a brief selection of their accounts, though one representative as to regions, time, and observer's nationality, can be given. For the sixteenth century no single title equals the value of two contemporary English collections. These are Richard Hakluyt's *Principall navigations* (London, 1598-1600) and Samuel Purchas' *Hakluytus posthumus; or, Purchas, his pilgrimes* (4 vol., London, 1625). Both print accounts by English travellers in the Americas, and translate Spanish or other foreign works. The first editions are rare, but later ones are found in most libraries. The Italian, Girolamo Benzoni, who visited most of Spanish America in the mid-sixteenth century, published an entertaining, if sometimes biased, description in *Storia del mondo nuovo* (Venezia, 1565), translated as *History of the new world* (London, 1857). Other descriptions for so early a date mostly appear incidentally to stories of the conquest. Among later writers, José de Acosta, *Historia natural y moral de las indias* (Sevilla, 1590 and later; several English and other translations), discusses conditions on both continents. Samuel Champlain visited ports in the Antilles, Mexico, and Panama, 1599-1600, and described Mexico City and the crossing of the isthmus, although he may not have gone inland. The best edition of his *Brief discours,* edited by H. P. Biggar as *Brief narrative of the most remarkable things observed* (Toronto, 1922), gives French and English text. Juan González de Mendoza, one of many missionaries to Asia who crossed Mexico, appended a valuable "Itinerary of the New World" to his *Historia de las cosas . . . de la China* (Roma, 1585, and later editions). This was first translated into English as *Historie of the great and mightie kingdom of China* (London, 1588).

For the seventeenth century, Pedro Ordóñez de Ceballos, *Viage del mundo* (Madrid, 1614; 2d ed., Madrid, 1691), covers most of tropical America. Thomas Gage, who lived in Mexico and Guatemala for twelve years, published the *English American* (London, 1648), commonly cited and reprinted as *A new survey of the West Indies*. Though religiously polemical, it is indispensable for other matters. Giovanni Gemelli-Careri, who crossed Mexico in 1698, wrote the *Giro del mondo* (6 vol., Napoli, 1699-1700). An English version, *Voyage round the world*, is in volume IV of Churchill's *Voyages* (London, 1744). Most of South America, in the early century, is described in two works: Reginaldo de Lizárraga, *Descripción breve . . . del Perú, Tucumán, Río de la Plata, y Chile* (best editions, Madrid, 1909 or Buenos Aires, 1916), and in a *Descripción anónima del Perú y Lima . . . por un judío portugués* which J. de la Riva Agüero edited in the *Actas y Memorias* (Madrid, 1914), of the Congreso de Historia y Geografía en Sevilla. Acarete de Biscay's account of his mid-century trip up the Plata to Peru can be read in Thevenot's *Relations des divers voyages* (Paris, 1696). The translation, "An account of a voyage up the river de la Plata" is in the *Voyages and discoveries in South America* (London, 1698) and reprinted as *A relation of Mr. R. M.'s voyage to Buenos Aires and . . . to Potosí* (London, 1716).

In the eighteenth century, South America was visited by many trained and methodical observers. The outstanding description resulted from the official trip (1735-1745) of Jorge Juan and Antonio Ulloa. Jointly, they published the *Relación histórica del viage* (4 vol., Madrid, 1748, and later editions), translated into English as *Voyage to South America* (2 vol., London, 1758, and later editions). It is indispensable for all economic subjects. The authors' *Noticias secretas de América* criticized Indian status and other affairs so stringently that it remained unpublished until stolen from Spain and printed in London in 1826. Religious intolerance caused its translations into English (*Secret expedition to Peru*, Boston, 1851; *Popery judged by its fruits*, Boston, 1878) but the versions, although abridged, are accurate enough. Ulloa alone wrote a *Noticias americanas* (Madrid, 1772), geographical and economic in subject matter, and less critical of Spanish policy. Foreign travellers include: Amédé F. Frezier, *Relation du voyage . . . 1712, 1713, et 1714* (Paris, 1716), translated as *Voyage to the South Sea and along the coasts of Chili and Peru* (London, 1717); Anton Z. Helms (a miner) *Tagebuch einer reise durch Peru von Buenos Aires an dem grossen Plata-flusse über Potosí nach Lima* (Dresden, 1798), abridged as *Travels from Buenos Aires to Potosí by Lima* (London, 1807); and William B. Stevenson, *Historical and descriptive narrative of twenty years residence in . . . Chile, Peru, and Colombia* (3 vol., London, 1825). Joseph Skinner's *Present state of Peru* (London, 1805), is pirated from the periodical *Mercurio Peruano* (Lima, 1791-1795).

Venezuela at the end of the colonial era is extensively treated in F. R. J. De Pons, *Voyage à la partie orientale de la terre ferme . . . 1801 . . . 1804* (3 vol., Paris, 1806), which in English is known as *Voyage to the eastern part* (New York, 1806) or *Travels in South America* (London, 1807); Alexander von Humboldt, *Voyage aux regions equinoxiales du nouveau continent* (12 vol., Paris, 1815-1826), translated into English as *Personal narrative of travels* (best edition, 7 vol., London, 1814-1829); J. F. Dauxion-Lavaysse, *Voyage aux îles de Trinidad, de Tabago, de la Marguerite, et dans . . . Venezuela* (2 vol., Paris, 1813), translated into English as *Statistical, commercial and political description of Venezuela* (London, 1820). The three only partially overlap as to region.

The best original English account of the Plata is J. S. Davie, *Letters from Paraguay, describing . . . Montevideo and Buenos Ayres* (London, 1805). Among several Spanish works, a very notable description occurs in the anonymous *Lazarillo de ciegos caminantes desde Buenos Aires hasta Lima* (Gijón, 1773, and Buenos Aires, 1908).

North America and the Antilles are better treated in Humboldt's studies of Mexico and Cuba, noted above, than in any distinctively travel narrative. For Española, about the same time, see William Walton, *Present state of the Spanish colonies, including a particular report of . . . Santo Domingo* (2 vol., London, 1810). Walton's specific facts on other regions evidently rest largely on the statements of De Pons, Humboldt, and other standard authorities.

D. *The People*

Population and emigration have not been much studied. The *Catálogo de pasageros á indias durante los siglos XVI, XVII, y XVIII. Tomo I (1509-1533)* (Madrid, 1900) will, when completed, afford a sound basis for investigation. Luís Rubio y Moreno, *Pasageros á indias. Catálogo . . . de las informaciones y licencias . . . 1492-1592* (Madrid, 1930 ff.), begins with 1534 and is incomplete even for the years it covers, but illustrates distribution and classes of emigrants. Data concerning the region of Buenos Aires appear in Emilio Ravignani, "Crecimiento de la población de Buenos Aires y su campaña, 1726-1810," in *Anales de la Facultad de Ciencias Económicas*, I (Buenos Aires, 1919), 405-416. Foreign elements can be glimpsed in José Toribio Medina's several works on the Inquisition, and in travellers' accounts. Special studies include: Ricardo de Lafuente Machain, *Portugueses en Buenos Aires. Siglo XVII* (Madrid, 1931), and in the study on the Jews in New Spain in the sixteenth century, which makes part of the *Precursores idealógicos de la guerra de independencia*, II (Mexico, 1932).

E. *Usages and Practices*

The land and labor systems have been treated chiefly as to legal aspects. Land is discussed in Cayetano Coll y Toste, "Propriedad territorial en Puerto Rico" in *Boletín Histórico de Puerto Rico*, I, 239-310; Carmelo Viñas Mey, "Régimen de la tierra en la colonización española" in *Humanidades*, X (La Plata, 1925), 71-126; and Helen Douglas-Irvine, "Landholding system of colonial Chile" in *Hispanic American Historical Review*, VIII, 449-495. Mariano Galván, *Ordenanzas de tierras y aguas* (Mexico, 1849), has much value for the colonial period. G. M. McBride's authoritative *Land system of Mexico* (New York, 1923), is largely on the period since independence.

Labor is usefully discussed by Carmelo Viñas Mey, "Derecho obrero en la colonización española" in *Humanidades*, VIII (Buenos Aires, 1924), 49-102. Despite its title, Louis Captain's *Travail en Amérique avant et après Colomb* (Paris, 1914), is not worth consulting for this study's purposes. The New Laws, of primary importance for Indian servitude, are reproduced in facsimile with an introduction in D. L. Molinari (ed.), *Leyes y ordenanzas nuevamente hechas* (Buenos Aires, 1923), and, with a translation added, in Henry Stevens and F. W. Lucas (eds.) *New laws of the indies* (London, 1893). An early code indicative of abuses of Indian labor rather than effective in correcting them, was edited by R. D. Hussey, "Text of the laws of Burgos, 1512" in *Hispanic American Historical Review*, XII, 301-326. Original sources for Indian status are printed in J. C. García Santillán, *Legislación sobre indios del Río de la Plata en el siglo XVI* (Madrid, 1928), and in Francisco Navas del Valle, *España y los indios del nuevo mundo. Documentos para su estudio hasta fin del siglo XVI* (Sevilla, 1925?). Secondary treatments in English include: Ruth K. Barber, "Indian labor in the Spanish colonies," in *New Mexico Historical Review*, VII (1932), 105-142, 233-271, 311-347 (also reprinted separately); H. C. Lea, "Indian policy of Spain" in *Yale Review* (old series) VIII, 1-19; L. B. Simpson, *The encomienda in New Spain . . . 1492-1550* (Berkeley, 1929). The early history is nowhere better handled than in José Antonio Saco, *Esclavitud de los indios* (Habana, 1932), which reprints an article by that title and another on the *encomiendas* to 1518 which originally appeared in the *Revista de Cuba*, volumes X through XIII. Other excellent accounts are Domingo Amunátegui Solar, *Encomiendas de indíjenas en Chile* (2 vol., Santiago, 1909-1910), and Carmelo Viñas Mey, *Estatuto del obrero indígena en la colonización española* (Madrid, 1929). The standard treatment of negro slavery is J. A. Saco, *Historia de la esclavitud africana en el nuevo mundo* (I, Barcelona, 1879, II, Habana, 1893); and for foreign aspects of the slave trade to 1714 is Georges Scelle, *Histoire politique de la traité négrière aux indes de Castille* (2 vol., Paris, 1906) introduction translated in *American Journal of International Law*, IV, 1910, 612-661. Elizabeth Donnan (ed.) *Documents illustrative of the history of the slave trade* (Washington, 1930 ff.) emphasizes foreign phases. Fernando Márquez de la Plata, "Documentos relativos á la introducción de esclavos negros en América" in *Revista Chilena de Historia y Geografía*, LVII, 226-249, LVIII, 286-304, LIX, 204-214, is valuable for the whole sixteenth century. Berber slavery in the first half of the sixteenth century is well, though not exhaustively treated in José Torre Revello, "Esclavas blancas en las indias occidentales," in *Boletín del Instituto de Investigaciones Históricas*, VI, No. 34, pp. 263-271. Organization of white labor in guilds is discussed by Ricardo Levene, "Los gremios durante la época colonial" in *Anales de la Facultad de Derecho y Ciencias Sociales*, 3a serie, II, 137-151; José Torre Revello, *El gremio de plateros en las indias occidentales* (Buenos Aires, 1932); Genaro Estrada's reprint of J. F. del Barrio Lorenzot, *El Trabajo en México durante la época colonial* (Mexico, 1920); Fernando Marquez Miranda, *Ensayo sobre los artífices de la platería en el Buenos Aires colonial* (Buenos Aires, 1933).

Representative contemporary viewpoints on involuntary servitude include the works of the humanitarians Las Casas (especially the *Brevíssima relación de la destrucción de las indias*, Sevilla, 1552, and later editions and translations), and Alonso Sandoval, *De instaurando Aethiopum salute* (Madrid, 1647), respectively outstanding on the Indian and the negro. Miguel de Monsalve, *Reducción universal de todo el Pirú y demás indias* (Lima?, 1604), is excellent on abuses in Peru, but excessively rare. For contrast to the humane viewpoint, see Bernardo Vargas Machucas, "Apologías y discursos," in *Colección de documentos inéditos para la historia de España*, LXXI, 201-311.

Communications on land are discussed for the Plata, and partly for other regions, in R. J. Cárcano, *Historia de los medios de comunicación y transporte en la república argentina* (Buenos Aires, 1893). The postal system in the same region is treated by Eduardo Olivera, "Correo en el Río de la Plata," in *Nueva Revista de Buenos Aires*, II, 10-48, 491-509, III, 3-24. Cayetano Alcázar, *Historia del correo en América* (Madrid, 1920), discusses the legal organization of the postal system, but hardly mentions American conditions. Ocean transport is well handled in Haring, *Trade and navigation* noted elsewhere. Other studies include: Cesáreo Fernández-Duro, *Disquisiciones náuticas* (6 vol., Madrid, 1876-1881); E. J. Hamilton, "Wages and subsistence on Spanish treasure ships, 1503-1660" in *Journal of Political Economy*, XXXVII, 430-450; P. S. Taylor, "Spanish seamen in the new world during the colonial period," in *Hispanic American Historical Review*, V, 631-661; and Federico de Castro y Bravo, *Las naos españoles en la carrera de las indias . . . en la segunda mitad del siglo XVI* (Madrid, 1927). The last, in spite of its unprepossessing appearance, is a work of real research.

Coinage is discussed in many general numismatic treatises. Special phases may be studied in: A. S. Aiton and B. W. Wheeler, "First American mint" in *Hispanic American Historical Review,* XI, 198-215; J. T. Medina, "Primera casa de moneda . . . en América" in *Revista Chilena de Historia y Geografía,* I, 353-366; Guillermo Subercaseaux, "Sistema monetario i la organización bancaria de Chile," in *Anales de la Universidad de Chile,* CXLVI, 199-316, 470-598, CXLVII, 3-154; Juan Alvarez, "Valores aproximadas de algunas monedas Hispano-Americanas, 1497-1771" in *Revista de la Universidad de Buenos Aires,* XXXV, 546-580. The last covers all Spanish America, giving values in Argentine gold.

F. *Agrarian and Manufacturing Pursuits*

A treatment of manufacturing fills volumes VII to XII of Ricardo Cappa, *Estudios críticos* (noted elsewhere). Volumes V and VI of the same work are devoted to agriculture and ranching. Some information on American conditions can be gleaned from: A. M. Camacho, *Historia jurídica del cultivo y de la industria ganadera en España* (Madrid, 1912); J. de la C. Mendoza, "Ganadería colonial en el siglo XVI" in *Revista de Derecho, Historia y Letras,* LXIII, 622-634; Julius Klein, *The Mesta* (Cambridge, 1920). Royal encouragement to agriculture, and transfer of crops to America, are discussed by: A. P. Whitaker, "Spanish contribution to American agriculture" in *Agricultural History,* III, No. 1; J. A. Robertson, "Some notes on the transfer by Spain of plants and animals to its colonies overseas" in *James Sprunt Historical Studies,* XIX, No. 2; Spain, Ministerio de Trabajo y Previsión, *Aportación de los colonizadores españoles á la prosperidad de América* (Madrid, 1929); and Bernabé Cobo, *Historia del nuevo mundo* (4 vol., Sevilla, 1890-1895). Cobo's book has original source character for Peru in the mid-seventeenth century. Localized studies include: A. L. Valverde, "Estanco del tabaco en Cuba (1698-1817)" in *Reforma Social,* III, 470-487; I. A. Wright, "Establecimiento de la industria azucarera en Cuba, 1523-1602" in *Reforma Social,* VII, 26-42; Joaquín García Icazbalceta, *Industria de seda en México (Obras completas,* I, Mexico, 1896, pp. 125-161).

G. *Mining*

Vicente Restrepo, *Estudio sobre las minas de oro y plata de Colombia* (Bogotá, 1888) and Irene A. Wright, "Orígenes de la minería en Cuba [1530-1647]" in *Reforma Social,* VII, 450-462, XV, 209-221 are the chief mining histories, and treat the less typical regions and metals. Legal aspects are well represented by: A. S. Aiton, "First American mining code" in *Michigan Law Review,* XXIII, 105-114; J. L. Mecham, "Real de minas as a political institution" in *Hispanic American Historical Review,* VII, 45-83; *Ordenanzas . . . del cuerpo de minería de Nueva España* (Madrid, 1783); *Ordenanzas reales de la minería de la Nueva España* (Madrid, 1783); Francisco Xavier de Gamboa, *Comentarios á las ordenanzas de minas* (Madrid, 1761), and in English as *Commentaries on the mining ordinances of Spain* (2 vol., London, 1830). J. A. Rockwell's *Compilation of Spanish and Mexican law in relation to mines and real estate* (New York, 1851) gives translations of Gamboa's *Commentaries* and of much other colonial law. José Rodríguez Carracido discusses mining technique in *Estudios históricos-críticos de la ciencia española* (Madrid, 1917), and in *Metalúrgicos españoles en América* (Madrid, 1892). Alvaro Alonso Barba, *Arte de los metales* (Madrid, 1640 and later; possibly first printed in 1600), is the standard contemporary treatise on the subject, and was widely translated.

The vexed subject of the amounts of bullion produced is discussed in: E. J.

Hamilton, "Imports of American gold and silver into Spain, 1503-1660" in *Quarterly Journal of Economics*, XLIII, 436-472 and *American treasure and the price revolution in Spain, 1501-1650* (Cambridge, Mass., 1934); C. H. Haring, "American gold and silver production in the first half of the 16th century" in *Quarterly Journal of Economics*, (XXIX, 433-479); Adolf Soetbeer, *Edelmetallproduktion . . . seit der entdeckung amerikas* (Gotha, 1879); and by Alexander von Humboldt in his *Essai politique* (noted elsewhere) and in his *Essay on the fluctuations in the supply of gold* (London, 1839).

H. *Trade*

Overseas trade prior to 1700 is thoroughly treated by C. H. Haring, *Trade and navigation between Spain and the indies in the time of the Hapsburgs* (Cambridge, 1918). G. Artiñano y Galdácano, *Historia del comercio con las indias durante el dominio de los Austrias* (Barcelona, 1917) has supplementary value. There are no broad studies relative to the eighteenth century reforms and conditions, but there is much pertinent data, and a chapter on the rise of free trade, 1700-1789, in Roland Dennis Hussey, *The Caracas Company, 1728-1784. A study in the history of Spanish monopolistic trade* (Cambridge, Mass., 1934). Legal aspects of the trade are set forth by José de Veitia Linaje, *Norte de la contratación de las indias occidentales* (2 vol., Sevilla, 1672), translated into English as *The rule of trade* (London, 1702); Joseph Gutiérrez de Rubalcava, *Tratado histórico, político y legal del comercio de las indias. Parte I* (Cádiz, 1750); and Rafael Antúñez y Acevedo, *Memorias históricas sobre la legislación y gobierno del comercio* (Madrid, 1797). Several scholarly periodical articles by W. L. Schurz amount to a book on Philippine trade. They are: "Mexico, Peru and the Manila galleon" in *Hispanic American Historical Review*, I, 389-402; "Voyage of the Manila galleon from Acapulco to Manila" in *Ibid.*, II, 632-638; "The Royal Philippine Company" in *Ibid*, III, 491-508; "The Spanish lake" in *Ibid*, V, 181-194; and "Acapulco and the Manila galleon" in *Southwest Historical Quarterly*, XXII, 18-37. Additional information appears in Manuel Azcárraga y Palmero, *Libertad de comercio en las islas filipinas* (Madrid, 1871).

Among useful papers on the foreign contraband trade are: A. S. Aiton, "Asiento treaty as reflected in the papers of Lord Shelburne" in *Hispanic American Historical Review*, VIII, 167-177; Adam Anderson, *Historical and chronological deduction of the origin of commerce* (London, 1764, and later editions); Vera L. Brown, "Contraband trade, a factor in the decline of Spain's empire in America" in *Hispanic American Historical Review*, VIII, 178-189; E. W. Dahlgren, *Relations commerciales et maritimes entre la France et les côtés de l'océan pacifique* (Paris, 1909). Anderson was clerk of the South Sea Company for many years. Other aspects of trade are described by: L. E. Fisher, "Commercial conditions in Mexico at the end of the colonial period" in *New Mexico Historical Review*, VII, 143-164; A. P. Whitaker, "Commerce of Louisiana and the Floridas at the end of the eighteenth century" in *Ibid*, VIII, 190-203, and the same author's *Documents relating to the commercial policy of Spain in the Floridas with incidental reference to Latin America* (DeLand, Florida, 1931). Domingo de Marcoleta, *Historia y descripción general de los intereses de comercio de todas las naciones de Europa* (4 vol., Madrid, 1772-1774) has many chapters on Spanish-American voyages and commerce.

Internal trade must be studied largely from original sources such as travel accounts and individual documents. Thomas de Mercado, *Suma de tratos y contratos* (Sevilla, 1571 and later revised editions), drew on American examples in discussing contemporary business practices. G. M. Wrigley, "Salta, an early commercial center of South America" in *Geographical Review,* II, 116-133 has considerable value for the colonial period.

II. PORTUGUESE AMERICA

A. *General History and Portuguese Policy*

Few economic studies of the Portuguese colonies exist. Paragraphs or chapters in the general narratives, and documents scattered through periodicals, must be sought by the student. So much of Portuguese policy was formed for Asia rather than Brazil that many treatises on the Portuguese East Indies are also valuable. Lannoy and Vander Linden, *Histoire de l'expansion* (noted elsewhere) and A. Zimmermann, *Kolonialpolitik Portugals und Spaniens* (Berlin, 1896) are among the better compilations. J. M. Pereira da Silva, *Historia da fundação do imperio brasileiro,* I (Rio de Janeiro, 1864), is devoted to conditions before 1808 and is exceptionally useful for the Portuguese background. J. Lucio d'Azevedo, "Politica de Pombal em relação ao Brasil" in *Tomo especial,* III, (1927), of *Revista do Instituto Historico e Geographico Brasileiro,* and reprinted in the author's *Novas espanáforas* (Lisboa, 1932), is the only study to consider Pombal's Brazilian policies alone.

B. *Specialized Treatises—Original Sources*

Original sources include several essentially geographical-economic accounts by native writers. All tended to exaggerate favorable conditions. The earliest is Pero de Magalhães de Gandavo, *Historia da provincia Sancta Cruz* (Lisboa, 1576 and later editions). The same writer's *Tratado da terra do Brasil,* written slightly earlier, is more valuable for specific economic data. It was first printed in 1827. Both have been translated by J. B. Stetson as *The histories of Brazil* (2 vol., New York, 1922). Father Fernão Cardim's *Narrativo epistolar de uma viagem . . . 1583-1590* (Lisboa, 1847), has been reprinted as part of the author's *Tratados da terra e gente do Brasil* (Rio de Janeiro, 1925). Gabriel Soares de Souza, a planter seventeen years resident in Brazil, wrote *Tratado descriptivo do Brasil em 1587* (Rio de Janeiro, 1851). Rodolpho Garcia has recently (Rio de Janeiro, 1930) reprinted the anonymous *Dialogos das grandezas do Brasil,* which described conditions in the early seventeenth century. Father Simão Vasconcellos, *Noticias curiosas e necessarias das cóusas do Brasil* (Lisboa, 1668), is more generally obtainable as the introduction to the author's *Chronica da Companhia de Jesu* (Lisboa, 1663, or Rio de Janeiro, 1864). The only important work on the period of transition from sugar growing to mining is A. J. Antonil, *Cultura e opulencia do Brasil por suas drogas e minas* (Lisboa, 1711; latest reprint, Rio de Janeiro, 1923).

Jesuit efforts to protect the Indians, and their other interests, make their writings valuable to economic historians. Collections of letters previously scattered are: Manoel da Nobrega, *Cartas do Brasil . . . 1544-1560* (Rio de Janeiro, 1886), and, for the seventeenth century, J. Lucio d'Azevedo (ed.), *Cartas do padre Antonio Vieira* (2 vol., Coimbra, 1925-1926). The instructions which two late viceroys left their successors cover especially the governmental and economic condition of the realm. Those of Lavradio (1779) and Vasconcellos (1789) are in volumes LXXVI and XXIII of the *Revista do Instituto Historico e Geographico Brasileiro.* The first is translated as *Secret instructions left by Marques de Lavradio,* in the appendix to volume II of Armitage, *History of Brazil* (London, 1836).

Foreign travel accounts are indispensable. The collections of Hakluyt and Purchas (noted elsewhere) contain much on Brazil, and most of the famous voyagers to the Pacific or about the world, such as Dampier, Shelvocke, Frezier, and Anson, left mention of a Brazilian call. Seventeenth century visitors include:

François Pyrard, *Discours du voyage* (Paris, 1611), translated into English as *Voyage of François Pyrard* (2 vol., London, 1887) ; and Richard Flecknoe, *Relation of ten years travells* (London, 1654). Four Englishmen give excellent data on conditions at the end of the colonial era : J. G. Semple-Lisle, *Life* (London, 1799) ; Thomas Lindley, *Narrative of a voyage to Brazil . . . and the imprisonment of the author and . . . crew* (London, 1805) ; Henry Koster, *Travels in Brazil* (2 vol., London, 1817) ; and John Mawe, *Travels in the interior of Brazil* (London, 1812). Koster, as manager of a sugar mill in Pernambuco, is chiefly valuable for agriculture. Mawe was one of the first travellers to penetrate and describe the interior mining areas.

C. *Specialized Treatises—Secondary Accounts*

Secondary accounts are few. For the Jewish elements of the population, see Lafuente Machaïn (noted elsewhere), and Solidonio Leite, *Judeus no Brasil* (Rio de Janeiro, 1923). Indian and negro servitude is discussed from an abolitionist and legalistic angle by A. M. Perdigão Malheiro, *Escravidão no Brasil. Ensaio historico-juridico-social* (3 pts., Rio de Janeiro, 1866-1867). The study is not essentially historical as to the negro. Evaristo de Maraes, *A escravidão africana no Brasil* (São Paulo, 1933), is historical and apparently authoritative, but has not been seen by this writer. Brazilian coinage is treated in J. X. da Motta, *Moeda do Brasil, 1645-1888* (Victoria, 1889).

Some information on agriculture, mining, and trade appears in : Oscar Schmieder, *Brazilian culture hearth* (University of California Publications in Geography, III, 1929, 159-198) ; E. O. von Lippmann, *Geschichte des zuckers* (Leipzig, 1890) ; W. L. von Eschwege, *Pluto brasiliensis. Eine reihe von abhandlungen über Brasiliens gold, diamanten und anderen mineralischen reichtum* (Berlin, 1833) ; and Adrien Balbi, *Essai statistique sur le royaume de Portugal et d'Algarve* (2 vol., Paris, 1822). Other data can be gleaned from certain essentially doctrinaire essays by Brazilians : José Veira do Couto, *Memoria sobre as minas da capitania de Minas Geraes* (Rio de Janeiro, 1842) ; J. J. Cunha de Azevedo Coutinho, *Discurso sobre o estado actual das minas do Brasil* (Lisboa, 1804) ; and the same author's *Ensaio economico sobre o comercio de Portugal e suas colonias* (Lisboa, 1794 ; revised edition, 1816). The last was translated as *Political essay on the commerce of Portugal and her colonies* (London, 1801). Bernardo de Jesus Maria, *Arte e diccionario do commercio e economia portugueza* (Lisboa, 1784), appears to be a Portuguese antecedent of Canga Argüelles' Spanish *Diccionario* (noted elsewhere), but the present writer has never seen a copy. Alan K. Manchester, *British pre-eminence in Brazil* (Chapel Hill, 1933), though somewhat too dependent on British sources, is invaluable for all trade, and useful for many other aspects of the economic life of Brazil.

CHAPTER TWELVE

COLONIAL INTERNATIONAL RELATIONS

Mare Clausum and the Theory of Effective Occupation

By John Tate Lanning

B Y THE application of the doctrine of *mare clausum* Spain theoretically closed the Americas and the American seas to all foreigners save the Portuguese. But Spain's inability to do so effectively produced a state which may be unconsciously described by mere reference to the Spanish Main. The doctrine was thoroughly scholastic and medieval in its authoritative division and monopoly of large portions of the world, but it was not without precedent. Venice had excluded traders from the Adriatic on a basis tacitly acknowledged by the excluded parties as legal. Spain and Portugal, too, had long established the framework for the partition of another world before the Admiral of the Ocean Sea was propelled by stormy winds into the Tagus and into the wrath of the king of Portugal. It was in the eighth article of the Treaty of Alcaçovas, negotiated in the memorable wedding year of Ferdinand and Isabella, that the Catholic Kings conceded to Alfonso V of Portugal the territory and trade of the Azores, Madeira, or any other islands that interspersed the sea from the Canaries to Guinea. In return, the Spanish sovereigns wrested from the Portuguese king an agreement not to disturb Castile in the exclusive possession of the Canaries. But the king of Portugal ordered the crews of all foreign 'ships captured in his own sphere to be cast into the sea! Thus the principle of partition and mutual exclusion was already laid down for further elaboration when the New World had been superimposed upon Europe. What is more, the principle had been entered into exclusively between Spain and Portugal—countries not always destined to be the determining factors in world peace. The intrusion of other powers into the areas appropriated, but not actually and strongly held, made of the international relations of the Americas little more than elaboration and variations upon the theme of effective occupation.

When America first became a problem to Europe, little of significance had been written on international law. The church was just emerging, however, from the epoch of its most Hildebrandic domination. It was only natural, therefore, that the institution of the *pax ecclesiae* should still be the highest authority in international affairs. Thus, when the problem of America revived the international rivalry allayed by the Treaty of Alcaçovas, it required more than a pontifical pronouncement to still the wrath of King John II of Portugal, who looked upon Columbus as a liar and upon the newly discovered territory as a part of Guinea, conceded to Portugal in the agreement of Alcaçovas. It was not papal presumption but the fear of impending war with John II and the realization that the Valencian Spaniard, Rodrigo de Borgia, then Pope Alexander VI, was dependent upon Spain for the perpetuation of his nefarious and grandiose schemes. The Catholic Kings, thus impelled, had wasted no time in laying their dilemma and their claim of sovereignty before the Papal Curia.

Contrary to the general belief, not one but four papal bulls were issued before their inadequacy was conceded by these two Hispanic powers. The anxiety of Alexander VI to please Spain led to the promulgation of the first bull, the *inter cætera,* in April 1493, which conceded to Spain the discoveries in the "ocean sea." So obvious and intense was the dissatisfaction of Portugal that it required only two months to procure the revision *(inter cætera II)* which is known as the papal line of demarcation. Thus an imaginary line was drawn one hundred leagues to the west of the Azores and Cape Verde Islands. Beyond that line Spain ruled supreme and exclusively on land and sea if they were not occupied by any Christian prince before Christmas of that year. The third document *(eximiae)* enlarged upon the concessions and delineated the *mare clausum* which the fourth bull, by removing the condition of foreign occupation by Christmas, rendered immediately effective.[1]

At the dawn of the modern era the position of pope as an international arbiter was not only waning, but John II considered these bulls neither satisfactory nor competent. Considering the papal efforts altogether one-sided, he proceeded to prepare his fleet in the Tagus while he prepared his briefs for direct negotiations. The ability of little Portugal, notwithstanding its maritime prowess, to intimidate the monopolistic Spain into important concessions has always appeared a little puzzling, but the same necessity which preserved the most punctilious observance of the terms of peace also led to their formulation. The Catholic Kings had their doubts about the pretentions of Columbus, who had nearly lost his chance through his braggadocian air before Isabella.

---

[1] A. P. Newton, *The European nations in the West Indies* (London, 1933), 2-7.

The state of Europe, moreover, required amicable Iberian relations. Such motives as these impelled the plenipotentiaries of Iberia to fore-gather and, supported by the widest available assortment of geographical knowledge, to sign the Treaty of Tordesillas in June 1494.[2] Running a line 370 leagues west of the Cape Verde Islands, by cutting exactly between the easternmost islands discovered by Columbus and the west-ernmost revealed by the Portuguese, was supposed to leave both satisfied. Just as a paucity of geographical knowledge had made the papal bulls possible, it was because Portugal did not realize the limitations of the line drawn at Tordesillas, or did not yet grasp its resillient qualities, that she acquiesced with a mere pinch off the great promontory of South America.

So long as Spain was not threatened by another European power her initial agreement with Portugal was scrupulously upheld, but with the advent of Charles V in 1520 a war with Francis I of France came in the next year. Almost immediately a new complexion was put on the international situation, and for the first time America began to suffer through the vicissitudes of European affairs. With Mexico yielding sheeny gold at the point of Cortés' lances, it had just begun to be per-ceived what the New World would mean to Spain. The realization only solidified a doctrine which she had been astute enough to proclaim twenty-eight years earlier. The first treasure of Mexico, secretly shipped to Charles V by Cortés,[3] arrived safely under the guardianship of Hernández de Portocarrero and Francisco de Montejo; but as con-spicuous sweets attract insects from all sides, the news was hardly her-alded around the ports of Europe before the seamen of three nations began to lay deep plots to taste the heart of this sweet gold. Vessels

---

[2] S. E. Dawson, "The line of demarcation of Pope Alexander VI, 1493, and the Treaty of Tordesillas," in *Proceedings of the Royal Society of Canada,* second series, V (1899), 467-546.

[3] This first shipment of Mexican treasure was minutely listed in a paper of the *Casa de Contratación* undiscovered until it was hit upon some two years ago by Dr. Earl J. Hamilton, Archivo General de Indias (hereinafter *A. G. I.*), 39-2-2/9, 1°. It is now being translated and edited by John Tate Lanning and Robert A. Smith. Two German estimates, based to a considerable extent upon printed works, Adolph Soetbeer, *Edelmetall-produktion und werthverhaltniss zwischen gold und silber* (Gotha, 1897), 49-60, and W. Lexis, "Beitrage sur statistik der edelmetalle nebst einigen bermerkungen über die werthrelation" in *Jahrbucher für National-ökonomie und Statistik*, XXXIV, 361-417, and also one by Clarence H. Haring, "American gold and silver production in the first half of the sixteenth century," in *The Quarterly Journal of Economics*, XXIX (1915), 433-479 have preceded the rela-tively exhaustive study of American treasure, by Earl J. Hamilton, entitled *American treasure and the price revolution in Spain* (Cambridge, 1934).

returning from America were soon beset by corsairs after they passed
the Azores and before they put in at the mouth of the Guadalquivir. In
1523 Jean d'Ango of Dieppe isolated and captured two of the richly
laden vessels in Cortés' treasure fleet of that year. Aside from gold,
the hides, logwood, and sugar taken in the other captured ships fore-
boded ill for trading security and an easy *mare clausum*. Just as this
Franco-Spanish war was ushered in with a significant capture, it was
ushered out with a still more sinister and prophetic blow, for in 1537
the Peruvian treasure fleet was assailed by corsairs and nine vessels
detached and taken. Those which successfully ran the gamut put in
with 10,582 ducats in precious metals. When the Truce of Nice
brought a temporary cessation of hostilities, Spain had been taught one
lesson. Every inch and every minute her commercial and territorial
exclusiveness in the New World would have to be defended by force
of arms. Just as Americans talked of armed neutrality in the trying
years between 1914 and 1917, so Spain talked of arming for the defence
of her ordinary commerce. Regular fleets of galleons to convoy the
American fleets were bound to come into existence.[4] It took twenty
years and the third French war to elicit the first royal decree for convoy
system (1543), and twelve years more for the convoy to take the shape
so commonly described.[5]

In the first years, when two fleets, sailing together to the West Indies,
there to part for separate voyages to Puerto Bello and Vera Cruz, assembled at Havana for a joint trip home through the Bahama Channel, the
French still constituted the principal menace. That stout old imperialist,
Pedro Menéndez de Avilés, as governor of Florida, proved spectacular
when he ruthlessly murdered a handful of Huguenots on Florida's shore
over whom he is alleged to have inscribed: "This we do not as to
Frenchmen, but as to Lutherans." The private voyage of Gourges to
Matanzas, where he surprised and butchered the Spanish garrison and
wrote over their swinging heads, "This we do not as to Spaniards, but
as to Marranos, traitors, and thieves," is still one of our classical examples of poetic revenge. But it was the crumbling of France in a

---

[4] Two works, Gernasio de Artinano y de Galdácano, *Historia del comercio con
las indias dominio de las Austrias* (Barcelona, 1917), and C. H. Haring, *Trade
and navigation between Spain and the indies in the time of the Hapsburgs* (Cambridge, 1918), give the most complete authoritative summaries of the fleet system.
The merchants paid a tax, the *avería,* on goods shipped, to support the convoy.

[5] See José de Veitia Linaje, *Norte de la contratación de las indias occidentales
. . .* (Sevilla, 1672).

series of factional wars that eliminated France, and the horizon of Menéndez's far-flung imperial strategy that were vitally and lastingly important. Recognizing the plain requirements of a New World converted into a *mare clausum* by sheer force against the will of all Spain's neighbors, Menéndez advised his sovereign that the great trade channels must first of all be adequately guarded. The settlement of Florida was incidental to that idea. The English could not be more perturbed about the English Channel than were the Spaniards about the Bahama Channel during the colonial period.

Unfortunately for Spain's quiet and exclusive enjoyment of half a world, the demise of one of her maritime enemies witnessed the rise of others in successions which dovetailed with disconcerting orderliness and regularity like filling the ranks of a well-disciplined regiment in battle.

The decline of the Age of Francis I and d'Ango in France corresponded with nicety to the advent of Elizabethan England, personified in Hawkins and Drake. But these newcomers apparently did not set out to distinguish themselves as robber barons—they sought favored nation advantages in trade and opportunities in the land of the setting sun. With some variations and even aberrations this theme of sharing in the profits of American trade (and later land) became the Holy Grail of British statesmen and the greatest discordant note in international affairs for little less than three hundred years. As much as the Elizabethan Englishman professed to know the Spaniard as a pious cutthroat and a grasping Shylock, these first intruders on the American scene expected the Spaniards to acquiesce in their trade ventures with inconsistent ease and naïveté. On no other basis can we explain Hawkins' apparent foolhardiness in running blithely into the principal Spanish ports of the New World and at last allowing himself to be ingloriously attacked and expelled from Vera Cruz. When at last it dawned upon these men that the principle of *mare clausum* was so deeply imbedded in Spanish national economy and in the imperial Spanish mind that there was no dislodging it, only then did they resign themselves to the example of robbery and national depredations set by the French. Obviously the French, the English, and the Dutch could not enter into an international agreement upholding the position of the Spaniards without defying the laws of nature. The Spaniards, on the other hand, could make no concessions in trade and navigation to these rivals. Concord on one of the greatest issues of modern times was, therefore, clearly impossible. Realities, however, have a way of requiring acknowledgment of their presence. The result was a tacit agreement not to mention navigation in American waters in any negotiations except to shroud them occasionally in convenient ambiguity. Nonetheless, after 1550, settlement of European affairs alone was not sufficient to insure equitable relations on that continent. Such, for example, was the case when Drake returned from a "robbing, sacking, and burning" [6] expedition through the Indies and the Florida Channel with nearly 2,000,000 in loot and 240 heavy guns which were used as ballast, and finally mounted and turned so effectively upon their original owners two years later in that historical and literary epic, the destruction of the Spanish Armada.

The coronation of James I in 1603 made possible a resumption of friendly relations with Spain—on paper and on the surface at least. When the Treaty of London[7] was signed the next year, thirty years of intense rivalry and twenty of open warfare were brought to an end. Only the pro-Spanish party, which for twenty years hampered the development of a vigorous American policy, professed to find much good in this treaty. They argued that the right of navigation and trade was guaranteed by the section which provided for

> "free commerce between Spain and the . . . King of England and the . . . subjects of each of them by land and sea . . . in all and singular their kingdoms, dominions, islands, and other lands, cities, towns, ports, and straits where commerce existed . . . according to the use and observance of the ancient alliances and treaties." [8]

The French followed the example of the English at Vervins in 1608 and the Dutch came around the next year, thus beginning a period of intermittent truces which afforded an opportunity for an elucidation of the unfolding principles upon which these powers were operating. Spain was found to be clinging tenaciously to the contention that discovery gave an ineluctable title and right of possession to all lands beyond the seas. This was a clean-cut revival of the pontifical and regal principle of *mare clausum* laid down in the papal bulls and in the Treaty of Tordesillas, and now maintained in Spanish quarters by reference to the precedent of the exclusive monopoly of the Adriatic by the Ve-

---

[6] *A. G. I.*, Sec. V, Audiencia de Santo Domingo, Información hecha en S. Agustín de la Florida, sobre la entrada que hizo en aquellas provincias, el cosario yngles francisco Draque, saquando, robando, y quemando el fuerte donde se hallaban las cajas y de bienes de difuntos. . . .

[7] For text of treaties see Lewis Hertslet, (comp.), *A complete collection of treaties and conventions* . . . (31 vols., London 1827-1925).

[8] Treaty of London, Article IX, quoted in Newton, 119.

netians. In the century after 1550, when American trade and land became a real international factor, those European powers wishing to share in the opportunities of the New World urged, with increasing frequency, that the only valid title to land or control of the sea was effective occupation.

At the close of Charles V's wars with France, the French had adduced this thesis, but by the pressure of more important points closer home and closer to the hearts of Frenchmen it fell into abeyance. Those wars were ended in 1559 by the peace of Cateau-Cambrésis. There the Spanish plenipotentiaries urged a doctrine from which they did not depart in essential particulars in the Convention of Pardo nearly two hundred years later. To the papal bulls, the Treaty of Tordesillas, and other confirmatory supports of the Spanish position were added arguments which, as far as they went, conformed to the thesis of effective occupation; that is, it was contended that Spain had spent blood, labor, and treasure in surveying America and in taking it over for civilization. Although the French and English on more than one occasion demonstrated an abysmal ignorance of geography long in Spanish diaries and archives, so early as 1559 the French knew that not all the land of America was effectively occupied by the Spaniards as their allegation of the costly reduction of America seemed to indicate. Accordingly, France refused to exclude Frenchmen from any ports, rivers, and lands not so held. If Spain would have admitted such a principle, which she would not do, it was clear that the power with the most force would give its own interpretation. As much at loggerheads as the powers could have been with Spain sixty-five years earlier, no agreement on the problem was possible; and since peace was imperative and eagerly sought, the whole matter of title and monopoly in America was omitted from the treaty of Cateau-Cambrésis. Moreover, fifty-one years later in the Treaty of Vervins the same omission was made, because Henry IV and Sully would not accept a clause renouncing America.

The wall-like barrier between Spain's *mare clausum* and her enemies' theory of effective occupation gave rise to a famous unofficial corollary rule—the tenet that the nationals of European powers could fight to their hearts' content "beyond the line" [9] without disturbing amicable relations between their courts in the Old World. Nothing was more natural, therefore, than the agreement that after the treaty of Cateau-Cambrésis corsairs in the Indies would have to fend for themselves and

---

[9] A concrete meridian was understood—that passing through the Azores and the Tropic of Cancer.

that their execution as pirates would not disturb the friendly and peaceful relations of the two countries in Europe. Thus was set the unfortunate fashion that made the Caribbean the vortex of international pillage. The Spaniards preferred this underhanded and perpetual war to raising European intrusions in her domains to the elevation of international concerns if, in so doing, they could not secure sanction of her old absolute exclusionist policy. Irresponsibility was the result, for every pirate knew that he could not be held accountable at the international bar for violation of treaties if he were so fortunate as to escape the Spanish garrote. Any ship overtaken and captured was as legitimate a prize as if taken in European waters in time of war.

Until France came under the tutelage of Richelieu and, especially, Colbert, trade and oceanic affairs were far more resounding in English and Dutch than in French ears. Every effort made by the English and the Dutch, whom the Spaniards addressed by the sobriquet of "rebels," to induce Spain formally to sanction their right to navigate and colonize in the Americas fell through. Imagine how far they were from success when Philip II in Spain's heyday, ten years after the Armada, forbade the Dutch subjects of his daughter, Isabella, and Archduke Albert to trade with the Indies on pain of confiscation of the ships and execution of the crew. Reverses and the appearance of formidable rivals, instead of lessening, only accentuated Spain's stubborn and dogmatic adherence to the idea on which she had held America for a century. In 1584 Philip II had made a desperate effort to coerce the rebellious Dutch by a strict prohibition of all trade with them and the confiscation of all Dutch vessels in Spain. It was the retaliatory decree of the States General against commerce with enemies that began to bring Dutch and Flemish vessels to America in large numbers by 1586—a migration which, to the surprise of Europe, lifted Zeeland and Holland to an ascendancy in the West Indies from which they later toppled almost as quickly as they had ascended. Dutch success meant that the Dutch took the place of the French in insisting upon freedom of trade in the New World and their inclusion in any treatise to that effect. Their overtures to France and England to join them in coercing Spain into this long-sought concession came to a sad and disappointing climax when the "scholarly . . . driveling" James I failed on the eve of the Treaty of London to urge free trade.

In order to avoid "all inconveniences that peradventure happen in places so remote, where the subjects of other princes shall fall in company with another where their laws and discipline cannot be so well executed," James I informed his envoys negotiating for the Treaty of London (1604) that he was willing to prohibit his subjects from repairing to places in which the Spanish and Portuguese were planted. On the other hand, he mentioned that his subjects should be permitted to repair to "seek their traffic" and to make discoveries, "whereof there are infinite dimensions of vast and great territories," where the Iberian states had no interest. In such a manner even this pro-Spanish Stuart king stood on the ground that the test of ownership was effective occupation, and that land not effectively occupied was his who took it. Despite the abortive efforts of Sir Walter Raleigh, James I and his envoys mentioned not colonization but trade; that point, too, was as readily denied by the Spaniards, who sought officially to establish that the English were excluded expressly or by unmistakable implication and that all Englishmen would trade in the Indies at their own peril. The English could not accept this exclusion as the French had done secretly and unofficially, but better relations at home were paramount to those in America and the objective prevailed. America—and it was more than a fashion now—by virtue of its very importance and difficulty was left unmentioned and unsolved. By sheer iteration, however, Spain's rivals were steadily building up a position, that of effective occupation, and just as assuredly as if they roamed the Caribbean by international agreement, the anarchy left in the wake of these nomads of the sea was beating down the tenet of Spanish exclusiveness.

When the French signed the Treaty of Vervins in 1608, only the Dutch were openly at odds with Spain. Thus placed at a disadvantage in warring alone against Spain and upholding the economic views of all of Spain's enemies, the Dutch were forced to make peace overtures. To avoid making it a suit for peace from a vanquished people, the Dutch threatened to duplicate their famous East India Company in the West Indies when William Usselincx became the promoter for a Dutch West India Company. The menace was thereby cleverly parried and thrown back into Spain's face. Nothing so alarmed the Spaniard as the prospect of organized and successful intrusions in the West Indies —the "apple of his eye" Hakluyt called them. Philip III, who proved so supine and inert when the London Company of Virginia was driving a wedge into Axacan, now gave his consent to negotiations in which actual possession was an admitted possibility. Apparently a decoy to facilitate the much needed peace, this unprecedented concession was more than counterbalanced by the demand that the Dutch should retire not only from the West but the East Indies. The Spanish envoys even refused a treaty such as that accorded France and England in which the baffling problem of America was left in unmentioned confusion. As if they were unchallenged throughout the whole world, the Spaniards desired an unmistakable renunciatory clause. With the fundamental tenets of the two negotiators poles apart after long months of diplomatic dickering, the English and French did mediate to secure a twelve-year truce after 1609. By many scholastic circumlocutions the Spanish recognized the presence and success, if not the rights, of the Dutch in the East. But on the suggestion that the Dutch should enter any parts of America in effective Spanish occupation—even to trade— the Spaniards were adamant. Thus by implication Spain had admitted, in saying that the Dutch could not enter her effectively occupied lands, that intruders could not be stopped from entering the unoccupied or ineffectively held territories. The principle of effective occupation now became an accepted axiom of international law—by those who stood to profit by its operation.[10] In a way, this rule of international law was made virtually as effective as any item of international law through its open and complete acceptance by all the maritime nations except Spain. Many islands and vast reaches of unexploited territory in the Americas, it was not perceived, lay open to colonization, which was beginning to become a partner as well as a concomitant of trade. England and France proceeded to establish American colonies almost from the very year of these agreements with Spain and without strong or successful opposition from Spain.[11]

As an example of the inability or disinclination of the Spaniards to incorporate an unpleasant fact into their intellectual fabrications, Virginia, which the English entered just as the new doctrine held the center of the stage, proved as unwelcome in principle as Jean Ribaut's bold intrusion on the Matanzas.[12] Every one knew that Virginia was claimed, not actually held, by Spain on the arrival of the Jamestown settlers. If Spain had really accepted the doctrine sometimes attributed to her, no

---

[10] As will be seen in the next chapter the Spaniards regarded it as an accepted principle as applied to any territory except such as she had formally conceded by treaty. As a basis for the occupation of territory not held by any power at the time of the last formal treaty concession, the Spaniards never embraced it.

[11] Newton, 128.

[12] Irene A. Wright, "Spanish policy toward Virginia, 1606-1612; Jamestown, Ecija, and John Clark of the Mayflower," in *The American Historical Review,* XXV (1919-1920), 448-479; Alexander Brown, *Genesis of the United States* (2 vols., Boston and New York, 1890), I, 42 ff.; John Tate Lanning, "A descriptive catalogue of some *legajos* on Georgia in Spanish archives," in *The Georgia Historical Quarterly,* XIII (1929), 410-421.

Spanish opposition would have resulted. Perhaps the Spanish government thought Virginia could be effectively held. In the uncertainty of
American geography, the Spanish ambassador, Pedro de Zúñiga, lamented that the king of England, in the supine explanation he made to
the Spanish, did not say how far the settlement was to be from His
Catholic Majesty's ships—the Bahama Channel, a strong item in Spanish imperial strategy since the days when Pedro Menéndez de Avilés
decided the only defence for the empire was control of the ocean channels. Success in Virginia would worry the Spanish trade and contaminate the faith in America. It was sufficient justification to exclude foreigners, urged Zúñiga, that this land was discovered for the crown of
Castile and lay within its demarcation.[13] It was tantamount to official
sanction of Zúñiga's views when the Council for War in the Indies repeatedly instructed the Spanish ambassador, who clearly saw what Virginia meant, to approach the king of England with the complaint that
he should not allow his vassals to disturb the seas, coasts, and lands of
his Catholic Majesty. To do so would encourage the "rebels" (Dutch)
or other nations to take advantage of the movement.[14] Moreover, the
Council of State advised the king that Virginia should be extirpated by
force—not salved with diplomacy—and all the culprits punished. This,
they told the Catholic Majesty, could be done "without disturbing the
peace." [15] That contention was an implicit denial of the principle that
European rivals could occupy unexploited American territories, but confirmed the old "no peace beyond the line." The Council of War in the
Indies advised raising a force large enough to turn the Virginians out,
or if attacked, to prevent defeat, but at the same time not so formidable
as to impel England to break the peace! The king of England once
explained to Spain that settlers were sent out to America "to get them
drowned in the sea," so now the Spaniards felt that if the Virginians
were only "finished off" smoothly enough, they would go unrevenged
and have only themselves to blame for ever taking up their abode in
Mosquito Land. Spanish officials spoke of "finishing off the survivors"
during "the starving time" in Virginia in even a more alarmed tone than
they used to refer to the extermination of buccaneers in Española. Only
one member of the Council for War in the Indies, like Philip III, thought
lightly of the Virginia settlement.

[13] Pedro de Zúñiga to the king, in Brown, I, 88-90.
[14] Junta de Guerra de Indias, 14 March, 1660, in Brown, I, 167; *A. G. I.*, Indiferente General, Junta de Guerra de Indias, 26 January, 1607, 8 July, 1608.
[15] Archivo General de Simancas, *legajo* 844, fols. 10-11.

It is commonly thought that the lethargy of Philip III, and his inactivity when his advisers counseled vigorous tactics against the Jamestown settlement, was born of a conviction that the Englishmen would starve themselves out if given time, but his seeming torpor could easily have sprung from the conviction that the English could not be kept out. Indeed, he so confided to his son. Spain never produced a more farseeing, able, and altogether convinced imperialist than Menéndez de Avilés, but "cleaning the seas" of foreigners had been too much for him.

Even in Philip III's day, a score of years after the defeat of the Armada, Spain had a fleet that could not be challenged by England with certainty of success. But even when overwhelming on the seas, the Spanish king was always anxious about the safety of his treasure galleons and the profits of the Indies trade. To guarantee that all-important contingency, the king of Spain was forced always to maintain a more powerful fleet than his enemies could muster at any one specific time, and the House of Trade seldom allowed a fleet to sail with a convoy that did not seem invincible. Those who have delved deep into the economic records in the Archives of the Indies come away with the conviction that the Spaniards had a right to expect their fleets to ward off attack and that any enemies who broke through to a treasure galleon, after all the elaborate precautions taken by the Spaniards, had well earned what they might seize.

But it was not alone in Virginia that the new theorem was subjected to a test. A group of islands swing in a crescent from the easternmost extremity of the Greater Antilles to Trinidad like pillars to bar the mouth of the Caribbean to European egress. Once having sailed past them with the winds, it was nearly impossible to sail (from the very heart of the Spanish power in America) back to them again. These islands, the Lesser Antilles, were unattractive to the Spaniard when such islands as Cuba, Española, and Jamaica lay ready for conquest. They did not even yield small returns in gold. Even in Española the mines and creek beds were early pitched upon and exhausted.. The smaller islands were either inhabited by Caribs, whose unconquerable determination made their capture too expensive, or by docile Indians whose seizure decimated and sometimes exterminated the population. Wooded and loaded with an invincible coppice, they were equally ill-adapted to stockraising which in importance always ranked near the top in the age of the conquerors. This natural neglect in the sixteenth century proved such an attraction and refuge to the northern powers that what ensued can only be described as "swarming." Thus the

Spaniards themselves, by leaving the Lesser Antilles like bait to hungry fish, laid the foundations for the greatest menace to their own territorial monopoly.

While the Dutch constituted the greater early trade threat, the English held the chief distinction as absorbers of land. After Sir Walter Raleigh had demonstrated the English interest some ten years earlier, Captain Charles in 1604 attempted the first English colony of forty-six members on the Wiapoco in Guiana to cut into the profitable trade the Dutch were conducting with the Indians and to find the inevitable gold mines. Dissensions and destitution and Frenchmen from Cayenne, however, so completely did their work that only four survivors, after a sojourn in St. Lucia, ever saw England again. Profiting by that lesson, Robert Harcourt sponsored the next English colony there under the auspices of the Dutch merchants, who understood and succeeded in that country. His expedition sailed in 1609 with the aim of planting tobacco. Despite the fact that the colony had completely run out by 1613, Harcourt attempted the organization of a Guiana joint-stock company for the continuance of his project. A French attempt in 1613 and a Dutch one in 1614 had gone the same way, but the Dutch under Captain Amos van Groenewegen with mixed Englishmen and Zeelanders did manage to hold out permanently on the Essequibo. If the alarmist Spanish reports are to be credited, tobacco was being grown both in Guiana and Trinidad. In confirmation of the Spanish alarums, the Dutch produced much tobacco in those parts. Moreover, upon the rapid rise of the Virginia tobacco industry after 1612, the English surrendered the Caribbean tobacco trade more and more to the Dutch.

In pursuance of the mercantilist view, Virginia tobacco was given an exclusive position in the English system. Consequently, certain entrepreneurs like Sir Walter Raleigh and Roger North, who went out with Raleigh in the expedition of 1617-1618, hoped to put their English colonial tobacco on the preferential list with that of Virginia. North's Amazon Company patent, however, was revoked in 1620 when he was already on his way out to the Indies. The fluctuations of policy between the pro-Spanish party and the nationalists made such business extremely risky, and with the growing ascendency of the Spanish ambassador, Count Diego Acuña Gondomar, quite impossible. Unfortunately, as Gondomar's success in London diminished the support at home, the Spaniards applied the pressure on the field in Guiana by ordering the Brazilian authorities to use force in the expulsion of the intruders in Guiana. With the death of Philip III in 1621 his policies of watchful waiting died with him; those of Philip II were revived and the Spaniards set out once again to be the exclusive mistress of the ocean sea. The Dutch alone thought to stand without truce and to fight without quarter. The doubtful project of a West India Company, which William Usselincx had advocated, was given its chance by this turn of events. Despite the national resentment aroused against the Spaniards, investments, which depend more upon the prospect of profit than upon national antipathies, were closed in 1623 with an investment of 7,000,000 florins, one million of which had been subscribed by the government.

The rise of the West India Company came at an inauspicious moment for Brazil, for Portugal was a part of Spain from 1580-1640, and everything Portuguese was afflicted by the enemies of Spain in the interval. The twenty-seven ships bearing sixteen hundred sailors and seventeen hundred regular soldiers under Admiral Jacob Willekens and Vice-Admiral Pieter Pieterzoon Hein which appeared at the Bahia de Todos los Santos were rewarded with the capitulation of that city in May 1624. It was not the booty alone which threw consternation into the breasts of Spaniard and Portuguese, but the possibility of a Dutch empire in the heart of their monopolistic area. A supreme effort was the response when Fadrique de Toledo appeared in 1625 to retake the city in April of that year, but like many another ambitious Spanish maritime venture, the elements appeared unfriendly to it and Don Fadrique's expedition was relentlessly battered and tossed before the arrival of the remnant at the close of 1625. The menace of a Dutch or French empire in Brazil was always a powerful and concrete menace to the Hispanic empires, but in this expedition the most significant item for Hispanic America was the education which it gave Piet Hein.[16]

But more than a Dutch attack and a Spanish counterattack witnessed the turn of this quarter of a century in America, for it saw the collapse of Spanish monopoly in the Antilles. Before Don Fadrique arrived in Spain, Captain John Jefferson had brought his *Hopewell,* with her holds full of tobacco, safely into London from St. Christopher Island, where Warner's men had begun planting in 1624. On September 13 of the next year Warner and his patron secured from Charles I the crown patent (with promise of protection) to settle and plant not only in St. Christopher, but in Barbados, Montserrat, and Nevis. Richelieu was a month and a half late when on October 31, he signed a similar grant to

---

16 S. P. l'Honoré Naber, and Irene A. Wright, *Piet Hein en de zilverlost bescheiden uit Nederlandsche en Spaansche archieven bijeenverzameld en uitgegeven door* (Utrecht, 1928).

d'Esnambuc and de Roissey for the establishment of Frenchmen in Barbados. It was on February 18 that the Earl of Pembroke granted to Sir William Courteen a patent to colonize in Barbados, Tobago, Trinidad, and nonexistent St. Bernard. It matters little for our purpose that Courteen began one of those classic English Caribbean disputes with Warner and his patron, Carlisle (backed by the Warwick group), about the jurisdiction in, and rights to, St. Christopher. Not even the Frenchmen under d'Esnambuc who began planting on the other end of the island could dislodge Warner's planters.

The convenient year 1625 was literally a great landmark in the settlement and international relations of America. The great Cardinal Richelieu, notwithstanding his preoccupations with making the Bourbons supreme in France and France supreme on the continent, was giving French enterprise that certainty of a sound base which Charles I and Buckingham were, after James I, supplying in England. The freedom to plunder proved a boon to the subjects of both countries. The governmental grants and sanctions which marked the turn of the century were far from mere gestures. In 1625 a Courteen ship commanded by John Powell put in at Barbados, took possession in the name of King James I, and upon returning to England the captain faithfully reported his discovery to Sir William Courteen. From that day until the conquest of Jamaica, Barbados held the center of the English Antilles. In 1627, therefore, Henry Powell, the brother of the discoverer, landed with eighty colonists. So rapid and characteristic was the rise of the population of Barbados that there was never any doubt about its permanency—two years sufficed to give it a population of eighteen hundred English souls.

Fully appreciating what was going on, the Spaniards looked impotently on. The seething in the pot of international politics rendered the situation uncontrollable even to the ambitious Philip IV of Spain and his adviser Conde de Olivares. Fully expecting to reduce all enemies except the implacable "rebels," the Dutch, to inaction by shrewd and conciliatory diplomacy, they only timed their efforts with a literal tidal wave from the north of Europe which ended only when, fifteen years later, the islands had taken on virtually the population which they maintained for a century and a half. The great colonizing ardor of the English and French coincided with the supreme maritime effort of the Dutch against Spain which proved so benumbing. The Dutch, who executed such a powerful rearguard action for these swarms of English and French settlers in the Caribbean, and who alone made the migration possible, won the least advantage from their efforts. The English and French colonies still thrust themselves under our eyes to crowd out the memory of the paramount rôle of the Dutch. This decade and a half not only served to nonplus the Spaniard, but it changed the Caribbean situation completely and permanently. Henceforth, in the *mare clausum* there was only a dogmatic scholastic sophistry.

Basic political motives in France and England made possible this epoch-making movement of European peoples. To Charles I's flippant war with Spain must be added the vigor and suppleness of Richelieu. The great decade of settlement, however, was cut across by a demonstration of the suppleness on the part of both of these men. Charles I effected a *volte-face* more characteristic of his son when the futility of the war with Spain became discernible and the pressure of the still surviving Spanish party again began to be felt. The upshot of both was that in January 1631, by the secret Treaty of Madrid, Charles I not only withdrew from the war with Spain but entered into an alliance with the Spaniards against the Dutch. With Richelieu temporarily engrossed in European affairs, both the French and the English settlers, therefore, were left for a few years to shift for themselves. When by 1636 the servility of the pro-Spanish party had brought no results, its members were so discredited that the adherents of the vigorous Elizabethan tradition gained the ascendancy and fell under the guidance of that alert trader, adventurer, and imperialist, the Earl of Warwick,[17] and the Earl of Holland, who hatched the schemes and gained the adherence of John Pym in enforcing them. One year before the triumph of the Warwick party in England, the Cardinal was again free to turn his attention to America. Two significant American projects resulted from this revival of governmental interest—the French organized the *Compagnie des Isles d'Amérique,* whose subsidiaries promoted the settlement of the two most important islands of the French Caribbean, Martinique and Guadeloupe. In 1635 settlers arrived in both. As for the other project, while it never unfolded as the Warwick faction planned, it was the "design" to create an English West India Company, inevitably copied from the Dutch. It was projected to serve a political as well as an economic purpose by supplying the cohesive element in all the English colonies with Providence as the advance guard and focus. Although the project was difficult, and as it proved, impossible, there

---

[17] W. Frank Craven, "The Earl of Warwick, a speculator in piracy," in *The Hispanic American Historical Review,* X (1930), 457-479.

were many enterprises of the Warwick faction in the six years before 1643 which cannot be explained otherwise. This ambitious scheme, moreover, apparently turned out to be the mother of the grandiloquent scheme, hatched between Oliver Cromwell and the ex-Jesuit Thomas Gage, which is ordinarily described as the "Western Design."

The Dutch, who had not depended so much on the slow money-making process of colonization and had naturally been making a good thing as the only unencumbered business men in the West Indies, came in for sharp reversals just as the English and French population reached its high peak. The Dutch slave traders inundated the area as indicated by the fact that the slave population of Barbados in the five years after 1645 increased from six to twenty thousand, leaving Barbados with the malodorous reputation of a penal colony among prospective white settlers and the suffering, displaced laborers already there.

Upon the begining of the Portuguese war of independence in 1640 (1640-1668) King Philip IV forbade all commercial relations with the Portuguese, destroyed the *asientos de negros,* and gave the whole slave business the stamp of illegality in all the Spanish dominions. The Dutch response was summary, for when at immense sacrifice of money, materials, and labor the Spaniards prepared to convoy 10,000 men in seventy ships to the rescue in Flanders, the Dutch Admiral Tromp ignored the asylum which the Spaniards sought in English waters, pursued them with impunity up the Thames and exacted his sweeping vengeance under the surprised eyes of the peaceful inhabitants of Deal. In the equally decisive battle of Itamaraca, the Brazilian fleet was eliminated in January 1640. The coincident attacks against Spain, and aggrandizements at her expense, rendered the empire vulnerable. To the victors now belonged the opportunity, which they soon seized, to fight among themselves for the fruits of an embarrassed empire.

But what territories did the European rivals hold in America at the beginning of the series of treaties in which Spain acknowledged the principle of effective occupation with reference to the lands won and held up to that time? At that juncture the perimeter of the Caribbean and the Greater Antilles, Cuba, Puerto Rico, Jamaica, and Trinidad, remained effectively in the hands of the Spaniards. The Lesser Antilles, with the exception of the Windward group in which the Caribs beat off even the European newcomers, were now held by a trio of Spain's European rivals. Besides Virginia, the English held Barbados, Antigua, Montserrat, Nevis, and a part of St. Christopher. Although they had surrendered the famous Providence along with 600 negroes and 500,000 ducats (after they had captured Truxillo and held it for a ransom of 16,000 pieces of eight in bullion and indigo), as a sample of the medicine the English doctors had been prescribing, they had nevertheless raided inland and done much trading along the Bluefields River and established many logwood-cutting settlements around Cape Gracias á Dios. Besides, certain Virginians and New Englanders had begun a plantation on Ruatan.[18] The French held Tortuga, a part of St. Christopher, Martinique, Guadeloupe, Marie Galante, Désirade, St. Lucia, and Grenada. The Dutch, not so land-minded, then conducted trading centers in Buen Aire, Curaçao, Orba, and held St. Eustatius and St. Martins.[19] The Dutch had failed in Brazil but on the Surinam and the Essequibo maintained a hold on Guiana (where the English and French had given up)—a hold from which they raided the Spanish missions where the padres had pushed in from the western shores.[20]

Despite the favorable decision of arms around 1640 the Dutch business men in the East and West India companies sought to maintain the state of war in which they had built up their system of profits to the detriment of the average Dutch citizen. Thus isolated in their motives, the companies lost so much influence that by 1648 they could not prevent peace overtures and negotiations, nor could they argue the Spaniards into freedom of trade in Spanish America—the only legal equivalent for what the Dutch had enjoyed. It was the old story. After two years of negotiations at Münster and Westphalia, the Peace of Münster omitted the items which the West India Company had sought and remained as noncommittal and ambiguous on American trade questions as

---

[18] See John Alder Burdon, *Archives of British Honduras* . . . (London, 1931).

[19] In the decade before the Peace of Westphalia in 1648, the year in which Spain first legalized any of these intrusions, the non-Spanish population in the Caribbean area was sometimes estimated as high as 100,000. As strange as it seems in a New World of vast unoccupied lands, the islands were overpopulated despite the high mortality figures. Barbados, the vortex of English settlement in the West Indies, numbered 36,500 souls in 1645 but, so eloquent of suffering and adversity are the figures, declined to 23,000 in a decade thereafter. Two hundred and seventeen persons are too many to eke a living out of each square mile of soil, and how much more was that true in an island covered with untillable mountains and world-famous for its planting estates and land monopoly! St. Christopher and Nevis also felt the exhausting impact of overpopulation. The opportunities remaining in Antigua and Montserrat did not atone for the lack of them elsewhere. With a possible population of seven thousand, the congestion was not so acute in the French islands. A population of something over a thousand sufficed to conduct the smuggling business of Curaçao.

[20] J. Fred Rippy and John T. Nelson, *Crusaders of the jungle* (Chapel Hill, 1935), *passim*.

had the truce of 1609 or the treaties signed in the same epoch with France and England. The Spanish position on trade, despite the lessons which had been taught since the wars with Francis I, remained as irrevocable as it was a hundred years before. The Treaty of Münster adopted the principle of effective occupation and permitted the signatory powers to retain the lands of which they were in actual possession, and all powers were guaranteed access to their subjects so located. Curaçao and St. Eustatius were now officially Dutch even in the Spaniards' eyes. Although the free access clause officially ended the privateering of the West India Company, the prohibition of trade between the Spanish and the Dutch left the old contraband in the hands of individual Dutch smugglers or merchants.

After the Peace of Westphalia, wherein Spain made her first formal concession of territory, the Dutch were still such successful traders that England and France joined hands to evict the Dutch from the island trade. While England and France were competing with the Dutch for the profitable illicit trade to the Greater Antilles and the shores of the Caribbean, there was developing between them what was to be the great imperial rivalry of the eighteenth century. The transition, becoming clearly visible after 1648, was the keynote after 1689. This transition in imperial rivalries underwent at least one major reversion to the Elizabethan tradition.

In April 1654, the Treaty of Westminster, which dampened the hope and dashed the prosperity of the West India Company, gave Cromwell opportunity and pause for other worlds to conquer. A policy of national aggrandisement did not, therefore, seem extraordinary to him. Imperial aggrandisement which went beyond the pale of trade was sure to be at the expense of France or Spain—most likely Spain. Cromwell had clearly open to him the possibility of an alliance with Spain, a problem dating from Henry VII, a tradition since James I, and even the policy in the later Elizabethan period. His object was the official recognition of the English colonies and a share in the Spanish colonial trade. Could both these objects be obtained by either war or alliance? Certainly the seizure of Cuba or some other important colony might be added to the two desired items if war were to be the method.

The Western Design which confronted Cromwell after 1649 was in part a continuation of a previous scheme which had been supported by the Earl of Warwick. When the majority of his council recommended this course of aggression, Cromwell turned to its execution with his customary vigor. It does not seem to have occurred to Cromwell that an attack in force on Spain in America would end friendly relations in Europe, but the old disorderliness in the West Indies had been giving away to law long before it was dealt a blow by the international agreement of the Treaty of Münster. Cromwell thought to have his expedition slip out to America leaving the world none the wiser, not only as a bit of good strategy, but in order that it might fight beyond the line as in the Elizabethan days. When the wives of two sailors approached him during a walk to know whither their husbands had gone, he responded, "Aye, both Spain and France would give a million each to know that." With Cuba invincible before a fever-ridden expedition, the palliative which Penn and Venables sought in Jamaica was nevertheless accepted by the Protector as another means of "smiting Spain and her dark Domdaniel to the heart." England had taken up in the Greater Antilles to stay.

The seven years after the restoration of the Stuarts saw many agonizing efforts of import to the New World enacted, rescinded, and reenacted. While the old Spanish-Dutch struggle was gasping its last in this seven-year interlude, the other powers were moving into position to take the field of the colonial carrying trade and imperial dominion. It was natural that the English should replace the Dutch when the wisdom and feasibility of pushing them aside became apparent; but almost simultaneously Louis XIV realized that his costly wars against Holland had only given Dutch business to England and promoted that antagonist. From the Peace of Breda in 1667 to the accession of William and Mary in 1689 the world waited for the new alignments to join battle. Henceforth, with a Dutchman on the throne of England, the ordinary requirement of the American scene—that France was to be the enemy—lifted much weight from the shoulders of Spain.

Almost immediately after the Restoration, agitation was set afoot in England for the establishment of legal and mutually beneficial trade with the Spanish Indies—only another example of the advantage of hope over experience. It is a well-known fact that Charles II looked to America to fill depleted royalist coffers, but less known that, after the exit of Clarendon, he resolved to promote the same end by reverting to his grandfather's policy of friendly agreement with Spain. Predatory war and buccaneering had to go. Treaties had to be made. Even Charles II's nefarious secret negotiations with Louis XIV could be placed on the footing that in the new order the Grand Monarch might look with favor upon Charles II as he assumed the Spanish American trade, or caught the Spanish colonies as they fell like ripe fruit upon the death of Charles II of Spain. Partly for that reason France and England declared war on the United Provinces in 1672.

The English had long looked upon the slave trade with envy, especially since the revolt of Portugal from Spain in 1640 had disqualified the Portuguese *asientistas* and left the Spanish colonies (whose slave marts were now more important than those of the sugar colonies) without legal means of acquiring slaves for twenty-three years. A clamor was set up in England by the merchants to replace the Portuguese. These merchants also knew that Dutchmen had been given this privilege by Spanish colonial governors. Accordingly, Sir Henry Bennet proposed an *asiento de negros* whereby some thousands of negroes would be brought to the Spanish colonies in English ships and Spain would pay a certain sum for each one. The Spaniards apparently knew more about the realities of business in the Caribbean than the English, for they pointed out that the English cared more for the profits of illicit trade than for the smaller licensed gains, and, indeed, when the South Sea Company attempted to carry out the *asiento* contract after the Peace of Utrecht by introducing 4,800 slaves yearly, they found that the surreptitous profits of smugglers were more profitable and begged to be excused from introducing the negroes in accordance with the contract! It is no wonder that the Council of the Indies saw in the proposal a villainous scheme (which the English perhaps did not contemplate) to break the Spanish trade monopoly by promoting a relaxation of Spanish trade in which the French and Dutch would also demand special privileges. But the Genoese merchants, Grillo and Lomelin, introduced by the Dominican Order, were given the exclusive *asiento* after 1663— much to the chagrin of the English who sought it. The new *asientistas* agreed to bring 24,000 *piezas de India*[21] obtained anywhere except from the friends of Spain. The revival of the Portuguese *asiento* at the end of the Portuguese rebellion forced the Dutch and the English still deeper into their slave smuggling. Becoming weary with the chaos and competition, the English made an English *asiento* a steady feature of their foreign policy until they were rewarded with success at the time of the Treaty of Utrecht (1713). It was the irony of an age of bitterness that the very smugglers on whom the English had depended made the contract for legal business unprofitable, and, with the Spanish *guarda*

---

[21] That is, 24,000 units; it might take several young or inferior slaves to make a *pieza de India*.

costa replacing the English buccaneer, embittered Anglo-Spanish relations until 1748.

For more than twenty years before the accession of William and Mary the English had been projecting a scheme of American trade which required friendly relations with Spain. Sir Thomas Modyford, dreaming of making the strategically located Jamaica into an emporium of Caribbean trade like Curaçao, a warehouse for goods, and a training ground for slaves destined for the Spanish mainland, proposed an international agreement.

It was in 1664 that Charles II, urged by West Indian merchants and worsted by the envoys of Louis XIV, sought a *rapprochement* with Spain, but not alone for the sake of the Indies. At that time Richard Fanshawe was sent to present the trade plan and to request that the Royal African Company be given an *asiento* contract in return for which he was to promise an alliance to guarantee the integrity of Spanish America against the Dutch and French. Indeed, after 1665 slaves came to the English not in Dutch but in English bottoms. Even if the suggestion had been consonant with Spanish policy, the fact that England refused to desert rebellious Portugal or return Jamaica kept Philip IV from considering the overture.

Even the English government acknowledged when these negotiations were undertaken that there were between 1,500 and 2,000 sea dogs plying Spanish commerce who were not only in possession of numerous fly-boats but some fifteen well-armed and equipped ships. Many of these rovers were French and Dutch, but, since they used Port Royal as a center, the Spanish naturally laid the blame on the English. When Sir Thomas Modyford, in order to convince the Spanish of the sincerity of the English, clamped down on the buccaneers with stringent regulations, the buccaneers took up in Tortuga. The Spaniards in America, hailing the day of the new order with gusto, sent more than a score of ships to Port Royal for negroes instead of buying them from the Dutch slavers. The new-sprung trade was ruined, and seemingly the honesty of the English impeached, when the buccaneers waylaid and captured these vessels on their return voyage. Even Modyford bowed to the inevitable, and the ideal of international comity on the Spanish Main collapsed again. In 1666 he received Mansfield, the pirate, as guilelessly as if he had been an admiral of the fleet. So, just as the English began to think in terms of order, the Spaniards were forced to go over to the idea of pillage and so aggravated the situation with their depredations that the anti-Spanish opposition policy gained weight while the plan of legal business vied with the old method in Parliamentary debates between 1663 and 1678.[22]

Instead of Jamaica humming with the fruitful processes of legal business, Port Royal became, contrary to the basic judgment and wishes of Modyford, an entrepôt of sea robbers. The best Modyford could do was to use them as a kind of Elizabethan free-lance fleet in the absence of regular naval ships and regiments of trained soldiers which had been established in Cromwell's time. International law had thus fallen narrowly short of becoming a reality. Basically guerilla war—with the approval of the government—reigned in the West Indies while peace prevailed in Europe.

The movement so vigorously and hopefully inaugurated by Charles II, Modyford, and Fanshawe produced indirect results, for the negotiations dragged on until 1667 when Lord Sanwich signed a treaty in 1667. Sir Thomas Modyford, in July 1667, in a disheartened moment made it clear that *mare clausum* was still the official Spanish ideal.

> "The Spaniards look on us as intruders wheresoever they find us in the Indies, and use us accordingly; and were it in their power, as it is fixed in their wills, would soon turn us out of all our plantations; and is it reasonable that we should quietly let them grow upon us until they are able to do it? It must be force alone that can cut in sunder that unneighborly maxim of their government to deny all access to strangers." [23]

The writer of this penetrating communication actually had word the year after the signing of the treaty that the Spaniards planned an expedition in force to retake Jamaica as they had retaken Providence. Such rumors did nothing of course to lessen the activities of the innumerable buccaneers who were again being harbored in Jamaica. The Treaty of 1667 had required England to enter no alliance with the enemies of Spain. In return Spain agreed to receive goods from the English colonies and factories and, apparently, for the first time conceded England the right to hold and colonize lands in America.[24]

Modyford seems to have undergone a change of heart since his early optimism, for he calmly ignored the treaty; and war beyond the line

---

[22] *Cf.* C. H. Haring, *The buccaneers in the West Indies in the XVII century.* . . . (New York, 1910).

[23] Sir Thomas Modyford to Secretary Arlington, in Newton, 261.

[24] Sir William Godolphin in negotiating the American Treaty three years later had orders to excuse the English government's recent connivance with buccaneers by the contention that the Treaty of 1667 did not refer to America—certainly that treaty was unsatisfactory.

went on. The Spanish Queen Regent's threat of war beyond the
Tropic of Cancer, if the depredations did not cease, indicates that the
European states were finally getting tired of anarchy in America and
were at last prepared to extend what international comity they enjoyed
to America. It was the uncertainty of the decade on these basic matters
which rendered the old type Treaty of 1667 inadequate and led to negotiations culminating in the most important treaty dealing with America
so far written. In 1669 England joined Sweden and the Netherlands
in the Treaty of The Hague in guaranteeing the integrity of the Spanish
dominions as the French had already done in the Treaty of Aix-la-
Chapelle. At last the field was reasonably clear for agreement on basic
points which had been left without solution for 188 years.

The culmination of the orderly processes in America, from the
Treaty of Münster to that of Nymwegen, was nothing more than the
simple extension of accepted principles of international law to America.
In the process the first Anglo-Spanish agreement of basic importance on
America was reached in 1670. Sir William Godolphin, the envoy
selected for this important mission, began negotiations late in 1669 to
pull together the loose threads which had been dangling for many
decades. Of paramount importance was that perennial British objective—"good intelligence for the future and a friendly reception of
English ships into the ports of Spanish America." A treaty providing
that boon must of course carry "amnesty for the past."

Both powers had come together again with each party in a peculiar
position. Godolphin did not lay down the condition of free trade
against which the Spaniards could be expected to stand inexorable, for
he did not wish his negotiations to break down, and free trade was less
important now that the English merchants had perfected a system of
consigning their goods through the merchants of Spain. Godolphin
was also prepared to dodge the only sharp claim against England—the
depredations of Jamaican buccaneers since 1667—on the ground that
the treaty of that year did not embrace America. That America, therefore, stood in sore need of treaty guarantees was all the more reason
why the pending negotiations should not be frustrated. It was not
clever diplomacy, for the Spanish statesmen saw that the proposed
treaty was potentially dangerous to the monopolistic system whose
adherents had thwarted all such previous attempts. It was Spain's loss
of advantage and her bankruptcy which brought her to terms. Accordingly, in July 1670, Sir William Godolphin had the pleasure of seeing
the conditions which the Spaniards regarded as hard accepted by the

plenipotentiaries of the Queen Regent. The American Treaty, as this document is called, was the only title Spain ever gave England to America, if we exclude the Treaty of 1667, and even in English eyes was regarded as a significant title deed.

In the preliminary articles England and Spain made agreements which would have done much for peace if private and national psychologies could be shifted as fast as national policy. They agreed to "forbear and abstain from all pillage, depredations, hurt and injury and any sort of molestation, as well by land as by sea or in fresh waters, in whatever part of the world." This negation of the old rule of "no peace beyond the line" forced the signatories to revoke all letters of marque or reprisal and to punish violators not only with the criminal penalty but with the indemnification of the injured subjects.[25]

It was perhaps Castilian pride which forced the Spaniards to insist on these provisions before actually writing England's title deed to America into the treaty, for the concession in the seventh article put an end to the ancient principle of *mare clausum*. That unyielding principle of undebatable and exclusive title now dead, there was no reason why international conduct in the West Indies should not be circumscribed and regulated by international agreement. Now on the brink of concord, the envoys even proposed to sweep the slate of memory clean in that famous seventh article.

> "VII. All offences, losses, damages and injuries which the English and Spanish nations have, for whatsoever cause or pretext, suffered from each other at any time past, in America, shall be buried in oblivion and completely effaced from memory, as if they had never occurred. Moreover it is agreed that the most serene King of Great Britain, his heirs and successors, shall have, hold and possess forever, with full right of sovereignty, ownership and possession, all the lands, regions, islands, colonies and dominions, situated in the West Indies or in any part of America, that the said King of Great Britain and his subjects hold and possess; so that neither on that account nor on any other may or should anything ever be further urged or any controversy begun in the future." [26]

Thus was the old contention of Spain that valid title rests upon discovery[27] formally thrown overboard for the argument developed by her

---

[25] The American Treaty, Articles II, III, and IV, and Hertslet, II, 196-199.

[26] Hertslet, II, 196-197.

[27] It cannot be said that Spain, or England for that matter, ever used the argument of prior discovery again.

assailants—the argument of concrete effective occupation. Thus Spain recognized England's title to Virginia and Carolina[28] on the mainland and to Barbados, Antigua, Jamaica, Montserrat, Nevis, and St. Christopher in the islands. It was not likely the intention of the Spaniard to concede title to the logwood-cutting settlements in Campeche and on Mosquito Coast, for they regarded that mainland area as in their effective control, and up to this point the nations preferred the control of trade in tropical goods to the actual acquisition of territory.

If the British authorities could excuse themselves after 1667 for the ruthless marauding of the Jamaican buccaneers on the ground that the treaty of that year did not embrace America, they could never logically present the same argument again. The American Treaty provided four months for the exchange of ratifications (completed by Spain, October 1670) but, due to the delays of transportation, extended the period to eight months for the proclamation of the agreement in the colonies. It is an ironic characteristic of the sad history of the Caribbean that the most barbarous piratical assault ever suffered by the Spanish colonists was delivered them from Jamaica during this interval of grace designed to demonstrate the good will of the signatory powers. So well-timed was it that it is nearly impossible not to attribute the raid to deliberate intention. It is known that Governor Modyford had tidings of the pending peace in August, but was impotent before Morgan or was a conniver in his base depredations. Indeed, it was Modyford who had conceived of Jamaica in the rôle of honest merchant to the Caribbean. It was in May 1671 that an emissary from the *Audiencia* of Santo Domingo arrived in Jamaica for the proclamation of the peace and the exchange of prisoners. An English convoy had gone to Cartagena in 1670 to exchange prisoners, but when the pirates and buccaneers of many nationalities refused to give up their lives of pillage and took up headquarters in Tortuga, it was irresistibly easy to attribute their every assault to the double-dealing governor of Jamaica. So reasoned the Spanish officials in Santo Domingo and Cartagena. Morgan's awful work was done, Panama lay desolate, and now the technicality of a time limit was used by the English to cover the worst crime in West Indian history.

To save their faces the English had to make a show of holding individuals responsible for this allegedly private crime since they did not

---

[28] The English later tried to rest their "effective occupation" at that time on the Carolina grants, one of which included St. Augustine! To the Spaniards Carolina only went to the Charlestown settlement.

wish to acknowledge it as an act of state. Yet the Jamaica Council on May 31, 1671 had tendered a formal vote of thanks to the commander of the expedition which had cost the Spaniards untold suffering and a loss, according to their estimates, of 6,000,000 crowns! The English dressed down the perpetrators of this high-handed business only in a perfunctory way. Sir Thomas Lynch, who was authorized to pardon any buccaneers who would begin the planter's life, was sent out as governor of Jamaica upon the revocation of Modyford's commission, but so lukewarm was the procedure that it took him from June to August to let Modyford know that he was to go back a prisoner of the state. Although sent to England in 1672 and to the Tower, Morgan was soon released, honored with knighthood, fêted in London, and even returned to Jamaica as lieutenant-governor, where, on the surface at least, he made a good record. If Morgan now had any connection with the buccaneers, as Lord Vaughan alleged, he encouraged them to use French papers and to keep their headquarters at Tortuga. Just as in the case of the American Treaty, those merchants who had learned to send their goods through Spain, and the planters of Jamaica who wanted another kind of prosperity than that improvident kind based on the intermittent gains of sporadic piracy, brought the pressure to bear which ended that official piracy known as buccaneering and, after Morgan, reduced sea robbers to "mere vulgar pirates." [29] From the first appointment of Lynch as governor of Jamaica, official England turned its back upon buccaneering and stopped the use of the British islands, particularly Jamaica, as bases of predatory operations against Spanish craft and the Spanish mainland. When Sir Thomas Lynch returned to Jamaica ten years after his first appointment to that post, he found the originally hostile Jamaicans in a different mood, and noted that instead of sullen hostility they, too, had come over to the government's point of view and responded to his efforts to thwart the outfitting of pirates. Jamaica was far from through as a center of smuggling to the Spanish mainland, but planting and other pursuits became more stabilized. In short, buccaneering had lost its glamour, its official favor, and, therefore, passed from sight.

Dickering was promptly set up or continued over items of trade and the right of navigation. Logwood had already lured the English onto the mainland, and so persistently did they pursue that valuable commodity that, next to sugar, it played the greatest commercial rôle in

---

[29] Newton, 275.

Caribbean history; politically, it was paramount. Sugar and tobacco could be grown on the French and British islands, negroes could be imported from Africa, but to get logwood the English had to make inroads into Española or the mainland in the vicinity of Campeche, regions generally admitted to be in the effective occupation of Spain. When, after 1670, piracy began to be seriously punished and became, therefore, unprofitable, the buccaneers joined the logwood cutters, making of the latter a hard-bitten, motley crew of business men and cutthroats. With the supply in Tortuga and Española almost exhausted before their arrival, these Jamaican logwood cutting adventurers betook themselves in increasing numbers to Campeche and Yucatan where they clustered around a place called Triste—an ominous symbol of the sinister fate that awaited them when a Spanish ship arrived or the Spanish infantry made a sally. On many creeks, and especially on the Belize River, from Guatemala to Honduras they were known. Spaniards protested against the wood stealing, but the governor of Jamaica knew the trade had supplanted buccaneering and would not restrain law-abiding cutters. The English ministers contended the region was not in effective Spanish occupation and that the men did not engage in piracy. After the American Treaty, Jamaica became the entrepôt not only of a lively trade in logwood, but other Brazil woods, and finally mahogany. The Spaniards now ironically turned the scales on two counts: they employed corsairs to extirpate the intruders, and the governor of Jamaica was forced to order them to go in fleets to avoid attack! Perhaps it was not this indignity to Spanish sovereignty that hurt so much as the fact that the English cutters also carved the price of legitimate Spanish logwood in twain.

But there was a legend in Europe almost as significant as these three commodities—the legend that the West Indian trade was a second El Dorado, one of the two or three great sources of wealth in the whole world. For this legend there was a basis in fact. European commerce at that time was narrowly circumscribed. Outside of the region which was once the Roman Empire, the world of trade was small in the seventeenth century. Africa was little beyond a source for slaves to increase American production, and then India and China bought few manufactured goods to pay for the many raw materials they offered. To pay the Orientals in bullion as was necessary, taxed stock, and, besides, ran sharply counter to the prevailing economic philosophy that the store of precious metals and the excess of exports over imports were infallible indices to the wealth of a nation. Hispanic America, on the other hand, furnished many raw materials badly needed in Europe and greedily gobbled up the finished goods with which the Europeans expected to pay, and made a hive of activity of the nation handling the business. For this reason, more than for their epochal success in the East, the Dutch were envied in the mid-century when they controlled the American trade and when, after the Restoration, the English found that to restore their old trade they must penetrate a Dutch monopoly. The Second and Third Dutch Wars were, much for this reason, fought with unusual bitterness.

It was a century after Spain began relaxing her all-inclusive rule of land monopoly before she bowed to the inevitable in trade. In 1670 Spanish restrictions were as severe as ever, but, as in the case of land, enforcement was being trod down with ever larger strides. The fleets sailing back from Vera Cruz and Puerto Bello could still protect themselves during their intermittent and inadequate trips and were seldom subjected to any depredations other than those of nature, but it has been said that more than six times the trade conducted through the legal portals of Sevilla and Cádiz was of a clandestine nature, especially before the Treaty of Münster when the Dutch could not live in Spain. Illicit trade had gained much of that complete control which it had from the Treaty of Utrecht to the Treaty of Aix-la-Chapelle. A memorial was submitted in 1680 to Colbert and Louis XIV, classic exponents of mercantilism, that the system was not working in Spain; that the complicated system of periodical sailings, fairs, and trade routes was a sham, ignored in American waters; and that Spanish merchants in Spain had been converted into mere agents for foreign ones.[30]

The fleet system, however, was well on its way to collapse for more reasons than swarms of interlopers. Although the sailings of the fleets were not as haphazard and infrequent as commonly thought, it is doubtful whether they could have supplied more than a small percentage (one-fifth) of the needed goods if they had not had the competition of the illicit trade after the middle of the seventeenth century. The French and English were not so free to exploit this situation, but the Hollanders whose primary interest was commerce, neglected planting. Occasionally, too, the French and British neglected the best interest of

---

[30] "All the merchandise that they send to the Indies, is loaded under the name of Spaniards who very often have no knowledge of it, in order to keep the business more secret. Only the supercargo knows about it, and he renders his account after his return from the Indies directly to the merchant who has entrusted the cargo to him in confidence without paying any attention to those in whose names the ladings were made." Quoted in Newton, 279.

the West Indian trade as well as the colonies for the sake of a broader contemporary adjustment in Europe or Asia.

Especially laggard were the European states in giving America the blessings of the same international comity accepted in Europe—war in America was encouraged, and sometimes enforced, during peace in Europe. The obliteration of "no peace beyond the line" was destined to die with the final acceptance of the theory of effective occupation. In 1673, three years after the American Treaty, the first treaty guaranteeing peace in America as well as in Europe was signed at The Hague. The English followed the Dutch in the Anglo-Spanish Treaty of Windsor, 1680, whereby both parties agreed to suppress depredations and to treat American troubles just as if they occurred in Europe. Such did not fit the suddenly imperialistic schemes of Louis XIV, which supported many designs in America and against the Spaniards beyond La Salle's celebrated explorations on the Mississippi. Beginning with the two Treaties of Nymwegen, August 1678, the French incorporated the idea of effective occupation by guaranteeing to the signatory powers what they then possessed in America, but in the second treaty freedom of navigation and commerce was accepted with relation to Europe alone. France was expectant of the most favored nation position. Moreover, the French refused to abandon the old device of leaving the Indies unmentioned when hostilities were banned. Louis and Colbert, however, tacitly recognized the decadence of the Elizabethan conduct when they took express pains to herald the fact that the Indies were not included in the peace pact. They even dispatched a naval expedition in 1678 to make a most flagrant reconnaissance—to report the sailings, routes, and calls of the fleets, size of the Spanish garrisons, and the French force necessary to reduce them.[31] The expedition under D'Estrées was repeated in 1679-1680. Indeed, it was French coöperation with privateering and buccaneering raids that forced Spain to concede special advantages to the exclusion of the English and Dutch.

Wherever possible the French prodded the Spaniards. An outrage against Spain in Vera Cruz was the culmination of a series of humiliations. Spain accepted war in 1683, just as she has many times heroically but despairingly accepted wars thrust upon her. Although Charles II of England was bound to support Spain, his whimsicality and the diplomatic finesse and influence of Louis XIV, kept him out. The war which followed is significant in American history, for the king of France

---

[31] Colbert to de Gabaret, 30 September, 1678, in Newton, 308.

was under the tutelage of the enthusiast for America, La Salle, Marquis de Seignelay, who planned to join the perimeter of the Gulf of Mexico to the Mississippi Valley. His recourse to the waning technique of American warfare in using corsairs from French Saint Dominique to reduce the Gulf region so late as 1684 made the French the last great enemies of international comity in America. When in 1684 the French signed the Truce of Ratisbon and restored the state established by the Treaty of Nymwegen, however, they recognized the principle that the same conditions must apply to the waging and settlement of war "beyond the line" that applied in Europe.

Thus by 1688,[32] the year of the death of Morgan, the principal states interested in America had at least shown a theoretical adherence to the principle of ordered and stable relations in the New World as well as in the Old. The French were late because it happened that they had schemes of aggrandizement after the English became convinced that piracy and anarchy were destructive not only of Spanish, but of their own commerce and prosperity. Responsible statesmen henceforth insisted upon the regulation of American affairs. If there must be a war, they felt it should be undertaken by officers who could discipline their men and hold them responsible to the state. It was on that basis that Vernon raided the Caribbean in the eighteenth century—a century in which the Spanish Main suffered as severely as ever before, but by fleets and armies organized in Hanover Square and not in some mangrove swamp or Tortugan cove. In a sense the practice of international relations went through a complete circuit from 1492 to 1688. Beginning by international agreement in papal bulls in the Treaty of Tordesillas, and in the first disciplined and responsible expeditions against Spanish America, the mantle of regulation and responsibility later fell down, not to be restored until near the eighteenth century.

In the last decade of that transition period three principles, long weighed in the international balances, suddenly emerged with unanimous approval. First, Spain at last accepted the maxim of the freedom of the seas. Her old position, *mare clausum,* was admittedly undermined by 1660, and thoroughly delineated in the eighth article of the celebrated American Treaty. Second, the doctrine that effective occupation rather than prior discovery was the basis of title to American territory was first conceded by the Spanish in the Treaty of Münster and made famous in the American Treaty. By the former the Dutch

---

[32] See George Herbert Guttridge, *The colonial policy of William III in America and the West Indies* (Cambridge, Eng., 1922).

came officially into possession of Curaçao and St. Eustatius and perhaps Guiana, while by the second the English were given Spanish sanction in their tenure of Virginia, the Carolinas as far as Charlestown, Barbados, Antigua, Montserrat, Nevis, and St. Christopher in the West Indies. To the French the new maxim meant security in Martinique, Guadeloupe, Marie-Galante, St. Martin, St. Bartholomew, Saint-Croix, and Grenada in the islands. The effective English occupation of the South Atlantic was yet to be established, as was a similar French title to the lower Mississippi. In some respects the third achievement, the ending of dualism in European and American hostilities, was the happiest of all. With the accession of William and Mary, agreements among the principal nations that peace and war should prevail simultaneously in Europe and the Indies had been reached. Thus America was at last rescued from the extra-legal position of unstable and savage international relations.

CHAPTER THIRTEEN

COLONIAL INTERNATIONAL RELATIONS

OGLETHORPE AND THE THEORY OF EFFECTIVE OCCUPATION

BY JOHN TATE LANNING

DESPITE the contemporary solemnity of the American Treaty and the importance attributed to it in current writings, it went abegging in every camp for three-quarters of a century. The Spaniards never accepted the theory of effective occupation as a working principle for the future, for such a position would have precipitated a race for the sparsely settled territory in the Spanish Empire. Instead, the Spaniards negotiated with reference to the past to stop processes then set in motion to prevent their operation in the future. The time limit of the American Treaty was extended to the death of Charles II of Spain which, unexpectedly, did not occur until 1700. The enemies of Spain, who were strong on land, alone could afford to apply the doctrine of effective occupation to the future—about the past there was for them no question. The doctrine was equivalent to that trite but malodorous tenet: might makes right. In short, the idea meant to the rivals of Spain that they were entitled to what they could seize and hold. Moreover, the geography of 1670, five years after Charles II had inadvertently included the city of St. Augustine in one of his munificent grants,[1] was exceedingly vague. What did each hold at that time? The English, directed by John Barnwell in South Carolina and James Oglethorpe in Georgia, were later willing to argue that they held as much of the Atlantic coast as they wanted by treaty agreements, but in the event that argument failed, they were quite prepared to "occupy, dissemble, and to hold." They blithely assumed, and remarked with calm assurance, that the burden of the proof rested on the shoulders of the aggrieved party. England neither hearkened to nor obeyed that part of the American Treaty which limited her trade—only that which extended her domain.

Even when they were compelled to give in, the Spaniards promptly forgot their international agreements when they held no advantage for them or did not conform to their political economies and philosophies.

---

[1] This provision was later struck out.

But before coming out with so crass a position, the English were prepared to try any advice. First, having brought Spain to agree never "to sell, yield, pawn, or transfer" any of her territory to France,[2] they settled down to take it for themselves during a half-century of negotiations in which they accepted no established principles save those that served their purpose. What were the limits established by the American Treaty? Were they determined by original discovery, royal grants, or effective occupation? The English attempted to sustain their case on all three counts. Long after forcing Spain practically to abandon prior discovery as a basis of title, the English were indefatigable in emphasizing the discoveries of Sebastian Cabot along the American coast, but it was curious that they had to conjure up the names of Peter Martyr, Oviedo, Herrera, Gómara, and Ramusio to lend credibility to that uncertain story. Indeed, a hundred years after the Spanish *Conquistadores* had traversed the south with the diaries of their predecessors in their hands, the English said that under the patronage of some gentlemen merchants in Cromwell's time a group of men "discovered all the coast of Florida from the Bay of Apalachy on the West Side of the Peninsula of Florida for about two hundred miles and within twenty leagues of the River Majchebee." [3] That Hernando de Soto had been buried in that river could quite conveniently be forgotten. The Spaniards were not dull enough to refuse the challenge on these grounds where they possessed such odds. In laying a foundation for title by right of discovery they recited the details of the expeditions of Juan Ponce de León, Hernando de Soto, and even the founding of St. Augustine.[4]

But this belated revival of prior discovery was peculiarly hollow even to its spokesmen. When devoid of all dissimulation and metaphysics, the question reduced itself to the ability of the contestants to seize and to hold—by force if necessary. Reasonably enough, especially in the light of the concessions of the Spanish in 1667 and 1670, the universal right to all America could not belong to the Spaniards merely for their being the first to get sight of the unknown land. The assumption was

---

[2] In the Treaty of Utrecht (1713). Article VIII established American boundaries as they stood in the reign of Charles II of Spain. Renewed in the treaty of 1721. Add. MSS., 33005, Diplomatic Papers, I, 220, 227, 271.

[3] Add. MSS., 15903, p. 117.

[4] M. Serrano y Sanz, ed., *Documentos históricos de la Florida y la Luisiana* (Madrid, 1912), 29-88; *Old England forever, or Spanish cruelty displayed; wherein the Spaniards' right to America is impartially examined and found defective. . . .* (London, 1740), 25.

the target of innumerable gibes. In passionate tones English imperialists assailed the already discarded title. Even Dr. Johnson in his *London* took time to put the question in rhyme:

> "Has Heaven reserved, in pity to the poor,
> No pathless waste, or undiscovered shore?
> No secret island in the boundless main?
> No peaceful desert, yet unclaimed by Spain?"

The author of *Old England forever,* summarily dismissing this theory, held: "It must then follow, that they ground their *Claim* upon actual *Possession;* and, if so, such *Claim* cannot extend to any Parts whereof they were never possessed." [5] And just there lay the argument. It was an opportune brand of ignorance. With astonishing lack of knowledge of the string of actual settlements which Spain maintained between 1566 to 1683 from St. Augustine to Port Royal Harbor, Oglethorpe and his supporters based their arguments to substantiate their alleged right by previous occupation on Sir Francis Drake's raid on St. Augustine in 1586! It was somewhat embarrassing to have to admit that Spaniards and not Timucuan Indians defended the city and remained in possession of it. Other evidence was therefore adduced: the charter of Charles I and II, the submission of the Indians, and the occupation of a small fortress on the Altamaha for a period, which no Englishman appeared willing to state, some time between 1670 and 1721. Detachments of English soldiers on the Altamaha during this indefinite time were reputed to have occupied the coast as far south as 30° 2'. The only question Oglethorpe would admit was whether or not the twenty-ninth degree, far to the south of St. Augustine, belonged to England or Spain.[6]

As bases for the claim to the Old Southwest the grants of Charles I were almost as singular as Drake's pillaging St. Augustine. A large grant of this land was made to the Earl of Arundel which was later assigned to Dr. Daniel Coxe who called the country Carolina. On the basis of that concession he sent out two hundred settlers in 1629 and planned to send out more and to appoint Sir William Welles governor. The hostility of the French, however, forced the abandonment of the project and the subsequent neglect of the granted territory.[7] The very

---

[5] *Old England forever, or Spanish cruelty displayed,* 39.

[6] Public Record Office, Colonial Office Papers (hereinafter *C. O.*), Georgia, 5/654, Oglethorpe's Memorandum on Georgia, 18 August, 1737.

[7] *C. O.* 5/384, Papers of Governor Bull to the secretary of state; Daniel Coxe, *A description of the English province of Carolina* (London, 1722), 116, *passim.*

year after this abortive plan Charles I gave to Sir Robert Heath a patent of all America from the St. Johns River, slightly north of the thirtieth degree, north latitude, extending from the Atlantic to the Pacific, territory held in the document not to be "in actual Possession of any Christian Prince or State." Although the concession embraced St. Augustine and New Mexico, this loophole maintained a semblance of legality.

It was in 1663 and again in 1665 that King Charles II of England, through letters patent, made grants to a distinguished group of his subjects and laid the permanent foundations of Carolina.[8] The first of these, to eight patentees, embraced the region from the thirty-first to the twenty-ninth degree of north latitude. These grants superseded those of Sir William Heath, but they were not to remain intact. Carved through the center of them was to run that thin slice of land granted to the Georgia Trustees. It appears in these later instances also that granting and effective occupation were synonymous. The Spaniards alleged that the Georgia charter was diametrically opposed to the seventh article of the Treaty of Utrecht, but, countered the English, by the eighth article of the same treaty the question could have no further retrospect than the death of King Charles II of Spain in 1700, thirty-five years after the last Carolina grant.[9] That argument could not be admitted by a contestant who recognized the incompatibility of granting what one did not have, a vulnerable position which no interested Spaniard failed to assail. At the price of great blood and immense expenditure of energy, they cried, the Spaniards were settled and in pacific effective possession of the country from the South Pole to the thirty-third degree—possession sealed by a solemn agreement between King Charles II of England and King Charles II of Spain who also agreed to cease depredations and live amicably together.[10] It was in the letter of the inadvertent thirty-five years leeway that England began to carve up Florida on technicalities. In the last resort international comity was cast aside. The issue was first clearly joined in 1721 by Jacinto Pozobueno, Spanish ambassador in London, and maintained by his successor, Tomás Geraldino, with pacific but troublesome

---

[8] See Verner W. Crane, *The southern frontier* (Durham, 1928), 4, 9, 207-208.

[9] *Great Britain's complaint against Spain* (London, 1740), 65-66.

[10] Don Iñigo Abad y Lasiera, *Relación del descubrimiento, conquista y población de las provincias y costas de la Florida,* 1785, in Manuel Serrano y Sanz, *Documentos históricos de la Florida y la Luisiana,* Siglos XVI á XVIII (Madrid, 1912), 89-93.

persistency until the debacle of 1739. It was, as Oglethorpe recognized, solved by domination.

Years of contact with English traders in the back country of Carolina and many English-led raids against the Spanish missions on the Golden Isles had thoroughly antagonized the Spaniards. But the use of the Yamasees, which recoiled upon the English with such devastating effect in the Yamasee War, forced the English to an open avowal of a policy they were to pursue to the end of the War of Austrian Succession. The fantastic buffer project of 1717 called Azilia, embracing exactly the region which subsequently became Georgia, found its way to the pigeon-hole;[11] but when Governor Francis Nicholson sent Colonel John Barn-well to build a fort at the mouth of the Altamaha, a point the Spaniards had occupied as well as claimed, a diplomatic battle was joined which ceased only when Spain was displaced in the Old South by the Treaty of Paris. Barnwell, the vigilant leader of the southern frontier, fre-quented the lodge of Governor Nicholson before he came out to America and convinced him that the frontier needed defense. When Barnwell came to write Nicholson's instructions, to give his argument additional force, he held that the "French particularly pretend a Right to the River May." As the English took up their posts on the Altamaha to control its navigation and to insure British domination in the region, no allu-sions were made to Spanish rights. Governor Antonio Benavides Bazán took umbrage at such aggressiveness and complained to the court at Madrid in 1720 against the constant excesses and hostilities of the English and Indians on the Florida-Carolina border—an old issue which embittered the delicate boundary question. The Spanish minister, Marqués de Grimaldo, took up the cue in energetic fashion and passed orders to Ambassador Pozobueno to present a vigorous memorial to the court at London.[12] When the English government transmitted these complaints to Governor Nicholson, he temporized. When Francisco Menéndez Marqués headed a mission to Carolina demanding friendly relations and the destruction of the offensive fort, Governor Nicholson countered with the characteristic evasions and sophistries of diplomacy on that frontier—first (after having led the Spaniards to believe other-wise) he admitted he had no power to make a treaty, then claimed

[11] *Dictionary of national biography*, XXXVIII, 321; Dorothy Brewster, *Aaron Hill; poet, dramatist, projector* (New York, 1913), 50-59; Crane, 210-214.

[12] Archivo Histórico Nacional (hereinafter *A. H. N.*), Papeles de Estado, *sec.* ix, *leg.* 1705, Benavides to the king, St. Augustine, 30 September, 1720; Grimaldo to Pozobueno, Madrid, 24 March, 1721.

all runaway slaves and prize vessels held by the Spaniards before issuing
a formal response to any overtures. No matter what the Spaniards
might demand of the English, and there were many missions from St.
Augustine to Charlestown and St. Simons, instead of answering they
always demanded to have back their slaves, sometimes doubtless when
the Spaniards were harboring none.[13]   The English could not stand
the life on the Altamaha, the fort was both abandoned and burned in
1727; and altogether the English did not maintain a firm hold on the
Altamaha until the arrival of Oglethorpe, but they never admitted,
despite numerous peremptory Spanish demands, that the fort was destroyed intentionally.[14]   The Board of Trade claimed the fort was in
Carolina, basing title to the region on the nebulous legal plea of the
charters, but they ended with a typically Oglethorpian hint:

> "We were rather induced to take this Method because his
> Majesty being in Possession it will certainly be incumbent on the
> Spaniards to produce Proofs of their Title before His Majesty can
> be under any necessity of justifying his own Right." [15]

The set of "Observations," drawn up in response to Carteret's demand for information in this crisis, became the argument of the Board
of Trade; and, indeed, the argument of the English never deviated from
it in twenty years of almost perpetual dickering. In short, the English
made no attempt to justify their position by international agreement at
the time, but passed silently by the American Treaty and stood firmly
on the Charter of 1665. They could not have thought that a mere
charter constituted effective occupation. Thus in an intense crisis these
negotiations were droned out from 1720 to 1729. The tediousness is
easily explained. Time worked for the English as the frontier rolled
southward, consequently they reversed their usual rôle and availed
themselves of every pretext for delay. Nicholson used the device by
taking leisurely trips to London, and even the energetic Oglethorpe
resorted to it.[16]

---

[13] *A. H. N.*, Papeles de Estado, *sec.* ix, *leg.* 1720, Pozobueno to Carteret, London,
6/17 November, 1722; Pozobueno to Grimaldo, London, 19 November, 1722, and
26 November, 1723.

[14] It was the theory of effective occupation as a basis of title which led the South
Carolina Assembly to vote £2000 for rebuilding it in the time of Governor Johnson.
The government in Westminster was even more concrete: "As possession gives
a right in this case, so the abandoning of what we have held so many years is
tacitly giving that right away." *C. O.* 5/233, Instructions to Governor Johnson.

[15] *C. O.* 5/382, fol. 35.

[16] Archivo General de Indias (hereinafter *A. G. I.*), Audiencia de Santo Domingo, 87-1-1, doc. no. 6, dated 2 June, 1726, *ibid.*, doc. no. 43A, including letters

Despite the growing vexation of the Spaniards with the Jamaica sloop trade, English logwood cutting in Campeche,[17] and English settlements in the Bahamas, and this trying fort that menaced the Bahama Channel, in 1728 negotiations looking to the Treaty of Seville began to brew.[18] When affidavits had been taken by the English from all settlers of experience in Carolina and by the Spanish in St. Augustine, the Board of Trade supplied the Duke of Newcastle with documents reiterating the old familiar thesis of the Carolina "Observations." The Duke of Newcastle, in preparing instructions for the English plenipotentiaries, Benjamin Keene, John Goddard, and Arthur Stert, argued that the occupation of one point preëmpted the whole province, and declared that on no other ground could Spain object to foreign settlements and claims outside St. Augustine. Literally, then, if both the English and Spanish had observed the terms of the American Treaty, the Spanish would have stood forever at St. Augustine and the English forever in Charlestown. The good Duke, however, did not have the facts on his side—he overlooked the farmers, soldiers, and missionaries sent scurrying by English raids. Newcastle and the Board of Trade were clearly perverting the historical meaning of the Treaty of 1670 when they endeavored thereby to establish title not only to the actual possessions at the time of the Treaty but also to the concessions like those of Coxe, Heath, and the Lords Proprietors which by no stretch of the imagination could have been effectively "held" in 1670 or even 1700. The Spaniards, the argument ran, had never proclaimed their opposition to these grants. Neither did the English proclaim their opposition to Virginia or London, but by such reasoning they proceeded to turn the tables on the Spaniards. If Spain would not subscribe to the theory that "planting one part of a Province secures the title to the whole, any Nation," the Board of Trade reasoned, "is at liberty and may settle the remaining part of Florida," with the generous exception of St. Augustine, over which Spain had—the English were loath to admit—remained

---

of President Arthur Middleton of the Council of South Carolina, Governor Benavides, and many Spanish affidavits signed by Juan Solano, notary public; *Ibid.* doc. no. 43.

[17] Sir John Alder Burdon, *Archives of British Honduras* (London, 1931), *passim.*

[18] Archivo General de Simancas, Secretaría de Estado, 396.7.634, "que es el tomo 1° de las memorias manuscritas de D. José de la Quintana, sobre la junta de comisarios españoles y engleses en Sevilla . . .; 397.7.635, otro: idem. tomo 2° de dichas memorias; 398.7.636, otro: idem. tomo 3° de dichas memorias." *C. O.* 5/360, C21, C22, C24, C25.

26

sovereign. After the Treaty of Seville,[19] the American boundary problems were still dangling. They were left for later and unwitting diplomats while the conspiracies to control the vicissitudes of the Creeks in the back country absorbed the attention of the Floridians and Carolinians, for here the skein of international intrigue was often entangled with the lesser one of inter-tribal politics. Out of these first diplomatic jousts came the English decision to hold the Altamaha. It remained for Oglethorpe's liberal interpretation to push the boundary down to the St. Johns.

When a group of opposition members of the British Parliament, then called "men of compassion and public spirit," and ever since simply "philanthropists," felt so little sympathy for the famous peace-loving Whig dictatorship of Walpole they could espouse the imperialism of the Carolinians, they wheedled the king into granting a charter by calling the new province Georgia. It could not have been a mere coincidence that the projected colony should embrace the territory between the rivers Altamaha and Savannah, and that its western confines should be the Pacific. This wide swathe, so deftly cut by King George, was just as presumptuous as Ferdinand's and Isabella's grant of all in the "Ocean Sea," or as inexplicable as the donation of St. Augustine by England's King Charles. It embraced great areas of Florida, Louisiana, and Texas, and ripped off the top of the Spanish Empire itself—New Mexico.

An incident of this nature could not go unnoticed, especially when Savannah, Frederica, and Darien rose rapidly almost under the muzzles of Spanish guns. Spain had made that mistake with Jamestown. In this last crisis a Spanish padre, Ramón Escudero, dispatched an historical appraisal to the Marqués de Monteleón, Spanish ambassador in London. The virtual silence maintained by Spain for the next two years is inexplicable. Yet when the furies broke under the pen of Tomás Geraldino, minister in London, Spanish diplomacy gained more than it had lost in vigor. There was no relaxation from the excitement until the climax of the War of Jenkins' Ear.[20] Perhaps the battle was joined by the decision to fortify the banks of the Altamaha and the Golden Isles to St. Simons.

With the southern boundary at the Altamaha, which the Spanish re-

[19] Hertslet, II, 225-229.

[20] For a detailed study of this whole question see John Tate Lanning, *The diplomatic history of Georgia: a chronicle of the epoch of Jenkins' Ear* (Chapel Hill, 1935), *passim*.

fused to relinquish, Oglethorpe might have expected a successful, if tacit, solution of his problem. But Oglethorpe, in many respects, never appeared to have a direct interest in Georgia beyond the play it gave to his buccaneering spirit and the field which it offered for his military inclinations. He was more than a Georgian; he was an Englishman— perhaps first of all an Englishman. He had ample latitude for his talents as one of the Georgia Trustees and as a member of the Royal African Company—one to traffic in souls and the other in slaves. When Oglethorpe came back to Georgia in 1735 he resolved to colonize to the Altamaha. If the Spaniards were bitter at the deliberate intrusion to this point fifteen years before, that ancient resentment was again properly aroused. Yet Oglethorpe, martial and imperialistic rather than humble and philanthropic, was a wily entrepreneur. Before leaving London he obtained from the Spanish minister a sanction of the appointment of a commissioner to act as an internuncio between himself and the governor of St. Augustine. For this purpose Charles Dempsey returned to America with Oglethorpe in the ship *Symond*.

In St. Augustine, Dempsey was received with great civility. To Governor Francisco Moral Sánchez this courtesy had another significance.[21] In the first place he was a Spaniard and could not suffer himself to be overshadowed in the Latin art of kindness and suavity, especially when so much was at stake. The commissioner's urbane and affable manner mingled with a lesser degree of haughtiness was not a little surprising in Florida. "I dispossess him," wrote Governor Moral Sánchez, "of his advantage and confuse him with kindness and sincerity, but I look upon his strange proceedings with suspicion." [22] Yet this was the man who was hanged in Spain for signing a treaty with Oglethorpe and Dempsey and in 1736 (later repudiated by the Spanish) for placing the southern boundary of Georgia at the St. Johns. A series of comic opera Spanish diplomatic expeditions to Georgia[23] were foiled in an effort to forestall that contingency. In this crisis Oglethorpe, now "Commander of the English Colonies," had said openly that although he should receive orders from his king and court to fix the boundary limits, he would delay the execution "so that there should never be a

---

[21] C. C. Jones, *History of Georgia* (2 vols., New York, 1883), I, 240.

[22] *A. G. I.*, Audiencia de Santo Domingo, 87-1-1, doc. no. 56, Moral Sánchez to Güemez y Horcasitas, St. Augustine, 26 October, 1736.

[23] Robert Wright, *Memoirs of General James Oglethorpe* . . . (London, 1867), 160-161; *C. O.* 5/690, Dempsey to the Trustees, London, 6 April, 1737; *A. G. I.*, Audiencia de Santo Domingo, 87-1-1, doc. no. 46; docs. nos. 48 and 58, Arredondo to Güemez y Horcasitas, St. Augustine, 31 August, 1736.

sign of those limits." Accordingly, he never even answered the letters
sent him from Florida. In judging this old Nicholsonian attitude as of
basic importance, and in recommending that it would be well to relieve
the colonies "of a gentleman whom it would be exceedingly troublesome
to manage," Governor Manuel de Montiano, successor to the deposed
Moral Sánchez, was eminently right. But what Spanish mouse would
trap this English cat? Already in 1736 the lines of communication between the Spanish embassy and Whitehall were hot with angry and, as
Keene said, "blustering memorials" of Geraldino.[24] Calling the English
sharply to task and reminding them of the terms of the American Treaty
and the Peace of Utrecht,[25] and seeking to prevent Oglethorpe's return
to America, the second memorial was much stronger and menacing in
tone.[26] Simultaneously a great and somewhat quixotic campaign was
on foot "to reannex all that formerly belonged to the Spanish monarchy." John Savy, Indian trader, carrying tatoo marks as a Yamasee
memento, who was charged with murder in the Carolina-Georgia country, and the vigorous Spanish secretary of state, José de la Patiño, were
the promoters of this project. Taking passage on the first loaded vessel
ever to sail from Georgia, Savy was put on shore at Dieppe, appeared
in Paris and so successfully presented himself there as an Irish Catholic
anxious to uproot Georgia and South Carolina (about which he professed so much knowledge) that he was taken up by the French and sent
to Spain by the Spanish ambassador. The Spanish secretary of state,
José de Patiño, was a man essentially militant, and the extravagance of
any visionary scheme did not act as a deterrent upon him. His decision
was to strike suddenly and with force in America and to lose none of
the advantages of diplomacy in Europe—the same longing to which
Cromwell had to revert to the discarded "no peace beyond the line." He,
therefore, fell in with the schemes of this adventurer. Savy was now
Captain Miguel Wall, Spanish recruiting officer extraordinary. Wall,

---

[24] *A. G. I.*, Audiencia de Santo Domingo, 87-1-1, doc. no. 69, Geraldino to
Torrenueva, London, 4 July, 1737. These papers are to be found in the archives
at Seville, and also at Simancas in the Spanish State Papers. Documents accessible
in this country are *Collections of the Georgia Historical Society* (9 vols., Savannah,
1840-1842), VII, Part iii, 16-18; Egmont, *Diary* (3 vols., London, 1920-1923), II,
300-304, 426-438; William Coxe, *Memoirs of the life and administration of Sir
Robert Walpole, Earl of Oxford* (4 vols., London, 1816), IV, 9; Wright, *op. cit.*,
Chapter x; H. W. V. Temperley, "The causes of the War of Jenkins' Ear, 1739,"
Royal Historical Society Transactions (third series, 17 vols., London, 1918-1934),
III, 197-236.

[25] *A. G. I.*, Audiencia de Santo Domingo, 87-1-1, doc. no. 53.

[26] Edgmont, *Diary*, II, 426.

being a man who liked to linger over his glass, and as his success thus far indicated, was extremely talkative. News about the ships and men assembling at Havana leaked out. Consequently, during the period in which memorials contesting the right of Georgia and complaining of the depredations of its inhabitants were being passed in London, the court of Madrid was kept busy answering embarrassing questions. Nothing could have made support for Oglethorpe more certain. By the time that seven thousand men and seven warships had been made ready there, Wall had been fêted in every town from Santiago to Havana. One of his alcoholic conversations fell upon the ears of the factors of the South Sea Company in Santiago, and gradually the Spanish authorities began to distrust him as a prospective guide. Upon the death of Patiño, Wall was ordered back to Spain under surveillance. By cunning he escaped through Portugal to England and there presented himself as an English spy extraordinary.[27] By now, under the guidance of José de la Quadra, Patiño's successor, the momentary menace to Carolina and Georgia died down.

The news of the Savy-Patiño menace played propitiously into Oglethorpe's hands. It was being noised abroad that in London he was devoting himself with much zeal and solicitude to the object of securing the regiment of seven hundred men which became so famous in Georgia. There were no dire pictures and artifices to which his friends did not resort in furthering the same end.[28] It was then that the desperate Spanish minister, knowing that Walpole was as docile as the pressure on him would permit, turned to Horace Walpole and implored him to intercede with his brother, Sir Robert, to stay the efforts of Oglethorpe and the Trustees. Sir Robert, however, could do little more than take care of himself and his own during these last critical five years of his reign. Oglethorpe was returned, with a more dignified title than ever, but for "defense only," and the troops he had demanded followed him.[29]

---

[27] C. O. 5/388, fols. 72, 73, 79, 80; State Papers, Foreign (hereinafter S. P. F.), Spain, 126, 127 passim; ibid., 246, fols. 2-6, 9, 19, 20, 29, 47, 55, 169; C. O. 5/638, fol. 14; ibid., 639, fols. 57, 58, 77; ibid., 654 passim; Add. MSS. 32794, N. P. (Newcastle Papers) CIX, 337-341; ibid., 32795, N. P., CX, 22-24, 90, 131-133, 303-309; ibid., N. P., CXI, 36-37, 46-48; S. P. F., Ministers, 59, fols. 58-65. See John Tate Lanning, "Don Miguel Wall and the Spanish attempt against the existence of Carolina and Georgia," in The North Carolina Historical Review, X (1933), 186-213.

[28] Add. MSS., 35909, Hardwicke Papers, DLXI, 74, Georgia Trustees to Walpole, London, 22 June, 1737.

[29] A. G. I., Audiencia de Santo Domingo, 87-1-1, doc. no. 71, Geraldino to Torrenueva, London, 18 July, 1737.

A second memorial from the unexpectedly bellicose Geraldino so terrified Sir Robert that he ventured to offer Oglethorpe a regiment in England in lieu of one for Georgia, but Oglethorpe fired back and demanded to know what sort of man Sir Robert thought him and whether he judged him capable of abandoning three thousand people whom he had taken out to Georgia for the sake of a regiment. He also demanded in unequivocal language to know whether Georgia was to be given up, "yea or nay." By this time every faction was thoroughly stirred up. If the new crisis brought consternation to the ministry it brought delight to the Prince of Wales and the war faction. In Spain, England's jovial fat minister, Benjamin Keene, was oblivious of these transactions, merely writing, "in the Gazets I find there is a notion that a blustering memorial has been presented by M. Geraldino upon the colony of Georgia, but as I have heard nothing of it from the office, I suppose it is without foundation." [30] His placidity, however, was of short duration. The London government redispatched Keene's servant to him in all haste with Geraldino's "very extraordinary memorial" and the answer made to it.

In the instructions to Benjamin there appeared, however, a note of mildness. In spite of the peremptory nature of the Spanish memorial, the English saw fit to conceive their answer in as moderate terms as were consistent with the support of the British title to Georgia and the resolution to defend and maintain British rights and properties. The cause of this moderation under duress is discernible in the instruction to the representative at Madrid to offer to settle differences by reference to commissaries, or in any amicable manner agreed upon by the two courts as La Quadra suggested. At Hampton Court the Duke of Newcastle expressed doubts about whether or not the limits of America had ever been determined—another reason for the appointment of commissaries. Unfortunately for the ministry when it came down to the concrete question the friends of Georgia would negotiate this question only on the grounds that the Spanish lost. On the other hand the Spaniards, who were now earnestly promoting a commission, were demanding evacuation and demolition of certain forts built by Oglethorpe in the disputed area. [31]

In this impasse wild rumours began to fly in London. Anxious eyes turned to France in dread expectation of the immediate operation of the *pacte de famille*. The English hastened to issue letters of marque and reprisal to both the English and the colonials. Newcastle dispatched

[30] *S. P. F.*, Spain, 128, Keene to Newcastle, Segovia, 16 September, 1737.
[31] *S. P. F.*, Spain, 247, Newcastle to Keene, Whitehall, 13 April, 1738.

information to Spain requiring all British merchants forthwith to withdraw ships and effects from the ports of Spain.[32] As midsummer approached, Spain still frantically tried to enlist the support of France and to frighten England with the shadow of the *pacte de famille*,[33] while Englishmen went deliberately about granting letters of marque and reprisal and ordering attacks on Spanish ships without the incidental declaration of war. Meanwhile, the diplomatic stage was cut across by a sincere effort of the friends of peace to effect a reconciliation in the Convention of Pardo—an attempt which revealed the real nature of his Majesty's opposition as well as that of the "Oglethorpians" among the Trustees. For a moment there was a truce—like the calm before a storm, for everyone knew that it might end with a rush of troops and fortifications to the frontier from both sides. Ambassador Geraldino, in trying to force the evacuation of Georgia and the retirement of Oglethorpe, had every hope that the English would show a supine deference to Spanish wishes as the English enemies of the reign of Walpole so fervently preached.

Into this restless, disturbed, and expectant state came news of the Convention of Pardo—the signed intention of the two courts amicably to adjust both their maritime and boundary troubles through a convention of commissaries. This resolve entailed a very exacting armistice on the Georgia-Florida boundary. And in this state things stood while those who wished peace awaited the materialization of the boundary question. Thus it happened that Oglethorpe's plan of dissimulation, coupled with activity, prevented a settlement of the essential issue and enhanced his opportunities for achieving glory. Since his spirit was essentially buccaneering, it is no wonder that the Spaniards saw in him and his every fomentation an eye adjusted solely to the plaudits contingent upon successful conquest.[34] But they could not deny that he had laid down the policy of his master—a policy which baffled all efforts at settlement. His was an irreconcilable and unreasonable policy. And, indeed, this much mooted question was brought to a termination only when Florida was ceded to England. Nothing else could have solved it on the foundations laid by Oglethorpe. Debarring the element of force as a justification or right of occupation, the English had as good a claim to St. Augustine as to the St. Johns River, and Oglethorpe himself did not have the temerity to claim the former.

[32] Add. MSS., 32798, N.P., CXIII, Newcastle to Keene, Whitehall, 1 June, 1738.
[33] A. Baudrillar, *Philip V et la cour de France* (6 vols., Paris, 1898), IV, 159.
[34] *A. G. I.*, Audiencia de Santo Domngo, 86-6-5, Montiano to the king, St. Augustine, 19 December, 1737.

CHAPTER FOURTEEN

COLONIAL INTERNATIONAL RELATIONS

FINAL TRIUMPH OF EFFECTIVE OCCUPATION AND THE FREEDOM OF NAVIGATION

By JOHN TATE LANNING

ENGLAND and Spain approached the diplomatic crisis of 1739 with statesmanship as docile as their problems were perplexing. In diplomacy the personal factor is always important, yet Spain was ruled by "three or four mean, stubborn people with little minds and limited understandings." [1] That pungent, uncomplimentary appraisal embraced La Quadra, secretary of state, Quintana, secretary of marine and Indies, and Uztáriz, first commissioner in the war office. José Patiño, secretary of state in the critical years before 1738, should more often be mentioned in the same breath with Alberoni. He possessed Philip II's ideas of national grandeur, and never refused to encourage a projector like Miguel Wall, let his schemes be ever so impracticable, "though he afterwards let the author of them starve in waiting for further orders and succor he promised him." [2] Queen Elizabeth Farnese, "the termagant of Spain," manipulated the court with an assertive hand. Montijo, president of the Council of the Indies,[3] was the most reasonable. When La Quarda shifted the onus of the Anglo-Spanish tension onto Torrenueva, the officious Keene called him "a weak, embarrassed, timid man, without any bad or good intentions toward us. . . ."

English officialdom was likewise unique. The prime minister, Sir Robert Walpole, was easy, good natured, and tremblingly desirous of peace. His, moreover, was an age in which standards of political corruption were different from, if not worse than, those of today. Walpole was at the head of the relentless Whig political machine about which there hinged a great deal of vituperative, if ineffective, criticism. The Duke of Newcastle, an efficient and well-balanced official, was the principal secretary of state. To anyone who probes beneath the surface of English affairs during the reign of Walpole, Newcastle's influence and

[1] Add. MSS. 32796, N. P., CXI, 241.
[2] Add. MSS. 32795, N. P. CX, Keene to Newcastle, Casa del Monte, 10 June, 1737.
[3] *Royal Historical Society Transactions,* third series, III, 204.

preponderance must appear more and more obvious. Newcastle[4] controlled the extreme royalists, and Walpole was a master of groups. Keene, the minister at Madrid, was fat, amiable, and agreeable, yet resolute and adroit enough when occasion required. The Spaniards and others whom he bribed and garnered into the English service in Madrid, and connected through "channels" (referred to unemotionally as just another fact in the day's work), were dubbed his "Purple Friend" or his "Friend No. 101." Keene, however, was an agent of the South Sea Company and at the same time a representative of the English Crown. Although such a position was aboveboard and not then considered incompatible with the performance of his duties, serving two public masters and another private one augmented Keene's difficulties.

One of the innate difficulties of the Spanish colonial system was that it ran counter to the tendency of trade to flow freely through the profitable channels of commerce. Naturally, the English continued to find one method or another around this highly monopolistic system. Since European merchants outside of Spain could not send goods to the Spanish West Indies on their own account, their goods were sometimes carried over under reputed ownership of Spaniards.[5] Precarious was a trade so dependent on individual honesty and so withdrawn from the sanctions of government. English merchants were occasionally divested of their goods in Spain, particularly wheat and barley of which the American fleets were frequently in dire need, without explanation or compensation. Seizure was the penalty upon proof of undeclared, or illegally declared, goods. Such business was discreditable, costly, and vexatious, and nothing short of one hundred per cent profit made it worth while. It, therefore, devolved upon England to infringe on Spanish trade and to tap the stream of wealth that flowed perennially and inexhaustibly from America. The English were left free to engage in illicit commerce with the Spanish coasts without interference from England. Defense was one of those many burdens of proof and action the English were quite content to let rest on Spanish shoulders.

Opportunely located and ever active, the Jamaicans led the fleets of elusive sloops that darted in and out of the Caribbean coasts, plying a highly remunerative trade. Of the same nature were the merchants of Barbados, the Bermudas, and the Bahamas. The Jamaican sloops, slip-

---

[4] For the formative years of his life see S. H. Nulle, *Thomas Pelham-Holles, Duke of Newcastle* (London, 1931), *passim*.

[5] *Memorials presented by the deputies of the Council of Trade in France* (London, 1736), 26.

ping out of Kingston or Port Royal, dropped suddenly into the mouths of streams between the Río de la Cacha and the Chagres. The Spanish fleet system had made disturbing centers of Cartagena and Puerto Bello, but runs between New Spain, Puerto Rico, Española, and Cuba widened the range of these enterprising merchants. Avoiding the numerous taxes imposed by the Spanish government upon legitimate trade, these men could naturally undersell competitors, effect a quicker turnover in flour, manufactured articles, and woolens. Not only in "shoes, ships, and sealing wax," but in negroes, they could undersell the market. Enthusiasm rose as one pamphleteer exclaimed "Jamaica will be the richest spot in the universe." [6] The *British Merchant,* inclined to moderation rather than exaggeration, estimated the Jamaica sloop trade at £200,000 to £300,000 per annum.[7]

In logwood cutting along the bays of Campeche and Honduras, where a party of Spanish soldiers at any moment might swoop down and blot them out or put them in chains, these resolute men from England, New England, and Jamaica cut blithely away, their arms close by prepared for any eventuality.[8] The Board of Trade was early petitioned to appoint a governor for the Bay of Campeche and to list it among the British colonies.[9]

For nine years before 1706, the galleons had not arrived a single time. Intervals of this kind made illicit commerce inevitable. Down by the gulf stream from the north there came a steady flow of interlopers from Maryland, Pennsylvania, New York, and New England. They sold provisions to the logwood cutters, provisions and marketable commodities to the Dutch at Curaçao, to the piratical Danish settlement at St. Thomas, to the French, and to the very Spaniards themselves. These interlopers the Jamaicans loved less than they did the Spanish officials— both were their enemies. But the Jamaicans themselves, in cutting through the ever-dear Spanish monopoly, were flying in the face of the American Treaty which was revived in the Treaty of Utrecht. When

---

[6] Charles Leslie, *A new and exact account of Jamaica* (London, 1740), 376.

[7] An official source fixed the sums as follows: "August, 1706-August, 1707, of which the most modest computation is 1,400 negroes at £56,000. 4,000 bayes at £48,000. 10,000 perpitts at £45,000. 8,000 sayes at £36,000. 4,000 scarletts at £20,000. 1,000 mixed serges at £3,500. In sundry goods as laces, worsted stockins, wax, hatts, lynnens of all sorts, by the lowest computation can't have been sold for lesse than £66,500. Total £275,000. Besides ye above goods we supply ye Spaniards with great quantitys of flower which brings in return only silver." *Calendar of State Papers* (hereinafter *C. S. P.*), Colonial, XXII, iii.

[8] Sir John Burdon, *passim.*

[9] *C. S. P.,* Colonial, fourteenth series, XX, 439-440.

the crisis came it was found impossible to curb these American traders. When the English sought to enter the South Sea Company legally in the trade about 1700, they found these self-reliant smugglers athwart their own economic path.   The spirit of the colonies was such that "neither the Laws of the Islands, nor the Laws of England, nor the Laws of other Nations, can restrain them from trading wherever they foresee Advantage."[10]   In short, Walpole admitted that the illicit trade was so profitable that Parliament could never be induced to outlaw it for legal trade.[11]

So the accumulated grievances other than Georgian which led to the Convention of Pardo can be traced directly to the Peace of Utrecht. Taking advantage of the general negotiations in 1713, the Spanish ministers at the behest of vast and discontented colonies, decided to sign the long-sought *asiento* compact with the eager Earl of Oxford.   This agreement involved the sending of forty-eight hundred slaves annually for thirty-eight years to designated ports in Spanish America and the right to unload one vessel of five hundred tons annually.   For this privilege the English in the South Sea Company were to pay thirty-three and one-half pieces of eight a head for the negroes on that number whether they imported them or not.   The actual shipment seldom reached half that figure.   Although both English and Spanish merchants opposed this treaty, they drifted on with their governments and helped lay the foundations for a diplomatic entanglement from which it was impossible to get free.   Although the South Sea Company was allowed two vessels as tenders, returns, as the other *asientistas* had learned, were disproportionate to the capital invested or to their expectation, so persistent had been the legend of the Indies trade.[12]   The profits were whittled to one-half by the required twenty-three eightieths to the Spanish Crown, and by the British and American interlopers.

The Jamaicans continued naturally and stubbornly to sell on the Spanish Main.   Undaunted by the Spanish authorities, why should they quail before the bureaucratic South Sea Company?   In the ensuing feud between the Jamaicans and the Company, the private trade, reduced to

---

[10] *Popular prejudices against the convention and treaty with Spain, examined and anshwer'd . . .* (London, 1739), 23.

[11] H. W. V. Temperley, "The relations of England with Spanish America," in *Annual Report of the American Historical Association for 1911,* (2 vols., Washington, 1913), I, 236.

[12] The French Guiana Company during the War of Spanish Succession had refused to labor under the burden.   *British Merchant,* (London, 1713), III, 209, 254-266.

peril by the Company's identification with the government, continued to cut the *asiento* profits. Soon, open charges that South Sea Company factors supplied the Spaniards with information were being hurled about. The Company itself, however, was hostile to Spain and kept up a running dispute with Madrid over its dues, and the South Sea ships *Prince Frederick* and the *Wool Ball* were seized and confiscated by Spain. Total Company claims presented at Madrid ranged upward of £250,000.

The Spanish governors frequently connived with schemers in order to supply the wants of the colonies. Soon, instead of the two tenders allowed the *asiento* vessel, whole flotillas replenished the lawful cargo as fast as it sold. Without a more direct communication with Madrid it was hard to control the Spanish privateers (from which the governors sometimes made profits) that swarmed the Spanish Main. The realization of high prices generally for contraband traffic made it difficult for Spain to control her governors and police craft. Unlimited foreign competition and the practical impossibility of retaining the American trade for her own galleons explains the eager adoption of monopolistic ideals in the political schools of Gerónimo de Uztáriz and Sebastián de la Quadra.

Although perhaps bearing no relation to that sovereign, during the reign of Philip V, Spain, taken with a new sense of her national dignity after the Peace of Utrecht so tightened her efforts at policing the American waters that only a national catastrophe, with which English imperialists were becoming more and more willing to accommodate her, would suffice to conform her ideas to her size. The Peace of 1721, ending one of the frequent, meaningless wars, resulted in mutual restorations, the king of England holding onto the *asiento* contract and the Spaniards gaining their codfishing rights around Newfoundland.[13] Besides, Uztáriz, whose first literary attempt at the rejuvenation of a nationalistic commercial policy appeared in 1724,[14] now stood high in Spanish councils—perhaps higher than his merits warranted. His work, far from being a detached, scholarly tome, passed beyond the range of a disquisition and became an exhortation to Spain to invigorate her navy, encourage manufacturers, reform customs, and promote trade. In perfecting his case, he made brilliant use of the mercantilism of Louis XIV and Colbert, analyzed what a group of Spanish thinkers superior to

---

[13] Board of Trade Papers, Plantations General, X, 140.
[14] *Teórica y práctica de comercio y de marina* (Madrid, 1724).

himself had done, and showed familiarity with the English navigation and trade acts. Although mild and ineffective wherever engaging any powerful institution, he pressed the case against England (in denying fishing rights to the Guipuzcoans and Biscayans in Newfoundland) far enough to advise asking the pope for a dispensation permitting another form of abstinence on fast days.[15]

Of first significance was the fact that the Spanish governors issued instructions to the *guarda costas* to guard the coasts against illicit commerce. By dickering with smugglers the Spaniards found a method of inveigling them. Sometimes these ships acted as pirates towards Englishmen while holding the credentials of the Spanish government. They often became careless in discriminating between smugglers and vessels plying in good faith between England and the English West Indies. Spanish courts confirmed the captures by condemning ships and cargoes and impressing English seamen.

As the crisis of 1718 precipitated the volcanic eruption of the Anglo-Spanish mixture in the Caribbean, Colonel Stanhope, member for Derby who had served as envoy to Spain, began to speak in bulk of English claims, relating that he had presented more than twenty-five memorials to the Spanish court without the slightest redress.[16] Looking upon so many documents as formidable, Stanhope began to present his protests in bundles. That was a distinction that also fell to the lot of Benjamin Keene. Depredations began to figure seriously in Anglo-Spanish affairs around 1726. Merchants inundated the House of Commons with petitions against Spanish maritime onslaughts. The House itself echoed with the stirring resolutions of indignant members.[17] The policy of the British government, already inert in the hands of the master, Walpole, who desired the fruits but not the costs of war, found expression in the memorable expedition of Vice-Admiral Francis Hosier to the perimeter of the Caribbean and the border of Spain's empire. He had instructions[18] to surprise and capture both fleets—the galleons and the *Flota*—and any isolated ships, and to inform the Spanish governors that he intended committing no hostilities unless it should be necessary in order to protect British property. His orders carried the peculiar provision

[15] For a revised opinion of the influence of Uztáriz see E. J. Hamilton, "The mercantilism of Gerónimo de Uztáriz: a reëxamination," in *Essays in honor of T. N. Carver* (Cambridge, 1935).

[16] *Parliamentary history of England from the Norman conquest in 1066 to 1803* (23 vols., London, 1812).

[17] *Journals of the House of Commons,* XXI, *passim.*

[18] Dated March 28, 1726.

that he was to use "his best Endeavours by Persuasion, or even by force, to get them and their Cargo into his Possession; declaring in the strongest manner to the Commander in Chief, that his orders were to carry them to a Port of Safety, and that his Majesty's Design was to restore to everybody what belonged to them. . . ." That, to the ribald Englishman of the eighteenth century, was the height of effeminancy, and he inquired with supreme irony to know whether "a *British Squadron* was ever fitted out before, at a vast Expense, for a long and hazardous Voyage, to play the *Pedants,* and *endeavour to* persuade." [19] Stanhope was next called upon to "endeavour to persuade," and accordingly went directly to Madrid where he required the service of Benjamin Keene. The Treaty of Seville[20] was the result of the negotiations, but the Parliamentarians were unsatisfied and it only augmented English vexations. Their harangues continued and, with regard to Carolina, one document merely replaced another as a basis for argument.

But there was a possibility that the sore spot of navigation and depredations would at last be healed. The king on April 2, 1730, commissioned John Goddard, Benjamin Keene, and Arthur Stert as commissaries to adjudicate differences. By the eighth of the same month Newcastle had designated the Board of Trade to receive claims of the British subjects. During April and May numerous advertisements of the Board appeared in the *London Gazette,* one informing the public that the claims, accompanied by Spanish translations, were to be authenticated in the Court of Admiralty at the expense of the king. When Goddard and Stert departed to join Keene in Spain, they left behind their secretary, John Crookshanks, to press matters. Soon, they received from that worthy one hundred and two claims, and seventy-two cases of lost ships. All this he did before the voluminous papers of the South Sea Company were ready. On December 21 the Spanish government had not yet appointed commissaries to review the English documents. When they were appointed, they frequently acted without conferring with the English. Newcastle droned out to Keene that far from the disorders ceasing,

"the Number of *Spanish* Privateers, or rather Pirates, under the Denomination of *Guardia costas,* increases daily; and that the gain which the *Spanish* Governors in *America* make by countenancing these unlawful Practices, and sometimes being ourselves Sharers

[19] Caleb D'Anvers, [Nicholas Amhurst], *Some farther remarks on a late pamphlet, entitled observations on the conduct of Great Britain* (London, 1729), 19.
[20] November 9, 1729.

in the fitting out of those Privateers is such a Temptation, that unless the Court of *Spain* takes some more effectual Method, as by punishing those who have most notoriously offended that way, and making them answerable for the *Disorders* and *Irregularities* committed by ships to which they grant Commissions, or which are harboured in their Ports with Impunity, there will never be an end of the unjustifiable, and, as it too frequently happens, barbarous Practices." [21]

A *cédula* of the king of Spain early in the next year commanding the governors not to permit any abuse to Englishmen or their ships sailing in the American seas was nullified by the proviso "as long as they keep their proper distances and are not concerned in any illicit trade. . . ." [22]

"Spanish insults and depredations" became the refrain of the faction which called Wolpole "that indefatigable Minister who, for many years hath rock'd the publick cradle, and endeavored to lull that forward Babe, the Nation, to rest." A lull in 1736 gave way to a new wave of depredations in 1737 as the Savy-Patiño expedition outfitted in Havana. [23] Ambassador Keene, therefore, abandoned remonstrances and peremptorily demanded cessation of the depredations and restitution of property lost. "Oh, England! At what a State of Contempt and Cowardice are you arrived? England that destroyed the *Spanish* Armada in 1588, and . . . is now in danger of being destroyed by Spanish Pyrates," came the Jeremiad from the wailing pen of "L. D." [24] But why all this diplomatic furore between England and Spain when the Dutch, who were also doing a lively business, made no protests? The answer is that the poor Dutch could not pretend that their captured smuggling vessels were plying legitimate trade, for they had no *asiento* contract. When they lost a vessel, the unfortunate Dutch could do nothing but wince.

So, after five years of relative quiet, the pot was beginning to boil again with war heat. The conniving Elizabeth Farnese, in trying to get England's assistance in the seizure of the Duchy of Tuscany, vented her disappointment upon Englishmen by issuing vindictive instructions for increasing the vigilance of the *guarda costas* in America. [25] Scores

[21] Newcastle to Keene, 18 November, 1731; Hugh Hume Marchmont, *A state of the rise and progress of our disputes with Spain*, 11; G. H. Rose (Comp.), *Marchmont Papers*, illustrative of events from 1685-1750, (3 vols., London, 1831).

[22] *Journals of the House of Commons*, XXII, 86.

[23] *Gentleman's Magazine* (253 vols., London, 1731-1883), X, 639.

[24] *Reasons for war against Spain* (London, 1737), 37.

[25] Statement of Horatio Walpole in William Coxe, *Memoirs of the life and administration of Sir Robert Walpole, Earl of Oxford* (4 vols., London, 1816).

of merchants entrusted their perplexing claims to his Majesty's justice as the overworked Keene presented bundles of petitions in Madrid. Merchants resented the disastrous implication that the discovery of logwood, cocoanuts, and pieces of eight (all of which could be found in the British possessions) meant illicit commerce, especially when the search was made in a way outlawed by the agreements of 1660 and 1667. There was a perplexing vestige of the old *mare clausum* in La Quadra's retort to Newcastle that Englishmen only had a right to the free commerce and navigation around their own islands and plantations when they steered a due course. Unnecessary altering of the route was provocation enough for Spanish seizure.[26] The inability of the Ministry to establish that characteristically tropical goods were not proof of illicit commerce forced Newcastle to admit that the situation was coming to a head when he observed that the trouble lay in the assumption of English merchants that unless they were actually taken in illicit commerce, despite proof of their having engaged in it having been found aboard, they were unjustly taken, and of the assumption of the Spaniards on the other hand that they had a right not only to seize ships continually trading in their ports, but to search them on the high seas for proof of fraud. Between these two opposing theses lay the perpetual embarrassment of the two governments.

Meanwhile, the signs of conflict grew more ominous. A truculent House of Commons began to make nationalistic demands. As the government issued letters of marque and reprisal a fleet under Admiral Haddock sailed for the Mediterranean, May 28, 1738. The twin problem of Georgia and navigation and depredations in America, the merchants by numerous petitions did not permit the government to forget. In the bellicose Parliament an outspoken and vehement resolution was offered against the Spanish maritime procedure, demanding the cessation of depredations, satisfaction for losses already suffered, and security for the navigation of British subjects in the future, and beseeching the king to use his utmost endeavors to that end. Unsympathetic ministers merely sanctioned the strong resolution, defeating by 163 to 224 a motion from the polemic faction to recommit.[27] In the midst of this exciting debate there appeared the screeching anti-Spanish motto of the opposition: "No search." Said Lord Carteret,

---

[26] La Quadra to Keene, 10/21 February, 1737. *Parliamentary History*, X, 1181-1182.

[27] *Parliamentary History*, XXIII, 135.

"There is a point in dispute, my Lords, betwixt us and the Spaniards, which, if adjusted, must either leave us in the quiet and uninterrupted exercise of navigation and commerce, or must leave to Spain an absolute and uncontrollable sovereignty of these American seas. The Spanish Court says, 'We have a right to search your ships;' but 'No search' are the words that echo from shore to shore of this island. This, my Lords, is what we ought to insist upon; for without this concession, all other concessions from the Spanish Court are to no purpose. . . . 'No search,' my Lords, is a cry that runs from the sailor to the merchant, from the merchant to Parliament, and from Parliament, my Lords, it ought to reach the throne." [28]

Montijo, who kept his head throughout the whole extraordinary agitation, put the Spanish case fairly and deftly, when he said:

"What would it avail . . . if we should hang up half a dozen of our governors in America to please you, or because they deserve it, if you [the English] do not treat your contrabandists with equal rigour? You only hear of your ships being taken, but give no attention to the damage we suffer essentially by your interlopers." [29]

On another occasion he was reported to have said that

"if Spain would accumulate all her grievances against us [the English], she might make as much to do as we did; that there are faults on both sides; our contrabandists ought to be punished and some of their governors, hanged." [30]

The friends of peace in both countries had expressed themselves as favoring good correspondence. Although each desired its contentions conceded as a preliminary to negotiations, after many delays and objections it was agreed to leave everything *in status quo* in Georgia and to take no new posts while plenipotentiaries met in Madrid to arrange both the baffling problems of navigation and Georgia. Although the hope of French succor served as a barrier to reconciliation, the desire of the Spaniards to attack Curaçao was an aid to the same end. But as the pacific faction worked for a convention, England nevertheless increased her seamen from ten to twenty thousand. Military and naval orders smacked of war. Parliament was prorogued and voted £3,750,000 for combating injuries. Walpole was still noncommittal when the opposition faction played an ace card. They produced Captain Robert Jenkins of the *Rebecca* in Parliament where he exhibited his detached

---

[28] *Parliamentary History*, X, 754.
[29] Add. MSS., 32800, N.P., CXV, Keene to Newcastle, Madrid, 16 March, 1739.
[30] *Royal Historical Society Transactions*, third series, III, 204.

27

and pickled ear, credit for its removal eight years before going without challenge to the Spanish Captain, Juan León Fandino. In the uncannily apt speech that he made he recalled how, after being manacled, he expected the threatened death and recommended his soul to God and the revenge of his cause to his country. Whether this speech was prearranged or not it was a happy one for the war faction. Excitement ran high in England as the House of Commons resounded to the cry: "Our countrymen in chains! and slaves to the Spaniards! is this not enough, Sir, to rouse all the vengeance of a national resentment?" [31] Just as the situation began to get out of control in England, Keene despairingly reported from Spain: "I am persuaded they have gone all the lengths they will go towards avoiding a war, and bringing on a reconciliation between the two crowns." [32] But in spite of all odds the Convention of Pardo for the amicable adjustment of American depredations and limits at Madrid within six months was signed and ratifications exchanged January 14, 1739. For Spain, José de la Quintana and Esteban José de Habaria were appointed as the Spanish plenipotentiaries, although La Quadra had fallen under the influence of Casimiro Uztáriz and neglected the sane counsel of Montijo.[33] For England, Benjamin Keene and Abraham Castres, consul-general in Madrid, were appointed commissioners. Both countries had a primary interest in the settlement: Spain to stop the English advance in Georgia, and England to stop the depredations in the Caribbean. The English plenipotentiaries hoped to settle the Caribbean problem mentioned in the second article of the convention and to sign the treaty before the affair of Georgia, in which Spain could demand concessions, could be broached and thereby deprive Spain of a great diplomatic advantage. Fearing that the Spaniard would make some difficulty in agreeing to this, Keene and Castres appealed to Newcastle for all the reports and papers relating to the English right to Georgia.[34]

In the instructions to the commissioners the old briefs were pulled out and recited. The debate in the English Parliament which followed the convention was the high peak of the pre-war diplomacy in England. The patriots and imperialists, including the Trustees of Georgia, were

---

[31] *Parliamentary History*, X, 572, 786.

[32] Add. MSS., 32799, N.P., CXIV, Keene to Newcastle, 13 October, 1738.

[33] *S. P. F.*, Spain, La Quadra to Keene, Madrid, 10 January, 1739; Add. MSS., 32800, N.P., CXV, Keene to Newcastle.

[34] Add. MSS., 32800, N.P., CXV, Keene and Castres to Newcastle, Madrid, 13 January, 1739.

resolved to ruin the effects of the convention before they had heard a word of its provisions, in which, according to a contemporary, "England was never more misled and unreasonable." [35]

The negotiations were complicated by domestic politics, by the interjection of the South Sea Company's affairs, and finally doomed by them. The Georgia faction was skillful enough to sell its support of the convention for an appropriation of £20,000 for Georgia. Walpole, however, soon realized that it would be a political mistake ruinous to himself as well as to the convention really to jeopardize the English possession of Georgia. He, therefore, turned about with a gesture of bravado, "called to Col. Bladen, and ask'd him whether England had a right to Georgia? yes, reply'd the Col? Can you prove it, said Sr Robert, and will you undertake it? the Col? answer'd he would. Then, said Sr Robert, By G—d the Spaniards shall not have it." [36]

On March 6, 1739, the House of Commons met to take into consideration the foredoomed convention. Interest and feeling in the matter were intense. The pleas of merchants blended with unscrupulous and vehement attacks on both the peace and the convention. Pitt deemed it

"a stipulation for national ignomy; an illusory expedient to baffle the resentment of the nation; a truce without a suspension of hostilities on the part of Spain; on the part of England a suspension as to Georgia of the first law of nature, self-preservation and self-defense; a surrender of the rights and the trade of England to the mercy of plenipotentiaries. . . ." [37]

Bolingbroke and Pulteney attempted to withdraw the opposition from the House of Commons and to create such a sensation all over England that Walpole would be scared into refusing the passage of the convention. Sir William Wyndam, in a defiant but despairing mood, appealed

---

[35] *Appeal to the unprejudiced concerning the present discontents occasioned by the late convention with Spain* (London, 1739), 6.

[36] *Colonial records of Georgia* (24 vols., Atlanta, 1904-1915, edited by Allan D. Candler), V, 121. Bladen lately wisely advised the English not to insist on the twenty-ninth degree of northern latitude (included in the second charter, embracing territory "only inhabited by some barbarous peoples, who have no knowledge of Almighty God," that incorporated St. Augustine as shown in Popples' map) and to rest on the first which, like the grant to Sir William Heath, placed the boundary at the St. Johns. "Here, therefore," he cautioned the Duke of Newcastle, "I would stop for how desirous soever Your Grace, or I may be to extend the British Dominions in America, yet I apprehend the best way of asserting our Right is to carry it no farther than our vouchers will support us." C. O. 5/654, fols. 205-207, Bladen to Newcastle, Albrohatch, 25 April, 1739.

[37] *Parliamentary History*, X, 962-1325.

to the future to judge him while the "insolence of enemies without and the influence of corruption within threaten the ruin of the constitution."

No such excitement had been seen since the Excise Bill and the South Sea Bubble. Indeed, no more extraordinary crisis ever faced the British Parliament. Outside of the House a veritable maze of pamphleteering, speaking, and letter writing confused the mind and inflamed the passions. Every pamphlet called out another.[38] The ministers carried the convention in the House with the precarious vote of 244 to 214.[39] In the House of Lords, Carteret repeated his "no search" doctrine, attacked the convention article by article, and contended with great plausibility that trade winds and the proximity of the islands of the West Indies compelled English craft to pass within sight of Spanish territory. Although the Lords passed the address of thanks for the convention, thirty-nine of these peers signed a resolute condemnation of it.[40]

The conferences in Madrid did not begin auspiciously. It was an unwonted complication that the French ambassador advised the Spanish government "no longer to have patience" with the English—an easy task since the English had not withdrawn their fleet under Admiral Haddock from the Spanish back door, as they promised to do upon Spanish suspension of military measures, and since Elizabeth Farnese had completely abandoned herself to France.[41]

When the plenipotentiaries met on May 5 for a formal reading of their full powers they were hard put to it to prove that Spain had not occupied territory to Santa Elena and to substantiate English possession below Charlestown at the time of the American Treaty. Newcastle, who knew that the English could not claim actual settlement of the uttermost limits of the grants on which the English rested their case, made the significant blunder of instructing his plenipotentiaries to hold that at that time "the Lands were not possessed or occupied [or claimed] by the subjects of any other Power" [42]—an error in fact which must have weakened the English case. Meanwhile, the presence of Haddock's squadron, Spain's refusal to pay the £95,000 in indemnities and her threat to suspend the *asiento* pact brought the negotiations to a most delicate point.

---

[38] Of these, probably the ablest was *Observations on the present convention with Spain* (London, 1739).

[39] *Journals of the House of Commons*, XXIII, 277.

[40] *Parliamentary History*, X, 1241-1243.

[41] Add. MSS., 32800, N.P. CXV, fols. 299, 338; *S.P.F.*, Spain, 133, Keene to Newcastle, 4 May, 1739.

[42] *S.P.F.*, Spain, 134, Newcastle to Keene and Castres, 8 May, 1739.

The point upon which the negotiations broke down completely lay entirely outside the merits of the issues. It was the old story of maneuvering. Spain wished to have the Georgia question (Article II) settled first; England that of depredations (Article I) which were mentioned first.[43] Upon the suggestion of Quintana and Habaria an exchange of memorials containing the reciprocal statements of pretentions was made. As was expected the English harped upon navigation and the loss of their ships; the Spaniards upon the loss of Georgia. Besides, they demanded the evacuation of all islands and lands not held by the English in 1670, and projected the issue of Providence Island into the debate. There was the arrogant element of force in the English contention that if Great Britain enjoyed the possession of any territory which could be disputed,

> "it is incumbent upon the Spanish Plenipotentiaries to produce proofs to the contrary supported by the Treaties; & not the business of those of His Majesty to produce the Titles, which they may have in their hands, to justify their Possessions; still less to abandon places where the King's subjects have made Settlements, as the Spanish Plenipotentiaries pretend. . . ."[44]

When Spain made absolute prerequisites of the payment of £68,000 due from the South Sea Company, the recall of Haddock from the Mediterranean, the dispatching of necessary orders to Carolina and Florida, and insisted that "Spain is obliged to insist on the stopping, visiting, and searching of all vessels which navigate in the American seas, as a right depending on, and inseparable from their preëminences in those seas,"[45] deadlock was reached. The last condition, which elicited a thunderous negative declaration in reply, doomed and practically ended the conference. Newcastle, thereupon, ordered the English to desist from the conferences.

With the breaking off of negotiations it became apparent that a state of war was the only alternative. All diplomacy having been rendered futile, the Georgia agitation merged with the veritable bedlam of 1739 in England. The English ministry had recourse to backhanded methods while it was supinely swept into war by the combined fever of Georgians,

---

[43] *S.P.F.*, Spain, 133, Keene and Castres to Newcastle, Madrid, 9 June, 1739; *A.G.S.*, legajo 7633, Antigua, *passim.*

[44] *S.P.F.*, Spain, 133, memorial of the English Plenipotentiaries of June 25, 1739.

[45] *A.G.I.*, *legajo* 7633, "Respuesta al papel dado por Yngleses en 1° de Julio de 1739." Address to Electors; *Ten years' transactions with Spain* (London, 1739),

merchants, imperialists, and jingoes. At this juncture, the beginning of
the War of Jenkins' Ear, the diplomatic story of Georgia becomes no
longer traceable. The threads can only be picked up and distinguished
at the conclusion of the War of Austrian Succession and the signing of
the Treaty of Aix-la-Chapelle in 1748. Oglethorpe's dictum to dissemble and to hold (by force if necessary) now became the exclusive
title whereby Georgia was retained in the British Empire. That title
had at least the virtue of accommodating itself to the inexorable facts of
the occupation of America by all the powers.

So imbedded was the Anglo-Spanish enmity that when it was proposed to remove the regiment from Georgia in 1748, the Trustees loudly
protested exposing the Englishmen and foreign protestants settled there
"to the Rage of their inveterate and irreconcilable Enemies." [46]

The secret Treaty of Aix-la-Chapelle provided for the restoration
of all conquests, including the West Indies.[47] The South Sea Company
was compensated for the interruption of its business during the war by
a renewal of the *asiento* contract. Since the general treaty, however,
did not deal adequately with Anglo-Spanish affairs, Keene signed a
separate treaty with Caravajal at Madrid, October 5, 1750. The *asiento*
contract was now deleted and all claims between the two crowns were
dropped. The South Sea Company was awarded £100,000 which it
probably never collected. Whereas "Don Benjamin" Keene in the
epoch of the Convention of Pardo had been held up to national oppro-
brium, he was now hailed as a national hero.[48]

In 1755 the lull on the Georgia-Florida border was interrupted by
English sallies southward. Despite Spanish protests and their own
promises, the English never withdrew. When Florida was exchanged
for the captured Havana in 1763, little had been achieved by diplomacy.
Apparently Georgia shared the usual fate of the American colonies in
European diplomatic stakes—restoration of all conquests. But merely
to be left *in status quo* was the crowning achievement of Oglethorpe's
policy—effective occupation at the point of the sword. Spanish diplomatic victory would have necessitated a great retrocession. Thus, while
the imperialists and merchants steadily infringed on the Spanish domain, ever nearing the sweeping and majestic claims of the English royal
charters, time was gained, and suspense not infrequently maintained by

---

[46] *C.O.* 5/668, fol. 299.

[47] *S.P.F.*, Treaty Papers, 103, *passim.*

[48] Sir Richard Lodge, *Private correspondence of Benjamin Keene* (London,
1933), 415.

diplomacy. It is little wonder that Spain in 1763 abandoned La Florida with few qualms.

Although the treaties after the War of Jenkins' Ear did not remove the old points of dispute, they died, as they usually do, of inanition and not of war. Irascible old Elizabeth Farnese was dead. And despite the fact that in 1739 Spain had been speaking of the right of search because of her "preëminence in these seas," the abandonment of the fleet system at the end of the War of Austrian Succession was a tacit admission on the part of Spain that a new era had dawned in the Caribbean and the New World—this time the right of navigation which had been gained on paper as early as 1660 became a reality. Spain was just a sister and no longer the mother of the Caribbean.

SELECTED BIBLIOGRAPHY

It has not been thought advisable to attempt a survey of all the international relations of Hispanic America. To do so in the space of three chapters would require such condensation as to make the story repetitive and hackneyed. But there is one theme around which it has been found possible to cluster the maze of early Caribbean relations: the *mare clausum* of Spain and the rival contentions of free seas and effective occupation. Although Professor A. P. Newton, *The European nations in the West Indies, 1493-1688* (London, 1933) has introduced this theme into his excellent summary (upon which the first chapter is based), it seemed necessary to attempt an interpretation of the first half of the eighteenth century when the theories opposed to *mare clausum* really triumphed. The same field of international relations in the second half of the eighteenth century has been covered by Miss Vera Lee Brown, *Anglo-Spanish relations in America in the closing years of the colonial era* (Baltimore, 1923, reprinted from the *Hispanic American Historical Review,* V, no. 3). In a measure, therefore, the first of these three chapters is designed to give a legalistic skeleton to colonial international relations, and the second and third, while still adhering to that purpose, to bridge the gap between the works of Professor Newton and Miss Brown through the use of source materials. To undertake a résumé of the border diplomacy of West Florida, the Mississippi Valley, and Texas would serve no useful purpose and require a sketchy duplication of such works as: F. J. Turner, "The diplomatic contest for the Mississippi," in *The Atlantic Monthly,* XCIII (1904); F. J. Turner, "The policy of France toward the Mississippi," in *The American Historical Review,* X (January, 1905), 268 ff.; Thomas Maitland Marshall, *The western boundary of the Louisiana purchase* (Berkeley, 1914); Herbert Eugene Bolton, (ed.), *Athanase de Mézières and the Louisiana-Texas frontier, 1768-1780* (2 vols., Cleveland, 1914); Herbert Eugene Bolton, *Texas in the middle eighteenth century* (Berkeley, 1915); Isaac J. Cox, *The West Florida controversy, 1798-1812* (Baltimore, 1918); and Herbert Bruce Fuller, *The purchase of Florida; its history and diplomacy* (Cleveland, 1906). If one follows the destinies of Spain's international relations in America until the final northward thrust, we find the story completely treated in William Ray Manning, "The Nootka Sound controversy," in the *Annual Report of the American Historical Association for the year 1904* (Washington, 1905), 283-478. Even Spanish diplomacy in the period of recognition has now been sketched out from the sources. See J. Goebel, *The recognition policy of the United States* (Columbia University Studies, LXVI, New York, 1915). See W. S. Robertson, "The policy of Spain toward its revolted colonies," in *Hispanic American Historical Review*, VI (1926), 21-46, "The recognition of the Spanish colonies by the motherland," *ibid.*, I (1918), 70-91, and "The United States and Spain in 1822," in *American Historical Review*, XX (1915), 781-800; and John Tate Lanning, "Great Britain and Spanish recognition of the Hispanic American states," in *Hispanic American Historical Review*, X (1930), 429-456. But to trace the relations of nations in the Caribbean into the eighteenth century, and to interrelate them with the Anglo-Spanish contest for the North American mainland, is not, of course, the whole story of the colonial international relations of Hispanic America. On the continent of South America a bitter contest went on between the Spaniards and the Dutch settled in Guiana. The Dutch, unlike the Portuguese, could not soften their relations with the Spanish *padres* on the frontier by means of a common religion and similar language. Their contacts, consequently, meant more than trading, or even slave catching expeditions—they meant Indian massacres, terror, and desolation. For a more complete insight into this question see: Joseph Gumilla, *Historia natural, civil y geográfica de las naciones situadas en las riveras del Río Orinoco* . . . (2 vols., Barcelona, 1791), I, 360-361; Alexander von Humboldt, *Personal narrative of travels to the equinoctial regions of America, during the years 1799-1804* (3 vols., London, 1852-1853), III 22-23, 77, 85-87; *The case of Venezuela, a reply to the British Blue Book* (3 vols., New York, 1897) *passim; The counter-case of the United States of Venezuela before the Tribunal of Arbitration to convene at Paris* (4 vols., New York, 1898), *passim;* and J. Fred Rippy and J. T. Nelson, *Crusaders of the jungle* (Chapel Hill, 1935), chapter xii. It is little wonder that the Spaniards referred to these neighbors as of the "diabolical sect of Calvin" and the "accursed heresiarch Luther." Of the French it has not been possible to treat at all. In the long run the effective occupation of the land came about just as it did in North America. The Portuguese in Brazil, with a vanguard of Paulistas cutting ruthlessly and relentlessly through, gained headway in the tractless interior, but at the same time that the North American rivalry came to a head, the climax was reached in South America and with identically the same legalistic technique. A treaty of limits was negotiated with Spain in 1750 by the Marquis de Pombal, based (with the exception of battle-scarred Colonia) upon actual occupation of lands. Another Treaty in 1777 duplicated that of 1750, except that the Seven Missions of Uruguay went to Spain. For a select bibliography of this question see Raul d'Eça, "The boundary settlements of Brazil," in A. Curtis Wilgus, (ed.), *Argentina, Brazil, and Chile since independence* (Washington, 1935), p. 447.

For the sporadic attacks of the English in La Plata region see P. Groussac, *Santiago de Liniers, Conde de Buenos Aires, 1753-1810* (Buenos Aires, 1907). Further bibliographical materials will be found in footnotes above.

CHAPTER FIFTEEN

THE MOVEMENTS FOR INDEPENDENCE. INTRODUCTION

By ALFRED HASBROUCK

I. POLITICAL AFFAIRS IN THE IBERIAN PENINSULA

IN 1807, when Napoleon was trying to fight England by excluding that country from the markets of Europe, he found himself unable to enforce successfully his so-called "continental policy" because the little kingdom of Portugal, loyal to its friendship for England, refused to close its ports to trade with that country. Therefore, the dictator of Europe determined to compel Portugal to obey his orders and to shut England out. In order to attack Portugal, he had first to march his armies through Spain. Having by the Treaty of Fontainebleau received from King Charles IV permission to do this, Napoleon, with his armies already on Spanish soil, treacherously took advantage of the weakness of King Charles, the dishonesty and intrigue of the minister Godoy, and the selfishness of the heir apparent, Prince Ferdinand.[1]

During a quarrel between the royal father and son, egged on by Godoy, Charles was forced to renounce his crown in favor of Ferdinand, who thereupon succeeded to the throne as Ferdinand VII, although later Charles regretted his hasty act, and withdrew his abdication. Promising to settle this quarrel to the satisfaction of all, Napoleon persuaded both to meet him at Bayonne. As soon, however, as they had crossed the border into French territory they were seized and made prisoners. It was an easy matter then for Napoleon to compel the weak old man to abdicate his throne and to grant to the French emperor the right of naming his successor, after Ferdinand had also been compelled to renounce his rights.[2]

In due season Napoleon appointed his brother, Joseph Bonaparte, "King of Spain and the Indies" and sent instructions to royal officials in the colonies to obey his orders. The people of Spain, however, did not sit back supinely and accept the deposition of their "dearly beloved" Ferdinand. Instead, the whole nation rose in arms against the new King

---

[1] A. Curtis Wilgus, *A history of Hispanic America*, 220; J. Fred Rippy, *Historical evolution of Hispanic America*, 139.

[2] Jules Mancini, *Bolívar et l'émancipation des colonies espagnoles*, 237.

Joseph, guerilla bands attacked the French troops, and aid was sought from England. The latter country sent a large army under Sir Arthur Wellesley (later the Duke of Wellington) to aid its new allies in driving Napoleon out of Spain and Portugal in the Peninsular War which resulted disastrously for Napoleon and Joseph.[3]

The Spanish people refused not only to accept Joseph as their king and to obey his constitution and laws, but they set up local *juntas* or councils of government in various parts of Spain to carry on their own government in the name of Ferdinand VII, their rightful sovereign. Among these *juntas,* the one at Seville took the lead and assumed jurisdiction for the whole of Spain, dispatching emissaries to the colonies to assert its authority there and to invite the colonists to send deputies to Spain.[4]

These events in Europe were the real and immediate cause of the movements for independence of the Spanish and Portuguese colonies in America. The Spanish colonists, like the people of Spain, refused to accept the king whom Napoleon had imposed upon them. They were loyal to the House of Bourbon and at first had no desire to detach themselves from the Spanish monarchy, but they were unwilling to admit the authority of the Spanish people, and declined to accept orders from the *Junta* of Seville. If each province in Spain might govern itself by means of a local *junta* there seemed no reason why each province in the colonies should not do likewise. There was all the more reason for it in the colonies, since they were distant from the mother land and their local interests were so different. Some sort of government must be maintained; why should they not do it for themselves? They would coöperate with the *juntas* in Spain to the extent of preserving intact his realm for their exiled and imprisoned King Ferdinand, but they would not take orders from *juntas* which were no more legitimate than their own. A few irreconcilables and advanced thinkers hoped for independence, but the majority of the colonists thought only of showing their loyalty to the rightful king of Spain by organizing temporary governments of their own to last only until he could be restored to the throne.[5]

II. JUNTAS AND PRECURSORS IN AMERICA

The earliest movements of the revolutionary era in Hispanic America, then, were no more than attempts to set up *juntas* for their home govern-

---

[3] Mancini, 236; J. M. Antepara, *South American emancipation,* 25, 221.

[4] Rodney and Graham, *The reports on the present state of the United Provinces of South America,* 71, 140.

[5] Rodney and Graham, 119; Mancini, 247-249.

ments, now that the royal officials had been deprived of their authority. Local *juntas* were established in each of the viceroyalties and in many of the provincial capitals, as will be described. They met opposition both from those who advocated independence and from those who declared themselves loyal to the government of the mother country. Among the latter were largely peninsular Spaniards, ex-officials, and the higher clergy, while among the former were the intelligentsia, members of wealthy Creole families, lawyers, teachers, and writers, who had absorbed ideas of independence from the success of the English colonies in North America or from the writings of the French philosophers, such as Montesquieu, Diderot, and Jean Jacques Rosseau, as well as from the revolutionary principles enunciated in the "Declaration of the Rights of Man." The majority of the thinking population wanted only to maintain a government for the colonies free from dictation by Napoleon or the Spanish *juntas,* and, therefore, found it easier to ally themselves with the independents or patriots than with the loyalists. Thus at first, and throughout most of the revolutionary era, the contests partook of the nature of civil wars between classes of colonists—between Creoles and Spaniards, between lawyers and higher ecclesiastics, and between patriots and loyalists.[6]

Among those advanced thinkers who hoped and worked for independence from the start were two who are now known as the "Precursors of Independence." These were Antonio Nariño, Precursor of New Granada, who popularized the principles of Liberty, Equality, and Fraternity by translating into Spanish the "Declaration of the Rights of Man and of the Citizen";[7] and Francisco de Miranda, the Precursor of Venezuela, or simply "The Precursor" as he is more often called. The latter, as an officer of the Spanish army, had given assistance to the revolting North American colonists, had fought as a general in the army of the French Revolution, and had then travelled throughout Europe in an effort to arouse sympathy for his native colony of Venezuela, especially in England, where he had tried to secure the promise of assistance in men and money for carrying on a revolution in the Spanish American colonies. At last, discouraged because international politics prevented English statesmen from acceding to his wishes, he departed for the United States, and there raised a group of filibusters for the purpose of liberating Venezuela. In 1806 Miranda sailed from New

---

[6] Wilgus, 217; Rodney and Graham, 119.

[7] Mancini, 84-85.

York with two hundred men for Coro on the north coast of Venezuela. This attempt, known as the *"Leander* expedition," from the name of the ship on which it sailed, was a complete failure because it was premature, and the people of Venezuela, upon whom Miranda relied to carry on the revolution which he started, failed to respond to his call. The Spanish authorities, warned in advance, met the little group of filibusters where they attempted to land and drove them away again after capturing and executing many of their number.[8]

These early attempts of Miranda must have had some influence on the minds of the patriots in Venezuela for they acted sooner and with more vigor than did those in the other colonies. When Napoleon's agents reached Caracas with orders to the colonists to accept Joseph as king, the citizens rejected their overtures and assembled in a *cabildo abierto* (open town meeting), where on April 19, 1810, a month before the people of Beunos Aires did likewise, a provincial *junta* of government was established, after the captain-general, Emparán, had been deposed. A week later the *cabildos* of the other towns of the captaincy-general were invited to send representatives to a federal congress which disavowed the Spanish regency, issued a declaration in favor of Ferdinand VII, and sent Andrés Bello, Luís López Méndez, and Simón Bolívar as commissioners to London to secure aid and recognition from the British government.[9]

Although the mission failed in its immediate purpose, it produced good results, for two of its members, Bello and Bolívar, induced Miranda who was still living in London, to return with them to Venezuela, and López Méndez, who remained in London, later did valiant service in securing English, Irish, and Hanoverian recruits for the patriot army.[10]

Immediately on his arrival at Caracas, Miranda took the lead in revolutionary activities by organizing the Patriotic Society of Caracas, modeled after the Jacobin Club of Paris, and by becoming a member of the Venezuelan Congress, where he vigorously urged that his native land should assert its independence. Thus, largely through the efforts of Miranda, the first declaration of independence of any of the Spanish

[8] William Spence Robertson, *The Life of Miranda* I, ch. xiv, 307-310; James Biggs, *The history of Don Francisco de Miranda's attempt to effect a revolution in South America.*

[9] Robertson, *Miranda* II, ch. xviii, 84-93; William Spence Robertson, *Rise of the Spanish American republics,* 61; Mancini, 285-288.

[10] Alfred Hasbrouck, *Foreign legionaries in the liberation of Spanish South America,* 29, 30, 45, 49, 164.

colonies was voted by the Venezuelan Congress at Caracas on July 5, 1811. The colors, red, yellow, and blue, which Miranda had used on his *Leander* expedition, were adopted as the flag of the Venezuelan Republic, and the new constitution provided for a federation of states modeled somewhat after that of the United States.[11]

God was angry at the disloyalty of the Venezuelans toward their king —so taught the priests who opposed independence—and took vengeance upon them by razing their cities to the ground. On March 26, 1812, a severe earthquake destroyed Caracas and other patriot towns leaving some of the loyalist districts comparatively unharmed. The terrified and superstitious people fell on their knees amidst the ruins of their homes to ask God to spare them further punishment and to forgive them for their sins. Many of them, especially those who had previously been lukewarm, deserted the patriot cause, and even those who were more staunch began to lose faith in their ultimate success, so that the patriots found it necessary to endow Miranda with dictatorial powers as commander-in-chief of the army of the republic, in order to check the royalists in their efforts to regain control.[12]

Perhaps Miranda was growing old; perhaps the odds against him were too heavy; but in this time of crisis he failed to come up to his reputation for generalship. When a vigorous policy might have won the victory before the royalists could consolidate their strength, Miranda procrastinated. Instead of attacking and driving the royaltists out, he waited to gather recruits and munitions, which might have been a wise policy under ordinary conditions, but which, under the circumstances, opened the way for further disasters. Through the treason of Bignoni, an Italian officer, the castle of Porto Cabello was betrayed to the enemy and that stronghold fell into the hands of the Spanish commander Domingo Monteverde. Miranda seemed to lose heart at this disaster and negotiated with Monteverde the Treaty of San Mateo wherein the patriots agreed to lay down their arms on condition that their persons and property be respected. Thus, July 25, 1812, the date of this treaty, saw the end of the First Venezuelan Republic.[13]

To many patriots this surrender of Miranda seemed unnecessary, premature, and cowardly; he was accused of treason, and of trying to enrich himself at the expense of his country. Charges that he accepted a bribe to sign the treaty have never been proved, but it is true that he

---

[11] Mancini, 369-370; Robertson, *Miranda* II, ch. xix, 104-119.
[12] Robertson, *Miranda* II, ch. xxi, 145-148; Rippy, 146; Wilgus, 238.
[13] Robertson, *Miranda* II, ch. xxii, 168-169; Rippy, 146; Wilgus, 239.

planned to take the public treasury out of the country with him. Whether he intended to use this money to continue the struggle for liberty at a more convenient season, or for his private purposes, is not known. However, his acts were bitterly resented by a group of his officers, among whom was Colonel Bolívar. When Miranda attempted to leave the country on an English ship, he was seized by these officers and turned over to Monteverde who, in violation of his promise in the treaty, shipped Miranda in chains to Spain where he died in prison.[14]

These events in Venezuela furnish in many respects prototypes of the revolutions elsewhere in the Spanish colonies. Although there were some earlier abortive attempts, the system of setting up *juntas* of government in practically all cases occurred in 1810. Within a month and a half after the events of April 19 in Caracas, *juntas* of government had been organized in nearly all the other capitals, some of which tried to establish federal unions centering in the *junta* at the provincial capital. However, in many cases a spirit of localism prevented the other departments of a province from accepting the dictation of the capital, and in nearly all cases there was civil war between departments, thereby jeopardizing seriously the success of many of the independence movements. This condition of affairs is well illustrated by events which took place in the Viceroyalty of New Granada.

When news came to Santa Fé de Bogotá, the capital of that viceroyalty, that commissioners were about to arrive from Spain, a *cabildo abierto* met and on July 20 elected a *junta* for the government of New Granada. The commissioners, seeing themselves forestalled, then proceeded to Quito, where their arrival was the signal for a renewal by the revolutionists of their activities, which had been temporarily put down the year before. This revolt of August 1810 was ruthlessly crushed with the aid of loyalists from other sections of the viceroyalty, the spirit of loyalty being especially vigorous in the mountainous districts of Popayán, Pasto, and Patía where the people were strongly influenced by their bishop and by General Sámano, their royal governor. These mountaineers not only aided in crushing the revolt in Quito, but rejected the overtures of the *junta* of Bogotá and fought attempts of patriot troops to enter their country.[15]

Although many towns in New Granada expressed their concurrence in the setting up of *juntas* of government, they would not consent to ac-

[14] Robertson, *Miranda* II, ch. xxii, 181-185, ch. xxiii, 213; Wilgus, 239.

[15] Wilgus, 243; Robertson, *History of the Latin American nations,* 165; Pilling-Mitre, *The emancipation of South America,* 22; Mancini, 429-430.

cept the invitation of Bogotá to join it in a federal union, electing instead *juntas* of their own and declaring themselves independent of the capital of the viceroyalty. Mompox, on August 16, declared its absolute independence from Bogotá, and was followed by Cartagena, which on September 19 published a manifesto openly hostile to the designs of the *junta* at Bogotá and invited the other provinces to unite with it in sending delegates to a federal congress at Medellín. Still another federation was formed by the towns of Cauca, Santa Marta, Chocó, Neiva, Casanare, and Tunja, while other towns also set up their own *juntas*. Some success might have been achieved by these various *juntas* had they consented to coöperate against the common enemy, but unfortunately the spirit of localism was too strong and each provincial town hoped to rule as the capital of an independent republic of its own.[16] Jealousy was especially keen between Cartagena and Bogotá. When the former organized its rival federation, the latter abandoned its pretentions to control the whole of the viceroyalty and declared itself the State of Cundinamarca (its Indian name) with a republican form of government to be maintained temporarily while the king was in captivity.[17]

The success in forming this centralized government of Cundinamarca was largely due to the precursor, Antonio Nariño, who on September 19, 1811, was appointed dictator. Nariño, who realized that coöperation by the patriots was essential to their success, conceived a new plan of centralization and tried to force the other provinces to join the "legal province" of Cundinamarca; but he was defeated at Paloblanco and Ventaquemada by the partisans of Tunja, while Santa Marta, which had been blockading Cartagena, furnished a refuge for a Spanish expedition which entered the valley of Cúcuta and threatened Bogotá. In the south, Nariño failed to force the submission of Socorro, but was successful in conquering Popayán. However, after having defeated the main body of the royalists at the difficult crossing of the ford of the Juanambú, he was in turn attacked by guerilla bands composed of loyalist mountaineers, his troops were dispersed, and he himself was captured. The precursor of the independence of New Granada was then sent in irons to Spain and thereafter that viceroyalty relapsed into a state of chaos, until a greater man came upon the scene to reorganize the patriot cause.[18]

In addition to the early separatist movement in Quito, the failure of which has been mentioned, another abortive attempt in that same year,

---

[16] Mancini, 431-432; Pilling-Mitre, 313.
[17] Mancini, 433; Pilling-Mitre, 319-320.
[18] Mancini, 437-440.

1809, was made by the Creoles of Chuquisaca in Upper Peru. These deposed the president of their *audiencia* and with the aid of the patriots of La Paz, organized a *junta* of their own. However, the combined royalist troops of the neighboring viceroyalties of Peru and La Plata were too much for the patriots, whose leaders were forthwith either killed on the field of battle or executed on the gallows. Yet, as one of their martyrs declared, they had lighted a fire "which shall never be quenched." [19]

The news that French soldiers were victorious in Spain and had driven the central *junta* to take refuge in Cádiz was proclaimed to the people of Buenos Aires by the Viceroy Cisneros on May 18, 1810. In this proclamation he urged that the colonies remain loyal to the Spanish monarchy and even intimated that the people of Buenos Aires might have to govern themselves if the central *junta* of Spain should be destroyed by Napoleon.[20]

Taking him at his word, the leaders of the more radical or patriotic element among the citizens asked the viceroy to call a *cabildo abierto* to decide on what form of government should be established in order to put into effect the purposes of his proclamations. Cisneros reluctantly granted their request, and on May 22 an open town meeting decided that the *cabildo* should assume the viceroy's powers, and combining them with its own, should take charge, although the deposed viceroy was to be president of a *junta* which was entrusted with the government. This sop to royal authority failed to meet the approval of the more radical patriots in the *cabildo,* which on May 25 excluded the deposed viceroy altogether from any share in the government and formed a new *junta* of nine members of which Colonel Cornelio Saavedra was president and Juan José Passo and Mariano Moreno were secretaries. The latter, who was in charge of political and military affairs and who had a vote in the *junta,* practically controlled that body in important matters of policy, most of which were within his jurisdiction, since the other secretary dealt only with financial affairs.[21]

---

[19] Pilling-Mitre, 22; Robertson, *History,* 164.
[20] José P. Otero, *La révolution argentine 1810-1816,* 139.
[21] Robertson, *Rise of the Spanish American republics,* 150; Otero, 148-154.

CHAPTER SIXTEEN

THE MOVEMENTS FOR INDEPENDENCE IN SOUTHERN SOUTH AMERICA

By Alfred Hasbrouck

I. Revolt of the Provinces of La Plata, Paraguay, and Uruguay

ALTHOUGH independence was not declared on May 25, 1810, that date is celebrated in Argentina because the formation of the new *junta* controlled by Creole patriots and free from the influence of royal officials marks a first step toward the eventual formation of an independent government.[1] Having deposed them from power, the *junta* decreed the deportation of the former viceroy and *audiencia* to the Canary Islands, and having established itself as the executive and legislative body of the capital, it attempted to extend its authority throughout the former Viceroyalty of La Plata. Calling itself "The Provisional Junta of the Provinces of La Plata River," it sent emissaries to the other provinces to secure their adhesion.[2] Many of the interior provinces accepted the new government, but Paraguay and the region on the eastern shore of the Uruguay River directly across from Buenos Aires (now known as Uruguay),[3] refused to do so.[4]

General Manual Belgrano had been sent in 1810 to what is now Paraguay to force that province to join the United Provinces. Although this campaign against Paraguay was a military failure, it was nevertheless a partial diplomatic success. His force of 1,000 men was better armed and equipped than that of the Paraguayans, yet the latter succeeded in drawing him further and further into their country by retreating before him until they had led him into a trap at Paraguarí where they turned upon him, defeated him, and captured 120 of his men. Belgrano fell back to Tacuari to await reënforcements, where he was again surprised in his camp by Colonel Cabañes, and refused to surren-

---

[1] Robertson, *Rise,* 152; Otero, 156-162.

[2] Robertson, *Rise,* 151; Rodney and Graham, 92-93.

[3] Before the establishment of the present republic of Uruguay, this region went by the name of "Banda Oriental" (Eastern Shore). To translate this as the "Oriental Republic," as is sometimes done, is not only absurd, but misleading.

[4] The attempts to conquer Upper Peru and to drive royalist influence out of the provinces of the northwest led to the campaigns of San Martín.

der but sent a flag of truce suggesting a suspension of hostilities until he could recross the Paraná and withdraw from Paraguay.[5]

This armistice was utilized to permit fraternization between the Paraguayans and the officers and troops from Buenos Aires and to spread propaganda. What Belgrano had been unable to do by force, he accomplished by kindness, for he offered to pay the Paraguayans for cattle which he had confiscated, and gave gold to support the widows of those who had been killed in battle; thus having gained their good will, he sowed the seeds of revolution in their minds. The Paraguayans, however, had been afforded the opportunity to learn that they could take care of themselves and that they needed no control or assistance from Spain or from anywhere outside their own boundaries.[6]

By craft Belgrano also won over Pedro Somellera, secretary to the governor, whom he induced to stir up internal strife. Although Governor Velasco, who was popular and well-liked, had been appointed by the legitimate king of Spain, he had declined to take sides between Joseph and Ferdinand. The people also had been satisfied with their present independent situation and had seen no reason to join Buenos Aires.[7]

Yet in spite of the willingness of the people to keep Velasco in power and to follow him in resisting the invasion of Belgrano, Somellera managed to stir up strife between him and the *cabildo* over the matter of accepting aid from Portuguese troops for defense against Buenos Aires. By a sudden *coup d'état* on the night of May 14, 1811, conspirators, led by two ignorant officers, Juan Pedro Cavallero and Fulgencio Yegros, chosen by Dr. Somellera, seized and occupied the barracks of the Asunción garrison and forced Velasco to resign.[8]

Then, in accordance with the usual procedure, a *junta* of government was formed. Naturally the two soldiers, Cavallero and Yegros, became members of this, but since they were too ignorant to transact the necessary business, a certain *tinterillo* (notary public), Dr. Gaspar Rodríguez de Francia, was designated to be the third member and do the clerical work. Dr. Somellera might have had this position but he preferred to turn it over to Dr. Francia, since he himself wanted to leave Asunción and return to his home in Buenos Aires.[9]

---

[5] Charles A. Washburn, *The history of Paraguay,* I, 141, 146-150.
[6] *Ibid.,* 153-156.
[7] *Ibid.,* 140.
[8] *Ibid.,* 157-8; Carlos Navarro y Lamarca, II, 810.
[9] Washburn, I, 159; Navarro y Lamarca, II, 811.

Had Dr. Somellera consented to remain in control, Paraguay might have thrown in its lot with the remainder of the viceroyalty, for the revolution at Ascunción had been made in the name of the ideas proclaimed by Buenos Aires in 1810. Left to himself, however, Dr. Francia called a hand-picked congress which met from June 17 to 20, 1810, to approve his plans, and issued a declaration of independence not only from Spain but from Buenos Aires as well. Congress then appointed a *junta* of five, consisting of Yegros as president, and Caballero, Dr. Francia, Dr. Fernando Mira, and a priest named Boyardín as members. Francia, fearing that he might lose control of this enlarged body, withdrew from it, well knowing that they could not get along without him, permitting Gregorio de la Cerda to be appointed in his place.[10]

When, therefore, in 1813 an envoy from Buenos Aires arrived for the purpose of making a treaty of commerce and amity and it was seen that no one in the *junta* was clever enough to prevent Buenos Aires from getting more than the Paraguayans were willing to concede, Dr. Francia seized this opportunity to convince the people that he was indispensable in their government. He won over the troops and forced his own reinstatement in the *junta* as a practical dictator. Cerda and Mira were dismissed from the *junta,* and Dr. Somellera, who was still in the country, was thrown into prison.[11]

A year later the *junta* convoked a congress of representatives from all the towns. This congress proved to be a farce, for it was dominated by Francia who induced it to abolish the *junta* and appoint himself and Yegros consuls. Having thus reduced the ruling power of the country to a board of two men, of which he shared half the power, Francia then outwitted the slow-thinking Yegros and forced the deputies to appoint himself dictator for three years. During these three years Francia made himself invaluable, so that his lease of power was extended from time to time and the three years grew into twenty-five. From 1814 to 1840, when he died, Dr. Francia ruled Paraguay with an iron hand. He succeeded in maintaining its independence, but he made it a hermit nation cut off from Buenos Aires and the rest of the world and ruled by the whims of its dictator.[12]

While Belgrano was fighting and negotiating in Paraguay, events on the eastern shore of the Uruguay River had become so complicated that

---

[10] Washburn, I, 186; Rodney and Graham, 96, 345-349; Mitre, *Belgrano,* I, 301-302; Mary W. Williams, *People and politics of Latin America,* 305.

[11] Washburn, I, 177-197.

[12] Navarro y Lamarca, II, 812-814.

they necessitated his attention, and in 1811 he was sent by the Buenos Aires *junta* to assist the Uruguayan patriots who at that time were besieging Montevideo in an attempt to wrest it from the royalists. Shortly thereafter, however, Belgrano was recalled to explain the failure of his recent campaign in Paraguay, and the command of the Buenos Aires troops was entrusted to his second-in-command, Colonel José Rondeau.

To explain why Buenos Aires was offering this help to the patriots of Uruguay, it will be necessary to go back three years to September 21, 1808, when a *cabildo abierto* at Montevideo, influenced by the royal governor, Francisco Javier de Elío, had refused to accept a governor sent by the viceroy at Buenos Aires and had declared the independence of the Province of the Eastern Shore from the viceroyalty. While this declaration was apparently an act of disloyalty, it was in reality an effort of the royalists in Uruguay to counteract the Creole influence of Buenos Aires, which was tending toward eventual separation from the mother country.

Montevideo, in fact, remained loyal to Spain after the events of May 25 in Buenos Aires and was, therefore, made the capital of the viceroyalty with Elío as viceroy. There were, however, a large minority of Creoles in this capital who resented the obedience of the new viceroy to the Supreme Council of Regency in Spain[13] and preferred to accept the invitation of the Revolutionary *Junta* to unite with the other La Plata provinces in supporting Buenos Aires in its war on the Spanish authorities. Secretly, many of these patriots organized themselves into a Nationalist Party plotting to overthrow the viceroy and supplant the royalists, but their efforts proved futile until a capable military leader was found in José Gervasio Artigas.

Artigas, who had grown up as an irresponsible *gaucho* chieftain, now held a royal commission as captain of *blandengues* (militia lancers) and was biding his time until he could join the patriots with whose ideas of home rule he had long sympathized.[14]

This opportunity occurred on February 28, 1811, when two patriots, Pedro Viera and Venancio Benavídez, declared their hostility to Spanish domination in the famous *Grito de Ascencio* (Battle Cry of Ascencio).

---

[13] The Supreme Council of Regency was the successor of the Central *Junta*, which claimed authority to rule all Spain and its colonies in the name of Ferdinand VII.

[14] Artigas recognized no other law than his own will, and if he accepted any superior authority, he did not give up the privilege of attacking or not attacking as he saw fit. F. A. Berra, *Bosquejo histórico de la República Oriental*, 406.

With a hundred followers they seized the towns of Mercedes and
Soriano, whereupon their numbers were rapidly augmented by patriots
from other towns and militia organizations of the departments.[15] When
the Cry of Ascencio echoed through the Eastern Shore, Artigas, who
was in communication with the Nationalist leaders, deserted from his
command and fled to Buenos Aires, whence he returned with an escort
of 150 *patricios*[16] who had joined him there.

On landing near Colonia, Artigas was acclaimed as the "First Chief
of the People of the Eastern Shore" and sent out eloquent proclamations
urging all Uruguayans to stand together and obey their patriot leaders.[17]
Having organized his troops and having set out from his headquarters
at Mercedes, he was marching toward Montevideo when at Las Piedras
on May 18, 1811, he met and defeated a superior force of royalists sent
against him by Elío.

The victory of Las Piedras not only aroused the enthusiasm of the
patriots and increased their confidence in their leader, but gave them
the military advantage of confining the royalist troops to their defenses
in Montevideo and Colonia, the latter of which Benavídez had been sent
to seize and establish as a base for easy communication with Montevideo, and around the former of which Artigas had drawn his lines of
investment. It was at this point that Belgrano and his successor, Rondeau, joined Artigas with their troops from Buenos Aires, ostensibly
to aid him, but actually to assume control of the operations against the
last Spanish viceroy. In spite of this blow to his prestige and self-
esteem, Artigas then displayed the nobility of his character by declining
an offer from Elío to promote him to be a general in the Spanish army
and to give him a large sum of money, if he would return to the royalist
army.[18] Immediately after assuming command, Rondeau increased the
activities of the patriot army against Montevideo by confiscating quantities of powder stored by the royalists on an island in the harbor, by
mounting additional guns, and by bombarding the city.

Elío, finding himself hard pressed, and looking about for a source
from which aid might come to raise the siege, was glad to welcome a
Portuguese army of 4,000 men under General Diego de Souza which in

---

[15] *Ibid.*

[16] A colonial militia organization composed of young men from the best families
of Buenos Aires.

[17] The prestige and popularity of Artigas among the *gauchos* of the provinces
attracted to his revolutionary columns large numbers of followers.

[18] A. D. de Pascual, *Apuntes para la historia de la República Oriental del
Uruguay*, 6-8.

July 1811 had invaded the Eastern Shore from Brazil, and, after having seized some border towns and forts, had advanced to Maldonado. This army had been sent to enforce allegiance by the Princess Joaquina Carlotta, sister of Ferdinand VII, who claimed that she was heir to the throne of Spain, now that her brother was unable to occupy it. It so happened that the Princess Carlotta was also queen of Portugal and with the king of that country had been driven out of Lisbon by Napoleon. The exiled Portuguese court having been established at Rio de Janeiro, it was a comparatively easy matter to send Portuguese troops from Brazil.

Because of reverses suffered by its army in Upper Peru, necessitating the concentration of its forces, the Buenos Aires government consented to withdraw its troops from before Montevideo and to recognize the authority of Spain over the Eastern Shore, provided the Portuguese troops also should be withdrawn.[19]

In spite of this agreement, however, General Souza did not immediately withdraw, but under the pretext of pacifying the country dispersed his men throughout the Eastern Shore, permitting them to devastate it and to commit every kind of atrocity, without meeting any opposition except that from the Uruguayan generals and troops which Artigas was able to detach for that purpose. Artigas himself, angered at the terms of this armistice by which Buenos Aires had abandoned the Uruguayans to the vengeance of the royalists, then marched toward the north with his main body, followed by the whole mass of inhabitants, amounting to nearly 16,000, who preferred to abandon their homes rather than again support the yoke of Spain. Even four hundred Charrua Indians joined in this emigration, which is known in history as the "Exodus of the People of the Eastern Shore" (*Exodo del pueblo oriental*).

When, however, after a new treaty had been made whereby the Portuguese agreed to evacuate the Eastern Shore, and Artigas had been persuaded to return and rejoin Rondeau in a renewal of the siege of Montevideo, it soon became evident that Buenos Aires was less interested in defeating the royalists than in trying to use Artigas for the purpose of regaining the allegiance of the Province of the Eastern Shore to the Plata confederation.

To forestall these maneuvers, when it became evident that the Spaniards must eventually withdraw, Artigas resolved to call an assembly for the purpose of organizing a national government. This First Na-

---

[19] For the provisions of this armistice see Pascual, I, 15-16.

tional Congress adopted a constitution, designated Artigas military governor and president, and agreed to recognize the National Constituent Assembly recently established in Buenos Aires on condition that the latter should respect the autonomy of Uruguay. Under the pretext, however, that the delegates sent by Uruguay lacked sufficient powers, their admission to the Buenos Aires Assembly was refused and a new congress was called by Rondeau, which elected new delegates unrestricted by conditions and deposed Artigas from his office of governor of the province.

Artigas, however, remained firm in his conviction that it was as important that the Eastern Shore maintain its independence of Buenos Aires as it was that it should win its independence from Spain, so he, convinced that Montevideo would fall to the besiegers sooner or later without his aid, led his troops out of their lines and deserted Rondeau on the night of January 20, 1814. Of this desertion Zorilla de San Martín says:[20]

> "If Artigas had remained in the besieging lines until the end of the siege; if he had resigned himself to enter Montevideo in the magnificent train of Alvear; if he had not saved in his own person, in his ideals, and in the army of Uruguayans which followed him, the idea and nucleus of resistance of the Uruguayan people against the spirit of skepticism of Buenos Aires; it is proved by every bit of evidence that neither this republic would have been born on the shores of La Plata, nor would we exist today as an independent people. We would be Portuguese!"

Thereafter, Artigas, proclaimed a traitor, openly fought Buenos Aires by crossing the Uruguay River and inducing the Paraná provinces of Corrientes, Entre Ríos, Santa Fé, and Córdoba to join a Federal League against Buenos Aires. So successful was Artigas in his military operations that he drove the Buenos Aires troops out of Montevideo, which had been occupied by them since the Spanish had surrendered to Rondeau on June 23, 1814. It was true that Spanish rule had been brought to an end on the Eastern Shore, but that was not enough for Artigas, who insisted on absolute independence from any foreign rule.

Prior to its loss of Montevideo, Buenos Aires, rather than yield to Artigas and the Federal League, had treacherously invited Portugal to renew its invasion of the Eastern Shore, and General Francisco Lecor, with 10,000 Portuguese troops, had marched across the Brazilian fron-

---

[20] Quoted by H. D., *Ensayo de historia patria*, 343-4, from *La epopeya de Artigas*.

tier. Having kept up a valiant fight against these new invaders for two years, Artigas and his generals met several disastrous defeats in 1816.

The bitterest blow came on November 19, when Fructuoso Rivera was overwhelmed at the battle of India Muerta, and Lecor succeeded in entering Montevideo on January 20, 1817. Nevertheless, Artigas for a whole year longer kept up hopeless opposition to the invaders in the north, until he was overwhelmed by superior numbers of the enemy at Tacuarembó.

Thereupon, his own allies from Entre Ríos and Santa Fé turned against him, and at last, when he had exhausted all his efforts, he was forced to yield to overwhelming odds and to give up the struggle. On September 23, 1820, Artigas with only forty followers, the last remnant of his former power, crossed into Paraguay and sought the hospitality of the dictator Francia. There, in lonely exile, Artigas remained until his death on September 23, 1850.

In June 1821 the Eastern Shore was annexed as the Cisplatine Province to Brazil, which had by that time secured its independence from Portugal. So resentful, however, were the inhabitants at Brazilian rule that they preferred to reconsider throwing in their lot with Buenos Aires.[21] Indeed, among the numerous Uruguayans living in exile at Buenos Aires were Juan Antonio Lavalleja and thirty-two others, the "Immortal Thirty-Three," who had visions of liberating their fatherland with the aid of Buenos Aires. On the 19th of April 1825 these men, under the leadership of Lavalleja, crossed the river and landed again on the Eastern Shore at the little port of Las Vacas. There they were joined by Colonel Fructuoso Rivera who commanded a regiment of Uruguayan cavalry in the service of Brazil but who, when he saw an opportunity to free his country from Brazil, deserted to the patriots and led his regiment after him. Small forces of Brazilians, taken by surprise, were cut off and besieged in La Colonia, and other minor successes rapidly followed, permitting the insurgents to organize a government, convoke a Provincial Assembly, and to declare independence. In return for aid sent by the Argentine Republic, the authority of the latter was recognized and on October 25, 1825, after the victory of Sarandí, the Province of the Eastern Shore was incorporated in the United Provinces of Río de la Plata.[22]

In the war which ensued between the United Provinces and Brazil

---

[21] Navarro y Lamarca, *Compendio de la historia general de América*, II, 804-805.
[22] *Ibid.*, II, 806-807.

the latter was defeated at the battle of Ituzaingó on February 20, 1827, and a treaty of peace was signed which left the Banda Oriental under Brazil. So unnecessary and unpopular was this treaty that President Bernardino Rivadavia of the United Provinces was forced to resign and war was resumed. In 1828, however, upon the intervention of the British minister, a treaty was agreed upon whereby neither Argentina nor Brazil retained sovereignty, but the complete independence of the Republic of Uruguay was recognized by both.[23] Thus, until the signing of this treaty, the independence of Uruguay, subject in succession to Spain, Buenos Aires, Portugal, and Brazil, was not effected until eighteen years after the *junta* at Buenos Aires had begun its efforts to secure the adhesion of the other provinces of the Viceroyalty of La Plata. To continue the history of La Plata it will be necessary to return to that period.

II. Argentina. San Martín and the Army of the Andes

After his failure to induce the people of Paraguay to unite their fortunes with those of Río de la Plata, and his recall from Uruguay, Belgrano was sent with his army into Upper Peru to wrest that province from the control of the viceroy of Peru. Although he received considerable assistance from the patriots there, he found that the towering bulwarks of the Andes gave most effective aid to the royalist troops who held them. In spite of success in the lower foothills in driving the royalists back, as he advanced further into the mountains he met a serious check at Vilcapugio in 1813 and was so badly defeated at Ayohuma that he had to abandon the campaign, his failure necessitating his relief from command and the substitution of a more skillful general to carry on his work.[24]

The government of the United Provinces of La Plata did not have far to seek, because just at that time a victorious general had returned from the campaign against the Eastern Shore to receive the plaudits of his fellow citizens in Buenos Aires. His recent victory at San Lorenzo was little more than a skirmish, but it was spectacular and it was a victory at a time when the patriots were discouraged by defeats. Its effect on the history of Argentina is out of all proportion to its real importance, for it gave to the cause of independence one of its two greatest

[23] *Ibid.*, II, 807; Wilgus, 362.

[24] Pilling-Mitre, 60-61; Bartolomé Mitre, *Historia de Belgrano,* II, 210-213, 241-249.

heroes. At this battle of San Lorenzo, José de San Martín, then colonel of the mounted grenadiers, defended the monastery of San Carlos near San Lorenzo on the Paraná and defeated a night attack by two hundred and fifty royalists landing from a ship on the river. During the *mêlée* San Martín nearly lost his life, for his horse was shot and fell on him, pinning him by the leg; but just as a Spanish soldier was about to bayonet him, one of the grenadiers, a negro (known in history and tradition as *El Negro Primero*), rescued him from his predicament, only himself to fall pierced by two mortal wounds. In this skirmish fifteen of his grenadiers were killed and twenty-seven were wounded, but San Martín had accomplished his mission of preventing the enemy from invading the territory of the United Provinces.[25] Such was the prestige won that he was promptly given command of two additional squadrons of mounted grenadiers, a hundred artillerymen, and a battalion of infantry and sent to Upper Peru to relieve Belgrano from command.[26]

San Martín found himself in command of only 2,000 men, mostly undisciplined recruits, called the Army of the North, which comprised the defeated remnants of Belgrano's army, patriots from Upper Peru under Arenales who had been more or less successful in holding their own against the royalists, and some Indians and patriots under Colonel Ignacio Warnes, governor of Santa Cruz de la Sierra, as well as his own troops from Buenos Aires.[27] This force was disorganized, short of officers, badly clothed, and unable to drive out of the mountains the royalist troops who were inured to that kind of fighting and who numbered about four thousand regulars and between two and three thousand mountaineers. San Martín, therefore, assumed the defensive, constructed an intrenched camp or citadel at Tucumán, and furnished aid to the patriots of the provinces at the portals of the road to Upper Peru, where he devoted most of his attention to stopping the desertion of his recruits and training his troops by means of strenuous drill and schools of instruction in the art of war.[28] By these methods he succeeded in putting up such a strong defense that he defeated an attempted invasion by the royalist general, Pezuela.[29]

Thus, although San Martín had again saved the government of the United Provinces and had checked the advance of the royalists through

---

[25] Pilling-Mitre, 54-60; Colonel Carlos Smith, *San Martín hasta el paso de los Andes*, 75, 80; Mitre, *Belgrano*, II, 278, 280.

[26] Pilling-Mitre, 62.

[27] *Ibid.*, 66-67.

[28] *Ibid.*, 72-73.

[29] Pilling-Mitre, 75-78; Smith, 91, 96-97.

Upper Peru, he had proved to himself that his own invasion of that province was impracticable, even though the destruction of the power of the viceroy in Peru was essential to the preservation of the safety of the revolted provinces. To secure the coöperation of as many provinces as possible against the power of Spain, the *junta* of the United Provinces of La Plata had sent envoys to neighboring provinces, even outside of the former Viceroyalty of La Plata. To spread the principles of self-government and to secure the alliance of the Captaincy-General of Chile which, although a near neighbor, formed part of the Viceroyalty of Peru, an envoy, Antonio Álvarez Jonte, had been sent to Santiago to arouse the patriots there.[30] Although the revolutionary government which had been set up in Chile, as will be described later, was weakened by internal dissensions and was tottering to its fall, San Martín had visions of utilizing the spirit of patriotism there which destined him to become the saviour of the independence of the whole of southern South America.

When he had come to the realization that he could not break through the mountain barriers of Upper Peru to defeat the viceroy's army, San Martín, with a strategical instinct far superior to that of any of the previous generals or statesmen of Buenos Aires, conceived of an alternative plan by which he might not only preserve the safety of the United Provinces of La Plata but also secure the liberation of Chile and Peru as well by destroying the power of the royalists in the Viceroyalty of Peru. This plan was to withdraw his army from Upper Peru, leaving only small detachments of mountaineers to block the passes into La Plata, and to reorganize his army with the purpose of crossing the Andes into Chile where less royalist opposition was to be expected; then, having aided the patriots in Chile to maintain their independence, he would secure their assistance to transport his army by sea for the liberation of Peru.[31]

Having secured the approval of the supreme director at Buenos Aires for this plan, San Martín was appointed governor of Cuyo, a border province on the eastern slopes of the Andes. To Mendoza, the capital of that province, he removed his headquarters where, having assumed both civil and military command, he devoted all his time, thought, and effort to the furtherance of his plan. He arranged with General Ber-

---

[30] Robertson, *Rise of the Spanish American republics,* 155.

[31] A. Stuart M. Chisholm, *The independence of Chile,* 122, 123, 127-129; Pilling-Mitre, 78, 82, 84-87; Smith, 97.

nardo O'Higgins, leader of the Chilean refugees, for their coöperation; he recruited large numbers of mountaineers from the vicinity for his Army of the Andes; he used his own regular troops as instructors and disciplinarians; and he secured funds by inducing the local *cabildos* to levy taxes by imposing forced loans upon Spanish and Portuguese residents, by fines for infractions of the law, and by voluntary gifts from enthusiastic patriots. Most of this money went to the support and equipment of his troops, but he spent enough on schools, irrigation, and other public projects, to keep the good will of the inhabitants. Fortunately for the success of the project, Juan de Pueyrredón, the supreme director of La Plata, who was a friend of San Martín ready to aid him to the utmost of his ability, gave orders increasing the monthly allowance to San Martín from 5,000 to 8,000 *pesos,* and also sent him experienced officers and reënforcements for the Buenos Aires regiments.[32] Another piece of good fortune was the presence in Mendoza of Fray Luís Beltrán, a young Franciscan brother who had educated himself in all branches of mathematics, physics, chemistry, and mechanics. Although he had entered the army as chaplain, he was detailed to organize the ordnance department and to establish an arsenal, which he did with such skill and success that he was able with three hundred laborers to construct whatever San Martín needed in the way of guns and their carriages and to keep worn-out small arms in repair.[33] San Martín, who was firm but just in all his dealings with his subordinates, made no man work harder than himself. From early morning until nightfall he was at his desk or else busy inspecting the progress of equipping and training of his troops. Although he generally retired early, if his chronic illness kept him awake he would pass the remainder of the night in further work on his plans. He ate sparingly and dressed simply in the plain uniform of the mounted grenadiers. He lived a lonely life, for he had few friends and confidants, yet he was respected by all who came in contact with him for his high aims and well-directed energy. He, like Washington and Bolívar, gained the highest position in the esteem of his compatriots by the nobility of his personal character and the firmness of his determination never to yield to obstacles.[34]

News of his doings must necessarily reach the royalists in Chile, but San Martín took care that any information about his plans which came to them might be distorted and misleading. By arranging that incorrect

---

[32] Bartolomé Mitre, *Historia de San Martín,* I, 558-560; Pilling-Mitre, 113.
[33] Mitre, *San Martín,* I, 534-535.
[34] Pilling-Mitre, 113-116.

despatches should fall into their hands, he frightened the royalist generals, Osorio and Marcó del Pont, with threats of immediate invasion of southern Chile, and caused them to scatter their forces and to strengthen the defenses of the southern passes. He gained information of their movements and spread false reports regarding his own by means of spies and secret agents whom he sent into Chile, for which purpose he often used Chilean refugees of prominence whom he had arrested on some charge of treachery and then aided to escape back into Chile.[35]

When Martín Rodríguez started an abortive revolution in the south of Chile which had no part in San Martín's plans, the latter wrote censuring him for attracting the royalist forces to occupy the passes in the south, sending this despatch in such a way that it would inevitably be captured by the royalist patrols. By these means San Martín drew the attention of the royalist commanders constantly to the south, while he himself made all his preparations to cross the Andes by the more difficult northern passes. In order to reconnoiter these passes, an aide-de-camp, Álvarez de Condarco, who was instructed to trust nothing to paper but to bring back in his head route maps of both passes, was sent by Los Patos pass to the governor of Chile with a copy of the Declaration of Independence of La Plata recently signed at Tucumán, for San Martín rightly expected that this paper would be unwelcome to the governor and that his messenger would be sent back by the other road, the Uspallata Pass, which was shorter.[36] As a further measure of mystifying Marcó del Pont, San Martín called a council of the Indians who lived on the eastern slopes of the southern passes, and bought from them, by means of presents, permission to march his army unmolested through their country. As had been anticipated, information of this treaty was soon brought to the ears of the royalist commander, causing him to scatter the forces which he should have concentrated for the defense of the capital.[37]

Still further to delude the enemy, San Martín's plan of campaign involved the use of six different passes. The main body was to cross through the Uspallata and Los Patos passes, while small detachments of militia and volunteers were sent into the northern provinces of Chile by other passes. The most northernly of these forces consisted of Chilean miners and about two hundred poorly armed and clothed volunteers under Nicolás Dávila and Francisco Zelada which was to set out

---

[35] Agustín Edwards, *The dawn*, 84-89.
[36] Pilling-Mitre, 129-130; Mitre, *San Martín*, I, 580-581.
[37] Pilling-Mitre, 134-135.

from Rioja in Argentina, cross the Come Caballo pass, and fall upon the district of Copiapó, a place reported to be weakly defended. The second column of invasion composed of seventy soldiers of the line, some four hundred militia of San Juan, and a patriotic legion of more than one hundred Chilean emigrées, well-armed and officered, was to start from San Juan under command of Lieutenant-Colonel Juan Manuel Cabot, cross through the pass of Azufre, advancing cautiously, not risking a serious fight, but taking advantage of any favorable opportunity, and was then to occupy La Serena.[38] Meanwhile, two more detachments were to threaten the royalists through the southern passes. Captain José León Lemus, in command of Fort San Carlos, was to take twenty-five soldiers of the line from his garrison and a small detachment of militia from Mendoza, cross by the pass of Pinguenes, and advance cautiously until he could be seen by the royalists who guarded the banks of the Maipú River. He should not risk a fight but should so maneuver as to deceive the royalists into believing that he was the advance guard of an army of invasion coming through this pass to attack Santiago from the south. Finally, in order to cause the enemy to concentrate in the south for the defense of that part of Chile, Major Ramón Freire with eighty mounted infantry and twenty-five mounted grenadiers was to make a raid through del Planchon pass, and aided by Chilean guerillas, make a feint against the towns of San Fernando, Curicó, and Talca.[39]

The only feature of the campaign which was left to chance was reliance on the patriotic population of Chile to aid these small detachments. All else was arranged with meticulous care. "This combination admirably prepared in all its details, presupposed the regular march of six corps of troops separated by distances more or less considerable, almost without communications between them, but advancing parallel and according to a uniform plan to scale the mountains and to arrive in the valleys of Chile at a fixed time on the same day."[40]

In order that these six different columns might operate as a single machine, San Martín gave to the leader of each column the most minute instructions. He prescribed the length of each day's march and indicated where food, forage, water, and firewood were to be obtained; he figured out in advance, from information based on preliminary surveys of the terrain, the time that would be lost in constructing bridges and in crossing difficult precipices, and his time-table foresaw and allowed for

---

[38] Barros Arana, X, 539.
[39] Ibid., X, 540.
[40] Ibid., 538.

all possible delays.[41]   In spite of these minute instructions, all divisions of the army were kept in touch with each other and with the commanding general by means of couriers selected from among trustworthy Chilean muleteers who knew every trail or possible footpath. The length of the march prescribed for each day was made short in order to give necessary rest to the troops, and although all the men were mounted on mules, the soldiers were expected to walk part way in order to rest their mounts and to limber their own muscles.[42]   In order to hide the movements of the main body from the enemy, its march was conducted with extra caution.

The Uspallata pass was chosen as the only one practicable for artillery and train. On this, a division of eight hundred men (one battalion of infantry, thirty grenadiers, and thirty artillerymen with two mountain guns) led the way. Then came the artillery pack and baggage train escorted by a squadron of militia from San Luís, accompanied by sappers and miners charged with the repair of the road where necessary. This whole force was under the command of Juan Gregorio de las Heras and was sufficient to begin action with any detachments of royalists it might find in the way, to take by assault the guard which held the exit of the pass, and to advance thence on Santa Rosa de los Andes at the time fixed in its instructions.[43]

San Martín himself, with his staff, rode over Los Patos, while the troops using the same road went in two divisions of about equal strength marching at an interval of one day's journey. The first division was commanded by General Soler, and the second by General O'Higgins. It was planned that both divisions should occupy the town of San Felipe de Aconcagua on the same day that Las Heras should take possession of Santa Rosa de los Andes.[44]

In ten days of marching Las Heras was to cover the sixty-three leagues between Mendoza and Santa Rosa, while in seventeen days the hundred and five leagues over Los Patos were to be accomplished.[45] The movement was so planned that in case the enemy tried to interpose himself between these two forces he would be struck simultaneously in rear and flank by forces amounting to about 4,087 men.[46]

---

[41] *Ibid.*, 541.

[42] *Ibid.*, 546, 548.

[43] *Ibid.*, 541.

[44] *Ibid.*, 541.

[45] Hans Bertling, *Documentos históricos referentes al paso de los Andes*, Doc. 97, annexo 2 and 3.

[46] Bertling, Doc. 102. This total comprised 241 artillery, 560 riflemen, 2795 infantry, 742 mounted grenadiers, and 209 officers of all arms.

To keep the enemy's forces engaged and to prevent them from falling upon the patriots on the mountain trails, Chilean guerillas were employed so that Marcó del Pont had to concentrate almost all his troops around Santiago and to abandon the Province of Concepción to its own resources. The independent marches of these six columns of the Army of the Andes were conducted with the synchronism of clockwork, and all San Martín's plans worked out to perfection.[47]

In the north, the royalist commanders were taken by surprise and were unable to cope with the uprisings of Chilean patriots who welcomed the invaders. On the night of February 12, the first column of invasion succeeded in capturing Copiapó by surprise and with little bloodshed.[48] On February 6, the column which had set out from San Juan had crossed its pass and was in the valley in a position to threaten La Serena, where in anticipation of this aid from across the mountains a patriot government had been set up by the local *cabildo,* and the royalist commander, Colonel Manuel Santa María, had been frightened into abandoning the city. On his retreat toward Santiago he was attacked and defeated by Colonel Cabot, who thereupon entered La Serena without further opposition. As a politician Colonel Cabot was not as good as he was a soldier, for he interfered in the newly established government and so disturbed the tranquillity of the Chilean patriots that he was later relieved of command and recalled. He had, however, accomplished his mission and northern Chile was in the hands of the patriots.[49]

In the south, although Captain Lemus with his little scouting party was at first successful in deceiving the royalist detachments guarding the southern pass, soon, however, before he had reached the exit of his pass, his weakness was discovered and he had to withdraw to Los Pinguanes. Colonel Freire, however, was fully successful and so magnified the importance of his two hundred men that reports were sent to Santiago that the invasion was coming from the south. On February 3, by a surprise night attack, he dispersed the royalist force defending Campeo, and then withdrew for four days into the mountains where he augmented his force with 600 Chilean guerillas, sent out patrols to harass the royalists, and spread reports that O'Higgins was coming. He sowed such confusion and alarm that royalist troops were aimlessly marched back and forth between Santiago and the south, until finally authentic news was received of San Martín's real invasion. Then, on February 7, all

[47] Barros Arana, X, 538.
[48] *Ibid.,* 562.
[49] *Ibid.,* 565-570.

royalist troops were ordered to concentrate on Santiago for the protection of the capital. This left Freire in control of the south where patriot governments were set up in San Fernando, Curicó, and Talca; and by February 12, all this region had refused obedience to the government of Marcó del Pont.[50]

In spite of the difficulties to be surmounted, the march of the main body over the two longest passes was carried out exactly as had been planned. The negro soldiers and those from the Argentine *pampas* suffered intensely from the cold and from the lack of oxygen at the high altitudes, but the Chilean and Argentine mountaineers, many of whom were in the army, knew how to relieve those who suffered from *soroche* (mountain sickness) by bleeding the patient, by giving him to eat certain vegetables (probably onions and garlic) which appeared to supply more oxygen to the body,[51] or by dosing him with brandy and wine, a supply of which had been laid in at Mendoza—all of which measures proved effective in stimulating the soldiers who suffered from cold and *soroche*.

Las Heras met some opposition in the Uspallata pass and had a successful skirmish at Potrerillos with a royalist scouting party which had driven in the patriot outpost at Picheuta.[52] The royalist guard detachments at Guardia Vieja in the Uspallata pass and at Guardia de Achupallas in Los Patos were easily overwhelmed and captured, although some of their members managed to escape and to carry reports of the invasion to Colonel de Otero, the local commander at San Felipe, who hurried off a messenger to Santiago calling for reënforcements.[53] When Putaendo had been occupied by the invaders who were welcomed by the peasants and aided with food supplies, a council of war was held by the royalist commander in San Felipe. Colonel Otero did his best to stand his ground, but when the council, fearing that the royalist troops would be cut off in the rear by peasants, decided to withdraw beyond the Cuesta de Chacabuco, a high range of hills south of San Felipe, he was forced to accede. His retreat soon became a rout, and by February 6 there was not a soldier left in San Felipe. Two days later San Martín and O'Higgins entered that city amidst the acclamations of the inhabitants. On that very same day Santa Rosa de los Andes was entered by Las Heras with little opposition. Las Heras immediately pushed on to

---

[50] *Ibid.*, 570-575.
[51] *Ibid.*, 548.
[52] Mitre, *San Martín*, X, 614-615.
[53] Barros Arana, X, 554-555.

occupy the hills of Chacabuco after having repaired the bridge which the royalists had destroyed on their retreat from San Felipe. As soon as this was completed, San Martín ordered the advance of the divisions from San Felipe, and that night (exactly as had been planned) the whole army was united and encamped at Curimón within sight of the enemy's camp fires.[54]

The successful execution of San Martín's plans can only be attributed to his careful preparations and the excellent discipline of his troops. To march an army across mountains 12,000 feet high over a narrow pass suitable only for mules and mountaineers on foot is in itself a remarkable proceeding; but to send that army by divisions through six different passes over a frontage of 1,300 miles and to retain such perfect control over it that the separate divisions were able to concentrate at the point selected and on the date fixed, seems unbelievable. Yet San Martín actually made his army do this. He lost 6,000 mules and two-thirds of his horses, but he brought all his guns across.[55] Even though it suffered intensely from the cold and from the rarefaction of the air, this army emerged from its hardships an effective fighting machine. The details of similar sufferings endured by troops in crossing the high Andes will be described in relating Bolívar's campaign in New Granada. Both Bolívar and San Martín deserve equal credit for their hardihood, determination, and inflexible will power in their crossings of the Andes, but the exploit of San Martín seems to excel, in that troops and commanders separated from his immediate supervision retained the discipline which he had instilled in them to such a degree as to carry out his plans without the slightest deviation in spite of difficulties and hardships which only grit and indomitable will power could overcome.

At Curimón San Martín rested and reorganized his troops, gathered supplies and remounts, and reconnoitered the trails through the ridge toward the *hacienda* of Chacabuco where the royalists were encamped. One of the spies whom he had sent into Santiago to learn the results of the movements of his other four columns returned with the information that all territory to the south between the Cachapoal and the Maule rivers was in revolt against royal authority, that the patriots were absolute masters of Comarco, that royalist forces had everywhere retreated to Santiago, that 2,000 troops had been sent north from the capital to Chacabuco, and that 1,000 more would start soon.

---

[54] *Ibid.*, 555-561.

[55] *Ibid.*, 142.

In order to forestall the arrival of these royalist reënforcements, San Martín hurriedly decided that he must make his attack at once and not wait until the 14th as he had planned. Thus, two days before schedule, on the night of February 11-12, he ordered his troops to advance to battle.[56]

For the battle of Chacabuco the Army of the Andes was formed in two divisions. The first division, 2,000 strong under O'Higgins, was to advance through the hills by means of a ravine leading directly to the *hacienda* of Chacabuco. It was to drive back the enemy outposts and then make a frontal attack, while the second division (1,400 men) under Soler was to follow another ravine which twisted around the hills and peaks, and was to strike the left flank of the enemy near the *hacienda*. San Martín kept only a small reserve of one hundred militia. The line of march of the two divisions, both of which contained artillery and capable guides, was separated by about two kilometers, so that, because of the darkness of the night, coördination of their movements was difficult.[57]

By 8 a.m. on the 12th of February, O'Higgins had driven in the royalist outposts under Major Marqueli and held the crest of the ridge. Thus warned, the royalist General Maroto occupied his prepared line of defense on the level ground in front of the *hacienda* where the ravines debouched from the hills—a very strong position, since both its flanks were protected by the hills and the enemy emerging from the ravines had little space in which to deploy. Another advantage enjoyed by the royalists was due to the presence of the reënforcements which had arrived from Santiago during the night.[58]

O'Higgins ordered his cavalry to charge the left flank of the enemy, but this proved impossible because of the roughness of the hilly ground. Likewise, the advance of the patriot infantry was slowed down by the difficulties of following the *barranca,* until a halt had to be ordered to repel detachments of the royalists which had been sent forward to harass the entangled patriots. San Martín, seeing the critical situation in which this division was involved, despatched urgent messages to Soler to hasten his advance. In spite of the oppressive heat which made further expenditure of effort on the part of any troops seem impossible, O'Higgins ordered a second charge at 10 a.m. He himself led the infantry, including many negroes who had been freed from slavery at Mendoza,

---

[56] Barros Arana, X, 592-594; Mitre, *San Martín,* I, 624.
[57] Edwards, 118.
[58] Barros Arana, X 598-600.

in a bayonet attack in which they fell on the enemy's line with shout
of victory. After another attack by patriot cavalry on the right flank
O'Higgins pushed on to victory. The royalists tried to form square
but just then Soler's men burst through the underbrush and fell on thei
left flank. The royalist troops could no longer defend their position
They broke and fled in disorder four leagues to the southward, wher
they scattered in all directions. Maroto himself was wounded, but man
aged to change horses and to escape to the capital. The royalists los
five hundred killed, while the patriots suffered only one hundred an
fifty killed and wounded although they captured seven hundred prisoners
two cannon, one thousand muskets, the flag of the Battalion of Chile
and all the royalist munitions.[59]

When on the night of February 12 the news of their defeat at Chaca
buco reached Santiago, Marcó del Pont and all royalist officials aban
doned the capital in the utmost haste and fled toward Valparaiso
O'Higgins, believing that this victory would gain all Chile, asked to be
allowed to lead a force to cut off the retreat of the royalists, but Sa
Martín preferred to keep the army together to resist another attack
Since this did not come, San Martín and O'Higgins together entered
Santiago two days later at the head of the victorious Army of the
Andes.[60]

San Martín placed himself and his troops at the service of the provisional government of liberated Chile, but declined to accept appointment
as chief of the state. Thereupon, an assembly of notables unanimously
acclaimed O'Higgins Supreme Director.[61] To understand the popularity
of O'Higgins, it will be well to review briefly his part in early movements for the independence of Chile.

III. The Independence of Chile

The captain-general of Chile in 1810, Francisco García Carrasco, a
stubborn headstrong man of limited intelligence and vacillating character, was influenced largely by his secretary, Dr. Juan Martínez de
Rozas, a liberal strongly inspired with new ideas of popular self-
government. In order to increase the importance of the *Cabildo* of
Santiago, Rozas induced his superior to add to that body twelve influential citizens who were men of advanced opinions. Although he had
followed the advice of his secretary, Carrasco promptly realized the

---

[59] *Ibid.*, 601-604.
[60] *Ibid.*, 608-628.
[61] Pilling-Mitre, 148.

inadvisability of what he had done and cancelled the appointments. The opposition thereby engendered was augmented by the arrest of three leading citizens for correspondence with the revolutionaries in Buenos Aires.[62]   Hostility to the captain-general resulted in the calling of a *cabildo abierto* which forced him to rescind his order for the arrest, and to agree to submit his official acts to the supervision of representatives of the will of the people.   In spite of his promise, however, Carrasco continued to hold the prisoners in jail until the threats of eight hundred armed and angry citizens forced him to resign his power into the hands of Zambrano, Conde de la Conquista, a prominent and highly respected Chilean noble.[63]   The appointment of Zambrano as captain-general was a matter of compromise, since the Spanish party hoped to control him because of his advanced age of eighty-five years, and the patriots, although not fully satisfied, expected to influence him through councilors whom they could trust.   As will be remembered, the attitude of the patriots in Santiago was fostered and encouraged by commissioners from the *junta* of the United Provinces of La Plata until they were aroused sufficiently to follow the example of Buenos Aires and to induce the old Count to call a *cabildo abierto*.   Thus, on September 18, 1810, overawed by the militia drawn up in the plaza and armed mobs in the streets, Zambrano resigned his office as captain-general.   The *cabildo abierto* thereupon elected a governing *junta* of seven members including the old Count and Dr. Rozas.[64]   Although no attempt was then made at declaring separation from Spain, this date—September 18—is now celebrated as Chile's independence day.

Martínez de Rozas, leader of the radicals who wished for independence, was the soul of this government *junta,* and he, like Mariano and Moreno in Buenos Aires, was the most valuable intellectual contributor to the revolution.   The one, however, who furnished the most dynamic force was Bernardo O'Higgins, a wealthy landowner of southern Chile who was a natural son of Ambrosio O'Higgins, a former viceroy of Peru.   O'Higgins had organized and commanded a band of soldiers whose services he offered to the patriot government, in order to strengthen which he and Dr. Rozas advocated the sending of delegates from all the local *cabildos* of Chile to a National Congress in Santiago.[65]

"The Chilean revolution resembled that of Buenos Aires in that it

---

[62] Chisholm, 122-126.
[63] *Ibid.,* 146-147; John J. Mehegan, *O'Higgins of Chile,* 40-41.
[64] Mehegan, 42; Pilling-Mitre, 82-86.
[65] Edwards, 24-26.

was parliamentary and legal, initiated and carried out within the precincts of the municipal forum. . . . Thus from the beginning the two nations were bound together by fraternal ties and by a common cause." [66]

Rozas responded to the calls for aid from Buenos Aires and sent a few troops to help in the subjugation of Montevideo, an act which aroused the hostility of the royalists and the moderate Creoles in the *cabildo* and was taken advantage of by a military adventurer named José Miguel Carrera, who advocated separation from Spain in order that he himself might seize the reins of government. By two *coups d'état,* one in September and the other in November 1811, Carrera, with the aid of his two brothers, overthrew the National Assembly and set up a *junta* consisting of himself, O'Higgins, Rozas, and MacKenna representing the three provinces of Santiago, Concepción, and Coquimbo. Thus had Carrera supplied the overwhelming impetus that destroyed the old régime and killed the hope of reconciling the desire for liberty with scruples of loyalty to the monarch.[67]

In December, Carrera again executed a *coup d'état* against congress and made himself dictator. O'Higgins resigned and was sent as an emissary to Concepción to adjust a dispute between that province and Santiago. Rozas, who had set up an opposition *junta* representing the radicals in the south, was arrested and exiled to Mendoza, where he died a couple of years later.[68]

Such discord within the ranks of the patriots naturally weakened their resistance to royal authority, so that in order to maintain their dictatorship the Carrera brothers had to fight not only disaffection in the ranks of the patriots, but a considerable armed force of royalists which revolted in the south and on the Island of Chiloé. To the aid of these troops the viceroy of Peru had sent an army under General Pareja, who had begun a reconquest of Chile. In this campaign the Carreras revealed their lack of military skill, but at the battle of El Roble on October 17, 1813, when the day was going against the patriots and Carrera had fled in panic, O'Higgins arrived with reënforcements in time to turn defeat into victory. "Just as the revolution of 1811 may be called the advent of the Carreras, the Battle of El Roble may be called the advent of O'Higgins." [69] The latter became commander-in-chief of

[66] Pilling-Mitre, 86.

[67] Edwards, 7, 35-37.

[68] Edwards, 39-43; Pilling-Mitre, 95.

[69] Edwards, 48.

the patriot army of Chile when the fugitive Carreras were taken prisoners by the royalists.[70]

Although O'Higgins was the better general and on more than one occasion was victorious over the royalists under Gainza, he failed to receive adequate support from the government at Santiago, which left him in the lurch by negotiating the Treaty of Lircay with a royalist emissary in 1814 by which it was agreed that Chile should return to the status of the year 1811 under the rule of a provisional *junta* subject to the Regency of Spain.[71]

As one of the outcomes of this treaty, the Carrera brothers who, as will be remembered, had been captured by the royalists, were released and had returned to Santiago. Taking advantage of the confusion, José Miguel Carrera fomented a revolt among the troops and reëstablished his dictatorship to carry out the terms of the treaty. When O'Higgins attempted to march his army back to Santiago, Carrera attacked him and drove him off; and when the viceroy of Peru failed to ratify the treaty and sent more royalist troops to Chile, O'Higgins was left to oppose them single handed. On October 1-2, 1814, he was surrounded by superior forces and shut up in Rancagua where, deserted by the Carreras, he maintained a stubborn defense until his ammunition was exhausted. Then with only three hundred men he cut his way out through the whole royalist army and escaped across the Andes to Mendoza in Argentina.[72] Carrera withdrew precipitantly to Santiago, destroyed all supplies, took the public money from the treasury, and fled. Somehow he lost the money in the mountains but managed to reach Mendoza, only to find that O'Higgins was there ahead of him. Instead of standing together in their adversity, Carrera assumed imperious airs, declared O'Higgins an interloper, and asserted his own right to represent the fallen government of Chile.[73]

Meanwhile, the patriot government had been completely suppressed, and royalist power was supreme in Chile. Osorio as governor of Santiago ruled with a heavy hand, favoring the Spaniards in every way possible, and discriminating harshly against the patriots, many of whom he deported.[74] The revolution in Chile had apparently been crushed.

This is the point at which the narrative of events in Argentina and

---

[70] Barros Arana, IX, 283, 288-289; Pilling-Mitre, 103.
[71] Pilling-Mitre, 105; Barros Arana, IX, 402-405, 453-457.
[72] Pilling-Mitre, 107; Barros Arana, IX, 462, 483, 509, 572-574, 605.
[73] Edwards, 60-66; Barros Arana, IX, 589-590, 515-516.
[74] Edwards, 73; Barros Arana, IX, 617-622.

Chile come together again. As has been seen, the presence of this small force of Chilean patriots at Mendoza had important influence on the plans of San Martín. That general saw through the pretensions of Carrera and forced him to leave Mendoza. With keen judgment he selected O'Higgins as the strong man among the Chilean patriots and gave him his support. It has already been shown how O'Higgins organized a Chilean contingent from among the emigrées in Mendoza; how this contingent was incorporated in the Army of the Andes; how he and San Martín together crossed the mountain barrier into Chile; how O'Higgins struck the decisive blow at Chacabuco; and how he was chosen as Supreme Director. Thus Chile rose again under O'Higgins with the aid of San Martín.

Although during the remainder of the year 1817 and part of 1818 Freire was successfully engaged in clearing the royalists out of Chillán, Concepción, Valdivia, and other strongholds in southern Chile,[75] further reënforcements under General Mariano Osorio, sent by the viceroy of Peru had disembarked at Talcahuano and were advancing toward Santiago. Inasmuch as it had been expected that these troops would land at Valparaiso, O'Higgins, who had gone there to oppose them, was forced to withdraw again toward Santiago, marching on roads more or less converging on those used by the royalists. San Martín, with the main patriot army which had marched southward for the protection of the capital, effected a junction with O'Higgins near San Fernando. These united forces, having driven back advanced detachments of the enemy, hastened southward by forced marches to surround the royalist army before it could recross the River Maule. The opposing forces met near Talca, a few miles to the northeast of which San Martín drew up his troops on the hills of Cancha Rayada. The patriots were resting after their strenuous marches of the past two days when suddenly, at 8 o'clock at night, the royalists moved out of the village in three columns. To check this advance and to cut off these troops from their base San Martín ordered his own division to change front across the Santiago road. The suddenness of this movement and the obscurity of the night caused the division of O'Higgins to mistake it for an attack, with the result that the sound of firing, the clatter of horses' feet, and the cries of alarm threw his men into such confusion that in the darkness they fired into those of San Martín. The latter replied, and the confusion, of which the royalists took advantage, became disastrous. Many of the

---

[75] Pilling-Mitre, 194-195.

patriots fled in panic, even the artillery abandoning their guns.[76] O'Higgins himself was badly wounded and had to retreat with his division and the reserve artillery to Santiago whither San Martín followed him. The royalist sympathizers, believing that their faction would soon be restored to power, wrote to the royalist commander-in-chief, Osorio, offering their assistance; but that officer delayed so much in following up his victory that San Martín was able to reorganize his shattered forces and perfect his plans for the defense of the capital.[77]

On the 3rd of April, 1818 Osorio crossed the River Maipú and encamped some distance from its north bank in the *hacienda* Espejo, less than ten miles south of Santiago in a position from which he could threaten that city and could either advance upon it by the direct highway or return by the Santiago-Valparaiso road. For the protection of the capital San Martín had encamped his army on a ridge called Loma Blanca about seven miles south of the city, a ridge from which he commanded all roads leading into Santiago from the south and west. The royalist troops occupied a triangular shaped elevation, the base of which fronted the Loma Blanca at a distance of about a kilometer.[78]

At dawn on April 5, the patriot outposts reported that masses of the enemy were advancing northwestward toward the road to Valparaiso. After San Martín had ridden forward to observe this movement he remarked to his staff: "Osorio is a bigger fool than I thought he was. The victory is ours today. That same sun which is now topping the mountains shall witness it." He then sent orders for his own army to advance along the Loma Blanca to a position threatening the right flank of the enemy's marching columns.[79]

When the royalist commander realized that his flank was threatened, he ordered his troops to halt and face the patriots, but his advance column under Primo de Rivera composed of eight companies of grenadiers and chasseurs, with four pieces of artillery, had already descended from the triangular ridge. When ordered to halt, Primo de Rivera formed his men on a small detached hillock from which he might oppose the patriot right flank. The two armies halted in these positions and remained immovable watching each other until midday.[80] Whichever first took the offensive would be at a disadvantage because it would have to

---

[76] Barros Arana, XI, 379-380.
[77] Barros Arana, XI, 385, 418-420; Pilling-Mitre, 170-173.
[78] Mitre, *San Martín*, II, 189-191.
[79] Barros Arana, XI, 440-441.
[80] Mitre, *San Martín*, II, 199-200.

descend into the plain between the two ridges and cross it under the concentrated artillery and musketry fire from the opposite heights; the royalists held the stronger position, but the patriots had more men; all depended on the genius of the respective generals.[81]

San Martín saw that the royalist left was extended so far forward as to leave his right unsupported and exposed, so that to resist an attack the left wing of the royalist army would have to close on its center and in doing so might be attacked while changing position. In order to draw their fire and thus locate the positions of the enemy's guns, four of the patriot guns opened fire. Osorio's horse was shot from under him, but otherwise the fire was not destructive, although it brought a return fire from the royalist artillery and gave the patriot commander the information he needed. San Martín saw at once the enemy's right was his weak point and ordered the signal for the attack to be given by raising a red flag between the Argentine and Chilean flags.[82]

While the patriot artillery on the ridge furnished a barrage of fire, the infantry charged across the plain against the enemy's position and struck the flank of the troops of Primo de Rivera, which, as San Martín had foreseen, were closing in to support the right. They, however, attempted a countercharge, temporarily checking the patriot advance. Instantly San Martín, who had ridden toward the foot of the royalist position, the better to observe the action, ordered up his reserve, thereby throwing Primo de Rivera's troops into confusion. His right, left unsupported, was driven back. The fighting, which was hand to hand, had developed all along the line, but everywhere the royalists were getting the worst of it. Even the patriot artillery was able to limber up and come down from the heights to fire at closer range upon the backs of the retreating enemy. This kind of fighting lasted for half an hour when Ordóñez, now in command, for Osorio had fled, seeing the royalists everywhere surrounded, ordered their withdrawal to the *hacienda* of Espejo.[83]

At this moment O'Higgins, who on account of his wounds and the fever resulting therefrom had been considered incapacitated for active duty and had been left behind in command of a thousand militia to preserve order in the city, rode on the field accompanied by his staff and bodyguard. When he had heard the sounds of battle, his impetuous courage would not permit him to remain out of action and, taking with

---

[81] *Ibid.*, 200.
[82] *Ibid.*, 201-202.
[83] Mitre, *San Martín*, II, 203-211; Barros Arana, XI, 443-447.

him such men as he could gather, he had ridden at full speed to the battlefield. His arrival was a magnificent gesture and probably did something to maintain the enthusiasm of the patriot troops, but its actual result was unimportant, for the battle had already been won.[84]

Ordóñez made his final stand behind the walls of the *hacienda* with four companies of fusiliers and the two guns which were all he could save from the disaster. But his position was untenable since it was commanded by higher ground all around, and he was forced to surrender to prevent further useless bloodshed. The number killed in this battle on each side was approximately the same—1,000; but the royalists surrendered 160 officers, 2,200 men, 3,850 muskets, twelve guns, four flags, and all their munitions and funds. The royalist army was wiped out.[85] The victory of Maipú definitely assured the actual independence of Chile, which had been voted by the Chilean people in November of the year previous and had been proclaimed by O'Higgins on January 1, 1818.[86]

IV. THE PROTECTOR OF PERU

The independence of Chile having been assured by the battle of Maipú, San Martín must have felt that his plans for completing the independence of the Provinces of La Plata were well under way. The next step in his plan, as will be remembered, was to assist the Peruvians to gain their independence so that the viceroy's army which threatened from that direction might be driven out. To transport his troops by sea to Peru, San Martín realized the importance of gaining command of the sea. Chilean warships were necessary for the purpose of capturing or destroying the ships of Spain and for convoying the patriot army; but Chile had no navy. O'Higgins gave his loyal coöperation toward the creation of a Chilean navy, sending commissioners to England and to the United States with money to buy vessels; a Spanish brigantine, lured into Valparaiso by the use of the Spanish flag, was captured and converted into a Chilean cruiser to attack and capture two other Spanish ships; and the artilleryman, Blanco-Encalada, who had served a year

---

[84] Mitre, *San Martín,* II, 212; Barros Arana, XI, 449-450. Barros Arana mentions, but does not give credence to the claim that the arrival of O'Higgins with the detachment of militia which accompanied him had a decisive influence in disconcerting the enemy. Mitre remarks at the end of his paragraph that "United they both [San Martín and O'Higgins] went on to complete the victory."

[85] Mitre, *San Martín,* II, 215.

[86] Pilling-Mitre, 167-168.

as a midshipman in the Spanish navy, was appointed rear admiral over this little squadron.[87]

Although Blanco-Encalada was successful in making further captures and increasing the Chilean fleet, nevertheless he enthusiastically welcomed to the command of the navy a former British admiral, Lord Thomas Cochrane, Earl of Dundonald, who, having been cashiered from the British navy for radical political activities, gladly accepted the offer of returning to active service presented to him by the agents of O'Higgins in London.   On March 28, 1818,[88] Lord Cochrane arrived at Valparaiso bringing other English officers with him.   Then, by a series of remarkable achievements and bold attacks on ships and fortified ports in Peru and southern Chile, notably in Callao and Valdivia, Cochrane drove from the Pacific coast most of the Spanish navy and captured enough of their ships to organize a fleet of sixteen transports and eight ships of war for convoying San Martín's army to Peru.[89]

Chile had nobly done its part to facilitate the carrying out of the plans agreed upon between San Martín and O'Higgins, but his own country was about to discredit its hero and to spoil San Martín's plans.   A government hostile to him which had come into power at Buenos Aires ordered him to give up his expedition to Peru and to bring the Argentine troops back to Buenos Aires.   San Martín was torn between loyalty to his own country and to Chile; between obedience to orders and keeping his promises to O'Higgins; between carrying out his own plans of liberating the whole of southern South America, and sacrificing those plans to become embroiled in factional quarrels.   If his troops were brought back to support the government which happened just then to be in power, it might result in an invasion of the royalist army through Upper Peru and the end of the independence of his country, for which he had been fighting.

Having received from O'Higgins assurances that he could count on being appointed a general in the Chilean army with 4,000 men to engage in the expedition to Peru, San Martín decided to disobey the orders which he had received from the supreme director of Buenos Aires.   Therefore, having assembled his officers, he explained the situation to them and then resigned his command.   In accordance with custom in such a

---

[87] Chisholm, 285-286.

[88] Thomas, Earl of Dundonald, *Narrative of services in the liberation of Chili, Peru and Brazil,* I, 1-4.

[89] Barros Arana, XII, 231, 247, 473, 512, 564-565; Pilling-Mitre, 201-209, 230-231; Anna Schoellenkopf, *Don José de San Martín,* 110.

contingency, the officers were permitted to elect their own commander and to decide where he should lead them. Thereupon, at Rancagua on April 2, 1820, a declaration was adopted that the authority which the general of the Army of the Andes had received to make war on the Spanish and to secure the happiness of the country, was essential to the safety of the people, and that, therefore, he should be reëlected to the command of the Army of the Andes and should continue to carry out the great task which had been entrusted to him.[90]

This "Act of Rancagua" was henceforth the only authority on which San Martín could base his command of the Argentine troops. "It was a revolutionary act which by vote of a military congress had sanctioned his disobedience of orders. It was a double act of insubordination which made him subservient to the will of the soldiers." [91] It did not, however, prevent him from being considered a deserter by the government at Buenos Aires, and it made him an exile in his old age.

Having thus cut himself off from Argentina and having received from Chile all that was necessary for carrying out his plans for liberating Peru, San Martín assembled his Liberating Army of Peru at Valparaiso and sailed from there on August 20, 1820, under the convoy of warships commanded by Lord Cochrane. The latter had been explicitly placed under the orders of San Martín who had been designated by O'Higgins as commander-in-chief with the rank of Captain-General of the army of Chile.[92]

The object of the proposed expedition may be learned from a proclamation to the Peruvian people issued by O'Higgins, and from orders to his troops by San Martín. The former stated that after the Peruvians had been liberated from Spanish domination they would be free to adopt any form of government which they thought best. The latter warned his soldiers thus: "Remember that you are come, not to conquer but to liberate a people; the Peruvians are our brothers." [93] Owing to the fact that large numbers of the Peruvians were still loyalists, war against the royalist army in that province would involve fighting against these brother Americans. San Martín, therefore, planned to win over to his side as many as possible of the Peruvian colonists before attacking the royalist troops, so that victory might be gained by diplomacy rather than by force of arms.

---

[90] Mitre, *San Martín*, II, 456-457.
[91] *Ibid.*, 459.
[92] Barros Arana, XII, 653-658; Pilling-Mitre, 230-231.
[93] Quoted in Pilling-Mitre, 231-232.

With this object in view, San Martín did not want to give battle to
the royalist forces but tried merely to prevent their concentration while
he induced the people to revolt and to set up a government of their own.
He did not wish to besiege Lima, but only to threaten it, so that the viceroy might withdraw. By landing troops north and south of the capital
with orders to converge upon it, this might be accomplished without
risking a serious engagement, while the fleet was blockading the coast.
To carry out this plan, a base of operations was to be established at Trujillo, the northernmost province of Peru; but to distract attention from
his purpose, by threatening the capital from the other side, he first put in
at Pisco, a small port one hundred and sixty miles south of Lima. There
he caused to disembark on September 8 the first division of his army
under General Gregorio de las Heras with instructions to threaten Lima
from the eastern highlands and then to effect a junction with the main
body, meanwhile flooding the country with proclamations and propaganda to induce revolt. San Martín then with the remainder of the
army proceeded northward to Huacho, ninety miles north of Lima,
where he disembarked and occupied a strong position in the valley of
Huara,[94] where he was in a position to cut off all communication between the northern provinces and the capital.[95]

On the way north, the squadron had entered the Bay of Callao and
remained there a few days during which time Cochrane tried to induce
San Martín to attack Lima. Finding himself unsuccessful in this, the
former directed and carried to a successful conclusion one of those
spectacular and daring exploits for which he was noted. During the
night of the 5th of November, with two hundred and forty sailors and
marines in small boats, Cochrane led an attack in two columns, through
its protecting boom, upon the Spanish frigate *Esmeralda*. This sudden
and well-planned attack took the Spanish officers by surprise. Before
the sentry on deck could fire a shot to alarm the crew, the two columns
of small boats had closed in upon the frigate and patriot sailors were
clambering over the bulwarks on both port and starboard sides. A
charge was made upon the crew as they rushed from their sleeping
quarters, and the officers were captured in their cabins. Cochrane, or
one of his captains, ordered the cables cut and the sails set. Under the
fire of the guns of the forts the *Esmeralda* sailed out of the harbor, a

---

[94] Schoellenkopf, 111; Gonzalo Bulnes, *Historia de la expedición libertadora del
Perú*, I, 425; John Miller, *Memoirs of General Miller* I, 274.

[95] Schoellenkopf, 111; Gonzalo Bulnes, *Historia de la expedición libertadora del
Perú*. I, 425; John Miller, *Memoirs of General Miller* I, 274.

prize of the Chilean navy to which it was added after its name had been changed to *Valdivia*.[96] The moral effect of this daring act was very great and aided San Martín in his plans for propaganda but did not cause him to change his determination not to attack.

Instead, he continued his military inactivity allowing only skirmishes between his scouting detachments and those of the enemy. As the patriots were generally successful in these minor engagements, many royalist soldiers including the troops of the Numancia Battalion, which was composed largely of Colombians, deserted to San Martín and were incorporated in his army. Prisoners of war were released and slaves given their freedom on condition that they enlist in the patriot army.[97] The Marquis of Torre Tagle, royalist governor of Trujillo, convened an open *cabildo* at which it was decided to maintain the independence of Peru. Torre Tagle then succeeded in forcing the disbandment of the royalist garrison in Piura and in bringing that city over to the patriot side. These decisions which were generally welcomed by the inhabitants of this region, enabled San Martín to utilize the northern provinces as a safe base from which to draw recruits and supplies. Thus in three months, without risking a pitched battle, San Martín had accomplished his purpose of inducing the people of northern Peru to resist the royalist government.[98]

This method of warfare without fighting did not satisfy the intrepid Cochrane and many of San Martín's officers who accused him of cowardice and inactivity. Nevertheless these methods resulted in the establishment of a provisional patriot government over the four departments into which northern Peru had been divided, and the outwitting of the viceroy who had permitted the patriot forces under Arenales, which had been landed in the south, to cross the mountains almost unopposed. These had seized the important cities of Tarma and Huamanga, occupied the Valley of Jauja, captured Cerro de Pasco from General O'Reilley, and finally on January 8, 1821, after a march of 840 miles through hostile territory, had effected the junction with the main body which San Martín had planned.[99] Meanwhile, bands of patriot guerillas organized by San Martín harassed the royalist outposts, and Cochrane starved the people of the capital by blockading its harbor. There was much sickness

[96] Pilling-Mitre, 237-240; Miller, I, 272; Cochrane, I, 85-88.
[97] Miller, I, 275-277.
[98] Pilling-Mitre, 243-244. For letter from San Martín to Torre Tagle, urging him to declare for independence, see Bulnes, II, 32.
[99] Bulnes, I, 449-451; Miller, I, 280-281; Mitre, *San Martín,* 603-606, 612.

in the city and among the royalist troops, and fever infested the patriot army at Huara and even attacked San Martín himself. When, therefore, an envoy arrived from the new liberal government of Spain to treat with the rebels, both sides were ready to accept the armistice which was proposed and signed at the farmhouse of Punchauca, fifteen miles outside of Lima.[100]

After the revolution of 1820 in Spain, the Liberals who had gained control there wished to conciliate the colonists in America. Instructions were, therefore, sent to their military commanders in the colonies to sign armistices with the rebel commanders in order that negotiations might be carried on. Thus the war was brought to a temporary pause in 1820 and 1821 by this armistice between San Martín and the representatives of the viceroy of Peru at Punchauca, and between Bolívar and Morillo at Trujillo.[101] Although this cessation of hostilities was welcomed by both contestants—by the patriots because they were worn out and needed time to rest and reorganize, and by the royalists because the army which had been assembled at Cádiz to reënforce them had revolted and refused to go to America—the negotiations were bound to fail since the commissioners of both sides stood firmly for principles which were diametrically opposed. Those sent from Spain demanded that the colonists swear to the Spanish Constitution of 1812 and accept the invitation to send delegates to sit in the *cortes* on equal terms with the delegates from Spain. The patriots, however, who had by this time lost their loyalty toward Ferdinand VII, and who now yearned for independence, demanded complete separation from the mother country. Therefore, no decisions could be arrived at except to cease hostilities temporarily while awaiting new instructions from Spain. In the north, as will be seen later, hostilities broke out again in less than five months, and in the south a peace, in which both sides were suspicious of each other, lasted only four weeks.

When the armistice came to an end on July 4, 1821, the Viceroy La Serna, evidently alarmed by San Martín's threats to attack the city, abandoned Lima amid wild confusion and marched his troops into the mountains. San Martín attempted neither to pursue the retreating enemy nor to occupy the abandoned city,[102] since he did not wish to seize the capital by force but rather to win over its people to his views. He is quoted by an Englishman who knew him as saying:

---

[100] Mitre, *San Martín*, II, 633-634; Miller, II, 288.
[101] Schoellenkopf, 113; Mitre, *San Martín*, II, 635-637.
[102] Bulnes, II, 174, 195; Mitre, *San Martín*, II, 674-675.

"People ask why I don't march to Lima at once; so I might and instantly would, were it suitable to my views, which it is not. I do not want military renown; I have no ambition to be the conqueror of Peru; I want solely to liberate the country from oppression. Of what use would Lima be to me, if the inhabitants were hostile in political sentiment? How could the cause of independence be advanced by my holding Lima, or even the whole country in military possession? Far different are my views. I wish to have all men thinking with me, and do not choose to advance a step beyond the march of public opinion." [103]

San Martín, therefore, placated the frightened citizens by keeping his regular troops outside of the city and by ordering the guerillas to cease operations. Reassured by this attitude, the people consented to the replacement of the royal arms over the doorways of the public building by the new escutcheon of Peru, bearing the words *Lima Independiente*.[104]

Cochrane, dissatisfied with this policy, insisted that attacks be made upon the royalists. His own plans to capture the forts at Callao were frustrated by the viceroy's secret service, and an expedition to the south was prevented by an outbreak of fever among the troops. Arenales, with whom this expedition was to coöperate, abandoned his campaign against the royalists in the mountains and, under orders from San Martín, retired upon Lima. Colonel John Miller, sent by Cochrane to effect a diversion in the south, had several initial successes and might have captured Arequipa had the strength of his detachment been greater.

Arenales, who had been forbidden by San Martín to attack the royalist column on its retreat into the mountains, had a much larger force than Canterac and occupied a superior position. Had he been permitted to attack at that time, Arenales would, according to Bulnes, in all probability have destroyed the viceroy's army and ended the war then and there with a signal victory. Mitre says that American historians, admirers of the unmistakable military genius of San Martín, have censured his attitude of inertness on this occasion.[105]

As will be seen, San Martín's neglect to push the campaign against the viceroy and his troops in the mountains was a serious mistake. Instead, he devoted his attention to establishing a government in the capital. On July 14 at his suggestion a convention of the principal citizens of Lima declared the independence of Peru. Two weeks later this was solemnly proclaimed amidst acclamations, pomp, and ceremony in the

---

[103] Reprinted from the *Journal of Captain Basil Hall* in Pilling-Mitre, 480.
[104] Mitre, *San Martín*, II, 677-678.
[105] Bulnes, II, 195; Miller I, 346; Mitre, *San Martín*, II, 679-681.

main plaza of the city.[106] On August 3, in response to repeated urgings from deputations of citizens, San Martín proclaimed himself Protector of Peru with supreme civil and military authority, and proceeded to name his cabinet. He then issued a decree confiscating the property of Spaniards who might work against the new republic, and other Spaniards, who refused to swear allegiance to it, he ordered into exile. Among the latter was the Archbishop of Lima, an old man who had exerted a beneficial influence in quieting the people after the abandonment of the city by the viceroy. A decree also liberated all children of slaves born after the declaration of independence and raised the status of the Indians to equality with the other races.[107] Although San Martín had been vested with almost absolute power by the people who wanted a strong government to reëstablish order, he failed to secure their loyalty, largely because they looked upon him as a foreigner.[108]

There was also the accusation that San Martín was trying to make himself sovereign, and there was some justification for this charge. He, like Bolívar, felt that the people were too ignorant to govern themselves and that they needed a ruler and an aristocracy to tell them how. "They should not have the best laws," he wrote, "but those most suited to their character, maintaining the barriers which separate the different classes of society, so that the most intelligent class may preserve its natural preponderance." [109] He not only allowed the members of the Peruvian nobility to keep their titles and to display their escutcheons, but even instituted "The Order of the Sun" by means of which he might confer distinction upon his supporters. To each of twenty of his favorite officers he distributed $25,000 out of a fund of half a million obtained from the confiscation of the property of exiled Spaniards, and likewise decreed to himself an annual salary of $30,000 which he spent largely in presents to his friends and in lavish displays of pomp and majesty.[110]

Meanwhile, many of the exiled Spaniards and their families had sought refuge in the castle of Callao which was still held by royalist troops under General José de la Mar; but unfortunately for the large number of refugees gathered there, the castle was not stocked with sufficient provisions. Inasmuch as this state of affairs rendered the withstanding of a protracted siege impossible, Canterac marched his

---

[106] Cochrane, I, 124-125; Bulnes, II, 206.
[107] Bulnes, II, 238-240.
[108] Pilling-Mitre, 275-277; Miller, II, 333; Cochrane, I, 126.
[109] Quoted in Pilling-Mitre, 285.
[110] Bulnes, II, 375; Mitre, *San Martín*, III, 125-128.

troops down from the mountains for its relief. When on September 2 this army was seen approaching Lima, great was the consternation in the city, until San Martín promised that he and his troops would shed their last drop of blood rather than be witnesses of the capture of the city. San Martín then posted his battalions in two lines behind mud walls for the protection of the city and utilized the services of volunteers from among the citizens—men, women, and priests—in building and defending these walls. Canterac, unable to use his cavalry because the River Rimac separated him from the defenders, made no attempt to attack, so that the two armies remained facing each other in this position until September 9.[111]

On the 10th Canterac suddenly executed a flank movement, passed along the whole front of the defense, and marched into Callao to relieve its beleaguered garrison. Although he succeeded in entering the castle, he accomplished nothing worth while, for he had no extra supplies to leave there and the presence of his own troops would only increase the number of mouths to be fed; therefore, all he accomplished was to secure some munitions which could be used by the viceroy's troops in the mountains.[112]

San Martín must have understood this condition of affairs for he allowed Canterac to enter Callao and then to withdraw again unopposed. The fact that the royalist army was allowed to march past the capital in this way and to return again unmolested aroused intense indignation among the patriots, who bitterly blamed San Martín for not attacking Canterac. It is true he had the superior force, but if by any chance he should have been defeated and Lima captured, the independence of Peru would have been delayed. Nevertheless, he was accused of supineness and lack of vigor, and not only the Peruvians but even his own subordinates began to lose faith in his energy and ability as a soldier.[113]

Cochrane did his best to try to persuade San Martín to attack the royalists, even offering himself to lead the cavalry, but was met with a curt refusal, until his loyalty, which had been steadily diminishing, now gave way completely. He suggested that now that San Martín was Protector of Peru, he no longer had authority over the Chilean fleet, and that he himself as admiral of this fleet was no longer subject to the former's orders, but only to those of the Chilean Director O'Higgins. There still exists in the public archives in Chile voluminous correspond-

---

[111] Bulnes, II, 244; Barros Arana, XIII, 474-475.
[112] Bulnes, II, 252-253; Pilling-Mitre, 278-281; Barros Arana, XIII, 476-477.
[113] Bulnes, II, 255; Barros Arana, XIII, 504, 506.

ence in English between Cochrane and O'Higgins, in which Cochrane complains bitterly of the treatment accorded him by San Martín and especially of the failure of the latter to carry out his promises to pay the crews of the Chilean ships. Cochrane stated that he feared mutiny unless his men were paid, and reported that he had seized some public moneys which San Martín had sent aboard a ship in the harbor of Ancón to be safe from capture by Canterac.[114]

Since he feared lest Cochrane might raise the blockade of Callao and sail away if he made any attempt to retake the money, San Martín had to content himself with giving preëmptory orders for its return, orders which Cochrane met with a flat refusal, saying that he must keep the money to pay his crews or else they would mutiny. Then San Martín told Cochrane to go back to Chile and report to his own government.[115] Although he refused to accept orders from San Martín, Cochrane sailed away and eventually returned to Chile after having searched the coast for the frigates *Prueba* and *Venganza,* the last of the Spanish navy to remain on the Pacific.[116] After his return to Chile, Cochrane relinquished his command in that navy and gave his services to Brazil, which by that time was struggling to maintain its newly declared independence from Portugal.[117]

This example of disobedience was not lost on the army. The situation there was rendered worse because of the fact that this was not a homogenious unit but was composed of detachments from four different nationalities. Those from Argentina were lacking in discipline because they knew that San Martín himself had disobeyed the orders of the Argentine government when he insisted on going with the expedition to Peru.[118] The Chileans felt that they should be at home fighting for their own hearths and feared that their absence in Peru was imperilling the independence of Chile. The Numancia Battalion, as will be remembered, was largely composed of Colombians who had repeatedly demanded that they be repatriated. Their officers were jealous of the efforts of San Martín to attach Guayaquil to Peru, since they felt that that province really belonged to Colombia. The Peruvians were torn

---

[114] Papers in the archives of Benjamín Vicuña Mackenna, National Library, Santiago; Mitre, *San Martín,* III, 171-173.

[115] Miller, I, 343; Mitre, *San Martín,* III, 175-176.

[116] Pilling-Mitre, 288-291; Barros Arana, XIII, 498.

[117] Cochrane, II, 7-9.

[118] Schoellenkopf, 108; Bulnes, II, 416.

by internal dissensions and nearly all of them, as has been said, looked upon San Martín as a foreigner.[119]

San Martín was at last aroused to the necessity of driving the royalists out of the mountains before the independence of Peru or the rest of America could be assured. He, therefore, sent General Tristan and Colonel Gamarra with 2,000 men to occupy the valley of Ica and threaten attack upon the viceroy's detachments. These generals, however, proved incompetent, abandoned Ica when they in turn were threatened, allowed their retreat to be thrown into disorder, and permitted themselves to be vanquished by Canterac with a force no larger than their own.[120]

The news of this defeat caused an impression of the utmost terror in Lima, so that it was all that the Society of Patriots could do to keep up the spirits of the populace and to prevent their giving way to despair at the magnitude of the disaster. On thè mind of San Martín the defeat at Ica worked havoc, for it revealed to him the dangers with which he was surrounded, and was a demonstration that the royalists in the mountains were still eager for a fight and that further military inaction would be risking the cause of independence.[121] The realization which had been growing in the mind of San Martín that he alone was not able to drive the viceroy out of Peru, an objective which would clinch the freedom of all American colonies, caused him to look for help to Bolívar who had just then brought to a successful end a campaign against Quito.

As will be fully described in its proper place, Bolívar, the liberator of northern South America, had freed Venezuela and New Granada and had invited them to form the Republic of Great Colombia. When he rescued Quito from Spanish control he joined this also to Great Colombia, thereby making that republic include all the provinces of the former viceroyalty of New Granada. Quito proper was a mountainous region occupying the high valleys and plateaus between the lofty ranges of the Andes, with its only access to the outside world through the strip of lowlands bordering the Pacific coast and centering around the Gulf of Guayaquil. Since this province had at various times belonged to each of the viceroyalties of New Granada and Peru, when the city of Guayaquil declared its independence, there arose two factions—one which felt that it should throw in its lot with the other provinces of the former Viceroyalty of New Granada, and the other which, when it learned that San Martín had declared himself Protector of Peru, hastened to claim

---

[119] Bulnes, II, 417-418.

[120] Bulnes, II, 250-251; Mitre, San Martín, III, 197-201, 202-205.

[121] Bulnes, II, 454-455; Mitre, San Martín, III, 208-210.

relationship with that viceroyalty and to throw itself under his protection. When, however, Quito was freed and annexed by Bolívar, the
Colombian faction in the port of Guayaquil naturally gained the ascendancy and welcomed Sucre, Bolívar's lieutenant, and finally Bolívar himself as their saviours.[122]   It was at this unpropitious time of factional
strife that the arrangement was made for a conference at Guayaquil
between the liberators of northern and southern South America.   Bolívar had the advantage, for he was already in occupation as the acknowledged choice of the Colombian faction.   As San Martín stepped ashore
from the schooner which brought him, he was welcomed to "Colombian
soil" by Bolívar.   During the three days in which San Martín remained
at Guayaquil he had several meetings with Bolívar.   For many years
this celebrated "Interview at Guayaquil" remained shrouded in mystery,
inasmuch as there were no eyewitnesses to other than their public ap-
pearances; and although these two heroes held long conversations alone,
no one recorded what they said.   Later, however, there came to light
certain letters of San Martín in which he stated his side of the controversy.

Both were working for the same end—the freedom of America; both
had risen unaided to pinnacles of success; one had liberated the northern provinces of South America, the other the southern; now they must
coöperate to complete their task by driving out the last royal authority
in America, the viceroy of Peru.   San Martín felt himself too weak
to accomplish this alone; he called upon Bolívar to help.   Bolívar
seemed to want to keep all the glory for himself.   In consequence San
Martín recognized the necessity of withdrawing in order that Bolívar
alone might finish that which was uppermost in the hopes of both.

San Martín first asked for three or four thousand Colombian troops
with whose aid he expected to be able to defeat the royalist army.
Bolívar reluctantly offered him three battalions.   Then San Martín
begged Bolívar to take charge with as large an army as he could bring,
offering himself to serve under him if Bolívar would do this.   Bolívar
declined this magnanimous offer, alleging that unless the Colombian
congress gave him authority to do so, he could not go outside of Colombian territory.   It was evident, then, that Bolívar's jealousy prevented
him from sharing any of the glory, so that he must be allowed to do the
job alone in his own way.   San Martín could not do it alone, but Bolívar

---

[122] Rippy, 205; Hasbrouck, 252.

believed he, himself, could; hence, there was nothing for San Martín to do but to withdraw from the scene.[123]

"The Conference of Guayaquil may be considered as the abdication of San Martín in behalf of Peruvian independence; it is the moment in which he sacrificed the rewards of his greatness on the altar of America, in which he, worn out and ill, yielded to his rival the government of Peru and gave him half of his own glory." [124]

The foregoing is Mitre's conception of this famous interview and is the one generally accepted as correct. Bulnes is not so sure as to what actually took place. He says that really it makes little difference what was said at the conference. Its importance lies only in the decision of the problem who should end the war, Bolívar or San Martín. Neither the victories of Bolívar in the north nor those of San Martín in the south could establish independence permanently in any of the colonies as long as a single Spanish viceroy remained in power on the continent. Whose duty would it be to drive out the viceroy of Peru? It was a practical question. Bolívar was in a better condition to end the war.

"Bolívar represented the democratic principles of the revolution in Colombia; San Martín, on the contrary, had supported political monarchy in Lima. . . . Bolívar counted upon the loyalty and devotion of the three peoples whom he had liberated; San Martín always worked alone; alone in Lima, alone in Chile, alone in Buenos Aires. . . . Bolívar had everything necessary to end the war; San Martín lacked everything." [125]

On the night of July 27-28, 1822, San Martín left a ball which was being held in honor of the two liberators, went aboard his ship, and ordered it to weigh anchor and return to Peru. After his arrival there he wrote to Bolívar:

"My decision is irrevocable. I have convened the first Congress of Peru; the day after its installation I shall leave for Chile, convinced that my presence is the only obstacle which keeps you from coming to Peru with your army.

"For me it would have been the height of happiness to have concluded the War of Independence under the orders of a General to whom America owes her liberty. Destiny has decreed otherwise, and I must resign myself to it."

---

[123] Pilling-Mitre, 423-424.
[124] *Ibid.*
[125] Bulnes, II, 476.

He concluded with "my sincere desire that you may have the glory of finishing the war for the independence of South America." [126]

This promise San Martín fully and promptly kept. On September 20, 1822, after the installation of the first Constituent Congress of Peru, he presented his renunciation of all future command and, after telling one of his friends that there was not room in Peru for both Bolívar and himself, sailed for Chile,[127] while from others he concealed the real reason for his departure. Many believed that he was provoked because factional quarrels among the Peruvians prevented them from supporting him and his ministers as loyally as he wished. To O'Higgins he wrote that the climate of Peru had broken his health and that he wished to spend his old age in peace and retirement.[128]

San Martín remained in Chile only two months until he had recovered somewhat from his illness. He then crossed to Mendoza where he learned of the death of his wife. On his return to Buenos Aires the faction in control there at the time accused him of desertion and received him with indifference and contempt. Embittered at this treatment and not caring to engage in factional quarrels, he took his daughter with him and in 1823 went into self-imposed exile in France. There, forgotten by his compatriots, whose descendants have raised hundreds of statues in his honor, he lived a peaceful but poverty-stricken old age, until he died at Boulogne on August 17, 1850.[129]

The duty and the glory of completing the liberation of the whole of South America was now left to Bolívar. How he accomplished this will be told in a subsequent chapter, but first it will be necessary to relate how he became the liberator of northern South America up to the time when at Guayaquil he was entrusted with the same duty in the south.

---

[126] Quoted in Pilling-Mitre, 425.
[127] Mitre, *San Martin* III, 668.
[128] Pilling-Mitre, 428.
[129] Robertson, *Rise*, 262; Schoellenkopf, 134.

CHAPTER SEVENTEEN

THE MOVEMENTS FOR INDEPENDENCE IN NORTHERN SOUTH AMERICA

By Alfred Hasbrouck

I. Simón Bolívar, the Liberator

RETURNING again to northern South America it will be remembered that the first Venezuelan republic collapsed in 1812 as a result of an earthquake and the ineptness of Miranda. After the latter had been sent into exile and imprisonment, one of those officers who had betrayed him, Simón Bolívar, grasped the reins which had fallen from his hands.

Having obtained a passport from the royalist commander, Bolívar escaped to Cartagena where he offered his sword to the independent government of that place, which accepted his offer and gave him a detachment of two hundred men with which he was to operate against the royalists along the Magdalena River. Bolívar, having embarked his little force in small boats and canoes, took by surprise the fortified point of Tenerife, and on December 27 occupied Mompox. There, having more than doubled his force by the addition of recruits, he continued his offensive operations, and by the first of January 1813 had seized the fortified towns of Guamal and Banco and, by the sixth, had established his headquarters at Ocaña.[1]

Although the forces employed were small and the engagements fought were of minor importance, this campaign opened communication between Cartagena and the interior of New Granada along the valley of the Magdalena, and it furnished Bolívar, at that time new to the art of war, with valuable experience. A serious breach of discipline committed by him at that early period in his military career, deliberate disobedience of the orders of his commanding officer, actually resulted beneficially.[2]

While at Ocaña, Bolívar conceived the bold plan of leading his little band of New Granadians across the mountains into Venezuela to destroy the royalist garrisons there and to liberate that province. In spite

---

[1] Eleázar López Contreras, *Bolívar conductor de tropas,* 28.
[2] Simón B. O'Leary, *Memorias del General O'Leary; narración* I, 99-100.

of the fact that Labatut, a French officer in command of the patriot army at Cartagena, was unwilling that his troops should be taken beyond the limits of his jurisdiction and forbade the execution of this plan, Bolívar went over the head of his commanding officer and secured the permission of the congress at Bogotá to undertake this expedition, and in violation of positive orders from Labatut, Bolívar began his march toward Cúcuta in February. On the twenty-seventh of that month he crossed the Zulia River and next day defeated the royalist troops under Colonel Correa, forcing them to withdraw from San José de Cúcuta, and preventing a royalist invasion from the north. In recognition of his services Bolívar was promoted to Brigadier General and given command of all patriot troops in the Province of Pamplona.[3]

Bolívar, then, with the approval of congress and with forces increased to five hundred and sixty men, felt himself free to cross into his native province to carry out his plan for its liberation. Although the strength of the royalists was ten times that of the patriots, Bolívar struck so rapidly and in so many places that his enemies were unable to divine his objective and permitted him to enter Mérida without serious opposition by the end of May. Detachments sent out toward the north, northeast, and northwest cleared the province of Mérida, outwitting the royalists and making it possible for Bolívar to continue his advance to Trujillo where he arrived with his staff and main body on June 14.[4]

While at Trujillo Bolívar issued his notorious proclamation of "War to the Death" for which he has been severely blamed by many historians. This was a proclamation which resulted in such orgies of retaliation and counter-retaliation by both sides that Venezuela was for six years drenched with the blood not only of prisoners of war but of civilians of all ages and sexes. In this decree of extermination of royalists, Bolívar proclaimed that "every Spaniard who does not conspire against tyranny in favor of the just cause, in the most active and efficacious manner, shall be held to be an enemy, shall be punished as a traitor, and shall be put to death."[5] The War to the Death thus begun in 1814 lasted until an armistice was signed at this same place in 1820.

The permission which Bolívar had received from the Congress of New Granada was limited to an invasion of the provinces of Mérida and Trujillo, but when this was accomplished, inasmuch as his own plans were as yet uncompleted, Bolívar again disobeyed orders, and de-

---

[3] Jules Mancini, *Bolívar et l'émancipation des colonies espagnoles*, 457-459.
[4] López Contreras, 30-35 and map 30-31.
[5] Quoted in Pilling-Mitre, 331.

cided to march on Caracas and drive the royalists from that capital. In accomplishing this plan, Bolívar fought six engagements in ninety days, defeated 4,500 of the enemy, and reconquered the whole of western Venezuela.[6] In these operations, Bolívar, efficiently aided by his subordinate commanders, Ribas, Girardot, and Urdaneta, had from beginning to end kept the strategic initiative and had prevented the various royalist corps from concentrating against him or furnishing each other mutual support. While this campaign of 1813 is criticized as necessitating too much audacity and temerity, it nevertheless taught Bolívar the importance of concentrating his forces, and resulted in brilliant success.[7]

On the sixth of August Bolívar entered Caracas in triumph and was acclaimed as the "Liberator," a title by which he is still known. He proclaimed himself dictator and reëstablished the republic, the weakness of which, however, soon developed owing to jealousy among its leaders. Santiago Mariño, the patriot commander in the east, had enjoyed supreme power in that portion of the republic which he had reconquered with his own army and, although union and coöperation between the east and the west was necessary for the welfare of Venezuela, he showed his jealousy of the upstart dictator in the west and refused to obey his orders.

Meanwhile, a new danger threatened from a hitherto unsuspected direction. In the plains (*llanos*) of the Orinoco the cowboys (*llaneros*), who cared little whether they fought on the patriot or the royalist side provided they were given plenty of loot and excitement, had formed themselves into a sort of irregular cavalry armed only with lances to fight against their helpless patriot neighbors. These *llaneros* had found an appropriate leader in the renegade Spaniard, Boves, who had already twice changed sides and was now employed by the royalist cause. The threat of attack from behind by Boves made it difficult for Bolívar to direct his attention to renewing the siege of the main royalist army in Puerto Cabello. He, therefore, directed Mariño to make an advance into the *llanos* and destroy the troops and resources of Boves; but Mariño, swayed by jealousy, neglected to coöperate with Bolívar in time to prevent the royalist forces under their new Captain-General Cajigal and his second in command, Ceballos, from establishing themselves in

---

[6] *Ibid.*, 333.

[7] López Contreras, 42-43.

strong positions at Barquisimeto and San Carlos, threatening Caracas from the west.[8]

In his haste to capture Caracas, Bolívar had passed by Puerto Cabello and had failed to pursue the defeated Monteverde into that stronghold, where the latter received reënforcements from Spain and was able to take the field again in September with one thousand six hundred men.[9] When Bolívar sent Colonels Urdaneta and Girardot and Major D'Eluyar against Monteverde, the royalist commander made the mistake of weakening himself by dividing his forces, was defeated in detail, and was driven back again into Puerto Cabello. But this victory was a sad one for Bolívar, since Colonel Atanasio Girardot had fallen shot through the head. This young and popular officer is still eulogized in Venezuela, for he was one of the first of those officers from New Granada who gave their lives for the liberation of the sister republic.[10]

Profiting by this lack of coöperation among the patriots, Boves was able to concentrate 4,000 cavalry and 2,500 infantry at Calabozo and to threaten the valleys of Arauca south of Caracas. At last Mariño had decided to bring his troops from eastern Venezuela to oppose Boves and had summoned General Piar to join him, thereby leaving a serious gap in the lines besieging Puerto Cabello. Nevertheless, Bolívar was able to concentrate his remaining forces at Valencia and to defeat Cajigal on the plains of Carabobo (First Battle of Carabobo, 1814), a short distance south of that city.[11] The capture of the enemy's artillery by General Urdaneta and a bayonet charge ordered by him contributed much to the winning of this victory which cost the royalists eight flags, all their artillery, five hundred muskets, and a great quantity of munitions and supplies of all kinds. After this victory Bolívar sent Urdaneta westward in pursuit of the scattered forces of Cajigal, and himeslf hastened eastward to support Mariño, who was hard pressed by Boves at La Puerta.[12]

Bolívar found Mariño defending himself in a most unfavorable position against superior forces of the enemy, for even after the arrival of Bolívar's troops the patriots numbered only 3,500 against nearly 8,000 under Boves. In spite of the odds against him, Bolívar ordered a simultaneous frontal and flank attack; but suddenly the patriot infantry was

---

[8] *Ibid.*, 52-54.
[9] Pilling-Mitre, 334-335; Mancini, 519-522.
[10] O'Leary, *Narración* I, 163.
[11] López Contreras, 52-54.
[12] *Ibid.*, 71-73.

charged by a concealed squadron of *llaneros,* and although one battalion formed square to resist the charge it was unable to hold its ground and stay the disaster of that fatal 14th of February, when the patriots left one thousand dead on the field and only four hundred escaped to follow Bolívar and Mariño into Caracas.[13]

Boves then advanced to Valencia, captured that place, cut off Urdaneta from returning to support Bolívar, and marched upon Caracas, spreading terror and destruction in his wake. Left with only a weak command, Bolívar realized that it would be impossible to defend Caracas, and determined to withdraw while he still had a nucleus of an army to unite with the troops which Mariño had left in the province of Oriente, and, therefore, on June 7 he evacuated the capital and began his retreat to the easwtard. The citizens, fearing massacre at the hands of Boves, would not permit Bolívar to desert them, but followed him on the march as long as their strength held out. The whole population of Caracas hastily gathered as many of their worldly possessions as they could carry and loaded them into carts or strapped them to their backs; the men seized a musket, a sabre, or a lantern, and the women snatched up their babies and followed their erstwhile defenders from the eastern exits of the city. Few had time to put on proper clothing; many were half naked before the long tramp was over; all lacked food; the weak and exhausted fugitives were racked with sickness; women, children, and old people formed a tragic procession. On this retreat, which lasted twenty days, many succumbed to exhaustion along the way. This abandonment of the city of Caracas by its inhabitants is known as "The Emigration of 1814." [14]

On arrival at Barcelona and Cumaná the fugitives received the protection of the few troops of Mariño which were there, but the leaders of these troops, Ribas and Piar, refused to recognize the authority of Bolívar. Bereft of followers, Bolívar and Mariño then set sail for Margarita Island, but having been refused admission there, continued their flight to Cartagena. Such was the inglorious end of the campaign of 1813 and of the second republic of Venezuela.[15]

The next three years in the career of Bolívar may be compared with the winter of Valley Forge in that of Washington. In those years Bolívar, like Washington, saw all his expectations of victory vanish; there was no ray of hope; all his resources were exhausted; he was so poor

---

[13] López Contreras, 71-73; O'Leary, *Narración,* I, 189-190.

[14] Pilling-Mitre, 23; José María Salaverría, *Bolívar, el libertador,* 120-121.

[15] Pilling-Mitre, 23; López Contreras, 74; Salaverría, 121.

that he had to beg alms from a friend;[16] patriotism seemed nonexistent among his followers; the enemy was welcomed by his fellow colonists; and the king's troops occupied his native land. All was black! Yet Bolívar, like Washington, never lost hope; he never gave way to despair; he bolstered up his own spirits and aroused enthusiasm in those about him. He continued to fight against fate; he was thrown down time after time, yet he always jumped up again smiling, ready to renew the fray. Had it not been for Washington's courage and determination, the thirteen colonies of North America might never have gained their independence. Had it not been for Bolívar's unbreakable will power, the colonies of South America might have been reconquered by Spain. We honor both Washington and Bolívar because they never yielded to despair. Neither of them acknowledged defeat; neither of them knew when he was beaten. So in the end both of them won.

During these three years Bolívar saw his own estates consumed and his fortune dissipated; he saw quarrels among his followers; he saw his friends desert his side; he saw the royalist cause grow stronger and stronger with the arrival of more and more reënforcements from Spain. He himself was an exile; he was in constant danger; once even an attempt was made to assassinate him. Yet in his exile he talked and wrote and persuaded, he built up an organization, he collected funds, he persuaded other patriots to join him, and he enlisted recruits. He worked through this long and discouraging process not only once, but three times. In the end his loyalty to his cause and his perseverance were rewarded with success.

On his escape from Venezuela after the collapse of the second republic, Bolívar, as will be remembered, sailed for Cartagena, hoping there to begin all over again the campaign by which he had become the liberator of Venezuela, but in which he had now lost all. On his arrival, finding civil war rampant in the provinces of New Granada, he was given a command by one of the factions which would have required him to fight other patriots in his effort to force them to make common cause against the royalists. Meanwhile, 10,600 Spanish troops, veterans of the Peninsular War, arrived under the command of General Morillo to overawe the patriots who were too weak to resist, even if they had put aside their jealousies and united to drive out the invader. Bolívar did not acknowledge that the odds for open warfare against these Spanish troops were too great, but he recognized that he could do nothing

---

[16] Salaverría, 134.

against the jealousy and secret opposition of his personal enemies. He knew that the patriots in Cartagena were willing to go down in defeat rather than coöperate against the common enemy; and he told them so. He then shook the dust of Cartagena from his feet and sailed for Jamaica.[17]

While Bolívar remained in his self-imposed exile in Jamaica during the year 1815, Morillo had had little difficulty in reducing to submission all the revolted provinces of northern South America. He first captured Margarita Island off the north coast of Venezuela and then took possession of Caracas, from which he made expeditions along the coast. One of these landed at Santa Marta for an advance against Cartagena, and having drawn siege lines about this latter port, supplies were cut off until three hundred people had died of hunger in its streets. At last, after one hundred and eight days of suffering, the garrison became so weak that on December 6 Morillo's troops were able to enter and take possession of the city. Columns of royalists sent out by Morillo occupied the three provinces of Pamplona, Socorro, and Antioquia, and at length one of them succeeded in entering Bogotá, where Morillo established a military government in the capital with instructions to imprison or execute all those citizens who should dare to speak or write anything against Spain or his government. Having thus crushed the revolution in New Granada, Morillo left Sámano as viceroy and crossed the mountains into Venezuela.[18] The suppression of the patriots in New Granada and Venezuela seemed complete.

Fortunately, however, for the patriots in Venezuela, although their leaders were unwilling or unable to coöperate, each in his own way was doing his best to keep alive the spark of resistance in his own district. Among these may be named especially Urdaneta, Piar, Bermúdez, Saraza, Montilla, Cedeño, and Sucre. There was also Arismendi in Margarita Island, who again aroused the people of that island to revolt, accepted the challenge of the royalist governor for war to the knife, and recaptured the capital as well as other important forts on the island.[19]

On the plains of Casanare a new leader had come to the front. This was José Antonio Páez, an uneducated *llanero* who, by his justice and daring and by his spectacular intrepidity, became the leader of the *llaneros* who craved excitement, yearned for danger, and knew they

[17] Pilling-Mitre, 355; O'Leary, *Narración*, I, 265-272.
[18] Pilling-Mitre, 357-364; O'Leary, *Narración*, I, 327-330.
[19] O'Leary, *Narración*, I, 277.

could always obtain it if they followed him. Many of those who had been fighting under Boves felt that there was more glory to be won under Páez and changed sides. For these *llaneros* cared little whether they were royalists or patriots, but since Páez was a patriot they, in accepting his leadership, fought for that side. So many of them flocked to him that by 1816 Páez had one thousand five hundred men in his Army of the Apure.[20]

Meanwhile, Bolívar had been busy. He persuaded the Dutch ship-builder Luís Brión of Curaçao, to invest funds in the patriot cause and to lend it seven armed schooners for the formation of a Venezuelan navy, of which Brión was made admiral. Alexandre Pétion, the mulatto president of Haiti, promised to furnish arms and money if Bolívar would abolish slavery in the lands which he might liberate.

The negro slaves in the western end of the island of Santo Domingo having revolted against their masters and having prevented the reconquest of their island by an expedition sent by Napoleon, had erected there the black republic of Haiti. To this land, which had established its freedom, flocked many of the defeated and exiled patriots of northern South America, among whom were Piar; Mariño who, as will be remembered, had failed Bolívar in his time of need; Montilla and Soublette, both from the eastern provinces of Venezuela; Francisco Zea, a lawyer; and the Scotch adventurer Gregor MacGregor. With these and others Bolívar, who had gone to Aux Cayes, Haiti, organized a small expedition and sailed from that port on March 16, 1816.[21]

With this little expedition of three hundred men Bolívar, having landed on Margarita Island, in coöperation with Arismendi announced the reëstablishment of a third republic of Venezuela and the installation of a national congress, and then proceeded to spread the good news to the north coast of the mainland. After disembarking at Ocumare, the patriot advance guard under Soublette was attacked and driven back by a superior force of royalists. Since it was rumored that a large force of the enemy was pursuing him into the town, munitions and stores were hurried aboard one of his ships under the protection of darkness, and then Bolívar with the rear guard sailed away to save them from capture, leaving Soublette and MacGregor on shore with instructions to retreat inland by a roundabout route and meet him at a designated point on the coast further east. These two officers succeeded in leading a

---

[20] Pilling-Mitre, 365-368.
[21] Pilling-Mitre, 368-369; O'Leary, *Narración*, I, 340.

masterly retreat through a region occupied by the enemy and in reaching the plains of Barcelona, where they effected a junction with Cedeño. Bolívar managed to reach Guiria on the peninsula of Paria, but having been accused of cowardice in deserting his troops, was in turn deserted by his subordinate commanders, was repudiated by the patriots of Margarita, and returned discredited to Haiti.[22]

Convinced by this failure that it was futile to attempt to hold the north coast and to drive the enemy out of Caracas, but still hopeful of eventual success in freeing his native land, Bolívar now decided to change his base of operations to the Orinoco valley where he could receive the assistance of Páez and could find ample supplies and open lines of communication for his own followers. The credit for this decision is largely due to Piar who had foreseen the importance of preserving the line of the Orinoco and had already established depots for gathering food, supplies, and recruits in the Province of Guayana along the lower reaches of that river. Other patriot leaders also urged Bolívar to come there, and Páez, who was besieging San Fernando, magnanimously offered to place himself under the Liberator's command. Brión also furnished important assistance, for with his fleet he entered the river and threatened Angostura, the headquarters of the royalists. This city which had held out so long against previous attack was now entered by Bolívar who established there in 1817 the capital of the fourth Venezuelan republic.[23]

The years 1817 and 1818 in Bolívar's career were marked by constitutional progress, military defeats, and preparation for victory. After establishing the capital of the fourth republic of Venezuela at Angostura, Bolívar organized both a High Court of Justice and a Council of State, to the latter of which he entrusted the management of civil affairs whenever he might be absent in the field. This of course was in line with constitutional methods and a step toward entrusting all civil government to a national congress which Bolívar hoped soon to be able to install.[24]

In the field, however, it was only the energy and intrepidity of General Páez which saved Bolívar and the republic from disaster, for Bolívar had not yet learned fully the lesson that while the patriots were strong in the interior along the Orinoco valley the royalists were likewise strong along the coast. Páez wanted to defend the republic in the *llanos* of

---

[22] Pilling-Mitre, 369-372.

[23] Pilling-Mitre, 375-379; O'Leary, *Narración*, I, 383.

[24] José Felix Blanco, *Documentos para la historia de la vida pública del Libertador*, VI, 151-152.

the Orinoco where his cavalry guerillas were more than a match for the royalists, but Bolívar still yearned to deliver Caracas, his birthplace, from the enemy and planned another campaign with that end in view. When Saraza, whom Bolívar had expected to join in retaking Caracas, had allowed himself to be surprised and defeated with the loss of one thousand two hundred men and all his guns and colors, Bolívar called upon Páez to coöperate with him in an advance on San Fernando. It was during this march that a most remarkable event occurred—an action between naval vessels and cavalry in which the horsemen won. In the course of their advance it became necessary to cross the River Apure, but the patriots had no vessels at hand for transporting their troops, whereas near the opposite bank could be seen a number of canoes and three armed *flecheras*[25] guarded by a royalist gunboat. After a short inspection of the enemy, Páez dashed into the water calling to the *llaneros* who formed his guard of honor: "Into the water, boys! Follow your Uncle!" Digging in their spurs, this little band of cowboys swam their horses across the river, charged with their lances, drove overboard the royalist crews, and captured fourteen of their boats, making it possible for Bolívar to use them in transporting the rest of his troops across the river.[26]

After investing San Fernando, Bolívar urged Páez to accompany him in a campaign against Caracas, in spite of the protest of the latter that this might endanger their control of the Orinoco valley if they left behind them royalist troops in occupation of San Fernando. Bolívar, having left Páez there, tried to cut his way to Caracas between the royalist forces of La Torre and Morillo, with only one thousand raw infantry and one thousand two hundred cavalry, when Morillo with the main royalist army suddenly fell upon the patriot troops as they were passing through the ravine of El Semen near La Puerta on March 15, 1818. This defeat was a disaster, for Bolívar lost one thousand men, all his flags, munitions, and baggage, and even his correspondence.[27] He himself barely escaped with his life and might have been captured or been forced to wander as a fugitive had not Páez by this time captured and held San Ferdinando, which furnished a haven of refuge until the coming of the rainy season forced the royalists to suspend operations and to relinquish pursuit of the patriot detachments which still held on.

---

[25] "Arrow boats," so-called because of their speed when propelled either by sails or paddles.

[26] Pilling-Mitre, 383; O'Leary, *Narración* I, 491-492, 539.

[27] O'Leary, *Narración*, I, 459-460, 465.

Again Bolívar was at a low ebb of his fortunes, but Páez stood by him faithfully in defending Angostura and the Orinoco valley. Again Bolívar showed his strength and determination in adversity. He did not for an instant lose hope, but set to work to raise fresh troops to take the place of the patriot infantry which had practically been wiped out.

Just at this time help was beginning to arrive from an unexpected or at least forgotten source. These reënforcements were "foreigners" from England and the continent who were being sent largely at his own expense by Luís López Méndez whom, as will be remembered, Bolívar had left in London in 1810 to serve as Venezuelan commissioner to England. López Méndez had established himself in the former home of Miranda from which he had sent out appeals to British and Hanoverian army officers and men to enlist in the cause of independence.[28]

After the Battle of Waterloo times were hard, as they generally are after the close of a long and bitter war, and there was much unemployment in England and many men mustered out of the army could not find jobs. The appeal of good pay to these men and the offer of increased rank to officers brought López Méndez many applications for service under Bolívar. From these applicants there was formed the nucleus of a first contingent of five shiploads of legionaries (most of them officers it is true), who set sail for Venezuela at the end of 1817. One of these ships was wrecked and lost with all on board, and on the arrival of the other ships in the West Indies many of the recruits deserted, so that in that year only four hundred and twenty of the foreign legionaries reached Venezuela. In 1819, however, larger contingents joined Bolívar so that by the end of that year he had 5,508 foreigners under his command.[29] Among these were the contingents under General English, Hanoverians under Colonel Elsom, Scotchmen under Mac-Gregor, and the Irish Brigade of General D'Evereux. Later came many other individuals seeking pay and excitement so that it is said that no fewer than 9,000 foreigners came at different times to Venezuela and New Granada to reinforce the rebel armies.[30] This number may be slightly exaggerated, and as it is known that these did not all come at once and that they were pretty well scattered, it is probable that the

---

[28] Vicente Dávila, *Investigaciones históricas,* 169.

[29] Carlos Navarro y Lamarca, *Compendio de la historia general de América,* II, 744.

[30] Mariano Torrente, *Historia de la revolución hispano-americana,* II, 462.

actual number present in any one campaign did not exceed one thousand two hundred.[31]

The exact number of the foreign legionaries is, however, not so important as the relative weight which they bore in the contending armies. These contingents, together with natives which the patriot generals had been able to recruit, brought the strength of the patriot armies up to approximately the strength of Morillo's forces in Venezuela. Hence, the arrival of these foreign legionaries by 1819 gave Bolívar a force of infantry strong enough for him to plan a new offensive.

His thoughts turned back to New Granada from which he had made his invasion for the liberation of the second republic of Venezuela. The patriots in New Granada were still struggling to win their independence; why could he not turn about and help them with an army led from Venezuela? Bolívar saw that this was possible now and that the liberation of New Granada would be such a severe blow to the royalists that it would help to preserve the independents of Venezuela. He could now carry out this plan for he had sufficient infantry to make the invasion of New Granada and could trust to the cavalry of Páez to protect his rear by keeping the royalists busy.[32] Bolívar, therefore, sent some of his recruits to reënforce Urdaneta, Bermúdez, and Mariño who were to make diversions along the coast against Caracas, ordered Páez to continue guerilla operations in the Orinoco valley and to interpose his cavalry between Morillo and the mountains; and he himself determined to lead his main force in an invasion of New Granada to liberate that province from royalist control.[33]

II. The Founding of Great Colombia

This plan for the invasion of New Granada Bolívar kept secret even from his own officers until one day in May 1819 he broached it to them at a council of war at which he had assembled less than a dozen of his generals, where, in a little ruined hut in the deserted village of Setenta, they were grouped about him reclining on the bare ground or sitting on the skulls of oxen whitened by the sun and rain. The infantrymen, especially the British commander, Colonel Rooke, were eager to follow him, but since it was decided to leave most of the cavalry behind to

---

[31] Hasbrouck, 388.

[32] Bingham collection of manuscripts in Yale University Library, Bolívar letters, 5, 6 and 7.

[33] O'Leary, *Narración* I, 541, 550.

protect the rear, the cavalrymen refused to risk their horses in the mountains.[34]

On May 26 the army, consisting of four battalions of infantry (one thousand three hundred men) and eight hundred cavalry, began its advance from Mantecal. The fact that this was the beginning of the rainy season was both an advantage and a disadvantage, for it was assumed, and rightly, that the royalists would withdraw into their garrisons and would not attempt to campaign during the rainy season unless forced to do so. The disadvantages to the patriots of going into the field at this time were many, and how the daily downpour hampered their movements can be appreciated only by one who has experienced a rainy season in the tropics. The rain fell in solid sheets almost obliterating the landscape from view until that landscape had disappeared under the rising waters. Small streams which were nothing more than arid gullies during the dry season now became rushing rivers, while real rivers became lakes and seas. The burned, dry, and dusty *llanos* soaked up the descending waters and became soft and oozy mud, then quagmires, then lakes, and finally a vast sea extending for miles and miles from the lowlands of the Orinoco valley to the eastern foothills of the Andes. In the dry season this region is a network of small rivers, affluents of the Apure and the Orinoco, but during the rainy season these rivers overflow their banks and spread out to cover the whole vast area of the *llanos,* over which ordinarily even the *llaneros* mounted on their horses did not at such times dare to operate. For infantry, campaigning over these submerged plains was impossible, but Bolívar did the impossible.[35]

For nearly a month Bolívar's troops were crossing the Province of Casanare, wading in mud and water. For a week the water was up to their belts and often to their necks, leaving so few high spots that often the men could find no place to rest after struggling for hours through the swollen waters. Their arms and ammunition and even their food were so wet as to be almost unusable; their clothing rotted on their backs and became torn into shreds and tatters. The weaker men and the women who followed their husbands were in constant danger of sinking beneath the waters and the stronger ones were in terror of the caymans and caribes, or of the man-eating fish which infested these streams. Such fish, atoning for their small size by their voraciousness and by their numbers, would fasten themselves in myriads upon the

[34] *Ibid.,* I, 477-478, 543-545.
[35] *Ibid.,* I, 547, 552.

legs of their victims and in a few seconds strip with their sharp teeth the living flesh from their bones. To be attacked by them meant sure death.[36]

Hesitating to venture into such infested waters might be excused even in the best disciplined soldier, but when a body of troops was once in, to retreat was as dangerous as to advance. To keep on going required more than discipline and courage; it required blind determination and implicit faith in one's leader. Only Bolívar's personality could have inspired this faith or could have resisted the tendency to give up. His men knew that he would not call upon them to do more than he himself would do, and they felt confident that he would help them whenever he could. He took the lead in overcoming danger and hardship, shared with the men his scanty rations, and time after time swam his horse back and forth across an especially difficult river to rescue from its swirling waters any who might become exhausted and need his assistance to carry them across.

On arrival at Tame a junction was effected with the New Granadian patriots under General Francisco de Paula Santander. Here, fresh provisions were at hand and the exhausted Venezuelans were permitted to rest in preparation for even more arduous marching.[37] After leaving Tame, the trail led up the foothills into the mountains and up the high Andes to the páramos, or passes, near the top and thence down again to the lofty plateaus between the highest peaks. Nearly a week was spent in struggling up these mountain ramparts to the Páramo of Pisba. The rough and narrow trail ascended by almost perpendicular and exhausting grades or swung around a corner on a dizzy shelf a thousand feet above the bottom of a gorge. Footing on both slopes and shelves was precarious, for the rains and the climbing feet converted the rocky soil into greasy mud, and in the upper heights films of ice formed along the footways. The cold biting winds penetrated the worn and flimsy clothing which was suitable as protection against the sun during the dry season, but now served only to retain the rain until it froze. As they climbed higher these men of the plains and lowlands began to suffer splitting headaches, nausea, and extreme drowsiness, until they foamed at the mouth and went mad, owing to the terrible soroche, or mountain sickness, caused by the rarified atmosphere of those extreme altitudes. To keep on climbing made the suffering more acute, yet to lie down and

---

[36] Campaigns and cruises in Venezuela and New Granada, 57-158; O'Leary, Narración I, 551-552.

[37] O'Leary, Narración I, 552.

give way to the *soroche* meant inevitable death. When a man showed a tendency to give up, his comrades beat and lashed him to keep him going, a seemingly brutal treatment, but the only way to keep him alive.[38]

The *Páramo* of Pisba is a pass or saddle between the higher peaks lying at 12,000 feet altitude far above the timber line. Nothing grows upon it except lichens and a tall species of mullen called *fraylajón,* so there is no wood or fuel of any kind. A drizzling mist is always falling and an icy draft howls across the stony plain.

The night spent in crossing this *páramo* was the worst in all that long nightmare of marches. The icy gale blew against them with such violence that they could scarcely make headway against it; ice from the drizzle formed on their clothing, their beards, and their eyebrows; they could not build a fire because there could be found nothing which would burn; their rations were spoiled or exhausted so that they had nothing to warm them inwardly; they could only huddle together to share the warmth of each other's bodies, hoping that they might survive this night of misery. Many of them did not; and when the long night was ended and the column moved on again there were not a few gaps in the ranks. The frozen corpses of the men who the day before had filled these gaps were left behind to guard their empty bivouac.

Fortunately this was the dawn of better days. Presently the beautiful mountain valley of Serinza lay before them, where the climate was milder, where food and supplies were furnished by the patriotic inhabitants, and where recruits were enlisted to fill the places made vacant by the hardships of this terrific march. Statistics of losses at this particular period are not available although it is known that one-third of the British perished on the march and not a single horse or mule survived.[39]

Little opposition from the enemy had been met on this march, for Bolívar had chosen the most difficult and dangerous trail and had thereby avoided the outposts which awaited him along the more usually travelled route. Likewise throughout the rest of this campaign Bolívar outwitted the royalist commander, José Barreiro, by marching around his prepared positions, attacking his defenses on the flank, leaving a small detachment to distract his attention, and then attacking suddenly where he least expected it. The strategy of Bolívar's campaign in New Granada, by its vigor, its unexpectedness, its secrecy, its sudden changes of base, its flank marches and attacks, strikingly resembled the equally successful strategy of Stonewall Jackson's famous Valley Campaign.

---

[38] *Ibid.,* I, 560-561.
[39] *Ibid.,* 561-566; *Documentos,* XVI, 411.

Barreiro's mission was to prevent Bolívar reaching Bogotá; Bolívar's aim was to get there. From his central position at Sogamoso, Barreiro might have held either of the two routes along the mountains. Bolívar deceived him into believing that he would advance by one road, drew him away from his strong position, and then countermarched and swung around to the other route.[40]

Although there were a number of skirmishes fought between detachments of the rival armies, only two battles need be mentioned. These were at the *Pantano* de Vargas and at Boyacá. When Barreiro thought that Bolívar was advancing by the road through Paipa, he allowed himself to be drawn from his position at Sogamoso and advanced as far as the narrow defile known as the *Pantano* (swamp) de Vargas. This was a strong position in which to make a stand, for Barreiro held the heights overlooking the road while Bolívar was limited in maneuvering ground by the swamps on his right. It looked as if Bolívar had been caught in a trap, but the valor of his troops not only saved him from disaster but weakened Barreiro's strength so materially as to take away his initiative, and force him to act on the defensive and wait for Bolívar to make the next move. In the infantry charge up the heights Colonel Rooke was mortally wounded and Anzoátigui's patriot infantry suffered severely, but in the cavalry charge along the road by Colonel Rondón and his small detachment of *llaneros,* the royalist cavalry was annihilated.[41]

After both sides had withdrawn to their original positions, Bolívar continued to make feints along the Paipa road. On August 3 he threatened to attack the royalist position of Sogamoso; but that night, under cover of darkness, countermarched his army, recrossed the Sogamoso River which he had crossed that afternoon when he was pretending to return to his encampment, and swung around Barreiro's position until he was between the royalists and Bogotá. That night the patriots were on their way to the capital, having captured by surprise the royalist arsenal at Tunja with all its supplies.[42]

Had the royalist scouts and patrols been properly active and efficient in keeping contact with the patriots, Barreiro would not have been outwitted in this way. As soon, however, as he became aware of the situation he hastened to retrieve matters by placing himself again between the patriots and the capital, and by marching south on another road fur-

---

[40] O'Leary, *Narración* I, 567, 568.
[41] *Ibid.,* I, 556, 571.
[42] *Ibid.,* I, 573; *Hasbrouck,* 203.

ther to the west which joined the road from Tunja at the bridge of Boyacá. Whoever should cross this bridge first would command the road to Bogotá. It was a race for the bridge, and Bolívar's troops had the start although he himself delayed in Tunja superintending the collection of the captured stores of munitions.[43]

At two o'clock in the afternoon of August 7, 1819, the advance guards of both the royalist and patriot armies met at the junction of the roads within sight of the bridge of Boyacá. In the skirmish which ensued the royalists made a short stand in a tile-roofed farmhouse near the road fork, but were soon driven out by an impetuous charge of patriot skirmishes and retreated across the bridge to occupy the heights on the south bank of the river. This was an initial advantage which Barreiro tried to make the most of by rushing his main body forward to join his advance guard at the bridge. In doing so he exposed his left flank to attack by the Second Division of the republican army under Anzoátigui which was following a short distance behind the patriot advance guard. The arrival of these troops checked the movement of the royalists toward the bridge and forced them to retire to some rocky ridges which commanded the road from Tunja. There they formed a defensive line about their artillery and held on against Anzoátigui's attack.

Meanwhile, the First Division of the patriots under Santander swung down the road toward the bridge where it was checked by fire from the royalist vanguard. Since he could not cross the bridge under such heavy fire, he sent his cavalry to find an old ford further downstream. Having crossed the river by this ford the patriot cavalry attacked the flank of the royalist position south of the river, occupying the attention of the enemy until Santander could cross the bridge and dislodge them from their position.

Anzoátigui's impetuous charges had by this time penetrated the lines of the royalists north of the bridge and had thrown them into a huddled confusion. Barreiro, realizing that his army was cut in two and that he could not retreat toward Bogotá, threw away his sword and gave himself up as a prisoner. Some of the royalist advance guard managed to escape toward Bogotá but the rest of it, as well as the main body, had to surrender. In a battle lasting less than two hours the royalist army defending New Granada was wiped out, its commander, thirty-nine officers and one thousand six hundred men were made prisoners, and all its arms, ammunition, guns, horses, colors, and baggage were captured.[44]

---

[43] O'Leary, *Narración*, I, 574.
[44] O'Leary, *Documentos*, XVI, 428-430.

The Battle of Boyacá was the decisive battle in the campaign, for it opened the road to the capital. On learning from the royalist fugitives that Barreiro's army had been surrounded and cut off and that the patriots had crossed the Boyacá and were on their way to the capital, the Viceroy Sámano hastily evacuated the city taking with him the four hundred men of his guard of honor, the members of the *audiencia,* and all the royalist civil and military employees.[45] On the 10th of August, therefore, Bolívar entered the capital in triumph and amidst the plaudits of the patriotic citizens who were happy at last to be freed from royalist domination. In spite of the enormous difficulties he had encountered and overcome, Bolívar had thus brought to a successful conclusion in only seventy-five days his campaign of New Granada.

Although other sections of New Granada, including the ports of Cartagena, Barranquilla, and Santa Marta, were still held by strong royalist detachments, the capital and the mountainous region of Cundinamarca contiguous to Venezuela was cleared of all organized opposition. The time was ripe, therefore, for Bolívar to declare New Granada freed and to unite it with its sister state of Venezuela in the Republic of Great Colombia. Consequently, after a hurried trip to Angostura to report his success and to induce the congress of Venezuela to accept his plan, Bolívar established his headquarters and the capital of the new republic at Cúcuta, a city on the eastern slopes of the Andes near the boundary of Venezuela and conveniently located for both the recently liberated states. A vice-president was chosen to head each of these states while Bolívar was elected president of the Republic of Great Colombia.[46]

III. CARABOBO AND LAKE MARACAIBO

It will be remembered that when the Liberals gained control in Spain, they were anxious to win back the colonies to the fold, and that their generals in America were instructed to arrange for temporary cessations of fighting while negotiations were in progress. Since, however, the patriots stood out for independence which the Spaniards refused to consider, the negotiations came to naught and the armistices were broken. In the north as in the south this outcome was inevitable, yet, whatever the immediate cause, each side blamed the other. On April 28, 1821, the armistice between Bolívar and La Torre (the Spanish general who had succeeded Morillo when the latter returned to Spain during the

---

[45] O'Leary, *Narración* I, 580.
[46] *Ibid.,* II, 19, 21-23.

armistice) was declared at an end, and both sides hastened preparations for a renewal of the campaign.[47]

During the armistice the royalists had held Caracas and most of the north coast of Venezuela while the patriots controlled the Orinoco valley with strong detachments at the Island of Margarita and the ports of Barcelona and Carúpano. Owing to the fact, however, that the patriots must live off the country, they had been scattered widely over this area, so that on the outbreak of hostilities it was necessary for Bolívar to effect their mobilization.

His plan was to concentrate the divisions of Páez and Urdaneta with his own near Guanare, to take the initiative as rapidly as possible, attack La Torre near his headquarters at Valencia, and drive him back to the sea. Bermúdez, with the patriot troops in Barcelona, should meanwhile create a diversion on the royalist flank in order to force La Torre to detach part of his forces for the defense of Caracas.[48]

Bolívar's plans worked out successfully. La Torre not only sent his second in command, Morales, to recapture Caracas from Bermúdez, but also a division under Colonel Tello toward San Felipe in the west to oppose a raiding party which Urdaneta had sent to create a diversion on that flank. Then La Torre had marched his main body a few leagues to the south of Valencia where he took up a position on the plains of Carabobo to observe the roads leading thither from the south.[49]

On the morning of June 24, 1821, Bolívar at the head of his troops looked down from the low range of hills through which passed his road to Valencia. On the vast plain of Carabobo below him he could see the white uniforms of the 5,000 royalist troops which were prepared to block his way. The guns of the enemy's artillery could be seen posted in such a position as to concentrate their fire on the exit of the narrow pass through which he must debouch upon the plain. Under such conditions a frontal attack would be hazardous.

Having received word from a peasant that there was another trail which led further to the westward and came out upon the plain beyond the right flank of the enemy's position, and obeying his usual instincts in favor of a flank attack, Bolívar ordered Páez with the First Division to follow the guide along this trail and charge the right flank of the enemy. Having cut their way through this tangled and winding trail

---

[47] José Antonio Páez, *Autobiografía*, I, 203; *Correo del Orinoco*, April 14, 1821.

[48] O'Leary, *Narración* II, 75, 78-79; Lino Duarte Level, *Cuaderno de la historia militar y civil de Venezuela*, 337-338.

[49] Colonel Arturo Santana, *La campaña de Carabobo*, 112.

for two hours the leading elements of the First Division came out upon the Carabobo brook. The *Bravos de Apure* jumped down and tried to rush across, but were met by such a withering fire that they were checked and forced to halt for shelter under the further bank. Then the British Battalion, following immediately behind, deployed along this bank and held the position with their fire until the *Bravos* could form on their left and other companies on their right. The whole short line then charged as well as they could up the steep hillside under a decimating fire, driving the royalist battalions back from the crest. At this juncture Páez at the head of the cavalry had emerged on the plateau from higher up the stream. Calling to his staff and to his guard of honor to follow him, he led a charge against the flank of the enemy, scattering the three infantry battalions and the cavalry which protected the right flank of La Torre's position. The battle was won by these charges of the First Division under Páez.[50]

When, however, the enemy's troops were seen to be in flight with only the Valencey Battalion forming square to protect the withdrawal of the artillery, the Second and Third Divisions of the patriot army charged down the road. Colonel Plaza, the heroic commander of the Third Division, fell mortally wounded and the charge was checked, but the royalists were forced to abandon two of their guns in the road and to withdraw rapidly in the direction of Valencia.[51]

Bolívar pursued the retreating enemy through Valencia and on to the coast where the Valencey Battalion and one thousand five hundred cavalrymen shut themselves up in Puerto Cabello. These were all of his army that La Torre was able to save, for on this day he had lost two guns, most of his flags and munitions, and forty per cent of his troops, while the patriots lost only two hundred men. The victory was so decisive that five days later Caracas capitulated, while all that was left of the royalist army was beseiged in Puerto Cabello.[52]

The fact that the patriots could surround this place only on the land side and that they did not have at that time any vessels to spare from their little navy to blockade its sea approaches enabled La Torre to maintain communication with the outside world to replenish his supplies as needed by means of the warships of Spain which then controlled the Caribbean. Indeed, as long as the royalists held Puerto Cabello they could threaten the independence of Venezuela. Even though the royal-

---

[50] Santana, 115; Páez, I, 205-206.
[51] Santana, 116.
[52] Páez, I, 207-208.

ists could not be starved out or driven away, this threat to the safety of Venezuela could be minimized by blocking all their exits toward the land side. The essential duty of stationing troops around Puerto Cabello for this purpose and of conducting siege operations was entrusted to General Páez, inasmuch as Bolívar had more important matters to attend to in the south.

Although this was a duty in which there was little opportunity for active guerilla operations and daring cavalry charges, his favorite method of fighting, Páez had to continue it for nearly two years. La Torre could have escaped by sea and did manage to send out detachments to make raids upon the coast of Venezuela, but he knew the importance of holding on to Puerto Cabello as long as possible since it furnished an essential base to which reënforcements might be sent from Spain in case reconquest should be attempted. Since siege duty is bad for the morale of troops, especially for cavalry, the *llaneros* pined for their active life in the saddle. And since they were now encamped near unhealthy coastal marshes, sickness spread among them and carried off so many that the patriot force was reduced by two-thirds. This condition of affairs convinced Páez that the siege was becoming too costly, and because it was ineffectual he violated his instructions and withdrew his lines.[53]

This transferred the scene of action to Lake Maracaibo, for Morales, who had been able to march out from Puerto Cabello, established a base in the city of Maracaibo from which he could threaten that region and the valleys leading to Cúcuta, the capital of Great Colombia. Although his position there, however, was not as strong as it was in Puerto Cabello, yet he constituted such a threat to the republic that strenuous efforts must be made by the patriots to dislodge him. To his protection came the Spanish fleet under Admiral Angel Laborde, and after the Spanish fleet, came in pursuit the patriot admiral, General José Padilla with all the ships which he could gather for the operation. These consisted of three brigantines, the same number as the Spanish, but only seven schooners and thirteen light craft, whereas the Spanish admiral had twelve schooners and seventeen small vessels under his command.[54]

Lake Maracaibo forms a landlocked harbor deep enough for the heaviest ships of those days, but its mouth is shut in by islands and shoals through which winds a narrow channel passable only at high tide. Furthermore, this channel was protected by strong forts under the guns

---

[53] *Ibid.*, I, 221.

[54] Florez Álvarez, "Acción de la marina colombiana en la guerra de independencia," *Memorial del estado mayor del ejército de Colombia*, No. 89, p. 141.

of which ships entering must pass at short range. Nevertheless, in spite of these dangers, Padilla determined to force this channel with his ships and attack the Spanish fleet which had already sought shelter inside the bar. In forcing the bar two of Padilla's largest ships ran aground. One of them managed to work itself off, but the other was battered to pieces by the guns of the forts as it lay helpless in the mud. The other vessels were brought through safely by removing guns and ballast, but so much time was lost thereby that the night was past before they were sailing on the lake. The Spanish admiral fled before them and refused to engage, so that it was not until July 24, 1823, that the Spanish ships were caught anchored in line near the city of Maracaibo to leeward of the patriot ships.[55]

Having the wind in their favor, the Colombian ships bore down on the helpless Spaniards, each ship picking out its opponent, grappling to its side, and pouring its crew upon its adversary's decks. It was a duel between ships, and each duel was fought by the sailors and marines hand to hand with the enemy's crew. Eleven of the larger vessels were captured, the others blown up, and the Spanish admiral was forced to strike his colors. A few days later Morales surrendered the city and its fortress, but was allowed to withdraw his troops to Cuba. The royalist troops left in Puerto Cabello, no longer supported by a fleet, yielded that stronghold when Páez attacked on November 7.[56]

The victory of Lake Maracaibo destroyed Spanish naval power on the Caribbean and prevented any further attempt to regain Venezuela. It completed the decision on the sea which Carabobo had won on land.

IV. BOLÍVAR'S FINAL CAMPAIGNS. LIBERATION ATTAINED

Having driven the enemy from New Granada and Venezuela, Bolívar was left free to assist the patriots in Quito to secure their independence and to unite that department as a third state in the Republic of Great Colombia. This was accomplished in 1822 by the Campaign of the South, the credit for the actual and successful execution of which, although it was Bolívar's genius which conceived and planned it, must be divided between him and his faithful subordinate, General Antonio José de Sucre. In order to secure the allegiance of the inhabitants of the southern department and to prevent their accepting the protection of San Martín and Peru, as will be remembered, General Sucre was sent

---

[55] *Ibid.*, 143, 144.
[56] Páez, I, 230.

to Guayaquil where he had to exercise infinite diplomacy as well as win victories in the field.[57]

In retrospect, the strategy of the Campaign of the South seems simple, for it was to catch and crush the royalist commander of Quito, General Melchor de Aymerich, between the two jaws of the military pincers which Sucre in the south and Bolívar in the north would close upon him. The execution of this maneuver, however, was not so simple, for Sucre, as has been said, had first to win over the inhabitants of Guayaquil and to secure the coöperation of the Peruvian General Santa Cruz; he must overcome factional dissentions and crush a naval revolt; finally, he had to prevent the junction of two Spanish divisions which had been sent against him. Bolívar summoned his scattered forces from Venezuela and the north coast and assembled them at Bogotá,[58] where they had been reëquipped by the efficient service of supply organized by General Santander, the vice-president. Then Bolívar had to march with them southward for more than seven hundred miles along the loftiest mountain range in America and over the steepest and most difficult trails in the world. He must fight sickness, hunger, desertion among his own troops, and the incessant attacks and ambushes from guerillas and partisans of the enemy. For the last third of the journey he was passing through country where the inhabitants were completely in sympathy with the royalist cause and showed that sympathy by destroying supplies and attacking, ambushing, and murdering Bolívar's men whenever they found an opportunity.[59]

Having marched into this hostile country, Bolívar at last found his way blocked by a strong force of royalist regulars under Basilio García who occupied an almost impregnable position along the further edge of a wooded ravine in the *hacienda* of Bomboná. In order to continue his advance on Quito it was necessary for Bolívar to break through this obstacle; so relying on the valor of his troops, the patriot commander gave the order to attack. By a long and difficult trail one division of the patriot army climbed the steep escarpment of the ravine and attacked the right flank of the royalist defense, while another division charged the center over a narrow bridge. The slaughter of those engaged in this frontal attack was compensated for by the fact that it held the royalists' attention until the flanking movement could be accomplished, so that the royalist commander, finding himself surrounded and cut off,

---

[57] O'Leary, *Narración* II, 118-120; Hasbrouck, 252, 259.
[58] F. B. O'Connor, *Independencia americana*, 56-59.
[59] O'Leary, *Documentos*, XIX, 249; *Archivo Santander*, VIII, 259.

was forced to surrender.[60]   Had García been able to check Bolívar's advance in this battle, he himself could have withdrawn to support General Aymerich who was then hard pressed in defending Quito.

Sucre advancing from the south had driven Aymerich back to his last stand before Quito.   On May 24, 1822, the two armies met on the slopes of the volcano Pichincha, where, if Sucre could outmaneuver the royalist commander, he might be able to close in upon the capital and threaten its safety.   By a night march Sucre gained the heights of the volcano, but when day dawned he was perceived by the royalist scouts and an attack was launched upon him.   The advantage rested with the patriots because they occupied the superior position and were able to drive back the attacking royalists before the reserve of the latter could come to their assistance.   Sucre's maneuver and his successful defense had left him master of the ground between the royalist army and its base;[61] yet had the expected reënforcements from García been able to arrive at this time, the results of the battle might have been different. As it was, Sucre entered Quito and secured the capitulation of Aymerich and his entire force.   Since there were no longer any royalist troops to defend it, the whole province of Quito was claimed by Bolívar when he marched into the capital from the north, and the liberated province was forthwith incorporated as a third state in the Republic of Great Colombia.[62]

Subsequent to, and as a result of, this action there took place the conference described previously between Bolívar and San Martín at Guayaquil.   Bolívar had then sent Sucre to Lima as his representative and to command the contingent of Colombian troops furnished to aid Peru in its efforts to gain independence.   With these Colombians Sucre sailed for southern Peru where he took part in what has been called the "campaign of the intermediate ports"; but since the Peruvian General Santa Cruz failed to keep Sucre informed of his plans or movements, the latter was unable to give him the coöperation that he needed, so that this campaign resulted in disaster for Santa Cruz.   Sucre himself lost heavily and was able to escape defeat only by a painful and masterly retreat across the deserts from Arequipa to the coast.[63]

[60] O'Leary, Narración II, 134-135; Documentos XIX, 237-239.

[61] O'Leary, Documentos, XIX, 287, 299; Recuerdos históricos del coronel Manuel Antonio López, 71-80.

[62] Carlos Cortes Vargas, Participación de Colombia en la libertad del Perú, I, 2-3, 34.

[63] O'Connor, 108-109; Miller, II, 76-79.

Now that San Martín was out of the way, Bolívar, having completed the consolidation of the three states of Great Colombia, and having received necessary permission from the congress, himself sailed for Peru in August 1823. On arrival there he was invested with supreme military and political authority, but had as much difficulty in maintaining the latter amid the bitter factional quarrels among the patriots as he had in winning the former against the royalists. In accordance with his orders large contingents of troops continued to arrive from Colombia, which together with Argentine and Chilean troops left behind by San Martín were incorporated with Peruvian troops in the "United Army of Liberation." It was this army which connected Bolívar's northern campaigns with San Martín's campaigns in the south and completed the liberation of all the Spanish colonies of South America by a final campaign ending in a decisive victory.

After the organization of this army Bolívar had determined to finish the war by leading it against the army of the viceroy, which was established in the high valleys of the Andes near Cuzco and held all the important passes. There the royalist troops were supplied and supported by the Indian inhabitants who as mountaineers lost no love for the inhabitants of the lowlands and coast, patriots though they might be. To oust the viceroy from this strong position, Bolívar ordered his own army to advance into the mountains in three divisions, each division ascending one of three valleys leading toward Cerro de Pasco and Cuzco, where the patriot divisions would converge upon the enemy. In the course of this advance the utmost difficulties and hardships were encountered and surmounted, inasmuch as the only roads were narrow trails used by the Indians for climbing on foot or for driving their llamas. These trails wound around and over the mountain sides and were often mere shelves cut into the perpendicular face of the rock, and in places were too steep even for loaded mules, so that the cavalry had frequently to dismount and lead their horses. Burdened as they were with their arms and equipment, the climb would anywhere have been exhausting, but at altitudes of 10,000 to 15,000 feet the thinness of the atmosphere made it torture. Not only did the troops suffer from the dread *soroche* but also from snow blindness caused by the reflection of the intense tropical sunlight from the vast snow fields which they had to cross near the mountain tops. On these bleak passes there was no shelter from winds and snow and no protection against the zero temperatures. Thus the month required to cross the cordillera was a period of torture to the soldiers of the United Army of Liberation.[64]

On approaching Cerro de Pasco the patriot army encountered the royalist cavalry sent to spy them out and to check them near the borders of the Lake of Reyes. On the narrow plain between the borders of the lake and the steep hillsides was fought on August 6, 1824, the Battle of Junín, a battle in which not a single shot was fired, since only lances and sabres were used, as the cavalry of the two armies charged each other back and forth across the plain. The fortunes of war favored first one side and then the other; but in the end, after less than an hour's whirlwind fighting, the royalist cavalry was put to flight. This was a severe blow to the viceroy for it destroyed the eyes and ears of his army and thereafter he had no efficient means for scouting or keeping informed of the movements of the patriots, especially after the royalist headquarters had been withdrawn from Cuzco and removed further into the mountains.[65]

After reaching Cuzco, Bolívar, having received news necessitating his return to Lima, entrusted the command of the army to Sucre with instructions to use his own discretion in concluding the campaign. Sucre, thereupon, decided that his duty was to pursue the royalist General Canterac and fight him to a finish. In pursuance of this plan both armies continued their march for several days along nearly parallel roads, eying each other from time to time, and each hoping to catch the other in a position where it might be unable to fight to the best advantage. At last Sucre caught up with Canterac who had established himself on the heights of Condorcanqui, at the foot of which was spread the plain of Ayacucho, 11,600 feet above the sea. Inasmuch as this plain was just broad enough to allow the deployment into line of the patriot army, while the flanks were protected by ravines where the plain terminated on both sides, this was an ideal defensive position for the patriots if the enemy would give up its commanding position on the heights and come down to attack. Strangely enough this is what the royalists did when, on the morning of December 9, 1824, the Spanish Viceroy José de la Serna led down from the heights four columns from the royalist center and left. He advanced too rapidly so that he did not allow time for the royalist right to cross the ravine and attack the partiots' left flank as had been planned. Thus unsupported, La Serna found himself attacked

[64] Miller, II, 121-125, 217-220.
[65] *Ibid.*, II, 130-134; O'Connor, 116.

by the whole patriot line, with cavalry charging against his exposed right. He himself was wounded and captured as the patriot troops swarmed up the hillside through his shattered lines. The commander of the royalist right wing attempted to withdraw, but was unable to regain the heights before the patriots had occupied them. The royalist headquarters were surrounded, while those who should have been its defenders were scattered in hopeless confusion in the plain and ravine below. Canterac was forced to surrender his entire army and as acting viceroy after the capture of La Serna, he was also compelled to consent to the capitulation of all royalist troops in the Viceroyalty of Peru.[66]

This victory meant the end of the war, since now the last viceroy of the Spanish colonies in South America had agreed to the withdrawal of his troops. As a reward for his victory Sucre was promoted Grand Marshal of Ayacucho. The Battle of Ayacucho is universally considered as the decisive battle which ended the wars of independence with victory for the patriots.

As a matter of fact, however, three royalist commanders refused to capitulate and kept the field in defiance of the orders of the viceroy. Of these General Pedro Antonio de Olañeta, who had asserted his independent authority in Upper Peru, was defeated in battle and killed by one of his own subordinates who had turned against him. Sucre took advantage of this situation, marched into Upper Peru and aided the patriots in establishing a government of their own. The republic which they founded in 1825 received its constitution from Bolívar and was named in his honor, Bolivia.[67]

On January 18, 1826, the royalists who had been holding out on the Island of Chiloé, near the southern coast of Chile, were driven therefrom by the Chilean General Ramón Freire. In the castle of Callao the royalist General José Ramón Rodil, defended himself for more than a year after the Battle of Ayacucho, resisting every bombardment and attack of the patriots; but at last, reduced by sickness and starvation, he was forced on January 23, 1826, to evacuate the fortress, marching out with the honors of war and lowering the last flag of Spain to fly on the South American continent. Thus 1826 may be considered as the final date at which all the republics of Spanish South America were secure in their independence from Spain. In South America the republics of Argentina and Chile were freed through the efforts of San Martín; of

---

[66] O'Connor, 145-148; Miller, II, 166-173; Cortes Vargas, II, 232-253.
[67] O'Leary, *Narración* II, 375; O'Connor, 166-167.

the five republics of Venezuela, Colombia, Ecuador (Quito), Peru, and Bolivia, Bolívar is called the Father.[68]

---

[68] Robertson, *Rise of the Spanish American republics*, 263-264, 311-312; Rippy, 153-159. It will be remembered that although Uruguay had gained its independence from Spain before 1826, it was not recognized as independent by Brazil or La Plata until 1828.

CHAPTER EIGHTEEN

THE MOVEMENTS FOR INDEPENDENCE IN MEXICO AND CENTRAL AMERICA

By Alfred Hasbrouck

THE statement that the wars for independence of the Latin American republics partook of the nature of civil wars is well exemplified in the case of Mexico (New Spain). In fact, there were in that viceroyalty two civil wars, the normal one between Creoles and Spaniards and a preliminary race-war between Indians and whites; yet both these contests were closely related and hinged on the resentment of the colonists, both white and Indian, at being ruled by the *juntas* in Spain.

When news came of the overthrow of the Bourbon monarchs by Napoleon and the setting up of the *juntas* in Spain, the viceroy of New Spain, José de Iturrigaray, at first commanded submission to the orders of the *Junta* of Seville. When this was refused by the *ayuntamiento* (city council) he proposed the establishment of local self-government by means of a *junta* composed of himself, the Archbishop of Mexico, and representatives from the army, the municipality of the capital, and the principal families. To this *Junta* of Notables, Creoles were to be admitted on equality with peninsular Spaniards.[1] Thereupon, there was set up a division of the colonists into two parties. The Creole party welcomed the proposal of the viceroy, for it not only gave them a better standing in the government but would, as they hoped, maintain more firmly the rights of King Ferdinand, while the Spanish party was inclined to favor the authority of the *Junta* of Seville. The Creoles were actually more loyal to the king than were the European Spaniards, since the latter, sometimes called the French party, plotted to defeat the plans of the viceroy, whom it suspected of attempting to establish himself as an independent ruler.[2]

On the night of September 15, 1808, Pedro de Garibay with a select group of Old Spaniards entered the viceregal palace, arrested Iturrigaray and shipped him a prisoner to Spain. Pending the arrival of the

---

[1] Philip Young, *History of Mexico*, 72.

[2] Arthur H. Noel, *From empire to republic*, 29.

new viceroy, Vanegas, Pedro de Garibay acted as viceroy.[3] But, never-theless, the Creoles were not satisfied with this turn of events and con-tinued to plan the setting up of a government of their own. They formed literary societies and correspondence clubs, and sent emissaries to the provinces and principal cities to inculcate their ideas among the people. These were everywhere welcomed by the Creoles and even by many of the clergy, who formed similar clubs in the provincial towns and cities.

Among these clubs were those at Querétero and Dolores. The presi-dent of the latter was the parish priest Miguel Hidalgo y Costilla, who took the matter in hand so actively that he persuaded many of his parish-ioners to plot independence and had arms prepared for their use. Even the date for the uprising was set for December 8. Unfortunately, how-ever, one of the conspirators in the club at Querétero, fearing that he was about to die of a sudden and dangerous disease, revealed the de-tails of the plot to the confessor who came to give him absolution, even including the names of the conspirators. Among those named were two officers of militia, Allende and Aldama, and the *corregidor* of Querétaro and his wife, Josefa Ortiz de Domínguez.[4] This *"corregidora,"* as she is known in history and tradition, having learned of the danger which she and her fellow conspirators were in, at the risk of further involving herself, sent a messenger to Allende to warn him. The latter hastened to the home of the curate Hidalgo and at two o'clock in the morning of the night of September 15-16, 1810, warned him that all had been dis-covered. Hidalgo, seeing that they must act at once, rang the bell of his church to summon his parishioners.[5] Instead, however, of celebrat-ing mass for the assembled crowd of Indians, he told them that now was their chance to rise against the masters who had stolen their lands from them, and to fight for their independence. The Indians eagerly acclaimed his plan with the *Grito de Dolores* (Battle cry of Dolores) and followed the lead of their white-haired priest. Bands of Indians came swarming in from the countryside to join the Army of Independence which, as it advanced, continued to swell in numbers. At the head of this throng marched the old curate waving the banner of the Virgin of Guadeloupe

---

[3] Young, 73.

[4] Noel, 39. A *corregidor* was a local official having to do with the protection of the Indians and the collection of taxes.

[5] Annually on September 15, the president of Mexico now steps out upon a bal-cony of the National Palace in Mexico City and rings the tocsin on this same bell in celebration of the anniversary of independence.

snatched in passing from the altar of the church of Atotonilco. Of the mob of 30,000 Indians who followed, only one thousand had muskets, the rest being armed with spears, *machetes,* and other homemade weapons which the conspirators had provided. City after city in the State of Guanajuato fell into their hands, for the attack came so unexpectedly that no one was prepared to resist. Everywhere the Indians rushed to join the standard of the Virgin, but the whites fled terror-stricken to escape indiscriminate looting and slaughter. Shouting the battle cry "Death to all Spaniards," the Indians failed to discriminate between Creoles and peninsular Spaniards so that the former who would gladly have espoused the cause of independence had to flee for protection to the support of the Spanish faction. Thus, what had begun as a civil war between Creoles and Spaniards was metamorphosed into a race-war between Indians and whites.[6]

Hidalgo had no wish to bring about this indiscriminate slaughter of the whites. Since his only aim was independence and the return of the lands to the Indians, he tried in vain to control his excited Indians, but was swept along helpless in the mad rush of his followers. The town of Celaya surrendered, and the regiment to which Allende belonged declared for independence. Hidalgo was acclaimed Captain-General and found himself at the head of 20,000 followers, the ardor of whom was not dampened at his excommunication by the Bishop of Michoacán.[7] They surrounded the city of Guanajuato and drove the defenders into a strong stone building called the *Alhóndiga de Graniditas,* used as an arsenal and storehouse for grain. When this was captured, its defenders were put to the sword and its contents were looted, while Hidalgo secured $5,000,000 for the support of his army and likewise confiscated additional large sums from the church treasury in Valladolid, a city which promptly declared for independence.[8]

The people of the capital were terror-sticken when it seemed probable that the Army of Independence would march upon Mexico. Colonel Truxillo with a small force was sent out to oppose the invasion, but was defeated at Monte de las Cruces in a victory which was costly for the patriots since the poorly armed Indians fell in heaps under the volleys of the regular troops. Consequently, although he was now within twenty-five miles of the capital, Hidalgo hesitated. Why he did not follow up his victory is not known; perhaps because the people of the

[6] Noel, 40-41.
[7] *Ibid.,* 40-41.
[8] *Ibid.,* 42-45.

city failed to rise in his favor.[9]   At any rate, he turned when his objective was in sight and retreated, a fatal move, for it cost him the
confidence of his troops, many of whom deserted, so that although
hitherto he had been uniformly successful, from now on he suffered
defeat after defeat.   At Aculco, the royalist General Calleja del Rey
caught up with him and administered a severe chastisement.   The Army
of Independence was scattered, but Hidalgo made a final stand at the
Bridge of Calderón near Guadalajara where, after having lost 30,000
men, he was again badly defeated by Calleja and forced to flee.   On
March 21, 1811, Hidalgo, Allende, and Aldama with their staffs were
betrayed by Captain Bustamente, one of their number, and were captured, all of them being later put to death.[10]   After Hidalgo had been
tried by the Inquisition, convicted of heresy and treason, and defrocked,
he was turned over to the civil authorities and was executed in prison
on July 31, 1811.[11]   Hidalgo was a sincere enthusiast, unselfish and of
noble motives, but he was too weak to control the mob which his elo-
quence had aroused to fury.   He had no military experience or ability,
and did not know how to profit by his victories which were won by the
enthusiasm of his men and their overwhelming numbers.   Although
Hidalgo is the popular hero of Mexican independence, at least one Mexican historian gives the credit to Allende for beginning the revolution
and for furnishing whatever leadership and military skill there was in
the Army of Independence.[12]   After the death of Hidalgo and Allende,
the war of independence continued as a class struggle of Indians against
Spaniards.

This contest lacked all semblance of a coördinated or unified movement, since those who claimed to be fighting for independence often
thought more of their own personal interests than of the welfare of the
nation; they might call themselves patriots but sometimes they were
little more than bandits.   Undoubtedly many fought for lofty and disinterested motives, but not all did so.   The insurgents carried on a
guerilla warfare in scattered bands without attempting to coöperate
against their common enemy.   Those who wished to fight for independence joined the band which was operating in their own neighborhood;
but these bands seldom combined for extensive operations since the

---

[9] Gutiérrez de Lara and Edgcumb Pinchón, *The Mexican people: their struggle
for freedom*, 36.
[10] Young, 84-85.
[11] Noel, 49.
[12] Francisco Bulnes, *La guerra de independencia. Hidalgo-Iturbide*, 96.

leaders were jealous of each other and each preferred to carry out his own plans.[13]

Among these patriot leaders in the Province of Valladolid was Ignacio Rayón, who was a good lawyer but an unsuccessful general. Disgusted at the brutality of this kind of warfare and having been deserted by his professed followers, he was forced to surrender the fort of Copero to the viceroy, and was captured and imprisoned until 1821.[14] Guadeloupe Victoria, with one thousand five hundred men, kept up guerilla warfare in the mountains of the Intendancy of Vera Cruz, where he was successful in his tactics and was kind and helpful to the inhabitants.[15] Osorno, who was inhuman and lacking in principle, with two thousand cavalry operated near the capital where in the guise of patriotism he and his lieutenant, Vicente Gómez, ever more cruel and licentious, plundered all parties, especially the wealthy Old Spaniards.[16] Juan Antonio Torres, who had an army consisting of one thousand Indians and *mestizos,* divided the Province of Guanajuato into subsidiary districts and allowed his subordinates to exercise unlimited sway over the lives and property of the inhabitants of their districts. He himself, although he had formerly been a curate, acted like a ruffian and levied contributions upon the civil population; yet, in order to keep up an appearance of acting under proper authority, he maintained correspondence with the Revolutionary Committee, the members of which were merely his tools.[17]

In addition to Hidalgo and Torres, other priests, among whom may be mentioned Dr. Cos and Mariano Matamoros, helped to keep alive the insurrection. But it was not until a real military genius, José María Morelos, also a priest, succeeded to the leadership of Hidalgo, that the patriot cause made any headway.

This priest, after whom the State of Morelos has been named, is revered as one of the most honored fathers of independence. Beginning in January 1812, he required but a few months to clear the enemy completely out of the zone between Acapulco and Cuautla, and conceived the project of marching on the City of Mexico, but was surrounded and besieged in Cuautla by a much superior force under Calleja. With only three thousand men Morelos repulsed all assaults upon his defenses and then one night broke through the ring of enemies which

[13] Noel, 50.
[14] *Ibid.,* 73.
[15] Young, 119.
[16] *Ibid.,* 122.
[17] *Ibid.,* 124-125.

hemmed him in and escaped with his whole force intact under the fire of artillery concentrated upon him from all sides. This evacuation of Cuautla, cited to show the military genius of Morelos, is called "unique in the history of all liberators and in the histories of all heroic peoples." [18] After this escape, Morelos advanced to Tehuacán, and in October 1812 took the City of Orizaba after a hand to hand fight in the streets. There he enrolled 5,000 men and marched upon Oaxaca, a city which he took by assault on November 25, 1812. The following August, after a protracted siege, Morelos received the capitulation of the castle of San Carlos at Acapulco, and eventually became master of the whole of the provinces of Oaxaca and Valladolid, as well as of a portion of Guadalajara.[19]

At Chilpancingo he convoked the first Mexican congress which proclaimed the declaration of independence of Mexico, abolished slavery, and established equality before the law. While meeting at Azpatzingán, forty members of this congress drew up a constitution and issued a declaration of the intentions of the patriots to be loyal to King Ferdinand, and proposed that the conditions of warfare be regularized and made more humane. If the viceroy should not accept these conditions, then only would the patriot commanders resort to retaliation.[20]

Morelos made a serious mistake in delegating to this congress his power as commander-in-chief, for thereafter he was hampered in all his movements by having to await the consent of congress. His military strategy was debated in the congress, and since many of the delegates were traitors and were in the pay of the viceroy, his secret plans were revealed to the royalists.[21] On the other hand, this congress was useful in giving a semblance of unity and furnishing an office to which the various patriot commanders might turn for instructions which, had they been willing to do more frequently, the several movements for independence might have been properly coördinated.

Morelos, being free no longer to carry into execution his brilliant tactical conceptions, suffered an unfortunate succession of reverses. In order to protect the government and to establish it more formally, he made an unsuccessful attempt to recapture the city of Valladolid, and was forced to retreat through the province of that name, pursued most vigorously by Colonel Agustín de Iturbide who, as will be seen, later

---

[18] Rafael Anzures, *Los héroes de la independencia,* 181.

[19] *Ibid.,* 182.

[20] Young, 100-103.

[21] *Ibid.,* 104.

deserted the royalist cause and became the leader of the revolution. At Puruándiro the latter overtook the rear guard of the patriots and disastrously defeated it, capturing its commander, Matamoros, and nine hundred of his men. Morelos continued his retreat but was hampered by the presence of the congress and a large number of women camp followers whom he had to protect. At Texmalca on November 5, 1815, he was again defeated and fell into the hands of the enemy,[22] was tried by the Inquisition, and convicted of atheism, materialism, and heresy. After having been defrocked, he was turned over to the secular authorities for execution, and on December 22, 1815, Morelos was shot in the back as a traitor. Thus ended the career of one of Mexico's most admired heroes of independence.[23]

Manuel Mier y Terán, who succeeded Morelos as commander-in-chief, dissolved the congress because it threatened to deprive him of command; this was an unfortunate move, for it ruptured the only tie which bound the other insurgent chiefs, the jealousies and lack of coöperation of whom were responsible for the failure of Mier y Terán to carry out his wise plan of occupying the Isthmus of Tehuantepec from coast to coast where it was only one hundred and thirty-five miles wide. His plan was to secure bases for supplying his forces by the occupation of the ports of Guascualco on the east and of Tehuantepec on the Pacific, but through the failure of Victoria and Osorno to unite their forces with his, Mier y Terán's march on Guascualco was interrupted. He was defeated at Playa Vicente, and when besieged at Tehuacán was forced to capitulate to the troops of the new Viceroy Apodaca.[24]

Meanwhile, operations were progressing independently in the north, where the Mexican insurgents in Texas were joined by American adventurers led by Lieutenant Magee of the United States Army, who invaded Texas and captured Nacogdoches and Goliad. Then the royalist General Salcedo in 1813 besieged the latter place and tried unsuccessfully to capture it. Colonel Kemper, who had succeeded to command after the death of Magee, during this siege, defeated Salcedo at San Antonio de Bexar, but resigned after his Mexican allies had executed prisoners to whom he had promised safety. Colonel Perry, who was then placed in command of the United States and Mexican volunteers, decisively defeated near Bexar the next royalist commander who had been sent to check his advance. But when he was deserted by his Mexi-

---

[22] Anzures, 183.
[23] Young, 108.
[24] *Ibid.*, 110-117.

can allies, he had to retreat to the border to save the remnant of his force of four hundred Americans and two hundred Indians.[25]

Another expedition from the United States, consisting of two vessels, two hundred infantry, and a company of artillery, mostly Americans, led by Francisco Xavier Mina, a former general in the Spanish army who had resolved to aid the patriots in Mexico, sailed from Baltimore on September 21, 1816.[26] In spite of the protests of the Spanish minister at Washington, the United States government did nothing effective to prevent the sailing of this expedition, which succeeded in landing at Soto la Marina near the mouth of the Río Santander (Province of San Luís Potosí). After having erected fortifications to protect his base, Mina started inland with the greater part of his force to effect a junction with Torres, and after marching six hundred and sixty miles in thirty-one days arrived at Sombrero, after which in the battle of Peotillas he defeated a royalist division of seven hundred Spanish infantry and one thousand one hundred Mexican cavalry and continued his invasion of Zacatecas as far as Guanajuato.[27]

The small garrison left behind at Soto la Marina was attacked and, although it put up a valiant defense, was forced to capitulate under promise of pardon and safe conduct, a promise which was broken when Americans as well as Mexicans after their surrender were sent as prisoners to do forced labor in Spain.[28] Mina then tried to aid Torres, who was surrounded at Los Remedios, by cutting off the besieging forces from communication with the southern provinces, but was surprised by an attack on his camp near Guanajuato, was captured, and was executed by a firing squad on November 11, 1817. When his ammunition was exhausted Torres had to abandon Los Remedios, although his attempt to escape by night was discovered and his entire force was annihilated.[29]

After this massacre at Los Remedios and the death of Mina the royalists appeared to have triumphed. The patriots, scattered in the mountains, could operate only in small parties without plan or cohesion. Torres, who had been degraded from the position of commander-in-chief by the *junta,* intrigued with other independents to betray the cause.

---

[25] *Ibid.,* 94-97.

[26] *Ibid.,* 129-130.

[27] *Ibid.,* 137, 142.

[28] *Ibid.,* 143-148, 167-169.

[29] *Ibid.,* 167-170; William Davis Robinson, *Memoirs of the Mexican revolution,* 282-283.

Guadeloupe Victoria, whose real name was Félix Fernández, made no attempt to keep together an organized force under his command. His men lived widely scattered in their own homes and responded to his summons only when he was about to make an attack on some royalist detachment, after which, whether this attack resulted in success or failure, they immediately scattered to their homes again. Although this method of warfare proved extremely effective in annoying the royalist commanders who were unable to find any orgnized body of insurgents to chastise, it was unimportant in influencing the general cause of the revolution. The inhabitants, even those who favored the patriot cause, soon grew tired of these raids and forays of the insurgents, and after 1816 Guadeloupe Victoria, deserted by his followers, had hidden himself all alone in the forests and mountains of the Province of Vera Cruz where he was hunted like a wild beast by detachments of royalist soldiers constantly alert to follow up any report of his appearance near an Indian village.[30]

The only leader of importance left was Vicente Guerrero who with scarcely eighty men had retired from the mountains of Misteca to Valladolid, where his group was constantly augmented by the arrival of refugees from the other patriot guerilla bodies. Guerrero, therefore, managed to hold the country along the Pacific near Valladolid in defiance of the royalist General Negrete, and to protect the other revolutionary chiefs who had retired to Zacatula.[31]

The new Viceroy Apodaca, who had replaced Calleja del Rey, was both energetic and conciliatory. He kept 5,000 Spanish troops and a large force of native soldiers constantly pursuing the guerillas, while at the same time he offered indulgence and forgiveness to all those who would return to their allegiance to Spain. In this way the enthusiasm of the revolutionists was destroyed and their former sympathizers began to look upon them merely as banditti, so that among intelligent people the cause of independence was no longer popular.[32]

The second phase of the movement for Mexican independence began in 1820 when, as will be remembered, a barrack revolt followed by a revolution in Spain made prisoner Ferdinand VII who had previously been restored to his throne, and established the popular and liberal *cortes* as the real ruler of the Spanish empire. This *cortes* proclaimed the restoration of the Constitution of 1812 with all its liberal provisions,

[30] Fay Robinson, *Mexico and her military chieftains,* 63-65.
[31] Young, 173-175.
[32] Fay Robinson, 74.

sequestrated the property of the church, and ordered the viceroy to put these orders into effect in New Spain. Apodaca, who was loyal to the king, resolved to resist the commands of the *cortes* and for this purpose hastened to assemble troops throughout the viceroyalty for the ostensible purpose of suppressing the rebels.[33]

These events in Spain also put the royalists and Old Spaniards in Mexico into an embarrassing position. Should they declare themselves obedient to the *cortes* (the representative of the Spanish nation), or should they remain loyal to the king? The choice involved acceptance of liberal ideas which they hated, or a separation from the mother country; for if they continued their adherence to Spain they would lose the much prized privileges of their class and would suffer the degradation of being governed by upstart bourgeoisie liberals like those who were ruling Spain. True royalists and other prejudiced persons, attributing this unsatisfactory state of affairs to the malevolent influence of liberal ideas and to the accursed constitution, devoted themselves to checking these threatening evils.[34] The Mexican church was especially hard hit, for if it obeyed the orders of the *cortes* it would lose not only its privileged position but would also suffer sequestration of its property. Thus, a decision had to be made which resulted in the anomaly of the clergy, the nobility, the wealthy Creoles, and the Old Spaniards as a whole, casting aside their loyalty to Spain and favoring a movement for independence. This state of affairs in Mexico should be noted as a striking contrast to the usual alignment of classes in the other Spanish colonies during their wars for independence.

The clergy, panic-stricken for fear that the viceroy would enforce the orders of the *cortes* for the sequestration of their property, led the way in plotting independence. The first meeting of the conspirators was held in Mexico City at the convent of La Profesa under the presidency of the Spanish priest Monteagudo and the Mexican Dr. Tirado, both of whom were members of the Inquisition and bitterly opposed to liberal ideas.[35]

These conspirators, aware of the favor with which the viceroy looked upon the church, yet uncertain what attitude he would adopt in this crisis, decided to use their influence with him to appoint a military commander who would aid them to carry out their plans. The officer whom they selected was Colonel Agustín de Iturbide, who recently had been

---

[33] Young, 179.
[34] Mariano Torrente, *Historia de la independencia de México*, 272.
[35] *Ibid.*, 273.

relieved of his command in disgrace and was now an idler in the city. During this leisure time, Colonel Iturbide had devoted himself assiduously to religious exercise and by the austerity of his practices had endeared himself to the priesthood. From his earliest entry into military service he had shown himself a violent opponent of the insurrection, had received his captaincy for valor in action against Hidalgo at Las Cruces, and had been rapidly promoted step by step to colonel, as he was nearly always on the field of battle against the rebels.[36] Such a record must have deceived the viceroy, even if he suspected the motive which actuated the conspirators.

At any rate, Iturbide was appointed to command the Army of the South with orders to provide for the protection of half a million dollars of public treasure which he would find at a place called Iguala, and then to attack Guerrero and crush the insurrection in the south. Whether the viceroy winked at the colonel when he gave him these orders is not known, but the latter paid no heed to their actual words; whether or not he suspected the sentiments of the viceroy, the colonel obeyed the instructions which he had received from the clerical conspirators. On arrival at Iguala, Iturbide confiscated the money which he was to protect and then opened correspondence with Guerrero, the enemy whom he was ordered to fight, in the course of which negotiations Guerrero rejected every proposition which did not include the granting of independence. Meanwhile, in order to make a pretense that he was carrying out his orders, Iturbide permitted his Lieutenant-Colonel Verdejo, who little suspected the perfidy of his commander, to carry on operations against the rebels.[37]

At length, Iturbide offered to Guerrero a document, called the Plan of Iguala, which had been provided by the conspirators. In order to conciliate all parties, the Plan of Iguala provided for the independence of the Mexican nation, the protection of the Catholic religion, and the union, without distinctions, between Americans and Europeans, thereby guaranteeing the protection of three desirables—independence, religion, and union. Further, the plan provided for a constitutional monarchy with Ferdinand VII as king, or the offer of the crown to another Bourbon or to a member of some other royal family, in case Ferdinand should fail to accept it, with a *junta* to carry on the government in the interim.[38]

---

[36] Alejandro Villaseñor y Villaseñor, *Biografías de los héroes y caudillos de la independencia,* II, 268.

[37] Torrente, 282.

[38] A full translation of the twenty-four articles of the Plan of Iguala is quoted in Young, 181-183.

Since this plan met the demands of the independents, Guerrero was glad to accept it, which he did on February 24, 1821, when he joined his troops with those of Iturbide in a combined force called the "Army of the Three Guarantees." [39]

Iturbide naïvely sent a copy of the Plan of Iguala to the viceroy who replied by declaring him a rebel and despatching General Liñan against him. Apparently Apodaca felt that he must continue to oppose the revolutionists as heretofore, but had he fully realized the change of sentiment among the clergy and aristocracy, he might have acted differently. Everywhere signs of disaffection showed themselves, and everywhere desire for independence was evident. The tricolor of independent Mexico, white, red, and green, signifying religion, independence, and union, was displayed in the streets and even painted on the walls of houses. [40] There was reason to believe that the royalist troops were disaffected; and even if they should remain loyal they were not sufficient to suppress sedition. [41]

The Army of the Three Guarantees was being daily augmented by the accession of members of guerilla bands and by the former patriot leaders. Herrera, Bravo, and Osorno threw in their lot with the new army; Bustamente and Cortázar joined with a division of 2,000 dragoons; Guadeloupe Victoria came out of hiding in the mountains and speedily raised a new detachment of volunteers; and in Vera Cruz a young officer, who later was much heard of, Antonio López de Santa Anna, took up the cry for independence. [42]

Leaving Guerrero in command of operations in the south, Iturbide marched with the greater part of the army across the country gathering in these reënforcements and receiving the acclamations of all classes of people, [43] until Apodaca became convinced that resistance to this wave of sentiment was no longer possible. Even the clergy came out openly against him, and through their intrigues caused him to be deposed and an officer of artillery, Francisco Novella, to be placed at the head of the government. Novella tried his best to stop the wave of insurrection but was utterly unable to do so, for in a campaign lasting seven months the independents were everywhere victorious. [44]

---

[39] Young, 184.
[40] Villaseñor, 418.
[41] Torrente, 289.
[42] *Ibid.*, 295.
[43] Rafael Anzures, 268.
[44] Young, 185.

In August 1821 the last viceroy of New Spain, General Juan O'Donojú, who had been sent by the *cortes* to supersede Apodaca, landed at Vera Cruz. O'Donojú saw at once the futility of attempting to check the revolution, since he had brought no new troops with him and would not have strength to force his way through hostile territory to join the loyal troops in the capital. He, therefore, made the best of the situation by agreeing to meet Iturbide at a conference at Córdoba. There on August 24, 1821, the Treaty of Córdoba was signed whereby O'Donojú accepted the Plan of Iguala and recognized the independence of Mexico. A month later, after the royalist troops had been withdrawn from the capital, Iturbide and O'Donojú entered the city together amid enthusiastic acclamation.[45] To carry on the government a regency of five was established of which Iturbide and the viceroy were the most influential members; but shortly thereafter O'Donojú died and Iturbide as president of the regency actually ruled the country.

A congress was assembled in which three parties became evident: the Borbonistas, who favored the strict enforcement of the Plan of Iguala with Ferdinand VII or some other member of the House of Bourbon on the throne; the Republicans, consisting largely of those patriots who had kept the revolution alive since the time of Hidalgo and who now favored the organization of a federal republic; and the Iturbidistas, who accepted the Plan of Iguala but who advocated conferring the imperial sceptre upon Iturbide.[46] This latter party consisted largely of those whose personal interests depended on the success of their patron. When, however, the Spanish *cortes* refused to ratify the Treaty of Córdoba or to permit Ferdinand to accept the throne of an independent Mexico, the Iturbidista faction was strengthened by the reception into its ranks of many of the former Borbonistas.

It was not long before the Iturbidistas felt that the time was ripe for staging a demonstration in favor of their idol, so they secured the assistance of a sergeant of the First Regiment of Infantry, named Pío Marcha, who on the night of May 18, 1822, led from their barracks a crowd of soldiers shouting "Viva el Emperador!" "Viva Agustín I!" This cry was taken up by the throngs in the streets and by those coming out of the theatres who had been aroused to a receptive mood by demonstrations in favor of Iturbide which they had just witnessed on the stage. When the enthusiasm of the crowds in the streets spread to the

---

[45] Noel, 84.
[46] *Ibid.*, 87.

galleries of the hall where congress was sitting, the members, half in
the infection of enthusiasm and half in terror of the mob, voted seventy-
seven to fifteen for the election of Iturbide as Emperor of Mexico.
Iturbide, evidently forewarned of what was in store for him, was ready,
and at once took the oath of office. On July 25 he was crowned Emperor at a lavish and imposing ceremony celebrated in the Cathedral.[47]

This First Empire in Mexico lasted less than a year. Since Iturbide
was not to the manor born, instead of devoting himself to the best interests of his subjects, he spent his time in devising pompous ceremonies
for his own aggrandisement and in ordaining empty honors for his
friends and members of his family. Those who had suffered and fought
for independence through the bitter years since 1808 were forgotten;
they received no rewards for their valuable services; and they were
passed over for promotion in favor of upstarts who had fought for independence only after victory had been assured by the acceptance of
the Plan of Iguala. Therefore, Guerrero, Bravo, Guadeloupe Victoria,
and other patriot generals joined the Republicans. The Old Spaniards
and the Creole aristocracy were aroused to indignation at the airs which
were put on by this middle class colonel, by the members of Iturbide's
family, and by the new aristocracy of the Order of Guadeloupe which
he had created.[48]

The Republicans in congress so vehemently opposed the emperor that
he arrested several of the most important of them and entrusted legislation to a *Junta* of Notables which he had established to take the place
of the congress dissolved by his order. With the connivance of this
junta, the emperor levied forced loans and issued a surplus of paper
money, thus destroying the credit of the nation. Although the revolts
which broke out in the north were suppressed, the Republicans flooded
the country with pamphlets advocating the establishment of a republic.[49]

At Vera Cruz in February 1823 General Santa Anna promulgated his
Plan of Casa Mata in which a republic was proclaimed, and he was soon
joined by many of the former patriot generals and by all the national
troops. Too late the emperor tried to placate the Republicans by re-
leasing the imprisoned deputies and reinstating congress. But this
restitution was in vain, for the popular opposition was too strong. In

---

[47] Torrente, 334.

[48] Noel, 92-93.

[49] Torrente, 335.

order not to involve the country in civil war Iturbide, on March 20, 1823, decided to abdicate.[50]

Iturbide was granted a pension provided he would remain in exile in Italy. After his departure, however, his partisans in Mexico plotted a restoration of the empire and wrote to him that his presence was necessary and that popular sentiment favored his return, although they neglected to tell him that congress had declared him a traitor and had condemned him to death if he should return to Mexico. In ignorance of this decree, Iturbide, professing that he was returning to give to his country the services which he alone could render, recrossed the ocean and landed near Tampico. But, shortly after his feet had touched Mexican soil, he was arrested and condemned to death by the provincial assembly. On July 19, 1824, he was executed at Padilla, after exhorting his fellow citizens to observe the religion, maintain the peace, and obey the laws of their country.[51]

Subsequent to the abdication and death of Iturbide, the government of Mexico was changed to that of a federal republic in imitation of the United States, its official name becoming the "United Mexican States." Guadeloupe Victoria was elected its first president, and Nicolás Bravo vice-president.[52]

One of the few partially successful accomplishments which can be credited to Iturbide's short reign was the annexation to the Mexican Empire of the greater part of the former Captaincy-General of Guatemala. In 1821, under the lead of its royal governor, Gavino Gainza, that captaincy-general had peacefully declared its independence from Spain at a meeting of a *junta* held at Guatemala City on September 15, a date which is now celebrated by all five of the Central American republics as their Independence Day. They did not, however, enjoy this independence long, for Iturbide seeing the opportunity to take advantage of political discords within the states of the former captaincy-general invited them to join his empire and sent an expedition under the command of General Filísola to enforce their acquiescence. Although he proclaimed their annexation to Mexico on February 21, 1822, he was not able at once to enforce the acceptance of this proclamation in all departments of Central America, inasmuch as Salvador refused to obey and drove out Filísola's army.

---

[50] Noel, 95-96.

[51] *Ibid.*, 100.

[52] Torrente, 340.

After the dissolution of Mexico's first empire, the Captaincy-General of Guatemala went its own way. The Province of Chiapas still adhered to the republic of Mexico, but the other five states, Guatemala, Salvador, Honduras, Nicaragua, and Costa Rica, on July 1, 1823, declared themselves an independent republic called the "United Provinces of Central America." [53]

---

[53] Dana G. Munro, *The five republics of Central America,* 24-29; W. H. Koebel, *Central America,* 132-135; Robertson, *History,* 180, 446; Wilgus, 264.

CHAPTER NINETEEN

THE MOVEMENT FOR INDEPENDENCE IN BRAZIL

By Alfred Hasbrouck

THE winning by Brazil of independence with little bloodshed and practically without warfare is a strange and interesting story somewhat different from that of the Spanish colonies. Influenced by the French Revolution and the establishment of the independence of the North American states there were, it is true, some early attempts to gain the independence of parts of Brazil by force of arms.

In Minas Geraes in 1789 some forty conspirators led by Joaquin José da Silva Xavier, rendered desperate because the Portuguese government insisted on the payment of taxes which the diminution of their mining profits precluded their paying, plotted to set up an independent republic. Their plans were discovered by the government and were nipped in the bud, and they themselves suffered severe penalties. Their leader, called by his admirers "Tiradentes" (the tooth-puller), was hanged, decapitated, and his body quartered, his head was exposed to public view, his house destroyed, and his children and grandchildren declared infamous.[1]

In 1801 negroes in Bahia organized a plot to gain their freedom, but were discovered and checked before they had a chance to put it into execution. Such attempts to gain independence were abortive and unsuccessful and were not even premonitions of what was to follow. Nor should they be considered as evidence of general discontent among Brazilians as a whole.

Although the examples of North America and France had something to do with encouraging hopes of independence, the historian must again turn to Napoleon as the immediate cause of the movement for independence in Brazil. It will be remembered that Portugal, bound to England by a treaty, had failed to close its harbors to British goods when ordered to do so by Napoleon, compelling the latter to invade that country in order to enforce his continental system of exclusion of British trade. While doing this he compelled the vacillating Prince Regent João to obey his orders and then frightened him into quitting Portugal and escaping to Brazil. This was a crafty move of Napoleon's by which he outwitted the British ministry, for he knew that England would sup-

---

[1] John Armitage, *The history of Brazil*, I, 11.

port the Portuguese ruler and that if this ruler established himself in his colony of Brazil, England would be prevented from seizing that colony.[2]

The British ministers, having fallen into this trap of Napoleon's, aided the escape of the Braganzas from Portugal to the extent that on November 29, 1807, convoyed by thirty-six sail, four British ships of the line left the Tagus with the Prince Regent, the whole royal family, and a retinue of nobles and courtiers, while Lord Strangford, the British minister, accompanied them until they were well on their way. "Thus the emigration of the court of Lisbon was planned by Napoleon and our ministers eagerly lost their heads to execute it." [3]

Shortly after the arrival of the Braganza family in Brazil, the royal court was established at Rio de Janeiro, and thus was brought about that extraordinary situation in which the capital of a colony became the capital of the mother country. The colony naturally benefited by this unusual state of affairs, for its ports which had previously been closed to all but Portuguese trade were now thrown open to foreign vessels, a national bank was founded at Rio, and courts of justice, royal libraries, and institutions of higher education were established.[4]

There were, however, certain disadvantages resulting from the transfer of the royal court to the colony, for the expenses of that court and the support of a large number of hangers-on and idle Portuguese nobility had now to be paid for by the colonists. To make matters worse, the increase in business, necessarily attendant upon the presence of the court, was given to Portuguese residents in preference to Brazilians; and these Portuguese, enjoying the favor of the court, began to treat the Brazilians with haughty arrogance, while the newcomers regarded their stay as only a temporary exile and failed to interest themselves in the welfare of the colony. Thus, since most of the official positions were filled by Portuguese, most of the acts of the government were dictated by motives not for the best interest of the colony.[5]

On the other hand, possibly as a sop to the colonists, when the Prince Regent on the death of his mother became King João VI of Portugal, he, by an edict of December 16, 1815, raised Brazil to the rank of king-

---

[2] Ralph Rylance, *A sketch of the causes and consequences of the late emigration to the Brazils,* 24-25.

[3] *Ibid.,* 21, 28.

[4] Armitage, I, 13-14.

[5] *Ibid.,* I, 15.

dom fully equal to that of his other domains, Portugal and Algarves.[6]
This may be considered the first step in the independence of Brazil.

The Kingdom of Brazil enjoyed five years of this quasi-independence when a liberal revolution broke out in Oporto, which attempted coöperation with the Republicans in Spain. The army joined the movement, and before the end of 1820 the whole of Portugal was in the hands of revolutionists, and a year later a *côrtes* was assembled at Lisbon which proposed to draw up a liberal constitution.[7]

The liberals in Brazil received with rejoicing this news from Portugal, and without knowing what the provisions of this constitution were to be, proceeded to advocate it, the Province of Pará being the first to act and form a *junta* of government, and a month later Bahia, the richest and most powerful province of Brazil, following suit. The troops stationed in Pará declared for the popular cause, and a mass meeting of the populace in Rio de Janeiro, attended by the troops and even by the royal princes, demanded that the king should accept the constitution. When the mob took the horses from the carriage of the king and dragged it into the city from his palace in the suburbs, João VI, thoroughly frightened by this manifestation of popular insubordination, swore to accept the new constitution of Portugal which had not even yet been written.[8]

Both Portuguese and Brazilians, in the exuberance of their desires for a more liberal government, had joined in this demand that the king should sign; but the Brazilians soon had cause for wishing that they had not done so, for when the completed constitution was received, it was found to portend the destruction of that independence which the colony was enjoying. The royal family was to be compelled to return to Portugal and the former Kingdom of Brazil was to be placed under the authority of the *côrtes* at Lisbon, although it was allowed to send a number of deputies to this *côrtes* in proportion to the size of its population. On the other hand, the previous virtual independence of Brazil was tacitly admitted, for provision was made whereby Brazil might accept or refuse this constitution as it saw fit;[9] and had it not been for their own precipitancy in forcing the king to accept the constitution before they knew its provisions, the Brazilians might have taken advantage of this last clause, have rejected the constitution, and gone their own

[6] Alphonse de Beauchamp, *L'indêpendance de l'empire du Brésil*, 9.
[7] Armitage, I, 23.
[8] Carlos Navarro y Lamarca, *Compendio de la historia general de América*, II, 798-799.
[9] Beauchamp, 17.

way to actual independence. Now it was too late, for João VI and his court must return to Portugal while all government of his three kingdoms would in the future be centered in Lisbon. The Brazilian party tried to prevent the king's departure and so profoundly influenced his mind that he worried lest there should be an increase of sentiment for independence and even for republicanism. Fearing that this part of his realm might before long be lost to the House of Braganza, when his ship was about to sail and he was taking adieu of his son, Dom Pedro, who was to be Prince Regent of Brazil during his absence, the old king embracing the youth for the last time said, "Pedro, Brazil will I fear, ere long separate herself from Portugal; and if so place the crown on thine own head, rather than allow it to fall into the hands of any adventurer." [10] This occurred on April 26, 1821, and may be considered the second step in the independence of Brazil.

Dom Pedro, left behind as Prince Regent, found his position none too happy, for the colony was torn between two factions: those who wished to maintain and those who wished to destroy the old institutions—the Brazilians and the Portuguese. The first group urged the Prince Regent to rule as though Brazil were still a kingdom equal to Portugal, while the second group advocated obedience to the *côrtes* at Lisbon. Bahia, the second city of the colony, refused to recognize the authority of the Prince Regent, and the Portuguese troops adopted an attitude hostile to him. The provinces would no longer contribute taxes to the central government, while the national bank, robbed by dishonest directors, found its vaults nearly empty. The commerce of Brazil received a deadly blow when the *côrtes,* in order to satisfy the demands of Portuguese merchants, again closed its ports to any but Portuguese trade; yet Pedro tried his best to overcome these difficulties. He displayed excellent sagacity in cutting down expenses and reduced the budget from fifty millions to fifteen millions; and he adopted economies for the royal household in every department. In his stables now stood only fifty carriage mules where formerly six hundred were maintained. But Pedro was not popular because he suffered from the faults of his ministers who were hated by the Brazilians because they belonged to the Portuguese party, and by the Portuguese because they were suspected of being too favorably disposed toward the Brazilians.[11]

Meanwhile, the *côrtes* in Lisbon proceeded to enact legislation affecting Brazil without waiting for the arrival of the delegates from that

---

10 Armitage, I, 36.
11 Beauchamp, 18-19.

colony. Even after they arrived, it treated them with contempt, and because their number was only half of that of the Portuguese delegates, passed legislation over their protests. Thus, having ruined the foreign trade of Brazil in order to benefit Portuguese merchants, the *côrtes* further to weaken the colony, decreed that the chancery court, the treasury, and the chamber of commerce, which had been created at Rio de Janeiro during the reign of João VI, were to be abolished; it directed that in the future the provincial governments should cease to respond to the jurisdiction of the former colonial capital and should correspond directly with the tribunals of Portugal; and to facilitate carrying out these regulations, ordered that the Brazilian troops should be incorporated in the army of Portugal in order that the Brazilians might be transferred to Portugal where they could not protect their friends and that their places might be taken by Portuguese troops sent to enforce these obnoxious laws on the Brazilians.[12]

Finally, the *côrtes* directed that the Prince Regent should return to Lisbon after having first made a tour incognito through England, France, and Switzerland under the guidance of certain persons appointed as his tutors by the *côrtes*. In spite of the humiliation of this last gratuitous insult, Dom Pedro was so discouraged by the bad state of affairs in his realm, by the insubordination of his troops, by the bitter party discords, and by the refusal of the provinces to obey his government, that he was willing to submit.[13] In fact, he wrote to his father, "I supplicate your Majesty, by all that is most sacred, to relieve me from these painful functions, beneath the burden of which I can no longer exist. . . . I conjure your Majesty to permit me as soon as possible again to kiss your royal hand, and to reseat myself on the steps of your throne." [14]

Fortunately for Brazil, however, he was dissuaded from abandoning his post by the action of a body of patriots in the City of São Paulo, led by the hero of the independence of Brazil, José Bonifacio de Andrada e Silva. José Bonifacio, at the time vice-president of the provincial *junta,* summoned a meeting of his colleagues at which it was decided to send an appeal to the Prince Regent to remain at his post, warning him that his departure would be the signal for Brazilian independence; and shortly after sending this address, José Bonifacio himself went to see the Prince Regent. Meanwhile, the Province of Minas Geraes sent a similar appeal, and the municipality of Rio de Janeiro drew up a mani-

---

[12] Armitage, I, 41, 51.
[13] Beauchamp, 19.
[14] Quoted in Armitage, I, 49.

festo signed by eight thousand persons urging the Prince Regent not to allow the enforcement of the decree of the *côrtes*.

Convinced by the arguments of Bonifacio and by these manifestations of popular will that failure to remain at his post, in spite of his own inclinations and the order of the *côrtes,* would jeopardize the rights of the House of Braganza to rule over Brazil, the prince hesitated. Remembering that his father had told him not to let anyone else seize the crown, he feared that if he left now, Brazil would declare its independence and probably become a republic. On January 9, 1822, to a deputation sent to receive his answer, Dom Pedro replied, "If it be for the good of all, and for the general felicity of the nation, tell the people that I will remain!" [15] This was the third step in the independence of Brazil.

This statement of his position was received with joy by the entire populace and gained for Pedro the esteem and affection of the Brazilians.[16] The general of the Portuguese garrison submitted his resignation and his troops became mutinous, but they were cowed by the overwhelming demonstrations of loyalty of the populace and by the threat of the Prince Regent that he himself would be the first to fire upon them if they did not at once embark and sail for Portugal. After the Portuguese troops had departed the municipality conferred upon Pedro the title of "Perpetual Protector and Defender of Brazil." He then appointed José Bonifacio his "Minister of the Interior, of Justice, and of Foreign Affairs," [17] and endeavored to insure Brazilian unity by the election of an assembly and a council of state. Pernambuco drove out its Portuguese garrison, and Minas Geraes and Espiritu Santo gave their adherence to the Brazilian system. The Brazilians demanded not only a separate legislature, local self-government, and central magistracies, but equal liberty in commerce as well.[18]

Having rejected all these demands, the *côrtes* replied by sending more troops to Brazil and by accusing the Prince Regent of acting despotically in convoking the national constituent assembly without its permission. It declared this convocation to be null, and the government at Rio de Janeiro to be illegal. It specifically revoked the authority of the Prince Regent and ordered him to return to Europe within four months under penalty of losing his hereditary right to the throne. Furthermore, it

---

[15] Armitage, I, 59-60, 62-64.
[16] Beauchamp, 20.
[17] Armitage, I, 65-67, 80.
[18] Beauchamp, 29-30.

threatened to hold his ministers and naval and military commanders responsible for his acts and to punish them if they obeyed the colonial government.[19]

This decree of the *côrtes* finally cut the knot which had bound the colony to the mother country. Even Bahia joined the other provinces, and the ruling faction in Montevideo, which until then had been considered an independent state, asked for annexation to Brazil. A Portuguese squadron was sent with troops to subdue Bahia, an attempt which proved only temporarily successful, as did similar undertakings against Pará and Maranhão.[20]

News of this decree reached the Prince Regent while he was on a hunting trip on the margin of the Ypiranga, a small stream near the City of São Paulo. Forthwith Pedro declared that he would not obey the order of the *côrtes,* removed the Portuguese cockade from his hat and cried, "Independence or Death." His followers dashed up to him tearing the red and green brassards from their sleeves and took up his cry. This *"Grito do Ypiranga"* marks the fourth and last step in the independence of Brazil. The day on which it occurred, September 7, 1822, is celebrated as the Independence Day of Brazil.[21]

On the 12th of October, Dom Pedro's birthday, he was offered the title of Constitutional Emperor of Brazil and agreed to accept the constitution of the new empire. On December 1, 1822, he was solemnly crowned Emperor.[22]

Meanwhile, the *côrtes* fulminated against him by decreeing that voluntary obedience to the new government would be accounted criminal; that the ministers who had signed the decree convoking the constituent assembly in Brazil had acted illegally and would be indicted accordingly; that the military commanders who obeyed the new government should be punished as traitors; and that the Prince Regent should be deprived of office and return to Portugal at once.[23]

The Andrada ministry headed by José Bonifacio took steps to defend the independence of Brazil against which the *côrtes* had threatened to send all its available troops and ships. All property in Brazil belonging to Portuguese subjects was sequestrated, and all those who would not accept the empire were ordered to leave the country within four months;

---

[19] *Ibid.,* 33.
[20] Beauchamp, 33-34.
[21] Navarro y Lamarca, II, 800.
[22] Armitage, I, 89, 97.
[23] *Ibid.,* 93.

preparations were made to expel the Portuguese garrisons; the marine force was increased; and Lord Cochrane, that Anglo-Irish admiral who, it will be remembered, had organized a navy for Chile, was invited to come and do likewise for Brazil.[24]

On his arrival, Admiral Cochrane found that he was to help defend the government in a civil war in which the Brazilian party which desired independence was trying to drive out the Portuguese party which advocated obedience to the *côrtes* at Lisbon. In Rio de Janeiro and the southern provinces the Brazilians were in control, but in the north the loyalists refused to support the new government, for they were protected by troops of the Portuguese army which held Bahia, Maranhão, and Pará, and by a formidable Portuguese squadron.[25]

With a hastily assembled squadron badly manned, Cochrane blockaded the Portuguese squadron and garrison in Bahia, shut off their supplies, and threatened the destruction of their vessels by means of fire ships which he was preparing. Such fear did his activities inspire in Admiral Mello and General Madeira that they decided to abandon Bahia and transport all their forces to Maranhão. While the unwieldy line of transports escorted by warships was en route to the latter destination, Cochrane, with not more than three ships and sometimes with only his own flagship, hung on to their flanks and by means of his superior dash and seamanship disabled many of them and captured fully "half of the enemy's army, ensigns, artillery and stores." Cochrane himself ingenuously states:

"Thus were the Northern provinces entirely rescued from the designs of this armament, which luckily for the consolidation of the empire—I had been enabled to frustrate; so that the cause of independence became free to develop itself throughout its whole extent. It is satisfactory to record the fact, that the whole military force was captured or dispersed, and its objects averted by a single ship—without the loss of a man on our part—or the additional cost of a dollar to the Imperial Government; though when we left Rio de Janeiro, it was believed that such objects could only be effected by costly naval and military expeditions combined."[26]

After the convoy of seventy ships had been reduced to thirteen and these and the warships were headed for Portugal, Cochrane abandoned further pursuit and entered the harbor of Maranhão. Having hoisted

---

[24] *Ibid.*, 89, 99.

[25] Cochrane, II, 2, 5.

[26] *Ibid.*, 55-58.

the Portuguese colors in order to deceive the garrison into the belief that his ship was bringing expected reënforcements, he was visited by a vessel sent out by the port authorities with despatches for the Portuguese admiral and congratulations upon his safe arrival. When the Portuguese captain stepped on the deck of Cochrane's flagship, he was arrested and his ship was seized, but they were both later released on the promise that they would carry back with them letters to the governor and *junta* of the city. The information impressed upon this captain and the letters sent by Cochrane contained "a fiction held justifiable in war, and indeed necessary under our peculiar circumstances," [27] that there was an imaginary number of vessels in the offing, accompanied by transports filled with troops, which the superior sailing of the flagship had enabled her to outstrip. Cochrane then reported his destruction of the Portuguese fleet and transports sent from Bahia and threatened to inflict the same treatment on the garrison of Maranhão if it offered resistance, while at the same time he magnanimously offered to let depart for Portugal all those Portuguese civilians and troops who wished to do so.

"The ruse was completely successful and proposals for capitulation were immediately returned. On the following day the Junta accompanied by the bishop came aboard and gave their adherence to the empire. Thus without military force or bloodshed was a second great province secured to the empire." [28] The Portuguese troops forming the garrison were peacefully embarked aboard vessels captured in the harbor and were shipped away. A provisional government was set up which on July 28, 1823 proclaimed a declaration of independence for the Province of Maranhão. On August 1 the inhabitants of Alcantara made a declaration of adherence to his Imperial Majesty.[29]

Captain Grenfell was then placed in command of one of the captured brigs and sent to Pará with instructions to use a similar ruse in demanding the surrender of that place. He was successful not only in securing that city but in capturing the new frigate (later renamed *Imperatriz*) which had just been launched there for the service of Portugal. With a single ship and less than a hundred men he had secured the adhesion to the imperial government of "a province greater in extent than France and England combined." The only bloodshed in the liberation of Pará was that of Captain Grenfell who was wounded by an assassin hired

[27] *Ibid.*, 61.
[28] *Ibid.*, 64.
[29] *Ibid.*, 67, 70.

by the Portuguese authorities after they had discovered how they had been duped.[30]

Thus, in a campaign lasting less than three months, and in which practically no blood had been shed, by September 1823 all Portuguese troops and ships had been expelled from Brazil and all the northern provinces had joined the southern in their adhesion to the empire.[31] In 1825, upon the promise by the emperor of the payment of a large indemnity, Portugal signed a treaty recognizing the independence of Brazil.[32]

SELECTED BIBLIOGRAPHY

Antepara, J. M. *South American emancipation. Documents historical and explanatory showing the designs which have been in progress and the exertions made by General Miranda for the attainment of that object during the last twenty-five years* (London, 1810).

A collection of documents published shortly after the events occurred to which they refer. Hence many of them have not been wisely chosen.

Anzures, Rafael, *Los héroes de la independencia. Colección de biografías de los principales héroes de la independencia de México* (Tlaxcala, 1909).

Too brief to be of much value except for reference.

Archivo diplomatico da independencia (6 vols., published by Ministro das Relações Exteriores, Rio de Janeiro, 1922).

Archivo Santander (22 vols., Bogotá, 1916).

A collection of well-edited documents essential to a clear understanding of the formation and dissolution of Great Colombia.

Armitage, John, *The history of Brazil, from the period of the arrival of the Braganza family in 1808 to the abdication of Dom Pedro I in 1831* (2 vols. London, 1836).

A convenient general history of this period, not especially well written.

Barros Arana, Diego, *Historia jeneral de Chile* (16 vols., Santiago, Chile, 1889). The standard history of Chile by a noted Chilean historian.

Beauchamp, Alphonse de, *L'indépendance de l'empire du Brésil* (Paris, 1824).

A clear exposition of events.

Belgrano, Manuel, *Documentos del Archivo de Belgrano* (5 vols., Buenos Aires, 1916).

A useful but not essential collection of documents relating to the early years of the independence movement in La Plata provinces.

Bertling, Hans. *Documentos históricos referentes al paso de los Andes efectuado en 1817 por el General San Martín* (Concepción, Chile, 1908).

This collection contains a few useful documents buried in a heterogeneous mass of unimportant ones.

Biggs, James. *The history of Don Francisco de Miranda's attempt to effect a revolution in South America* (Boston, 1808).

A quaint and vivid account by a participant.

---

[30] Cochrane, II, 84.

[31] Navarro y Lamarca, II, 802.

[32] William Spence Robertson, *History of the Latin American nations*, 192.

Bingham, Hiram. *Journal of an expedition across Venezuela and Colombia in 1906-7; an exploration of the route of Bolívar's celebrated march of 1819 and of the battlefields of Boyacá and Carabobo* (New Haven, 1909).

By following the route of Bolívar's march, the author proved to himself the difficulties surmounted by the Liberator in his New Granada campaign.

Blanco, José Felix y Azpurúa Ramón, *Documentos para la historia de la vida pública del Libertador* (14 vols., Caracas, 1877).

A very useful collection of documents but not conveniently arranged or indexed.

Boletín de historia y antigüedades, República de Colombia, Bogotá.

The various numbers of these bulletins, especially for the years 1902 to 1917, contain numerous scattered documents of historical interest.

Bulnes, Francisco, *La guerra de independencia. Hidalgo-Iturbide* (Mexico, 1910).

Philosophical discussions of the importance of Hidalgo and Iturbide in the winning of Mexican independence.

Bulnes, Gonzalo, *Historia de la expedición libertadoro del Perú (1817-1822)*, (2 vols., Santiago de Chile, 1887).

Contains some valuable extracts from documents, but devotes too much attention to unimportant military details.

Campaigns and cruises in Venezuela and New Granada, and in the Pacific Ocean, 1817-1820 (3 vols. in 2, London, 1831).

An interesting account of his own experiences by an anonymous Englishman who served under Bolívar as one of the foreign legionaries.

Cartas del Libertador (10 vols., Caracas, 1929). Published by the government of Venezuela, and edited by Dr. Vicente Lecuna, the world's foremost authority on Bolívar.

Chisholm, A. Stuart M. *The independence of Chile* (Boston, 1911).

Popular and superficial.

Cortes Vargas, Col. Carlos, *Participación de Colombia en la libertad del Perú* (3 vols., Bogotá, 1924).

An exhaustive well-documented account of military operations by a scientific military historian. Contains useful maps and illustrations.

Dávila, Vicente, *Investigaciones históricas* (Caracas, 1923).

A collection of unusual short historical essays based on documents in the National Archives of Venezuela by the Director of those Archives.

Documentos del Archivo de San Martín. Comisión Nacional del Centenario (Buenos Aires, 1910).

Dundonald, Thomas, Earl of, *Narrative of services in the liberation of Chili, Peru and Brazil from Spanish and Portuguese domination* (2 vols., London, 1859).

A somewhat egotistical and prejudiced account of Lord Cochrane's own experiences written by himself from memory in his later years.

Edwards, Agustín, *The dawn: being the history of the birth and consolidation of the republic of Chile* (London, 1931).

Evidently written from source material by an intelligent Chilian historian.

García Calderón, Francisco. *Latin America: its rise and progress* (London, 1913).

Although written by a Peruvian, this philosophical history deals rather harshly with the Latin Americans.

Gutiérrez de Lara, and Edgcumb Pinchón, *The Mexican People: their struggle for freedom* (Garden City, N. Y., 1914).

This leaves the impression that it was intended for purposes of propaganda for land reform in Mexico.

Hasbrouck, Alfred, *Foreign legionaries in the liberation of Spanish South America* (New York, 1928).
    A monograph describing the services of the foreigners who fought under Bolívar.

H. D. [Hermano Damaseno], *Ensayo de historia patria* (5th ed., Montevideo, 1923).
    A textbook used in Uruguay.

Koebel, W. H. *Central America* (London, 1917).
    This like other volumes in *The South American Series* is descriptive rather than historical. Only two of the chapters are devoted to history.

Level, Lino Duarte, *Cuadros de la historia militar y civil de Venezuela* (Madrid).
    Contains good essays on the military history of Venezuela.

López Contreras, Eleázar, *Bolívar conductor de tropas* (Caracas, 1930).
    An excellent critique of Bolívar's tactics and strategy by a thoroughly competent military historian. Contains valuable maps and battle plans.

López, Manuel Antonio, *Recuerdos históricos del coronel Manuel Antonio López; Colombia y Perú 1819-1826* (Bogotá, 1878).
    Detailed accounts of campaigns in which the author took part as an adjutant of the general staff. Useful battlefield maps.

Mancini, Jules, *Bolívar et l'émancipation des colonies espagnoles; des origines à 1815* (Paris, 1912).
    A well-documented scholarly work. Especially useful for early independence movements in New Granada and Quito.

Mehegan, John J., *O'Higgins of Chile* (London, 1913).
    A popular and superficial biography.

Miller, John, *Memoirs of General Miller in the service of the republic of Peru* (2 vols., London, 1828).
    Interesting account, by the brother of General Miller, of the events in which the latter played a leading part. Practically source material.

Mitre, Bartolomé, *Historia de Belgrano* (2 vols., Buenos Aires, 1859).
    A standard history of the early years of the Argentine revolution as well as a reliable biography of the hero.

Mitre, Bartolomé, *Historia de San Martín y de la emancipación Sud-Americana* (4 vols., Buenos Aires, 1890).
    Begins as a biography of San Martín, but covers the whole of the wars of independence not only under San Martín, but under Bolívar as well. A reliable history by a famous Argentine historian.

Monro, Dana G., *The five republics of Central America* (Published by the Carnegie Foundation for International Peace, New York, 1918).
    Probably the best historical and descriptive account in English of these five republics.

Navarro y Lamarca, Carlos, *Compendio de la historia general de América* (2 vols., Buenos Aires, 1913).
    A brief but compact and reliable compendium of the histories of all the Latin American nations written from the Spanish point of view.

Noll, Arthur Howard, *From empire to republic—the story of the struggle for constitutional government in Mexico* (Chicago, 1903).
    Probably the most complete history of this period in English.

O'Connor, F. Burdett, *Independencia americana* (Madrid, n. d.).
    The memoirs of General O'Connor written in Spanish. First-class source material on Sucre's campaigns.

O'Leary, Simón B., *Memorias del General O'Leary* (30 vols., Caracas, 1883).
    This collection of 26 volumes of documents, 2 vols. of narration, and 2 vols.

of appendices is the fountain from which all historians of Bolívar must sooner or later drink.

Otero, José P., *La révolution argentine, 1810-1816* (Paris, 1917).
Detailed account of events day by day, supported by frequent quotations from contemporary documents.

Páez, José Antonio, *Autobiografía del General José Antonio Páez* (2 vols., New York, 1871).
Good source material for events in which Gen. Páez took part.

Petre, Francis Loraine, *Simón Bolívar, el libertador; a life of the chief leader in the revolt against Spain in Venezuela, New Granada, and Peru* (London, 1919).
Probably the best biography of Bolívar in English.

Pilling, William, *The emancipation of South America* (London, 1893).
A condensed translation into English of Mitre's work on San Martín. Cited as "Pilling-Mitre."

Priestley, Herbert Ingram, *The Mexican nation, a history* (New York, 1923).
An excellent general history of Mexico, accurate and interesting. More than a textbook.

Rippy, J. Fred, *Historical evolution of Hispanic America* (New York, 1932).
The most up-to-date general textbook on Hispanic American history so far published.

Robertson, William Spence, *History of the Latin American nations* (New York, 1930).
The second textbook in English on Latin American history. Revised in 1930.

Robertson, William Spence, *The Life of Miranda* (2 vols., Chapel Hill, 1929).
By far the best life of Miranda ever written. Based on lifelong study and on Miranda's own journals discovered by the author.

Robertson, William Spence, *Rise of the Spanish American republics as told in the lives of their liberators* (New York, 1921).
A reliable and interesting series of biographies of the heroes of the Independence Era, in whose lives the story of this period may be found.

Robinson, Fay, *Mexico and her military chieftains from the revolution of Hidalgo to the present time* (Hartford, 1851).
Brief but conveniently arranged and useful.

Rodney, Caesar and John Graham, *The reports of the present state of the United Provinces of South America, drawn up by Messrs. Rodney and Graham commissioners sent to Buenos Aires by the government of North America, and laid before the Congress of the United States* (London, 1819).
Contemporary account of conditions in the rebellious La Plata provinces by official observers.

Rylance, Ralph, *A sketch of the causes and consequences of the late emigration to the Brazils* (London, 1808).
A contemporary tract revealing discontent with the attitude of the British ministry toward the Braganza dynasty in Portugal.

Salaverría, José María, *Bolívar, el libertador* (Madrid, 1930).
An attempt by a literary biographer to depict the character of Bolívar. A knowledge of his history being presupposed, the latter is touched on very briefly.

Santana, Col. Arturo, *La campaña de Carabobo* (Caracas, 1921).
A clear and detailed description of this campaign by a skilled military historian. Its many maps and battle plans are indispensable.

Schoellenkopf, Anna. *Don José de San Martín, 1778-1850* (New York, 1924).
   A superficial popular biography.

Shepherd, William R. *Hispanic nations of the new world.* Chronicles of America Series, vol. 50 (New Haven, 1921).

Shepherd, William R. *Latin America.* Home University Library of Modern Knowledge, No. 78 (New York, 1914).
   Both of these little books by Professor Shepherd are exceedingly readable and give sympathetic introductions to the study of the history and culture of Latin America.

Smith, Col. Carlos. *San Martín hasta el paso de los Andes* (Buenos Aires, 1928).
   A brief handbook of military events in the early years of the revolution of La Plata provinces.

Torrente, Mariano, *Historia de la independencia de México* (Madrid, 1918).
   A standard history, but lays too much stress on minor military events. Written from the Spanish point of view, it is unsympathetic toward Mexico.

Washburn, Charles A., *The history of Paraguay with notes of personal observations and reminiscences of diplomacy under difficulties* (2 vols., Boston, 1871).
   A fascinating account of the dictators of Paraguay by the American minister to that country. The first volume based on official documents deals with the career of Dr. Francia; the second based on personal acquaintance describes Francisco Solano López and his acts.

Wilgus, A. C., *A history of Hispanic America* (Washington, 1931).
   A reference handbook of Hispanic American history indispensable to teachers and advanced students.

Williams, Mary W., *The people and politics of Latin America* (Boston, 1930).
   An exceedingly readable general history and textbook with chapters on economic and social conditions.

Young, Philip, *History of Mexico; her civil wars, and colonial and revolutionary annals from the period of the Spanish conquest to the present time, 1847* (Cincinnati, 1847).
   A very full, detailed, and useful account.

Villeseñor y Villeseñor, Alejandro, *Biografías de los héroes y caudillos de la independencia* (2 vols., Mexico, 1910).
   Rather full biographies with portraits of the heroes of Mexican independence.

APPENDIX A

THE CATHOLIC CHURCH AS AN ECONOMIC FACTOR IN COLONIAL SPANISH AMERICA

By ALMON R. WRIGHT

I N THE period of the old colonial movement, from the fifteenth to the nineteenth centuries, Spanish imperialism was based upon the doctrine of mercantilism. This policy, which in theory called for the control of individual effort by the state for the benefit of the nation as a whole, was by no means an unmixed good. In practice, the national interest was interpreted to be the profit of the mother country or even a relatively small part of the population of the home land. To the large majority of the colonists, therefore, mercantilism was a selfish exploitation of themselves for the benefit of the commercial and industrial interests of Spain. In the economic control of the church the mercantilistic practice of constant government supervision and intervention was present as in the commercial and industrial world. On the other hand, the Spanish economic policy in the religious sphere was not designed to benefit any one class or the mother land at the expense of another class or the colonies. Many instances of unscrupulous and heartless conduct on the part of royal and ecclesiastical officials are recorded, but the general attitude of the Spanish sovereigns was one of benevolent interest in the church, the colonists, and the Indians.

I

Although the economic supervision of the church by the state was in accord with the mercantilistic practices of the age, the Spanish rulers were continuing a policy which had been followed by their medieval predecessors. In the seventh century the Gothic kings of Spain, having accepted the faith of the Roman Church, displayed great generosity in renovating Arian churches and in founding new ones.[1] From the eighth to the fifteenth century the Mohammedan invaders occupied much of the peninsula, but during the same period a crusade of reconquest was intermittently carried on. The kings of the new Christian states, established in the recovered areas, provided the economic means for con-

---

[1] Matias Gómez Zamora, *Regio patronato español é indiano*, 178; Hector D. Esquivel, *Régimen eclesiástico argentino*, 12.

verting the Moorish mosques into Christian churches or founded and endowed new establishments.[2]   Such pious generosity on the part of the lay authorities, which frequently meant the difference between survival and death of the churches, gave royalty a powerful means to control these religious institutions.   Upon this economic base rested the claim to the patronage of ecclesiastical offices by the Spanish sovereigns. Royal munificence by no means precluded the acquisition of property from other sources by the churches.   But such gifts were subject to royal approval.   The Gothic kings readily granted the clergy the right to obtain and enjoy the uses of property.[3]   The Christian lords of the reconquest likewise encouraged gifts to the church.[4]   They permitted the institution of mortmain to develop even to the point that the economic progress of Spain was threatened.[5]

Although the bulk of the church revenues was derived from gifts of land, a considerable proportion had its source in fees charged for spiritual ministrations.   The clergy abused its privileged position by exploiting the layman.   The national councils of ecclesiastics which met under the patronage of the king at Toledo during the seventh century attempted to restrain the greed of the clergy.   The bishops were enjoined from reserving for themselves more than the third of the revenues to which they were entitled.[6]   On the other hand, in the eleventh century, Sancho, king of Castile and Navarre, took pains to restore the income of the bishop and the lower clergy.[7]

Prior to the late thirteenth century, tithes were not generally levied in the Spanish states.   Only by special permission of the kings and only in certain regions were the clergy maintained by this form of taxation. Alfonso the Wise extended the tithe to all of those portions of Spain over which he ruled.   The new tax was applied not only to the larger part of Spain, but it touched nearly all classes of the population from the king to the prostitute.   Even non-Christian Jews and Moors did not escape.   Some of the military religious orders, such as the Templars and Hospitalers, were exempted.   The tithe was due from the products of the earth and trees, from the wages for personal service, and from

  [2] Gómez Zamora, 186-188.
  [3] Council of Toledo, VI, canon 15, in G. D. Mansi, ed., *Sacorum conciliorum nova et amplissima collectio*, X, 668; H. Florez, ed., *España sagrada*, VI, 179.
  [4] Gómez Zamora, 190.
  [5] Esquivel, 17, 18; A. K. Ziegler, *Church and state in visigothic Spain*, 164.
  [6] Councils of Toledo, VII, canon 4, XI, canon 8, in Mansi, X, 768-769, XI, 142; *España sagrada*, VI, 185, 208, 229.
  [7] Gómez Zamora, 190-191.

the profits and gifts derived from war.[8] The lower clergy were permitted to collect the revenue under the supervision of the bishops' representatives. Alfonso's code of laws also specified the manner of distributing the income from the tithes. The proceeds were apportioned in accordance with the local custom of dividing ecclesiastical revenues. In some dioceses half the income was assigned to the maintenance of the church building and the support of the poor; the other half was divided evenly between the bishop and the parish priests. In other dioceses a threefold distribution was followed, the portion for the poor being omitted as a separate item.[9] The royal legislation provided in either case that the parishioners receive back a considerable part of their tithes in the form of poor relief or of wages for work on the church premises.

II

With the conquest of the New World in the sixteenth century, Spain did not depart from the policy of attempting to control the economic power of the church. As the medieval kings claimed title to lands reconquered from the Moors, so in the early modern age the Spanish Crown maintained that the original title to all the soil of the Indies belonged to itself. The possession of any portion of it by an individual, or a group of persons, or a corporate body rested upon the direct or tacit consent of the monarchy.[10] On this basis the governing agencies might employ their regulative powers on church property. The latter was classified into three groups: first, that which was consecrated for divine worship, including churches, cemeteries, and sacred utensils used in religious services; second, the temporal possessions which provided the clergy with a living; and third, the private patrimony of ecclesiastics, considered as individuals.[11] Members of the regular orders were not permitted by the Council of Trent to hold property, but those organizations as corporate bodies were allowed to acquire vast holdings.[12] This

---

[8] *Las Siete Partidas*, part I, title xx, laws 1, 3, 4, in Martínez Alcubilla, ed., *Códigos antiguos de España*. . . .

[9] *Ibid.*, part I, title XX, laws 7, 10, 19.

[10] *Collección de documentos inéditos relativos al descubrimiento, conquista, y organización de las antiguas posesiones españolas de América y Oceania*, XVIII, 234-235, (hereinafter cited as *Doc. Inéd. descub.*); V. G. Quesada *Derecho de patronato* . . . , 107.

[11] Gómez Zamora, 633-634.

[12] James Waterworth, ed., *The canons and decrees of the . . . Council of Trent*, 237-238.

conciliar pronouncement was speedily sanctioned by Philip II.[13] At the close of the eighteenth century, however, the crown was endeavoring to prevent monks and nuns from making wills and inheriting from one dying intestate.[14]

The alienation of church properties, according to the canons, was justified in certain instances. Such procedure was permitted when the sustenance of the ministers, the repair of churches, or the payment of debts could be provided in no other way. An exchange of distant possessions for properties close at hand was sanctioned. The churches might divest themselves of ownership, if the sale was for the purpose of relieving the poor.[15] These were instances where upscrupulous bishops attempted to capitalize on the popular idea of mortmain by prohibiting bequests by any of the clergy.[16] Both Charles V and Philip II required the higher prelates to allow prebendaries and canons to make wills and to distribute their estates freely, whether acquired from a benefice and ecclesiastical rents or from their parents.[17]

The bishop's estate was a matter of special legislation by the civil authorities. By ancient custom, these properties, known as *espolios,* belonged to the Apostolic See, but the Spanish monarchs refused their recognition to the claim.[18] Nevertheless, the papacy did concede bulls which authorized the holder to receive the *espolios,* and the kings demanded that these be collected and sent to the Council of the Indies.[19] The procedure for administering the estate of the bishop required the taking of an inventory of the properties placed in the custody of the vice-patron.[20] The inspection of the estate was to be made by the prelates and by representatives of the royal *audiencia* jointly.[21] To safeguard the heirs, the law prescribed the deduction from these resources of the properties which, according to a prior inventory, the bishop possessed before entering upon the duties of a diocesan.[22]

---

[13] *Recopilación de las leyes de indias,* I. Boix, ed., *lib.* i, *tít.* xiv, *ley* 50, (hereinafter cited as *Recop. leyes Ind.*).

[14] *Ibid., lib.* i, *tít.* xiv, *ley* 50 n.

[15] Gómez Zamora, 637-638.

[16] *Colección de documentos inéditos relativos al descubrimiento, conquista, y organización de las antiguas posesiones españolas de ultramar,* X, 394-395 (hereinafter cited as *Doc. inéd. ultramar*).

[17] *Recop. leyes Ind., lib.* i, *tít.* xii, *ley* 6.

[18] Dalmacio Vélez Sarsfield, *Derecho público eclesiástico,* 141-143; Esquivel, 102.

[19] *Recop. leyes Ind., lib.* i, *tít.* ix, *ley* 4; *Doc. inéd. descub.,* XVIII, 412-413.

[20] *Recop. leyes Ind., lib.* i, *tít.* vii, *ley* 37.

[21] *Ibid., lib.* i, *tít.* vii, *ley* 39.

[22] *Ibid., lib.* i, *tít.* vii, *ley* 38.

III

Of the revenues upon which the colonial church depended for its daily maintenance, the tithes were most important. In the latter part of 1501 Pope Alexander VI, in recognition of the pious design of Ferdinand and Isabella to exalt the faith in the New World and in reply to their solicitation, conferred upon them and their successors the privilege of levying and collecting tithes.[23] According to its customary diplomatic practice the Holy See imposed a condition upon this grant to the effect that ". . . an endowment be given and assured by you and your successors from your properties and theirs, sufficient for the churches which may be built in the said Indies with which their prelates and rectors may be suitably maintained. . . ."[24] This condition imposed by the papacy gave the crown its justification for a vast body of economic legislation. "The true pontiffs," according to an Argentine historian, "of the Hispanic American Church, then, were the kings because they were the owners of the revenues of ecclesiastical origin and because they filled all the vacancies."[25] Pope Gregory XIII, in July 1569, broadened this concession to include the increase in the tithes attributable to the development of the colonies over a space of seventy years.[26]

Ferdinand and Isabella did not wait for the bull of Alexander VI granting the tithes before promulgating an elaborate schedule to go into effect in the Indies.[27] Of all the grains and vegetables, the producer was compelled to pay one measure in ten without first withdrawing his seed or an amount for the payment of rent. If the rice farmer sold his crop without turning over the legal proportion, the obligation was thereby transferred to the purchaser. A tithe was due from those who raised livestock even though the animals were consumed by the household of the farmer. In the case of the tithe on lambs, the ten per cent tax benefited the parish where they grazed and not that where the owner resided. This same provision applied to the products of livestock, to milk, cheese, butter, and wool. The law specified the time at which colts, calves, young pigs, and mules were subject to this tax. To avoid double taxation, pine cones and acorns which were fed to the pigs were exempt

---

[23] Francisco J. Hernáez, ed., *Colección de bulas, breves, y otros documentos relativos á la iglesia de América y Filipinas*, I, 20-21.

[24] Gómez Zamora, 290-291.

[25] Ricardo Levene, *Lecciones de historia argentina*, I, 294.

[26] Gómez Zamora, 662.

[27] *Recop. leyes Ind.*, lib. i, tít. xvi, *ley* 2.

from the tithe on the products of trees. Olive oil and grape juice were subject to this assessment.[28]

As the colonial agricultural and industrial occupations became more diversified, the crown broadened the base for the decimal tax. Flax and cotton or their textile products were added to the list of tithable goods. As wine was manufactured from the native sumach instead of the grape, the interested parties evaded the letter of the law until their new product was specifically included. The crown attempted to clarify the provisions concerning grains and fruits by defining that stage of the growth of these products when the tithe was due.[29] Early in the sixteenth century the colonists founded the dye industry, in consequence of which indigo and cochineal were made subject to the financial needs of the church.[30] A year later, 1540, the emperor took cognizance of the growing sugar industry. The tax was to be paid on this product before any division of the proceeds was made between the laborers and the owners of the refineries. Apparently the latter had a choice of paying five per cent on sugar partially purified or four per cent on the refined white product.[31]

Many of the nobility who emigrated to the colonies, long accustomed to many privileges, were specifically included among those from whom the tithe was payable. The knights of the military orders, such as those of Santiago, Calatrava, and Alcántara, were required to turn over one-tenth of their profits in the same manner as any other resident.[32] Those who held *encomiendas,* or concessions for the labor of Indians, were ordered to tithe all the products, maize, cacao, cotton, which they received from their native laborers.[33] Even the properties of the crown were subject to the duty of financial support of the church, and royal officials were commanded to observe the law in behalf of their royal superiors.[34]

The Spanish government made some exceptions, however, to the general assessment of the tithe. In 1511 gold was excluded from the schedule.[35] Charles V extended this reservation to include silver, pearls, and

---

[28] *Ibid., lib.* i, *tít.* xvi, *leyes* 2, 7, 8.
[29] *Ibid., lib.* i, *tít.* xvi, *ley* 2.
[30] *Ibid., lib.* i, *tít.* xvi, *ley* 4.
[31] *Ibid., lib.* i, *tít.* xvi, *ley* 3.
[32] *Ibid., lib.* i, *tít.* xvi, *ley* 17.
[33] *Ibid., lib.* i, *tít.* xvi, *ley* 12.
[34] *Ibid., lib.* i, *tít.* xvi, *ley* 16.
[35] *Cédula* of 1511 in *Doc. inéd. descub.,* XXXII, 118.

other precious stones and metals.[36] The sense of justice of the Spanish monarchy is revealed in its attempt to safeguard the owner, lease holder, and renter from being assessed three times for the same product.[37] At least two industries, those of hunting and of fishing, were favored by total exemption from the tithe.[38]

The distribution of the tithes was determined by the crown. The broad basis for the division was decreed in royal laws applicable to all the Indies. But the detailed specifications for individual cathedrals were set forth in articles of erections, which were chartars of government, formulated at the creation of a diocese by the first bishop and passed upon by both the pope and the king. A fundamental law was issued in 1541 to regulate the division of the tithes.[39] In each diocese fifty per cent of the total of these revenues was to be set aside for the bishop and the cathedral chapter. The remaining half of the tithes of the diocese was to be divided into nine parts. Of these, two were reserved to the crown, or about eleven per cent of the whole. Three-ninths, or nearly seventeen per cent, were destined for the upkeep of the church and the hospital. The remaining four-ninths, or approximately twenty-two per cent, were to be used for the salaries of the curates and as the articles of erection specified. The cathedral chapter, from the twenty-five per cent allotted to it, was responsible for the salaries of its own members such as the dignitaries, canons, and prebendaries.[40] The system of distribution was applicable not only to the cathedral churches, but the same proportions were to be observed in the financial management of the parish churches.[41] The royal ninths were to be withdrawn before the other allotments were distributed.[42]

In accordance with the obligation which Pope Alexander VI stipulated in his concession, the crown made provision to supply any expenditures for the maintenance of the church not covered by the tithes.[43] The civil authority assumed the right to define the minimum needs for the ecclesiastical officers. Charles V agreed to make up any deficiency

---

[36] *Recop. leyes Ind., lib.* i, *tít.* xvi, *ley* 14.

[37] *Ibid., lib.* i, *tít.* xvi, *ley* 19.

[38] *Ibid., lib.* i, *tít.* xvi, *ley* 18.

[39] *Ibid., lib.* i., *tít.* xvi, *ley* 23; this was by no means the first law on the subject, see a *cédula* of 1511, *Doc. inéd. descub.,* XXXII, 122.

[40] *Recop. leyes Ind., lib.* i, *tít.* xvi, *ley* 23; "Relación . . . de esquilache" in R. Beltrán y Rózpide, ed., *Colección de memorias ó relaciones que escribieron los virreyes del Perú . . .,* I, 288.

[41] *Recop., leyes Ind., lib.* i, *tít.* xvi, *ley* 23.

[42] *Ibid., lib.* i, *tít.* xvi, *ley* 25.

[43] *Ibid., lib.* i, *tít.* xvi, *leyes* 22, 23; *lib.* i, *tít.* xiii, *ley* 20.

in the revenues of a bishop if these fell below 500,000 *maravedís* annually.[44] For minor ecclesiastical offices the amounts were naturally much smaller: for a missionary priest 50,000 *maravedís,* and for a sacristan 25,000 *maravedís* yearly.[45]

The administrative machinery for the tithes was complicated and overlapping. The collecting and spending of the two-ninths belonged to the treasury officials of the colonial government. By law and custom these funds were employed for religious purposes.[46] If the tithes proved insufficient for the needs of a diocese, the clerical hierarchy paid for the royal assistance by handing over the entire control of this source of income.[47] In the seventeenth and eighteenth centuries the crown incorporated into the civil law the claim to control the revenues of a vacant ecclesiastical office from that of an archbishop to the lowest prebendary, and according to this ordinance, such funds might be used as any other moneys of the state.[48] Even in those dioceses where the prelates were conceded the right to manage the tithes, the crown insisted upon choosing subordinate officials who had immediate supervision over the tax collectors. Thus Philip III and his successor instructed their vice-patrons to fill the office of sacristan and collector-general, both of which were financial positions.[49] In the latter part of the eighteenth century a new administration for the tithes under civil officials was established.[50]

IV

Over a period of three centuries and in such a wide extent of territory, complaints of corruption were to be expected in the enforcement of the system of the tithes. Violations of the laws were committed by all parties concerned. In 1523, while Española was still the center of Spain's colonies, a royal *cédula* revealed a serious objection to paying a tithe on bricks and tile for church buildings.[51] In the same year Charles V commanded his own representatives in the Indies to tithe the

---

[44] *Ibid., lib.* i, *tít.* vii, *ley* 34; *lib.* i, *tít.* xvi, *ley* 22.

[45] *Ibid., lib.* i, *tít.* xiii, *ley* 21.

[46] *Ibid., lib.* i, *tít.* xvi, *ley* 24.

[47] *Ibid., lib.* i, *tít.* xvi, *ley* 23.

[48] "Ordenanzas de intendentes de Buenos Aires," *ordenanza* 178, in *Documentos referentes á la guerra de independencia . . . de le república argentina,* I, 69-71 and n., (hereinafter cited as *Doc . . . indep.*); "Relación . . . esquilache," Beltrán y Rózpide, I, 289.

[49] *Recop. leyes Ind., lib.* i, *tít.* vi, *leyes* 21, 22.

[50] *Ordenanzas* 150, 151, *Doc. . . . indep.,* i, 63-67.

[51] *Cédula* of July 4, *Doc. inéd. ultramar,* IX, 181-182.

royal income.[52] A decade later complaints were directed at the bishop who was reported to have levied a tithe on gold and to have neglected to tax grain, both contrary to the royal will.[53] Later in the century, as settlement moved southward, difficulties in collecting tithes became more widespread. The Bishop of Cuzco reported that there was a reluctance to yield the tax on the plea that the land of the colonists was new, or on the claim that their products were exempted.[54] Since the monarchy was obligated to provide for the deficiency in the tithes, there was resistance from the laboring class and lethargy or dishonesty from those administering the tithes. One observer claimed that if honestly managed, the tithes amply covered the clerical needs for which they were intended.[55] Considerable disorder and exploitation in the collection of the tax was reported by another.[56] A viceroy of Peru, the Count of Superunda, declared that on the pretext of collecting the tithe, the clergy molested the Indian population.[57] The division of responsibility between civil and ecclesiastical administrators inevitably led to incessant attempts of one party to injure the other.[58] A perplexing problem arose as to whether the tithe was due on products raised on property acquired by the regular orders from laymen.[59] Payment of the tithes was made in kind, a proceeding which led to attempts at manipulating the price levels. In 1803 Buenos Aires experienced a failure in the wheat crop due to floods which made the roads impassable. The collector of tithes advanced the price on grain in storage from nine and one-half to eleven *pesos*. The civil *cabildo* took steps to compel the ecclesiastical authority to maintain the old price level, but the collector justified his action on the ground of increased costs of transportation and storage and the reduced supply.[60]

The clergy derived a living not only from the tithes and the royal bounty but from the fees which were imposed upon their congregations for religious services. In this field, as in so many others, the regulative power of the state was employed. The Spanish monarchs, however, re-

---

[52] *Cédula* of July 4, *Ibid.*, IX, 183.
[53] *Ibid.*, X, 174.
[54] *Doc. inéd. descub.*, III, 97.
[55] "Memorial de Miguel Sánchez de la Parra," in *Colección de documentos inéditos para la historia de España*, CIV, 281, (hereinafter cited as *Col. doc. inéd. España*).
[56] "Memorial para el buen asiento y gobierno del Perú," *ibid.*, XCIV, 177-178.
[57] "Relación de . . . Superunda," Beltrán y Rózpide, I, 125.
[58] *Ordenanza* 150, *Doc. . . . indep.*, I, 63n.
[59] "Relación de . . . Mendoza y Luna," Beltrán y Rózpide, I, 154
[60] *Documentos para la historia argentina*, IV, 319ff.

quired at least the coöperation of the ecclesiastical authorities in drawing up schedules of the amounts to be asked of the parishioners. In
the middle of the sixteenth century the vice-patrons were instructed to
assemble the prelates in conferences for the purpose of arranging the
detailed specifications.[61] There is one record, on the other hand, of a
royal *audiencia* issuing such regulations.[62] In a *cédula* of April 1538,
the crown stipulated that the fees should not exceed amounts equal to
three times the fees charged in the Archbishopric of Seville.[63] Philip II
insisted on the same rule, but about a century later the government demanded that the canons of the Council of Trent be obeyed in the fixing
of fees.[64]

The temptation to extort high prices for the services of Christian
consolation and blessing was too strong for the frontier clergy. But
their parishioners were not disposed to suffer in silence. Reports of excessive charges for various religious services reached Madrid prior to
1538 when the emperor instructed the viceroy to take steps to remedy
the evil.[65] Apparently little good came from that royal order, for in
1559 Philip II required the *Audiencia* of Lima to enforce existing
schedules of those fees.[66] Frequently, particular impositions were sin-
gled out for complaint. The visits of the higher prelates were reported
to have been occasions for the collection of offerings, and doubtless
those occasions were unnecessarily multiplied. The ecclesiastical judges
were guilty of asking compensations larger than litigants could afford
to pay.[67] Philip IV, in 1631, requested the prelates of the regulars to
forbid their members to receive stipends for preaching on certain days
of the church calendar.[68]

Perhaps the occasions of funerals and interments offered the clergy
the best opportunity for profit. To the layman the price of their aid
to secure heaven's blessings was high, if not prohibitive. The crown
was somewhat responsible for this extortion. A royal *cédula* of 1528
permitted prelates to make arrangements for masses to be said at the
burial of one who died intestate, or of one whose heirs were absent.

---

[61] *Doc. inéd. ultramar*, X, 409.
[62] "Memorial para . . . gobierno del Perú," in *Col. doc. inéd. España*, XCIV,
185.
[63] *Recop. leyes Ind.*, lib. i, tít. viii, *ley* 9.
[64] *Doc. inéd. descub*, XIX, 44; *Recop. leyes Ind.*, lib. i, tít. vii, *ley* 43.
[65] *Doc. inéd. ultramar*, X, 409.
[66] *Doc. inéd. descub.* XIX, 44.
[67] *Col. doc. inéd. España*, XCIV, 185, 203.
[68] *Recop. leyes Ind.*, lib. i, tít. xiv, *ley* 79.

The elaborateness of the ritual depended upon the amount of property left by the deceased, and the executors were commanded to pay the proper fee for the services.[69]   The exploitation of the families and relatives became so serious, however, that Philip II twice issued a caution against injury of the heirs through clerical burial charges.[70]   These decrees were forgotten.   Two centuries later Viceroy Armendaris reported an instance of a popular tumult aroused by the complaints of a widow whose meagre properties were, in considerable part, demanded by the clergy.[71]

If the funeral fees were most burdensome, the Indian inhabitants were most exploited.   The civil authorities repeatedly attempted to prevent the collection of any fees from the natives, no matter how small, for the administration of any of the sacraments, particularly for the marriage and funeral rituals.[72]   Ecclesiastics who visited the Indian towns were forbidden to demand money or food or promises to pay.[73]   The crown threatened to deduct from the revenues of the priests of the missions an amount equal to that which they took illegally from the natives, and informed them of its intention to accept from any source information concerning such abuse.[74]

Closely connected with the funeral fees were the bequests which the clergy induced laymen to make in their wills for the benefit of the church.   Both regular and secular clergy were encouraged by the crown to employ the pulpit and the confessional to induce the people to make some provision for ecclesiastical establishments as well as to remember the poor and their creditors.[75]   But in the execution of wills the crown preferred that the secular rather than the regular clergy have supervision.   In 1540 two of the regular orders were interdicted from seeking or demanding bequests from those making wills or from exacting property from the estates of those dying intestate.[76]   Philip II issued a mandate upon the viceroys, *audiencias,* and governors forbidding their intervention in the execution of wills by the archbishops or bishops.[77]

---

[69] *Ibid., lib.* i, *tit.* xviii, *ley* 5.
[70] *Ibid., lib.* i, *tit.* xviii, *ley* 2.
[71] "Relación de . . . Armendaris," in M. A. Fuentes, ed., *Memorias de los virreyes que han gobernado el Perú . . .* III, 339.
[72] *Ibid.,* II, 21, 31; *Recop. leyes Ind., lib.* i, *tit.* xviii, *ley* 10; *lib.* i, *tit.* vii, *ley* 15.
[73] *Ibid., lib.* i, *tit.* vii, *leyes* 23, 24.
[74] *Ibid., lib.* i, *tit.* xiii, *leyes* 8, 12.
[75] *Ibid., lib.* i, *tit.* xviii, *ley* 4.
[76] *Ibid., lib.* i, *tit.* xxi, *ley* 4.
[77] *Ibid., lib.* i, *tit.* vii, *ley* 35.

The safeguarding of the Indians from spoliation became an object persistently attempted by the crown. Late in the sixteenth century the Spanish monarch commanded that the natives be permitted freely to will and dispose of their properties. Some years later, acknowledging the baneful intervention of the mission priests, the crown appealed to the secular clergy and the civil authorities to prevent excesses.[78] The frequency of the legislation indicates the failure to discover any real solution for the problem.

V

The tithes, fees, and wills were matters in which the crown exercised its powers of supervision. More directly controlled by the government were the collection and spending of monies derived from the successful candidates for ecclesiastical offices and from the preaching of indulgences. Pope Urban VIII permitted the kings the rights of the *mesada* of the lesser church offices.[79] As the name suggests, this consisted of a fee equal to the revenue for one month of the church office. It was payable whenever a candidate was presented to a position. The amount of the fee of the benefice was established by a calculation of the revenues of that position over a period of five years prior to the presentation of the new candidate.[80] The concession which Pope Urban made was renewed from time to time, usually for five-year periods, by his successors.[81]

It might seem that such a law imposing a tax of eight and one-half per cent on the first year's revenue would have deterred the clergy from desiring to move from one place to another. When such a result appeared probable, however, Philip IV accommodatingly made exceptions. The clergy in frontier missions were not required to pay the tax more than once in five years no matter how often the incumbents in those offices were changed. Nor was any priest in this field compelled to pay the fee more than once if he remained at his station more than five years.[82] Nevertheless, there was a disposition on the part of some kings to employ this requisition as a means of controlling the clergy. Royal decrees specified that a new occupant of an office pay the sum asked

---

[78] *Ibid., lib.* i, *tít.* xiii, *ley* 9.

[79] V. Salva, ed., *Novísima recopilación de las leyes de España, lib.* i, *tít.* xxiv, *ley* 7.

[80] *Recop. leyes Ind., lib.* i, *tít.* xvii, *ley* 1; *Ordenanzas* 187, 190, *Doc.* . . . *indep.*, I, 75-77 and n.

[81] Alcubilla, 849 n. 7.

[82] *Recop. leyes Ind., lib.* i, *tít.* xvi, *ley* 5.

before his induction could be considered complete and legal. But such attempts to compel prompt payment were not successful.[83]

In 1752 Pope Benedict XIV granted the request of the Spanish sovereign to impose an obligation upon ecclesiastics to pay the crown a sum equal to half of a year's salary. This half of the annate was not to be applied to church offices in which the income was less than three hundred *pesos* for the year. Ferdinand VI, to whom the papal grant was addressed, did not make use of the privilege, but his successor in 1775 issued the enforcement decrees.[84] The half annate was assessed, like the *mesada* tax, on the basis of the value of the office over a period of five years prior to the initiation of the candidate into his new position. Title to such an office was withheld until some guarantee of payment was furnished.[85]

The administration of the annates was one of the less important functions of the general commission of the crusade.[86] In the Indies an ecclesiastical hierarchy was developed for the purpose of distributing the papal bulls of the holy crusade. Among other favors, these certificates conferred indulgences upon the possessor. The origin of the practice of granting remissions of sins is said to go back to the twelfth century when Urban II granted this singular favor upon the warriors engaged in the sacred campaign to rid Spain of the infidels.[87] The sixteenth century popes were especially liberal in authorizing the preaching of the bulls of the holy crusade. In the first quarter of the century Julius II and Adrian VI permitted the practice in Spain. Fifty years later, just prior to the celebrated battle of Lepanto, Pius V, sorely beset by Turkish squadrons, extended the bull of the crusade with other favors to Philip II for the naval aid which that monarch gave to him.[88] The bull of Gregory XIII promised plenary indulgence to those enlisting and to those who provided the stipend for the soldiers. Each member of the higher clergy and of the court was expected to pay the expenses of ten soldiers, while poor people might combine to supply the needs of one warrior.[89] In 1718 Clement XI revoked the bull of the crusade in all the Spanish dominions because the proceeds of their distribution were used for carrying on war with Christian princes; but

---

[83] *Ordenanza* 190, *Doc. . . . indep.*, I, 77.
[84] *Ordenanza* 182, *ibid.*, I, 72.
[85] Viélez Sarsfield, 186.
[86] *Ordenanza* 182, *Doc. . . . indep.*, I, 72.
[87] Hernáez, I, 705-706.
[88] *Ibid.*, I, 709, 710, 711, 712.
[89] *Doc. inéd. descub.*, XVIII, 397-398.

two years later the suspension was lifted.[90]   In pursuance of these provisions, the crown dispatched orders to the viceroys to extend the benefits of the bulls of the holy crusade to the colonists.[91]

Members of the regular orders were permitted to preach the bulls
of the crusade early in the sixteenth century, but the widespread and
powerful hierarchy of officials seems to have developed late in that
century.   Tribunals were established in the more important towns to
supervise the administration of the preaching and the collections.   The
crown contrived to fill these offices with royal appointees.[92]   The scope
of authority of these tribunals was extensive since all disputes in which
indulgences were involved belonged to these courts for adjudication.
Thus, cases concerning the dispensation of the laws governing marriage,
the innumerable disputes involving payment for the bulls, and the frequent charges of graft and fraud in the collections were included in the
jurisdiction of the tribunals of the crusade.[93]   The coöperation of civil
officials in the administration of the system of indulgences was essential
from the first.   The House of Trade in Seville was authorized to deal
with ship captains in order to provide for the transportation of the bulls,
while treasury officials in the Indies were empowered to receive them.
The civil authorities were also charged with the duty of supplying transportation facilities for the long journey from one place to another in
the New World.[94]   In the latter part of the eighteenth century, the
crown officers possessed almost exclusive management of the system
of indulgences.[95]

Since to remit sins, directly or indirectly, touched the sphere of activity of the ordinary ecclesiastical officers, these were in everlasting
conflict with the agents of the Holy Crusade.   The civil authorities attempted to arbitrate between them.   Frequent, also, were the disputes concerning the extent of the jurisdiction of the distributors of indulgences
over royal governors.[96]   The greed of the former became notorious as
they sought to inherit or to extort properties from their sinful subjects.
So lucrative were the offices connected with their tribunals that the
crown repeatedly sought to prevent their sale.[97]   The efforts of the

[90] Hernáez, I, 748.
[91] *Doc. inéd. descub.*, XVIII, 397-398.
[92] *Recop. leyes Ind., lib.* i, *tít.* xx, *ley* 1.
[93] *Ibid.; Hernáez*, I, 773-774.
[94] *Recop. leyes Ind., lib.* i, *tít.* xx, *leyes* 25, 26.
[95] *Ordenanzas* 147, 148, *Doc. . . . indep.*, I, 62-63; Fuentes, IV, 258-259.
[96] *Recop. leyes Ind., lib.* i, *tit.* xx, *ley* 15.
[97] *Ibid., lib.* i, *tít.* xx, *ley* 18; Hernáez, I, 741-754.

monarchs were directed also toward preventing foreigners from engaging in such a profitable business.[98] The intervention of foreigners took a different form, occasionally, as when Elizabethan seamen interrupted the transportation of the bulls of indulgence from Spain to the colonies. In 1593 an English vessel commanded by Thomas White seized a Spanish ship carrying, according to the Englishman's report, two million of such papal certificates.[99]

VI

In general the kings of Spain attempted to prevent the clergy from engaging in ordinary business occupations. The *audiencias,* or colonial courts, were instructed to proceed against members of the regular orders who maintained shops and stores. The clergy were forbidden to interfere with the driving of livestock to the towns, or in any other way to interrupt the food supply of the civilian population.[100] The government was insistent upon preventing the clergy from engaging in any mining industries.[101] There was evidence to prove, however, that the spiritual fathers openly flaunted this prohibition.[102] Again, the Spanish law held that their participation in the pearl fisheries was indecent.[103] But the clergy evaded these injunctions by using intermediaries which the crown, always a step behind, then prohibited.[104] To enter commercial activities on a business scale for profit was forbidden by both canon and civil statutes, but the government, aware that the revenues of the church were largely in kind, permitted a certain amount of exchange and even of exportation of colonial products.[105]

VII

The Spanish government not only attempted to restrict the clergy's participation in colonial trade and industry, but also to limit expenditures for purely religious objects. In conducting the funeral ceremonies the clergy were advised to spend with moderation.[106] There appears to have been considerable extravagance in building churches. A royal *cédula* of 1601 mentioned the unfortunate grandeur with which the

[98] *Ordenanza* 149, *Doc. . . . indep.,* I, 63.
[99] R. Hakluyt, *Principal navigations, voyages . . .,* VII, 103 ff.
[100] *Recop. leyes Ind., lib.* i, *tit.* xiv, *ley* 82.
[101] *Ibid., lib.* i, *tit.* xii, *ley* 4.
[102] *Col. doc. inéd. España,* XCIV, 202.
[103] *Recop. leyes Ind., lib.* i, *tit.* xii, *ley* 3.
[104] *Ibid., lib.* i, *tit.* xii, *leyes* 2, 5.
[105] *Ibid., lib.* i, *tit.* vii, *ley* 46.
[106] *Ibid., lib.* i, *tit.* xviii, *ley* 5.

cathedrals at Lima and Cuzco were begun and left unfinished. The crown counseled the viceroy to insist upon less extravagant plans.[107]

The responsibility of the government to maintain the church included not only the duty to make up any deficiency in the tithes, as has been explained above, but also an obligation to give aid in the building of churches and in furnishing utensils and supplies for the service.[108] The crown boldly claimed the credit for bearing the expense of building the first churches in the New World, but royal decrees placed a portion of the burden upon others. The costs of construction were to be divided into three parts according to a law of Philip II. The royal treasury was made responsible for one-third; the *encomenderos,* or landed proprietors, were required to shoulder a third of the burden; and finally, upon the natives was imposed an equal share.[109] Juan de Mendoza y Luna, viceroy from 1607 to 1615, informed his successor that in Indian towns where no private individual had a concession of the native labor, the crown was obliged to pay two-thirds of the costs of building churches.[110] The government assumed, likewise, a part of the burden of erecting monasteries.[111] The regular orders received royal licenses for the land upon which their cloisters were constructed. If the land was not used by them, the title to it reverted to the king.[112] Such establishments were not to be built closer than six leagues from each other.[113]

The Spanish claim to founding, building, and maintaining churches was to prove embarrassing in its application to earthquake country. In 1687 the Andean countryside was visited by earth tremors. The damage to the cathedral at Lima was reported to have reached 60,000 *pesos.* The churches at Callao and Arequipa suffered to the extent of 40,000 and 20,000 *pesos* respectively.[114] According to the viceroy's report, some 200,000 *pesos* were expended by the crown in repairs for these and other churches of the viceroyalty. Perhaps the clergy felt that the divine wrath was directed at the civil authorities, for they seemed to believe that the government should be responsible for the whole cost of the rebuilding. The viceroy bemoaned the unfortunate precedents which were created by this generosity of his royal master, for he had reason

---

[107] *Doc. inéd. descub.,* XIX, 128.
[108] See above.
[109] *Recop. leyes Ind., lib.* i, *tít.* ii, *leyes* 2, 3.
[110] Beltrán y Rózpide, I, 146.
[111] *Recop. leyes Ind., lib.* i, *tít.* iii, *ley* 5.
[112] *Ibid., lib.* i, *tít.* iii, *ley* 3.
[113] *Ibid.*
[114] "Relación de . . . Navarra y Rocaful," in Fuentes, II, 4.

to believe that the future would experience many more earth tremors.[115] In the latter part of the eighteenth century, the crown contributed 6,000 *pesos* annually for the reconstruction of the cathedral in Buenos Aires. From 1758 to 1777 this subsidy approached the 100,000 *pesos* mark. In 1779 the royal officials awoke to the fact that the local officers were rendering no accounts of their expenditures.[116]

VIII

Royal beneficence was especially noteworthy in the financial support afforded to the emigrating regulars. As early as 1510, the House of Trade ordered that every member of these orders embarking for the Indies receive a coat and two blankets.[117] In the following year the royal representatives in Española were required to give the newcomers further help.[118] As the American continent was colonized during the sixteenth century, royal subsidizing of the emigrating monks became more extensive. The administration of the bounty was accompanied by misappropriation of funds. The House of Trade was instructed to prevent those who had received assistance from remaining in Spain.[119]

Early in the seventeenth century, Philip III promulgated several detailed laws to facilitate the emigration of members of the clergy. The selection of desirable monks and friars was to be placed in the hands of commissioners designated for the purpose by the regular orders. These agents were required to give a full report to the Council of the Indies of every individual selected for mission work in the colonies, and present these certificates approved by the council to the House of Trade before the clergyman could receive the allowance for food and clothing.[120] The missionaries were enabled to reach Seville from their homes in various parts of Spain by the royal provision of a beast of burden and six *reales* a day for travelling expenses.[121] According to the law of 1607, the subsidy allowed them for the voyage from Seville to the Indies was to be paid in two installments. The House of Trade furnished the ecclesiastical commissioners with the funds necessary for food and clothing on the ocean trip, and the royal agents in the Indies were authorized to pay the ship captains for passage after a safe arrival.

[115] *Ibid.*, II, 4-5.
[116] *Documentos para la historia del virreinato del Río de la Plata*, II, 117.
[117] *Doc. inéd. ultramar*, V, 243.
[118] *Ibid.*, V, 249.
[119] *Recop. leyes Ind.*, lib. i, tít. xiv, ley 7.
[120] *Ibid.*, lib. i, tít. xiv, ley 4.
[121] *Ibid.*, lib. i, tít. xiv, ley 6.

The sum payable to the latter was fixed by the crown at a uniform figure of 18,326 *maravedís* for every passenger.[122] The subsidy granted for the necessities of the voyage, on the other hand, varied with the different orders. Each member of the Augustinian Order received 1,049 *reales* for this purpose, while to each Dominican was allotted about 960 *reales*. The crown assigned 817 *reales* for each member of the Order of Mercy with which his superior furnished the vestments and paid his freight charges. The Franciscans were less favored with money to pay for the necessities of the voyage. The decree of 1607 allowed them 796 *reales* each, but to the barefoot monks of that Order, approximately 714 *reales* were assigned for clothing and food.[123] Two years after the enactment of this law the estimated expenditure by the crown for the passage of monks and friars to the Indies was 12,000 ducats.[124]

The members of the regular orders in the colonies frequently found serious difficulties in obtaining subsistence for themselves and in fulfilling their religious obligations. In the less populated and poor regions, the government occasionally permitted the representatives of the regulars to obtain supplies at the expense of the local royal governors.[125] More frequently the civil authorities furnished oil and wine for the service of mass in the convents. The governors were cautioned to permit such aid to be given in cases where divine services would cease without it. Philip III advised that only reasonable prices be paid for these supplies.[126]

IX

The presentation of some of the economic aspects of the ecclesiastical system of the Indies shows that the influence of the Spanish clergy in the colonies was often detrimental to the welfare of the inhabitants. On the other hand, the beneficial effects of much of the missionary activity is admitted by the unbiased investigators. The cleric, like his fellow colonist, was greatly affected by the frontier. The distant and vague authority, both of the bishop and of the civil governor, frequently gave the priest a practical immunity from punishment for misconduct.

---

[122] A *maravedí*, for a long time an obsolete coin, is said to have been worth one-third of a cent.

[123] *Recop. leyes Ind., lib.* i, *tít.* xiv, *ley* 6.

[124] "Presupuesto de ingresos y gastos de 1609," *Col. doc. inéd. España*, XXXVI, 558. The ducat was valued at from 2.12 to 4.13 *pesos;* ordinarily one *peso* equalled 8 *reales*.

[125] *Recop. leyes Ind., lib.* i, *tít.* xiv, *ley* 22.

[126] *Ibid., lib.* i, *tít.* iii, *ley* 7.

The temptation to extortion and vice was too great for a large number of the ecclesiastical hierarchy as for many of the laymen. The Spanish sovereigns persistently attempted to curb the evils as they arose, but they were usually a step behind. The economic control of the church by the Spanish government was no more successful than the political and economic supervision by the crown in the non-religious sphere.

APPENDIX B

THE EARLY FRANCISCANS IN FLORIDA AND THEIR RELATION TO THE COLONIZATION OF THE SPANIARDS

By Maynard Geiger

THE early history of Florida from 1513 to 1574 is fairly well known through the works of Lowery, Bourne, Smith, Shea, and others who have unfolded the story of the discovery, the attempts at colonization, and the final conquest under Pedro Menéndez de Avilés in 1565. Up to recent years, however, the long period of Spanish domination from 1574 to 1763 has been to most Americans a *terra incognita*. Miss Mary Ross has well said that "among the silent places in American history, the story of seventeenth century Guale, or the record of the golden age of Franciscan labor in the region now known as eastern Georgia, is notable." Parenthetically, it might be added, that what holds for eastern Georgia, is equally true of Florida, western Georgia, Alabama, and a part of South Carolina. A vital impetus has been given to this study in recent years through the collection and publication of documents relative to the period, notably by the Florida State Historical Society. Also excellent work has been done by Dr. H. E. Bolton, whose insistence that the Spanish borderlands are part of our cultural heritage has not only aroused interest in the Florida field but has been the occasion of new endeavors. In connection with such labors in the past and at present must be included the names of Dr. James A. Robertson, Dr. George Johnson, Miss Jeannette Connor, Miss Irene Wright, Miss Mary Ross, and a host of other writers.

Omitting the names of the Franciscan friars who accompanied Pánfilo de Narváez and Cabeza de Vaca, as well as De Soto, it may be stated that the members of that Order labored in Florida for over a century and a half beginning with the year 1573 until the destruction of the Spanish missions in the beginning and middle of the eighteenth century. The seventeenth century saw mission activity in flower. The Florida of that day might be appropriately designated, as was our great southwest, "The New Kingdom of St. Francis." Considering the actual activity of the friars and the extent of territory involved, the peaceful conquest of Florida may without exaggeration be called the

Franciscan conquest. This was already the opinion of Fray Luís Jerónimo de Oré, who shortly after 1616 wrote concerning his fellow friars: "It is we who are bearing the burden and the heat; it is we who are conquering the land."

While Florida history is intensely fascinating during this early period from 1573 to 1616, to which this paper is limited, yet it is a slow moving and conservative type of history. The historian working in this field must be a patient sort of being and must have the capacity of being intensely interested in small details, taking for his motto the Scotch saying: Many a mickle makes a muckle, or translated into Spanish, which is more apropos, *Muchos pocos hacen un mucho.* He will find himself becoming a sort of spiritual shock absorber, listening to all the complaints and miseries which were part and parcel of the lives of the people in that forlorn colony. And one can only understand the difficulties under which the friars labored when one becomes thoroughly acquainted with the condition of the colony.

Poverty and depression are the constant theme songs that run through all the records of this early period. From the governor down to the meanest soldier, the perennial complaint was insufficient pay. The unmarried soldier might get along, but what of those with families? And what of the widow and orphan? Even at that the soldiers' pay was often in arrears. The friars received their daily sustenance, but at best it was on a starvation basis. The *presidio* of St. Augustine was poorly located. The bar allowed only the smallest ships to enter. The town was in danger of being inundated, while fire was an ever present scourge. The houses were built of the rudest material. Swamp land abounded. There was little or no agriculture or cattle raising. No mines in the region had been opened. Florida was entirely dependent on the outside for her very necessities. These were supplied by Mexico and the islands of the Caribbean. Prices were enormous. Travel was slow. It took about a week to get to Havana. Most of the travelling in Florida itself had to be done by canoe or frigate. There was a notable lack of skillful pilots for the dangerous coast, with the consequent loss in lives, ships, and cargo. Repeatedly in the documents occurs the refrain: the land is poor and off the beaten track of commerce. Hostile Indians took their toll of human lives among soldier and missionary—five of the latter were killed in 1597 while one was held in captivity for a period of ten months. Fear of the foreign corsair made Florida desolate in her loneliness—witness the destruction of St. Augustine by Drake in 1586. Besides the worry of feeding themselves, the military and religious elements of the colony had to placate the Indians with numerous gifts. Then, it seems, the officials often lacked the spirit of initiative where standing on one's own feet was a prime requisite. Yet let one not judge them too harshly; they were part of the bureaucratic system which placed the whole colonial system in one grand regimentation and which canonized meticulously. When a friendly Indian received a Spanish hat gratis, that was noted down. When Fr. Baltasar López became ill because of his unhealthful surroundings and needed more and better food for his convalescence, a requisition had to be made to the governor, who in turn called a meeting of the officials. These left the decision to the governor. He in turn called in two doctors who declared that the three *reales* which Fr. López had been receiving for his daily sustenance were not enough to sustain a well man, much less for curing a sick man. Thereupon, the governor acted and the king was notified and beseeched for further assistance. The reports burgeon forth with details as to how every *maravedí* was spent, often accompanied with whys and whereases as to the spending. It is very true that the king was generous, but he had other and more important colonies to look after. However, the financial system as it operated in regard to Florida wrought great hardship to all concerned.

It will be recalled that by virtue of the *patronato real* the Catholic Kings of Spain, who had the privilege of appointing ecclesiastics, likewise had the duty of supporting the spread of Christianity in the New World by maintaining the religious personnel as well as building the necessary churches, friaries, and other institutions. In colonizing the New World, Spain organized all her agencies, political, commercial, and religious, in order to employ them along a unified plan and regular method. Part and parcel of this systematic penetration and colonization was the mission system instituted in behalf of the evangelization and gradual civilization of the natives. A certain field was given to a religious order to evangelize. As the confines increased, new fields were opened under the auspices of the same or another order. The religious in most cases were given military protection. Mandate upon mandate was given out by the Spanish kings to the effect that the native be kindly treated, indoctrinated, and civilized. No unbiased historian denies this or questions the sincerity of the decrees. Vast sums of money were spent for this purpose. And in Florida, it should be remembered, it brought no direct financial returns to Spain. It is basic to understand Florida's position in the whole scheme of Spanish colonization. In brief it is this. Repeated attempts had been made to colonize Florida, but all failed. Philip II ordered the abandonment of further attempts. Then the French settled on the very spot, a direct thrust at the heart of Spanish commerce. Philip reversed his decision. Menéndez de Avilés conquered Florida. How was life to be made secure, property safe? Spain must have friendly Indians as neighbors. They must be converted and civilized, that is, Hispanicized. Besides, if Spain desired to reap the commercial and political benefits, was she not also bound to undergo the necessary expenditures for the Christianization of the Indian? That was part of the understanding. To convert the Indian, missionaries were needed. The Franciscans were called. These, Spain supported and encouraged. They in turn gave to Spain friendly Indians and ampler territory. And early in the seventeenth century, when there was talk of abandoning St. Augustine, a Franciscan argued along the following lines: The Indians are here and have been converted, and I cannot consent to their being removed to Española. The Indian is adverse to changing his natural habitat. On the other hand, he cannot be abandoned. Since the Indian cannot be moved, and Spain cannot move him and be just, or what would be worse, abandon him, the Indian must remain and St. Augustine must continue to function as a *presidio*.

The Franciscan Order was ruled by a Minister-General with headquarters at Rome. The Order was divided into provinces, each ruled by a provincial. When Franciscan activity relative to the Indies began to take on such great proportions, modifications in organization began to take place. In 1572 a Commissary-General was instituted at Madrid who had complete charge of all Franciscan activities relative to the Indies. This officer was to all intents and purposes the General of the Order as far as the Indies were concerned. He dealt with the king and the Council of the Indies. If the king ordered twelve friars to go to Florida, the Commissary-General was notified. A commissary was appointed to recruit the friars, prepare them for the journey, or even accompany them to their destination. At that time Spain had a large standing body of religious, but still there was a drain on their ranks for their activity in the missionary field covered North, Central, and South America, as well as the East Indies. In America, where a small group of friars was working in an alloted field, the district was known as a *custodia* at the head of which was a *custodio*. A *custodia* was a province in the process of formation and development. When the field appeared to be permanent, the personnel larger, and the scope of activity more widespread, the *custodia* became a *provincia,* or a province, which equalled then the fully developed provinces of Europe. Thus, Florida, together with Cuba, formed a custody until 1612 when it became the Province of Santa Elena. In America, likewise, commissaries were appointed to look after a group of provinces. These were to visit the provinces, the friars, and the localities in which they labored. Thus, Fray Luís Jerónimo de Oré was appointed Commissary for Cuba and Florida. He made two visitations, one in 1614 and another in 1616. The term commissary was used also in other senses. Thus, there was in St. Augustine a commissary of all the friars in Florida who looked after their temporal welfare and stated their needs to the governor, who in turn referred them to Madrid. A commissary was also a friar delegated by special commission for an important investigation or some other work of like nature.

When the religious sailed from Spain, or came into one of the large ports of the Indies, a housing problem was created. Fray Alonso Escobedo tells us that when he and his companions came to San Lúcar, the port of Seville, he could find no quarters in the Franciscan convent there because of the presence of a hundred other Franciscans all awaiting embarcation for the Indies! In the latter years of the sixteenth century, the Franciscans and Dominicans of Havana made insistent appeals to the king to amplify their convents there so as to be able to give shelter to the friars when the fleets came in, for at such times the number of friars was quadrupled. From Havana the friars spread fan-like to Florida, Mexico, Central America, and Venezuela.

It is interesting to read the royal *cédulas* of the period to see how the Spanish government provided in detail for the friars going to the Indies. From these records it may be learned that the books and clothing of the friars were transported from their convents to Seville, thence to America. Every day each friar remained at Seville awaiting embarcation, he received three *reales* a day for his support. Special orders were given that decent and commodious quarters be provided for them aboard ship. One *cédula* stated that if any of the friars had to remain in Cuba en route to Florida, for instance, by reason of sickness, he was to be given medicine and other necessities. In Florida itself each friar received three *reales* a day for his maintenance, besides clothing and necessary religious articles for his own use or for divine service, while the government built the monasteries and churches, and provided the friars with transportation into the interior and freight service at stated times. Relative to the Franciscans, it is necessary to state that according to the Franciscan rule, the vow of poverty was stricter than that of the other religious orders. Moreover, there was the prohibition against having or using money in the ordinary sense. This was done for them by civilians, called syndics, for the province and the local monastery. The friars in Florida, likewise, had their syndic. The money destined for them went through his hands.

From 1573 to 1595 the missionary work went on rather slowly. At times there were only a few friars in Florida, and these were engaged as chaplains at the forts in St. Augustine and Santa Elena, or as parish priests in the former town. A few friars came to Florida under Fray Alonzo de Reinoso in 1584. He brought another band in 1587. Fray Juan de Silva brought a group of eleven in 1595. Seven new missionaries came in 1605. In 1612 Governor Rodríguez de Olivera could write to the king that twenty-one friars had come to Florida. In 1617 there were thirty-five Franciscans laboring in Florida, while twenty more were requested as being necessary. In 1626 Fray Alonso de Pesquera received permission to bring sixteen; in 1631 Fray Francisco de Jesús brought twelve. Ten came with Fray Francisco Alonso de Jesús in 1635, and so on.

Of course, there was depletion in the ranks of the friars in Florida, and this resulted from various causes. Some who came with Fray Baltasar López in 1587 found the work strenuous beyond their endurance and went to New Spain. Five were killed in the Guale rebellion in 1597, and one had to retire because of the hardships endured during ten months of captivity. Fray Blas de Montes was forced to return to Spain by reason of illness, and Fray Baltasar López was given leave to go to New Spain for the same reason. At times, too, friars were withdrawn from Florida for service in Cuba. After 1612, however, the number of permanent friars in Florida was greater. At the height of activity there were fifty friars in forty-four mission centers working for the welfare of thirty thousand converted Indians. This was the Golden Age.

One cannot here go into details as regards the individual missions. It is sufficient to point out that the first work among the Indians was at Nombre de Dios and San Sebastián near St. Augustine. Very important missions were opened among the Timucuans at San Juan del Puerto at the mouth of the St. John's River and at San Pedro in southern Georgia. Then there was what was known as the Salt Water District along the Georgia coast where the inland waterway divided the mainland from the islands that fringe the coast. There were found such towns as Guale, Ospo, Obdalquini, Tupiqui, Talaxe, and others. South of St. Augustine was the Fresh Water District between St. John's

River and the sea. There were found the Indians of Ais and Sorruque. West of the Fresh Water District was Potano in north central Florida and west of that, Apalache. All these districts entered into the picture before 1612.

When the friars came to St. Augustine, after a rest from the long overseas journey, the superior appointed them to new stations or to vacancies in the old stations. The Franciscan superior consulted with the governor, at least in 1595, as was right and necessary, for, after all, the governor wanted to know where his Spanish subjects were, since he was responsible for their safety and had to provide them with the necessities of life. In 1595 Governor Domingo Martínez de Avendaño himself accompanied some of the missionaries to their new posts. To impress upon the Indians the sacred trust granted to the friars, as well as the exalted position they held, the governor knelt down and kissed the hand of the religious before the assembled Indians. The question would naturally rise in the Indians' minds: Who are these men whose persons the governor himself reverences? Fray Francisco Marrón then visited the friars and found them separated at a distance apart, ill-provided in the things considered necessary for Divine service according to Catholic practice. At this time there were about 1,500 Christian Indians in the entire land.

Once a friar arrived at his mission, life began in earnest. He no longer enjoyed the benefits of conventual life as he once did in Spain, nor the spiritual and intellectual companionship that permeates a religious community. He came into a totally different environment ranging from savagery to barbarism. To win the Indian he had to undergo much personal discomfort. The friar had to grow accustomed to Indian ways of life and habits of thinking. One of his first endeavors was to learn his language. Fray Baltasar López spoke Timucuan well. Fray Francisco Pareja has left us a grammar in the Timucuan language. The friars in Guale spoke the native tongues. The new doctrine he taught had to be unfolded gradually. Often the Indian language lacked words to adequately express Christian ideas. The work of Christianizing the natives in Florida was a very slow and systematic, though thorough, piece of work. The records leave no doubt that the natives were not baptized until they were fit to enter into the duties of Christian living. The note of hurry in this regard is totally absent from the Florida field. Throughout the period from 1597 to 1616, request upon request came in from the Indians themselves for friars to reside among them. Frequently there was none to spare, but the friars visited such Indians occasionally. Thus on one occasion, Fr. López spent three months with the Indians in the interior. Pagan Indians frequently visited the Christian settlements and thus came into direct association with their Christian fellow men. The Christian Indians were allowed to visit their pagan relatives in the interior, after having obtained the necessary permission. Some of the *caciques* used their influence in bringing other chiefs under Spanish and Christian influence. In the beginning the Christian had to bear the taunts and persecution of the pagan; at a later date the friars had to restrain their well-meaning but overzealous Christians in their reaction against the pagans. Fr. Oré says that when he visited the Florida Indians, many of the old superstitions had been wiped out and in some cases forgotten, and that the younger generation laughed at the older one for its practices.

The documents frequently describe a certain Indian as *muy españolado,* thoroughly Hispanized. At some places the Indians are described as adept pupils. Some learned to read and write even in the early period. Fr. Oré writes that some learned these arts in the brief span of two years; that some as old as forty thought it worth the while to take advantage of the opportunity offered them, and that they wrote letters to one another in their own tongue. The Indians of Guale were taught the art of singing by Fray Pedro Fernández de Chozas, for which they greatly esteemed him. Fr. Oré, who visited Florida not only as the representative of the Order but as delegate of the Bishop of Cuba, everywhere examined the Indians carefully as to their knowledge and progress in Christian doctrine and found that in some cases they excelled even the Spaniards themselves.

Usually a friar had a central station where he lived and where the principal church was located. The Indians of the outlying districts would come in for the principal feasts and for the celebration of Holy Week. At other times the friar would go to their villages. At times he went to other districts where his presence was desired but where no friar, for lack of numbers, was stationed. Then there was always the possibility of a sick call to some distant place to minister to a dying person. The journey was made either on foot or by canoe.

The Indians, everywhere in the records, are described as poor and the friar had to share their poverty. Roads were practically nonexistent; swamp land abounded along the coastal district. It is recorded more than once that the missionaries, in order to supply themselves and their Indian charges with things necessary for the becoming celebration of Christian services, deprived themselves of a part of their daily ration.

When the missionary became sick there was no other alternative but to go to St. Augustine for a while to recuperate. In 1599 the friars' convent, together with part of the city, burned. They had to take temporary shelter in the city hospital which, by the way, was the first hospital within the present limits of the United States. The physical toil and, at times, the mental sufferings of these friars are understandable only in the light of the exalted idealism that motivated their activity.

The temporal gain that accrued to Spain as a result of this mission activity was very great. The Timucuans, north and west of St. Augustine, proved very friendly and never rose in rebellion after they were converted to Christianity. In times of hunger and starvation at the *presidio* they helped gratuitously the helpless Spaniards. They aided Spain, likewise, by their influence over neighbor chieftains. During the Guale outbreak, San Pedro formed the first line of defense for the *presidio* in the south. The Guale Indians, after killing the friars, descended on San Pedro with the avowed intention of not desisting until every Spaniard, his cattle and crops were wiped from the land. Faithful San Pedro, under the guiding hand of Fray Baltasar López, stopped the attack.

The Indians of Ais and Sorruque submitted to Spanish authority in 1605. This was a most important gain. Many ships had been lost or stranded along the coast of Cape Cañaveral so that it was most important to have friendly Indians there. Prior to that year it was unsafe for soldier, friar, or voyager to set foot on the land, for death was almost the inevitable result. When these Indians submitted, owing to the very prudent handling of the affair by Governor Pedro de Ybarra, they came into the *presido* city. He took them over to see the friars. The whole procedure, as well as the words spoken on that occasion, has been preserved to us in documentary form.

Fray Martín Prieto was among the western Timucuans in 1605 and subsequent years. The Indians of Apalache to the north were warring against them and they expressed their concern to the friar. He conceived the bold proposal to go with some friendly Timucuans into the Apalache territory to make overtures of peace. In this he was successful. Minute details of this great event may be had for the mere reading.

Besides their accomplishments in the mission field, the friars were in the front line with the leading citizens for the progressive development of the country. In 1600 Philip III asked for a statement on Florida conditions. The reports of the friars are not only illuminating but comprehensive. The mission phases may be passed over. But what should be pointed out is their progressive spirit and foresight in civil matters. The reports referred to are those of Fray Baltazar López, Fray Francisco Pareja, Fray Pedro Bermejo, and Fray Pedro Ruiz. They are all dated September 1602. Fray Pedro Bermejo suggested that the Indians in the very small towns be united with those in the larger ones so that the Indians would be better provided for spiritually and economically. This was the reduction system on a small scale. He furthermore suggested that the governor visit all the Indian villages once a year to encourage the good and threaten the evildoers. Fray Pedro Ruiz charged the governor with laxity in this regard, the governor holding that there was no punishment for the Indians after having accepted Christianity. This, of course, was a situation which neither the Indian chiefs nor the friars cared for. The chiefs wanted their subjects punished for violations of the law. They complained that they had a harder time making their subjects obey than in previous times. The governor would not inflict just punishment, and the Indian chiefs feared to do so because of the governor. In one instance when an Indian ransacked a house in St. Augustine, the governor let the crime go unpunished so that the respectable Indians were ashamed of the act and declared that if the Spaniards were not there, they themselves would punish the crime. Fr. Ruiz had this to say:

"Things are going topsy-turvy here. When we see Indians committing an excess worthy of punishment which we cannot remedy, and if we ask the governor to correct it, he overlooks it and so the Indians look upon him as their father and upon us as accusers. This is just the contrary of what it should be: since the governor's duty was to punish them and we were to do the supplicating for leniency and thus they would hold us for their fathers and the governor for a just judge."

At this time the friars urged the king to move the *presidio* from St. Augustine to Guale or Georgia for the benefit of all concerned. But this was not an abandonment of the Florida field; it was a plan of radiating from a different and more practical center. Neither was it a question of the removal of the Indians. The greater number of converted Indians were in Guale, and better work could be accomplished there by the spiritual and temporal agencies. They enumerated the dangers of St. Augustine from fire and flood, the unserviceableness of the bar, the scarcity of wood for building material, and the absence of a place to plant or graze. Furthermore, the populace was in constant poverty. Journeys that had to be made to Guale by land, when ships could not go by reason of unfavorable weather, sapped the strength of the most hardy. They pointed out that in Guale there were better ports and bars for ships, apt places for raising cattle, an abundance of fertile land for the culture of grain and fruits, plentiful material for construction purposes, and the presence of clay for making tiles and bricks. All these advantages, they said, would serve to ameliorate the economic condition of all concerned. It was even suggested that the Spanish populace and the Indians could profitably enter into commercial relations.

Finally, a word should be said concerning the activity of the friars along intellectual and scientific lines. In 1597 Fray Pedro Fernández de Chozas and Fray Francisco de Verascola, with the permission of the governor and their religious superior, explored the interior of Georgia as far as Tama. Gáspar de Salas and some Guale Indians accompanied them. Friendship was established with the chief of Tama. Moreover, the land was found to be very fertile and there were indications of the presence of precious metals. On the basis of this exploration, Governor Gonzalo Méndez de Canzo a few years later suggested to the king that a Spanish colony be planted at Tama because of its favorable location, and so that he might use it as a base to cross the country and come into contact with the Spaniards who a few years before had reached New Mexico! Another friar, who must be mentioned as a contributor to *belles lettres* and history, is Fray Alonso de Escobedo, who came to Florida in 1587. He has left us a history of his experiences in the form of a narrative poem entitled *La Florida,* a work that is hardly known in the United States. The manuscript is preserved in the *Biblioteca Nacional* in Madrid and covers 449 folios. It has never been printed entirely, even in Spanish, although the writer has seen two larger portions of it edited by the Franciscans in Madrid. The poem abounds in facts relative to the period, and is a mine of information for geographers, anthropologists, and students of mission history. Though in verse, it is most exact in historical detail as has been proved by checking it against independent sources in prose in a number of instances. Thus, from a Franciscan has come a contribution that deserves the most careful scrutiny of historians and students of literature.

One of the most eminent missionaries in Florida during the early period was Fray Francisco Pareja, the great scholar in the Timucuan language. His *Arte y pronunciación en lengua timuquana y castellana* was made known to a surprised assembly of Americanists in France during the latter part of the nineteenth century. This work was printed in Paris in 1886, based on the only known copy of the 1614 edition of

Father Pareja's work which was printed in Mexico City. Fr. Pareja was the author of four other works in Timucuan, and these constitute most of what is known today of that Indian language. Later, Fray Gregorio de Mobilla had printed in Mexico City in 1635 a translation into Timucuan, the *Explanation of Christian doctrine* of Cardinal Bellarmine, a classic work of the period.

In 1616 Fray Luís Jerónimo de Oré came to Florida for his second official visitation. He has left us a *Relación de los martires que han vido en las provincias de la Florida,* wherein may be found abundant historical matter pertaining to the early period. An excellent feature of the work is that Fr. Oré had the true historical sense. When he is not sure of a thing, he says so. Moreover, he gives the sources of his information. Then, frequently, rather than give a digest of documents, he includes his sources verbatim and often at length. He travelled through the entire Florida mission field, knew the friars, the Indians, and the Spaniards. Thus, he has preserved for us the original account of the captivity of Fray Francisco de Ávila among the Indians at the time of the Guale rebellion. Fr. Ávila wrote this account at the command of his superiors. The document was preserved in the Havana archives after Fr. Ávila's death. Thus historians know the sources of Father Oré's information. Furthermore, the statements of Fr. Ávila can be checked by many other independent documents of the period, both secular and religious, all of which tend to confirm his declarations. The *Relación* of Fr. Oré was not printed until 1931 when Fr. Atanasio López, O.F.M., of the *Archivo Ibero-Americano,* edited a limited edition. No other printed edition is known to exist.

SELECTED BIBLIOGRAPHY

This brief discussion has endeavored to give, in a most compact manner, the history and activity of the early Franciscans in Florida. In doing so there has been no intention to obscure or belittle the work of the Dominicans and Jesuits prior to the coming of the Franciscans. Nor would it have served any purpose to present here a discussion of the mission field in general, for this has been done in many excellent treatises by scholars secular and religious. The writer has preferred rather to select one territorial unit of the Spanish colonial field, and one religious unit which worked within that field.

Among the materials used in the preparation of this paper, the following are of importance:

Abad y Lasiera, Don Íñigo, *Documentos históricos de la Florida y la Luisiana, siglos XVI al XVIII* (Madrid, 1913).

Bolton, Herbert E., *Arredondo's historical proof of Spain's title to Georgia* (Berkeley, 1925).

Bolton, H. E. and Mary Ross, *The debatable land: a sketch of the Anglo-Spanish contest for the Georgia country* (Berkeley, 1925).

Cárdenas y Cano, Gabriel (Barcía), *Ensayo cronológico para la historia general de la Florida* (Madrid, 1923).

Chapman, Charles E., *Colonial Hispanic America: a history* (New York, 1933).

Connor, Jeanette Thurber, *Colonial records of Spanish Florida* (2 vols., De Land, 1925-1930). Publications of the Florida State Historical Society.

Documents on Florida from 1573 to 1621 (photostats in Washington). Florida State Historical Society Collection.

Engelhardt, Zephyrin, O. F. M., "Missionary labors of the Franciscans among the Indians of the early days," in *Franciscan Herald,* (Teutopolis, Ill., Jan. 1913-Sept. 1914).

López, Atanasio, O. F. M., *Relación histórica de la Florida, escrita en el siglo XVII* (2 vols., Madrid, 1931-1933).

Lowery, Woodbury, *The Spanish settlements within the present limits of the United States* (2 vols., New York, 1901-1905).

Ross, Mary, "The restoration of the Spanish mission in Georgia" in *Georgia Historical Quarterly,* (Savannah, Sept., 1926), 171-199.

Ruidíaz y Caravia, Eugenio, *La Florida, su conquista y colonización por Pedro Menéndez de Avilés* (2 vols., Madrid, 1893).

Velasco, Juan López de, *Geografía y descripción universal de las indias* (Madrid, 1894), J. Zaragoza, editor.

Wright, I. A., *The early history of Cuba, 1492-1586* (New York, 1916).

APPENDIX C

COLONIAL BRAZIL AS AN ELEMENT IN THE EARLY DIPLOMATIC NEGOTIATIONS BETWEEN THE UNITED STATES AND PORTUGAL, 1776—1808

By RAUL D'EÇA

THE subject of the diplomatic relations between the United States and Brazil has already been studied by able historiographers who have also, as was to be expected, devoted some space to the period from 1808, when Rio de Janerio became the seat of the Portuguese monarchy, to 1822, when Brazil declared herself independent from Portugal.[1] In this paper it is proposed to put together some scattered notes concerning Brazil as an element in the diplomatic negotiations which took place between the United States and Portugal from the year of the American Declaration of Independence to 1807 when the Portuguese royal family, fully understanding the wisdom of the saying that discretion is the better part of valor, took to the ships anchored in the Tagus and sought in Brazil a safe place of abode.

It will be recalled that the news of the American Revolution was received with various degrees of sympathy or antipathy by the old courts of Europe. In Portugal, ruled at the time in the name of His Majesty Dom José I by the all-powerful minister of state, Sebastião José de Carvalho e Mello, later Count of Oeiras and Marquis of Pombal, as soon as news of the outbreak reached Lisbon, a royal decree was issued prohibiting the entrance of American ships in Portuguese ports and ordering those found there to leave within eight days. This decree, published in Lisbon on July 5, 1776, declared as a sort of introduction and justification that the pernicious example set by the American colonists should interest even the most indifferent princes, leading them to deny all favor and help, direct or indirect, to vassals who were publicly and formally in rebellion against their natural sovereign.[2]

---

[1] Helio Lobo, *Cousas diplomaticas* (Rio de Janeiro, 1918), Part III, "Uma velha amizade internacional; Brasil-Estados Unidos," 83-112; Joseph Agan, *The diplomatic relations of the United States and Brazil* (Paris, 1926). I, "The Portuguese Court at Rio"; and Lawrence F. Hill, *Diplomatic relations between the United States and Brazil* (Durham, 1932).

[2] José Ferreira Borges de Castro and later Julio Firmino Biker, *Collecção dos tratados, convenções, contractos e actos publicos celebrados entre a coroa de Portu-*

At that time Pierre de Beaumarchais, the devoted friend of Americans and of the American Revolution, had already incorporated in Paris his notorious firm of Rodríguez Hortález et Cíe., with a capital of two million *livres* furnished by his secret partners, their Majesties the Kings of France and Spain, and was actively furthering the interests of the thirteen American colonies in rebellion against their mother country. In one of his letters to the Committee of Secret Correspondence (September 15, 1776) commenting on the decree above mentioned, Beaumarchais declared that "the blunder Portugal has lately fallen into, of shutting their ports with still more imprudence than haughtiness, seems to be an act of Heaven in your favor of which you cannot too soon avail yourselves." He then went on to advise Congress to declare war against Portugal and send a fleet to "the Brazils," which, in his opinion would engage Spain to do likewise, thus making the United States "in some sort" the ally of Spain.[3]

Whether Beaumarchais thought that an American fleet could then conquer Brazil or any part of it, is doubtful. He probably felt that by harassing the Portuguese there, Congress might compel the government of Lisbon to revoke its decree of July 5, 1776, besides, of course, securing the advantages resulting from Spanish recognition if American and Spanish ships were to take part side by side in war against the Portuguese.

The same advice was repeated by Silas Deane, no doubt under Beaumarchais' influence.[4] Congress, resenting the action of the Portuguese government, directed its agents in France to inquire whether the news was true and, if so, to remonstrate in the firmest tone with the Portuguese ambassador to Versailles.[5] But besides such remonstration,[6] nothing else seems to have happened, except the seizure of a Portuguese ship bound from Brazil to the Island of Fayal, which however was ordered restored to her owners by the admiralty court of Massachusetts.[7]

As to the Portuguese policy towards the American Revolution, it was

---

gal e as demais potencias desde 1640 até ao presente (12 vols., Lisbon, 1856-77), 366-67.

[3] Francis Wharton, *The revolutionary diplomatic correspondence of the United States* (6 vols., Washington, 1889), II, 146-47.

[4] Wharton, II, 148, 169.

[5] *Journals of Continental Congress, 1774-1789*, edited by W. C. Ford, G. Hunt, and J. C. Fitzpatrick (Washington, 1906-35), VI, 1035.

[6] Wharton, II, 307.

[7] *Journals of Cont. Cong.*, XI, 484-88; XVII, 528-30; XIX, 75; XXI, 900.

not changed even after the dismissal of Pombal as a result of the death of his master and friend, Dom José I, on February 24, 1774, and the accession to the throne of Dona Maria I. The governments of both France and Spain endeavored after 1780 to have the court of Lisbon either enforce its neutrality against all the belligerants or open the Portuguese ports to all. But in spite of repeated promises, Portuguese neutrality continued to be weakly enforced in favor of British ships.[8] And it was not until February 15, 1783, that the decree of July 5, 1776 was repealed and the independence of the United States duly recognized by Portugal.[9]

Immediately after recognition, the Portuguese diplomatic representatives in France and the Netherlands showed marked attention to the American plenipotentiaries then in Europe and, just as so many other representatives of European powers, began to talk about a treaty of commerce.[10] John Adams, while in France, had a conversation with the Portuguese ambassador at Versailles and asked him whether American ships would now be admitted to the ports of Brazil. To this the Portuguese representative replied that such a privilege could not be granted since it was the traditional policy of the Portuguese government to reserve for Portuguese citizens the right to trade in Brazil. Adams then asked whether one of the Azores Islands could not be made into a depot for such Brazilian produce as sugar, coffee, cotton, cocoa, etc., which American ships then could get there, presumably in exchange for American products.[11]

In this, Adams evidently followed instructions he had received from Congress. For a fact, Jefferson, Gerry, and Williamson, reporting as a committee to Congress, had advised that in the drafting of treaties of commerce with nations holding American colonies, direct intercourse between the United States and such colonies should be sought. However, if that were not possible, at least direct intercourse between the United States and certain free ports in such possessions should be secured.[12]

Adams had also a long interview with the Portuguese envoy at The Hague. To understand this sudden interest of Portugal in negotiating

---

[8] José Maria Latino Coelho, *Historia politica e militar de Portugal desde os fins do XVIII seculo até 1814* (3 vols., Lisbon, 1784), II, 38.

[9] *Ibid.*, II, 46.

[10] Wharton, VI, 480.

[11] *Ibid.*, VI, 568.

[12] *Journals of Cont. Cong.*, XXV, 821-28.

a treaty of commerce with the United States, we must remember that
the Portuguese government was then anxious to secure new markets
for Portuguese wines, fearing that the treaty of commerce then being
negotiated between England and France might give French wines such
privileges as to greatly reduce the sale of Portuguese wines in England.
The American diplomat in the course of this conversation asked if England or any other foreign nation had the right to send its ships to Brazil.
Informed that at the time foreign ships were not allowed in the ports
of Brazil, Adams did not insist but again spoke of having one of the
Portuguese islands in the Atlantic made into a depot for the produce of
Brazil. The Portuguese representative liked the idea and promised to
write home about it. But apparently nothing came out of this conversation, although at about the same time the draft of a treaty was prepared and sent to Lisbon by Benjamin Franklin.[13] One might observe
at this time that it is unfortunate that such a scheme was not tried since
its results for all parties concerned might have been of great value.

The negotiations for a treaty of commerce between the United States
and Portugal did not start in earnest until John Adams was transferred
to London in 1785. Luiz Pinto de Souza Coutinho was then Portuguese Envoy Extraordinary and Minister Plenipotentiary at the British
court. A lieutenant-colonel of artillery, Pinto de Souza had been
governor-general of the Matto Grosso Province in Brazil, and was
familiar with the general interests of that country, as well as those of
Portugal. He had been away on a long leave of absence, but returned
to London in that year. Upon several occasions, he told John Adams
that his government had instructed him to confer with the American
representative on the draft treaty sent to Lisbon by Franklin in 1783.
When the two men at last met at John Adams' house, Pinto de Souza
declared at once that his government was sincerely anxious to negotiate
and sign a treaty of commerce with the United States but that there
were things in the draft sent to Lisbon which it could not accept. Thus,
for instance, the ports of Brazil could never be opened to American
ships. Those of other nations, even the British, were then excluded,
and the United States could not expect an exception made in their
favor. There were, however, many Brazilian products which Portugal
could furnish to the United States, such as sugar, cocoa, cotton, tobacco,

---

[13] *The Works of John Adams*, edited by C. F. Adams, (10 vols., Boston, 1851-
56), VIII, 126-28, quoting letter to Secretary Livingstone, August 1, 1783.

etc.[14] The negotiations continued and were somewhat fostered by the desire of the American Congress to enter into some kind of an alliance with Portugal against the Algerian pirates as recommended by Secretary Jay.[15]

Thomas Jefferson, then in Paris, upon hearing from Adams how the negotiations were progressing with the Portuguese envoy, wrote to Adams expressing his pleasure and sending him some remarks on different points which might be taken into consideration during the negotiations. Jefferson suggested, for instance, that besides sugar, cocoa, cotton, and coffee, the United States might buy from Portugal ginger and spices produced in Brazil. Of the Brazilian sugar, he declared that it was esteemed in America more than any other. In his opinion the United States should, however, strive to secure direct access to the Portuguese possessions in America. He felt that the treaty should be so worded as to allow American ships under stress of weather, or wanting supplies of provisions or other refreshment, to enter Portuguese ports in America, the object of this being to obtain leave for American whaling ships to refit and obtain provisions on the coasts of Brazil—"an object of immense importance to that class of our vessels," he added, since in time it was hoped that other privileges would be secured and thus a *pied à terre* obtained in Brazil.[16]

At last, on April 25, 1786, a treaty was signed by the Portuguese envoy and by Adams and Jefferson, as American plenipotentiaries, with provisions quite similar to those of the treaty signed between the United States and Prussia the previous year.[17] But the American diplomats had failed to secure any special advantages in Brazil, for which they were sorry, Jefferson declaring in a letter to Carmichael (May 5, 1786) that "we wished much to have had some privilege in their [Portuguese] American possessions; but it was not to be effected." [18] The general license to trade granted to American ships was restricted to those places where any foreign nation was admitted.

---

[14] The Papers of the Continental Congress, Manuscript Division, Library of Congress, quoting letter of John Adams to Secretary Jay, Nov. 5, 1785, vol. LXXXIV, n. 717.

[15] *Journals of Cont. Cong.*, XXIX, 833-34, quoting letter of Secretary John Jay to Congress, Oct. 13, 1785.

[16] *The writings of Thomas Jefferson* (20 vols., Washington, 1904-05), V, 222-228.

[17] The Thomas Jefferson Papers, Manuscript Division, Library of Congress, n. 49, quoting letter to Dumas, May 6, 1786.

[18] *Ibid.*, n. 54, quoting letter to Colonel Humphreys, May 7, 1786.

The treaty was then sent to Lisbon. From there, unfortunately, word was never received by the American plenipotentiaries of it having been ratified or rejected. This was probably due to several factors: the renewal of friendly relations between Portugal and Great Britain after certain strained relations due to complications during the war of the American Revolution; the insistence of American representatives to secure the right of free importation of American flour in Portugal; and the failure of the American Congress to send a diplomatic representative to Lisbon.

When in 1788 Pinto de Souza, the Portuguese envoy in London who had signed the treaty, was called back home and appointed minister of state for foreign affairs, Jefferson entertained a hope that the treaty might at last be ratified by the Portuguese government. But as to the admission of American ships in Brazil, a matter of great potential importance for the United States, he did not think it probable then. In a letter to Secretary Jay he declared, however:

> "I think, myself, that it is their interest to take away all temptations to our coöperation in the emancipation of their colonies; and I know no means of doing this, but the making it our interest that they should continue dependent, nor any other way of making this our interest, but by allowing us a commerce with them. However, this is a mode of reasoning which their Ministry, probably could not bear to listen to." [19]

It may be interesting to recall here that during the previous year Jefferson had had an interview with a young Brazilian student at Montpellier, France, and, although professing that the United States wished very particularly to cultivate the friendship of Portugal, with whom the Uniter States had an advantageous commerce, Jefferson, nevertheless, had told him that a successful revolution in Brazil could not be uninteresting to the United States.[20]

The matter of a treaty of commerce, together with that of the admission of American ships to the ports of Brazil, continued to receive the attention of American diplomats thereafter for several years. In 1791 Colonel David Humphreys became the first minister resident from the United States to Portugal, his mission lasting until November 1794. In a dispatch to Humphreys (from Philadelphia, April 11, 1791) Jefferson, then secretary of state, instructed him to "procure us all the

---

[19] *The writings of Thomas Jefferson,* VII, 298.
[20] *The writings of Thomas Jefferson,* VII, 113.

information possible as to the strength, riches, resources, lights, and dispositions of Brazil," adding that "the jealousy of the Court of Lisbon on this subject will of course inspire you with due caution in making and communicating these enquiries." [21]   It is interesting to note that in his report on Brazil, Humphreys declared that although the natives of Portugal were by no means deficient in points of genius, yet Brazilians were "allowed to be a more shrewed & penetrating People," having more "books, more instruction, & particularly more knowledge on the subject of Government than the People of Portugal." [22]

In the instructions sent by Secretary Pickering to John Adams, who in 1796 was appointed minister to Lisbon but who later was sent to Prussia instead, the latter was desired to inquire as to the possibility of direct trade between the United States and Brazil and other Portuguese colonies. As yet there had been no direct intercourse between the United States and Brazil, said Pickering; however, the "climate and produce of at least a very large portion of that extensive country must be such as to render supplies of some species of provisions, particularly bread, as necessary to the inhabitants, as to those of the West India Islands." Secretary Pickering declared that little information existed in the United States on this matter and that the subject should merit the attention of the newly appointed minister.[23]

In 1797, William Loughton Smith was sent to Lisbon as minister resident. In the matter of a treaty of commerce he was no more successful than his predecessor. Secretary Pickering wrote him (March 22, 1800) that "unless Portugal would permit a commercial intercourse with her American colony, the Brazils, a treaty would seem to be of no great moment." [24] In Smith's opinion the lack of interest on the part of Portugal in this matter was actually due to fear of the entrance of Americans in Brazil.[25] In 1801 the American mission in Lisbon was discontinued, both for the lack of results favorable to the United States and reasons incident to American internal politics.

Until 1808, the ports of Brazil continued closed to American ships, except for occasional encroachments by United States whaling vessels

---

[21] State Department, Archives, Instructions to Ministers, Vol. I.

[22] State Department, Archives, Dispatches from Ministers, n. 41, Vol. III, from Lisbon, Dec. 23, 1791.

[23] State Department, Archives, Instructions to Ministers, Vol. IV, dispatch of Feb. 17, 1797.

[24] State Deparement, Archives, Instructions, V, n. 18.

[25] State Deparement, Archives, Dispatches IV, n. 32 and 36.

on the whale fisheries along the coast from Santa Catharina Island to
the Río de la Plata, a number of which were reported in a dispatch sent
by Joseph Rademacker, Portuguese chargé d'affaires in Philadelphia,
dated March 16, 1807, to Secretary James Madison, protesting against
such encroachments.[26]   During this interim no American diplomatic
representative resided at the Portuguese court until Henry Hill, an
American merchant, was sent to Rio de Janeiro as consul.   He presented
his credentials on May 5, 1808.

---

[26] State Department, Portuguese Legation, Vol. I.

APPENDIX D

SPANISH ROYALISTS IN THE UNITED STATES, 1809-1821

By PHILIP COOLIDGE BROOKS

MUCH has been written upon the aid given by citizens of the United States to the rebelling Spanish American colonies. It has even been shown that the government, or certain of its officials, at times gave clandestine sympathy and encouragement. The purpose of this paper is to illustrate by examples the reverse of that narrative, the efforts of the Spanish royalist agents in this country to offset the work of the insurgents. Diplomatic histories have barely mentioned the chief of these agents, and probably few students are aware of their large number and the complicated extent of their activities.

This is a discussion which involves at once the increasingly futile defensive measures of Spain, the desperate intrigues of the revolutionary agents, and the relation to Spanish America of the only American state which then had any claim to being a power. The very complex nature of the narrative is the chief difficulty in presenting it. The outstanding royalist representative, Luís de Onís, was an unrecognized minister for the first six years of his sojourn in this country, and most of the others who worked with him were secret agents whose activities are not easily followed. The period was one of opportunity for all sorts of adventurers and plotters, who used all the arts of intrigue. Several of them served Spain at one time or another, but their loyalties shifted so that even their contemporaries did not always know their true positions.

There is ample material with which to study these men and their work. The major collection of Onís' correspondence, in the *Archivo Histórico Nacional* in Madrid, comprises more than ten thousand pages. These can now be perused by means of photographs in the Library of Congress. They include instructions sent to Onís, his despatches, and accompanying documents such as selections from correspondence between him and other Spanish officials in the Americas. Besides these there are in Seville and in Mexico many more thousands of pages of correspondence of colonial officials in Cuba, the Floridas, the Provincias Internas, and Mexico which deal with this subject.

The very extent of these records is one evidence of how important the United States was considered during the Spanish American uprisings. Those revolutions form a part of one of the great world movements, the separation of the Americas from European political domination. Dr. Herbert E. Bolton stresses their vital relation to the United States by referring to the whole episode from 1776 to 1825 as "the American Revolution." This viewpoint makes it easier to appreciate the position of this country in the last, the Spanish, phase of that development. Not only as the pioneer in independence, but also as the only nation in the hemisphere which had diplomatic and military authority, the nation was one for the favor of which the contestants desperately vied.

The Spanish position was largely a defensive one, inasmuch as the sympathies of the United States were quite naturally with the insurgents. One can trace the development of the Spanish policy from confident arrogance to despair through the activities of Onís and his associates. In that gradual change there appears an interesting view of the Spanish attitude toward the revolutions as a whole.

This country's policy was conditioned upon its long-standing entanglements in European diplomacy and its friendliness toward Napoleon. Through the embarrassments resulting from the Anglo-French wars the governing party of Jefferson and Madison had developed a distinctly pro-French attitude. For reasons too complex for narration here they believed Napoleon to be the lesser of the two evils, and were on the point of war with England. This put Spain in a difficult position. She had signed in 1809 the alliance with England on the basis of which Wellington fought the Peninsular campaign. Still there were definite reasons why she must not unduly antagonize the United States. For one, the allied troops in Portugal and Spain were in great measure fed on grain from North America. For another, it was easy to see that if Spain allowed herself to enter what was to be the War of 1812 on the side of England, the United States could at once attack her through her colonies.

In previous pages reference has been made to the establishment of Joseph Bonaparte on the throne of Spain in 1808, and to the patriot uprisings which soon made his throne untenable. It is, therefore, unnecessary to relate the organization of the patriot *Junta Suprema Gubernativa del Reino* (Supreme governing body of the kingdom) at Aranjuez, which carried on in the name of Ferdinand VII, then a captive of the French. This group, continuing its sittings at Seville and Cádiz, held the fealty of the royalist authorities in the colonies until the restoration of Ferdinand in 1813.

The *junta* viewed with alarm many developments in the Americas. Relations with the United States were most uncertain. This country voiced ambitions of conquering not only Canada but also the Floridas, and was rapidly expanding in the Mississippi Valley region. Tension between England and the United States threatened to create an embarrassing situation. French plotters were rampant, spreading hostile propaganda. And now the colonies themselves began to rebel and to court the favor of their North American neighbor. To observe and to try to head off these dangers, a strong diplomatic agent at Washington became a necessity. For this position the *junta* in the summer of 1809 chose Don Luís de Onís.

Onís was a career diplomat of service extending back to the days of the great foreign minister, Floridablanca. He had been for many years chargé d'affaires in Saxony, and more recently senior official in the foreign office. Specialization in Franco-Spanish relations had given him valuable practical training, and his education was of the best.

Onís arrived in Washington in October 1809, not long after James Madison assumed office as president. He met with a major obstacle at the outset. In his first interview with Robert Smith, secretary of state, he was told that he would not be officially received. The United States chose to consider the troubles in Spain as a civil war, and declined to acknowledge either Joseph Bonaparte or the *junta* as the real ruler. Accordingly, it could not receive diplomatic agents of either. Onís then remained unrecognized until 1815.

Despite such a discouragement, there was still much for Onís to do. He was instructed to find some roundabout means of dealing with the United States government, and to avail himself of all possible ways of favorably influencing public opinion in this country.[1] Most important, he was to keep the flow of commerce between the two countries moving, and to observe and offset the actions of French and colonial revolutionary agents.

Onís at once assumed an important position as a sort of clearing house for information of all Spanish interests in the Americas. He maintained such an extensive correspondence with other royalists in this country, in Mexico, in Cuba, and in other places that he kept two copyists busy much of the time. Previous to his arrival, two lesser authorities, Valentín de Foronda and José Viar, had bitterly disputed the

---

[1] Bardaxi (Spanish foreign minister) to Onís, April 21, 1810, in Archivo del Ministerio de Estado (hereinafter cited as *A. M. E.*), Madrid, *legajo* 217.

rights and duties of the position of chargé d'affaires. Onís accepted the appointment as minister only on condition that both of them be dismissed and that the office of consul general be suspended. He then undertook a complete reorganization of the Spanish consular system in the United States, and maintained close supervision over it. This arrangement gave him, perhaps, as complete a picture of the whole narrative of Spanish interests, at least in North America, as any one person could have. One result was that he constantly worried over an almost overwhelming number of obstacles, intrigues, and rumors of others that never materialized. His despatches and his letters to other colonial officials are full of warnings against the ambitions of the United States and the insurgents, and of pleas for the defense of the frontiers of the colonies.

Onís spoke bitterly of the Democratic administration and of its friendship for France. One letter, written in that tone to the captain-general of Caracas, was intercepted and published, much to his chagrin. It accused the United States government of standing in a position of "serville meanness . . . in relation to their oracle, Bonaparte," and went on to say that nothing could be obtained from this country except "by energy, by force, and by chastisement." [2] The document fell into the hands of a revolutionary agent, was delivered to Monroe, and officially communicated to Congress.

This incident clinched the antagonism between the Spanish minister and the Democratic Party. It is important to note that his bitterest diatribes were issued against that group, rather than against the United States as a whole. In fact, he tried to make friends with the Federalists, capitalizing on their enmity toward the administration in power. He had retired to Philadelphia when told he would not be recognized, and there had set about his task of gaining advocates for the Spanish cause. This proved difficult in view of the general sympathy for the rebelling colonies, but there were some persons whom Onís considered his friends.

One association that he made he probably overvalued. That was with Alexander J. Dallas, then United States district attorney for eastern Pennsylvania, who served as an unofficial "contact man" between Onís and Monroe. "Mr. Dallas," the Spaniard wrote, "is like all those of the Democratic Party, but is a man of much talent and admitted in the society of the Federalists. I was already in friendly relations with

---

[2] Onís to the captain-general of Caracas, February 2, 1810, in *American State Papers* (Washington, 1832-1861), Series I, Foreign Relations, III, 404.

him." [3] It should be noted, though, that Dallas soon after this served in a similar capacity between Monroe and the arch rebel, José Álverez de Toledo, then an ardent conspirator against Spain.

This connection with Monroe was one of several which Onís used to transmit complaints, and which Monroe employed for abortive efforts to obtain the Floridas. No agreement resulted. The difficulties of the situation increased considerably when the United States declared war on England. It has been shown that among the dominant reasons for that act was the ambition of the westerners to conquer Canada from England and the Floridas from England's ally, Spain. During the war, in fact, the British used the Floridas as bases of operations, and Spain looked to the English fleet to protect the Spanish colonies against the United States.

Throughout the entire period of Onís' service, the Floridas were a focal point of attention, and in a way they fit into the narrative of the Spanish colonies. There were the distinctions, though, that their population was largely made up of adventurers from the United States, their commerce was in large measure controlled by British firms, and Spanish rule was hopelessly weak before the revolutionary movement started. Nevertheless, the uprisings in West Florida in 1810 and the filibustering which harassed East Florida throughout the decade might be called parts of the Hispanic American revolutions. These difficulties, with the absorption of West Florida by the United States and the invasions of the Floridas by Andrew Jackson in 1814 and 1818, form major items among the complaints made by Onís at Washington. These territories continued to hold international attention until the execution of the treaty of 1819, Onís' greatest achievement, by which the Floridas were ceded to the United States.

Onís had begun spreading propaganda soon after his arrival in 1809. The following year there appeared a widely circulated pamphlet signed by one "Verus," a pseudonym used earlier by Spanish Minister Irujo. This one, which was written by Onís, spoke of the United States government as "our government," and urged that it recognize the Spanish claims regarding the disputed possession of the Floridas, Louisiana, and Texas. Two later pamphlets, written by Onís or one of his coworkers, appeared in 1812 and 1817.

Numerous persons are mentioned by the Spaniard as aiding him officially or otherwise. First of the subordinate officials to be of consid-

---

[3] Onís to Bardaxi, Oct. 31, 1810, in Archivo Histórico Nacional (hereinafter cited as *A. H. N.*), Madrid, Sección de Estado, *legajo* 5636.

erable aid were Juan Bernabeu, consul at Baltimore, and Pablo Chacón, vice-consul at Alexandria, Va. Having official status as agents, they served as intermediaries carrying protests and other communications between Onís and Smith and Monroe. Bernabeu engaged in some important but futile conversations which were the only means of communication between the two governments. His chief worries, however, were over the active if supposedly secret aid given to the colonial rebels at Baltimore itself. The fitting out of ships and supplying of munitions in that port formed one of the most conspicuous examples of North American sympathy for the insurgents. Bernabeu served for some time, but eventually Onís lost faith in him. Fearing that Bernabeu's American wife of obscure background and her seven or eight children might have weakened his zeal for Spain, Onís recommended that he should not be given the post of consul-general when it was revived.

Other consular representatives in Boston, New York, Charleston, Savannah, and New Orleans faced the same problem of maritime conspiracy in lesser degree. All reported their difficulties to Onís. In the Louisiana region vice-consuls were disturbed by land activities such as the Gutiérrez-McGee invasion of Texas in 1813. From New Orleans, Natchez, Natchitoches, and St. Louis they communicated at length to Onís and to the captain-general at Havana.

At Washington, Onís had a staff of four or more, including copyists and those who served as messengers to and from Spain. Chief of these was José Heredia, Onís' son-in-law and the brother of an important foreign office official in Madrid.

Most interesting, however, were the unofficial aides the minister used for various purposes. He began as soon as he arrived by sending one Gaspar Moylana ahead of him to verify a report that Mrs. Madison and Mrs. Monroe could be influenced by means of gifts. He had heard that the French minister obtained preferred attention at the capital in that manner, and thought of using it himself. This plan, like one of Onís' to get one or two members of Congress under his pay in 1817, proved unworkable.[4] In addition, both were in time vetoed on account of expense by the Spanish foreign office.

The next secret agent of interest was one Diego Correa, sent from Spain to serve as spy for Onís. Under the name of Gorbalán, he went to Baltimore and conferred with the veteran intriguer, James Wilkin-

---

[4] Onís to Garay (Spanish foreign minister), Nov. 16, 1809 and Dec. 27, 1809, in *A. H. N.*, Estado, 5635. Onís to Pizarro (Spanish foreign minister), Feb. 2, 1817, in *A. H. N.*, Estado, 5642.

son. The former associate of Aaron Burr now offered to join the Spanish service in Mexico with four of his military officers. The ministry at Madrid figuratively threw up its hand in horror at this suggestion, forbidding Onís to give Wilkinson any money or to permit him to enter Mexico under any circumstances. Typical of the procedure of the time, however, is the letter in which these instructions were sent. Onís was told to encourage Wilkinson to think his offer might soon be accepted, using this encouragement to obtain whatever papers and information he might have.[5]

Correa, like Bernabeu, incurred Onís' distrust. The minister came to believe he was pro-French, and a long dispute ensued. Apparently it was smoothed over, for in 1817 we find Correa's son Segundo going with the Mina expeditions to Mexico as a spy for Onís. The younger Correa escaped in the debacle of that enterprise, and some years later appeared as a Spanish teacher in Massachusetts.

Throughout this period Spain cherished the dream of regaining Louisiana, which it felt had been taken from it by trickery in the French and American dealings of 1800 and 1803. The Spanish minister had in 1804 officially withdrawn objection to the Louisiana purchase, but years later the complaints were heard again. In this connection various plans were brought forth, none perhaps better worked out than that of Luís Clovet, a former vice-consul at New Orleans. He submitted to Onís a detailed program of attack, in which three armies were to advance simultaneously.[6] In nearly all such cases there was a *quid pro quo* desired for the trouble of drawing up the plan. Clovet wanted permission to settle in Spanish America at a time when such authority was granted sparingly. Whether or not he obtained it is uncertain. He was sent to Spain to present his plan to the government, and there he is lost track of.

Other secret agents were numerous in the Mississippi Valley, the hotbed of international rivalry and intrigue. One of the most useful to Onís was an aged priest, Padre Antonio Sedella, who reported developments there and served as negotiator with various rebels who turned royalist. Among the men he helped to bring into the fold were Juan Mariano Picornell and José Álverez de Toledo.

---

[5] Papers relating to Correa, in *A. H. N.*, Estado, 5553, *expediente* 50. Bardaxi to Onís, June 29, 1811, in *A. M. E.*, 218.

[6] Onís to Luyando (Spanish foreign minister), June 8, 1814, and Clovet to Cevallos (Spanish foreign minister), Dec. 7, 1814, in Archivo General de Indias, Sevilla, Indiferente general, *legajo* 1603.

Picornell was a conspirator of old, who had twice been sentenced to death for plots against the crown.[7] The first time was in Madrid in 1795, the second in Caracas, where he had been spreading seditious literature, in 1799. He remained in the West Indies and Venezuela region for some time, leaving early in the revolutionary period. He appears to have had some connection with the Gutiérrez-McGee Texas enterprise of 1812 and 1813. When that failed he offered his services, through Sedella and the vice-consul at New Orleans, to the royalists. The foreign office warned Onís against Picornell, but the minister found a way to make sure of him, and found him quite useful.

Picornell's greatest service was in upsetting the plans of Toledo, who in 1816 was still a rebel. From Washington, P. Gual, a revolutionary emissary, sent letters to Toledo and other leaders reporting upon the ease with which expeditions for Mexico could be fitted out at Baltimore. This was evidently part of the background of the adventure of Francisco Xavier Mina, with which Toledo was at first associated. Two of the letters were given by Gual to the famous Gulf pirate, Jean Lafitte, who was to deliver them. He did so, but not to the persons intended, for he had previously made an agreement by which he turned them over to Picornell. From him they went to Onís, and thence to Spain. Picornell eventually was pardoned for his previous plots by the Spanish government.

Within a year from that incident Toledo had also joined the royalists. This colorful, if somewhat elusive figure, was a Cuban who was sent as a representative of the colonies to the liberal Spanish *cortes* in 1810. He became too vociferous there and left for the United States in the next year, soon joining the Gutiérrez-McGee conspiracy. He discussed matters unofficially with Dallas, Monroe's representative, and actually received money for travelling expenses from him. During this period Toledo came secretly to Onís with an offer to betray the scheme, for a consideration.[8] Onís distrusted him, and gave him no money. Toledo went on with the plot, and in 1813 succeeded to the military leadership of the invading army in Texas. Following the failure of that effort he became interested in the Mina enterprise. He was apparently disuaded

[7] Papers relating to Picornell, *A. H. N.*, 5558, *expediente* 46.

[8] Onís to Labrador (Spanish foreign minister), 1812, and Labrador to Onís, Dec. 8, 1812, in *A. M. E.*, 219. See also *A. H. N.*, Estado, 5554, *expediente* 30, and Joseph B. Lockey, "The Florida intrigues of José Álvarez de Toledo," Florida Historical Society, *Quarterly*, XII (1934), 145-178.

from proceeding with that group at least partly through the work of Picornell.

Toledo came to Washington and became a valuable aide to Onís. He was pardoned by the government in 1817. His memoranda on the relations with the United States and on the possible reconquest of the colonies were of influence in the state councils at Madrid. Before long, Toledo himself went to Spain, and 1819 was sent on what was planned to be a secret mission to England involving considerable responsibility.

From the early patriot organizations at Cádiz came another of Onís' most prized assistants. Miguel Cabral de Noroña, a Portuguese by birth, edited a liberal newspaper there and in some way incurred the disfavor of the patriot government. He came to the United States in 1811, intending to join Toledo. Very soon, however, he was prevailed upon to serve as a translator for Onís, for a consideration (which Onís was never permitted to call a salary).[9] His duties expanded to the point where he wrote one of the "Verus" pamphlets circulated by Onís, and later tried, unsuccessfully, to found a newspaper. He eventually earned official recognition, and in 1819 was sent by the government to England, where he published a Spanish propaganda newspaper called *El Observador* (The Observer).

These maneuvers characterized the work of Onís while he lived in Philadelphia as an unrecognized minister, although he had to continue them after that in addition to diplomatic duties. He was finally recognized as a minister in December 1815, and his task was considerably changed. From then on his attention was largely taken up with the treaty which he finally concluded with Adams in February 1819.

This meant Onís was to be more busy than ever, because the insurgent agents became more and more numerous, sympathy for them in the United States increased, and the revolutions themselves became marked with notable successes, such as the independence of Argentina and the victories of San Martín and Bolívar. Thus his activities in those lines had to be enlarged, in addition to the management of a great treaty negotiation.

By 1817 representatives of the rebelling colonies appeared openly in Washington, and caused no end of trouble for the Royalists, even subjecting them to personal insults. In that year a storm arose over an attack on Don Diego Morphy, the long faithful vice-consul at New Orleans. Morphy was hit over the head and seriously injured in a

---

[9] Papers relating to Noroña, in *A. H. N.*, Estado, 5555, *expediente* 60.

street of that city by an aide-de-camp of Mina, following an argument
over the seizure of some of Morphy's letters.[10]   Onís pled with his
government for proper protection and vigorous action, and with the
United States for more safeguards for foreign diplomatic representatives.

The next year, Onís came to Secretary of State John Quincy Adams
with complaints that he had been insulted by revolutionary agents who
threw stones at his house in Washington, finally breaking the lamp on
the porch.   Adams said they must have been thrown by playful children,
but Onís insisted that they represented a conscious insult to the Spanish
monarchy.   He was even more sure of that when a few days later he
found a dead chicken hanging to the bell cord, signifying as he interpreted it the weakness of the Spanish Crown.

At about this time a notable figure appeared in Washington in the
person of Manuel Moreno, brother of the great Argentinian revolutionary leader and himself a prominent patriot.[11]   Onís immediately
wrote home that he thought he could buy Moreno's services, but this
plan proved impracticable, like many others of its type.

French conspirators in this country and in Mexico provided another
cause of worry for the royalists.   When Onís first came, agents of
Joseph Bonaparte were using this country as a rendezvous for their
efforts to obtain influence in the Spanish colonies.   Some years later
Joseph Bonaparte himself was here as an exile, and certain of Napoleon's veteran officers were plotting to revolutionize Mexico.   They
actually conducted an invasion of Texas, with the alleged aim of setting
up Joseph as king of Mexico.   The Spanish and French royalist ministers in Washington were greatly disturbed.   But the colony soon dis-
integrated, and a force of 1,500 Spanish troops marched to the Trinity
River just too late to wipe it out.   The disappointed generals fled to
Galveston Island where they put themselves under the protection of the
"governor," Lafitte.

Pirates, privateers, and munitions sellers proved a major diplomatic
problem for Onís.   Reference has been made to the notorious alacrity
with which persons in the United States assisted in the fitting out of
ships to aid the insurgents, particularly in Baltimore.   This activity,
while generally popular, put the administration in a delicate position,
and was especially objectionable to such a meticulous diplomat as
Adams.

[10] Onís to Pizarro, May 9, 1817, in *A. H. N., Estado*, 5642.
[11] Onís to Pizarro, July 18, 1817 in *A. H. N., Estado*, 5642.

The policy of the United States toward the revolutions was theoretically one of neutrality, based on the view that the conflict constituted a civil war within the Spanish empire. This angered the Spaniards in much the same way the British attitude during our war between the states offended the United States government. Our attitude practically meant a recognition of the belligerency of the rebelling colonies, which according to Spain had no legal status. Under this policy the government did nothing effective to curtail insurgent plotting in this country. With the additional factor of wide popular sympathy for the patriot forces, it was natural for the Spanish royalists to charge that the United States favored the colonies.

Partly due to the almost incessant and certainly voluminous protests of Onís, a revised neutrality act was passed in March 1817. It included the statement that it was illegal for any citizen to aid in making war on a power with which the United States was at peace. This act was not sufficiently drastic to please the Spaniards, and was not effectively enforced. Although it was called a treaty of peace between Spain and the port of Baltimore, it was widely disapproved in this country on the ground that it favored Spain. It did Spain little good, in fact, but Onís was unable to get any further satisfaction on the point.

The Treaty of 1819 was far the most important factor in the relations of this country and Spain in the years immediately preceding that date. The problem of the colonies figured definitely in Onís' viewpoint on that subject, and his attitude merits attention. He was seeking, in addition to innumerable claims arising out of the aid given the insurgents, a clear boundary line between the United States and the northern Spanish colonial frontier. To him the delineation of a specific line, which theoretically could be fortified, would provide a means of defense against the intrusions of all sorts of adventurers and filibusters. To the same end he constantly pled for increased fortifications for the Floridas and the Provincias Internas. The boundary defense idea was perhaps even more important to the ministers at Madrid, who in 1819 were still blindly confident of reconquering the colonies.

The recognition of the independence of the new republics also figured prominently in the treaty diplomacy. Onís had been instructed as early as 1811 to do everything in his power to prevent recognition by the United States. The Spanish foreign office knew that such acknowledgment would be one of the greatest possible gains for the insurgents, and to some extent conditioned their whole policy on that fact. Onís was at times authorized to make considerable concessions in the boundary, involving the relinquishment of half of Texas, if by them he could obtain a nonrecognition promise.[12]

The minister knew, however, that this country would never make such a promise, and he wisely withheld the offer of that compromise. Despairing over the growth of sympathy for the insurgents, he was greatly disturbed over the effort of Henry Clay to put a bill through the House of Representatives providing for the recognition of the United Provinces of La Plata. At this time, only war directly between Spain and the United States was considered a more disastrous possibility by the Spanish foreign office. Thus it was with real relief that Onís recorded the defeat of Clay's motion, on March 30, 1818, by one hundred and fifteen to forty-five votes.

This postponed the issue for a time, to the satisfaction also of Monroe and Adams who were anxious to continue the treaty negotiation. Within a year from that date the document was signed. It was intended to put an end to the controversies between the two nations dating back to 1795. It defined the boundaries from coast to coast, and provided a major step in our expansion.

Possibly the insurgents regretted this rapprochement between the two countries. If so, their fears were short-lived, for the treaty aroused great consternation in Spain, and its ratification was delayed for two years. In the meetings of the council of state at Madrid, objections arose because the territorial concessions were too great, because of some Florida land grants which were disputed, and because there was no guarantee that the United States would not recognize the new Hispanic American republics. Persons at that time, and historians since, have believed that the land grant scandal was the chief obstacle. Study of the council's work shows, though, that this argument was simply used as a pretext, and that the other two objections were the major ones.[13]

Thus, the question of recognition, which previously had been held off by the United States for the treaty negotiation, now became the most important reason for Spain's delaying the ratification of the treaty. Late in 1820 the Spanish government simply realized the futility of further efforts, and the ratifications were exchanged at Washington on February 22, 1821.

Meanwhile, Adams and Monroe, knowing that any steps toward recognition would further endanger ratification of the treaty by Spain,

---

[12] Irujo (Spanish foreign minister) to Onís, Oct. 10, 1818, in *A. H. N.*, Estado, 5643.

[13] *Acta* of the *Junta de Ministros*, July 1, 1819, in *A. H. N.*, Estado, 5661.

had continued to allow no steps to be taken. After Spain's capitulation removed that obstacle it was not long until diplomatic representatives were officially sent to Mexico, Colombia, and the United Provinces of La Plata. Onís had left in 1819 and had become ambassador to England. Certain royalist officials remained after him, but the final failure of their efforts in connection with the revolutions was evident in the recognition of the new republics by the United States.

Recent studies of early United States have showed that this country made its gains at the expense of embarrassed European nations.[14] This was certainly true of relations with Spain up to 1821. Here in one of her most crucial periods, when the empire which made her great was falling away, Spain's resources were exhausted by the Napoleonic wars, and her people were disillusioned by the blind absolutism of an incompetent monarch. There were few diplomatists and soldiers of international experience who saw the realities of the situation and the concessions Spain must make. Some of these succeeded in establishing temporarily a liberal government, from 1820 to 1823. But by then it was too late. The valiant efforts of the insurgents, the very considerable though clandestine aid of other powers, and the disorganization of Spain's political, military, and naval systems had allowed the empire to be lost, and with it Spain's position as a major power.

SELECTED BIBLIOGRAPHY

This paper has been prepared largely from manuscript materials in the Spanish archives examined in the course of a study now in preparation for publication entitled "United States diplomacy and the Spanish borderlands; the Adams-Onís treaty of 1819."

The major manuscript collections are as follows:

Archivo General de Indias, Sevilla, Indiferente general, *legajo* 1603, and Papeles procedentes de Cuba, *legajos* 104, 1708, 1837, 1898, 1944, and 1945.

Archivo Histórico Nacional, Madrid, Sección de Estado, *legajos* 5635-5646, 5553-5554, 5555, 5558, 5661.

Archivo del Ministerio de Estado, Madrid, *legajos* 216-225, 227, 228, 237.

Some of the more useful published materials on this particular topic are the following:

Bemis, Samuel Flagg, ed., *The American secretaries of state and their diplomacy* (10 vols., New York, 1927-1929), Vol. III, "Robert Smith," by Charles C. Tansill and "James Monroe," by Julius S. Pratt; and Vol. IV, "John Quincy Adams," by Dexter Perkins.

Cox, Isaac J., "Monroe and the early Mexican revolutionary agents," American Historical Association, *Annual Report* (1911), I, 197-215.

---

[14] Especially Samuel Flagg Bemis, *Pinckney's treaty; a study of America's advantage from Europe's distress, 1783-1880* (Baltimore, 1926).

Gayarré, Charles, *History of Louisiana,* Volume III, entitled "Spanish domination" (New Orleans, 1854).

Lockey, Joseph B., "The Florida intrigues of José Álvarez de Toledo," Florida Historical Society *Quarterly,* XII (1934), 145-178.

Onís, Luís de, *Memoria sobre las negociaciones entre España y los Estados Unidos de América, que dieron motivo al tratado de 1819* (2 vols., Madrid, 1820).

Wilgus, A. Curtis, "Some activities of United States citizens in the South American wars of independence, 1808-1824,"*Louisiana Historical Quarterly,* XIV (1931), 182-203.

Wilgus, A. Curtis, "Some notes on Spanish American patriot activity along the Atlantic seaboard, 1808-1822," *North Carolina Historical Review* (1927), 172-181.

Wilgus, A. Curtis, "Spanish American patriot activity along the gulf coast of the United States, 1811-1822," *Louisiana Historical Quarterly,* VIII (1925), 193-215.

APPENDIX E

SIXTEENTH CENTURY HISTORIES AND HISTORIANS OF HISPANIC AMERICA[1]

By A. Curtis Wilgus

WHEN the Iberians, after several centuries of fighting the Moslem, launched upon the conquest of America they little knew what was before them. But their religious zeal and their desire for gold and glory overcame all obstacles, and during the sixteenth century they conquered or claimed more than two-thirds of the Western Hemisphere. The mechanical process of conquering two continents resulted inevitably in the recording of experiences, in speculation concerning the land and its people who were found in a state of nature, in letters, memoirs, reports, and in relations, histories, etc.

I. General Works

Among the earliest and most frequently quoted of the histories concerning America, or as it soon came to be called, the Indies or the New World, is that by Gonzalo Fernández de Oviedo y Valdes (1478-1557) whose *Historia general y natural de las indias* was published at Sevilla in 1535. This had been preceded by another brief work, now excessively rare, entitled *Sumario de la natural y general historia de las indias* (Toledo, 1526). The work of 1535 containing nineteen books or parts was continued in 1557 at Valladolid when the twentieth book appeared. The entire manuscript written by Oviedo seems never to have been published in its entirety, although fifty books were printed at Madrid in four volumes 1851-55. Various abidged editions in foreign languages have been published, the first English translation appearing at London in 1555, the work of Richard Eden (ca. 1521-1576) under the title *General history of the West Indies*. Oviedo derived many of the facts for his history from direct observation since he spent twenty-four years in America, returning to Spain as a gray-haired man.

Another work frequently cited, but of indifferent value because it is

---

[1] This and the following bibliographical discussions are based on the writer's *Histories of Hispanic America* (Pan American Union, Washington, 1932). The original material has been revised, corrected, and augmented. Many helpful suggestions have been made by Dr. Philip Ainsworth Means, Dr. C. K. Jones, Dr. James A. Robertson, and Dr. Raul d'Eça. Miss Catherine Phelps has rendered invaluable assistance.

based on hearsay rather than upon documents, is that by the Priest Francisco López de Gómara (1511-ca. 1560) entitled *La historia de las indias y conquista de México* published in two parts at Zaragoza in 1552. The history describes the conquests of Peru and Mexico, and its circulation was prohibited soon after publication. In 1596 the first translation in English appeared at London made by Thomas Nicholas in 1578. This, however, dealt only with the portion relating to Mexico as noted below. The author was never in America, and he was accused by his contemporaries of fabricating many facts. In 1932 at Madrid the first part of this work dealing with Peru appeared in two volumes.

One of the most impassioned writers of history in this century was Bartholomé de las Casas (1474-1566), the "Apostle of the Indies." His chief works, which because of their nature are not always trustworthy, are the *Brevíssima relación de la destrución de las indias* (Sevilla, 1552) ; the *Historia de las indias* (6 vols., Madrid, 1875-79) taken from the original manuscript begun by Las Casas in 1520 and completed in 1561; and the *Historia apologética de las indias* (Madrid, 1867) copied by E. G. Squier (1821-1888) from the author's unpublished manuscript completed about 1550. A great number of editions of these volumes were subsequently published in foreign languages, particularly by the French and Dutch who used the books as propaganda against Spain. What appears to be the first English edition of the *Brevíssima relación* was published at London in 1583 as part of a now very rare book entitled *The Spanish colonie,* etc.

An historian of greater authority is José de Acosta (ca. 1539-1600) whose *Historia natural y moral de las indias* was published at Sevilla in 1590, although an earlier edition of books one and two had been printed in Latin in 1588 and 1589 at Salamanca. The first English edition was printed in 1604 at London while the best English edition can be found in the Hakluyt Society publications, volumes LX and LXI (original series, 1878-79). Acosta spent seventeen years in Peru as a Jesuit official, and his history is marked by religious coloring and philosophical treatment.

A work of considerable value frequently referred to is *De orbe novo* by the Italian churchman and courtier, Pietro Martire d'Anghiera (ca. 1455-1526), usually called Peter Martyr, who is generally considered the first historian of America. The first three decades of this work were published in Latin at Alcalá in 1516. The first complete edition of the eight decades to appear was that of 1530 at the same place. An excellent English edition in two volumes was edited by F. A. MacNutt

(1863-1927) and published at New York in 1912. The first English edition was published at London in 1555.

Another Italian, Girolamo Benzoni (1519-ca. 1572), brought out at Venice in 1565 a superficial work, somewhat prejudicial to the Spaniards, entitled *La historia del mundo nuevo,* an English translation of which may be found in the Hakluyt Society publications, volume XXI (original series, 1857). The work has been translated into several other languages but never into Spanish. The author went to America at the age of twenty-two and stayed fourteen years collecting material for his volume. The illustrations in the book are from the author's own sketches.

A pretentious undertaking written in Italian is *Le relationi universali,* published at Venice in 1579. It constitutes a general history and description of the principal parts of the world, and the author was Giovanni Botero (1540-1617). In 1748 a Spanish edition appeared at Gerona with the title frequently encountered, namely, *Descripción de todas las provincias, reynos, estados y ciudades del mundo.* This had been translated by the churchman, Jayme Rebullosa, who has often been misnamed the author. What appears to be the first English translation was published at London in 1603.

Another type of general work is that by Juan López de Velasco, entitle *Geografía y descripción universal de las indias.* It was written probably between the years 1571 and 1574, but was not published in book form until the nineteenth century when it appeared in 1894 or 1895 at Madrid. The author compiled the volume largely from documents in Spain which were placed at his disposal by the Council of the Indies.

Another geographical work which did not appear until the nineteenth century is the *Relaciones geográficas de indias* (Lima, 1885) by Lorenzo Suárez de Figueroa. The manuscript was written in 1586.

A rare and valuable work also descriptive of America, as well as of other parts of the world, is that by Martín Fernández de Enciso (1470-1528) entitled briefly *Suma de geografía* (Sevilla, 1519). The material on America was largely written from personal knowledge.

A work of a descriptive nature concerning the west coast region of South America which seems to have been written at the end of the century is *La descripción y población de las indias,* by the Bishop and Dominican, Reginaldo de Lizárraga (ca. 1540-ca. 1612), who lived in Peru from 1555 to 1599. Two copies of this manuscript are extant, one in the library of the University of Zaragoza and the other in the library of the University of San Marcos at Lima. The latter manuscript was hurriedly edited by Carlos A. Romero (b. 1863) and published in *Revista Histórica* at Lima in 1907. This was reprinted in book form the next year at the same place. The Zaragoza manuscript was edited by Manuel Serrano y Sanz (1868-1932), and published at Madrid in 1909. Dr. Philip Ainsworth Means (b. 1892) considers this work more informative than that by Benzoni.

Another descriptive work, valuable especially for the early history of the Peruvian and Mexican Indians, was written by the Augustinian Friar Jerónimo de Román y Zamora (ca. 1536-1597). The author never went to America, but as an adviser to Philip II he was in a position to use a great amount of documentary material. His chief work is entitled *Repúblicas del mundo . . .* , published in two volumes at Medina del Campo in 1575. The second edition (three volumes at Salamanca) contains more material on America. A new Spanish edition was published at Madrid in two volumes in 1897 under the editorship of D. L. d'Orvenipe (1865-1921). It was called *Repúblicas de indias.*

In 1591 was published at Mexico City the first part of a work intended to be a treatise on universal knowledge. It was entitled *Primera parte de los problemas y secretas maravillosas de las indias.* The book lacked in scientific observation, and no further parts were published. A second edition appeared at Mexico City in 1913. The author was Juan de Cárdenas (b. 1563).

Two works of an historical nature but dealing with medicinal plants in the New World are of great value to the student of the sixteenth century. The first to appear was by Nicolás Monardes (ca. 1512-1588), entitled *Primera y segunda y tercera partes de la historia medicinal de las cosas que se traen de nuestras indias occidentales que sirven de medicina.* This was published in an incomplete edition at Sevilla in 1565. The whole work was issued at the same place in 1574 and 1580. It was published in many other languages, the first English edition being that at London in 1596, which bore the title *Joyful news out of the new found world.* Another somewhat similar work of this century, but dealing chiefly with Spanish North America, was by Francisco Hernández (ca. 1517-ca. 1587), who was sent by Philip II to study the medicinal plants of New Spain. The work, which was illustrated with some twelve hundred colored drawings of plants, bore the title *Cuatro libros de la naturaleza y virtudes de las plantas y animales de uso medicinal en la Nueva España.* It first appeared at Mexico City in 1615. In 1888 a new edition was published at Mexico City. In 1926 at the same place appeared a facsimile edition of his *De antiquitatibus Novæ Hispaniæ* treating Indian medical history to 1519. Because many of the plants which he describes appear in other parts of the Indies, his work has considerable value to the historian of the colonial epoch.

An exceedingly valuable volume describing the military organization of the Indies in the sixteenth century is Bernardo de Vargas Machuca's (1557-1622) *Milicia y descripción de las indias* published at Madrid in 1599. This was republished in a second edition at Madrid in 1892.

A work of an entirely different nature appeared in Italian in three volumes at Venice between 1550 and 1556. It bore a long title briefly cited as *Navigationi et viaggi* and was by the historian and geographer, Giovanni Battista Ramusio (1485-1557). Volume III particularly relates almost exclusively to the New World, but its value has been debated.

A somewhat similar work was published at London in 1555 under the editorship of Richard Eden with the title *The decades of the new world or West India*. This was an adaptation of parts of Peter Martyr's eight decades with additions made by the enthusiastic editor and compiler. The work was augmented and rearranged by Richard Willes and published at London in 1577 in one large volume.

A third collection of voyages was begun by Theodore de Bry (1528-1598) under the title *Americæ sive peregrinationum in indiam occidentalem,* the first two volumes of which appeared at Frankfurt in 1590. In the following years to 1634, forty-two more volumes were printed at the same place.

A fourth collection, in imitation of that of De Bry, is the *Sammlung von sechs und zwanzig schiffahrten* by Levinus Hulsius (d. 1606), published in twenty-six volumes at Nüremberg and Frankfurt between 1598 and 1650. Only part of this work, however, deals with America.

A fifth collection describes the first French voyages to America, particularly to Florida and Brazil. The work is entitled *Les trois mondes* and was compiled by Le Seigneur de la Popellinière (1541-1608). It was published at Paris in 1582.

A sixth collection dealing largely with English explorations was compiled by Richard Hakluyt (ca. 1552-1616), entitled briefly *The principal navigations, voyages, traffiques and discoveries of the English nation*. This was published at London in three volumes from 1598 to 1600, the last volume particularly relating to America. This work had been augmented largely from his *Divers voyages touching the discovery of America and the islands adjacent* (London, 1582) and from his *The principal voyages and discoveries of the English written in the compass of 1500 years* (London, 1589).

A record of a single voyage of importance is that by the Venetian Antonio Pigafetta (1480-1534) who as an eyewitness told the story of Magellan's voyage around the world in his *Il viaggio fatto dagli Spagnuoli atorno al mondo* published in an incomplete edition at Venice probably in 1534 or 1536. An English edition appeared at London in 1555 in Richard Eden's *The decades of the new world*. The best English edition is that edited and translated by James Alexander Robertson (b. 1873) under the title *Magellan's voyage around the world* (3 vols., Cleveland, 1906).

II. SPECIAL WORKS

Among the works of the sixteenth century are a number which deal particularly with geographical regions. It is obviously impossible to mention all such references and in consequence only those of greatest value or interest are here cited.

Brazil

Three sixteenth century general works dealing exclusively with Brazil are usually considered of importance largely because there are no others of great merit. The first is by Pedro de Magalhães de Gandavo (b. 1540), who aimed to stimulate migration to Brazil, and is entitled *Historia da provincia de Santa Cruz*. It was published at Lisbon in 1576, and is the first general history of Brazil. An English translation in two volumes under the title *The histories of Brazil* was printed at New York by the Cortes Society in 1912. The second work bears the title *Tratado descriptivo do Brasil* and was written by Gabriel Soares de Souza in 1587 but it was not published in an accurate edition until 1851, when, under the editorship of Francisco Adolpho de Varnhagen (1816-1878), it appeared at Rio de Janeiro. The third work, written by Fernão Cardim (d. 1625) in three parts at the end of the sixteenth century, is descriptive of the country, the natives, and the Jesuit missions. It appeared finally in print at Rio de Janeiro in 1925 under the title *Tratados da terra e gente do Brasil*.

A work of considerable value for its description of the Indians of eastern Brazil was written by Hans Staden (ca. 1520-ca. 1557), who went to Brazil in 1547. Two years later his vessel was wrecked off São Vicente and Staden was captured by the Indians, with whom he remained until 1555. His story was told in his *Warachtige historie*, published at Marburg in 1557. An English edition was published by the Hakluyt Society at London in 1874 as Volume LI, first series.

A second valuable autobiographical account is that by Alvar Núñez Cabeza de Vaca (ca. 1490-1564), famed in North America as a walker, who wrote, after his experiences in Brazil and Paraguay, *La relación y comentarios . . .* , which was published in one volume at Valladolid in 1555. In 1891 the Hakluyt Society published at London an English translation as part two of Volume LXXXI of its first series.

Another work which deals in part with Brazil was begun by João de Barros (1496-1570) and continued into the next century by Diogo do Couto (1542-1616). It bore various titles but it is usually cited as *Da Asia*. It was divided into decades, the first being published in one volume at Lisbon in 1552. This was followed by the second decade in a second volume published the next year also at Lisbon. The third decade appeared at the same place in 1563. The fourth decade did not appear until it was published at Madrid in 1615. The work was finally completed in twenty-four volumes; the best edition, and the first complete one, was published at Lisbon between 1778 and 1788. This work constitutes the best account of the early Portuguese discoveries in existence and treats of the Portuguese discovery and conquest of Brazil very thoroughly. The whole work is based upon archival materials.

A lesser work of Portuguese explorations appeared at Lisbon in 1563 under the title *Tratado que compôs o nobre e notavel capitão Antonio Galvão. . . .* This appeared in an English edition published by the Hakluyt Society at London in 1601.

Mexico

A number of notable works concerning Mexico or New Spain were written in this century, although several did not appear until later centuries. Among the latter are the *Historia eclesiástica indiana* by Fray Gerónimo de Mendieta (d. 1604) which did not appear until it was published at Mexico City in 1870; the excellent and widely known *Historia verdadera de la conquista de la Nueva España* by Bernal Díaz del Castillo (1492-1584) which appeared in a corrupt form at Madrid in 1632, but which was published in a much more accurate Spanish edition of two volumes at Mexico City (1904-05) under the editorship of Genaro García (1867-1920), and in an excellent five-volume English edition under the editorship of A. P. Maudslay (b. 1850) by the Hakluyt Society (1908-16) as Volumes XXIII-XXV, XXX, XL (second series); the *Sumaria relación de las cosas de la Nueva España,* containing among other information an account of the descendants of the conquerors and early inhabitants of New Spain, written probably about the end of the sixteenth century by Baltasar Dorantes de Carranza (ca. 1550-ca. 1604) but not printed until 1902 at Mexico City; the long lost *Crónica de la Nueva España* by Francisco Cervantes de Salazar (ca. 1514-1575) begun in 1560 but not published until it appeared at Madrid in 1914; the extremely valuable *Historia general de las cosas de Nueva España* by Bernardo Sahagún (d. 1590), the first eleven books of which appeared in three volumes at Mexico City in 1829 and 1830, and the twelfth book of which appeared finally at Mexico City in 1840 under the title *La aparición de Nuestra Señora de Gaudelupe*—an English translation was made by Fanny Bandelier entitled *A history of ancient Mexico* (Nashville, 1932); the account of Hernando Cortés (1485-1547) contained in his five letters which have appeared in several languages in many editions, one of the best English editions being *The letters of Cortés* edited by F. A. MacNutt (2 vols., New York and London, 1908); the *Noticias históricas de la Nueva España* by Juan Suárez de Peralta (b. 1536) dealing with Mexico from earliest times to the period of Drake, but not published until 1878 at Madrid; and the *Relación de algunas cosas que sucedieron al padre Alonso Ponce en las provincias de Nueva España* dealing not only with Mexico but with Cuba and parts of present-day Central America, and written about the Franciscan probably by his spiritual brothers, Alonso de Ciudad-Real and Alonso de San Juan.

An excellent picture of the advance of the Mexican frontier to 1584, as well as an interpretation of the significance of the frontier, was written by Baltasar de Obregón (b. 1544). It is entitled *Historia de los descubrimientos antiguos y modernos de la Nueva España*. It was written in 1584 but was not published until it appeared at Mexico City in 1924. An English translation was made by George Peter Hammond (b. 1896) and Agapito Rey and was published at Los Angeles in 1928.

A sixteenth century account of the Indians of Mexico bore the title *Historia de los indios de Nueva España*. It was written by Toribio de Benavente Motolinía (b. 1568), as he is usually called. It first appeared at Barcelona in 1914 as Volume I of Joaquín García Icazbalceta's (1825-1894) *Colección de documentos para la historia de México*.

Two volumes, both written and published in this century, should be noted. In 1595 at Madrid was printed the first part of Agustín Dávila Padilla's (1562-1604) *Historia de la fundación y discurso de la provincia de Santiago en México* which constitutes a valuable account written from the documents of the earliest missions in America. The second part of this work was completed by Alonso Franco y Ortega (b. 1616) in 1645 but was not published until 1900.   In 1554 Gómara published his *Historia de México* at Antwerp, which was in reality a reprint of the second part of his general history.   This was translated into English by Thomas Nicholas and printed for the first time at London in 1578 under the title *The pleasant history of the conquest of the West India.*

Florida

Three valuable works deal with Florida in this century.   The first is *La relación y comentarios* of Alvar Núñez Cabeza de Vaca, already mentioned, which was first published in 1555 at Valladolid, describing personal adventures in Florida and parts of New Spain and South America.   The part of the *Relación* dealing with regions in New Spain, however, was first published in 1542 and there are now only two known copies in existence.   The best English editions of the whole work are by Buckingham Smith (1810-1871), published in 1851 (and a better edition of 1873), and by Fanny Bandelier (1905).   The second work to appear dealt with Soto in Florida.   It was written in Portuguese and briefly entitled *Relação verdadeira.*   The author is known only as the "Gentleman of Elvas" and the book was printed first at Evora in 1557. The first English translation was made by Richard Hakluyt and was published at London in 1609 under the caption *Virginia richly valued,* which in 1611 was changed to a more appropriate title.   The most recent and best English edition is that by James Alexander Robertson (New Haven, 1932-33), published in two volumes with a facsimile of the original manuscript.   The third work is laudatory, frequently fanciful, and not entirely trustworthy.   It is by the Inca Garcilaso de la Vega (1539-1616) and bears the title *La Florida del Inca.*   It was completed perhaps in 1591 but was first published at Lisbon in 1605 and records the adventures of Hernando de Soto as seen mainly by an eyewitness who gave the story to Garcilaso.

West Indies

A curious volume dealing with the discovery of the West Indies and neighboring regions was written in 1524 by a friend of Columbus, Alexander Geraldinus (ca. 1455-1525).   This account, however, was not published until it appeared in Latin at Rome in 1631 briefly entitled *Itinerarium ad regiones sub æquinoctiali.*   The author as papal legate of Alexander VI traveled widely, and his work is in consequence very valuable because he came into intimate contact with many of the early discoverers.

Tierra Firme

Another region frequently treated by Spanish histories of this century is Tierra Firme. It was in this period that Pascual de Andagoya (ca. 1495-1548) wrote his complaining and inaccurate *Relación de sucesos de Pedrarias Dávila en las provincias de tierra firme* which, however, was not published until the nineteenth century, the first Spanish edition appearing at Madrid in 1829. The best English edition is by Sir Clements R. Markham (1830-1916), published in 1865 by the Hakluyt Society as Volume XXXIV (original series). Another work not printed until later is that by Pedro de Aguado. About 1581 he wrote a manuscript which was first published in three volumes at Bogotá in 1906 under the title *Recopilación historial.* This appeared in a new edition of two volumes at Madrid in 1916 and 1917 under the title *Historia de Santa Marta y nuevo reino de Granada,* and in a three-volume edition at the same place in 1930. A second manuscript by the same author, completed in the sixteenth century, was published at Caracas in two volumes (1913-15) under the title *Historia de Venezuela.* A new edition of this work appeared at Madrid in two volumes in 1918 and 1919.

A work of entirely different nature and of considerably less value is a heroic poem containing some 150,000 lines. It is entitled *Elegías de varones ilustres de indias* and the author was Juan de Castellanos (1522-1605) who spent much of his life in compiling biographies of the early *Conquistadores* and then turning their stories into verse. The work is in four parts, the first of which appeared at Madrid in 1589, while parts two and three appeared first in 1850, and part four appeared first in 1886 under the title *Historia del nuevo reino de Granada.* The whole work deals with the conquest and settlement of the Caribbean area.

Peru

Peru was treated by several authors of the sixteenth century. Among the chief was Agustín de Zárate (ca. 1492-1560) whose *Historia del descubrimiento y conquista de la provincia del Perú* was published at Antwerp in 1555. The first edition printed in Spain appeared at Sevilla in 1577. An English translation may be found in Robert Kerr's (1755-1813) *A general history and collection of voyages* (Edinburgh, 1824). The author went to Peru in 1543 as a royal official and became embroiled in the civil wars there. Upon his return to Spain, probably in 1545, he wrote these volumes from his notes made in America.

A second very valuable history of the conquest was written by a secretary of Pizarro, Francisco de Xeres (b. 1504), under the title *Verdadera relación de la conquista del Perú,* published at Sevilla in 1534. An Italian translation was published in 1535 at Venice. The best English edition was published by the Hakluyt Society at London in 1872 (Vol. XLVII, original series). The history was written in Peru at the request of Pizarro and can be considered virtually the official published record of the conquest.

Another work by a secretary of Pizarro, Pedro Sancho, was written in manuscript and lost, but not until Ramusio had made an Italian translation which he published in his previously mentioned *Navigationi et viaggi* at Venice in 1556. A Spanish translation was made from this by Joaquín García Icazbalceta and published in 1849 as an appendix to the Spanish edition of Prescott's *History of the conquest of Peru.* The work has appeared elsewhere, but this particular account was translated into English by Philip Ainsworth Means and published by the Cortes Society at New York in 1917 under the title *An account of the conquest of Peru.*

Still another record of the conquest is by the cousin of Francisco Pizarro, Pedro Pizarro (ca. 1515-1571). His manuscript, *Relación del descubrimiento y conquista del Perú,* is doubtless the most careful and authentic account of the activities of the Conqueror of Peru. The work itself, completed in 1571, has never been entirely published, but a part of it appeared in 1844 in volume V of the *Colección de documentos inéditos para la historia de España.* William H. Prescott (1796-1859) used the manuscript to prepare his *History of the conquest of Peru.* The work has been edited by Philip Ainsworth Means and printed in English by the Cortes Society (2 vols., New York, 1921).

Another important descriptive work dealing with Peru, particularly valuable for Inca culture, is by Pedro de Cieza de León (1518-ca. 1560). It is entitled *La crónica del Perú* and was written in four parts, the first only being published at Sevilla in 1553. An English translation of parts one, two, and four of this work appeared in the Hakluyt Society publications, volumes XXXIII and LXVIII, second part, original series (1864 and 1883) and in volumes XXXI, XLII, and LIV, second series (1913, 1918, and 1923). Part three has never been found. The author lived in Peru for sixteen years, beginning his history at Popayán in 1541 and completing it at Lima in 1550. It is interestingly written and is based largely upon observation.

A valuable work dealing with Peru, of which the first part appeared at Lisbon in 1609, is briefly entitled *Comentarios reales de los Incas*. The author was one of the foremost Peruvian chroniclers, the Inca Garcilaso de la Vega. In 1617 at Córdoba appeared the second part of the *Comentarios* under the title *Historia general del Perú*. Both of these works were written from Inca records and certain Spanish chronicles, particularly the *Historia del Perú* (now lost) by the Jesuit Blas Valera (ca. 1551-1597), of which Garcilaso had a fragment of the manuscript. These works by Garcilaso have been considered by some scholars as excellent authority for the early history of the country. The first English translation of the *Comentarios reales* was published at London in 1688 in two volumes under the title the *Royal commentaries of Peru*. The best English edition was published by the Hakluyt Society as volumes XLI and XLV (original series) in 1869 and 1871. The first part of the work gives an account of Inca history and civilization while the second part is the story of the Spanish conquest of Peru.

Another work dealing with Inca affairs is entitled *Suma y narración de los Incas*. The author was Juan de Betanzos (1510-1576), who came to Peru with Pizarro and married a daughter of Atahualpa. With the knowledge of the Quichua language he became official interpreter to the viceregal government, and Antonio de Mendoza ordered him to compile the history of the Incas, which was completed in 1551. The book was written from the native standpoint, and with considerable accuracy. The first two chapters of the manuscript were copied by Friar Gregorio de García (ca. 1560-1627) in his *Origen de los indios* (Valencia, 1607), but the complete manuscript seems never to have appeared in print, although a portion was edited by Marcos Jiménez de la Espada (1831-1898) and published at Madrid in 1880.

Between 1583 and 1613 the Indian, Felipe Huaman Poma de Ayala wrote his *Nueva corónica y buen gobierno*. This work of 1179 pages containing hundreds of illustrations was discovered by Dr. Pietschmann, librarian of the University of Göttingen, in the Royal Library at Copenhagen in 1908. The work is chiefly valuable for its illustrations of contemporary life and customs. The manuscript has not yet been published.

A work of considerable reputation but in reality an inaccurate and prejudiced account of the Peruvian Incas is found in the manuscript entitled the *Segunda parte de la historia general llamada índica* by the famed seaman, Pedro Sarmiento de Gamboa (1532-ca. 1582). This work was written in Peru in 1571 and 1572 but it was not published until it appeared in Spanish at Berlin in 1906 under the German title *Geschichte des inkareiches* with a German introduction. The next year the first English edition was published at London by the Hakluyt Society as volume XXII (second series). The first and third parts to this work were apparently never written.

A valuable but diffuse work, written probably near the end of the century, but not published in complete form until the twentieth century, was by Pedro Gutiérrez de Santa Clara (ca. 1520-ca. 1603). It finally appeared in six volumes at Madrid between 1904 and 1929 and bore the title *Historia de las guerras civiles del Perú y de otros sucesos de las indias.* José Toribio Medina (1852-1930) had earlier published a fragment in volume XXVII (Santiago, 1901) of his *Colección de historiadores de Chile.*

One of the greatest writers dealing with the early Indians of Peru, and at the same time one of the least known, was Father Miguel Cabello de Balboa (b. ca. 1535) whose extensive manuscript entitled *Miscelánea antártica* belongs to the New York Public Library. The work has never been completely translated into any language, but in 1840 at Paris Henri Ternaux-Compans (1807-1864) edited and published a brief part of the manuscript under the title *Histoire du Pérou.* This was translated into Spanish and published at Madrid in 1920 under the title *Historia del Perú bajo la dominación de las Incas.* The author went to America in 1566, stopping first in Nueva Granada where he began his study of the natives and their origin. His manuscript was begun in 1576 and was completed at Lima in 1586.

A history based in part upon the author's experiences and compiled after considerable careful research is by Diego Fernández (b. ca. 1510). It is entitled *Primera y segunda parte de la historia del Perú,* and was published in two volumes in one in 1571 at Sevilla. It relates chiefly to the civil wars in Peru from 1543 to 1556, and in consequence the Council of the Indies forbade its being sent to America before 1729 and after 1731. The first part of the work appeared in a new edition of two volumes at Madrid in 1913 and 1914.

La Plata

A work dealing with La Plata region appeared in 1555 in Spanish under the title *Viaje al Río de la Plata* which recorded a journey made by the author, Ulrich Schmidel (ca. 1510-ca. 1579), during the years 1534 to

1554, part of which time he served as a soldier under Pedro de Mendoza. The volume describes the conquest of the region and the activities of Cabeza de Vaca. The first German edition appeared at Frankfurt-am-Main in 1567 under varying titles, one of which was *Warhafftige und liebliche beschreibung etlicher furnemen indianischen landtschafften und insulen*. An English translation may be found in volume LXXXI (original series, 1889) of the Hakluyt Society publications.

Chile

An interesting and, if properly used, a valuable historical account of the Araucanian wars in Chile may be found in the epic poem *La araucana*, written by Alonso de Ercilla y Zúñiga (1533-1594), a noble who as a youth had been a page at the marriage of Philip II to Mary Tudor and who later served under García Hurtado de Mendoza in the conflicts with the Araucanian Indians. The first part of the work was published at Madrid in 1569 and the second part appeared at the same place in 1578. The third part was first published in conjunction with the two preceding parts in 1590, also at Madrid. The poem was continued in two more parts by Diego de Santisteban Osorio (Madrid, 1735), but its historical importance diminished with its numerous extensions. The poem has never been completely translated into English, but a very small part was translated by William Hayley (1745-1820) and H. Boyd and published at New York in 1808.

Another epic poem of a similar nature covering the same subject but supplementing *La araucana* and emphasizing the military aspects, is the *Primera parte de arauca domado* by Pedro de Oña (b. ca. 1570) published at Lima in 1596. A more recent edition is that which appeared at Santiago, Chile, in 1917. The second part was never written.

APPENDIX F

SEVENTEENTH CENTURY HISTORIES AND HISTORIANS OF HISPANIC AMERICA

By A. Curtis Wilgus

WORKS relating to America written in the seventeenth century assumed a different character from those of the previous century, and dealt more with biography, description, religious accounts, and travel than previously. The Spanish and Portuguese by 1600 had very nearly reached the limits of their colonial holdings, and the respective governments began to consolidate their territories politically, economically, socially, and religiously, while at the same time they made vigorous efforts to defend their rich possessions from the attacks of jealous foreign aggressors. For this was a century when the English, French, Dutch, and Swedes took considerable interest in the New World, and their rivalry with the Iberian states resulted in freebooting, buccaneering, and open warfare. Travelers from Europe began to go to America for pleasure or profit and some of them recorded their experiences in frequently biased accounts, so that many of the so-called histories were in reality travel and descriptive accounts.

I. General Works

Among the noteworthy general histories of this century which dealt with the Hispanic American world was the *Historia general de los hechos de los castellanos en las islas y tierra firme del mar océano* by Antonio de Herrera y Tordesillas (ca. 1549-1625). This work appeared at Madrid in eight volumes in four between 1601 and 1615, and the story was carried to the year 1555. The work is founded upon considerable documentary research since the author had been commissioned by Philip II to write the treatise. Yet certain parts of the history are taken literally from Las Casas. An English edition by John Stevens (d. 1726) was printed at London in 1725 and 1726 in six volumes. The best Spanish edition was published in eight volumes at Madrid in 1725. A new Spanish edition of eight or ten volumes is at present being published by the Academy of History at Madrid under the joint editorship of Antonio Ballesteros Beretta (b. 1880) and Angel de Altolaguirre y Duvale.

Another valuable and comprehensive work frequently cited is by Juan de Solórzano Pereira (1575-1655) usually given the title *De indiarum jure*, which appeared in Latin in two volumes at Madrid, the first volume being published in 1629 and the second in 1639. The first Spanish edition was published at Madrid in 1648 under a 275-word title briefly cited as *Política indiana*. The work is generally descriptive of the Indies and still constitutes a useful digest of laws and decrees applicable to the Spanish colonies.

A book of great erudition and of considerable interest to many because it brings together all of the theories concerning the origin of the American natives, but which at the same time is of little actual value, is the *Origen de los indios del nuevo mundo* by the Dominican Gregorio García, which was first published at Valencia in 1607. The author spent about twelve years in America as a missionary and came to the conclusion that the natives came originally from Asia and parts of the Old World. His writings and ideas are based partially upon his own observations and partially upon a manuscript written by a companion of Francisco Pizarro, Juan de Velanzos, which has never been published. García's volume was reprinted at Madrid in 1729, being edited by Andrés González Barcia Carballido y Zúñiga.

A very excellent and comprehensive work written in Peru between 1642 and 1653, but not published until 1890-95 when it appeared in four volumes at Sevilla, bore the title *Historia del nuevo mundo*. Its author was Bernabé Cobo de Peralta (1582-1657) who at the age of fourteen went to America to seek his fortune. In Peru he became a Jesuit and subsequently traveled widely collecting from observation many facts which he used in this history.

In 1625 appeared at Leyden a general descriptive treatise under the title *Nieuwe wereldt ofte beschrijvinghe van West-Indien* by Joannes de Laet (1593-1649), or Jean de Laet d'Anvers, as he is frequently called. The volume dealt with the natural history of America, with native customs, and with the establishment of colonies in the Western Hemisphere, all of which were treated in a careful manner. The book was republished in Latin at Leyden in 1633 under the title briefly cited as *Novus orbis*. It seems probable that the whole work was based upon the manuscript *Historia da America*, now lost, written by the Jesuit Manoel de Moraes (1586-1651).

A book biographical in nature is that by Francisco Pizarro y Orellana (d. ca. 1652) entitled *Varones ilustres de nuevo mundo* which appeared at Madrid in 1639. The author, who claimed to be a great-grandson of Francisco Pizarro, undertook this literary venture in order to defend the activities of the Pizarros in Peru and to solicit financial assistance for their descendants. Besides dealing with the conquerors of Peru, his book also tells the story of Cortés, Columbus, and others.

A work indispensable to economic and political historians, for it contains an abstract of the laws of the Indies, was published in two volumes at Sevilla in 1672 under the title *Norte de la contratación de las indias occidentales.* The author was José de Veitia Linaje (d. 1688). An indifferent English translation was made by John Stevens and published at London in one volume about 1700 under the title *The rule established in Spain for trade in the West Indies.* . . .

Another work of general nature, but of considerable importance, is the *Memorial noticias sacres y reales del imperio de las indias occidentales* by Juan Díez de la Calle published at Madrid in 1646. Somewhat similar in nature, but of greater length, is a volume by Alonso de la Peña Montenegro (d. 1688) entitled *Itinerario para parochos de indios* (Ambreses, 1698).

A general work with a misleading title is the *Reducción universal de todo el Perú* by the Dominican missionary, Miguel de Monsalve. This volume was written for the information of the Spanish king and was printed privately at Lima in 1604. Today only one copy is known. The author lived for thirty-seven years in Mexico, the West Indies, and South America, and no corruption or governmental defects seem to have escaped his attention.

A volume specialized in character is that by Antonio Rodríguez de León Pinelo (d. 1660) entitled *Tratado de confirmaciones reales de encomiendas oficios i casos* published at Madrid in 1630.

A work containing considerable tabulated information was published at Valencia in 1689 under the title of *Tablas cronológicas.* The author, who wrote under the pseudonym of Juan Eusebio Nieremberg, was Claude Clement (1594-1642), or as he is frequently called, Claudo Clemente. This work was based upon three separate publications (Zaragoza, 1676), one dealing with the Portuguese and two dealing with the Spanish discoveries and conquests to the year 1642.

A volume studied by all Spanish royal officials who went to America in the latter part of this century and in the one following was edited by Gaspar de Escalona y Agüero (d. 1659) under the title *Gazophilatium regium Perubicum.* It was published at Madrid in 1647 and was a compendium, written partly in Latin and partly in Spanish, of useful information about America. A second edition appeared in 1755.

German and Dutch accounts of the colonies are comparatively numerous. In 1612 at Cologne appeared a German work describing the discovery and exploration of America which bore the title *Indiæ occidentalis historia*. In 1618 the book was reprinted at the same place. The author was Gaspar Ens (b. ca. 1570). Another German work, by Johan Ludwig Gottfried, a collaborator with De Bry, was published at Frankfurt in 1655. Its title, running into nearly two hundred words, may be briefly cited as *Newe welt und americanische historien*.

A Dutch account, written by a person who used the pseudonym Athanasius Inga, appeared at Amsterdam in 1624 under the brief title *West-indische spieghel*. Another Dutch work entitled *Spieghel der australische navegatie* is by Jacob Le Maire (1585-1616) and was published at Amsterdam in 1622. A third Dutch account is by Arnoldus Montanus (ca. 1625-1683), who published at Amsterdam in 1671 his *Denieuwe en onbekende weereld* which treats mainly of the early discoveries made in America with special emphasis upon North America, the West Indies, and Brazil. An English volume based in part upon this book appeared at London the same year, its compiler being John Ogilby (1600-1676) and its title stated briefly is *America: being the latest and most accurate description of the new world*. This latter work was illustrated by fifty-seven plates and maps of considerable interest and value.

In 1604 at Madrid was published Pedro Ordóñez de Ceballo's (b. 1550) *Historia y viage del mundo,* a part of which relating to America was translated into Dutch and published at Amsterdam in 1621 under the title *Eyghentlijcke beschryvinghe van West-Indien*.

Some of the religious aspects of the conquest of America may be found in a work by Gaspar Plautius, an Austrian abbot, written anonymously under the title *Nova typis transacta navigatio* published in 1621, the place unknown.

A volume treating particularly the activities of the church in America and the conversion of the natives is entitled *Historia eclesiástica de nuestros tiempos*. The author was Alonzo Fernández and the book was printed at Toledo in 1611.

A volume containing much interesting and valuable information concerning the early religious establishments in the Spanish colonies and the native Indian creeds is that by Gil González Dávila (1577-1658) entitled briefly *Teatro eclesiástico*. The first volume was published at Madrid in 1649 and the second at the same place in 1655.

Among the chief and most familiar English works of the seventeenth century which concern Hispanic America is that by the English Dominican and later Protestant, Thomas Gage (d. 1656), usually entitled *A new survey of the West Indies*. However, when the book was first published at London in 1648 it appeared under the title *The English-American, his travail by sea and land*. Subsequent editions of this work have appeared at intervals, one of the most recent being at New York in 1929. The book deals not only with the West Indies but with Spanish North and South America, the author having spent twenty-four years in the Indies.

Another type of English publication of value to historians, which became especially popular in the next century, was the compilation of accounts of voyages to various parts of the world. One of the briefest of these dealing with America appeared at London in 1699. It was edited by William Hacke and bore the title *A collection of original voyages,* some of which concerned Hispanic America.

An earlier and even more important collection of voyages made by Englishmen and others to America and elsewhere appeared in five volumes at London in 1625 and 1626 under the title *Hakluytus posthumous, or Purchas his pilgrimes*. The editor was Samuel Purchas (ca. 1577-1626). The fourth volume and parts of the third and fifth relate to voyages to America. Volume V had first appeared in 1613 under the title *Purchas his pilgrimage,* and it constituted in part an interesting account of the religions of the peoples of all countries. The whole work is an important yet miscellaneous assembly of accounts, some of which are of indifferent value. The most recent edition of this work in English appeared at Glasgow in twenty volumes from 1905 to 1907.

A French collection of voyages was made by Melchisedech Thévenot (ca. 1620-1696) under the title *Relations de divers voyages curieux* and was published in two volumes at Paris between 1663 and 1696. Four accounts contained in part four of the work relate to Spanish America, one of which had never before been published.

Among the volumes written in this century which deal with pirates, freebooters, and gentlemen adventurers in Hispanic America is the near-classic history by Alexandre Olivier Esquemelin (1645-1707), or John Esquemelin as he is often called (whose real name may have been Henrick Smeeks), which was first published at Amsterdam in 1674, or more probably in 1678, under the title *De americænsche zee-roovers*. This book has appeared in perhaps as many editions as has any book which deals with America. The first English edition was printed at London in two volumes in 1684 and 1685. One of the best English editions was published at London in 1893. The first Spanish edition appeared in 1681 at Colonia Agrippina and was followed by a second edition at the same place the next year.

A work of somewhat similar character, but dealing largely with piratical activities in the Pacific, appeared at Paris in 1689 or 1690. It was by Raveneau de Lussan (b. 1663) and bore the title *Journal du voyage fait à la mer de sud*. The best and most recent English edition was published at Cleveland in 1930.

II. SPECIAL WORKS

Brazil

Several volumes dealing with Brazil should be cited. The first appeared at Valladolid in 1603 under the title *Historia general de la india oriental*. It was the work of the Benedictine monk, Antonio de San Román de Ribadeneyra, and dealt with the discovery and conquest of Brazil and other parts of the world in the sixteenth century. It constitutes one of the best records of the Portuguese explorers and their relations to contemporary events.

A second work was published in two volumes in one in 1628 at Madrid under the title *Epítome de las historias portuguesas*. The author was the poet and historian, Manuel de Faria e Sousa (1590-1648). His volumes treat Portuguese colonization to 1628 in Brazil as well as in the East, and are considered an excellent reference.

A third work appeared in 1627, the place of publication unknown, under the title *Historia da custodia do Brasil,* the author being the churchman Vicente do Salvador (ca. 1564-ca. 1639), the first historian of Brazil to be born there. In 1918 a new edition was published at São Paulo under the title *Historia do Brasil*.

A fourth work, which contains much valuable information, was written in 1634 by Pedro Cudena but first appeared in 1780 at Braunschweig in German under the title *Beschreibung des portugiesischen Amerika*. The translator and editor was Christian Leiste.

A fifth work of importance, written by a Jesuit to show that the gold of Peru could be brought to the Atlantic by way of Brazil, is entitled *Nuevo descubrimiento del gran Río de Amazonas*. The author was Father Christóbal de Acuña (1597-1675), and the book appeared first at Madrid in 1641 but was soon suppressed by Philip IV for fear the Portuguese would use the idea. What seems to be a partial plagiarism appeared in French in 1655, and in English in 1661 at London under the title *An historical and geographical description of the great country and river of the amazones in America.* The first English translation of the whole work appeared at London in 1698 under the title *Voyages and discoveries in South America.* The Hakluyt Society published a translation as part of Volume XXIV, first series (London, 1859).

A sixth work, concerning the Dutch in Brazil, appeared at Paris in 1651 under the title *Histoire des derniers troubles du Brésil entre les Hollendois et les Portugais.* The author was Pierre Moreau.

A seventh work of narrow scope covering the decade 1634-1644 and written from material furnished by the Dutch governor, Maurice of Naussau, was by Gaspar Barlaeius (1584-1648), or Kaspar van Boerle as he is often called, and it bore the title *Rerum per octennium in Brasilia et alibi gestarum.* The book was published at Cleves in 1660 and formed the basis of all subsequent histories of this period.

An eighth work is entitled *Noticias curiosas e necessarias das cousas do Brasil,* and was written by the Jesuit Simão de Vasconcellos (ca. 1611-1671). It appeared at Lisbon in 1668 but it contained much of the material found in his earlier and more important work entitled *Chronicas da Companhia de Jesus na provincia do Brasil* (Lisbon, 1663).

A ninth volume treating of the discovery and early history of Brazil is Francisco de Brito Freyre's (1620-1692) *Nova Lusitania,* published at Lisbon in 1675. Part of the book, which dealt with the Dutch in Brazil, was written from observations made while the author served as admiral of the Portuguese fleet.

A tenth work, by the Benedictine Raphael de Jesús (1614-1693) entitled *Castrioto lusitano,* was published at Lisbon in 1679 and dealt thoroughly with the Dutch in Brazil between 1623 and 1654. Only the first part of the work has ever been published.

An eleventh volume which summarizes the occupation and spiritual domination of a large part of Brazil bears the title *El Marañon y Amazonas* (Madrid, 1684). The author was Manuel Rodríguez (1633-1701), the Jesuit Procurator General of the Indies at Madrid, who wrote his account from the documents found in the government archives of that city.

A twelfth work of extreme value for the student of early seventeenth century conditions in Brazil is the anonymous *Dialogos das grandezas do Brasil,* written in the form of conversations between two persons living in the country. An incomplete edition was published serially in *Isis* (January 1848 to June 1849) at Rio de Janeiro. João Capistrano de Abreu (1853-1927) published a new and better edition in the *Diario Official* at Rio de Janeiro (February to March 1900). The best edition appeared at Rio de Janeiro in 1930, being edited by Rodolpho Garcia.

Mexico

Mexico, or New Spain, was the subject of many historical and descriptive treatises in the seventeenth century, only a few of the most important of which can be cited. Either in 1613 at Madrid or in 1615 at Sevilla the three-volume *Monarquía indiana* by the Franciscan Juan de Torquemada (1550-1625) was published dealing with the natives and antiquities of New Spain. The best edition of this work with changes and corrections appeared at Madrid in three volumes in 1723.

An account of the conquest of New Spain written in this century is by the literary but rather inaccurate historian, Antonio de Solís y Rivadeneyra (1610-1686), whose *Historia de la conquista de México* was first published at Madrid in 1684 in one volume which carries the story to the capture of Guatimozin. The work was continued in a second volume to the death of Cortés by Ignacio de Salazar y Olarte (d. 1786) under the same title (Córdoba, 1743). One of the best two-volume editions was published at Madrid in 1785. An English translation of the first volume was published at London in 1724.

In 1637 appeared at Mexico City the *Relación universal legítima* by Fernando de Cepeda which, after the corrections and additions made by Juan de Alvarez Serrano, dealt with the founding of Mexico City and described that country during the years 1553 to 1637.

A work following somewhat the same theme bears the title *Obediencia que México, cabeza de la Nueva España, dió á la majestad católica del rey D. Felipe de Austria*. It was written by Arias de Villalobos (b. ca. 1568) and was published at Mexico City in 1623. An edition edited by Genaro García appeared in 1907.

A general descriptive account of New Spain can be found in Agustín de Vetancourt's (b. 1620) *Teatro mexicano* published in 1697 or 1698 in two volumes at Mexico City. A four-volume edition of this work appeared at Mexico City in 1870 and 1871.

A valuable account of the activities of the Jesuits in New Spain, particularly in Sinaloa, California, and Florida, and with their conversion of the natives, is by the Jesuit Andrés Pérez de Ribas (d. 1655) who wrote the *Historia de los triunfos de nuestra santa fé entre gentes las más bárbaras y fieras del nuevo orbe*. It was published at Madrid in 1645. Another account of Jesuit activities in the region is given by the prolific writer, Francisco de Florencia (1619-1695), under the title *Historia de la provincia de la Compañía de Jesús de Nueva España* published at Mexico City in 1649.

An account of the Augustinians in New Spain and particularly in Michoacán is found in the *Historia de la provincia de San Nicolás de Tolentino de Michoacán* by Diego Basalenque (b. 1577), the chronicler of the Order, who died in 1651. His work, however, did not appear until 1673, the place of publication being unknown.

A work dealing with the Franciscans in Michoacán was written by Pablo de la Purísima Concepción Beaumont, a Franciscan. It was entitled *Crónica de la provincia . . . de Michoacán,* and was first published in five volumes at Mexico City in 1873 and 1874. A new edition in three volumes appeared at the same place in 1932.

A general work dealing with religious and other matters is the *Historia de las indias de Nueva España y islas de tierra firme* written by Diego Durán (b. ca. 1588) probably early in the century but not published until it appeared in two volumes at Mexico City between 1867 and 1880.

A number of works which deal in part with the conquest of the Indians were written in this century, some of which, however, did not appear in print until later. Among these is a curious work in praise of the American natives and in particular of the natives of New Spain somewhat in the manner of Las Casas. It is by Bishop Juan de Palafox y Mendoza (1600-1659) entitled briefly *Virtudes del indio* and was published perhaps at Madrid probably in 1650. The book was addressed to the king in order to show him the nature and extent of the Spanish mistreatment of the Indians. It was printed secretly. A second small edition was published at Zaragoza in 1661 under the title *Historia de las virtudes del indio.* A recent edition appeared in Madrid in 1893.

In 1828 at Mexico City appeared the seventeenth century work entitled the *Horribles crueldades de los conquistadores de México,* by Fernando de Alva Ixtlilzochitl (ca. 1568-1648).

A work in French entitled *Histoire du Mexique,* written in this century by Fernando Alvarado Tezózomoc, appeared at Paris in two volumes between 1847 and 1849. It deals mainly with the origin of the natives of New Spain. A Spanish edition appeared at Mexico City in 1878.

In 1914 at Madrid was published Diego Luís de Motezuma's (1619-1699) seventeenth century *Corona mexicana, ó historia de los nueve Motezumas.*

The story of the conquest of New Mexico, together with an excellent description of the native inhabitants, may be found in the *Historia de la Nueva México* by Gaspar Pérez de Villagrá (d. 1620), published at Alcalá in 1610 and at Mexico City in two volumes in 1910. An English translation of this account was made by Gilberto Espinosa and printed by the Quivira Society at Los Angeles in 1933. A religious history of the same region is the *Crónica* by the Franciscan Balthasar de Medina (1635-1697), published at Mexico City in 1682 giving numerous biographies of Franciscan martyrs in Mexico.

Of seventeenth century histories dealing with Yucatan mention may be made of those by Bernardo de Lizana (d. 1631) entitled *Historia de Yucatán* (Mexico City, 1633), and by Diego López de Cogolludo (1610-1686) entitled *Historia de Yucatán* (Madrid, 1688). Of the two works the latter is much the better since the author had the use of considerable documentary material.

Central America

One of the chief works dealing with Central America in this century is the *Historia de la provincia de S. Vicente de Chyapa y Guatemala* which deals with religious and other matters. It was written by Fray Antonio de Remesal (1570-1639) and appeared at Madrid in 1619. A new edition of this work with the 1619 title page appeared at Guatemala in two volumes in 1932. In 1620 at Madrid appeared an edition of the 1619 work with a title page reading *Historia general de las indias occidentales.* . . . Another important work written in this period but not published until later was the *Historia de Guatemala* by Francisco Antonio de Fuentes y Guzmán (1643-ca. 1699), two volumes, Madrid, 1882 and 1883.

West Indies

A work dealing largely with the natives of the West Indies and particularly with the Caribs is that by Guillaume Coppier (ca. 1600-1670) entitled briefly *Histoire et voyage des indes occidentales* published at Lyons in 1645. An English volume dealing with the West Indies appeared at London in 1655 under the initials N. N. and the title *America: or an exact description of the West Indies.* The aim of the author seems to have been to advertise to English readers the history and importance of the Spanish islands.

Tierra Firme

Tierra Firme was treated in this century by Lucas Fernández de Piedrahita (1624-1688) in his careful and eloquent *Historia general de las conquistas del nuevo reyno de Granada,* the first part of which appeared at Antwerp in 1688 and carried the account to the year 1563. The volume is written largely from the manuscripts left by Gonzalo Jiménez de Quesada (ca. 1500-1579) which have never been completely published.

An earlier book which dealt with the same territory is entitled *Primera parte de las noticias historiales de las conquistas de tierra firme en las indias occidentales* by Pedro Simón (b. 1574). It was published at Cuenca in 1627. Parts two and three of this work were not printed entirely until they appeared at Bogotá in 1882. In 1891 and 1892 parts one, two, and three were published at Bogotá in four volumes. Part four was lost and never printed.

Peru

The most important work in any language dealing with the conversion of the Indians of Peru is that by the Jesuit Pablo José de Arriaga (ca. 1562-1622), entitled *Extirpación de la idolatría del Perú,* published at Lima in 1621. This earliest edition of the book, of which there are only two copies known, contains 156 pages and the Cortes Society, before it expired, planned to publish an English translation. The author went to Peru about 1583 and became one of the leading educators in the colony.

A valuable work dealing with the activities of the Augustinian Order in Peru is by Antonio de la Calancha (1584-1654) entitled *Crónica moralizada del orden de San Augustín en el Perú, con sucesos ejemplares* (Barcelona, 1638). The work, however, is not exclusively confined to Peru proper but includes present-day Chile, Ecuador, and Colombia, and deals also in a somewhat confused manner with economic and political affairs of historical importance from 1551 to 1593. The work was continued later to 1657 by Bernardo de Torres (d. ca. 1660) in his *Crónica de la provincia peruana del orden de los ermitaños de S. Augustín* (Lima, 1657).

A Jesuit historian about whom there is much controversy concerning the accuracy of his work is the credulous and naïve Fernando Montesinos (b. ca. 1600), who went to Peru about 1629 and remained until at least 1642. Generally he seems to have repeated many facts as they came to him with little or no investigation. However, he preserved much valuable information in his *Memorias antiguas historiales y políticas del Perú* (Buenos Aires, 1870) which deals with the pre-conquest period, and in his *Los anales del Perú* (2 vols., Madrid, 1906) which covers the post-conquest period. The first work appeared in French at Paris in 1840 as Volume XVII of Henri Ternaux-Compans' *Voyages . . . ,* and was published in English translation by the Hakluyt Society in 1920 as Volume XLVIII (second series). A Spanish edition edited by Marcos Jiménez de la Espada was published at Madrid in 1882. The complete work as planned by the author under the title *Ophir de España* has never been printed in any language.

Still another work dealing with religious affairs in Peru in particular and with political conditions etc. elsewhere in South America was published at Rome in three volumes in 1681 and 1682 under the title *Tesoros verdaderos de las indias en la historia de la gran provincia de San Juan Bautista del Perú, de el orden de predicadores.* The author was Juan de Meléndez, a native-born Peruvian.

La Plata

Paraguay as a center of Jesuit activity was treated by Nicolás del Techo (1611-1680) in a book entitled *Historia provinciæ Paraguariæ societatis Jesu,* first published in Latin at Leodii (i. e., Liége) in 1673. An abridged English translation appeared in 1704 in Volume IV of Awnsham Churchill's (d. 1728) *A collection of voyages and travels.* Another volume dealing with the same region and the same subject was by the Jesuit Antonio Ruíz de Montoya (ca. 1593-ca. 1652) entitled *Conquista espiritual hecha por los religiosos de la Compañía de Jesús en las provincias del Paraguay* (Madrid, 1639). The author, who converted over 100,000 Indians, bitterly criticizes the Spaniards for their treatment of the natives. His book is written from memory and in an ill-arranged fashion, but is nevertheless of great value.

Still another volume dealing with the Paraguay district is entitled *Insignes misioneros de la Compañía de Jesús en la provincia del Paraguay.* The author was Francisco Xerque, honorary chaplain of the Spanish king, rector of Potosí, and a Peruvian judge. His book was published at Pamplona in 1687.

Chile

The chief historical and descriptive work relating to Chile written in this century bears the title *Histórica relación del reyno de Chile* and the author is Alonso de Ovalle (d. 1650). It was published at Rome in 1646 at the same time that an abridged Italian edition appeared there. The Spanish edition contains twenty-one engraved portraits of important Spaniards connected with early Chilean history, and treats of the activities of the Jesuits in the region. Part of the work (the first six books out of eight) was translated into English and printed at London in 1703 in Churchill's *A collection of voyages and travels.*

EIGHTEENTH CENTURY HISTORIES AND HISTORIANS OF HISPANIC AMERICA

By A. Curtis Wilgus

THE eighteenth century saw the publication of an ever increasing number of works relating to Hispanic America, a large portion of which were description and travel accounts (here generally omitted for lack of space), many of them of the sixteenth and seventeenth centuries and printed for the first time. These were almost invariably edited and compiled in collections numbering several volumes. General histories were numerous but they were frequently contentious and partisan; particularly is this true of religious accounts and of works treating nationalism. The French and English became sufficiently interested in Hispanic America to write histories in increasing numbers, while the Germans, Dutch, and Italians lost some of their interest in America.

During the century numerous European controversies which were both the cause and result of economic, social, and political theorizing, affected the literary output of both Europeans and Americans. Besides, the approach of revolutionary changes likewise affected published views and opinions in histories and pseudo-histories. In consequence a judicial use of certain eighteenth century works is obviously necessary.

I. General Works

Among the general works relating to Hispanic America the following should be mentioned. Between 1768 and 1770 Antoine Touron (1686-1775) published his fourteen-volume *Histoire générale de l'Amérique depuis sa découverte*. A few years later a five-volume comprehensive work entitled *Diccionario geográfico-histórico de las indias occidentales ó América* by Antonio de Alcedo y Bexarano (1736-1812) was printed at Madrid between 1786 and 1789. The work was translated into English and published at London in five volumes in 1812-15.

A careful work, written from the documents but never finished, is that by Juan Bautista Múñoz (1745-1799) entitled *Historia del nuevo-mundo* which appeared at Madrid in 1793. Four years later (1797) an English edition was published at London.

Another valuable volume which is in reality a preliminary sketch of a larger one never written is that by Lorenzo Boturino Benaducci (ca. 1702-1750) entitled *Idea de una nueva historia general de la América septentrional,* published at Madrid in 1746. The book deals largely with the natives of Mexico, and is based upon many manuscripts contained in monasteries of that country, where the author resided for eight years.

A work of less importance is that briefly entitled *Investigaciones históricas* by Cristóbal Cladera (1760-1816) published at Madrid in 1794, which describes the principal sea discoveries made by the Spanish in the fifteenth and the early sixteenth centuries.

Another author of this century often referred to is Antonio de Ulloa (1716-1795) whose *Noticias americanas* published at Madrid in 1772 is considered a storehouse of facts regarding Spanish America, and particularly Peru and Ecuador. An important volume of a different nature appeared at Madrid in 1748 by Jorge Juan y Santacilia (1703-1773) entitled *Observaciones astronómicas y físicas.* This work usually appears in conjunction with Ulloa's four-volume (Madrid, 1748) *Relación histórica del viage á la América meridional hecho de orden de S. Magestad.* An English translation in two volumes is dated 1758 and was published at London under the title of *A voyage to South America.* A special treatise jointly prepared by the authors for the king under the title *Noticias secretas de América* which gives a most thorough picture of colonial affairs was kept in the royal archives until it appeared in modified form in print at London, two volumes in one, in 1826. Later editions of this work have frequently appeared under the title *Popery judged by its fruits.*

A number of general works relating to Hispanic America were written by Englishmen in this century. Of these *The history of America* by William Robertson (1721-1793) published at London in two volumes in 1777 stands at the forefront. Two other volumes of less merit are by William Russell (1741-1793) entitled *The history of America* (2 vols., London, 1777-78) and an earlier volume by Richard Rolt (ca. 1725-1770) which bore the title *A new and accurate history of South America* (London, 1756). A projected second volume by the last author dealing with North America did not appear. A fourth work, attributed to Edmund Burke (ca. 1729-1797), was published in London in two volumes in 1757 under the title *An account of the European settlements in America.* Only a part of the account (part three and chapters VII-XI) deals with Spanish America.

A volume earlier than these, appearing in London in 1741 or 1742, bore the title *A concise history of the Spanish America.* The author is supposed to have been Dr. John Campbell (1708-1775). The book is comprehensive in treatment but with special emphasis upon trade and commercial conditions.   •

Two anonymous works whose authorship has not been definitely fixed are *An account of the Spanish settlements in America,* published at Edinburgh in 1762, and *A description of the Spanish islands and settlements on the coast of the West Indies,* published at London in the same year. The latter work is usually attributed to Thomas Jefferys (d. 1771) who aimed to call England's attention to rich Spanish possessions at a time when the two countries were at war with each other.

A different but interesting and valuable book for historians is entitled *The American atlas: or a geographical description of the whole continent of America,* published at London in 1778. It was the work of a number of collaborators.

Works dealing with more special aspects of Hispanic American history are numerous in the eighteenth century. In 1749 at Cádiz appeared a volume entitled *Tratado histórico* by José Gutiérrez de Rubalcava which concerned all aspects of Spain's commerce with the Indies. At Amsterdam in 1770 appeared the four volumes of the Abbé Guillaume Thomas François Raynal (1713-1796) entitled *Analyse de l'histoire philosophique et politique des établissements et des commerces des Européens dans les deux indes.* An English edition in four volumes was published at London in 1776 while a Spanish edition in five volumes appeared at Madrid between 1784 and 1790. Another work treating matters of a commercial nature appeared at Madrid in 1797. It was entitled briefly *Memorias históricas* and was written by Rafael Antúñez y Acevedo, a pseudonym for João Antonio Andreoni (1650-1716). Still another work, more theoretical in nature, was by Gerónimo de Uztáriz (d. ca. 1750) published at Madrid in 1724 under the title *Teórica y práctica de comercio.* A work both critical and suggestive of the economic and social conditions in the Indies was published at Madrid in 1789, although it had been written in 1748, under the title briefly cited *Nuevo sistema de gobierno económico para la América.* The author was José del Campillo y Cosío (1693-1743).

An interesting work of a different nature in three volumes is that by Andrés González Barcia Carballido y Zúñiga entitled briefly *Historiadores primitivos.* It was published at Madrid in 1749 and consists of a collection of relations, histories, etc., of the Spanish conquest in America.

A great many books in this century dealt with the treatment of the natives, and with their history, origin, etc. Many of these were naturally controversial or theoretical in nature. Such a work originally written in Italian by Giovanni (or Juan) Nuix (1740-1783) under the title *Reflessioni imparziali* was translated into Spanish by Pedro Varela y Ulloa (1748-1795) under the title *Reflexiones imparciales sobre la humanidad de los españoles en las indias* (Madrid, 1782). This work aimed mainly to defend the Spaniards from the calumnies of their enemies.

In this century, too, many volumes were written concerning religious matters, and particularly about the Jesuits who were expelled by the Portuguese in 1760 and by the Spanish in 1767.

The most extensive history dealing with ecclesiastical affairs appeared at Paris in fourteen volumes in 1768-70. It was the *Histoire générale de l'Amérique* by Antoine Touron, already referred to.

A volume indispensable to the student of the church and the *patronato real* in America is the *Manuel compendio del regio patronato indiano* by Antonio Joaquín de Ribadeneira y Barrientos (b. 1710) which contains all of the papal bulls relating to this subject from the time of Alexander VI to the date of its publication at Madrid in 1755. A second work very similar in nature, with edicts and decrees of the Spanish kings and of the popes concerning ecclesiastical administration in the Spanish colonies, is the *Fasti novi orbis et ordinationum apostolicarium ad indias pertinetium brevarium cum adnotationibus* by the Jesuit Domingo Muriel (1718-1795) who wrote under the pseudonym of Cyriac Morel. The book was first published at Venice in 1776 and is considered an excellent source for the secular as well as church legislation in the Indies.

Among the works dealing particularly with the Jesuits several should be mentioned. In 1741 at Madrid appeared the *Historia de la provincia de la Compañía de Jesús* by José Cassani (1673-1750) which treated the activities of the Order in northern South America. Some years later, in 1783, appeared the *Gobierno de los regulares de la América* by Pedro José Parras (d. 1787), the rector and chancellor of the University of Tucumán. It was published at Madrid in two volumes and deals largely with the Jesuits in southern South America. A German account of the Jesuits under the title *Reisen einiger missionariem der gesellschaft Jesu in Amerika* appeared at Nürnberg in 1785. The author was Christoph Gottlieb von Murr (1733-1811).

An Italian work dealing with the Jesuits in Paraguay is that by Ludovico Antonio Muratori (1672-1750). It contains a long title frequently cited as *Il Cristianesimo felice nel Paraguai* (2 vols., Venice, 1743-49). This is based upon two earlier accounts by the same author never before published together. The work was translated into English under the title *A relation of the missions of Paraguay* (London, 1759). The author and compiler was not a Jesuit, and the work has been considered by many as impartial for that reason.

Two works in Spanish dealing with the Jesuits in Paraguay may be mentioned. The first appeared at Madrid in two volumes in 1726 under the title *Relación historial*. The author, who was Juan Patricio Fernández (1661-1733), gives considerable information concerning the activities of the Jesuits and of the character of the Chiquitos Indians. The work has been widely translated. A second, and far better though little known, work is entitled *Historia de la Compañía de Jesús en la provincia del Paraguay*. It was also published at Madrid in two volumes during 1754 and 1755. The author was the Jesuit Pedro Lozano (d. ca. 1752), one of "the most prolific and trustworthy" of the Jesuit writers on Paraguay. His work covers only twenty-eight years of the region's history ending in 1614, and it seems to have been based in part at least upon two volumes of a work now lost written by Father Pastor (d. 1658).

The best and most authentic account of the Franciscans in America which appeared in this century is the *Crónica de la seráfica religión* by José Torrubia (ca. 1700-ca. 1768). This volume contains the important "Book One" of the ninth part of the author's chronicle and deals with the activities of the Order chiefly in America. The work was published at Rome in 1756. The author served as a missionary in both the Philippines and New Spain, and wrote his history from observations and documents largely from the missionary point of view and, in consequence, with some prejudice.

The eighteenth century saw the compiling of many histories and collections of travels and voyages. The following are given in the order of their appearance but do not, however, constitute a complete list.

In 1704 at London Awnsham Churchill published the first four volumes of *A collection of voyages and travels* previously mentioned. In 1732 were added two more volumes. In 1744 the work was revised and brought down to date in six volumes, while the next year saw the addition of the Osborne or Oxford collection to the original Churchill edition to make it more complete. A competing series was issued at London in 1705 by John Harris (1667-1719) in two volumes under the title *Navigantium atque itinerantium bibliotheca*. It was reprinted at London from 1744 to 1748 with additions and revisions. It differed from Churchill's largely because it was a history of travels rather than a collection of travels.

In 1706 and 1707 at Leyden, Pieter van der Aa (d. 1730) issued his *Naaukeurige versameling der gedink-waardigste zee en land-reysen na oost en West-Indiën* in 127 volumes containing accounts of voyages to all parts of the world. These have all been issued separately. In the same year (1707) M. du Perier published at Paris his *Histoire univer-selle des voyages*. This collection appeared in English at London in 1708, but in 1710 it was given a new title and the author was called the Abbé Bellegarde whose full name was Jean Baptiste Morvan de Belle-garde (1648-1734). The volume related to Spanish voyages to America and consisted of accounts taken from Spanish authors.

Another pretentious collection bore the title *The world displayed*. It was published at London in twenty volumes between 1759 and 1761 and it contained the accounts of the early discoveries of the Spanish, Portuguese, French, and English in America and other parts of the world.

A briefer collection of voyages was compiled by the English buccaneer, William Dampier (1652-1715), under the French title *Collection de voyages* which was published at Paris in five volumes in 1715, and in English at London under the title *A collection of voyages*. Each of the volumes contains material on Hispanic America. The best English edi-tion was published at London in four volumes in 1729. These volumes are based upon Dampier's *New voyages round the world* (London, 1697) and upon accounts written by others.

Three other collections may be noted. In December 1708 there began to appear monthly *A new collection of voyages and travels* compiled under the editorship of John Stevens. By 1710 the collection included two volumes. In 1770 and 1771 at London appeared in two volumes *An historical collection of the several voyages and discoveries in the south Pacific Ocean* by Alexander Dalrymple (1737-1808), the first vol-ume of which contained accounts of a number of Spanish voyages. In 1756 Charles de Brosse (1709-1777) brought out in two volumes at Paris his *Histoire des navigations aux terres australes* which was trans-lated into several languages, the first English edition appearing in 1766 under the title *Terra australis cognita*.

II. Special Works

Brazil

Histories concerning Brazil are numerous but are frequently of no great importance in this century. The chief general treatise, however meagre and inaccurate, although based upon much documentary material, is the *Historia da America portugueza* by the Brazilian Sebastião da Rocha Pitta (1660-1738), published at Lisbon in 1730. This work, shortly suppressed by the Portuguese government, covered the period from 1500 to 1724. Another work, which has a misleading title, is the *Histoire des découvertes et conquêtes des Portugais dans le nouveau monde* by the Jesuit Joseph François Lafitau (ca. 1670-ca. 1740) published at Paris in two volumes in 1732. This work deals almost exclusively with the Portuguese in Asia and Africa, although it does concern early Portuguese voyages to America. The same work was republished at Paris in 1734 in four volumes.

A volume frequently considered of great value in Brazilian history but of narrow scope is the *Annaes historicos do estado do Maranhão* by Bernardo Pereira de Berredo (d. 1748), published at Lisbon in 1749. The author was governor of Maranhão between 1718 and 1748 and his history covers the period from the discovery to 1718.

Another brief account is by José Joaquim da Cunha de Azevedo Coutinho (ca. 1743-1821) entitled variously *Ensaio economico sobre o commercio de Portugal e suas colonias* and *Analyse sobre a justiça do commercio*. It was published at Lisbon in 1794, and deals with the trade and economic conditions of Brazil. An English translation appeared at London in 1807 under the title *An essay on the commerce and products of the Portuguese colonies in South America, especially the Brazils*.

Another economic treatise of considerable excellence appeared at Lisbon in 1711. It was written by João Antonio Andreoni, who wrote under the pseudonyms of André Antonio Antonil and Rafael Antúñez y Acevedo, and bore the title *Cultura e opulencia do Brasil por suas drogas e minas*. So revealing was this volume of the colony's wealth that the Portuguese government suppressed it and all but a few copies were destroyed. The latest edition in Portuguese was published at São Paulo and Rio de Janeiro in 1923.

An extensive and valuable work dealing with the country in eleven volumes appeared at Lisbon between 1789 and 1806. It bore the title

O fazendeiro do Brasil and was by José Mariano da Conceição Velloso Xavier (1742-1811).

A large but anonymous work is entitled *Historia dos descobrimentos e conquistas dos Portuguezes no novo mundo.* It was published in four volumes at Lisbon in 1786 and 1787 and covers the period from Manoel I to João IV.

The most valuable accounts of the Franciscans in Brazil are the *Primazia serafica na regiam da America* by Appollinario da Conceição (1692-ca. 1760) published at Lisbon in 1733, and the *Orbe serafico novo brasilico* by Antonio de Santa Maria Jaboatão (b. 1695), the chronicler of the Order, published at Lisbon in 1761. The second part of this work finally appeared in a complete edition with the first part at Rio de Janeiro between 1858 and 1862. It was in five volumes.

A valuable ecclesiastical history of Brazil from the viewpoint of the Jesuits is the *Brasilia pontificia* by the Jesuit Simón Marques (b. 1684), published at Lisbon in 1758. The author went to Brazil in 1702 and held a number of important positions, including that of rector of the Jesuit college at Rio de Janeiro.

A military history of the Portuguese colony was written by José de Mirales under the title *Historia militar do Brasil.* It was completed in 1762 but was not published until 1900 when it appeared at Rio de Janeiro. The book covers the period from 1549 to 1762.

Mexico

Of the histories of New Spain in this century only a few need be named for, as in the case of Brazil, many are of indifferent quality. In 1770 at Mexico City Archbishop Francisco Antonio Lorenzana (1722-1804) published his *Historia de Nueva España* which contained the second, third, and fourth letters of Cortés and other documents of value for the study of the conquest of Mexico.

An earlier work entitled *Teatro americano,* which is statistical in nature, was published at Mexico City in two volumes in 1746. The author was José Antonio de Villa-Señor y Sánchez, the official cosmographer and accountant-general for New Spain, and his writings have been considered very valuable for social and economic facts.

A third and later work was by the Italian Jesuit and antiquarian, Francisco Javier Clavijero (1731-1787), entitled *Storia antica del Messico,* published at Cesena in 1780 and 1781 in four volumes. The work was illustrated with many maps and plates and is a mine of archæological information. An English translation appeared at London in two volumes in 1787.

A three-volume work treating the early period is the *Historia antigua de México* by Mariano José Fernández de Echeverría y Veytia (1718-1779) which, however, was not published until it appeared at Mexico City in 1836.

A volume dealing with the missionary activities of the Franciscans in New Spain and northern Central America, and containing much useful information concerning the Indians of the same region, is the *Crónica apostólica y seráfica* by Fray Isidro Félix de Espinosa (1679-1755) published at Mexico City in 1746.

A work concerning Jesuit activities appeared in 1754 at Barcelona under the title *Apostólicos afanes de la Compañía de Jesús*. The author is thought to be José de Ortega (1700-1768) and his volume deals with the Jesuits in New Spain and particularly in Pimería Alta.

Another work covering missionary activities was written by Francisco Ximénez (1666-ca. 1722) and bore the title *Historia de la provincia de San Vicente de Chiapa y Guatemala*. It was edited by J. A. Villacorta (b. 1879) in three volumes at Guatemala City, 1929-31. This work should not be confused with one of similar title written early in the seventeenth century by Remesal, to which reference has already been made. The volume edited by Villacorta was based upon a manuscript copy made in the years 1848 to 1875 from an earlier manuscript. The original manuscript is lost.

A curious and valuable work in the form of an annual yearbook or *gaceta* which, however, soon suspended publication, appeared at Mexico City between 1728 and 1734. The first three issues appeared under the title *Compendio de noticias mexicanas* and the last four under the title *Compendio de noticias americanas*. The author and compiler was Juan Francisco Sahagún de Arévalo. These accounts contained current historical facts from North and South America, the West Indies, and the Philippines and aimed to record valuable material which might otherwise be lost in the archives.

Florida

An excellent work covering Spanish Florida as well as parts of the present United States is by Andrés González Barcia Carballido y Zúñiga entitled *Ensayo cronológico para la historia general de la Florida*. It was published in one volume at Madrid in 1723 and dealt in a comprehensive manner with events between 1512 and 1722.

California

An interesting and most excellent work dealing with California is that by Miguel Venegas (1680-ca. 1764) entitled *Noticia de la California*. It was published in three volumes at Madrid in 1757, and deals with the temporal and spiritual conquest of that territory to the middle of the eighteenth century.

In 1789 at Venice appeared the two-volume *Storia della California* by Francisco Javier Clavijero which, like his history of Mexico, was based upon documentary materials, and particularly upon the manuscripts of the Jesuits Michael del Barco (1706-1790) and Lucas Ventura, both of whom had lived in the territory.

The chief account of California missions to 1784 is found in the *Relación histórica de la vida . . . del venerable padre fray Junípero Serra* by Francisco Palóu (1723-1789) which was published at Mexico City in 1787. An English translation was published at Pasadena in 1913, and in 1926 Professor H. E. Bolton (b. 1870) published at Berkeley in four volumes Palóu's *Historical memoirs of New California*.

A volume concerning the region written in this century but not published until the next is the *Historia de la Compañia de Jesús en Nueva España* by Francisco Javier Alegre (1729-1788). It appeared first in three volumes at Mexico City in 1841 and 1842 and was continued by José Mariano Dávila y Arrillaga (1798-1869) in two volumes published at Puebla in 1888 and 1889.

Central America

Among the volumes dealing with Central America, one in particular should be mentioned. It is the first part of the *Historia de la conquista de la provincia del Itza,* written by an advocate of the Spanish Royal Council, Juan de Villagutierre Soto-Mayor, and it appeared at Madrid in 1701. A second edition appeared at Guatemala City in 1933. No further part of the work has ever been published but even as it is, it constitutes one of the important works dealing with the early history of Yucatan and Guatemala.

West Indies

A work concerning the West Indies which is interesting and frequently used was published in two volumes at London in 1793 under the title *The history of the West Indies,* the author being Bryan Edwards (1743-1809). In 1819 a five-volume augmented edition was published at London. Another excellent historical and descriptive account of the region is contained in *The West-Indies atlas* by Thomas Jefferys, published at London in 1775.

An extensive account of the Island of Haiti based largely upon the manuscript memoir of Jean Baptiste le Pers (1675-1735) was published in four volumes at Amsterdam in 1723 under the title *Histoire de l'île espagnole ou de St. Dominique.* The author was Pierre François Xavier de Charlevoix (1682-1761).

A two-volume work published at Paris in 1776 and 1777 is entitled *Considérations sur l'état présent de la colonie française de Saint-Dominique.* It was by Michel René Hilliard d'Auberteuil (1751-1789).

Another general two-volume work dealing with Santo Domingo bore the title *Description topographique, physique, civile, politique, et historique de la partie française de l'île Saint Dominique....* It was published at Philadelphia during 1797 and 1798, and the author was Médéric Louis Élie Moreau de Saint-Méry (1750-1819).

A brief Spanish work based upon documents collected over a period of twenty years is the *Idea del valor de la isla española* by Antonio Sánchez Valverde (d. 1790). It was published at Madrid in 1785.

Tierra Firme

Northern South America received attention in a number of histories. In 1723 José de Oviedo y Baños Sotomayor (b. 1674) published at Madrid the first part of his *Historia de la conquista y población de la provincia de Venezuela,* which was written from many early documents (since lost) in the archives at Caracas. It was not until 1885, however, that the whole work in five volumes appeared at Madrid.

In 1741 at Madrid the Jesuit José Gumilla's (1690-ca. 1758) *El Orinoco ilustrado* appeared. This was reissued at Barcelona in two volumes in 1791 under the title *Historia natural, civil y geográfica de las naciones situadas en las riberas del Río Orinoco.* The work was based in part upon facts gleaned during thirty years in the Orinoco region and in part upon the manuscript accounts of Fathers Ribera and Mercado. Another generally descriptive work of value to historians is the *Descripción exacta de la provincia de Venezuela* by José Luís de Cisneros which was published probably at Valencia in 1764. Still another good descriptive work, which includes history and religious activities, is *Cualidades y riquezas del nuevo reino de Granada.* Although written in this century it was not published until it appeared at Bogotá in 1930. The author was Basilio Vicente de Oviedo (b. 1699).

A work entitled *Historia corográfica, natural y evangélica de la Nueva*

Andalucía written by the missionary Antonio Caulin (b. 1718) and published at Madrid in 1779, gives many valuable details concerning the natives of northern South America and the activities of the missionaries among them, and also an account of the products of the region.

Another work dealing with the Indians of South America but particularly with those in the Orinoco region is the *Saggio di storia americana* by Felippo Salvadore Gilii (1721-1789), which was published in four volumes at Rome between 1780 and 1784.

A volume dealing with religious activities in northern South America is the *Historia de las misiones de los llanos* by Juan Rivero (1681-1736), written in 1736 but not published until 1883 when it appeared at Bogotá.

A comprehensive work describing the history, geography, political conditions, etc., of the same locality, as well as of Peru and Chile, was printed at Madrid in 1740 under the title briefly cited *Aviso histórico*. The author was Dionisio de Alcede Ugarte y Herrera (1690-1777). An English edition with many travel accounts added appeared at London in five volumes in 1812. A Spanish edition also with additions was published at Madrid in 1883.

Peru

At Lima, Peru, in 1723 appeared an interesting two-volume history of the founding of that city and of the struggles which immediately followed. The account is in the form of a heroic poem and is entitled briefly *Lima fundada*. The author was Pedro de Peralta Barnuevo Rocha y Benavides (1663-1743), the official cosmographer of Peru, and a scientist and writer of note.

In 1789 an important manuscript was prepared by the Jesuit Juan de Velasco (1727-1819). Two known copies exist at present, both being in Madrid. The title of the manuscript is *La historia del reino de Quito en la América meridional*. It was first published in an incomplete form in two volumes at Paris and Quito in 1837 and 1839. The work may have been based upon a manuscript now lost by Fray Marcos de Niza (ca. 1500-1558) who was in the region before he went to New Spain. In 1840 at Paris Henri Ternaux-Compans edited an incomplete two-volume edition. The most complete edition, however, is that edited by Agustín Yerovi (d. 1903) which appeared at Quito in three volumes between 1841 and 1844. This work bears the title *Historia del reino de Quito,* and deals with the ancient history of Ecuador to the time of the Spanish conquest, which the author divides into three periods.

A work of great value for the historian of the later colonial period in Peru is the five-volume *Guía política, eclesiástica y militar del virrey-nato del Perú* by José Hipólito Unánue (1755-1833). The work appeared at Lima between 1793 and 1797 and covered the same years in the form of an annual publication.

La Plata

A volume describing the Gran Chaco was published at Córdoba, Argentina, in 1733, under the title *Descripción corográfica*. The author was Pedro Lozano and his account, which is the earliest of the region, is very comprehensive and includes much history and biography as well as geography. The same author wrote an account of the conquest of southern South America under the title *Historia de la conquista del Paraguay, Río de la Plata y Tucumán*. This work, however, was not published until it appeared in five volumes at Buenos Aires between 1873 and 1875.

A history of Paraguay frequently cited is that by Pierre François Xavier de Charlevoix entitled *Histoire du Paraguay,* published at Paris in four volumes in 1756 and 1757. It has been translated into many languages including English (2 vols., Dublin, 1769).

A valuable historical and ethnological work on Paraguay written in this century but not published until 1910 in two volumes at Buenos Aires is *El Paraguay católico* by the Jesuit José Sánchez Labrador (b. 1717).

A German work entitled *Geschichte von Paraguay* by Bernard Nusdorfer was published at Frankfurt in 1769. This book dealt largely with the activities of the Jesuits in the territory.

Argentina and the neighboring regions are described in two accounts by the missionaries, Thomas Falkner (1707-1784), who lived among the Patagonian Indians from 1740 to 1767, in his *Description of Patagonia and the adjoining parts of South America* published at Hereford in 1774; and Martin Dobritzhofer (1717-1791) in his three-volume *Historia de Abiponibus,* published at Vienna in 1784. An English edition of this latter work appeared at London in three volumes in 1822. This is in part a memoir of eighteen years among the natives, and it constitutes one of the most extraordinary descriptions of savage life ever published. Dobritzhofer entered the Jesuit Order in 1736 and went to South America as a missionary in 1749, spending many years among the Indians.

Chile

One of the chief eighteenth century works concerning Chile was written in Italian by the Chilean Jesuit Juan Ignacio Molina (ca. 1737-1829) under the title *Saggio sulla storia naturale del Chili* and was published at Bologna in 1782. For some time after the book appeared it was generally believed to be the work of Felipe Gómez de Vidaurre (b. 1740). In 1787 the second part of the work appeared at Bologna under the title *Saggio sulla storia civile del Chili*. The first English edition of Molina's account was printed in two volumes at Middletown, Connecticut, in 1808, and the next year a two-volume edition appeared at London. An earlier anonymous work by the same author had been published at Bologna in 1776 under the title *Compendio della storia, geographia, naturale e civile del regno del Chili*. This was printed in Spanish at Madrid in two volumes between 1788 and 1795. These three works have often been confused.

Another work concerning Chile which appeared toward the end of the century is briefly cited as *Chilidugu*. It was written by the Jesuit missionary, Bernardi Havestadt (ca. 1708-1781), and was printed in Latin in two volumes in Westphalia in 1777.

APPENDIX H

NINETEENTH CENTURY HISTORIES AND HISTORIANS DEALING WITH COLONIAL HISPANIC AMERICA

By A. Curtis Wilgus

THE nineteenth century, which was disturbed by nationalism, imperialism, and industrialism, saw many works produced dealing with colonial Hispanic America. At the beginning of the century Hispanic America succeeded in breaking away from the deadening influence of the mother countries and in winning independence. The consequent disturbances in America and the concurrent disturbances in Europe resulting from the activities of Napoleon and Metternich brought new interest in democracy to the peoples of America, while the Monroe Doctrine concentrated attention upon the Western Hemisphere. With the rise of dictators in Hispanic America party rivalry and political struggles tended to continue to attract the attention of European nations. All of these circumstances produced in literature partisan accounts and controversial histories, and at the same time stimulated travel by European visitors who published the records of their experiences. Yet in this century German dilettantism had its influence upon historical production, and even in Hispanic America the hyper-critical historian found material for his pen, as did the more robust and dependable scholarly writer of erudite history. Of the vast number of historical works of this century dealing wholly or in part with the colonial era, only a few outstanding examples are here given.

I. General Works

One of the most extensive of the general histories of this century was that by Guiseppe Compagnoni (1754-1833), who, continuing the work of the Conte di Segur (1756-1805), published the *Storia dell'-America* in twenty-nine volumes at Milan in 1820.

In 1823 the first of the four-volume *Geografía general* edited by Feliciano Montenegro Colón (d. 1853) appeared at Caracas. The last volume was published in 1837. Taken as a whole this work, despite its name, is more historical than geographical.

Between 1864 and 1866 Gil Gelpi y Ferro (1826-1894) published at Havana his two-volume *Estudios sobre la América*. Meanwhile, in

1865 at Santiago, Chile, appeared the *Compendio de historia de América* in two volumes by the justly famous Diego Barros Arana (1830-1907).

In 1875 Miguel Lobo y Malagamba (d. 1876) brought out in three volumes at Madrid his *Historia general de las antiguas colonias hispano-americanas.* Two years later in 1877 at Caracas was published the *Biografías de hombres notables de Hispano-América* in four volumes written by Ramón Azpurúa. This work is particularly of value to the historian of the independence period.

Another work of great value to historians, which contains many early relations of a descriptive and geographic nature largely dealing with Peru, was published by the Ministerio de Fomento of Peru in four volumes at Madrid between 1881 and 1897 under the title *Relaciones geográficas de indias.*

In 1883 there appeared at Bogotá the *Biografía de hombres ilustres* by Soledad Acosta de Samper (1833-1913), a woman novelist and editor. This work was used as a historical textbook in Colombian schools. In 1888 Adolfo Flórez (d. 1895) published at the same place his one-volume *Estudio cronológico.* The same year at Barcelona appeared the first part of the *Historia general de América desde sus tiempos más remotos* (two volumes in one). The author, Francisco Pi y Margall (1824-1901), was a lawyer and newspaper man. He never completed his work, which was written at the request of a Madrid publishing company. The study deals with pre-Columbian history. An earlier preliminary edition appeared in 1878.

From 1889 to 1897 Ricardo Cappa (1800-1897) published at Madrid his extensive *Estudios críticos acerca de la dominación española en América* in twenty volumes, the first part of which had appeared at Madrid a few years before. While this work was being published there appeared in 1892 at Barcelona the excellent and well-illustrated three-volume *América* by Rodolfo Cronau (b. 1855) covering the period from the earliest times, but placing most emphasis upon the age of discoveries. During 1894 and 1895 the *América* of José Coroleu é Inglada (1840-1895) appeared in four volumes at Barcelona covering the whole scope of Hispanic American history.

Among general French works written in this century one of the earliest to treat Hispanic America was that by Alexander von Humboldt (1769-1859) who with Aimé Jacques Alexandre Bonpland (1773-1858) travelled through South America between the years 1799 and 1804. Their works were published in twenty-three volumes between 1805 and 1834. Sections of this work have been reprinted at various times, and between

1836 and 1839 at Paris five volumes were reprinted under the title *Examen critique de l'histoire de la géographie du nouveau continent* containing considerable valuable information for historians. This work had been preceded by an account translated into English in seven volumes (London, 1814-29) entitled *Personal narrative of travels to the equinoctial regions of the new continent, during the years 1799-1804.*

Between 1875 and 1894 Jean Jacques Élisée Reclus (1830-1905) brought out at Paris his *Nouvelle géographie universelle* in nineteen volumes, of which Volumes XV to XIX treated the geography and history of America. From 1890 to 1893 an English edition in three volumes containing the material on North America was published at New York, while during 1894 and 1895 two volumes dealing with South America appeared at the same place. All of these volumes were edited by Augustus Henry Keane (1833-1912) and given the title *The earth and its inhabitants.*

In 1876 at Paris appeared the *Histoire de l'Amérique du Sud* by Alfred Joseph Deberle (1835-1877). The third French edition (1897) was translated into English and published at London in 1899. This work dealt with Hispanic America from the time of the conquest. In 1932 a new edition of this book was published at New York.

Among German works dealing in general with Hispanic America one of the earliest was the three-volume *Amerika* by Franz Jakob Kutscher (d. 1821), published at Schleswig in 1803, which was concerned largely with the natives of Spanish America. Another German work was published at Frankfurt-am-Main in two volumes in 1850. It was entitled *Geschichte der colonisation Amerika's* by Franz Justus Kottenkamp (1806-1858).

In 1885 at Leipzig appeared the third edition of Wilhelm Georg Friedrich Roscher's (1817-1894) *Kolonien . . .* which contained an excellent sketch of the Spanish colonies in America. This discussion was translated and edited by E. G. Bourne (1860-1908) under the title *The Spanish colonial system* (New York, 1904). This little study is doubtless the best brief statement concerning the subject in the English language.

A Dutch work of description and travel published in two volumes at Amsterdam in 1828 bore the title *Beschrijving der niewe staten van Amerika.* The author was Johann Gottfried Sommer (ca. 1782-1848).

A comparatively large number of general histories or near-histories of Hispanic America were published in English in the nineteenth century. In 1808 Abeil Holmes (1763-1837) published at Cambridge,

Massachusetts, for the first time *The annals of America* in two volumes which constituted a concise work containing much useful information. The volumes were reprinted subsequently in both England and America.

In 1818 at London appeared Sir Richard Henry Bonnycastle's (1791-1848) *Spanish America* in two volumes. The first volume dealt with Spanish North America and New Granada, and the second volume treated the remainder of Spanish America. The work is descriptive, geographical, and historical.

In 1823 H. C. Carey (1793-1879) and I. Lea (1792-1886) published at Philadelphia *The geography, history, and statistics of America and the West Indies,* and in 1825 at New York the two-volume work by John Milton Niles (1787-1856) appeared under the title *A view of South America and Mexico.*

In the decade of the forties two useful works appeared. One, of limited historical value, was Charles Darwin's (1809-1882) *Geological observations* published in three parts at London between 1842 and 1846 and later republished in Spanish at Santiago, Chile, in 1906. The other study was brought out in 1848 by Samuel G. Goodrich (1793-1860) at Louisville under the title *History of South America and the West Indies.*

From 1856 to 1868 Sir Arthur Helps (1813-1875) published at New York his four-volume work entitled *The Spanish conquest in America.* This had been preceded by *The conquerors of the new world and their bondsmen* (2 vols., London, 1848-52), treating of the enslavement of the negroes in the West Indies and on the mainland.

In 1877 E. J. Payne (1844-1904) published at London his volume on the *History of European colonies* which was followed by two volumes entitled the *History of the new world called America* (Oxford, 1892-99). This work, however, was never finished and in consequence did not get beyond the treatment of aboriginal America.

In 1878 at London Henry W. Bates (1825-1892) edited a volume entitled *Central America and the West Indies and South America.* This work had been translated by A. H. Keane from the German and is sometimes referred to as *Stanford's compendium of geography and travel.* The original work upon which these volumes are based is Friedrich Anton Heller von Hellwald's (1842-1892) *Die erde und ihre völker* (2 vols., Stuttgart, 1877-78).

In 1880 appeared the first edition of Antonio Carlo Napoleone's *South America* which was published at London. In 1884 R. G. Watson published at the same place his two-volume *Spanish and Portuguese South America during the colonial period.* Between 1884 and 1889 at

Boston was published Justin Winsor's (1831-1897) coöperative and monumental *Narrative and critical history of America* in eight volumes which dealt at some length with Hispanic America.

In 1891 Theodore Childs brought out at New York *The Spanish American republics* which was also published the same year in French at Paris. In 1893 Charles F. Lummis published at Chicago his excellent little volume on *The Spanish pioneers*. In 1898 Hezekiah Butterworth (1839-1905) published at New York his *South America* which dealt largely with the independence movement, and in 1900 at Akron, Ohio, appeared a volume entitled *South America* by F. G. Carpenter (1855-1924) which described society, politics, economic life, etc.

General histories on special topics are numerous. Among the volumes dealing with the American natives written in this century several are worthy of note. In 1878 and 1879 appeared *Die culturländer des alten Amerika* by Philip Wilhelm Adolf Bastian (1826-1905). It was published in three volumes in two at Berlin.

In 1810 the beautiful and excellent *Vues des cordillères, et monuments des peuples indigènes de l'Amérique* by Alexander von Humboldt was published at Paris. Four years later this appeared at London in a two-volume English translation entitled *Researches concerning the institutions and monuments of the ancient inhabitants of America.*

Another important volume dealing with native cultures is *L'Amérique préhistorique* by Jean François Albert du Pouget, Marquis de Nadaillac (b. 1818) published at Paris in 1883. This was translated into English and printed at London in 1885 under the title *Prehistoric America.*

A still indispensable work, which appeared at London in nine volumes (1830-48) is the *Antiquities of Mexico* by Lord Kingsborough (1795-1837). It is illustrated by more than 1,000 plates, many of them colored, showing early Mexican picture writing, architecture, and art, and it constitutes a mine of archæological information.

Another work dealing with early Mexican art and archæology is the *Monumentos del arte mexicano antiguo* by Antonio Peñafiel (b. 1831) published in three volumes (one volume text and two volumes portfolio) at Berlin in 1890. The illustrations are handsomely done.

Still another important contribution to this subject is the *Histoire des nations civilisées du Mexique et de l'Amérique Centrale* by the Abbé Charles-Etienne Brasseur de Bourbourg (1814-1874) published at Paris in four volumes between 1857 and 1859. The work is based upon an immense amount of research and deals with native cultures before the time of Columbus.

A brief English volume frequently cited is *The American race* by Daniel G. Brinton (1837-1899) published at New York in 1891, which describes the linguistic and ethnological characteristics of the Indians of North and South America.

Two brief works of limited value to the student of Hispanic America are George Catlin's (1796-1872) *Letters and notes on the manners, customs, and conditions of the North American Indians* published in two volumes at London in 1841; and Thomas Francis Gordon's (1787-1860) *The history of America* published in two volumes at Philadelphia in 1831, which carries the story only as far as the destruction of the Aztec empire. In 1832 at Philadelphia appeared two more volumes with the title *The history of Mexico* covering the same period and based chiefly on Clavijero's work.

One of the most elaborate works from the standpoint of illustrations is that by Johann Wilhelm Reiss (1838-1908) and Alfons Stübel (1835-1904) entitled *The necropolis of Ancón* in Peru which was published in English at Berlin in three volumes between 1800 and 1887. Another elaborate and classic work dealing with the highland civilization of the Peruvian coast is *Die ruinenstætte von Tiahuanaco* by Alfons Stübel and Friedrich Max Uhle (b. 1856). This was published at Leipzig in two parts in 1892.

In 1889 and 1890 a two-volume work of extreme value to the student of the South American Indian, and particularly of the Peruvian Indian, was issued at Berlin. It was entitled *Kultur und industrie Südamerikanischer völker* and was the work of Max Uhle in collaboration with Alfons Stübel, Johann Wilhelm Reiss, and P. Koppell.

Two other works dealing with Incan life should be consulted by all interested in the subject. The first is *Antigüedades peruanas* (one volume and atlas, Vienna, 1851) by Johann Jakob von Tschudi (1818-1889) and Mariano Eduardo de Ribero y Ustáriz (1795-1857). This work was translated into English and published at New York in 1853 under the title *Peruvian antiquities*. New editions appeared at the same place in 1854 and 1855. The second study is also by Tschudi. It bears the title *Culturhistorische und sprachliche beiträge zur kenntniss des alten Peru* (Wien, 1891). A two-volume Spanish translation appeared at Lima in 1918 entitled *Contribuciones á la historia, civilización y lingüistica del Perú antiguo*.

On the discovery period several books should be mentioned. In 1892 at Boston, Massachusetts, John Fiske (1842-1901) published *The dis-*

covery of America in two volumes. While not always accurate, this has been considered one of the chief guides to the subject in English.

The volumes of Henry Harrisse (1830-1910), *Les Corte-Real et leurs voyages au nouveau-monde* (2 vols., Paris, 1883), *Americus Vespuccius* (London, 1895), *Fernand Colomb, sa vie, ses œuvres* (Paris, 1872), *Christophe Colomb* (2 vols., Paris, 1884-85), and *The discovery of North America* (London, 1892), the latter an admirable cartographical essay, are all of value to the student of this period.

In 1828 Washington Irving (1783-1859) brought out at London and New York his four-volume *History of the life and voyages of Christopher Columbus* which soon after was translated into most European languages.

The greatest work dealing with Columbus and the period of discoveries in any language is the *Raccolta di documenti e studi* published in fifteen volumes by the Italian government at Rome between 1892 and 1894. This work is, however, very scarce as the edition was limited to 560 sets.

A scholarly and valuable study, although only thirty pages in length, of the Portuguese discoveries and their explorations before the time of Columbus is the very brief *Navegaciones y descubrimientos de los portugueses* written by Joaquim Pedro Oliveira Martins (1845-1894) and published at Madrid in 1892. A work more familiar to American students is *The golden age of Prince Henry the navigator,* translated from his *Os filhos de D. João I* and printed at London in 1914.

An account of the discovery of America by the Norsemen was printed in a collection of documents in Dutch at Hafniae (i. e., Copenhagen) in 1837 under the title *Antiquitates Americanæ sive scriptores septentrionales rerum ante-Columbianarum in America.* In 1839 there appeared in English at London another work on the Norse discoveries entitled *The discovery of America by the Norsemen* which aimed to prove the truth of the claims. The author was Joshua Toulmin Smith (1816-1869) and he brought out at Boston in the same year the same volume with the title *The Northmen in New England.*

A volume dealing with negro slavery in America is entitled *Historia de la esclavitud de la raza africana en el nuevo mundo y en especial en los países américo-hispanos* (Barcelona, 1879). The author was José Antonio Saco (1797-1879) and this book is generally considered a supplement to his history of slavery published at Paris in three volumes between 1875 and 1877. A new edition was printed at Havana in two volumes in 1932 with an introduction by Fernando Ortiz (b. 1881).

General works dealing with the independence period and with military matters are numerous. Between 1864 and 1867 at Paris appeared the *Annales historiques de la révolution de l'Amérique latine* in five volumes written by the famous internationalist, Carlos Calvo (1824-1906). The text was in Spanish and it covers the period from 1808. At the same time appeared the author's *Recueil complet des traités,* etc., published at Paris in eleven volumes between 1862 and 1869. Another but earlier work published at Paris was by Pierre Joseph Spiridion Dufey (1770-1854) entitled *Résumé de l'histoire des révolutions de l'Amérique méridionale.* It was printed in two volumes in 1826.

In 1858 and 1859 Bartolomé Mitre (1821-1906) brought out at Buenos Aires the first two volumes of his *Historia de Belgrano y la independencia argentina.* A third volume was added in 1876 and the work was published in four volumes in 1902. In 1890 was published the first edition of his *Historia de San Martín y de la emancipación de Sud-América* at Buenos Aires in four volumes. This was partly translated into English by William Pilling and published at London in 1893 in one volume under the title *The emancipation of South America.*

A work dealing with the independence period from the Spanish point of view was written at the command of Ferdinand VII and published at Madrid in three volumes in 1829 and 1830. It was entitled *Historia de la revolución hispano-americana* and the author was Mariano Torrente (1792-1856). Parts of the work dealing especially with the independence movements in Chile and in Mexico have been republished under various titles.

Another Spanish work bears the title *Las glorias nacionales* and was written by Fernando Patxot y Ferrer (1812-1859) to show the relations between Spain and Spanish America. The work was published in six volumes at Barcelona between 1852 and 1854.

As in the previous century collections of voyages and travels are numerous and frequently constitute valuable sources of historical information. Among the most important of such works the following should be mentioned in the order of their appearance.

Between 1803 and 1817 there began to appear at London a five-volume work entitled *A chronological history of the discoveries in the South Seas or Pacific Ocean.* The author was James Burney (1750-1821), a careful compiler. The first volume dealt with the period to 1579; Volume II (published in 1806) continued the story to 1620; Volume III (1813) treated the years 1620-1688; Volume IV (1816) covered the years 1688-1723; and Volume V (1817) carried the work to 1764. These volumes are very useful for the student of early California history.

Meanwhile, at Paris in 1808 appeared in six volumes another work of considerable value to the historian of the discovery period under the title *Bibliothèque universelle des voyages,* of which part five is devoted to America. The author was Gilles Boucher de la Richarderie (1733-1810).

From 1808 to 1814 at London appeared seventeen volumes under the title *A general collection of the best and most interesting voyages and travels in all parts of the world.* The editor, who was John Pinkerton (1758-1826), put into this collection the accounts of a number of early voyages hitherto unpublished in English.

From 1811 to 1824 Robert Kerr's *General history and collection of voyages and travels* appeared at Edinburgh in eighteen volumes, the last volume of which contained a bibliography of voyages and travels compiled by W. Stevenson.

Between 1825 and 1837 there appeared at Madrid the five-volume *Colección de los viages y descubrimientos que hicieron por mar los españoles desde fines del siglo XV* by Martín Fernández de Navarrete (1765-1844). This included various documents concerning Columbus, Vespucci, Magellan, and others, and dealt with the Spanish establishments in America. The work was never completed as planned because of the compiler's death.

In 1833 there began to appear at Paris the *Bibliothèque universelle des voyages par mer ou par terre dans les divers parties du monde* which covered the period from the earliest times. The work was completed in forty-six volumes and an atlas in 1837. The editor was Albert Montémont (1788-1861).

In this latter year (1837) there was published at Paris the first of a series of ten volumes entitled *Voyages, relations, et mémoires originaux pour servir à l'histoire de la découverte de l'Amérique.* In 1840 appeared ten more volumes at Paris. The editor was Henri Ternaux-Compans and the collection contained many Spanish accounts written before 1700, some of which were translated from the Spanish manuscripts and all of which were published for the first time in French.

The greatest undertaking of the nineteenth century in the realm of collecting, editing, and translating of earlier accounts was by the Hakluyt Society which in 1847 began to issue its first series of voyages and travels in one hundred volumes (London, 1847-98). A second series of seventy-five volumes (London, 1899-1935) continued the admirable work begun in the first series.

II. SPECIAL WORKS

Histories dealing with specific portions of Hispanic America became increasingly numerous during this century as each state won and maintained its individual freedom.

Brazil

The independence of Brazil and its vicissitudes during the period of the empire and the early republic attracted the attention of writers in most of the European countries. In 1808 Andrew Grant published his *History of Brazil* at London which was intended not only as a history but as a guide for those who contemplated a journey to that country.

In 1810 the first volume of Robert Southey's (1774-1843) well-known *History of Brazil* was published at London. The second volume appeared in 1817 and the third and last in 1819.

Meanwhile, in 1815 there appeared at Paris the comprehensive three-volume *Histoire du Brésil* by Alphonse de Beauchamps (1767-1832) covering the years from 1500 to 1810; in 1817 appeared the *Corografia brasilica* (two volumes at Rio de Janeiro) by Manuel Ayres de Casal (b. ca. 1754) from which James Henderson (ca. 1783-1848) compiled his *History of Brazil* (1 vol., London, 1821); and in 1819 at Frankfurt was published the valuable two-volume *Reise nach Brasilien* during the years 1815, 1816, and 1817, by Maximilian, Prinz zu Wied-Neuwied (1782-1867). The first volume of the latter work was translated into English and published at London in 1820.

In 1821 a Frenchmen, Jean Ferdinand Denis (1798-1890), published at Paris his history and travel account, *Le Brésil*. Eight years later, in 1829, at Dresden appeared the *Geschichte von Brasilien* in two volumes by Ernst Münch (1798-1841). Between 1826 and 1830 appeared in four parts the incomplete *Historia dos principaes successos politicos do imperio do Brasil* by José da Silva Lisbôa, who was commissioned by Dom Pedro I to write the official history of the independence movement. Meanwhile there appeared in three volumes (München, 1823-31) the valuable *Reise in Brasilien,* covering the years 1817 to 1820, by Johann Baptiste von Spix (1781-1826) and Carl Friedrich Philipp von Martius (1794-1868).

An extensive work in four volumes which dealt with the Province of Bahia was published at the city of Bahia in 1835. It bore the title

Memorias historicas e politicas and the author was Ignacio Accioli de Cerqueira e Silva.

In 1836 John Armitage (1807-1856) published at London his two-volume *History of Brazil* which was intended to be a continuation of Southey's work, and carried the story from 1808 to 1831. In 1839 Francisco Solano Constancia (1777-1846) brought out his *Historia do Brasil* at Paris in two volumes which traced the history of the country from the earliest times to the abdication of Dom Pedro.

Between 1842 and 1876 appeared at Paris (18 volumes in 13) the *Quadro elementar das relações politicas e diplomaticas de Portugal* by Manoel Francisco de Barros, Visconde de Santarem (1791-1856). The work is indispensable to the student of the external relations of Brazil. From 1842 to 1853 at Paris appeared from the pen of the same writer his *Atlas . . .* , which is the chief source for the study of Portuguese colonial expansion.

In 1843 the two-volume work of the revolutionary and adventurer, José Ignacio de Abreu e Lima (1796-1869), appeared at Rio de Janeiro under the title *Compendio da historia do Brasil.* This was followed at Pernambuco two years later by his *Synopsis* containing the chief facts in Brazilian history.

Between 1854 and 1857 Francisco Adolpho de Varnhagen brought out his comprehensive *Historia geral do Brasil* in two volumes at Rio de Janeiro. This was followed in 1871 at Vienna by his *Historia das lutas com os Hollandezes no Brasil desde 1624 a 1654.* He is also the author of a number of other works of a more special nature.

In 1857 Daniel P. Kidder (1815-1891) and James C. Fletcher published at Boston their profusely illustrated *Brazil and the Brazilians,* describing the country and its people, and summarizing its history. In 1860 at Berlin was published the large one-volume *Geschichte von Brasilien* by Heinrich Handelmann (1827-1891). This work was translated into Portuguese and issued at Rio de Janeiro in 1931 under the contracted title *Historia do Brasil.* . . . Between 1864 and 1868 appeared at Rio de Janeiro the monumental seven-volume *Historia da fundação do imperio brasileiro* by João Manoel Pereira da Silva (ca. 1819-1898), who was the author of numerous other extremely valuable works on the same period. In this connection should be mentioned another source of great help to the student of diplomatic history, entitled *Apontamentos para o direito internacional . . .* (4 vols., Rio de Janeiro, 1864-69), edited by Antonio Pereira Pinto (1819-1880).

From 1871 to 1873 there appeared at Rio de Janeiro the two-volume

Historia do Brasil . . . by Alexandre José de Mello Moraes (1816-1882) which covered the period between 1808 and 1871. This work had been preceded at Rio de Janeiro from 1858 to 1863 by the five-volume *Corographia historica . . . do imperio do Brasil*. In 1889 at Rio de Janeiro was printed the very useful *Historia financeira e orçamentaria do imperio do Brasil desde sua fundação* by Liberato de Castro Carreira (b. 1820). In 1896 at São Paulo was published the two-volume *Compendio de historia do Brasil* by Raphael Maria Galanti (b. 1840).

Between 1898 and 1900 there appeared at Lisbon two volumes entitled *Trabalhos nauticos dos Portuguezes nos seculos XVI e XVII*, written by Francisco Marques de Sousa Viterbo (1845-1910). In 1899 at Leipzig appeared the comprehensive one-volume *Brasilien* by Oskar Canstatt (b. 1842), and in 1900 an advanced textbook entitled *Historia do Brasil* was published at Rio de Janeiro by João Baptista Ribeiro de Andrada Fernandes (1860-1934).

Mexico

Histories dealing with Mexico in this century were very numerous and of considerable value. In 1811 there appeared at Paris the five volumes of Alexander von Humboldt entitled *Essai politique sur le royaume de la Nouvelle Espagne* which had first been published as part three of the *Voyage de Humboldt et Bonpland* (23 vols., Paris, 1805-34). A Spanish edition appeared at Paris in 1822 in five volumes and an English edition was printed at London in four volumes in 1811. Because of the extreme value of this work most subsequent writers on Mexico have found it necessary to refer to it.

In 1813 at London appeared the two-volume *Historia de la revolución de Nueva España* by José Servando Teresa Mier Noriega y Guerra (1765-1827).

Between 1821 and 1823 at Rio de Janeiro was printed the two-volume *Historia do descubrimento e conquista do imperio mexicano* by Antonio Vicente Dellanave. Between the latter year and 1832 there appeared at Mexico City the six-volume *Cuadro histórico de la revolución de la América mexicana* by Carlos María de Bustamante (1774-1848). This work was written in the form of letters dated from 1823 to 1832. In 1824 Nicholas Mill's *History of Mexico* was published at London covering the period from the earliest times and dealing with all phases of national life, but particularly stressing the mineral wealth of the country which he hoped British capital would exploit.

In 1831 and 1832 appeared at Paris the first edition of Lorenzo de Zavala's (1788-1836) two-volume *Ensayo histórico de las revoluciones de México desde 1808 hasta 1830.* In 1836 *Méjico y sus revoluciones* by José María Luís Mora (1794-1850) was published at Paris in three volumes. Between 1836 and 1838 the four-volume work by Andrés Cavo (b. 1739) entitled *Los tres siglos de México durante el gobierno español* was printed at Mexico City.

In 1843 appeared the first edition of William H. Prescott's classic *History of the conquest of Mexico* in three volumes at New York. This was followed the next year by an edition published at London. Between 1849 and 1852 Lucas Alamán (1792-1853) brought out his five-volume *Historia de Méjico* covering the period since 1808.

In 1852 and 1853 appeared Brantz Mayer's (1809-1879) *Mexico,* a historical and descriptive work dealing with the whole field of Mexican history. It was published in two volumes at Hartford, Connecticut. In 1862 Francisco Carbajal Espinosa brought out his *Historia de México* (2 vols., at Mexico City) which covered the history of the country from the earliest times to the middle of the nineteenth century.

An important work for the historian appeared at Mexico City in two volumes (1862-65) under the title *Cuadro descriptivo y comparativo de las lenguas indígenes de México.* The author was Francisco Pimentel. Another valuable work by the same author (Mexico City, 1883) bore the title *Historia crítica de la literatura y de las ciencias en México desde la conquista hasta nuestros días.*

A work reprinted in several languages appeared in 1863 at Paris under the title *Le Mexique, ancien et moderne.* The author was Michel Chevalier (1806-1879). A two-volume English edition was published at London in 1864 and a one-volume Spanish edition appeared at Madrid two years later (1866).

An extensive work in six volumes by Ignacio Alvarez (1833-1904) entitled *Estudios sobre la historia general de México* was published at Zacatecas from 1869 to 1877. An even more detailed study, although only in four volumes, was published at Madrid in 1871 and 1872. It was entitled *Méjico desde 1808 á 1867,* and the author was Francisco de Paula de Arrangoiz y Berzábal (d. 1889).

The first four volumes of a reference work which, however, was never completed, was published at Mexico City in 1874 and 1875 under the title *Diccionario geográfico, estadístico, histórico, biográfico,* etc. The author was José María Pérez Hernández and the volumes covered the letters A to C only. Another special work of historical value is entitled *México pintoresco, artístico y monumental* by Manuel Rivera Cambas and it was published at Mexico City in 1880.

In 1883 at Guadalajara appeared the *Compendio de la historia de México* by Luís Pérez Verdía. Between 1884 and 1888 appeared at Lagos a three-volume essay briefly entitled *Principios críticos* by Agustín Rivera y Sanromán (1824-1916) which dealt largely with the colonial and revolutionary periods. From 1888 to 1891 at Mexico City was published the valuable five-volume *Diccionario geográfico, histórico y biográfico de los estados unidos mexicanos,* the work of Antonio García Cubas (b. 1832).

Two valuable works of a special nature appearing in the decade of the eighties were the *Historia de la medicina en México desde la época de los indios hasta la presente* (3 vols., Mexico City, 1886-88) by Francisco A. Flores, and the *Geografía y estadística de la república mexicana* (12 vols., Mexico City, 1889-92) by Alfonso Luís Velasco.

In 1891 an important pioneering study by Frank Wilson Blackmar (b. 1854) was published at Baltimore as a volume in the historical and political science studies of Johns Hopkins University. It bore the title *Spanish institutions in the southwest.* Also in 1891 there appeared at Mexico City the first of two essays under the general title *Época colonial* by Luís González Obregón (b. 1865). The second volume was published in 1895 at the same place. A corrected and enlarged edition of these was published in one volume at Mexico City in 1900.

A brief but valuable work of 110 pages appeared at Mexico City in 1893 under the title *El arte en México en la época antigua y durante el gobierno virreinal.* The author was Manuel Gustavo Antonio Revilla (b. 1863). A second edition was published at Mexico City in 1923.

The most extensive work on Mexican history in this century is that by Niceto de Zamacois (d. 1886) entitled *Historia de Méjico desde sus tiempos más remotos hasta nuestros días.* It appeared in twenty-two volumes in twenty-three at Mexico City between the years 1876 and 1902 and is based upon considerable research.

The largest work in English dealing with Mexico published in this century is *The history of Mexico* (Volumes IX-XIV of his *Works)* by Hubert Howe Bancroft (1832-1918). This appeared at San Francisco between 1883 and 1888 in six volumes. His *History of the north Mexican states and Texas* (Volumes XV and XVI of his *Works)* was published at the same place in two volumes between 1886 and 1889, while his *History of California* (Volumes XVIII-XXIV of his *Works)* was published in seven volumes at San Francisco from 1884 to 1890.

One of the most valuable of nineteenth century works concerning Mexico is that edited by Vicente Riva Palacio (1832-1896) under the title *México á través de los siglos*. It was published at Mexico City in five volumes between 1887 and 1889. In this treatise all phases of Mexican history and civilization are covered from the earliest times to the date of publication.

Central America (Guatemala)

Histories of Central America, frequently referred to as "Guatemala" in colonial days and occasionally in the early nineteenth century, are very numerous. In English, Hubert Howe Bancroft's *History of Central America* was for a long time considered a standard treatise. It was published in three volumes at San Francisco between 1882 and 1887, being Volumes VI-VIII of his *Works*.

In Spanish one of the best and most comprehensive works is the seven-volume *Reseña histórica de Centro-América* written by Lorenzo Montúfar y Rivera Maestre (b. 1823). It was published at Guatemala City between 1878 and 1888.

An earlier work is that by Francisco de Paula García Peláez (1785-1867) entitled *Memorias para la historia del antiguo reyno de Guatemala* published in three volumes at Guatemala City in 1851 and 1852. This history treats the region to the year 1821.

A work covering about the same period (from 1502 to 1821) is the *Historia de la América-Central* written by José Milla y Vidaurre (1827-1882), the first volume of which appeared at Guatemala City in 1879.

A work dealing with a portion of Central America in the colonial period and one which contains the text of many historical documents from the Archives of the Indies is entitled *Costa Rica, Nicaragua y Panamá en el siglo XVI*. It was edited by Manuel María de Peralta (b. 1844) and was published at Madrid in 1883.

One of the earliest works of this century dealing with Central America is entitled *Compendio de la historia de la ciudad de Guatemala* which, however, covers more of the history of Central America than is indicated by the title. It was written by Domingo Juarros (1752-1820) and was published at Guatemala City in two volumes between 1808 and 1818. An abridged English translation appeared at London in 1823 under the title *A statistical and commercial history of the kingdom of Guatemala*.

A more recent work in Spanish is the *Compendio de historia de la América Central* by Agustín Gómez Carrillo (b. 1842) which was published at Madrid in 1892.

Two Spanish works dealing with the independence period in Central

America should be mentioned. The first is the *Memorias para la historia de la revolución de Centro-América* by Manuel Montúfar which was published at Jalapa in 1832; and the second is the *Bosquejo histórico de las revoluciones de Centro-América* by Alejandro Marure (1809-1851) published at Guatemala City in two volumes in 1837. This latter work deals specifically with the critical period from 1811 to 1834.

Honduras

A work in two volumes dealing with Honduras was published at Tegucigalpa in 1882 and 1883 under the title *Compendio de la historia social y política de Honduras.* The work was by Antonio R. Vallejo and was intended as a text for colleges and secondary schools.

An earlier work is by Ephraim George Squier entitled briefly *Honduras* published at London in 1870. This volume is in reality a revised edition of the author's *States of Central America* (New York, 1858) which in turn had been based upon his *Notes on Central America* (New York, 1855).

Nicaragua

At Managua in Nicaragua in 1889 appeared the *Historia de Nicaragua* by José Dolores Gámez (b. 1851). This is a comprehensive treatment of the story of the country from the earliest period to 1860 and gives at the same time the country's relations with Mexico, Central America, and Spain. A fair English volume covering a wide variety of subjects but ineffectually written is entitled *Nicaragua.* The author was Peter F. Stout and the book appeared at Philadelphia in 1859. A much better English work is *Nicaragua,* etc., by Ephraim George Squier, published at New York in 1852.

Costa Rica

In Costa Rica Francisco Montero Barrantes (b. 1864) brought out in two volumes at San José (1892-94) his *Elementos de historia de Costa Rica* dealing with the period from 1502 to 1890. A volume by León Fernández (1840-1887) treating the history of Costa Rica from 1502 to 1821 is entitled *Historia de Costa Rica* (Madrid, 1889). This book was written while the author was compiling his *Colección de documentos para la historia de Costa Rica* (10 vols., San José, 1881-1907).

West Indies

Among the general works dealing with the West Indies in this century the following should be mentioned. In 1808 the three-volume *His-*

tory of the West Indies by Thomas Coke (1747-1814) was published at Liverpool dealing largely with missionaries and Methodist missions in each of the islands. In 1827 Thomas Southey's *Chronological history of the West Indies* was published at London in three volumes. Ten years later (1837) at London appeared *The West Indies* by Sir Andrew Halliday (1781-1839) which is of greater value than its size would indicate. In 1847 and 1848 Adrien Dessales published at Paris his five-volume *Histoire générale des Antilles*. In 1880 a volume entitled *The West Indies* by Charles H. Eden (1839-1900), was published at London.

Cuba

Several works dealing with Cuba should be mentioned. In 1826 at Paris appeared as a separate publication the two-volume *Essai politique sur l'île de Cuba* by Alexander von Humboldt. An English edition, with omissions, was published at New York and London in 1856. In 1838 there appeared also at Paris an elaborate work entitled *Histoire physique, politique et naturelle de l'île de Cuba* in two volumes and an atlas. The work, although coöperative, was largely the production of Ramón de la Sagra (1798-1871).

In 1842 Jacobo de la Pezuela y Lobo (1811-1882) published at New York City his *Ensayo histórico de la isla de Cuba* which was followed between 1863 and 1866 at Madrid by his *Diccionario geográfico, estadístico, histórico de la isla de Cuba,* and between 1868 and 1878 by his four-volume *Historia de la isla de Cuba* published at Madrid and New York simultaneously.

During 1865 and 1866 at New York appeared in two volumes the *Historia de la isla de Cuba* by Pedro José Guiteras (1814-1890). A second edition was printed at Havana in three volumes in 1927 and 1928.

In 1876 and 1887 the first two volumes of the *Naturaleza y civilización de la grandiosa isla de Cuba* were published at Madrid which covered the story to the year 1602. The author, Miguel Rodríguez Ferrer (1815-1889), left two further volumes unfinished when he died.

From 1895 to 1898 Antonio Pirala y Criado (1824-1903) published at Madrid his three-volume *Anales de la guerra de Cuba* which dealt with the Ten Years War (1868-1878). In 1896 at Chicago Murat Halstead (1829-1908) brought out his *Story of Cuba* which was concerned mainly with the struggle for liberty against Spain, and in 1899 James Morton Callahan (b. 1864) published at Baltimore his carefully written *Cuba and international relations.*

Haiti and Santo Domingo

Because of local disturbed conditions in the island of Haiti or Santo Domingo, many writers turned their attention to this region. In 1801 Bryan Edwards and Sir William Young (1749-1815) published *An historical survey of Saint Domingo* at London. Four years later appeared at the same place *An historical account of the black empire of Hayti* by Marcus Rainsford. This work dealt with Haiti under France to the year 1804.

In 1826 at Paris appeared the *Histoire politique et statistique de l'île d'Hayti* by a person using the pseudonym Placido Justin (b. 1777). The same year and the following was published in three volumes at Dresden the *Geschichte des freistaats von St. Domingo* by Karl Ferdinand Philippi. In 1837 Jonathan Brown published in two volumes at Philadelphia his delightful *History and present condition of St. Domingo*.

In 1846 at Paris was printed in two volumes Romuald Le Pelletier de Saint-Remy's (1809-1882) *Saint Dominique, étude et solution nouvelle de la question haitienne*. In the following two years (1847-48) there appeared at Port-au-Prince Thomas Madiou's *Histoire d'Haiti* in three volumes dealing with the story of the island from 1492 to 1807. A second edition of this work was published at Port-au-Prince in three volumes in 1922 and 1923. In 1853 at Havana appeared the first volume (600 pages) of the *Historia de Santo Domingo desde su descubrimiento hasta neustras días* by Antonio del Monte y Tejada. Between 1853 and 1858 appeared at Paris the eight-volume illustrated *Étude sur l'histoire d'Haiti* by B. Ardouin (1796-1865).

In 1867 or 1869 at Santo Domingo City appeared José Gabriel García's (1834-1910) *Compendio de la historia de Santo Domingo* which carried the story of the island to 1865. In 1873 Samuel Hazard's (1834-1876) *Santo Domingo past and present, with a glance at Hayti* was published simultaneously at New York and London. In 1884 a popular volume entitled *Hayti or the black republic* was published at London, the author being Sir Spencer Buckingham St. John (1825-1910). Two years later the book was translated into French and published at Paris. In 1884 also appeared at Madrid a detailed two-volume study entitled *Anexión y guerra de Santo Domingo* by José de la Gándara y Navarro (1820-1885). Two years later Jacques Nicolas Léger (b. 1859), one of the foremost Haitian writers, published at Paris his *La politique extérieure d'Haiti*. In 1899 there appeared at Paris the *Histoire mili-*

taire de la révolution de Saint Dominique by Isidore Henry de Poyen-Bellisle (b. 1839).

Puerto Rico

A comprehensive work dealing with Puerto Rico was published at London in 1834 under the title briefly cited *An account of the present state of the island of Puerto Rico.* The author was George Dawson Flinter (d. 1839).

Colombia

Works dealing with Colombia are both numerous and valuable. In 1822 there was printed at London a two-volume work by Alexander Walker entitled *Colombia, being a geographical, statistical, agricultural commerical, and political account of that country.* At the same time the work was indifferently translated into Spanish in two volumes and also published at London. Three years later, in 1825, Francis Hall (d. 1833) brought out his popular *Colombia: its present state . . .,* at London. A second edition appeared two years later.

In 1827 at Paris appeared in two volumes and an atlas the monumental *Historia de la revolución de la república de Colombia* by José Manuel Restrepo (1781-1863). The next year Ernst Münch published at Dresden in two volumes his *Die geschichte von Colombia.*

In 1848 appeared at Paris Joaquín Acosta's (1799-1852) *Compendio histórico* which dealt with the discovery and colonization of New Granada in the sixteenth century. A second edition did not appear until 1901 at Bogotá.

In 1869 at Bogotá was published the three-volume *Historia eclesiástica y civil de Nueva Granada* by José Manuel Groot (1800-1878). A second edition in five volumes appeared at Bogotá between 1889 and 1893.

In 1872 at Poissy appeared the two-volume *Historia de la Compañia de Jesús en la Nueva Granada* by José Joaquín Borda (1835-1878).

In 1882 at Barranquilla appeared the first 225 pages of the *Historia de Colombia* by Carlos Benedetti. A second and complete edition was published in 1887 at Lima. In 1883 at Bogotá a work of considerable value to historians by Soledad Acosta de Samper appeared, entitled *Biografías de hombres ilustres o notables de la época del descubrimiento é colonización de Colombia.* During the next two years (1884-85) there appeared in a third edition at Bogotá the three-volume *Leyendas históricas* by Luís Capella Toledo. The date of the first edition is unknown.

In 1896 and 1898 appeared at Valladolid the three-volume history of *La Compañia de Jesús en Colombia y Centro-América después de su restauración* written by Rafael Pérez (1842-1901). The next year, in 1899, at Santiago, Chile, José Toribio Medina published his *Historia del tribunal del santo oficio de la inquisición de Cartagena de las indias* which constitutes a companion volume to his work dealing with the same subject in Peru.

Venezuela

Of the works dealing with Venezuela the following may be noted. In 1806 at Paris appeared three volumes briefly entitled *Voyage à la partie oriental de la terre-ferme* by François Raymond Joseph de Pons (1751-1812), often incorrectly spelled Deponds. The author spent the years 1801 to 1804 in the territory and gives the history of the country in connection with his observations. An English edition in two volumes appeared at London in 1807, and an excellent Spanish edition was published at Caracas in 1930.

In 1841 the three-volume *Resumen de la historia de Venezuela* of Rafael María Baralt (1810-1860) and Ramón Diaz was published at Paris in two sections, the first in one volume covering the period to 1797 and the second section in two volumes covering the period from 1797 to 1837. In 1887 at Curaçao appeared a new three-volume edition of this work.

In 1875 at Paris was printed a volume by Miguel Tojera (b. 1848) entitled *Compendio de la historia de Venezuela* covering the subject to about 1870. This was followed by two volumes (Paris, 1875-78) entitled *Venezuela pintoresca é ilustrada* dealing with the same period.

During 1890 and 1891 Arístides Rojas (1826-1894) brought out at Caracas his *Historia patria. Leyendas históricas de Venezuela* in two volumes. In 1891 appeared at the same place his *Estudios históricos* dealing with the origins of the country.

One of the best works on military history in the early national period is the *Bosquejo de la historia militar de Venezuela en la guerra de su independencia,* the first volume of which was published at Valencia in 1857.

Ecuador

In Ecuador Pedro Fermín Ceballos (b. 1814) brought out in five volumes his *Resumen de la historia del Ecuador* in 1870. The work was published at Lima, and covered the history of the country from the earliest times to 1845. The author intended to issue a sixth volume but because of errors it was suspended and did not appear until 1888 at Lima and then with the title *Geografía de la república del Ecuador.*

In 1881 at Quito appeared the brief *Historia eclesiástica del Ecuador* by Archbishop Federico González Suárez (1844-1917) covering the period from 1520 to 1600.

Peru

Among the writings in this century on Peru is the classic *History of the conquest of Peru* by William Hickling Prescott, published in two volumes at New York and Paris in 1847 and in many other editions subsequently.

In 1858 José de la Riva Agüero (1783-1858) under the pseudonym of P. Pruvonena published his important explanatory *Memorias y documentos para la historia de la independencia del Perú* in two volumes at Paris.

At Lima in 1863 Ricardo Palma (1833-1919) published his classic volume entitled *Anales de la inquisición de Lima*. Among his other productions should be mentioned his *Perú. Tradiciones* first published at Lima in two volumes in 1875-77, and followed by a second edition in six volumes in 1883.

Between 1868 and 1874 at Lima appeared the three-volume *Historia del Perú independiente, 1822-1827* by Mariano Felipe Paz Soldán (1821-1886). This work was reprinted at Lima in two volumes in 1919. In 1929 a new three-volume edition was published at the same place with additions to the year 1833.

In 1874 at Lima was published the brief secondary textbook entitled *Historia del Perú* written by Agustín de la Rosa Toro. In the same year at Lima appeared the first volume of the indispensable *Diccionario histórico-biográfico del Perú* by Manuel de Mendiburu (1805-1885). This was completed in eight volumes, the last being published at Lima in 1890. In 1931 the first volume of a new edition of the work appeared at Madrid also to be completed in eight volumes. In 1874, also, appeared at Lima the first of six volumes (1874-1911) entitled *El Perú* which constituted an historical geography of that country. The author was Antonio Raimondi (1826-1890), a widely known Peruvian geologist.

In 1879 and 1880 at Caracas appeared the nine-volume *Memorias* of General Florencio O'Leary (b. 1801), volumes XXVII and XXVIII of which bear the title *Bolívar y la emancipación de Sur-América*. These volumes were republished at Madrid in 1915. The first volume covers the period from 1783 to 1819 while the second treats the years 1819 to 1826.

In 1886 Ricardo Cappa published at Lima his secondary text entitled *Historia compendiada del Perú* in two volumes. The next year at Santiago José Toribio Medina brought out his scholarly two-volume *Historia del tribunal del santo oficio de la inquisición de Lima* which deals with the subject between the years 1569 and 1820.

In 1894 at Lima appeared the brief but valuable *Estado social del Perú durante la dominación española* written by Javier Prado y Ugarteche (b. 1871). Three years later at Madrid was published the brilliant two-volume *Bolívar en el Perú* by Gonzalo Bulnes (b. 1851) which dealt with the Liberator's last campaigns in that country. This work had been preceded by his two-volume *Historia de la expedición libertadora del Perú* (Santiago, 1887-88) which covered the years 1817 to 1822. In 1899 appeared at Lima the *Resumen de historia del Perú* by Carlos Wiesse (b. 1859) which has come to be considered the best general secondary textbook published in Peru.

The best general work in English on Peruvian history is by Sir Clements Markham entitled *A history of Peru* published at Chicago in 1892.

One of the leading historians of Peru in this century was Sebastián Lorente (d. 1884). Among his writings are the *Historia antigua del Perú* (Lima, 1860), the *Historia de la conquista del Perú* (Lima, 1861), the *Historia del Perú bajo la dinastía austriaca, 1542-1598* (Lima, 1863), the *Historia del Perú* (Lima, 1866), and the *Historia del Perú bajo los Borbones, 1700-1821* (Lima, 1871).

Bolivia

Among works dealing with Bolivia written in this century two may be noted. In 1896 appeared the *Compendio de historia de Bolivia* by José María Carnacho, and in this and the two following years Gabriel René Moreno (1834-1908) published at Santiago, Chile, his *Últimos días coloniales en el Alto-Perú* (two volumes in one).

Paraguay

Of the works about Paraguay in this century one of the earliest is that published at Paris in 1809 in four volumes and an atlas under the title *Voyages dans l'Amérique méridional* by Félix de Azara (1746-1821). This work, which dealt chiefly with the natural history of the whole La Plata region, had been enlarged by other writers from the previous editions of 1801 (2 vols., Paris), 1802 (2 vols., Madrid), and 1805 (3 vols., Madrid).

In 1827 at Paris appeared another French work of some importance by Johann Rudolph Rengger (1795-1832) and R. de Longchamp under the title *Essai historique sur la révolution du Paraguay*. The volume deals at considerable length with the dictator Francia. An English edition appeared at London the same year as the French. Still another French volume appeared at Marseilles in 1867 under the title *Le Paraguay moderne* dealing with the history and geography of the country and containing considerable statistical information. The author was Benjamin Poncel (1807-1872). A fourth French work is entitled *Le Paraguay*. It was written by A. P. F. Lambel (1814-ca. 1900) and it appeared at Tours in 1878. A fifth work written by a Frenchman, who became a Brazilian citizen, bore the title *Historia da republica jesuitica do Paraguay*. The author was João Pedro Gay (b. 1815), and his study appeared in book form in 1881 at Rio de Janeiro, after being published serially. A sixth work originally written in French by E. de Bourgade La Dardye (b. 1854) is entitled *Le Paraguay*. It was published at Paris in 1889. In 1892 it was translated into English and published at London under the title *Paraguay, the land, and the people*, etc.

An important work in Spanish which bears the title *Historia de los gobernantes del Paraguay* was published at Buenos Aires in 1887. The author was Antonio Zinny (1821-1890) and his volume deals with the history of the country from 1535 to 1887.

A work in English of value for the historian is in two volumes, written by Charles A. Washburn (1822-1889), and published at Boston in 1871 under the title *The history of Paraguay*. It is based upon studies, personal observations, and reminiscences of the author's diplomatic activities and is somewhat biased.

Argentina

Argentine history was the subject of numerous treatises in the nineteenth century. One of the earliest was published in three volumes at Buenos Aires in 1816 under the title *Ensayo de la historia civil del Paraguay, Buenos Aires y Tucumán*. The author was Gregorio Fúnes (1749-1830). A second edition of this work appeared at Buenos Aires in two volumes in 1856.

A still earlier work, but considerably shorter, is that by Samuel Hull Wilcocke entitled the *History of the viceroyalty of Buenos Aires* (London, 1807) which was written while the English held the city. The subject matter covered is varied and comprehensive, and the author considers the region a British colony.

In 1825 at London appeared in both Spanish and English editions Ignacio Benito Núñez's (1792-1846) *Noticias históricas* dealing with the United Provinces of the Río de la Plata. This work was published in the form of a letter of 323 pages which aimed to inform the British ministry of the Brazilian usurpation of Uruguay.

In 1839 appeared at London the first edition of Sir Woodbine Parish's (1792-1882) *Buenos Aires and the provinces of the Río de la Plata*. Since the author was an explorer his account contains much geographical and anthropological information.

In 1861 at Buenos Aires appeared the *Historia argentina* by Luís L. Domínguez (b. 1810) which covered the period from 1492 to 1820.

Between 1879 and 1882 the *Historia de los gobernadores de las provincias argentinas* by Antonio Zinny was printed at Buenos Aires in three volumes. This covered the period from 1810 to 1881. In 1920 and 1921 the work was reissued in a revised edition of five volumes at Buenos Aires. The same author published at Buenos Aires in 1875 his valuable *Bibliografía histórica de las provincias unidas del Río de la Plata* which covered the period from 1780 to 1821.

From 1883 to 1893 at Buenos Aires appeared the *Historia de la república argentina* in ten volumes by Vicente Fidel López (1815-1903). Because of the author's death the work was never completed and the story ended with the year 1829. In 1896 the author's *Manual de la historia argentina* was published at Buenos Aires.

In 1887 appeared in a definitive edition (3 vols., Buenos Aires) Bartolomé Mitre's *Historia de Belgrano y de la independencia argentina*. In the two following years (1888 and 1889) the three-volume *Historia argentina* of Mariano A. Pelliza (1837-1902) was published at Buenos Aires.

In 1892 appeared at Buenos Aires the five-volume *Historia de la confederación argentina* by Adolfo Saldías (1850-1914). This is the second edition which had been revised and corrected and covers about the years 1817 to 1870. An entirely new edition of the work was published in nine volumes at Buenos Aires in 1929 and 1930. The original edition of the work had appeared at Paris in three volumes between 1881 and 1887 under the title *Historia de Rosas y su época*.

In 1899 at Buenos Aires Martín García Mérou (1862-1905) published his *Historia de la república argentina* in two volumes, the first of which carries the story to 1800. Shortly before this volume appeared Francisco Ramos Mejía (1847-1893) wrote his *Historia de la evolución argentina* which, however, was not published until after his death when the first volume appeared at Buenos Aires in 1921.

Uruguay

Of the histories of Uruguay several should be mentioned. In 1864 at Paris were published two volumes of the *Apuntes para la historia de la república oriental del Uruguay desde el año de 1810 hasta el de 1852* by Antonio Deodoro de Pascal. The work seems never to have been completed and the story was carried only to the year 1829.

In 1879 and 1880 appeared a work of considerable aid to historians with the title *Rasgos biográficos de hombres notables de la república oriental del Uruguay*. It was written by Isidoro De-Marie (1815-1906) and was published in three volumes at Montevideo.

In 1881 at the same place was published the *Bosquejo histórico de la república oriental del Uruguay* in its third revised edition, the first printing being at Montevideo in 1866. This covers the history of the region from the discovery to 1830. The author was Francisco A. Berra (b. 1844).

In 1886 Eliza J. M. Clemens published at Philadelphia *La Plata countries of South America*. Two years later at Montevideo appeared a volume entitled *Apuntes sobre la historia de la república oriental del Uruguay* by Julian O. Nuranda (b. 1854). Between 1912 and 1916 the work was published in two volumes as a textbook.

In 1892 at Montevideo was published Victor Arreguine's (1865-1924) *Historia del Uruguay*. Eight years later, in 1900, the short *Historia de la república oriental del Uruguay* by Pablo Blanco Acevedo was published at Montevideo.

Among the most important works dealing with this region is the three-volume *Historia de la dominación española en Uruguay* written by Francisco Bauzá (1851-1899) and published at Montevideo from 1880 to 1882. The first edition carries the story to the year 1817. A second edition of three volumes published at Montevideo between 1895 and 1897 continues the story to 1830. In 1929 a third edition was published at the same place.

Chile

Chile produced some of the most prolific historical writers of the nineteenth century. Among these are Benjamín Vicuña Mackenna (1831-1886), José Toribio Medina (1852-1931), Miguel Luís Amunátegui (1828-1888), and Diego Barros Arana (1830-1907).

Among the nineteenth century works of Vicuña Mackenna should be mentioned his *Historia jeneral de la república de Chile* (5 vols., Santiago, 1866-83, written in collaboration with others), *Chile: relaciones históricas* (2 vols., Santiago, 1877-78), *La guerra á muerte* (Santiago, 1868), *Chile: episodios marítimos* (Santiago, 1879), *Los orígenes de las familias chilenas* (Santiago, 1903), and numerous biographies, etc.

The chief historical writings of Medina in this century are his *Los aborígenes de Chile* (Santiago, 1882), *Cosas de la colonia* (2 vols., Santiago, 1889 and 1910), *Historia del tribunal del santo oficio de la inquisición en Chile* (2 vols., Santiago, 1890) which amplifies his similar work on the Inquisition in Lima published at Lima in two volumes in 1887, *Descubrimiento del Río de las Amazonas* (Sevilla, 1894) which was translated by Bertram T. Lee and published in English by the American Geographical Society at New York in 1934, *Juan Díaz de Solís* (2 vols., Santiago, 1897), and *Historia de la literatura colonial de Chile* (3 vols., Santiago, 1878).

In this century Amunátegui published his one-volume *Compendio de la historia política y eclesiástica de Chile* (Valparaiso, 1856), *La crónica de 1810* (3 vols., Santiago, 1876-99), *Los precursores de la independencia de Chile* (3 vols., Santiago, 1870-72), *La dictadura de O'Higgins* (Santiago, 1853), *Descubrimiento i conquista de Chile* (Santiago, 1862), *La reconquista española de Chile en 1814* (Santiago, 1851), *Ensayos biográficos* (4 vols., Santiago, 1893-96), etc.

The largest single historical work on Chile in the nineteenth century is that in sixteen volumes by Diego Barros Arana entitled *Historia jeneral de Chile* (Santiago, 1884-1902). This began to appear in a second edition at Santiago in 1930. The same author's *Historia jeneral de la independencia de Chile* (4 vols., Santiago, 1854-58) is also of great value.

A number of other important works of considerable value should be mentioned. In 1850 appeared at Valparaiso the three-volume *Historia eclesiástica, política y literaria de Chile* by José Ignacio Victor Eyzaguirre. A French edition of this work was published in three volumes at Lille in 1855.

During 1877 and 1878 there appeared at Valparaiso the three-volume *Historia general de el reyno de Chile* by Diego de Rosales.

In 1891 at Barcelona was printed the two-volume *Historia de la Compañía de Jesús en Chile* by Francisco Enrich (1817-1883). An earlier and even more important and extensive work upon religious activities in Chile is the *Storia della missioni apostoliche dello stato del Chile* published in four volumes at Rome in 1827. The author was Giuseppe Sallusti.

In 1893 a work on Chile appeared in English with the title *A history of Chile*. The author was Anson Uriel Hancock and the book was printed at Chicago.

In 1899 at Valparaiso Daniel Riquelme brought out his *Compendio de historia de Chile*. The next year was published the two-volume *Historia natural, militar, civil y sagrada del reino de Chile* at Santiago by José Pérez García which carried the account from the earliest times to about 1800. The work had been written almost a century before it appeared in print.

TWENTIETH CENTURY HISTORIES AND HISTORIANS DEALING WITH COLONIAL HISPANIC AMERICA

By A. Curtis Wilgus

I N THE twentieth century, and particularly after the first decade, an increased interest was centered in Hispanic America by the nations of the world and especially by the people of the United States. With this condition came an earnest attempt to understand and to interpret the colonial and recent history and civilization of these peoples both in popular works and in scholarly histories and school textbooks. The people of Hispanic America themselves became aware of their growing importance in world affairs and have in a comparatively short period of time produced many valuable historical treatises.

I. General Works

Among the general treatises written in this century in English are many volumes which can be, or have been, used as textbooks for students in the United States. The following may be cited as of some importance. In 1901 at New York were published Henry William Brown's (1858-1906) *Latin America,* which concerned religious affairs; the *South American republics* by W. L. Markwick (1848-1911) and W. A. Smith (b. 1866); and Julian Hawthorne's (b. 1846) *Spanish America.* In 1903-04 at New York appeared in two volumes the very helpful *South American republics* by Thomas C. Dawson (b. 1865). A most important work, published in 1904, is *Spain in America, 1450-1580,* by Edward Gaylord Bourne.

In 1912 C. R. Enock (b. 1868) published *The secret of the Pacific* at New York, which gave an account of the early civilizations of the area. This was followed by *The republics of Central and South America* (New York, 1913), and *Spanish America* (two volumes, London, 1920).

In 1912 W. H. Koebel (1872-1923) published at London his *South America,* which was followed by *The South Americans* (London, 1915). In 1913 at Cleveland, the somewhat fantastic yet thought-provoking *History of South America* by W. F. Griewe (b. 1852) was published. The year following, the valuable essay by W. R. Shepherd (1871-1934) entitled *Latin America* was printed at New York, and in 1921 his equally valuable and popularly written volume entitled *The Hispanic nations of the New World* was printed at New York.

In 1919 the first true college textbook was published at New York under the title *History of Latin America* (revised in 1929). The author was W. W. Sweet (b. 1881). This text was followed by a second in 1922 when W. S. Robertson (b. 1873) published at New York the first edition of his *History of the Latin American nations* as a text for colleges. The most recent edition, with some added material, appeared in 1932. In 1923 at New York appeared a college text entitled *The republics of Latin America* by H. G. James (b. 1887) and P. A. Martin (b. 1879). The next strictly college text did not appear until 1930, when Mary W. Williams (b. 1878) published at New York her volume entitled *Peoples and politics of Latin America*. The next text appeared in 1931 in a preliminary edition entitled *A history of Hispanic America* by A. Curtis Wilgus (b. 1897). This, unlike the previous volumes, was intended as a textbook handbook for college students. The most recent text is that by J. Fred Rippy (b. 1892) published at New York in 1932 under the title *Historical evolution of Hispanic America*. A supplement to these textbooks is *Readings in Hispanic American history* by N. Andrew N. Cleven (b. 1874), published at Boston in 1927.

In recent years a number of important works have appeared dealing with Hispanic America in general but at the same time treating special phases of its history and civilization.

In 1901 at London, Robert Gallnigad Bontine Cunninghame Graham (b. 1852) published *A vanished Arcadia* which treated the history of the Jesuits in Paraguay between the years 1607 and 1767. In the following years appeared his *Hernando de Soto* (London, 1903), *Bernal Díaz del Castillo* (New York and London, 1915), *The conquest of New Granada* (London, 1922), *The conquest of the River Plate* (New York, 1924), *Pedro de Valdivia, conqueror of Chile* (New York and London, 1927), and other volumes.

Between 1901 and 1905 appeared in two volumes at New York and London the scholarly and indispensable *Spanish settlements within the present limits of the United States* by Woodbury Lowery (1853-1906).

In 1902 Henry Vignaud (1830-1922) published his critical and careful study on *Toscanelli and Columbus* at London. The next year the work appeared at the same place in a new edition of two volumes in one, which contained many of the author's letters on the subject to Sir Clements Markham and C. Raymond Beasley.

In 1902-03 there appeared at Berlin in English Arthur Baessler's (1857-1907) *Ancient Peruvian art*. The German edition was published the same year at Leipzig.

In 1907 Lewis Spence (b. 1874) brought out the first of a series of volumes dealing with early native cultures and civilizations. In that year appeared at London his *Mythologies of Mexico and Peru*. This was followed by *The Popol Vuh* (London, 1908), *Civilizations of ancient Mexico* (New York, 1912), *Myths of the North American Indians* (London, 1914), *The Gods of Mexico* (London, 1922), *The magic and mysteries of Mexico* (London and Philadelphia, 1930), and many other books.

In 1908 Bernard Moses (1846-1930) published at New York his *South America on the eve of emancipation*. This work had been preceded in 1898 by *The establishment of Spanish rule in America*. In 1914 he brought out at New York the two volumes entitled *The Spanish dependencies in South America*, which were followed in 1919 at Berkeley by *Spain's declining power in America*, in 1922 at New York by *Spanish colonial literature in South America*, in 1926 at New York by *The intellectual background of the revolutions in South America*, and in 1929 at New York by his *Spain overseas*. These volumes are extremely useful and are so well done that their author won a reputation as a leading authority in the field.

In 1908 H. C. Lea (1825-1909) published his classic work entitled *The inquisition in the Spanish dependencies* at New York as part of his general history of the Inquisition.

In 1910 at London Sir Clements Markham published his scholarly volume entitled *The Incas of Peru* which was followed two years later at the same place by his *Conquest of New Granada*. Also in 1910 C. H. Haring (b. 1885) brought out at London and New York *The buccaneers in the West Indies in the XVII century*. This was followed by an even more valuable book based upon scholarly research entitled *Trade and navigation between Spain and the indies in the time of the Hapsburgs* (Cambridge, Mass., 1918).

In 1912 at New York was published the first of several careful treatises on American archaeology by Thomas A. Joyce (b. 1878) entitled *South American archaeology*. In 1914 at London appeared his *Mexican archaeology*, and in 1916 at London was published his *Central American and West Indian archaeology*.

In 1913 Francisco García Calderón (b. 1883) published at London and New York his thought-provoking essay entitled *Latin America, its rise and progress.* In 1914 a well-written work dealing with the Norse discoveries of America was published at New York. It bore the title *The voyages of the Norsemen to America* and contained eighty-three illustrations and seven maps. The author was George William Hovgaard (b. 1857). Two years later Alfred Coester (b. 1874) published the first edition of his invaluable *Literary history of Spanish America* at New York. It was translated into Spanish and published at Madrid in 1929.

In 1915 Professor H. E. Bolton, one of the leading scholars in the field of Hispanic American history in the United States, published at Berkeley his *Texas in the middle eighteenth century.* This dealt with the Spanish colonial administration in the region. The next year at New York he brought out a volume entitled *Spanish explorations in the southwest, 1542-1706.* In 1921 appeared *The Spanish borderlands* (New Haven) which dealt with the Spaniards in Florida and the southwest. Many other volumes of a more special character have since come from his facile and scholarly pen.

In 1922 at New York and London Clark Wissler (b. 1870) published his valuable and indispensable volume on *The American Indian.*

In 1926 appeared Miss Lillian Fisher's (b. 1891) *Viceregal administration in the Spanish American colonies* at Berkeley, and in 1929 appeared at the same place *The intendant system in Spanish America.* A more localized volume by the same author is *The background of the revolution for Mexican independence* (Boston, 1934).

Also in 1926 a specialized treatise in English entitled *The economic geography of South America* by R. H. Whitbeck (b. 1871), was published at New York which treated the geographical and economic aspects of history. A somewhat similar volume by an Englishman, E. W. Shanahan (b. 1882), entitled *South America. An economic and regional geography with an historical chapter* was published at New York in 1927. Three years later Clarence F. Jones (b. 1893) brought out at New York his valuable work entitled *South America,* showing the interrelations of history and geography. In 1928 Alfred Hasbrouck brought out through the Columbia University Press his misentitled *Foreign legionaries in the liberation of Spanish South America,* written as a doctoral dissertation.

In 1930 at London the Hakluyt Society (Volume LXV, second series) published the first of four contemplated volumes by Cecil Jane (1879-1932) entitled *Select documents illustrating the four voyages of Columbus* which contained a brilliant introductory essay concerning the historical setting of the voyages and the psychological make-up of the discoverer. This work had been preceded by the brief and thought-provoking *Liberty and despotism in Spanish America* (Oxford, 1929).

In 1931 appeared at New York and London a highly specialized and scholarly volume by Philip Ainsworth Means entitled *Ancient civilizations of the Andes.*

A book long needed concerning Portuguese explorations appeared in 1933 under the title *The Portuguese pioneers.* It was written by Edgar Prestage (b. 1869) and was published at London as part of *The pioneer histories* edited by V. T. Harlow (b. 1898) and F. A. Williamson. Three other volumes in this series of outstanding importance for the student of Hispanic America are *The explorers of North America, 1492-1806,* by J. B. Brebner (b. 1895), New York, 1933; *The Spanish conquistadores* by F. A. Kirkpatrick (b. 1861), London, 1934; and *The European nations in the West Indies, 1493-1688* (London, 1933) by Arthur Percival Newton (b. 1873).

A highly important work of a specialized nature appeared during 1934 under the title *Church and state in Latin America.* The author was J. Lloyd Mecham (b. 1893) of the University of Texas, and the book was published at Chapel Hill. During this year also were published the following books of value to the historian of Latin American life and civilization: *Education in Latin America* (New York) by Henry Lester Smith (b. 1876) and Harold Littell; *Latin American music past and present* (Santa Ana, California) by Eleanor Hague; *Ores and industry in South America* (New York) by H. Foster Bain (b. 1872) and Thomas T. Read (b. 1880); and *American treasure and the price revolution in Spain, 1501 to 1650* (Cambridge, Massachusetts) by Earl Jefferson Hamilton (b. 1899).

Two extensive general works dealing with the Spanish American colonies and with the mother country appeared in this century. The first was published at Barcelona before 1920 (the date is not known) in twenty-five volumes under the title of *Historia de España y de las repúblicas latinoamericanas.* The author was Alfredo Opisso (b. 1847). The second work is by R. B. Merriman (b. 1876) and is entitled *The rise of the Spanish empire in the old world and the new* (4 vols., New York, 1918-34).

Among the general works in languages other than English which deal with Hispanic America are many of considerable value. Doubtless the best known is that by the Mexican historian, Carlos Pereyra (b. 1871), entitled *Historia de América española*, published at Madrid in eight volumes between 1920 and 1926.

From 1902 to 1923 at Berlin appeared Eduard Seler's (1849-1922) great work entitled *Gesammelte abhandlungen zur amerikanischen sprach und alterthumskunde* which constitutes an exhaustive treatment of Mexican and Maya life and speech with some discussion of the Incas. Many other important works have come from the pen of this great scholar.

In 1908 at Santiago, Chile, José Toribio Medina brought out in two volumes his *El veneciano Sebastián Caboto* which sketches the lives of the explorer and his companions and reproduces many important documents. In the same year appeared at Santiago his *Algunas noticias de León Pancaldo,* who attempted to reach Peru by way of the Strait of Magellan, *El portugués Esteban Gómez al servicio de España,* and *Los viajes de Diego García de Moguer al Río de la Plata.* Among his other important works of an historical nature are *El descubrimiento del océano pacífico* (four volumes, Santiago, 1913-20); *La primitiva inquisición americana* (two volumes, Santiago, 1914); *El piloto Juan Fernández* (Santiago, 1918); *Bartolomé Ruíz de Andrada, primer piloto del mar del sur* (Santiago, 1919); and the innumerable and invaluable histories of the press and printing in various part of Hispanic America.

Between 1908 and 1916 there was published at Santiago, Chile, the sixteen-volume *Obras completas* of the revered historian, Diego Barros Arana, who died in 1907. These volumes contained his historical writings.

Between 1910 and 1913 at Buenos Aires Carlos Navarro y Lamarca's *Compendio de la historia general de América* was published in two profusely illustrated volumes. In 1912 there appeared the first of seven volumes at Madrid entitled *Historia de la Compañía de Jesús de la asistencia de España* by Antonio Astraín (b. 1857). The last volume was published in 1925. The whole work contains much valuable information about the Jesuits in America.

In 1917 Juan Ortega y Rubio (b. 1845) brought out at Madrid his illustrated *Historia de América* in three volumes giving the history from the earliest times to the present.

During 1918 to 1920 at Buenos Aires was published the *Historia diplomática latino-americana* in three volumes by Vicente Gaspar Quesada (1830-1913). This work had been preceded by other volumes of historical importance, notably his *La vida intelectual en la América española durante los siglos XVI, XVII y XVIII* (Buenos Aires, 1910), the *Derecho público eclesiástico* (Buenos Aires, 1910), the *Historia colonial argentina* (Buenos Aires, 1915), etc.

In 1927 appeared at Buenos Aires in two volumes the *Nacimiento de las repúblicas americanas* by the prolific historical writer, Gonzalo Bulnes, whose *Bolívar en el Perú* (two volumes, Madrid, 1919) and his works on the War of the Pacific had won him international fame. Two years later at Paris, Jean Toussaint Bertrand brought out his two-volume *Histoire de l'Amérique espagnole* which traced the history of Hispanic America from the earliest times.

Two geographical works valuable for the historian appeared at Paris in the important collection, *Géographie universelle,* edited by Paul Vidal de la Blache (1845-1918) and L. Gallois. The first work bore the title *Amérique du Sud* and was published at Paris, two volumes in one, as Volume XV of the series. The author was Pierre Denis. The second work was entitled *Mexique: Amérique centrale* and was Volume XIV of the series (Paris, 1928). The author was Maximilien Sorre.

Among the shorter works of a general nature the following should be cited. In 1911 Ernst Robert Daenell (b. 1872) published in Munich and Berlin a volume entitled *Die Spanier in Nordamerika von 1513-1824.* In 1912 at Madrid appeared Rafael María de Labra y Cadrana's (1843-1919) *España y América 1812-1912* tracing international and constitutional relations between the two regions. This work was followed at Madrid in the same year by his *América y la constitución española de 1812.* Also in 1912 at Paris Carlos A. Villanueva (b. 1865) brought out his two-volume *La monarquía en América* which dealt with Bolívar and San Martín, and the relations between Ferdinand VII and the new states. The next year at Paris appeared his one-volume *Résumen de la historia general de América.* In 1912 at Berlin and Leipzig there appeared the first volume of the *Geschichte Sudamerika* by Hermann A. L. Lufft (b. 1880). In 1913 Francisco García Calderón published at Paris *La creación de un continente* dealing with Pan Americanism, Iberianism, and society in Hispanic America.

In 1917 there appeared at Barcelona the comprehensive but diffuse *Historia del comercio con las indias durante el dominio de los Austrias* by Gervasio de Artiñano y de Galdácano. This work was followed in 1920 at Madrid by his *La arquitectura naval española.*

In 1920 at Madrid was published a scholarly and documentary two-volume work, valuable for an account of the discovery and exploration of the Straits of Magellan, by the Jesuit Pablo Pastells (b. 1846) under the title *El descubrimiento del Estrecho de Magallanes.*

In 1922 Rufino Blanco-Fombona (b. 1874) brought out at Madrid his interpretive essay entitled *El conquistador español del siglo XVI.* This had been preceded by numerous other works of a literary and historical nature.

In 1926 José R. del Franco published at Madrid his excellent *Nociones de geografía é historia de América* which deals with the whole continent and which contains much valuable material for historians. The next year Pedro Aguado Bleye (b. 1884) brought out at Bilbao his *Manual de historia de América* which appeared in a third enlarged edition two years later at the same place. In 1927 *El nacimiento de la América española* appeared at Tucumán. The author was Juan Bautista Terán (b. 1880). A French edition appeared at Paris in 1930 and an Italian edition was published at Bari in 1931. The book deals with Spanish America to 1600.

In 1928 a German work entitled *Deutschland und Amerika* appeared at München. The author was Karl Heinrich Panhorst, and his book dealt with Germans in America before 1600 and particularly with the Fuggers and the Welsers.

In 1929 at Madrid Enrique de Gandía brought out his interesting one-volume work on the *Historia crítica de los mitos de la conquista americana.* In the same year at Madrid also appeared the comprehensive summary entitled *Compendio de geografía, historia y constituciones de América* by Francisco de Arce, while in the same year at Zaragoza appeared the brief essay on *España en América* by Juan Fernández Amador de los Ríos.

The year following at Madrid Carlos Pereyra published his one-volume *Breve historia de América.*

In 1931 at Madrid was published the *Historia de España en América* by the Ecuadorian Nicolás Espinosa Cordero (b. 1902) which dealt with the pre-Columbian and colonial periods. Also in 1931 Adolf Rein (b. 1885) brought out an excellent comprehensive essay on geographical discoveries, colonization, and world politics which treats the Spanish colonial system. The book bears the title *Die europäische ausbreitung über die erde* and contains 262 text illustrations and twenty-two plates. It was published at Potsdam.

The next year at Leipzig the geographer, Oscar Schmieder (b. 1891), published an historical geography describing the evolution of South American areas under the title *Länderkunde Südamerikas.*

II. Special Works

Brazil

Several important works dealing with Brazil should be cited. The most extensive treatise was published in ten volumes at Rio de Janeiro in 1905 under the title *Historia do Brasil*. The author was José Francisco da Rocha Pombo (b. 1857) and his work is indispensable to the student of Brazilian history. Another work with the same title *Historia do Brasil*, appeared in five volumes at São Paulo between 1910 and 1913. The author was Raphael Maria Galanti.

A work of value to all writers on Brazil is the four-volume *Livro do centenario, 1500-1900*, published at Rio de Janeiro from 1900 to 1902 by the Association for the Fourth Centenary of the Discovery of Brazil. This contains contributions from many leading Brazilian scholars.

One of the most widely known of Brazilian historians was Manoel de Oliveira Lima (1865-1928) who in 1901 at Rio de Janeiro published his *Historia diplomatica do Brasil*. Two of his brief but important works consist of published lectures. In 1911 he published at Paris a series of lectures delivered at the Sorbonne under the title *Formation historique de la nationalité brésilienne*. This was reprinted in Spanish and published at Madrid in 1918. In 1914 a series of lectures delivered at Stanford University was printed by the University under the title *The evolution of Brazil compared with Spanish and Anglo-Saxon America*. This was also translated into Spanish and published at Madrid in 1919. A larger work of great value is *Dom João no Brasil, 1808-1821* (two volumes, Rio de Janeiro, 1908). A briefer study is his *O movimento da independencia, 1821-1822* (São Paulo, 1922).

In 1904 appeared at Rio de Janeiro an important treatise entitled *Religiões acatholicas no Brasil, 1500-1900* by José Carlos Rodrigues (1844-1922).

In 1906 there appeared at Rio de Janeiro the first volume of the *Historia territorial do Brasil* written by Felisbello Firmo de Oliveiro Freire. The next year the first volume of his *Os Portuguezes no Brasil* was printed at the same place. In 1912 José Manoel Cardoso de Oliveira brought out at Rio de Janeiro a two-volume work which he edited entitled *Actos diplomaticos do Brasil*. . . . In 1914 at Bogotá in Colombia appeared *El Brazil á través de su historia* by Gustavo Arboleda (b. 1881).

In 1921 was published at Porto the first volume of the monumental *Historia da colonização portuguesa do Brasil*, compiled under the direction of Carlos Malheiro Dias. The third volume appeared in 1923 at the same place. Also in 1921 was published at Rio de Janeiro the widely used school history of Brazil by Mario da Veiga Cabral, entitled *Compendio de historia do Brasil.*

The history of music in Brazil is told in Italian in the excellent work entitled *Storia della musica nel Brasile . . .* by Vincenzo Cernicchiaro. It was published in 1923 at Milan.

In 1930 João Pandiá Calogeras (1870-1934) brought out at Rio de Janeiro his *Formação historica do Brasil,* first published as a series of lectures the previous year. In the same year and at the same place was published *O Brasil na America* by Manoel José do Bomfim (b. 1868) which dealt with the foundation of Brazil, and *O descobrimento do Brasil* by João Capistrano de Abreu, one of the leading Brazilian historians. Both of these men have written numerous other works on Brazilian history. Also in 1929 appeared at São Paulo the interesting *Historias que não vêm na historia* by F. Assis Cintra. This had been preceded by his *D. Pedro I e o grito da independencia* (São Paulo, 1921) and *Tiradentes perante a historia* (São Paulo, 1922).

In 1931 at Barcelona appeared an excellent historical summary by Gonzalo de Reparaz (b. 1860), entitled *La época de los grandes descubrimientos españoles y portugueses,* while in the same year at Rio de Janeiro, Jonathas Serrano (b. 1885) brought out his valuable illustrated one-volume *Historia do Brasil* as a textbook for secondary schools.

In 1932 at Rio de Janeiro appeared the important and profusely illustrated *O Rio de Janeiro no tempo dos vice-reis, 1763-1808,* by Luís Edmundo.

In 1933 Max Fleiuss brought out at Rio de Janeiro his *Apostilas de historia do Brasil* as a special volume published by the Instituto Historico e Geographico Brasileiro. This comprises a series of valuable essays which give an outline of Brazilian history. In this connection attention should be called to the *Diccionario historico, geographico e ethnographico do Brasil* which is being brought out by the Instituto. The first two volumes appeared at Rio de Janeiro in 1922. The work is indispensable to the student of Brazilian history.

Mexico

A number of important works dealing with Mexico have appeared in this century. From 1900 to 1902 at Mexico City appeared a work in three volumes edited by Justo Sierra (1848-1912) under the title *México, su evolución social.* An English edition appeared in two volumes in three at Mexico City, 1900-04. This work constitutes a veritable handbook of Mexican affairs.

In 1902 Nicolás León (1859-1929) brought out at Mexico City his *Compendio de historia general de México* covering Mexican history from the earliest times to 1900. An improved second edition appeared at Mexico City in 1919. In 1905, at Santiago, Chile, José Toribio Medina published his *Historia del tribunal del santo oficio de la inquisición en México*.

In 1907 at Philadelphia Alcée Fortier (1856-1914) and John Rose Ficklen published their *Central America and Mexico* as Volume IX of the *History of North America,* edited by G. C. Lee (b. 1862) and F. N. Thorpe (b. 1857), twenty volumes, published at Philadelphia from 1903 to 1907.

In 1909 W. H. Koebel published his one-volume *Mexico* at London and C. R. Enock brought out at the same place his single volume under the same title. In this year, also, at Mexico City appeared the two-volume *Historia del pueblo mejicano* by Carlos Pereyra which dealt with the political organization of the country. The year following Alberto Leduc published at Mexico City his large and valuable *Diccionario de geografía, historia y biografía mexicanas*.

In 1911 at Paris, Maurice, Comte de Périgny (b. 1877) brought out his *Les états-unis du Mexique*. In 1923 at Mexico City the *Historia nacional de México,* dealing with the period from the earliest times to the present, appeared from the pen of Enrique Santibáñez (b. 1869).

In 1920 appeared at both Mexico City and Paris *La evolución histórica de México* by Emilio Rabasa (b. 1856). The next year *México hacia el fin del virreinato español* by Gregorio Torres Quintero was published at Mexico City. In 1923 at Madrid was printed the very useful two-volume autobiographical dictionary compiled by Francisco A. de Icaza (b. 1863) under the title *Conquistadores y pobladores de Nueva España*. The same year the best one-volume history in English concerning Mexico was published at New York under the title *The Mexican nation*. The author was Herbert I. Priestley (b. 1875). Also in 1923 at Mexico City appeared the first edition of Jesús Romero Flores' *Historia de la civilización mexicana*.

In 1926 at Mexico City Alfonso Toro (b. 1873) brought out in three volumes his *Compendio de historia de México* which covered the period from earliest times to the present. Also in 1926 Ernest Gruening (b. 1887) brought out at New York his comprehensive *Mexico and its heritage*. This appeared in a new edition in 1930.

In 1930 at Durham, Charles S. Braden published his *Religious aspects of the conquest of Mexico.* Three years later at Paris appeared a work on the same subject by Robert Ricard entitled *La conquête spirituelle du Mexique.* This shows the methods and measures of the conquest from 1523 to 1572.

Central America

Among the general works dealing with Central America two in English may be mentioned. In 1914 at New York appeared W. H. Koebel's *Central America* which was reprinted at London in 1917; and D. G. Munro's (b. 1892) *The five republics of Central America* was published at New York in 1918.

In Spanish several works may be cited. In 1915 there appeared at Guatemala City the first volume of a series entitled *La América Central ante la historia* by Antonio Batres Jáuregui (b. 1847). In the same year J. Antonio Villacorte brought out his *Curso de historia de la América Central* (Guatemala City, 1915) for use particularly in normal schools. This work was followed in 1922 by his *Elementos de historia patria* in two volumes at Guatemala City. In 1927 the same author, together with Carlos A. Villacorte, brought out the *Arqueología guatemalteca.* In 1924 the *Vida militar de Centro-América* by Pedro Zamora Castellanos was published at Guatemala City. In 1925 at San José appeared *Nuestra tierra prometida* by Alejandro Alvarado Quirós (b. 1876). In 1930 at Guatemala City was published the first of a series entitled *Estudios de historia militar de Centro-América* by José N. Rodríguez.

In French at Paris (ca. 1911) Maurice, Comte de Périgny brought out his well-illustrated *Les cinq républiques de l'Amérique Centrale.* . . .

Honduras

In 1927 at San Pedro, Honduras, appeared a volume bearing the title *Bosquejo histórico de Honduras, 1501 á 1921.* The author was Rómulo Enrique Durón y Gamero (b. 1865).

Nicaragua

In Nicaragua Bernardo Portas published at Managua in 1918 his brief *Compendio de la historia de Nicaragua.* Another brief and earlier work is the *Geografía descriptiva é histórica de Nicaragua* published in 1908 at Managua.

Costa Rica

In Costa Rica one of the most important historians is Ricardo Fernández Guardia (b. 1867) who published the following works: *Historia de Costa Rica* (San José, 1905) dealing with the period of discovery and conquest, which was translated into English by H. W. Van Dyke (b. 1872) under the title *History of the discovery and conquest of Costa Rica* (New York, 1913); *Crónicas coloniales* (San José, 1921) dealing with the colonial period; and *La independencia y otros episodios* (San José, 1928).

A French work on Costa Rica appeared in Paris in 1918 under the title *La république de Costa Rica*. The author was Maurice, Comte de Périgny.

Salvador

A work written from the documents dealing with Salvador is the *Historia moderna de El Salvador* by Francisco Gavidia (b. 1864) published at San Salvador in two volumes in 1917. The title, however, is misleading, for nearly the entire work treats of the period of independence. Another work in two volumes appeared between 1914 and 1917 at San Salvador and is entitled *Historia de El Salvador*. It is the work of Santiago Ignacio Barberena (1851-1916) and it deals with the pre-Columbian and conquest periods.

Panama

In Panama Juan B. Sosa published at Panama City in 1911 his *Compendio de historia de Panamá,* which is in reality a textbook for schools and colleges. A book in English of some value is *Old Panama and Castilla del Oro* (Washington, 1911) by the army physician, Charles L. G. Anderson (b. 1863).

West Indies

Cuba

Works dealing with Cuba are of considerable importance. In 1918 at Havana appeared a three-volume work entitled *Historial de Cuba* by Ricardo V. Rousset which comprised a local history of the several provinces. In 1920 a five-volume *History of Cuba* by Willis Fletcher Johnson was published at New York. In 1921 at Havana appeared the first volume of *La historia de Cuba* by Ramiro Guerra y Sánchez (b. 1880) which treated the period from 1492 to 1555.

The early history of Cuba from 1492 to 1586 is well covered by Miss Irene Aloha Wright (b. 1879) in a volume entitled *The early history of Cuba* published at New York in 1916.

The colonial period is treated by Francisco Figueras (b. 1853) in his *Cuba y su evolución colonial* (Havana, 1907).

The independence period has been treated by Vidal Morales y Morales (1848-1904) in his *Contribución á la historia de la independencia de Cuba* published at Havana in 1901. In 1931 was published at Havana the three-volume *Iniciadores y primeros mártires de la revolución cubana* by the same author.

The general diplomatic relations of Cuba are treated by Manuel Márquez Sterling (1872-1934) in his *La diplomacia en nuestra historia* published at Havana in 1909. An important episode in Cuban history and diplomacy is presented by the well-known Cuban scholar, Herminio Portell Vilá, in his *Narciso López y su época,* the first volume of which was published at Havana in 1930.

Among the textbooks are the *Nociones de historia de Cuba* (Havana, 1903) by Carlos de la Torre y Huerta (b. 1859), who also in the same year revised his *Manual de historia de Cuba;* and the *Historia de Cuba* (Havana, 1925) by Juan M. Leiseca.

Santo Domingo

Chief among the works dealing with Santo Domingo are the *Historia moderna de la república dominicana* (Santo Domingo, 1906) by José Gabriel García; the *Bosquejo histórico del descubrimiento y conquista de la isla de Santo Domingo* by Casimiro N. de Moya who brought out the first volume of this work at Santo Domingo City in 1913; the *Resumen de historia patria* (Barcelona, 1922) by Bernardo Pichardo; and *Naboth's vineyard: the Dominican republic* (two volumes, New York, 1928) by Sumner Welles (b. 1892).

Haiti

One of the best works in this century on Haiti is by Jacques Nicolas Léger whose *Haiti, son histoire et ses détracteurs* was published at New York in 1907. The same year an English edition appeared at New York and Washington under the same title translated into English.

Other works of value in French are the *Manuel d'histoire d'Haiti* (Port-au-Prince, 1924) by J. C. Dorsainoil; and the *Histoire d'Haiti* by Auguste Magloire, the first volume of which appeared at Port-au-Prince in 1910.

Among the works in English are *The French revolution in Santo Domingo* (New York, 1914) by Theodore Lothrop Stoddard (b. 1883), and *The Haitian revolution, 1791-1804* (New York, 1914) by Theophilus Gould Steward (b. 1843).

Puerto Rico

The *Historia de Puerto Rico* by Salvador Brau (1837-1912) published at New York in 1904 is of value for the study of that country. A later volume by the same author is entitled *La colonización de Puerto Rico* and it was published at San Juan in 1907. In 1922 at New York appeared the comprehensive *Historia de Puerta Rico* by P. G. Miller (b. 1875).

Colombia

The following histories concerning Colombia may be mentioned. In 1909 and 1910 there appeared at Bogotá the two-volume *República de Colombia* written by Soledad Acosta de Samper containing a valuable treatment of the independence and modern periods. In the two following years (1911-1912) the two volume *Historia de Colombia* by Jesús María Henao y Gerardo Arrubla was published at Bogotá as a textbook for secondary schools. In 1929 the work was published in a single volume of 811 pages.

From 1917 to 1919 at Bogotá appeared the two-volume *Descubrimiento y conquista de Colombia* by Ernesto Restrepo Tirado (b. 1862). In 1929 appeared at Sevilla his two-volume *Historia de la provincia de Santa Marta,* while in 1934 at Buenos Aires was published his brief *Gobernantes del nuevo reino de Granada durante el siglo XVIII.* Meanwhile in 1918 Gonzalo Uribe Villegas brought out his valuable church history under the title *Los arzobispos y obispos colombianos* which covers the period from the foundation of the colony to the present.

In 1921 appeared the first volume of *El nuevo reino de Granada en el siglo XVIII* (Madrid, 1921) by Jerónimo Bécker (1857-1925) in collaboration with José María Rivas Groot. This work had been preceded at Madrid in 1920 by Bécker's *La política española en las indias,* a comprehensive essay on Spanish colonial policy. In 1923 at Bogotá was published *Los fundadores de Bogotá* by Raimundo Rivas.

In 1928 the first volume of the *Compendio de la historia de Colombia* was published at Bogotá by José Alejandro Bermúdez (b. 1886). In 1930 at Guayaquil, Ecuador, was printed the *Proceso histórico de Colombia* by Luís Enrique Navas Prada which covered the period from the earliest times to 1832.

Venezuela

A work dealing with both Colombia and Venezuela appeared at Paris in 1921. The author was Jules Humbert (b. 1867) and the book was entitled *Histoire de la Colombie et du Vénézuéla dès origines jusqu'à nos jours*. This work had been preceded by *Les origines Vénézuéliennes* published at Bordeaux in 1905.

Works dealing entirely with Venezuela are numerous. In 1907 José Gil Fortoul (b. 1862) brought out at Berlin his two-volume *Historia constitucional de Venezuela*. This was followed at Madrid in 1916 by his *El hombre y la historia* which concerned the social history of Venezuela.

In 1911 Lino Duarte Level published at Caracas his *Historia patria* which covers the history of Venezuela from the conquest through the war of independence. The next year (1912) at London was published the volume entitled *Venezuela* by L. V. Dalton (b. 1887). In 1913 the first volume of Bartolomé Tavera Acosta's (b. 1865) *A través de la historia de Venezuela* was published at Ciudad Bolívar. Six years later appeared *Capítulos de la historia colonial de Venezuela* (Madrid, 1919) by Arístides Rojas.

In 1923 at Caracas was published the *Investigaciones históricas* of Vicente Dávila (b. 1869) dealing with the colonial period and independence of Venezuela. This was followed the next year by his two-volume *Diccionario biográfico de ilustres próceres de la independencia*, published at Caracas.

Ecuador

Among the chief works concerning Ecuador is the three-volume *Compendio de historia patria* by Belisario Quevedo (d. 1907) which was issued in three volumes at Quito in 1931. Another extensive work is the *Historia de la república del Ecuador* by José Le Gouhir y Rodas, the first two volumes of which appeared at Quito in 1920.

Three local textbooks concerning the country are entitled *Ecuador. Estudios históricos* (Vol. I, Guayaquil, 1913) and the *Compendio de la historia del Ecuador* (Guayaquil, 1915), both by Camilo Destruge; and the *Historia del Ecuador* (Quito, 1929-32, in 2 vols.) by Emilio Uzcátegui García.

A brief work of interest on a special subject is *La escultura en el Ecuador* by José Gabriel Navarro, printed at Madrid in 1929. His briefer *El municipio en América durante la existencia de España* (Madrid, 1930) is also of value.

The chief book in English is by C. R. Enock, published at London in 1914 under the title of *Ecuador*.

Peru

The largest and most extensive work dealing with Peru published in this century is that by Nemesio Vargas entitled *Historia del Perú independiente* (eight volumes, Lima, 1903-17).

A volume of special nature dealing with the historiography of Peru is entitled *La historia en el Perú* and the author is José de la Riva Agüero, the younger (b. 1885). It was published at Lima in 1910. Another volume containing important information for the historian is the *Diccionario biográfico de peruanos contemporáneos,* edited by Juan Pedro Paz-Soldán (b. 1869) at Lima in 1917.

In 1919 appeared volume one of Pedro Dávilos y Lisson's (b. 1863) *La primera centuria*. This work is to be completed in eight volumes. The second volume appeared in 1922 and the third volume in 1934. All were published at Lima.

In 1921 at Lima appeared the first volume of Manuel C. Bonilla's study of the period of independence entitled *Epopeya de la libertad, 1820-1824*. A thought-provoking work for the social historian is the two-volume *La iniciación de la república* published at Lima in 1928 and 1929. The author is Jorge Basadre, librarian and professor of history at the Universary of San Marcos.

A record of military events in Peru's history may be found in the two-volume *Historia militar del Perú* (Lima, 1931) by Carlos Dellepiane.

Two valuable textbooks written in this century by the widely known Carlos Wiesse are entitled *Las civilizaciones primitivas del Perú* (Lima, 1913) and *Historia del Perú colonial* (Lima, 1918). Other volumes by the same author are *Historia del Perú y de la civilización peruana* (Lima, 1917), *Historia del Perú independiente* (Lima, 1925), and *Historia del Perú* (four volumes, Lima, 1925-28).

Two recent volumes dealing with the Inca civilization are *El imperio incaico* (Lima, 1931) by Horacio Urteaga (b. 1887), and *L'empire socialiste des Inka* (Paris, 1928) by Louis Baudin.

English works which might be added to this list are C. R. Enock's *Peru* published at London in 1908; Marie Wright's *The old and new Peru* (Philadelphia, 1908); and Philip Ainsworth Means' *Fall of the Inca empire* (New York, 1932).

Bolivia

There have been a number of first-class histories of Bolivia written in this century. In 1905 Daniel Sánchez Bustamante published at La Paz his volume of miscellaneous essays on various subjects dealing with the history and civilization of Bolivia entitled *Opiniones y discursos.*

In 1912 appeared at La Paz the *Bosquejo de la historia de Bolivia* by Manuel Ordóñez López. In 1917 appeared at Madrid *La creación de Bolivia* by Sabino Pinilla (1851-1907) which was left uncompleted by the author's death and which carried the story to the year 1828. Two years later, 1919, the two-volume *Historia general del Alto Perú* by Luís Pez was published at Sucre.

Between 1920 and 1924 at La Paz, Alcides Arguedas (b. 1879), the foremost historian of Bolivia, published his four-volume *Historia de Bolivia* which dealt with the foundation of the Republic to about 1864. His one-volume *Historia general de Bolivia,* treating the period since 1809, was published at the same place in 1922, and appeared in French at Paris in 1932. In 1921 at Madrid appeared his *La fundación de la república.*

In 1925 at La Paz was published the first volume of a series entitled *Los primeros cien años de la república de Bolivia* by José Agustín Morales. This work includes many biographies of prominent Bolivians.

Paraguay

Paraguay has received limited treatment at the hands of historians. In 1902 José Segundo Decoud published his *History of Paraguay* through the medium of the Government Printing Office at Washington. In 1906 at Asunción, Cecilio Báez (b. 1862) published his *Cuadros históricos y descriptivos.* In 1910 his *Resumen de la historia de Paraguay* was published at Asunción, and in 1926 his *Historia colonial del Paraguay* appeared at the same place. In 1911 appeared at Asunción Volume I of the *Estudio sobre la independencia del Paraguay* by Fulgencio R. Moreno (b. 1872).

In 1912 at London W. H. Koebel brought out his book entitled *In Jesuit land* which gave an account of the Jesuit missions, and in 1916 at London he published his *Paraguay.*

The international relations of Paraguay have been comprehensively treated by Luís Alberto de Herrera (b. 1873). From 1908 to 1926 appeared at Montevideo his five-volume *La diplomacia oriental en el Paraguay,* which chiefly concerns relations with Argentina and Uruguay.

This had been preceded by his *La revolución francesa y Sud América* (Paris, 1905).

Argentina

Of the works dealing with Argentina the following should be mentioned. In 1902 and 1903 appeared at Madrid in two volumes the *Historia de la Argentina* by Juan García Al-Deguer (b. 1855). In 1907 the *Lecciones de historia argentina* by Vicente Gambón (b. 1857) appeared in two volumes at Buenos Aires.

In 1912 a history in French by Roberto Levillier (b. 1881), an Argentine diplomat, was published at Paris under the title *Les origines argentines*. A Spanish edition appeared at the same time and place under the title *Orígenes argentinos: la formación de un gran pueblo. . . .* In the same year also an interesting work of a special nature was published at Barcelona under the title *Influencia del clero en la independencia argentina.* The author was Agustín Piaggio.

In 1913 at Buenos Aires Ricardo Levene (b. 1885), the widely known historical scholar and later president of the University of La Plata, published a two-volume work on the revolution and the period immediately following under the title *Lecturas de historia argentina.* A fourteenth edition of this work appeared in 1932. During 1920-21 his *Ensayo histórico sobre la revolución de mayo y Mariano Moreno* was published in two volumes at Buenos Aires. In 1927 and 1928 appeared at Buenos Aires a two-volume edition of his *Investigaciones acerca de la historia del virreinato del Plata,* first published in one volume in 1915 at Buenos Aires.

In 1917 appeared the first volume of the illustrated *Manual de historia de la civilización argentina* edited by Rómulo D. Carbia. Among several other valuable works is his *Historia de la historiografía argentina* (Buenos Aires, 1925).

An extremely valuable work for those interested in the history of the evolution of Argentine culture is *La literatura argentina . . . ,* by Ricardo Rojas (b. 1882). This appeared in four volumes at Buenos Aires between 1917 and 1922, and in eight volumes at Buenos Aires (1924-25) as Volumes VIII to XV of his *Obras.*

In 1918 José Ingenieros (1877-1925) brought out at Buenos Aires his extremely important two-volume work entitled *La evolución de las ideas argentinas.*

In 1920 Julio Cobos Daract (b. 1883) published at Buenos Aires his two-volume *Historia argentina* which covers the Republican period. The next year at Buenos Aires appeared the *Nuevo diccionario geográfico histórico de la Argentina* by Javier Marrazza, which constitutes a useful handbook. In 1921 and 1922 the *Historia argentina y americana* by Julián Rivera Campos was published in two volumes at Buenos Aires.

In 1925 at Buenos Aires (?) the Argentine sociologist, jurisconsult, and historian, Ernesto Quesada (1858-1934), published his chief historical work entitled *El ciclo cultural de la colonia.* This had been preceded and was followed by other works of a biographical, diplomatic, and philosophical nature.

In 1926 the *Historia de la república argentina* by Emilio Vera y González appeared at Buenos Aires in three volumes, beginning the story of the country in 1817 and carrying it to the date of publication. In 1926 also Roberto Levillier published the first volume of a series which he edited entitled *Nueva crónica de la conquista del Tucumán* (Madrid and Buenos Aires) which concerns Argentine history from 1535 to 1617.

In 1932 Enrique de Gandía at Buenos Aires brought out his specialized *La historia de la conquista del Río de la Plata y del Paraguay . . . , 1535-1556.* In the same year and at the same place appeared the monumental and much needed four-volume work by José Pacífico Otero entitled *Historia del libertador Don José de San Martín.*

A fair work in English is the *Argentine Republic* (London, 1922) by Pierre Denis, while the most recent volume is entitled *A history of the Argentine Republic* (Cambridge, England, 1931) by Frederick Alexander Kirkpatrick.

Uruguay

The chief history of Uruguay in this century is by Pablo Blanco Acevedo published in six volumes at Montevideo between 1901 and 1913 under the title *Historia del Uruguay.* Another valuable work for the historian of the country is the *Diccionario popular de historia de la república O. del Uruguay* by the exceedingly productive scholar, Orestes Araújo (b. 1853), published in three volumes at Montevideo between 1901 and 1903. In this latter year and the next at Montevideo appeared the second edition of the same author's two-volume *Gobernantes del Uruguay.* This was followed in 1907 by his *Historia compendio de la civilización uruguaya* printed at Montevideo in two volumes. Three years later appeared his *Nueva historia del Uruguay* in two volumes at the same place. In the latter year (1910) Juan Zorilla de San Martín (b. 1855) brought out at Montevideo his two-volume *La epopeya de Artigas* which dealt with the contemporary epoch of that hero.

In 1916 was published at Montevideo the first volume of the *Manual de historia de Uruguay* by Eduardo Acevedo (b. 1858). In 1919 appeared the valuable *Historia de la dominación portuguesa en el Uruguay* covering the years from 1810 to 1830. The author was Mario Falcao Espalter (b. 1892) and the book was published at Montevideo.

In 1930 appeared at Montevideo the first volume of the *Historia de la república oriental del Uruguay* by José Salgado (b. 1875) while the next year at the same place was published the two-volume *El Uruguay entre dos siglos (apuntes para un programa de la nueva etapa)* by Manuel Bernárdez (b. 1868).

Chile

Among the productive scholars of twentieth century Chile is Domingo Amunátegui y Solar (b. 1860). From 1901 to 1904 he published at Santiago, Chile, his *La sociedad chilena del siglo XVIII* in three volumes. In 1909 and 1910 appeared at Santiago his two-volume *Las encomiendas de indíjenas en Chile*. In 1915 he brought out his *Bosquejo histórico de la literatura chilena* at Santiago. In 1923 appeared at the same place his two-volume *Bajo la dominación española* covering Chilean history to 1808. In 1925 he published at Santiago his *Historia de Chile* in one volume and in 1930 appeared *Los próceres de la independencia de Chile* (Santiago, 1930) and the *Nacimiento de la república de Chile* (Santiago, 1930) dealing with the period from 1803 to 1833. In 1932 appeared the first volume of his *Historia social de Chile* at Santiago.

In 1901 and 1902 at Santiago José Toribio Medina published his two-volume *Relaciones de Chile* based upon early chronicles of the Indies. This prolific and scholarly historian continued up to the time of his death in 1930 to publish many valuable works including histories of printing, biographies, bibliographies, and works of a more general nature.

At Santiago in 1903 Alejandro Fuenzalida Grandón brought out his *Historia del desarollo intelectual de Chile (1541-1810)*. In 1906 at the same place he published *La evolución social de Chile (1541-1810)*. Both of these works contain valuable material for the historian.

In 1906 and 1907 Luís Galdames published at Santiago his illustrated two-volume *Estudio de la historia de Chile* and in 1925 appeared at Santiago the first volume of his *Historia de Chile, la evolución constitucional*.

Between 1908 and 1913 there appeared at Santiago the three-volume *Los conquistadores de Chile* which was the work of Thomás Thayer Ojeda (b. 1877). In 1910 Benjamín Vicuña Subercaseaux (b. 1876) published his *Crónicas del centenario: la colonia—la patria vieja* at Santiago which traced Chilean history to 1821, and during 1911 and 1912 his *Historia de Chile,* which dealt with Chilean history to 1810, was published in two volumes at Santiago.

In 1911 the famed internationalist, Alejandro Álvarez (b. 1868) published at Santiago his *Rasgos generales de la historia diplomática de Chile, 1810-1910,* and in 1916 at the same place was published his *Diplomacia de Chile* covering the years 1810 to 1824.

In 1924 there was published at Madrid the public school textbook by Indalecio Téllez under the title *Historia de Chile.* The next year at Santiago appeared the *Historia eclesiástica de Chile* by Bishop Carlos Silva Cotapos which dealt with the activities of the Catholic Church and its clergy. Between 1925 and 1927 at Santiago was printed the two-volume *Historia de Chile* by Thomás Guevara Silva (b. 1865) covering only the prehistoric civilizations.

A history of Chile by a literary man is entitled *Histoire du Chile.* It was published at Paris in 1927 and dealt with history and literary criticism. The author was Leonardo Peña.

Among the most widely known contemporary historians of Chile is Agustín Edwards (b. 1878). In 1929 at London appeared the first of six volumes dealing with Chilean life and history. It is entitled *Peoples of old* and treats the colonial period. The second volume was published at London in 1931 under the title *The dawn* and at Valparaiso the same year under the title *El alba.* This work deals with the birth and consolidation of Chile in the decades immediately following 1810.

INDEX OF AUTHORS

MENTIONED IN APPENDICES E, F, G, H, I

GENERAL INDEX

Prepared by
RAUL D'EÇA

GENERAL INDEX